TRADITIONAL DANCING IN SCOTLAND

THE SHAMIT REEL.
A Foursome Reel at a wedding in the Elgin district,
from John Grant's *The Penny Wedding* (1836).

TRADITIONAL DANCING IN SCOTLAND

by

J. F. and T. M. FLETT

With an Appendix

DANCING IN CAPE BRETON ISLAND NOVA SCOTIA

by

F. RHODES

Nashville, Tennessee

VANDERBILT UNIVERSITY PRESS

Published in the United States of America 1966
by Vanderbilt University Press
Nashville, Tennessee, U.S.A.
and in Great Britain
by Routledge & Kegan Paul Ltd
Broadway House, 68-74 Carter Lane
London, E.C.4

Library of Congress Catalog
Card Number 64-54967

Printed in Great Britain

Contents

Preface

SOME fifty or sixty years ago, the older social dances of Scotland, the Reels and Country Dances, were gradually losing the place they had once held in our social gatherings. Their decline was accelerated by the disruption of social life caused by the First World War, and by the introduction of jazz, so that, by 1920, they were rapidly dying out. The story of the formation of the Royal Scottish Country Dance Society and of its success in reviving interest in these dances is well known, but little has been written about social dancing in Scotland during the period prior to the formation of the Country Dance Society. In this book an attempt is made to give a picture of social dancing in Scotland before the First World War.

Our picture is based primarily on the recollections of people in many parts of Scotland who have told us what they remember of dancing in their younger days, and the period covered by the book is therefore from as far back as living memory extends up to about 1914. In order to make the book reasonably complete in itself, we have sketched the early history of the different dance-forms which were known in Scotland within living memory, but we must stress that the book is in no sense a complete history of social dancing in Scotland, and we give historical references only where we wish to establish the antiquity of the customs and usages which we have recorded from our informants.

The first part of the book, Chapters I–IV, gives the general social background against which the dances are set, and in the remaining chapters we record some of the various dances and steps which were in use within living memory. It has become obvious in the course of our work that the most universal and the most national dance-form in Scotland was the Reel, and in the dances given in the second part of this book we have emphasized this intrinsic importance of Reels by collecting together all the dances of this form which we have recorded from living memory. We give complete descriptions here, not necessarily to revive these dances, but because we feel that anything less than complete descriptions would be of no real value as a record.

The most technical part of the book is Chapter V, where we give descriptions of Reel and Country Dance steps. This chapter is designed primarily for the interested dancer who wishes to learn these steps, but we hope that the historical details which we have added will be of sufficient interest to cause the general reader at least to skim the chapter rather than to skip it.

In selecting the dances which we have described in this book, we have, with one exception, limited ourselves to those which we, or our collaborator Dr Frank Rhodes, have collected personally from informants who have first-hand knowledge of them, that is to say from informants who have themselves either taken part in these dances or witnessed them. We therefore make little reference to the work of previous collectors, but we wish to take this opportunity of paying a tribute to the valuable work done in this field by the late I. C. B. Jamieson, who collected some forty Country Dances from oral tradition among the country people of the Border counties, and by Mrs Mary Isdale MacNab of Vancouver, who has collected in a similar manner among the descendants of Scots in north-west Canada. With them, we would also couple Dr Hugh Thurston, whose pioneer historical researches, later embodied in his book, *Scotland's Dances*, initiated our own research over twelve years ago.

Most of the dances given in the later part of the book are performed either to particular tunes which are well known, or to any tunes of certain types, and where either is the case, we give no music. The exceptions to this are three dances from the Western Isles, for which we give appropriate pipe-settings, and some of the Shetland dances, for which we give a suitable selection of tunes. For these we are indebted to Pipe-Major Donald Adam who arranged the pipe-settings, to Mr Tommy Anderson of Lerwick, who very kindly made his recordings of Shetland fiddle music available to us, and to Mr and Mrs H. K. Larsen, who transcribed the fiddle tunes. We are indebted also to Mr Anderson's sources for permission to reproduce these tunes.

We gratefully acknowledge the very considerable debt which we owe to Dr Frank Rhodes of the University of Southampton. The whole book has gained a great deal from his valuable criticisms, and much of the technique of step-description which we have used was evolved with his help. He has collaborated with us in some of our investigations, and has made available to us his own findings in the Western Isles (so that in the following pages 'we' may refer either to one or both of the authors, to Dr Rhodes separately, or to Dr Rhodes and T.M.F.). He has also contributed in the form of an appendix the results of his own independent researches among the descendants of Scottish emigrants in Cape Breton Island, Nova Scotia, a contribution which adds materially to the picture presented by this book.

It would be impossible to list all the people who have given us information, but they are essentially the authors of this book, and to all of them, whether mentioned in the book or not, we express our deep gratitude for the manner in which they have welcomed us into their homes, and given us not only information, but also such kindly hospitality. We wish also to express our indebtedness to the many other people who have helped us to find our sources, have given us hospitality, or have in other ways assisted in the preparation of this book. In particular, we thank Mr William Adamson, Kingskettle, Fife; Dr J. L. Campbell of Canna; the Rev. Fr Joseph Campbell of Moidart; Mr Francis Collinson and Professor S. T. M. Newman of the University of Edinburgh; Mrs E. Creoll, Samalaman House, Glenuig; Mr Robin Johnstone, Gilmanscleuch, Ettrick; Miss Kathleen Jones, Mr and Mrs A. Grant and Mr and Mrs F. Morgan of Wallasey; Mrs Griselda MacFarlane and Mr Neil MacFarlane of Forfar; Mr and Mrs D. G. MacLennan, Edinburgh; Mr and Mrs Farquhar MacNeil, Jedburgh; Mr and Mrs A. G. Reid, Balnakilly, Strath Ardle; Mr Stewart F. Sanderson of the University of Leeds; Miss Elizabeth Wallace of Kilmarnock; Mr Jimmy Watson of Lauder; in Orkney, Mr and Mrs W. H. Forrest of Flotta, Mr and Mrs Roy Scott of Rendall, and Mr Jack Tait of Dounby; and in Shetland, Mr John Graham, Mr T. A. Robertson, and Mr Tommy Anderson of the Shetland Folk Society, and Captain John Hay of Hayfield. To these Dr Rhodes would add the Rev. Mgr MacKellaig and Dr Alasdair MacLean of Daliburgh, S. Uist; Mr and Mrs Archie Kennedy, Dunvegan, Cape Breton Island; and Major Calum I. MacLeod of Halifax, Nova Scotia.

We wish also to thank Archibald Campbell of Kilberry, Lieutenant-Colonel J. P. Grant of Rothiemurchus, Mrs I. C. B. Jamieson, and Mrs E. J. Maginnis for their kind permission to reproduce extracts from various manuscripts, Sir Compton MacKenzie and Messrs Chatto and Windus for kindly allowing us to reproduce the extract from *Whisky Galore*, and the Editor of the *Orkney Herald* for allowing us to reproduce material published in his paper. In addition we thank the Librarians and staffs of the many libraries we have consulted, and particularly of the Harold Cohen Library of the University of Liverpool, for the help they have rendered. Finally, we acknowledge our indebtedness to our own dancing-teachers, Pipe-Major David Taylor and Mr Jack McConachie, whose teaching made this book possible, and to the members of our own demonstration team, the Marlowe Scottish Dancers, who have given us such pleasure in performing these old dances.

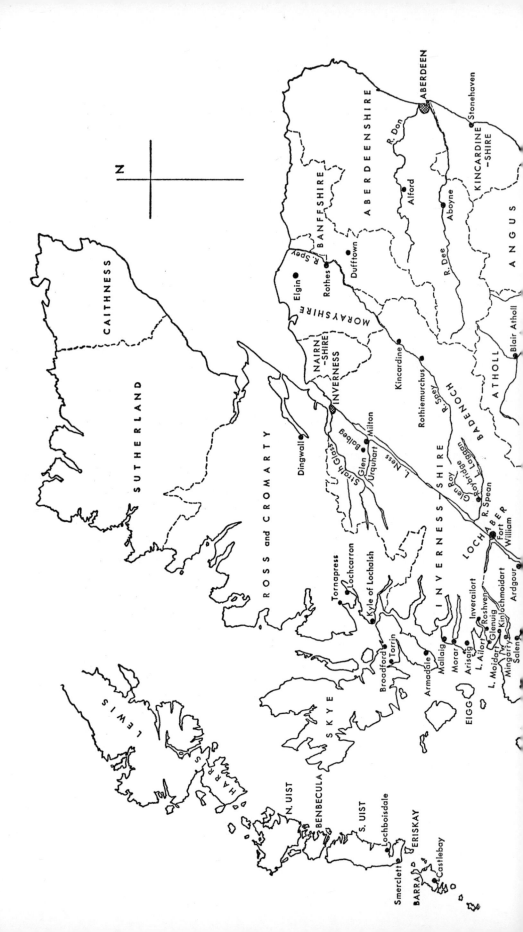

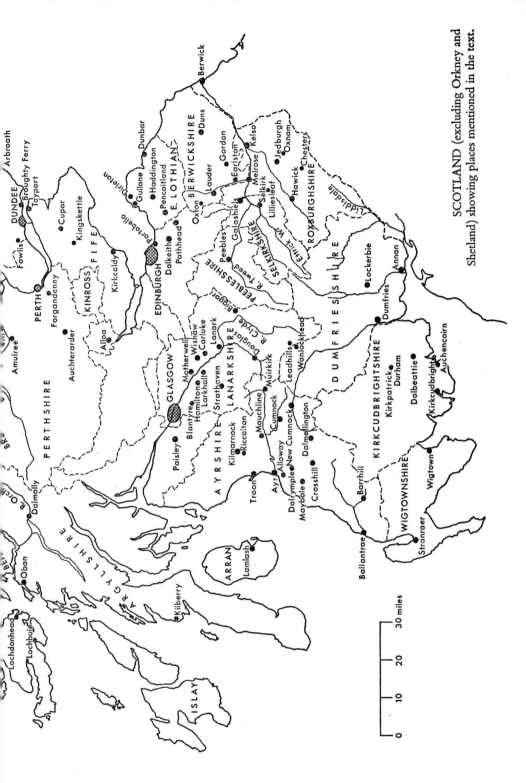

SCOTLAND (excluding Orkney and Shetland) showing places mentioned in the text.

NUMBERS in parentheses appearing in the text refer to the list of informants and the bibliography at the end.

In the diagrams illustrating the figures of dances circles are used to denote men and squares to denote ladies.

CHAPTER I

Of the Dances, and How They Were Taught

FROM the beginning of the period covered by living memory up to the early years of this century, four main types of social dance were in use in Scotland, namely Reels, Country Dances, Square Dances, and Circle Dances. Today, the distinctions between these types of dance have become blurred, but to older people in Scotland the four types were clearly differentiated, and each had its special characteristics.

A true *Reel* consists of setting steps danced on the spot, alternated with a travelling figure—the setting steps can be as varied as the dancers please, while the travelling figure is usually the same throughout the dance. In many Reels there is also a change in musical rhythm in the course of the dance, an unusual feature in social dances. A typical example of a true Reel is the Scotch or Highland Reel, a dance now more commonly known as the Foursome Reel; in this, the setting steps are performed with the dancers in line, and the travelling figure is in the form of a figure 8 with a third loop added. This particular Reel also displays the change in rhythm, for it is usually begun to a strathspey, and in the course of the dance the music changes to a reel.[1]

In addition to the true Reels, the general class of Reels also includes a few dances, not constructed in the manner of the true Reels, but performed in the same style as them; the best known of these dances is the modern Eightsome Reel, which was composed about 1870–80.

The term *Country Dance* today covers many different forms of dance, but to older people in Scotland it means a dance in which the dancers form two parallel lines, and each couple progresses down the set in turn. The progression can be made either one place at a time, as in the well-known Petronella and Flowers of Edinburgh, or directly from the top to the bottom of the set, as in Haymakers Jig and Strip the Willow.

[1] A brief account of the different types of dance tunes used in Scotland is given in Chapter V. It should be noted that we use Reel with a capital R to mean a dance; for a reel tune we use a small r.

The term *Square Dance* also has several meanings nowadays, but among dancers in Scotland before 1914 a Square Dance meant a dance of Quadrilles type, performed by four couples, with the dancers standing initially in the form of a square; typical examples are the Quadrilles, the Lancers, and La Russe.

Circle Dances are the progenitors of our modern ballroom dances. The oldest Circle Dance is the Waltz, and this is typical of the whole class of Circle Dances in that each couple performs the dance independently of the other couples. Other old Circle Dances are the Polka, the Common Schottische, the Highland Schottische, La Varsovienne (sometimes mistranslated as 'The Waltz of Vienna'), and Pas de Quatre; all of these were in common use in Scotland at one time or another.

In this book we shall use the terms Reel, Country Dance, Square Dance, and Circle Dance with the meanings given here; in particular, we stress that the term Country Dance will mean a dance of the 'longways' form described above.

In addition to the dances of these four types, there were a few miscellaneous dances in use which did not fit into this classification, for example the Bumpkin, the Waltz Country Dance[1] (also known as the Spanish Waltz or the Guaracha Waltz), Circassian Circle, La Tempête, Dashing White Sergeant, and the Ninepins (sometimes also known as the Ninepins Reel). There was also a kissing dance, most often known as Babbity Bowster, Bee Bo Babbity, or The White Cockade, but with a host of other names as well.

Of our four main types of dance, only Reels are truly indigenous to Scotland. Reels of one sort or another were known in every district of Scotland, in all classes of society, and were particularly popular in the crofting regions; in these latter regions most dancing took place in the kitchens of the croft houses, and Reels, with their compact travelling figures and well-contrasted periods of vigorous stepping, were ideally suited to the restricted dancing-spaces available.

Throughout the mainland of Scotland and in the Western Isles, the commonest Reel within living memory was the Scotch (Foursome) Reel.[2] Indeed, up to about 1880–90 this dance was so popular among the ordinary working people of the Central and West Highlands and the Western Isles that in these regions it was often almost the only dance in the local repertoire. For example, in Glen Roy in Lochaber about 1885

[1] Within living memory this dance was performed in a circular formation, with couples meeting couples round the room. It was, however, originally danced in 'longways' formation, and this explains the use of the name 'Country Dance' in its title.

[2] We should add that this name covered a number of different Reels for four; the differences are explained in Chapters VI and VII, but for the moment we ignore them.

the dances performed during an evening's dancing would be 'mostly Reels' (88). 'It's very few dances they had [in those days], just the Scotch Reel, the Polka, and the Highland Schottische. . . . They might have had Flowers of Edinburgh and Petronella, and that's all they had' (87). This applied particularly to the dancing that took place in the crofts in the upper stretches of Glen Roy, but even at the formal Volunteer Balls which took place in the Volunteers' hall[1] at Roy Bridge 'there was . . . Scotch Reel upon Scotch Reel, . . . with the Highland Schottische, and perhaps Flowers of Edinburgh and Triumph, but chiefly these Reels all the time' (89). As another example—equally typical—we may cite the little crofting township of Balbeg in Glen Urquhart. There, the programmes at wedding dances about the turn of the century consisted only of the Scotch Reel (known there as the Highland Reel), the Polka, the Highland Schottische, and the Country Dance Petronella; moreover, though some of the younger people in the community at that time may have known other dances, the older people knew only these dances, and no others (91).

Similar remarks apply also to the Western Isles. For instance, in Skye in 1954 a man of 84 told us that there the people of his parents' generation would happily spend an entire evening dancing Scotch Reels, and would have nothing to do with Country Dances, Quadrilles, and Lancers (113). Again, in Eriskay about the year 1895 'they were not keen on Country Dances at all. Give them Scotch Reels and the Highland Schottische all the time' (120).

It might be thought that only the use of a considerable variety of setting steps would give interest to an evening of Reels, but this was not so. In the warm intimate atmosphere of a crowded croft kitchen, with the noise of the dancing bouncing back off the walls and the low ceiling —the loud 'heuchs', the crack of finger and thumb, the thud of the dancers' feet, and, above all, the inspiriting music of the fiddle—it did not really matter how many or how few steps one knew, for the joy in dancing a Reel under these conditions was not the pleasure obtained from intricate stepping, but the sheer joy of vigorous rhythmic movement to exciting music.

Reels were also popular in the Lowlands, but there they shared the dance programmes with a wider range of other dances, and thus formed proportionately a smaller part of an evening's dancing. Before 1914 most dance programmes in the country districts of the Lowlands included at least one or two Scotch Reels, and at the kirns in the Border counties there would be at least three and sometimes five or six Scotch

---

[1] The Volunteer Regiments were the predecessors of the Territorials.

3

Reels in the course of the evening (23, 69)—'if things got a bit quiet, they had a Scotch Reel to liven things up' (75).

The other three types of dance, Country Dances, Square Dances, and Circle Dances, are foreign introductions to Scotland.

Country Dances came to Scotland from England, and were first introduced into Scotland about the year 1700. Within a few years of their arrival in Scotland there were Scottish contributions in the form of new figures inspired by the native Reels, and from about 1740 onwards Country Dances incorporating these Scottish figures seem to have been much more popular in Scotland than the more typically English dances. However, in spite of such Scottish contributions, Country Dances continued to be regarded in Scotland as 'English' dances right up to the end of the eighteenth century, and even later.

When Country Dances were first introduced to Scotland, they were essentially a dance of the upper classes, but as time went on they spread to other classes of society, and by about 1775–1800 they had become generally accepted throughout the Lowlands and the adjacent parts of the Highlands. In the remoter parts of the country, however, the spread of Country Dances among the ordinary working people was much less rapid than in the Lowlands. Thus in the West Highlands and the Western Isles it was not until about 1880 that Country Dances were everywhere accepted; even today old people in the Outer Hebrides speak of Country Dances, together with Square and Circle Dances, as 'modern dances', and it is probable that Country Dances first reached these districts about 1850. In Glenuig in Moidart (a tiny glen still accessible only by water or by hill tracks impassable to vehicles), the introduction of Country Dances is even more recent, for they were first performed there about 1875. In Glenuig, the grandparents of people living now knew only four dances, the Scotch Reel, the Reel of Tulloch, a Reel for eight called The Eight Men of Moidart which was peculiar to Glenuig, and the Highland Schottische (see p. 163).

The other two types of dance came from the Continent. Quadrilles, the earliest of the Square Dances, were brought to Scotland directly from Paris in 1816, after the end of the Napoleonic Wars. Originally, a set of Quadrilles consisted of four, five, or six different figures chosen arbitrarily from a large number of available figures, but certain fixed combinations of figures became particularly common, the most popular of these combinations being known as the 'First Set of Quadrilles'— doubtless because it was essentially the same as the first set of Quadrilles ever to be performed in Britain. Later on, new sets of Quadrilles consisting of definite sequences of figures were composed, and by the

middle of the nineteenth century all the various sets of Quadrilles in use
—some dozen in all—had a more or less fixed form.

After the middle of the century, the number of Quadrilles in use
decreased, and by the beginning of the period covered by living
memory only three sets of Quadrilles remained in favour, namely the
original First Set of Quadrilles, the Lancers Quadrilles (a mid-century
revival of a set of Quadrilles first published about 1817), and the
Caledonian Quadrilles (first published between 1820 and 1830). With
the disappearance of all other Quadrilles, the titles of these three sur-
viving dances were then simplified, the last two becoming known
simply as 'The Lancers' and 'The Caledonians', while the First Set of
Quadrilles became simply 'the Quadrilles'.[1] Among older people in
Scotland today, the term 'the Quadrilles' means a more or less standar-
dized version of the First Set, and in the sequel we shall use the term in
this sense.

Quadrilles, like Country Dances, were first introduced among the
upper classes in Scotland, but spread rapidly among the ordinary people
of the Lowlands and the less remote Highlands. There was, however, a
considerable lapse of time before they reached all parts of Scotland, and
there are still many people alive today who can recall the first introduction of Quadrilles to their districts. For example, in Benderloch in
Argyllshire these dances were first introduced about 1885 (109–10).

The only other Square Dance which was widely popular within
living memory was La Russe, a single-figure Quadrille dating from
about 1840. This dance was confined mainly to the Lowlands and the
less remote Highlands, and was unknown in the west and north-west of
Scotland.

The earliest of the Circle Dances, the Waltz, was imported from the
Continent soon after the beginning of the nineteenth century, shortly
before the introduction of Quadrilles. For some years the Waltz remained the sole example of its type, and initially it achieved little
popularity in Scotland. A similarly lukewarm welcome was given to
the Galop (or Galopade) and the various forms of Mazourka which
followed the Waltz, and it was not until the advent of the Polka in 1844
that Circle Dances began to achieve real popularity.

Following the introduction of the Polka there was a steady flow of
new Circle Dances, a flow which became almost a flood in the early
years of the present century. Among the immediate successors of
the Polka were the (Common) Schottische, introduced about 1849, the

[1] For a fuller account of the history of Quadrilles, see P. J. S. Richardson, *The Social
Dances of the Nineteenth Century in England* (303).

Polka Mazourka and La Varsovienne, introduced about 1853, and the Highland Schottische, which appeared about 1855. This last dance was a combination of the Common Schottische with an old Reel setting step, and became an immediate favourite in Scotland, spreading into even the more remote parts of the country with remarkable rapidity. Later Circle Dances which achieved widespread popularity were the Barn Dance, or Pas de Quatre, which was introduced from America about 1890, and the Veleta, which was composed in England in 1900.[1]

In the Lowlands, the introduction of the various Square Dances and Circle Dances in the first half of the nineteenth century had only temporary effects on the popularity of the already established Reels and Country Dances, and effectively the new dances were simply assimilated into the existing dance-programmes. After about 1870, however, the Square Dances and Circle Dances began to oust Reels and Country Dances from the dance-programmes in the larger Lowland towns, and by 1900 the programmes in these places consisted almost entirely of Square Dances and Circle Dances, together with an occasional Scotch Reel, and a few Country Dances such as Petronella, Flowers of Edinburgh, Rory O'More, and Strip the Willow, which still retained their popularity. With the advent of jazz after the First World War, the older dances—Reels, Country Dances, and Square Dances—were entirely swept away in the towns, and even the most recent of the Circle Dances had to yield their place to the newer ballroom dances, the Foxtrot and Onestep, and their successors, the Slow Foxtrot, Quickstep, and Tango.

In the country districts, on the other hand, changes in fashion took place more slowly, and Reels and Country Dances remained popular right up to the start of the 1914–18 War (though some of the older dances had begun to disappear before 1914). After the end of the war, the young men who had been the dancers of pre-war days came back to marry and settle down, their dancing days over, and the new generation who took over the village dances in 1918 turned to the new couple dances which accompanied the modern jazz, rather than to the old Reels, Country Dances, and Square Dances. Within a few years of the end of the First World War, the victory of the couple dances over the older dances was virtually complete, and the modern era of dancing had begun.

Nowadays we have come to think of Reels and Country Dances as

[1] The history of most of the Circle Dances mentioned here is given in the book by P. J. S. Richardson cited above.

'National Dances', and they are regarded as being on a different plane from ordinary ballroom dances. But for the proper understanding of the history of social dancing in Scotland, it is essential to realize that, for as far back as living memory extends, Reels and Country Dances were regarded as being on exactly the same footing as Square and Circle Dances. Moreover, in common with all the other social dances which were in current use, Reels and Country Dances were taught by professional dancing-teachers in the normal course of their classes.

It is essential to realize also just how thoroughly the teachings of professional dancing-teachers permeated the structure of social dancing in Scotland, for before 1914 most young people in Scotland attended dancing classes at some time or other.

In the bigger towns there were permanent dancing academies. In Glasgow, for example, the best-known teachers about the year 1900 were James Orr Robertson, Joe Diamond, James B. MacEwan, and J. D. MacNaughton, and all of these either owned their own dance halls or had the permanent hire of such a hall—these halls corresponded to the studio of the present-day dancing-teacher.

In Edinburgh, Mr D. G. MacLennan was the leading teacher of his time. He taught all branches of dancing—ballroom, ballet, stage, and Highland. His Highland dancing was learnt from his elder brother William MacLennan and from John McNeill senior,[1] both of whom were among the finest Highland dancers of their day, and he himself competed in Highland Games from 1898 until 1910, being one of the principal prizewinners during this period. His ballroom dancing and much of his stage dancing were learnt from his brother William, and his knowledge of ballet dancing was acquired from the distinguished Danish Maître de Ballet Alexander Genée, under whom he studied for ten years. Up to his retirement a few years ago, he was a member of the Grand Council of the Royal Academy of Dancing, and of its Executive and Technical Committees.

Among the ballroom dances which Mr MacLennan taught in his early days were the Scotch Reel and the half-dozen or so Country Dances which had remained in favour in the towns, such as Petronella and Flowers of Edinburgh. In more recent years he also taught all the various couple dances which have so largely replaced the older dances, and it was in fact he who brought the Foxtrot to Britain.

[1] John McNeill senior was a dancing-teacher in Edinburgh, where he taught ballroom and Highland dancing, and in his day was one of the foremost teachers of Highland dancing in Scotland. He died in 1890 at the age of 56 (39).

William MacLennan died in 1892 at the age of 32. A short account of his life can be found in Mr D. G. MacLennan's book *Highland and Traditional Scottish Dances* (239).

Sometimes the teachers in these urban schools also served the smaller towns and villages around them. For instance, David Anderson, who was one of the principal dancing-teachers in Dundee from about 1870 until about 1910, held dancing classes also in Brechin, Broughty Ferry, Tayport, and some of the smaller villages about Dundee. In Anderson's time, Country Dances were still in favour in such places, and there he taught Country Dances which he had long since discarded at his central school in Dundee. Indeed, even as late as 1900 he was still composing new Country Dances for the rural communities in his neighbourhood.

Such teachers also held classes in towns far away from their head-quarters. Mr D. G. MacLennan, for instance, has taught as far afield as Broadford in Skye, and David Anderson had schools in Alford, Ding-wall, and Inverness.

The country districts also had their professional dancing-teachers. In general such teachers made their homes the centre of their own territory, and travelled from home each day to the places where they held their classes. For example, the whole of East Fife was served in this way by two teachers, Alexander Adamson and his son William, who resided at Kingskettle.

Alexander Adamson was born in 1859, and began his working life as a miner in the Cowdenbeath district of Fife. He was an enthusiastic dancer, and in his spare time seized every opportunity to attend the classes of an old dancing-teacher, Andrew Doag,[1] who taught in the Cowdenbeath and Lochgelly districts. From Doag, too, he learnt to play the fiddle. At about the age of 20 Alexander Adamson set up in business himself as a dancing-teacher, made Kingskettle in Fife his head-quarters, and from there taught all over East Fife. He retired in 1927 at the age of 68, and died in 1939.

Mr William Adamson, Alexander Adamson's son, was born in 1880. He was taught to dance and to play the fiddle by his father, and com-menced his career as a dancing-teacher at the age of 16 or 17 by assisting at his father's classes. When he was 20, he started holding classes by him-self, though still working in partnership with his father. After his father retired, he continued in business on his own, and he himself retired in 1953.

Mr William Adamson has given us a very vivid picture of the day-to-day activities of a country dancing-master; this picture is in fact not only that of his own life but also that of his father's, for Mr Adamson ran his business on exactly the same lines as his father had done before him.

Mr Adamson's territory covered parts of Fife, Kinross-shire, and

[1] Doag died about 1900–10.

Perthshire; it was bounded by the Tay to the north and by the sea to the east, and extended westward as far as Forteviot, Muckhart, and Crook of Devon, and southward as far as Thornton, Leslie, and Largo. Within this territory, he has held classes in over seventy-two different places.

Map showing the region covered by Mr Adamson
(The boundary of his territory is marked with a dotted line)

In any particular place Mr Adamson's classes consisted of one meeting a week for fourteen weeks, always on the same day of the week. The last of these fourteen meetings was the 'full-time ball', when his pupils displayed their newly acquired knowledge to their parents and friends. There was also a 'half-time ball' in the seventh week which was a shorter and less elaborate version of the full-time ball. The remaining twelve meetings were devoted entirely to tuition. Normally Mr Adamson ran classes in five different places at the one time; these five sets of classes were held one each evening from Monday to Friday, and usually all five sets commenced in the same week.

9

The class-nights were divided into two sessions. The 'juveniles' session' took place from 6 p.m. until 7.45 p.m., and was attended by school-children, their ages ranging from 5 to 13 or 14. The 'adults' session' lasted from 8 p.m. until 10 p.m., and the majority of those who attended this were in their teens. Step-dancing was included in the juveniles' session, but not in the adults' session, the latter being devoted entirely to social dancing. For those adults who wished to learn step-dancing, Mr Adamson gave extra classes, either immediately before or immediately after the ordinary adults' session.

When Mr Adamson began to teach, the fee for the twelve classes was 6s.; the balls were extra, 1s. 6d. for the half-time ball and 2s. 6d. for the full-time ball, and there was also an extra charge for the step-dancing classes for adults. It was by no means uncommon for Mr Adamson to have about a hundred people present on each night, and it requires very little calculation to show that the profession of dancing-teacher gave him a very reasonable livelihood indeed.

To encourage the parents of large families to send their children to him, Mr Adamson only charged fees for the first three of any family, the remaining members of the family being admitted free. This was sound psychology, for parents who could not afford the fees for all their children might well have preferred to allow none of them to attend the classes, rather than to allow one or two to attend and to deny the rest the opportunity. Mr Adamson also sometimes admitted free a few former pupils who were good dancers; in return they assisted him by dancing with pupils who were slow to learn.

The five classes held in any one week were often in widely separated districts. In his early days Mr Adamson cycled out each afternoon to the place where that evening's class was to be held, and cycled back home after the class was finished, often a distance of eighteen miles each way. However, when he taught in the coastal districts, at Anstruther, Cellardyke, Upper Largo, Pittenweem, and St Monance, he stayed at Colinsburgh for the duration of those particular sets of classes, returning home each week-end. In more recent years he used a motor-bicycle, and latterly a car, and then he returned home each night from all his classes.

Usually Mr Adamson tried to hire a local hall or schoolroom for his classes. Where neither hall nor school was available, he generally obtained the use of a farm granary. On most Fife farms the granary is placed over the cartshed, and has a stout wooden floor. In the old days the grain was stored loose in the granary, and when it was about to be sold it was gathered up with large wooden scoops and put in sacks. In the course of time the floor of the granary acquired a smooth surface from the constant rubbing with the scoops, and the addition of a little 'Slipperine' (a substance similar to French chalk) turned it into an excellent dance floor. Mr Adamson has also held classes in a barn with a stone or concrete floor, and there he rubbed scrapings from candles on to the floor.

In any given place, he first made arrangements about a hall or a suitable substitute, and then set about publicizing the forthcoming classes. He had a standard printed notice advertising his classes, with spaces left for the date and place of the meetings, and when he had made the necessary arrangements he completed these notices and put them up in the local shops. In country districts he also cycled round all the farms within a radius of three or four miles, and at each farm gave a notice to several of the young people there and asked them to tell everybody else on the farm about the classes; often he spent a whole day cycling round the farms in this way. Then, on the Friday prior to the commencement of his classes, he inserted an advertisement in the *Fife Journal*.

He had no regular round for his classes, but simply went where there was a demand. Often pupils attending his classes from a distance would ask him to give them a set of classes in their own district. For example, when he taught at Dairsie there would generally be people present who had travelled over from Guardbridge (between three and four miles away), and they might ask him to come next to Guardbridge and give them a class there. It also happened that someone would write to ask him to visit a particular district which he had not visited for some time.

The Reels which Mr Adamson taught in his early years were the Scotch (Foursome) Reel, the Reel of Tulloch, and the Eightsome Reel, while the Country Dances in his repertoire included Petronella, Flowers of Edinburgh, Triumph, Haymakers Jig, Rory O'More, Strip the Willow, Blue Bonnets, Cumberland Reel, The Nut Country Dance, Brown's Reel or Duke of Perth (these were alternative names for the same dance), Corn Rigs, Royal Albert, and the Quadrille Country Dance. The Square Dances which he taught were the Quadrilles, the Lancers, and La Russe, while the Circle Dances included the Waltz, Polka, La Varsovienne, Pas de Quatre, Veleta, and many others. He also taught a number of the miscellaneous dances such as Circassian Circle, the Inverness Circle Dance, and the Waltz Country Dance.

He always kept his repertoire up to date, and in recent years he taught all the popular ballroom dances of the day, such as the Quickstep, Slow Foxtrot, and Tango. Latterly, he 'didn't go in for many Country Dances, because young people were trying to get more modern dances', but he was still teaching two or three of them to adults, and more than this to juveniles, even just before his retirement. In the old days, of course, 'the whole night went on Reels, Country Dances, Quadrilles and Lancers, and Circle Dances'.

In addition to all these social dances, Mr Adamson had a wide repertoire of step-dances, including not only the standard Highland solo dances, but also such dances as the Skirt Dance and Tambourine Dance which come under the general classification of 'stage' or 'fancy' dances.

Mr Adamson commenced the first class of each series with the step for the Polka, 'one, two, three, hop', first from side to side, and then with a turn. He demonstrated the step while playing on his fiddle—he could play and dance simultaneously—and then made his pupils do it by themselves. Those who found difficulty with it were given further demonstrations until eventually all had mastered it, and then he arranged them all in couples and taught them the Polka itself. After this the Waltz was taught in the same manner, and then followed some of the other dances.

In addition to the steps and figures of the various dances, Mr Adamson also taught his pupils (both juvenile and adult) 'deportment and etiquette'. The girls had to sit on one side of the room, and had to have their hands clasped in their laps, right hands on top; the men and boys had to sit on the other side of the room, and had to place their hands on their knees; no one was allowed—or ever dared—to sit with legs crossed.

The men and boys were taught how to ask a girl to dance with them, and how to escort her to her seat at the end of the dance. They had to walk over to the girl with whom they wished to dance, stand in front of her with heels together, bow, and then ask her formally to dance with them: 'May I have the pleasure of this dance?' If she accepted, they had to offer her an arm and take her on to the floor. For a Reel, a Country Dance, or a Square Dance, they went straight to their places in the dance, and when the music struck up the man bowed and the girl curtsied. For a Circle Dance they had to walk round the room arm in arm until the music began. At the end of the dance each man or boy had to offer his arm to his partner and take her to her seat, and, when she was seated, bow and thank her. This strict code of etiquette was taught no matter where the class was held, whether in village hall or stone-floored barn.

If his pupils did not mix sufficiently of their own accord, or if there were more men than girls (as was frequently the case), Mr Adamson numbered the men and gave No. 1 man first choice of the ladies, No. 2 man second choice, and so on. For the next dance he would call the numbers in reverse order, or perhaps start from the middle number and work outwards, and similarly for the succeeding dances. Halfway through the evening he would allow the men a free choice of partners for one or two dances, and then would begin again with the numbers.

The full-time balls were the culmination of the classes, and usually Mr Adamson provided a small band for these—often composed of his father, his daughter, and himself. Both the juveniles and the adults had to choose their own partners for these balls. Parents were invited to watch the proceedings, and were usually given one or two dances in the course of the evening.

The juveniles' ball took place from about 6 p.m. until 9 p.m. The invited parents were seated at one end of the hall, and the children sat on the remaining three sides. The programme commenced with some simple social dances in which all the children in the class took part, for instance, Circassian Circle, the Country Dance Rory O'More, and perhaps the Polka. Four or five of the younger children would then perform a simple step-dance, possibly Highland Laddie, after which all the children would take part in another social dance or two, perhaps Petronella and the Quadrilles. After these dances, another four or five children might perform the Highland Fling—this particular step-dance was usually performed twice during the evening, by different groups of children. After this second step-dance, there would be further social dances and then again a step-dance, perhaps a Skirt Dance or a Tambourine Dance, then further social dances, then perhaps a Clog Hornpipe, and so on until the end.

The 'Night Ball' for the adults started at 9 p.m. and went on until 3 a.m. or even later. This ball was not restricted to those who had attended the classes, and it was usual for former pupils and complete outsiders to attend. Most of the ladies wore white dresses, with flowers given them by their partners. In the old days it was quite common for a man who was courting his ball partner to buy her ball shoes for her. The men wore their best suits, and had to provide themselves with white gloves—Mr Adamson insisted on this.

The 'Night Ball' began with the Grand March, and the men in the class drew lots for their places in this. Mr Adamson led the march, playing on his fiddle, while the spectators watched from the end of the hall. The Grand March was followed by a Waltz or some other Circle Dance, and then perhaps by an Eightsome Reel. This would be followed by another Circle Dance, such as the Veleta, after which there might be an exhibition of step-dancing, possibly the Liverpool or Lancashire Hornpipe.

Between 10 and 11 o'clock, there was an interval for refreshments.

Sometimes during this interval the dancers performed the kissing dance Bee Bo Babbity, singing the accompaniment to themselves; they always asked Mr Adamson's permission before dancing this, for he never taught it in his classes. In the old days there might also be some songs or recitations during the interval, but these ceased with the introduction of entertainments tax, since their inclusion in the programme brought the ball within the scope of this tax.

After the interval the ball continued as before, step-dances alternating with general dancing. The last dance of the evening was always a Scotch Reel and Reel of Tulloch, and was usually encored until the musicians were too tired to play any longer.

Most men wore black patent leather dancing shoes both for the balls and for the classes (the alternative was ordinary outdoor shoes or boots), while the girls wore light shoes with moderately high heels. It must be emphasized that the light Highland dancing shoes so commonly worn today for Country Dances were, in the days before the First World War, worn only by professional Highland dancers at the Games. Indeed, Mr D. G. MacLennan has told us that in his younger days so few people wore Highland dancing shoes that there was only one shop in all Scotland where these shoes could be obtained. We stress this matter of footwear particularly, for the type of shoe worn by a dancer has a profound effect on the style of his or her dancing.

There were many other dancing-teachers who organized their classes on more or less similar lines to Mr Adamson's. The most famous of these was undoubtedly James Neill of Forfar, who died in 1920 at the age of 86.[1]

James Neill (better known throughout Angus and Perthshire as 'Dancie' Neill[2]) was born on the Glamis estate in the parish of Kirriemuir. A newspaper interview which he gave in 1908 tells how he came to be a dancing-teacher:

'I came of a musical race. My grandfather played the flute, my father and one uncle both played the violin, and . . . another uncle . . . the clarionet. I was always anxious to learn the violin when I was a boy going to school, but my parents tried to get me to turn my attention from the instrument. My grandfather, however, sympathized with my musical inclinations. "Never mind them, laddie; I'll bring ye a penny

---

[1] Our sources for information about the various dancing-teachers mentioned here and elsewhere are given in the list of informants on p. 286, under the name of the dancing-teacher concerned.

[2] 'Dancie' was a common nickname for a dancing-teacher in Angus, Kincardineshire, Aberdeenshire, and Banffshire.

whistle oot o' Kirriemair", he said, and he did. With this I practised assiduously going and coming from school till I was able to play a few tunes, and then my grandfather substituted for the tin whistle a flute, which was also my companion on the road to and from school. When my parents saw that they could not prevent me from learning the violin they gave way and I started to work hard.

'It then became a question whether I would adopt music or dancing for a profession, and I finally decided that it should be the latter. I went to Perth to get lessons from Mr John Lowe, who, along with his brother, was at the head of the profession at the time.'

In Perth, the young James Neill not only studied dancing under John Lowe, but also learnt to play the violin under John Lowe's brother. In 1855 he started in business as a dancing-teacher in Auchterarder and Forgandenny, and after some time there moved to Fife, where he spent the next two years. He then returned to Angus and settled in Forfar, where he remained until his death. He retired from teaching at the age of 84, on March 30th, 1918. His diary for that date bears the sorrowful comment 'no more classes'.

After James Neill came to Forfar, his territory seems to have covered a region within a radius of roughly fifteen to twenty miles from his home. We do not know how he arranged his classes in his early days, but his diaries show that from at least 1881 onwards he worked very much to a regular pattern. In January, February, and March he taught in Forfar itself. Then as the summer came on he began to go afield, his most distant classes being held during the summer months. In the autumn, as the weather deteriorated, he started to work nearer home, his nearest classes being in Kirriemuir in December. For example, in 1881 his classes in Forfar began in the middle of January and lasted until the end of March. From the beginning of April until mid-May of that year he taught daily in Kingoldrum, and then from mid-May to the end of June he taught on alternate days in Eassie and Alyth. Throughout July and part of August he taught in Airlie, Loyal, and Ruthven, and after that he held classes in Lindertis and Lintrathen until mid-September. In the second half of September and throughout October he taught in Blairgowrie, while in November he taught in Newtyle and Coupar Angus. Finally in December he held his usual classes in Kirriemuir.

Mr Neill travelled home each night from his classes, no matter the distance, and in his early years as a teacher he walked to and from those of his classes which were not accessible by rail. In later years he used a bicycle, and even right up to his retirement he thought nothing of cycling ten or fifteen miles each day to and from his classes.

In most places where he held classes, he taught on two or three days a week. He had a class from 3 p.m. until 4 p.m. for children who were under school age, and then took the schoolchildren from 4 p.m. to 6 p.m. The adults' class, for those who had left school, began at 7.30 p.m. and ended at 10 p.m.

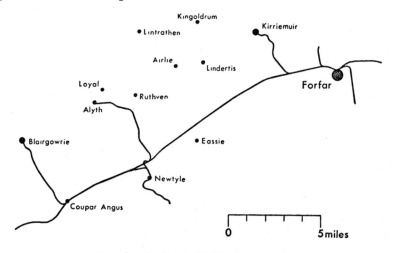

Map showing James Neill's classes in 1881
(Railway lines are indicated by continuous lines)

During the periods when he was teaching in Forfar, Mr Neill held public classes on Mondays, Wednesdays, and Fridays. He also held semi-private classes in the afternoons on Tuesdays, Thursdays, and Saturdays, for the children of those upper middle-class parents who preferred their children not to attend the ordinary public classes.

During this same period when he was teaching in Forfar, Mr Neill also held classes there for the violin—these took place in the evenings on Tuesdays, Thursdays, and Saturdays. He was himself a very fine violinist, and was noted as a player of reels and strathspeys. Through his pupils—and their pupils in turn—he exerted a strong influence on the style of fiddle-playing in his district. However, his music lessons were by no means confined to Scottish dance music, and, for instance, at a concert given by his music pupils in Forfar in 1891 we find such pieces as 'Intermezzo' (Downs), 'The Joyful Peasant' (Schuman), 'Nocturne' (Field), and 'Extract from Overture in D' (Haydn).

In addition to all these public and semi-private classes, Mr Neill had a very extensive private practice as a dancing-teacher among the county families of Angus and Perthshire, and indeed there was hardly a country house in these regions at which he had not given lessons. For instance, he taught the Queen Mother at Glamis Castle when she was a girl; he also taught three generations of the Atholl family at Blair Castle. In 1908, his ex-pupils presented him with a silver cup and a cheque as a mark of their regard for him, and the list of subscribers reads like a page from Burke or Debrett.

Mr Neill regarded himself primarily as a teacher of Highland dancing, and the Scotch (Foursome) Reel, the Reel of Tulloch, and (in more recent years) the Eightsome Reel figured prominently in his lessons. In spite of this, however, he wore a kilt whilst teaching only when he gave private lessons at Blair Castle, and his normal dress for his classes consisted of black jacket and black striped trousers, and patent leather dancing shoes of the usual evening type. Never at any time did he wear Highland dancing shoes, nor were these worn by his pupils. Most of his girl pupils wore patent leather slippers fastened with a strap round the ankle and with a heel about one inch high, while most of the men and boys at his classes wore patent leather dancing shoes similar to his own.

We have already mentioned the Reels which Mr Neill taught. He had a quite small repertoire of Country Dances, typical of that of a dancing-teacher in a near-Highland area—Petronella, Flowers of Edinburgh, Triumph, Haymakers Jig, Rory O'More, Strip the Willow, Brown's Reel (i.e. Duke of Perth), Speed the Plough, and Jacky Tar. His repertoire of social dances included also the Quadrilles, the Lancers, Waltz Cotillion, La Russe, La Tempête, Dashing White Sergeant, and the Waltz Country Dance.

Like Mr Adamson, he taught all his pupils the normal etiquette of the ballroom, and he also taught 'callisthenics'. The latter subject was an inheritance from the Lowes, and included a marching drill exercise and various physical exercises.

All Mr Neill's series of classes ended with a 'finishing assembly'. Here, for instance, is a newspaper account of one of his finishing assemblies at Airlie in 1893.

'Mr Neill's pupils held their finishing assembly at Mains of Airlie. . . . A long list of dances and exercises was performed to the delight of a large number of parents and friends. The boys danced the Highland Fling and Reel with great spirit, and in capital time. Four girls were very much admired by their tripping of the 'Seann Triubhais', but the principal feature in the programme, we think, was the marching drill exercise, which was most efficiently performed, the various movements being done with great precision. The juveniles finished about eight o'clock, when Mr Neill announced that the cake presented by the Dowager-Countess of Airlie in honour of the birth of an heir to the Airlie estates would be distributed amongst them. . . . The youngsters were then served with refreshments, and after a brief interval dancing was resumed, and joined in by the adult pupils and friends.'

James Neill's successor in Angus and Perthshire was 'Dancie' Reid of Newtyle. 'Dancie' Reid, who taught from about 1890 until his death in 1942, was principally a pupil of James Neill, though he had also taken lessons from a teacher in Dundee, possibly David Anderson. He made his headquarters in Newtyle, and held classes throughout a territory bounded roughly by Kirriemuir and Forfar to the north, by Auchter-house and Fowlis to the south, by Pitlochry and Blair Atholl to the west, and by the sea to the east. Although part of this territory was shared with Mr Neill until the latter's retirement, the two teachers were not in serious competition with each other for there was ample business for both. Like Mr Adamson and Mr Neill, 'Dancie' Reid used a bicycle to reach his classes in his younger days, though latterly he used a car. Whenever possible, he returned home each night after his classes.

Mr Reid taught in the towns in his territory in the winter and in the country districts in the summer, and had a definite annual round of places in which he held classes. In any particular place his classes con-sisted of two meetings a week for six weeks, and he normally ran classes in two different places at the one time. His usual practice was to hold his dancing classes on the first four evenings of each week, and then on Friday evenings he took engagements to play for private or public dances, either by himself or with an orchestra which he led, while on Saturdays he gave lessons on the violin. He was famous as a player of reels and strathspeys, and had won the Gold Medal for fiddle-playing at the Highland Mod.

Mr Reid's dancing-classes were divided into two sessions, one for schoolchildren from 4 p.m. to 6 p.m., the other for adults (i.e. those who had left school) from 8 p.m. to 10 p.m. His charge was 7s. 6d. for the twelve nights—this included admission to the 'finishing ball' which was held on the twelfth night. If more than two children in a family attended, only the first two paid, and the rest were admitted free.

Mr Reid taught four Reels, namely the Scotch (Foursome) Reel, the Reel of Tulloch, the Eightsome Reel, and the Sixteensome Reel. The Country Dances in his repertoire included all those taught by Mr Neill, and also Blue Bonnets, Meg Merrilees, Scottish Reform, The Rock and the Wee Pickle Tow, Torryburn Lasses, and My Love She's But a Lassie Yet. In addition to these Reels and Country Dances he also taught the Quadrilles, the Lancers, La Russe, Circassian Circle, Waltz Country Dance, Dashing White Sergeant, Ninepins, and many Circle Dances. He also taught various step-dances in his general classes—these were available to all his pupils without extra charge.

Like Mr Adamson and Mr Neill, Mr Reid taught the normal etiquette of the ballroom, and he also taught the children 'callisthenics', exactly as did Mr Neill. In all his teaching he was very strict, and a pupil who misbehaved was liable to receive a rap on the head with the fiddle bow.

His 'finishing balls', for which his orchestra provided the music, were held on the last night of the set of classes, the children's ball from 7 p.m. to 9 p.m., and the adults' ball from 9 p.m. until midnight. The children's parents were sent invitations to the children's ball, and seats were provided for them round the hall. When the parents were gathered, the girls entered from one side and the boys from the other, each child curtsying or bowing before sitting down, and the programme then commenced with 'callisthenics'. After this the dancing began, the first dance usually being a Polka or some other Circle Dance; each boy formally requested the dance from one of the girls, and all the children took part. After the opening dance, eight or nine of the children usually performed a step-dance, possibly the Highland Fling (of which Mr Reid had several different versions), and then followed several general dances, then another step-dance, perhaps the Skirt Dance or the Skipping Rope Dance, and so on. The programme ended with a Maypole Dance in which the children plaited ribbons round a maypole—there were occasionally some 'awfu' mix-ups' in this, with Mr Reid 'nearly tearing his hair' (53).

Some of the parents stayed to watch (and probably take part in) the adults' ball. This was purely a social dance, though sometimes Mr Reid and his daughter gave exhibitions of the latest new dances. His pupils could bring their own partners to the ball, though those who did not belong to the class were charged a small fee for admission.

Mr Reid insisted that the men should wear patent leather evening shoes for all his classes, and for the ball white gloves were also necessary.

Another teacher of similar type to Mr Adamson and Mr Neill was Mr George Maxwell, who taught throughout East Lothian from about 1880 until about 1914. His headquarters were in the vicinity of Haddington, and in Haddington itself he taught once weekly from October to Easter, his fee for the classes being one pound. Outside Haddington his normal classes consisted of one meeting a week for twelve weeks, followed by a final ball, and here his fee for the set of classes was ten shillings. Like most of the old country dancing-masters, he was a fiddler and could both play and dance simultaneously.

Mr Maxwell's repertoire of Country Dances included Petronella, Flowers of Edinburgh, Triumph, Haymakers Jig, Rory O'More, Strip the Willow and Drops of Brandy (these have the same figures, but Strip the Willow is danced to a 6/8 tune and Drops of Brandy to a schottische), Glasgow Highlanders, Cumberland Reel, Corn Rigs, Merry Lads of Glasgow, and Royal Albert. He also taught the usual Reels, Square Dances, and Circle Dances, together with a few of the miscellaneous dances.

There were also teachers in Lanarkshire and Ayrshire of similar type to Mr Adamson and Mr Neill, for instance the Muir family in Motherwell, Mr Blackley in Lanark, and the Wallace family in the Kilmarnock district.

The Muir family served the districts of Motherwell, Hamilton, Blantyre, Belshill, Wishaw, Carluke, and Strathaven. The first member of the family to take up the profession of dancing-teacher was John (Paddy) Muir. Born about the year 1837, he was brought up in Maybole in Ayrshire, and spent some time in America before he set up in business in Motherwell as a dancing-teacher. His principal classes were in Motherwell and Wishaw, and in each of these places he held two sets of classes every year, each set consisting of one class a week from October until April or May. The class-nights were divided into two sessions, one for 'juveniles' from 5.30 p.m. to 7.30 p.m., the other for 'adults' from 8 p.m. to 10 p.m., and normally he had about forty children and about fifty adults in each class. In addition to his regular classes in Motherwell and Wishaw, John Muir held classes each winter in two of the smaller towns in his district. In each of these towns he would teach once a week for three months—from October to Christmas in the one, and from the New Year to Easter in the other.

The social dances in John Muir's repertoire included the usual Reels and Square and Circle Dances, while the Country Dances which he taught included Petronella, Flowers of Edinburgh, Triumph, Haymakers Jig, Pease Strae, Meg Merrilees, Paddy O'Rafferty, St Patrick's Day, and Cumberland Reel. He also taught the usual Highland step-dances, and a number of 'fancy dances' for children, including some of his own composition.

John Muir's son, James D. Muir, and two of his daughters, followed him in his profession of dancing-teacher. They began by assisting him in his classes and then took over from him when he retired about the year 1895, some five years before his death. It is pleasing to record that James Muir's son, Mr Jack Muir, has carried on the family business, and is now teaching dancing in Motherwell.

Mr Blackley of Lanark, better known as 'Professor' Blackley, was a pupil of John Muir. He began to teach about 1880, and established a very big connection in Lanarkshire and Dumfriesshire. For the first part of each winter, from October until the New Year, he ran five or six sets of weekly classes in different places in Lanarkshire, while after the New Year he held a weekly class in Lanark for about eight weeks, and also four sets of weekly classes in Dumfriesshire, in Dumfries, Annan, Lockerbie, and Kettleholm. These latter four sets of classes lasted until Easter, and he travelled down to Dumfriesshire for them each Monday, returning home to Lanark on the Friday. These were the regular classes which he gave every year, and in addition he also held classes in the spring and early summer in various other districts of Lanarkshire and Ayrshire, such as Carmichael, Wanlockhead, and Leadhills. After about 1920, his daughters assisted him in his classes, and sometimes took classes on their own.

Mr Blackley died in 1942 at the age of 83. He continued to hold some classes up to a month before his death, but for the last few years of his life the major part of his practice was handled by his daughters. After his death his daughters carried on his business, and they still have a thriving practice in Lanark.

The Country Dances which Mr Blackley taught in his early days included Petronella, Flowers of Edinburgh, Triumph, Haymakers Jig, Rory O'More, Blue Bonnets, Pease Strae, Glasgow Highlanders, Paddy O'Rafferty, Soldier's Joy, St Patrick's Day, The Rock and the Wee Pickle Tow, Corn Rigs, Queen's Welcome, Highland Laddie, Linton Ploughman, and Merry Lads of Ayr (the last mainly in Dumfriesshire). He also taught the Foursome Reel and Reel of Tulloch, and various Square and Circle Dances, including La Russe. He composed a number of Circle Dances, of which the best known was the Baden-Powell Schottische. This last dance earned him a special award from the British Association of Teachers of Dancing, an association of which he was an early member.

The Wallace family of Kilmarnock is yet another family where the profession of dancing-teacher has been passed on from one generation to another. The first of the family whom we know to have practised as a dancing-teacher is Joseph Wallace the elder, who taught in the countryside just south of Kilmarnock. He died about 1900, and we know nothing of his teaching. His son, also named Joseph, was born in 1856 and began his career as a dancing-teacher in the Riccalton district. At the age of 20 he moved into Kilmarnock, and thereafter he taught in Kilmarnock itself and throughout the surrounding districts.

The younger Joseph Wallace had a large and unusual repertoire of Country Dances, including Petronella, Flowers of Edinburgh, Triumph, Haymakers Jig, Glasgow Highlanders, Duke of Perth and Pease Strae (these had the same figures, but were performed to different tunes), Meg Merrilees, Torryburn Lasses, Jessie's Favourite, The Thistle, Quadrille Country Dance, Queen Victoria, Royal Albert, Dandy Jim, Bonnie Dundee, Football Favourite (one of David Anderson's compositions), and Stewarton Lasses. The last was composed by Joseph Wallace's uncle, Sandy Porter, who was also a dancing-teacher around Kilmarnock; it went under several names, including Kilmarnock Lasses and Troon Lasses.

In addition to his normal classes, the younger Joseph Wallace held special classes for those who wished to specialize in the dancing of Reels. The Reels which he taught in these special classes consisted only of the Foursome and Eightsome Reels and the Reel of Tulloch, but for these three dances he taught some forty different setting steps.

The younger Joseph Wallace died in 1932, but here again the family business has been carried on, for his daughter Miss Elizabeth Wallace is very well known today as a dancing-teacher.

Apart from the numerous teachers who made their headquarters in some particular place, there were several teachers who seem to have been truly itinerant. One of these was a Mr MacDougall, who taught in the West Highlands and on several of the islands from at least 1890 onwards—we have records of his classes from Moidart, Arisaig, Morar, Mallaig, Skye, Tornapress (near Lochcarron), South Uist, and the Orkney island of South Ronaldshay. Mr MacDougall was an Argyll-shire man, born about 1850, and he taught until about 1912, when he retired to live in Fort William. He was a fiddler as well as a dancing-teacher, and in Orkney at least gave lessons on the violin.

Mr MacDougall had no fixed system for his classes, but varied them to meet local circumstances. For instance, in two successive years about 1898–9 he held classes in Glenuig and Roshven in Moidart, and on each occasion he stayed for four weeks, teaching in the two places on alternate nights. He lodged in each place on the night of his class there, and walked backwards and forwards between them during the daytime. In both places he gave special lessons in step-dancing for half an hour before his general class began. He charged six shillings for the general class for the month, and four shillings for each step-dance taught in the special classes.

Another teacher who seems to have been truly itinerant was 'Professor' R. F. Buck, who taught in the Border Counties from at least 1895 until shortly before the Second World War. Most of his teaching was done in Roxburghshire, Berwickshire, Selkirkshire, and Peebleshire, but he also travelled as far north as Pencaitland in East Lothian and as far west as Wigtownshire. He usually stayed in one village for ten weeks, holding classes there on two evenings a week, and at the same time he would also teach in neighbouring villages on the other evenings of the week, using a bicycle to return each night to his temporary base. On other occasions he made a round of three classes and stayed each night in the place where he held his class—for instance, nearly every year he held classes concurrently in Hawick, Lilliesleaf, and Selkirk, teaching in Hawick on Mondays and Thursdays, in Lilliesleaf on Tuesdays and Fridays, and in Selkirk on Wednesdays and Saturdays.

In Selkirk and Hawick he taught the usual Reels, Square Dances, and Circle Dances, and a few of the commoner Country Dances. In country districts, on the other hand, he included many more Country Dances in his lessons, in particular, Blue Bonnets, Cumberland Reel, Duke of Perth, Meg Merrilees, Corn Rigs, Speed the Plough, Roxburgh Castle, Bottom of the Punchbowl, Jessie's Hornpipe, Rifleman, and Duchess of Gordon. In his early years he also taught a further set of Quadrilles, the Land of Burns Quadrilles, and the Old Lancers, a single-figure Quadrille quite different from the ordinary Lancers.

In his classes generally, Mr Buck always tried to pair off the better dancers with the beginners, so that his pupils virtually taught each other. He also held the view that it was unnecessary to teach more than half a dozen or so Country Dances, because his pupils could easily learn all the other Country Dances in his repertoire just by taking part in them. Accordingly, he included in his lessons a number of Country Dances which he did not teach formally; there were always some former pupils present at his classes, and for these particular dances he made them take the top places in the sets, so that the newer pupils learnt the dances simply by watching the top couples. Mr Buck also introduced at his finishing balls further Country Dances which had not been performed in his lessons.

In his early days as a dancing-teacher, Mr Buck took lessons from Mr D. G. MacLennan of Edinburgh. However, these lessons were only to improve his own dancing, for he had already acquired his repertoire of

Country Dances before this, presumably from someone with a wide knowledge of the dances peculiar to the Borders.

We have been unable to trace a full-time teacher in the Border counties prior to Mr Buck, but we have records of a number of part-time teachers who taught there before Mr Buck's time.

At the head of Ettrick there was Mr James Laidlaw, who lived with his brother-in-law at Potburn Farm. Mr Laidlaw had a wasted right arm, but he could still hold a fiddle bow and was both a gifted fiddler and an excellent teacher of dancing. His repertoire included many uncommon Country Dances, such as Bottom of the Punchbowl, Falkland Beauty, Rocks of Gibraltar, Duchess of Gordon, Keep the Country, and The Lover's Knot, and he taught most of these dances, together with the usual Reels, Square Dances, and Circle Dances, in various classes in Ettrick from about 1875 to about 1890. The Lover's Knot and Keep the Country were regarded as rather difficult dances and may not have been taught in his general classes, but he taught them to his brother-in-law's family and to various friends. He died between 1890 and 1895, at the age of about 50 or 55.

Another part-time teacher who taught in the Borders was a Mr Fletcher, a shoemaker in Pathhead. Mr Fletcher held classes in Oxton in West Berwickshire in 1892 and 1894, his session being two nights a week for six weeks.[1] Unlike the majority of the country dancing-masters, he was not a musician, and had to hire the local fiddler to play for his classes. His repertoire included two unusual Country Dances, Loch Erichtside and My Love She's But a Lassie Yet, and also one of the less common of the miscellaneous dances, La Tempête.

One teacher who seems to have differed from the norm was Scott Skinner, who was a professional dancing-master before he achieved fame as a fiddler. He taught in the North-east, and had a repertoire typical of that region, containing relatively few Country Dances. It did, however, include a longways progressive Country Dance called Dashing White Sergeant.

Scott Skinner stopped teaching about 1885, and we have a record of only one of his schools, at Rothes, where he stayed for four weeks, teaching six evenings a week. His classes on Mondays, Wednesdays, and Fridays were for the well-to-do and his fee for these was a guinea for the four weeks. For the classes on the other nights, which were attended by the ordinary working people of the district, his fee was only 7s. 6d. Both sets of pupils, however, were taught exactly the same set of dances.

Our informant, Mr David Grant, a lad of 17 at the time, was coach-

[1] He probably taught elsewhere, but we have no other records of his classes.

24

man to an advocate in Elgin and drove his employer's family to the guinea classes. His employer paid for him to attend these classes, but when Mr Grant first entered the room where the classes were held, Scott Skinner approached him and suggested that perhaps he would be more at home on the other evenings. However, when Scott Skinner learnt that his fee was being paid by his employer, Mr Grant was accepted without further demur. By attending the guinea classes, Mr Grant was put to the expense of obtaining white gloves—these would not have been essential for the classes on the other evenings.

Scott Skinner was rather hasty-tempered, and, like 'Dancie' Reid, did not hesitate to rap an erring pupil on the head with his fiddle bow. He was completely democratic in this—the guinea pupils were just as likely to receive a rap as the seven and sixpenny pupils.

All the dancing-teachers of whom we have records taught their pupils the normal etiquette of the ballroom, no matter whether their classes were held in the grandest assembly-room or an earthen-floored barn. The girls were taught how to curtsy, and the men and boys were taught how to bow, how to ask a girl to dance with them, and how to escort her back to her seat at the end of a dance. As one old man put it, 'ye had to be verra mannerly when lifting your pairtner, no' likes as if ye were drawing a hog oot o' a ditch' (82). And as another told us, 'after the dance you had to take your partner back to her seat, no' throw her away like a hot potato' (64).

In spite of such strictness, these old dancing-teachers do not seem to have put great emphasis on technique. They regarded it as more important to learn the figures of the dances, and, whilst they taught steps, they were not greatly worried if their pupils did not attain great precision or polish. For instance, one of our informants who attended a good many of Mr Buck's classes told us that 'Mr Buck wasna' fussy as long as you were there to take your place' (16). Again, Mr Blackley of Lanark taught the travelling step for Country Dances as simply 'hop, step, close behind, and step'; he did not specify the exact position in which the one foot closed behind the other 'and was quite pleased if you got it behind, without worrying exactly where it was' (8). The same was true of James Muir of Motherwell. When we asked his son, Mr Jack Muir, about this, Mr Muir pointed out that in the old days there was no need to be very precise, for there were no medal tests or competitions in ballroom dancing. Indeed, when one remembers that these teachers frequently had classes of a hundred or more pupils, and that they had at their disposal only a dozen or so evenings in which to teach a fair selection of Reels, Country Dances, Square Dances, and Circle Dances (and often step-dances as well), one could not have expected them to attempt to aim at a high standard of individual performance in the steps.

Some of the professional dancing-teachers published little pocket *aides-mémoire* containing instructions for all the common dances of the day. David Anderson of Dundee, for instance, published a series of very complete ballroom guides, the earliest which we have been able to trace being entitled *D. Anderson's Ballroom Guide. With full tuition in the art of dancing without the use of French terms* (Dundee, c. 1886). However, this was itself a 'New, Enlarged, and Complete Edition', so that presumably there was an earlier edition. There were also two later editions published about 1891 and 1894, each containing a little fresh material. About 1899, Anderson revised the book more thoroughly, and published it under the title *The Universal Ball-room and Solo Dance Guide*, and this also ran into two further editions, published about 1900 and 1902, both with fresh material added. The 1886 edition of David Anderson's *Ballroom Guide* contains descriptions of the Scotch Reel and Reel of Tulloch, an early version of the Eightsome Reel, sixty-four Country Dances, fifteen Square Dances, fourteen Circle Dances, and a number of dances of miscellaneous types. In subsequent editions a few of the Square Dances are omitted, but in compensation further Country Dances and Circle Dances are added.[1]

Other teachers who published small ballroom guides of this type were William Smith of Inverness (224; c. 1889), J. N. MacLeod of Kirkcaldy (225; 1897), Scott Skinner (229; c. 1905), A. C. Mitchell of Aberdeen (230; c. 1905), and William Robertson, who taught around Brechin (231; c. 1905). Yet other teachers published books dealing with particular aspects of dancing; for instance W. Grahamsley Atkinson of Edinburgh published in 1900 an excellent book on Reels (226), while Graham MacNeilage of Alloa and another teacher, D. R. MacKenzie, both published books containing descriptions of the Eightsome Reel and some step-dances (227, 232). One very valuable work, by James Orr Robertson of Glasgow, occurs at the end of Kerr's *Collection of Reels and Strathspeys* (228; c. 1900). Here, within the compass of a few pages, are given very clear and precise descriptions of eighteen Country Dances with their appropriate steps. As a guide to the style of the professional dancing-teachers of about 1900, this work can hardly be bettered.

All these books were simply the continuation of a long series of

[1] We should add here that the presence of a particular dance in Anderson's books does not necessarily indicate that he ever taught that dance in his classes, for he endeavoured to make these books as encyclopaedic as possible (4).

similar ballroom guides published by dancing-teachers in Scotland during the nineteenth century. The study of these, however, would take us beyond the period of living memory, and we shall not discuss them here.

The various ballroom guides mentioned above were occasionally the means by which a dance spread from one place to another. As an example of this, we may cite The Royal Visit, a Country Dance composed by David Anderson of Dundee. This dance was performed for several years on the island of South Uist, where it had been taught by someone who had learnt it from a copy of Anderson's *Universal Guide* sent to him by a friend in Fife (40). However, on the whole these ballroom guides had very little effect on local repertoires, for most people seem to have used them as *aides-mémoire* for dances already learnt, rather than as sources from which to learn new dances. Before the First World War, the dissemination of a particular dance throughout a region was almost entirely a matter of oral transmission, and some dances, for example Rory O'More and Strip the Willow, achieved an extraordinarily widespread distribution well before their first appearance in print.[1] And in the oral transmission of dances, there can be no doubt that the professional dancing-masters played by far the major part.

It must be stressed that professional dancing-teachers serving all classes of society have existed throughout Scotland since at least about 1770. They were numerous enough in Edinburgh at about that time to cause Major Edward Topham, an English soldier stationed there, to write:

'I do not know any place in the world where dancing is made so necessary a part of polite education as in Edinburgh. For the number of inhabitants I suppose there are more Dancing-masters than in any other city, who gain large fortunes, though they instruct on very moderate terms, from the number of scholars who constantly attend them. In general they may be said to be very good ones, as well those of their own Country as Foreigners from most of the polite parts of Europe' (249; 1776).

[1] So far as we know, Rory O'More was first published in the 1894 edition of David Anderson's *Ballroom Guide*, yet before this date we have records of it from Perthshire (c. 1885), Kincardineshire (c. 1890), Aberdeenshire (c. 1890), Inverness-shire (c. 1891), Mainland of Orkney (c. 1888), and the islands of Flotta (c. 1891) and Rousay (c. 1892). Again, Strip the Willow was first published in Kerr's *Collection*, c. 1900, but we have records of it prior to this date from Perthshire (c. 1885), Kincardineshire (c. 1890), Aberdeenshire (c. 1890), Banffshire (c. 1895), Inverness-shire (c. 1891), Mull (c. 1893), Benbecula (c. 1891), Mainland of Orkney (c. 1898), and Rousay (c. 1892).

Such dancing-teachers were not restricted only to Edinburgh. Robert Burns attended a dancing school in Alloway in 1776, and Dr Currie, the biographer of Burns, gives a description of such a school which is clearly drawn from Currie's own experience, probably from the time of his youth in Dumfriesshire, c. 1773 (254):

'That dancing should also be very generally a part of the education of the Scotish peasantry, will surprise those . . . who reflect on the rigid spirit of Calvinism with which the nation is so deeply affected. . . . The winter is . . . the season when they acquire dancing. . . . They are taught to dance by persons generally of their own number, many of whom work at daily labour during the summer months. The school is usually a barn, and the arena for the performers is generally a clay floor. The dome is lighted by candles stuck in one end of a cloven stick, the other end of which is thrust into the wall. Reels, strathspeys, country-dances, and hornpipes, are here practised. The jig so much in favour among the English peasantry, has no place among them. The attachment of the people of Scotland of every rank, and particularly of the peasantry, to this amusement, is very great. After the labours of the day are over, young men and women walk many miles, in the cold and dreary nights of winter, to these country dancing-schools; and the instant that the violin sounds a Scotish air, fatigue seems to vanish. . . .'

An even better description of a country dancing-school has been left to us by MacTaggart in *The Scottish Gallovidian Encyclopedia* (263; 1824). This description probably refers to MacTaggart's native country-side round Kirkcudbright, about the year 1820:[1]

'A *light heel'd souter*[2] is generally the dancing dominie; he fixes on a barn in some *clauchan* to show forth in; he can both fiddle and dance, at the same time; he can cut double quick time, and *trible Bob Major*; he fixes on, and publishes abroad when his *trial night* is to come on, so the young folk in the neighbourhood doff their *clogs*, and put on their *kirk-shoon*, these being their *dancing-pumps*; off they go to the trial, which, if it be a good turn-out, he tries no more, but begins teaching directly; if not, he has a second, and even a *third* trial; . . .

'Commonly the first step dancing masters teach their pupils . . . [is] Peter a Dick's Peatstack, . . . performed by giving three *flegs*[3] with the feet, and two stamps with the heel alternately; . . . the noise the feet

---

[1] We have inverted the order of the first two paragraphs in this quotation. In all other respects the quotation is as in the original.

[2] Shoemaker.

[3] *Fleg*, a swinging blow with the foot (MacTaggart, op. cit.).

make seems to speak . . . *Peter a Dick, Peter a Dick, Peter a Dick's Peat-stack*. . . . When the scholars become tolerable at *beetling it*, they are next taught to fleup[1] through the side-step; then *Jack on the Green, Shawin-trewse*, and other *hornpipes*, with the *Highland Fling*, mayhap; these dances are all got pretty well by the feet in the *first month*, with sketches of *foursome*, eightsome reels and some country dances; but if the scholars attend the *fortnight* again of another *month*, they proceed at great length into the labyrinths of the art.

'They learn the "Flowers of Edinburgh", mayhap; *Sweden* and *Belile's Marches*, with other hornpipes, and country dances many; such as *Yillwife and her Barrles—Mary Grey—The Wun that shook the barley*, &c. with the famous *Bumpkin Brawley*; yes, and they will even dare, some times to imitate our Continental neighbours over the water, in their *waltzing, alimanging*, and *Cotillion trade*; ay, and be up with the Spaniards too, in their *quadrilles, borellos*, and *falderalloes* of nonsense; so out-taught, they become fit to attend *house-heatings, volunteer* and *masonic-balls*, and what not.'

It is interesting to note that the system followed by MacTaggart's 'light-heel'd souter', with a preliminary 'trial night', was still used within living memory by two dancing-teachers in Galloway, Peter Marshall of Kirkpatrick Durham, and his pupil Thomas Shanks.

Peter Marshall was born about 1860 and taught dancing from about 1880 until about 1923, covering Kirkcudbrightshire, Wigtownshire, and parts of Dumfriesshire. He died at some time before 1930.

In any particular place where he proposed to hold classes, Mr Marshall first had a 'trial night', in the form of a free dance for the young people of the neighbourhood.[2] This was advertised—by notices in the local shops—as a preliminary to the proposed classes. During this free dance, Mr Marshall would go round all those present and take the names of those who wished to attend his classes, and if he obtained sufficient names to make the classes worth while he would begin to teach on the following night. He would have already made a provisional booking of the local hall—or of a suitable substitute—and would either confirm or cancel this booking when he knew the result of his trial night. Usually he tried to obtain the use of the hall for five nights a week for six weeks, though he might, of course, have to make way for some other event. In any case, where his trial night was successful he would teach for thirty nights, the last night of all being the 'final ball'. If he did not obtain enough names to make the classes in that place worth while, he simply

[1] *Fleups*, broad feet (MacTaggart, op. cit.).
[2] Mr Marshall himself did not use the term 'trial night'.

went elsewhere and tried again. The number of pupils required for a class naturally depended on his expenses for the hall and his lodgings.

This same system was also followed by Mr Marshall's pupil Thomas Shanks, who held classes in Wigtownshire for some years between about 1910 and 1930.

The dancing-master's 'finishing ball' also goes back to at least 1770. Topham wrote that 'dancing-masters balls' were in Edinburgh

'as . . . much frequented, and in general more crowded than the . . . public assemblies. . . . You know 'tis a custom in London for some of the principal Dancing-masters to have balls [to exhibit their scholars to the public] . . ., but here it is a general thing, from the one most in vogue, to the humble teacher of a reel to the drone of a bagpipe. Each has his ball . . . in the Assembly-room; where each endeavours to show his own excellence and skill as a master, by the execution and performance of his scholars. It is incredible the pleasure and satisfaction the inhabitants of this City take in this diversion. They seem to enjoy it much more than dancing themselves' (249).

Here again, there was no essential difference between the teachers in Edinburgh and those in the remote country districts. Colonel Thornton, an Englishman who toured the Highlands about the year 1804, has left us the following description of a dancing-master's ball held at an inn in Dalmally where he was staying (256).

'They were dancing a country-dance when we entered. The company consisted of about fourteen couple, who all danced the true *Glen Orgue kick*. I have observed, that every district of the Highlands has some peculiar cut; and they all shuffle in such a manner as to make the noise of their feet keep exact time. Though this is not the fashionable style of dancing, yet, with such dancers, it had not a bad effect.

'But I shall never forget the arrogance of the master; his mode of marshaling his troops, his directions, and other maneouvres, were truly ridiculous; he felt himself greater than any adjutant disciplining his men, and managed them much in the same manner.'

However, Colonel Thornton approved in principle: '. . . it gave me great pleasure to see these poor people as innocently amused, and to observe with what spirit they danced, after the fatigues of the day, which evidently proved the strong inclination the Highlanders have for this favourite amusement. How much more rational is this conduct than that of our labourers in England, who, in their way, would be intoxicated and riotous'.

CHAPTER II

Of the Dancers, and the Occasions
When They Danced

I n the days before the First World War, public and private dances of
one sort or another played a more significant part in social life than
they do today, for they provided almost the only social occasions on
which young people of both sexes could mix freely. In those days, too,
such dances were more of an event than they are at present, for they
took place rather less frequently than nowadays, and few alternative
forms of public entertainment existed.

In most towns there were usually public dances at least once a fortnight throughout the winter, and these would be attended not only by
the townspeople but also by the people from the surrounding countryside. The majority of the country people would have to walk or cycle in
to the dances, though a few might have their own pony and trap, or
would hire one for the occasion. Country buses were, of course, nonexistent in those days, and people thought nothing of walking five miles
or more for an evening's entertainment.

In the smaller country towns, where public dances were not too
plentiful, this process was also often reversed, for not only would the
people from the surrounding countryside come in to the dances in the
town, but the townspeople would also go out to the dances in the
nearby villages. The town of Douglas in Lanarkshire may be quoted
here as typical of many of the smaller country towns of south-west
Scotland. Set in a good arable and dairy farming district which is dotted
with small mining villages, it serves as a centre for both the agricultural
and mining communities around it. Before 1914, public dances were
held in Douglas once a fortnight or so throughout the winter, and these
were attended not only by Douglas people but also by people from the
neighbouring farms and villages. The younger people in Douglas, in
addition to attending the dances in the town, also attended those in the
villages round Douglas, and made light of the four or five miles walk to

these places. Moreover, not only would they walk to one of these villages and dance there until 5 a.m., but on the way home they would stop and dance at the various crossroads, eventually arriving home just in time to have breakfast and go to work (10, 80).

In more remote country districts, as, for example, in the Lowland sheep country, the dances in the nearest towns were beyond the reach of all but the most enthusiastic dancers, and most people were limited to the dances held in the villages within walking distance (or perhaps cycling distance) of their homes. As in the neighbourhood of the towns, a five mile walk to a dance was not regarded as excessive, and here people would not necessarily keep to the roads, but would just as cheerfully walk five miles over a rough hill track to a dance in some neighbouring valley.

In spite of the fact that the people in these more remote country districts were almost wholly reliant on the entertainment provided locally, the number of public dances held in any one place in these districts was usually small. The upper part of Ettrick furnishes a good example here. The valley of Ettrick stretches south-west from Selkirk for some twenty-three miles, and the only place in the upper half of the valley where public dances were held was Ettrick Kirk, about six miles from the top of the valley. Before about 1905, when the present hall at Ettrick Kirk was built, the public dances there were held in the school hall, and this was let for only one dance a year, the Curling Club Ball. This Curling Club Ball was a 'real ball' to which one could not go without a partner, and the standard of etiquette and behaviour at it was as strict as that taught by the country dancing-masters. In addition to this one ball, there were also two or three concerts a year in the school hall, and after each of these there would be informal dancing until 2 or 3 a.m.

For the people in the upper part of Ettrick, the nearest places other than Ettrick Kirk where public dances were held were St Mary's Loch in Yarrow, the school at Roundstonefoot on Moffat Water, and Eskdalemuir on the White Esk (see the map below). All these places had their one or two public dances a year, and the younger people from the upper part of Ettrick regularly walked over the hills—four miles or more—to attend these dances. Public dances were also held at Ettrickbridge End in the lower part of Ettrick, but these were just too far away for the people in the upper part of the valley to attend unless some conveyance was available (62, 64).

In districts such as this, public dances were normally arranged at the time of the full moon, so that people could see their way over the hills; this had, of course, some effect in limiting the number of dances which could be held each winter. The time of the full moon was also the time for a much more informal type of dancing which took place in these districts, for on moonlit nights there would sometimes be dancing out of doors. For example, in the Tima valley, which runs down into Ettrick at Ettrick Kirk, the shepherds and farm girls used to dance in the road-way beside the river (66).

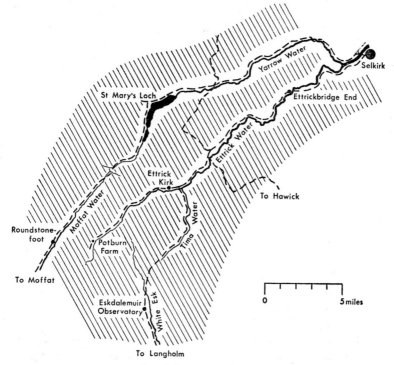

Ettrick and the surrounding district
(Continuous lines represent the principal rivers, dotted lines represent roads, and the shaded regions represent hilly land)

Some of the events which provided opportunities for social dancing in the old days, such as the 'hiring fairs' which were held in the Lowland counties, are now things of the past.

Until some time between the two World Wars, most Lowland farm-workers, both men and women, were on yearly or half-yearly engage-ments, and these engagements were made at the hiring fairs (or 'feeing fairs') in the various country towns. At these fairs, the business of hiring was conducted in the streets, and farmers in search of staff mingled with farm-workers in search of jobs until both were suited. The hiring fairs were also fairs in the more conventional sense, for the crowds provided a ready market for travelling salesmen, and the streets were lined with stalls selling goods of all kinds.

The hiring fairs were just as much social gatherings as business events, and almost invariably there was public dancing in one of the local halls throughout the day of the fair. For instance, at the hiring fairs at Biggar in Lanarkshire about 1920, there was a dance in one of the local halls which began at 3 p.m. and went on until 4 a.m., with a short break for tea. The charge for this dance was half a crown, and the doorkeeper stamped the 'ticket of admission' on the dancers' hands with a rubber stamp. In order that men and girls who had not secured engagements could enliven their search for a job with an occasional dance, the dancers were allowed to leave the hall and come back in again as often as they pleased, with no extra charge. Since the 'tickets' were obviously non-transferable, there were no difficulties over people lending their tickets to others. Most of the younger men and girls among the farm-workers spent some time at this dance during the day, as did also some of the townspeople. If a man had several dances with a girl, custom demanded that he should present her with 'her fairin'', a box of sweets purchased from one of the sweet stalls, and by the end of the evening some of the girls had four or five such boxes as evidence of their popularity (27).

In the Border counties, the dancing at the hiring fairs went on from midday until midnight, and latterly this period was divided into three sessions, for each of which the dancers paid separately. At one time in the Borders, however, the dancers were charged a penny or twopence for each dance that they took part in. For instance, at a dance at the hiring fair at Peebles, as late as 1906, the men had to pay a penny for themselves and a penny for their partners each time they took the floor —the money was collected by two men who came round with leather bags of the type used by bus-conductors. There was a special charge of twopence per person for the two longest dances, the Quadrilles and Lancers, and these were put on only if more than a certain minimum number of couples would take part (16). This system of payment was, of course, ideal for those who wished to take part in only one or two dances, but it was expensive for the more enthusiastic dancers. At the hiring fairs at Duns and Earlston, dances run on this system were known as 'Penny Reels', and there they went out of vogue about 1900 (67, 69).

'Penny Reels' were also held at the annual feeing fair at Kilmarnock in Ayrshire, and there they were run by Joseph Wallace senior, the local dancing-master. He used to hire a hall for the occasion, and he and his son played for dancing there throughout the day, charging the dancers a penny per dance.

Such dances were also known in Ayrshire in Burns' day, though the one of which we have a record took place on a race-day instead of at a hiring fair:

'There was a race at Mauchline in the end of April, and there it was customary for the young men, with little ceremony, to invite such girls as they liked off the street into a humble dancing-hall, where a fiddler had taken up his station to give them music. The payment of a penny a dance was held by the minstrel as guerdon sufficient' (269).

Another occasion for social dancing which has now fallen into disuse is the farm 'kirn' or 'harvest home'.

Before 1914, 'kirns' were held throughout the arable farming regions of Scotland to celebrate the completion of the harvest. They took place in the barns or granaries on the farms, and invariably began with a supper, after which there was dancing until the early hours of the morning.

In the Carmichael district of Lanarkshire, for example, about the year 1900 each farm had its own kirn. The farm-workers were allowed to invite their friends from nearby villages and farms, and the farmer himself would have a few personal guests from among the neighbouring farmers. Everything was completely free, the supper and other refreshments being supplied by the farmer.

The task of clearing and cleaning the granary in preparation for the kirn was undertaken by the farm-workers. If any grain was left from the previous year's harvest, it was put in sacks and stored out of the way. Then the dust and cobwebs which had accumulated since the last kirn were removed, and the granary floor, already worn smooth by the wooden scoops used for gathering up the grain, was treated with French chalk or candle scrapings to give it that extra smoothness required for dancing. Seating was provided by planks supported on chairs at each end and covered with sacking, and the big oil lamps from the byre and the stables were brought and hung from the roof beams to provide light. Usually, too, the granary was decorated with evergreens, and perhaps a cornsheaf or two.

The kirn began with supper, usually at about 7 or 8 p.m. One of the essential items in Carmichael—and in any dairy district—was curds and cream. No whisky or beer was provided, though some of the men might bring a bottle of whisky in their pocket (in those days whisky was half a crown a bottle). After everyone had eaten their fill, the remains of the supper were cleared away and the dancing began, the first dance of the evening usually being Circassian Circle. The music was normally provided by a fiddler, who sat at one end of the room, and the dancing went on, with intervals for refreshment, until 3 or 4 a.m. After the last dance, the head worker on the farm would bring the evening to a close with a short speech of thanks to the farmer (9).

This picture of a kirn is fairly typical, though there were minor variations from one district to another. In Roxburghshire and West Berwickshire, the first dance after the supper was invariably the Country Dance Triumph, led off by the farmer and the grieve's wife followed by the grieve with the farmer's wife. Here there were also various songs in the intervals between the dances. Most of the people who were called on to sing a song had one which was recognized as their particular 'party piece', and the M.C. would usually ask them to sing that particular song; from long usage, the audience were familiar with the words, and would join vigorously in any chorus. In these counties, too, a kirn usually did not finish until about 6 a.m., and the farm-workers would go home, change into their working clothes, have breakfast, and return at once to the farm to begin the day's work (23, 61, 68).

In Fife, the programme of dancing was interspersed not only with songs but also with recitations, and sometimes exhibitions of step-dancing. There were also a few games, for instance Hunt the Slipper and Forfeits, the latter involving a good deal of kissing (1).

In East Lothian, after about 1910, a kirn usually took the form of a more or less ordinary dance, and the farmer simply granted the use of his barn and gave three or four pounds to pay for the refreshments for his own workers. The 'making of the kirn' on any particular farm was entrusted to two or three of the workers there, and they would visit the neighbouring farms and invite enough people to 'fill up the kirn'. The kirn was free to all the workers on the farm where it was held, but there was a charge for outsiders; in 1914 this was about two shillings a couple, but between the two wars it rose to seven shillings or even nine shillings (78). In East Lothian kirns lingered on until about 1939, but in most other districts they died out shortly after the First World War.

The dancing at the kirns was more boisterous than that at the balls and dances in the village halls. 'Heuching' was general, and the ladies might be lifted off their feet in the basket figures of the Quadrilles and Lancers. In the Borders you would hear the leader of a set in a Country Dance cry out 'Best set in the hall', bringing a response of 'Easy' from the remainder of his set and a shout of 'Aye, efter this yin' from some-one in another set (289). Best Sunday shoes were the usual footwear, with sometimes working boots for the men. And as the evening wore on, jackets came off and the men 'linkit at it' in their shirt sleeves.

There were, of course, no kirns in the sheep-farming districts, but here their place was taken to a certain extent by 'dance-parties' held in the kitchens of the farmhouses. In the upper part of Ettrick, for example, most of the farms had at least one such party a year, when the farmer and his family entertained their friends from the neighbouring farms. Generally there was a fiddler in the house to provide the music for the party, for in the old days there was a fiddler in nearly every family in the valley (62, 64).

The programmes at the kirns often included some of the older Reels and Country Dances which were no longer performed in the nearby towns and villages. For example, the kirns held round the town of Lauder in West Berwickshire about the year 1900 included in their programmes five Country Dances, Duchess of Gordon, Mason's Apron, The Cuckoo's Nest, Dundee Reel, and Dumfries Lasses, which were not performed at the ordinary public dances in Lauder at that time (67, 70).

The reason for these differences in the dance-programmes at these various functions is to be found in the fact that, before 1914, one's dancing days ended with marriage, at least so far as attendance at public dances was concerned. This was a matter of public opinion; there was a general feeling that it was slightly improper for a woman to go to public dances after she was married, and this feeling, though vague, was nevertheless sufficiently strong to keep most married couples away from these dances. On the other hand, this suspicion of impropriety concerned only public dances, where people met solely and explicitly for the purpose of dancing, and there was nothing improper in a married couple's attending a kirn, or any other social gathering which was not explicitly for the purpose of dancing.

This distinction was in turn reflected in the dance programmes at these different kinds of gatherings. The public dances in the country towns and villages were attended only by the younger unmarried people, who tended to follow the latest changes in fashion, and accordingly the programmes at these dances tended to favour the newer Circle Dances at the expense of the older Reels and Country Dances. On the other hand, the farm kirns were attended by people of all ages, and the programmes normally included some of the older dances which had already fallen out of use in the village halls. The kirns were in fact one of the last strongholds of outmoded dances, and when the kirns disappeared after the 1914–18 War, many of the older dances disappeared with them.

So far, we have been concerned mainly with the Lowlands and the adjacent parts of the Highlands. In the more remote Highlands and the

Western Isles the situation was somewhat different, for here public dances were much less frequent than in the Lowlands, and informal dancing—at fireside ceilidhs and out of doors—seems to have been much more common.

Fireside ceilidhs in the croft houses were, of course, an integral part of the social life of the Highlands and the Western Isles. Usually in each small district there was one particular house which was the 'ceilidh house' for that district, where people were accustomed to gather during the winter evenings. There was no invitation needed; anyone who wished to come was welcome. There was, too, no knocking on the door; people just entered and quietly joined the circle by the fire, without interrupting whatever conversation was taking place at the time. 'You never knocked going to the house; you just walked in' (88). 'They just come into the house without knocking; they open the door and walk in—you never know who they are until they are on the floor' (90). Sometimes the older people played cards while the younger people sat and talked. At other times the company would gather round the fire and the man of the house would call on each person in turn to tell a story, or sing a song. The ceilidh was not only entertainment; it was the means by which the largely oral culture of the Gaelic-speaking people of Scotland was transmitted and preserved.

When young people were present at such a ceilidh there would generally be some dancing towards the end of the evening. Sometimes there would be a fiddler or piper to supply the music, or perhaps a melodeon-player. If no instrument were available, then someone would deedle the tune, or sing puirt-a-beul, the old Gaelic dancing-songs, often to the accompaniment of a Jew's harp or paper-and-comb.

In Glen Roy in Lochaber, a lady whose childhood home was the 'ceilidh house' in the township of Bohuntine recalled to us how the people of the district, both young and old, used to gather in her home in the winter evenings, usually nine or ten at a time, perhaps as many as a dozen. They would start to come in at about six o'clock—this was when it was dark at four or five o'clock in the afternoon—and six of the older people would settle down to a game of cards while the others sat and talked. About nine o'clock, some of the older people would go off to their homes, and on most nights the youngsters would bring out the melodeon and dance for an hour or so. The dances on these occasions were the Scotch Reel, the Reel of Tulloch, the Highland Schottische, and the Polka. The younger people knew other dances, for most of them had attended the classes of one or more of the dancing-teachers who taught locally, but they did not perform them at the ceilidhs (88).

In most districts of the Highlands such informal ceilidhs are now things of the past. An old lady in Benderloch—her father was a piper, and her home had been the ceilidh house of the district—sadly summed up their passing: 'now neighbours rarely drop in, and when they do, they rap on the door'.

In the Highlands and the Western Isles, there was also dancing out of doors on moonlit nights. At Milton in Glen Urquhart, for example, the usual place for such outdoor dancing was a bridge on the road by Little Milton. About the turn of the century, a noted family of pipers lived in a farm near this spot, and in the evenings one of them would come to the end of the farm steading and strike up a tune on his pipes as a signal for the young people of the village to gather at the bridge. The popular dances on these occasions were Reels, Country Dances, and Square Dances—Circle Dances were not done (92). In the Western Isles, this outdoor dancing usually took place on the roads. Each district had its favourite spot, sheltered from the prevailing winds, where the roadway was worn smooth and packed down hard by generations of dancing feet,[1] and on any fine moonlit night during the winter the young people of the neighbourhood would dance there to the music of a concertina, or perhaps to their own puirt-a-beul. In Barra, dancing on the roads was still a regular occurrence up to at least 1935 (130), while in certain parts of Lewis it still survives (118).

The ceilidhs and the outdoor gatherings in the West Highlands and the Western Isles gave young people there plenty of opportunities for social dancing. On the other hand, in these regions formally arranged public dances were very infrequent, and in sparsely populated districts people would come to a dance from a very wide area, often travelling long distances on foot. The dances in Glenuig, for instance, were attended by people from Inverailort and Kinlochmoidart;[2] those who came from Inverailort had either to travel nine miles down Loch Ailort by boat, or to walk down the lochside along a rough track, while those from Kinlochmoidart had to walk by an equally rough track along the shore of Loch Moidart and up over the head of the Glen, a distance of seven miles or more. As in the Lowland sheep country, the dances were normally arranged at the time of the full moon, so that people could see their way over the hills, and if the night happened to be wet, the dance had to be postponed for an hour while the girls' dresses were dried and pressed (95).

[1] Few roads in the Isles had a metalled surface until the Second World War.
[2] At one time the public dances in Glenuig were held in the boathouse there; in more recent years they have been held in a hall.

There were, of course, no kirns in the Highlands, but the annual ball given in some districts of the Highlands by the local laird for his tenants and neighbours was in certain respects a substitute. Here again, young and old people danced together, and again the programmes preserved many of the older Reels and Country Dances. At Lochbuie in Mull, for example, the summer balls given by the laird of Lochbuie House for his tenants have within the last few years included the Foursome and Eightsome Reels and the Country Dances Petronella, Flowers of Edinburgh, Triumph, Haymakers Jig, Rory O'More, Strip the Willow, Cumberland Reel, Glasgow Highlanders, and The Young Prince of Wales. All these Reels and Country Dances have been performed without a break at Lochbuie since at least 1900, when they were taught there by a Mr Dudgeon, a Lowland gardener at Lochbuie House who held dancing classes in his spare time (116).

Another gathering of this kind was the Kilberry Ball, held annually up to 1914 at Kilberry in Argyllshire. Archibald Campbell of Kilberry has sent us the following description of the Kilberry Balls as he knew them, from about 1887 to 1914. His description shows once more the extreme popularity of the Scotch (Foursome) Reel in the Highlands before the First World War; it gives also an extremely vivid picture of the kissing dance, which was known in Kilberry as The Bonny Lad.[1]

'The Kilberry Ball was a dance for the country people of a remote district, a unique entertainment, an invitation to which was highly prized. It was held in the granary of the home farm, within a couple of days of the old New Year (12th January).

'The party from the "big house" was in evening kilt and ladies' dinner frocks. One or two of the pipers were in the kilt. The rest of the company wore their Sunday clothes—Sunday clothes one year would be working clothes in a subsequent year. Shoes of any kind were not owned [i.e. by the men]; they wore their Sunday boots, which would subsequently become their working boots. Women, being women, would wear the lightest shoes they could afford. . . . Later on, the younger working man might turn up at the ball in a pair of patent leather shoes instead of boots . . . the girls showed increasing tendency towards evening frocks as the years went on.

'[The ball] . . . lasted from 9 p.m. till about 6 a.m., and sometimes later. There was no programme and no M.C., the principle being that the piper was in control of the proceedings, and whatever he chose to

[1] This description was sent to us in the form of two letters. We have here combined the contents of the two letters, and in consequence have had to make slight alterations in the original wording.

play the company had to dance. Sometimes there was a tune by a fiddler, but reels, polkas, and schottisches were always played on the pipes, for in those days pipers were tolerably numerous in the locality.

'There were no intervals between the dances, beyond time for one piper to replace another and to strike up a few bars to show what the dance was to be. The number of dances performed during the evening has been estimated at no fewer than sixty, and sometimes, perhaps, more. The greater number were the old Highland reel of four, usually strathspey and reel, but sometimes reel only, sometimes reel followed by strathspey, sometimes strathspey, reel, and reel of Tulloch—whatever the piper chose to play. The Reel of Tulloch was never danced unless the piper played the actual tune. The modern fashion of dancing the Reel of Tulloch to any reel tune was taboo. . . . In the 1880's the Reel of Tulloch did not seem particularly popular, and an indigenous piper never played it unless asked specially to do so. There were signs of its having been a novelty not many years back. . . .

'Other dances were a few polkas, a few schottisches, and a few country dances (e.g. Flowers of Edinburgh, Petronella, Triumph, Rory O'More, Speed the Plough), but never the Eightsome Reel, Quadrilles, and Waltzes.

'The Bonny Lad was the finale of the ball. The company sat round the walls of the ballroom, and the man selected to "lead" the dance (often a middle-aged man of some local standing) was given a handkerchief. The piper struck up The White Cockade; other pipers stood by to relieve him. The "leader" pranced round the room on a tour of selection, waving the handkerchief, sometimes indulging in such antics as dancing in front of a lady and then turning away from her. Finally, he selected a lady, spread the handkerchief in front of her and knelt on it, then invited her to kneel on it opposite to him, and, when she did so, kissed her (that lady was regarded as "the Belle of the Ball"). The two then rose to their feet, and the man marched round the room with the lady following behind him carrying the handkerchief. She in turn selected a man, and, as often as not, coyly flung the handkerchief to him. He sprang up, pursued her, flung the handkerchief round her neck, and kissed her. The lady then joined the "leader", and arm in arm with him processed round the hall, while Man No. 2 came behind waving the handkerchief. After a few antics, Man No. 2 selected a lady, and either went through the kneeling ceremony, or simply threw the handkerchief round her neck and kissed her. He then joined the procession leaving lady No. 2 to follow him carrying the handkerchief. She in turn selected a third man, and either threw him the handkerchief or perhaps, more boldly, flung it round his neck—anyhow, they kissed. Lady No. 2 then joined man No. 2 and arm in arm they made the second couple in what eventually was a long procession. Pipers relieved each other, and nothing but The White Cockade was played.

'In theory, when everyone present had been "lifted", but actually when the procession had become unwieldy and consisted of thirty or more couples, the dancers halted and joined hands in a large ring round the room, with the last person to be "lifted" standing in the middle, holding the handkerchief. This last person then selected and kissed one of the opposite sex and left the dance floor. The person kissed then did the same, and so on until either the ring was exhausted or until it was reduced to three or four couples. The piper then stopped and almost immediately struck up a final reel to which all the dancers stood up, generally (but not necessarily) partnered as in the Bonny Lad. . . . This finished the ball.

'The Bonny Lad may have taken an hour or more, and by the end, the first couple had had a long tramp on the top of several hours dancing.'

The kissing dance described above was once very widely distributed in Scotland, and went under a host of different names. In the Borders and Aberdeenshire it was known as Babbity Bowster (Bob at the Bolster), in Fife and Lanarkshire as Bee Bo Babbity, in the Highlands and Western Isles as Ruidhleadh nam Pòg (The Kissing Reel), Dannsadh nam Pòg (The Kissing Dance), Ruidhleadh Mòr (The Big Reel), Blue Bonnets, The Bonnet Dance, The Bonny Lad, Pease Strae, and The White Cockade, and in Orkney as either the Lang Reel, The Swine's Reel, The Reel of Barm, or again as Babbity Bowster. It is still occasionally performed in the Hebrides, but has not been danced elsewhere for many years. Perhaps Orkney retained it longer than anywhere else other than the Hebrides; in Flotta, for example, it was still performed until about 1925. In all districts of Scotland it was almost invariably performed as the last dance of the evening, and in some districts there was a convention that each man should escort the girl whom he selected to her home after the dance.

There were a number of variations in the kissing dance from one place to another. In the Central and West Highlands and the Western Isles, the oldest version appears to have included a few steps of the Sword Dance Gille Callum at the beginning. Before commencing his tour of selection round the room, the 'leader' twisted the handkerchief into a 'rope', then laid it on the floor and danced a few steps round and over it, just as in the Sword Dance (132). In the Central Highlands and the Western Isles this 'Sword Dance' was omitted from the kissing dance after about 1895, but in Skye and around Lochcarron it survived as an integral part of the dance until about 1905. This use of a few steps of the Sword Dance as a prelude to the kissing dance explains an obscure remark by Logan in *The Scottish Gael* (266; 1831), that in the Highlands the Sword Dance 'was usually introduced as a finale to a ball, in the manner of the "bob at the bolster" of the Lowlands'.

In most parts of the Highlands and Western Isles, the 'ring figure' in which the dancers leave the floor has not been included in the dance within living memory,[1] and the dancers simply formed up for a Scotch Reel as soon as all the people present had been 'lifted' by means of the handkerchief. The tune used for this Scotch Reel was often 'Pease Strae', a fact which explains one of the alternative names for the dance. The tune 'The White Cockade' was invariably used for the processional part, and this explains yet another of the alternative names.

In Barra and South Uist the kissing dance was always performed to the pipes, and, when the couples kissed, the piper would play the phrase 'pòg an toiseach' ('kiss first') several times. Sometimes, when the piper

felt that a couple had been somewhat perfunctory over their kiss, he would repeat the phrase until they gave each other a kiss which satisfied his standards of thoroughness.

Outside the Highlands there was no 'Sword Dance' at the beginning of the kissing dance, and there were many different endings to the dance. In some places the dance just terminated with the 'ring figure'; in other places—in particular, in the Borders—the 'ring figure' was omitted, and when all present had been 'lifted' with the handkerchief, the dancers then performed a Circle Dance such as a Waltz or Polka.

When the dance was performed to the fiddle (as was generally the case outside the Highlands), the fiddler usually signalized the kisses by drawing his bow backwards and forwards across his strings above the bridge, making a high-pitched squeaking sound. Sometimes in the Borders the fiddler just played a continuous note on the high string whilst running his finger up and down the string (15).

There is an early description of the dance from the Lanark district,

[1] In this region we have records of the ring figure only from Barra, Lochaber, and Kilberry.

given in Alexander Fordyce's poem *A Country Wedding . . .* (258; 1818), and in this the squeak on the fiddle is mentioned.

> '. . . but custom is pressing
> That Bob at'e Bowster be danced ere you go
> We must close in the door, tho' constraint be distressing,
> Bestman, let us see where the napkin you'll throw:
>
> That's plenty o' capers, come, kiss and be done, Sir,
> Another, another, and round, round you go
> The circle increases; that squeak in the tune, Sir,
> Is meant, by the fidler, more kissing to show.'

In the notes to the poem, Fordyce amplifies this description:

'The bestman takes a pocket handkerchief, and after cutting a number of capers round the barn, to a particular tune, catches a girl, kisses her, and gives her the handkerchief. She must follow him round the barn, and then throw it at another man—he kisses her, follows round the ring, and then takes up another woman—moving round in a circle, and repeating this till the whole is in motion. Some one is then placed in the middle, and the circle reduced by the same process.'

It is interesting to note the line

'We must close in the door, tho' constraint be distressing.'

In South Uist, one of the men always stood with his back to the door to stop reluctant girls from fleeing (126).

It is probable that the kissing dance goes back to very early times indeed. One form of it was popular in Court circles in England in the seventeenth century under the name of Joan Sanderson, or the Cushion Dance. A description of this 'society' form of the dance is given in the seventh edition of Playford's *The Dancing Master* (244; 1686), and this description agrees substantially with that of The Bonny Lad given above. In the Cushion Dance, a cushion replaced the handkerchief; it was laid in front of the selected partner, and both partners knelt on it to kiss.

One of the Scottish names for the kissing dance, Babbity Bowster (Bob at the Bolster), is a survival from the days when a bolster or pillow was used instead of a handkerchief. We ourselves have met no one who remembers this use of a pillow, but a writer in *Notes and Queries* (270) has recorded that in the Paisley district a pillow was still employed in the dance in 1851. The transition from a pillow to a handkerchief was probably made via a pillow-case, for a reference to the dance from Lass-wade near Dalkeith in 1811 mentions a 'bolster or pillow-case, which at a particular stage of the dance was thrown by the fair maiden to her partner, or *vice versa*' (274).

The use of a bolster or pillow may have been an oblique reference to the bridal bed, and it is interesting to note in this connection that the tune 'Pease Strae', which in certain places was associated with the dance, has words which run:

'The best bed, the feather bed
The best bed ov a'
The best bed i' wor hoose
Is clean pea straw.'

In Northumberland, where the kissing dance was known as either The Cushion Dance or Pease Straw, these words were actually sung by the dancers (265, 277).[1]

In the old days the kissing dance was not the only occasion for kissing during an evening's dancing, for it was once the common custom in the country districts of Scotland to kiss one's partner at the beginning and end of every dance. For instance, Sir Aeneas Mackintosh of Mackintosh, writing of weddings in the parish of Moy *c.* 1783–4, states that 'at the commencement and finishing of each Reel or Dance the Swains kiss their Nymphs' (276). And in the Duke of Gordon's verses to the tune 'Cauld Kail in Aberdeen' (250; 1788), we find

'Now piper lad, bang up the Spring;[2]
The Countra fashion is the thing,
To prie their mou's[3] 'ere we begin
To dance the Reel of Bogie.'

We have met two men in the North-east who can remember this custom of kissing one's partner before a dance—it died out there about 1895. In the Alford district, when the dancers were in position for a Reel, 'the band-leader would cry "kissing time", and skirled wi' his fiddle, striking it aboon the bridge—kee, kee, kee, kee, . . '. The kissing time was sometimes very short, sometimes 'a guid whilie'; it occurred several times during the evening, always immediately before a Reel (86). In Banffshire, in the Dufftown district, the dancers would themselves call for 'kissing time', again before a Reel. Here the fiddler just kept his bow trembling on the high string while the kissing time lasted (48).

---

[1] For some other descriptions of the dance from Scotland see (295) and references given there.
[2] i.e. strike up a tune. [3] i.e. kiss.

The custom also survived within living memory at Smerclett, in the extreme south of South Uist. In 1956 a lady of 80 who had been brought up in Smerclett recalled to Dr Rhodes that in her young days the piper used to play 'pòg an toiseach'—'kiss first'—before every dance (125). The custom was also known in Orkney and Shetland, and there it survived right up to the First World War.

We have yet to mention one other stronghold of old dances, namely the country wedding. Here again people of all ages danced together, and the older dances were well represented. Here, too, the dancing tended to be boisterous, though perhaps less so than in the kirns.

Usually the wedding festivities were held in a barn, or in the bride's house, and in the latter case dancing would take place both in the house and out of doors on the grass nearby. In Glen Roy in Lochaber about 1885 the dancing at weddings was sometimes wholly out of doors, and at Bohenie in the lower part of the Glen there is a flat-topped hillock behind the house which is still known as Tom-na-Banais (the wedding knoll), from its use as the dancing-place for weddings (87, 89).

Certain dances played a special part in weddings. In Roxburghshire and West Berwickshire up to about 1895–1900, the Country Dance The Bonny Briest Knots was always performed as the first dance after the wedding supper, the bride and groom leading off the dance with the best man and bridesmaid (16, 289). It may be this use of the dance The Bonny Briest Knots which is referred to in the song 'The Briest Knots' (251; 1790), when, following the wedding breakfast,

> 'Syne off they got a' wi' a fling,
> Each lass unto her lad did cling,
> And a' cry'd for a different spring,
> The bride she sought the breast-knot.'[1]

In the West Highlands and the Western Isles the first dance after the wedding supper was a Scotch Reel called the 'Wedding Reel' or 'Ruidhleadh na Banais'. This was danced by the bride and groom, best man, and bridesmaid, and was watched by the rest of the company. The Wedding Reel is still performed in all the islands of the Outer Hebrides, and there it is followed by further Scotch Reels—often as many as six in succession—in which the bride and bridesmaid dance with other men. In South Uist and Benbecula it used to be said (119) that the man who had the honour of partnering the bride in the first Reel after the Wedding Reel would be the next in the company to be married, but now all

---

[1] The dance The Briest Knots has been known since about 1770 (201).

the men in the company, both married and unmarried, vie with each other for this honour.

In Barra, Eriskay, South Uist, and Moidart (133), there was another special Reel just before the bridal couple were put to bed. This also was danced by the bride and groom and the best man and bridesmaid. We feel we cannot improve on Sir Compton MacKenzie's description of this in his book *Whisky Galore* (291). In the words of Father MacAlister of Little Todday:

'After they've been dancing [this Reel] for a while you'll see a couple of the girls come in and steal away the bride and another girl will take her place. That's to cheat the fairies in case they took it into their heads to steal away the bride themselves. They'll think the bride is still dancing.... Then in a minute you'll see the bridegroom look round and find that the bride has vanished, and two or three friends of his will come along and lead him away to where she is, and somebody else will take his place to cheat the fairies again.'

Sometimes the bridesmaid and best man were also stolen away, but this was less common. In Barra the Stealing Reel, 'Ruidhleadh Ghoid', is still performed, but in Eriskay, South Uist, and Moidart, it seems now to have disappeared.

The last dance at a country wedding, whether in the Highlands or the Lowlands, was almost invariably the kissing dance. At weddings the best man usually took the part of the leader, though in Orkney the dance was occasionally begun by the bride. Alexander Fordyce's poem quoted above shows that this use of the kissing dance is at least as old as 1818, and it is probable that it goes back much farther than this.

The most popular instrument for social dancing in Scotland before 1914 was undoubtedly the fiddle, and at that time there were first-class dance fiddlers in every district in Scotland. These men, however, are fast dying out, and fiddling is now in danger of becoming a lost art.

The style of the dance fiddler is, of course, very different from that of the classical violinist. The essence of good dance fiddling was once very succinctly stated by an old Orkney fiddler, Danny Rosie. At a dance on the island of Flotta about 1920, a young fiddler playing with Danny Rosie stumbled over a difficult part of the music and fell out of time with the dancers. Afterwards, Danny Rosie commented on this and told the young player 'never lose time by trying to get in a note—the dancers won't notice if you leave it out. There are only three things which are important when you are playing for dancing, time, sound, and dird.' The young fiddler never forgot the advice, and it was he, now nearing sixty, who told us of the remark (145). 'Dird' is the accent given to the notes—that extra something that makes the onlookers' feet tap and gives life and lift to the dancers.

In the countryside before 1914, the music for kirns and weddings and for the smaller dances in the villages was usually supplied by one or two fiddlers. Only at 'balls' was a band provided. Other instruments in use in more recent years were the melodeon and concertina, and latterly the piano accordion. In the Highlands and the Western Isles the pipes were used, but even here the fiddle was generally preferred. In these regions there was also puirt-a-beul, and sometimes just deedling.

In the countryside, the repertoire of dances performed in any particular locality was usually relatively small. Since gatherings at which dancing took place were comparatively infrequent, a large repertoire of dances was unnecessary, and it was enough that people should know sufficient dances to fill a programme for one evening, with some of the more popular dances being repeated once, twice, or even three times during the evening. In particular, in the Highlands and the Western Isles, where the favourite dances were Reels, the repertoire of any given locality might be very small indeed.

Before we close this chapter we must mention one other type of gathering where some of the older Reels and Country Dances still survive, namely the big Highland balls—the Northern Meeting Ball at Inverness, the two Perth Hunt Balls, the ball of the Argyllshire Gathering at Oban, the two balls of the Skye Gathering, the Forfar Ball (now the Angus Private Subscription Dance), and the Aboyne Ball. The programmes at these balls can have altered little in the last fifty years, and both the dances and the style of dancing seen there have remained surprisingly unaffected by the Country Dance revival.

The Reels performed at these balls are the Scotch (Foursome) Reel and the Eightsome Reel. At most of the balls the Eightsome Reel is danced three or four times during the evening, and on each occasion it is followed immediately by the Scotch Reel—the dancers remain on the floor at the end of the Eightsome Reel, and each set of eight simply splits into two sets of four. At the Northern Meeting Balls this combination of the Eightsome Reel with the Scotch Reel has been customary since about 1894 (222).

The Country Dances performed at the Highland Balls are relatively few in number. The most unusual of them is the Perth Medley, which within living memory seems to have been peculiar to the Perth Hunt Balls. The first half of the Perth Medley is also danced as a separate dance under the titles Speed the Plough and The Inverness Country

48

Dance, and under the latter title is invariably included at the Northern Meeting Balls. The Perth Hunt Balls and the Argyllshire Gatherings still preserve the dance Scottish Reform, which was once common throughout Perthshire and Argyllshire, and almost all the balls still include Duke of Perth in their programmes (at the Forfar Ball this goes under its Angus name of Brown's Reel). Petronella also was popular at all these balls, but is at last beginning to disappear from the programmes (83).

CHAPTER III

Dancing in Orkney

T HE islands of Orkney belong to the crofting regions of Scotland, and in the old days the favourite dances there, as elsewhere in the crofting regions, were Reels. Indeed, as recently as 1880 the only dances in use in the country districts of the Mainland of Orkney and on most of the smaller islands were three Reels, the Foursome, Sixsome, and Eightsome Reels, and the ubiquitous kissing dance, usually known in Orkney as Babbity Bowster or 'Bobadebouster'.

Of the three Reels, the Foursome Reel is identical with the Scotch (Foursome) Reel of the mainland of Scotland; the Sixsome and Eightsome Reels, on the other hand, are peculiar to Orkney. Like the Foursome Reel, these Sixsome and Eightsome Reels are true Reels, that is to say they consist of setting steps danced on the spot, alternated with a travelling figure. They are danced by three and four couples respectively, and in both of them the setting steps are performed with the dancers placed in two parallel lines, the men in one line with their partners opposite to them in the other. In the travelling figures in both dances, each couple moves as a single unit, with the lady leading and the man following immediately behind her; in the Sixsome Reel the track followed by the dancers is a simple figure 8, and in the Eightsome Reel it is a figure 8 with an additional loop. Both dances also display the change in musical rhythm which is a common feature in Reels, for each is danced to a combination of strathspeys and reels.

A native of Orkney, writing in 1910, has left us a vivid description of the manner in which these Reels were performed during the second half of the nineteenth century (284). Among other things, this description shows that the formal etiquette of the professional dancing-masters of the south had not affected the country districts of Orkney at the time of which the author wrote.

'. . . the young men made a dash for the centre of the floor, and invited their partners, not by polite bow and offer of the arm, but by a

50

shout of "come awa', lass", and a snap of the fingers; or, if with sim-pering modesty the maiden seemed slow in stepping forward, she got a tug of the elbow which took her twirling to the floor. All the dances were reels—none of your modern polkas, schottisches, quadrilles, etc.— there were the foursome or two couple reel, the sixsome or three couple reel, and the eightsome or four couple reel. Those were the days when dancing was engaged in with a vigour and abandon which would be considered rude in the ballroom of the present day. The men, with per-spiration streaming down their faces, threw off both coat and waistcoat and "tripped it" in their "sark sleeves", while the women tucked up their wide skirts, or spread them out on either side, as they assumed a variety of pose and airs worthy of a professional exponent of the skirt dance. When the music changed from slow to quick time, not a step nor a beat was missed, but in heavy walking shoes they "toed it and heeled it" with perfect precision. The measure was accented by a loud tap of the iron shod heels and a snap of the fingers. What a storm of sound arose! The men, waving hands and arms and shouting like people all "possessed" made the rafters ring with many a "Heeuch" and "Yeeuch", in which the women did not disdain to join.

'The fiddler marked the conclusion of the reel by a prolonged screetching, produced by drawing the bow rapidly across the strings behind the bridge of the fiddle. This was the signal for each gallant to seize his partner in his arms and give her a resounding smack [i.e. kiss]. This he called his *mooter* or payment for the pleasure of the dance. If this salutation was submitted to in an impassive manner the young lady was deemed lacking in propriety, so she usually made a rush for her seat as soon as possible, but if caught before the end of the fiddler's coda, a scuffle ensued, from which she emerged with dishevelled hair. But amid even such scenes of wild hilarity certain rules of etiquette and deport-ment were observed, the infringement of which never failed to bring down on the culprit sharp reproof.'

The term 'mooter' mentioned in this account is derived from *multure*, the toll paid to a miller in return for his services in grinding oats, usually taken in the form of a portion of the oats or of the ground oatmeal. The custom of exacting 'mooter' at the end of every dance began to fall into disuse in Orkney just before the end of the nineteenth century, but right up to the First World War, in all parts of Orkney, the fiddler still made his squeak for 'mooter' once or twice during the course of an evening's dancing, usually just before a Foursome Reel.

The same writer also gives a good description of one form of the kissing dance as it was performed at an Orkney wedding. Here, as elsewhere in Scotland, it was the last dance of the evening:

'As soon as the fiddler struck up the tune the best man threw down his cap on the floor and danced round it for a minute or two; then he threw his handkerchief on the best maid, who joined hands with him for a short time. She then threw the handkerchief to the bridegroom, who joined the ring, and he in turn threw it to the bride. She passed it to some favoured gentleman friend, who then took his place in the centre of the ring formed by the previous four joining hands. Those in the ring danced . . . round the other, who showed off his finest steps in the centre. After a minute or two of this he chose a partner, who ducked under the arms of the others to join him, and the two danced for a while. He then joined the ring, and she, in the centre, went through the same proceedings as he had already done. This went on till every couple in the room had joined the moving circle. . . . A chair was then placed in the centre of the ring, and the best man took his seat thereon, while the others danced round as before. The bride's-maid then stepped forward and took his hand to raise him from the chair. After kissing her he ducked under their clasped hands, and took his seat outside the ring of dancers. His partner now took the chair, when the same ceremony was gone through, and so on till each one had kissed his partner out of the ring.'

We ourselves have met a very similar form of the kissing dance among old people in Orkney, together with several other forms of the dance which more closely resembled The Bonny Lad described in Chapter II. Within living memory the use of a chair in the manner described above appears to have been peculiar to Orkney, but it is of interest to observe that in one of the later editions of Playford's *The Dancing Master* (245; 1721) a note mentioning just such a use of a chair was added to the description of the Cushion Dance given in the earlier editions.

When the newer dances from the south—Country Dances, Square Dances, and Circle Dances—were brought to Orkney, they were introduced first into Kirkwall and Stromness, and there they very soon displaced the old native Orkney Reels. The programme of a dance given by the Kirkwall St Magnus Football and Athletic Club in 1884 (300) shows this very graphically. In twenty-one dances, there were only two Reels, and even one of these was a recent introduction to the islands, namely the Reel of Tulloch. The Lancers was performed three times during the evening and the Quadrilles no fewer than four times, and the remainder of the programme consisted of Country Dances (Triumph, Rory O'More, and the Milanese Country Dance), Waltzes, and Polkas.

In the country districts of the Mainland of Orkney and on the other islands, the old Reels still remained the principal items at dances long after they had been ousted from the dance-programmes in Kirkwall

The Isles of Orkney

and Stromness. One old lady who was brought up in Kirbuster on the Mainland of Orkney told us that when she first went dancing, in 1877 or 1878, the only dances in use in her district were the Foursome, Six-some, and Eightsome Reels, and Babbity Bowster. She remembered very distinctly how, in 1881 at the age of 20, she was extremely irri-tated by a young man from Kirkwall who bragged that he knew the

E

Quadrilles, the Lancers, Petronella, and various other dances, all unknown in Kirbuster at that time (135).

Again, as recently as 1895, the principal dance used at social occasions at Birsay on the Mainland of Orkney was the Foursome Reel. At that time the Quadrilles and the Lancers had already begun to be introduced into neighbouring townships, but although the young girls in Birsay had quickly acquired these new dances, the young men of the district had found them more difficult to learn, and in consequence they were rarely included in the local dance-programmes. This difficulty was resolved when an instructor to the local Volunteers offered to teach the new dances to his Volunteers after their weekly meetings. The offer was eagerly accepted, and for the next few weeks each Volunteers' meeting ended with a practice session. The sets were all-male, with the 'ladies' distinguished by white handkerchiefs tied round their arms, but in spite of such difficulties the figures were soon learnt. Thereafter, the young girls of Birsay no longer found their partners unwilling to take the floor when the Quadrilles and Lancers were announced—and indeed they found that the men not only knew what to do themselves, but also knew what the girls should do! (65).

However, it must not be thought from instances such as this that the new dances were welcomed by everyone. Indeed, in the same township of Birsay the older people were violently opposed to their introduction, and at dances there some of the older people still insisted on dancing Foursome Reels while the younger people were trying to dance their newly acquired Square Dances (65).

It is interesting to compare the situation in Birsay in 1895 with that in Edinburgh in 1816, when Quadrilles were first introduced to Scotland from France. Elizabeth Grant (279) wrote of this earlier occasion:

'It was the first season of the quadrilles, against the introduction of which there had been a great stand made by the old-fashioned respectables. Many resisted the new French figures altogether, and it was a pity to give up the merry country dance, in which the warfare between the two opinions resulted; but we young people were all bit by the quadrille mania, and I was one of the set that brought them first into notice. We practised privately by the aid of . . . Finlay Dun [who] had been abroad and imported all the most graceful steps from Paris, and having kept our secret well, we burst upon the world at the White Melville's, the spectators standing on the chairs and sofas to admire us . . . the rage for quadrilles spread, the dancing-master was in every house, and every other style discarded.'

Thus on this earlier occasion also it was the younger people who welcomed the innovations, while the older people resisted them.

The earliest recollections of a dancing-teacher in Orkney are of a Mr Chalmers, who held classes in Kirkwall, Stromness, and Holm on the Mainland, and on the islands of Burray and South Ronaldshay. Mr Chalmers was already an old man by about 1890, and was presumably the teacher who taught the young braggart from Kirkwall. The dances in Mr Chalmers' repertoire included the Foursome Reel, the modern version of the Eightsome Reel, Petronella, Flowers of Edinburgh, Triumph, Haymakers Jig, Rory O'More, Glasgow Highlanders, Cumberland Reel, the Quadrilles, Lancers, Circassian Circle, Highland Schottische, Jacky Tar Schottische, and the Spanish Galop. He did not, however, teach the old Orkney Sixsome and Eightsome Reels (139).

Orkney also had occasional visits from dancing-teachers from other parts of Scotland. For example, the West Highland itinerant teacher Mr MacDougall made at least three visits to South Ronaldshay between 1892 and 1900. The dances which he taught there included all those taught by Mr Chalmers, together with the Queen Victoria Country Dance and a number of Circle Dances.

On those islands which were apparently not visited by dancing-masters (at least within living memory), the new dances from the south still arrived at about the same time as on the Mainland of Orkney. In Rousay, for example, a few Country Dances such as Petronella and Flowers of Edinburgh were already established by 1890, and the Quadrilles and Lancers were introduced soon after that date (146).

The island of Burray is worthy of special mention, for Burray people have a reputation as fine dancers among the older people of Orkney. Mr Chalmers no doubt contributed to this reputation, for he held classes regularly on Burray. Another reason for this reputation is that Burray was one of the first places in Orkney to have its own hall (this was built about 1895) and regular dances were held there throughout the winter, thus providing the islanders with frequent practice (139). Such regular dances were most uncommon in Orkney in the old days, for in most districts dancing took place only at weddings, at harvest homes ('inhames'), at the annual Volunteers' Balls, and at New Year time. Sometimes people held fireside dances in their own homes, but in general it was unusual for Orkney people to dance more than three or four times a year.

We were unable to visit any of the North Isles of Orkney, but we learnt something of dancing on North Ronaldshay from people from

55

this island now living on the Mainland of Orkney. North Ronaldshay has a very fine Eightsome (or 'Axum') Reel which has the most intricate travelling figure of all Scottish Reels. This dance, which does not seem to have been known elsewhere in Orkney, is still occasionally performed at weddings on the island. The Sixsome Reel was also performed on North Ronaldshay, though it has not been danced there for some years now. A schoolteacher on North Ronaldshay, a Mr Mackenzie, taught dancing there about 1882, and he seems to have introduced a number of southern dances to the island (149).

We have left till last the island of Flotta, which is unique in our experience. There, until about 1890, the islanders knew only *one* dance, the Orkney Sixsome Reel. This sounds almost unbelievable, but was confirmed by all the older people on the island.

One elderly lady on Flotta recalled a wedding held in her own home about the year 1888, at which there were about twenty couples present. The only dancing space available was a room about 12 feet by 15 feet, and here the company danced six at a time, with the fiddler sitting in one corner. When all had had their turn, the first set began all over again (142).

There was no hall in Flotta at that time, and the islanders had therefore to dance in their own homes, where usually only six people could dance at one time—as at the wedding mentioned above. The restricted repertoire on Flotta at this time thus becomes much more understandable when we realize that dancing only took place three or four times a year, and that even then each member of the company danced only one dance out of every seven or so.

This simple state of affairs ended in 1890 or 1891 when a dancing-teacher from Inverness, Mr William Smith, visited the island. Just at that time there was a house on the island in the process of being built, everything being complete except for the internal dividing walls,[1] and Mr Smith was able to obtain the use of this. Part of the floor was of wood and part was of stone, but this was a minor detail. Mr Smith stayed on Flotta only for a fortnight, but held classes every evening except on Sundays. In the twelve evenings available to him he taught the Foursome Reel and Reel of Tulloch, Petronella, Flowers of Edinburgh, Triumph, Haymakers Jig, Rory O'More, the Quadrilles, Lancers, Waltz, Highland Schottische, Dutch Polka, and the Ninepins Reel. It must have been a very intensive fortnight!

When he was on Flotta, Mr Smith also sold some copies of a little ballroom guide which he had published, and after he had gone the

---

[1] In the old croft houses, the internal walls are of wood.

young men and girls on the island met on the grass by one of the farm-houses, and learnt further dances from this book.

Until the advent of Mr Smith, dances on Flotta had been leisurely affairs, with plenty of time between dances, and the fiddler was not over-worked. At the New Year's Dance after Mr Smith came, all this was changed, and the fiddler was so overworked that he wore the skin off the fingers of his left hand fingering the strings. There was, indeed, such a craze for dancing on the island following Mr Smith's visit that the lads would even practise the step for 'running the reel' when follow-ing the plough (144).

In spite of the popularity of the dances introduced by Mr Smith, the Sixsome Reel survived on Flotta until about 1912. Until that date it was invariably danced as the 'Bride's Reel' at a wedding; this was the first dance after the wedding supper, and was performed by the bride and groom, the bridesmaid and best man, and the 'honest folk'. The last were a married couple, usually related to the bride; at the actual wed-ding ceremony they accompanied the bridal couple, the honest woman playing much the same role as a Matron of Honour today, and the honest man attending the bridegroom in a similar manner.

We also met this usage of the Sixsome Reel as the 'Bride's Reel' on South Ronaldshay. On the other hand, on the Mainland of Orkney, Burray, Rousay, and North Ronaldshay, the 'Bride's Reel' was an ordinary Foursome Reel, performed by the bride and groom, the brides-maid, and the best man. In these places we met no one who remembered the 'honest folk'.[1]

After Mr Smith's visit to Flotta, other dances were brought to the island by the islanders themselves, including the Threesome Reel danced with handkerchiefs, and the kissing dance, under the name of The Swine's Reel [Swain's Reel?].

During the First World War, hundreds of troops came to Flotta, and they brought with them the current Circle Dances from the south. The programme of a dance held on Flotta about 1920 lists several of these Circle Dances which remained after the troops had departed—the

---

[1] It is interesting to compare this use of the Orkney Sixsome Reel with the use of a Sixsome Reel as the first dance at Highland weddings c. 1822:

'The dinner being over, the "shemit reel" [i.e. shame-faced reel] is the next object of attention. All the company assemble on the lawn with flambeaux and form into a circle. The bridal pair and their retinue then dance a *sixsome* reel, each putting a piece of silver into the musician's hand. Those desirous may then succeed and dance with the bride and the two maids of honour; and are gratified at the commencement and termination of a reel by the usual salutes' (262).

This Sixsome Reel was presumably for three couples, since the account mentions specifically the bride and two maids of honour.

Maxina, Boston Two-step, Winking Polka, French Minuet, Hesitation Waltz, and the Eva Three-step. Surprisingly, the Sixsome Reel still appears on the programme for a last brief revival before it finally disappeared. And last, but not least, there still the kissing dance.

CHAPTER IV

Dancing in Shetland

THE islands of Shetland lie over 100 miles from the mainland of Scotland, some 50 miles beyond the most northerly point of the Orkney group. Like Orkney, Shetland is one of the crofting regions of Scotland, and the majority of the population outside the towns of Lerwick and Scalloway live in the typical small croft houses.

Most Shetland crofts are placed close to the sea, usually within easy reach of a safe anchorage, for in the old days the easiest method of travel between one district and another was by boat. Before 1914, the lack of good roads on the islands and the relative difficulty of transport by sea in winter tended to make the social life in each crofting township more or less self-contained, and in consequence there were considerable variations in social customs from one township to another.

Our information about dancing in Shetland is derived principally from the Mainland districts of Walls, Skeld, Cunningsburgh, and Sandwick, and the islands of Whalsay, Burra, and Papa Stour. The dancing in these places seems to have been fairly typical of that in Shetland as a whole, but we must emphasize that local variations in social customs are greater in Shetland than in most other regions of Scotland.

Prior to about 1900 most dancing in Shetland took place in the croft houses. In most districts there were one or two particular houses, generally the homes of fiddlers, where the young people were accustomed to gather and dance in the winter evenings. These evenings of dancing were completely informal, and everyone was welcome. Usually the young men present paid the musician a small sum for his services, and both the young men and the girls provided a little food and drink for refreshments during the evening. In those days there were few formally arranged public dances in the country districts of Shetland, and indeed such dances only became regular occurrences with the erection of public halls in the early years of this century. The introduction of regular public dances generally brought the informal evenings of dancing in the croft houses to an end, but in those districts where no

The Shetland Isles

hall was available these croft dances continued until some time between the two wars.

In the days of the croft dances the music for dancing was invariably supplied by a fiddler. The style of fiddle-playing in Shetland is distinctive, and is perhaps more akin to that of Ireland than to that of the rest of Scotland. There is a considerable body of native Shetland fiddle music which is of very high quality, and in addition many of the older tunes brought from the mainland of Scotland have in the course of time acquired a characteristic Shetland flavour.

Until about 1900, the principal dances in Shetland were 'Shetland Reels'. These Reels existed in a variety of forms—we have met one for two couples, three for three couples, and two for four couples, and there are almost certainly others.

A three-couple Reel of one form or another seems to have been known in every district of Shetland, but two-couple and four-couple Reels were more local in their distribution. We met the two-couple Reel only in Walls and Skeld, and four-couple Reels only in Skeld, Cunningsburgh, Sandwick, and Burra Isle. In the Walls district, where there were both two-couple and three-couple Reels, the two-couple Reel seems to have been the more popular form, but in the other districts where several forms were current the most popular form was one or other of the three-couple Reels.

All these various Shetland Reels are true Reels, consisting of setting steps danced on the spot, alternated with a travelling figure. In all the three-couple and four-couple Reels the setting steps are performed with the dancers in two parallel lines, and in the travelling figures each couple moves as a single unit, with the lady leading and the man following immediately behind her; in the three-couple Reels the track followed by the dancers in the travelling figures is a figure '8', and in the four-couple Reels it is a figure '8' with a third loop added. The two-couple Reel is exceptional; in this the setting steps are performed with the dancers placed roughly at the corners of a square, and the travelling figure consists of a simple 'four-hands across'. The three-couple and four-couple Shetland Reels are markedly similar to the Orkney Sixsome and Eightsome Reels; the two-couple Reel, however, has no analogue in Orkney.

Unlike the majority of Reels, these Shetland Reels are danced at the same tempo throughout. The strathspey tunes so common on the mainland of Scotland and in Orkney do not seem to have reached Shetland, and the only tunes used for the various Shetland Reels are reels and Scotch measures.[1]

[1] In Shetland both types of tunes are known as 'reels'.

In the old days the men danced the Shetland Reels with great vigour, accompanying their steps with loud 'heuchs' and the cracking of finger and thumb; sometimes the fiddle was hardly audible above the noise of the dancing. A large range of setting steps was not necessary for the enjoyment of these Reels, for in the circumstances under which they were danced the enjoyment lay primarily in vigorous rhythmic movement. This type of enjoyment, however, is strongly dependent on the right atmosphere. The Shetland Reels were ideally suited to the intimate atmosphere of a crowded croft kitchen, but when transplanted to the more impersonal conditions of a public hall they lost much of their appeal. Thus it happened that when the evenings of dancing in the croft houses came to an end, the old Reels disappeared with them.

The only other dance which was widely current in Shetland in the old days was the 'Auld Reel'. This again had many local variations, and there existed forms for three and four couples. The dance is essentially similar to a three-couple or four-couple Shetland Reel from which the setting steps are omitted, and consists of a simple travelling figure which is repeated over and over without pause, each couple dancing as a single unit, with partners either side by side or one behind the other. The Auld Reel is a less energetic dance than a Shetland Reel, and in the old days it was normally performed in the later part of an evening when the dancers were beginning to tire, 'just as a kind of light dance'.

Dances from the mainland of Scotland seem first to have arrived in the country districts of Shetland shortly after about 1890. On Whalsay, for example, before the year 1890 the only dances in use were a three-couple Shetland Reel (with a local variant for men only, known as The Drunken Skipper) and a version of the Auld Reel (187, 197). The first dances from the mainland of Scotland to be introduced to the island were the Scotch Reel, the Country Dance Haymakers Jig, the Waltz, and the Polka, all of which arrived between 1890 and 1900. Even at the latter date, however, the Shetland Reel still remained the principal item in an evening's dancing, though it was beginning to lose ground to the newcomers. The Auld Reel, on the other hand, had by 1900 almost entirely disappeared as a separate dance, and survived only in combination with the Shetland Reel. The Quadrilles and Lancers did not arrive on Whalsay until about 1907—their arrival more or less coincided with the building of the first hall on the island (192, 194–5).

Again, in Walls the only dances in use about 1890 were two Shetland Reels, a version of the Auld Reel, the Shaalds o' Foula,[1] and Haymakers

[1] The Shaalds o' Foula is better known today under the title 'The Foula Reel'.

Jig (170). By 1900, the Reel of Tulloch, the Irish Washerwoman,[1] Highland Schottische, Polka, and the Seven-step Polka had been added to the local repertoire, and the Waltz arrived shortly after this date. Here the Quadrilles and Lancers were first introduced about 1904 (172, 174–175).

The situation elsewhere was similar. For instance, in Wester Skeld the local repertoire in 1900 consisted of three Shetland Reels, a dance of Auld Reel type, the Shaalds o' Foula (performed in this district since at least 1870 (167)), the Jig, Highland Schottische, and Polka (165–6). Again, in Sandwick about 1897 the only dances in use were two Shetland Reels, the Scotch Reel, the Reel of Tulloch, and the Highland Schottische. The Waltz and the Polka were brought into Sandwick between about 1897 and 1901, and the Quadrilles and Lancers arrived after 1901 (161). And again, on Burra Isle, the local repertoire between about 1900 and 1905 consisted only of two Shetland Reels, the Scotch Reel, the Reel of Tulloch, and the Highland Schottische. The Quadrilles were introduced here about 1906 when the local hall was built, and the Lancers came later still (177–8).

The dances from the south seem to have been brought to Shetland by the fishermen and the fisher girls who came from the mainland of Scotland and the Hebrides to work in Shetland for the herring season.

About the beginning of this century, Shetland was one of the main centres of the herring industry. In 1901 there were 1380 herring boats based on Shetland, employing nearly 9,000 fishermen and boys. The total catch landed in Shetland that year amounted to about 637,000 barrels of herring, and nearly half a million barrels were exported to Europe. To deal with this catch, there were fish-curing stations in no fewer than twenty-six of the Shetland ports—thirteen on the Mainland, five on Yell, three on Unst, and one on each of Burra Isle, Papa Stour, Bressay, Whalsay, and the Out Skerries—and between them these stations employed nearly 5,000 girls as gutters and packers (282).

The girls employed as gutters and packers at the fish-curing stations were for the most part drawn from the mainland of Scotland and the Hebrides, but there were also a fair number from various parts of Shetland. During the herring season, all these girls lived in the various ports, in large tarred wooden huts known as 'barracks' or 'tarry temples', and in the evenings, after the day's work was over, there was often

[1] In the Irish Washerwoman, the couples form two parallel lines, with the men in one line and their partners opposite them in the other. Partners first set to each other, then swing each other and return to places, then set again, then swing again, and so on (174). This dance seems to be the same as the 'Jig', which we noted from Wester Skeld and Reawick, and is probably a simplified version of the 'Hullachan Jig' (see p. 148).

impromptu dancing in these huts. Sometimes the girls danced just among themselves, but more often they danced with the local Shetland lads or the men from the boats. In those days, when the boats were in harbour, it was a recognized custom for the younger members of the crews to spend the evenings in the huts dancing with the girls—there was usually no lack of music, for on most of the boats at least one member of the crew could play the fiddle or the concertina. In the course of these evenings of dancing in the huts, the Shetland girls learnt a number of the mainland dances from the men and girls from other parts of Scotland, and when the Shetland girls returned to their homes at the end of the season, they took these mainland dances with them.

The fishermen and the fisher girls from other parts of Scotland seem first to have come to Shetland in any numbers about the years 1890–5, and, as we have seen, it was during these years and the period immediately following them that the dances from the south were introduced to the country districts of Shetland. The dances which were introduced to Shetland in this way were naturally those which were currently popular in the parts of Scotland from which the fishermen and fisher girls were drawn—mainly the Morayshire, Banffshire, and Aberdeenshire coasts, and the island of Lewis in the Outer Hebrides. The dances brought in included the standard Reels, Square Dances, and Circle Dances, all of which were popular in one or more of these regions, but included very few Country Dances, for on the North-east coast Country Dances had lost their popularity by this time, while on the island of Lewis they had never attained much popularity. Thus of Country Dances only a few hardy favourites—Petronella, Haymakers Jig, Cumberland Reel, and Strip the Willow—reached Shetland.[1]

The country districts of Shetland, unlike those of Orkney, do not seem to have been visited by dancing-masters from the mainland of Scotland. It is possible that the Shetland lairds employed a dancing-teacher to teach their children when they were residing in Lerwick, but any dances which may have been introduced in this way do not seem to have spread to the ordinary people of Shetland. The importation of dances from the south to Shetland was thus almost entirely a matter of the dances being passed on from one person to another, without the intervention of professional dancing-teachers.

The custom of kissing one's partner at the end of a dance was fairly

[1] Mr Peter Henry, of the Shetland Old-time Dance Society, has kindly presented us with a list of all the mainland dances known to have been performed on the Mainland of Shetland within living memory, and the only Country Dances included are the four named above.

common in Shetland in the old days, and is still not unknown at weddings. According to a description of a Shetland wedding written in 1859 (271), the custom was at that time observed at the end of each dance, but within living memory it took place only two or three times in an evening's dancing, generally at the end of a Shetland Reel. In Walls and Skeld the fiddler sometimes signalized the kisses by running his bow backwards and forwards over the high strings, but elsewhere it was usual for one of the men to shout 'kiss the lasses' just as the Reel was coming to an end. The reaction of the girls to this custom is nicely described in an account of a wedding which took place in the Scousburgh district in 1837 (275):[1]

'Now the reel ends. "Kiss the lasses," exclaims the lad with the hairy bonnet, and four loud smacks are instantly heard, the lasses giving a twist or two in the arms of their partners, just for appearance sake, . . . this piece of hypocrisy is no fault of theirs, but arises from the tyranny of fashion. Poor things, why should they not like a kiss as well as the other sex? and when we all know so well that they do, how absurd that fashion should force them to appear as if they didn't.'

In the days of the croft dances most Shetland men danced in their Sunday boots, while ladies wore light shoes with a heel about one inch high. Shoes were worn by some men, but patent leather evening shoes were unknown in the country districts until the dances were transferred to the public halls.

At some time prior to about 1850 some of the women in the country districts of Shetland danced in their stockinged feet—they had special 'tatted socks' for dancing which had thicker soles than usual. We were told of these 'tatted socks' by a man of 75 who had heard of them from a lady somewhat older than his father. This lady had in turn been told of them by an aunt—the aunt was talking one day of the festivities which took place at Yule-time in her youth, and she mentioned the number of 'tatted socks' which she had worn out in dancing during the period of Yule (175). In the old days the festivities at Yule-time were kept up for several weeks. The actual date was calculated by the old Julian calendar, so that Yule itself—Christmas day—was celebrated on January 6th, and New Year's Eve on January 12th.

One of the great occasions for dancing in Shetland in the old days was a wedding. Here young and old alike joined in the dancing, and the old Shetland Reels were well represented. Even those people whose religious

[1] The account was actually written in 1890 by someone who had been present at the wedding. An abridged version is given by Ursula Venables in her *Life in Shetland* (301).

scruples prevented their taking part in an ordinary dance (that is, 'a dance set up for no reason except to dance') could happily join in the celebrations at a wedding, for they felt they had Scriptural sanction in the presence of Jesus and his mother at a wedding at Cana in Galilee (152).

A Shetland wedding usually took place on a Thursday, since Thor has a special blessing for brides and bridegrooms (152).[1] On the Saturday before the wedding, the bride and bridegroom visited the minister to ask for the wedding to be proclaimed at the Church next day, and then returned to the bride's home, where their more intimate friends and relatives had gathered for the 'Contract'. Here the final arrangements for the wedding were made and the invitations written out. These tasks completed, the company then sat down to a large supper, and afterwards joined in dancing until about 11 or 12 o'clock (152, 157).

On the Sunday, the wedding was proclaimed at the Church, and then on the Monday the bridegroom and his best man delivered the invitations. In Whalsay, outside living memory, the invitation to the fiddler— 'the fiddler's bid'—was delayed until the night before the wedding, when it was delivered by the bridegroom in person. The bridegroom then took the fiddler back to his own home where a few of his friends were gathered to celebrate his last night as a bachelor, and the fiddler stayed the night there, playing for entertainment whenever required (192).

The arrangements on the actual day of the wedding were in the charge of the 'married folk', who were usually a married lady from the

[1] The description of a Shetland wedding which follows is a composite one. Our principal sources of information here were Mrs Catherine Laurenson of North Delting, now living in Lerwick (152), and Mrs Laura Malcolmson of Cunningsburgh (157). Mrs Laurenson's account refers to North and South Delting in her younger days, about the year 1910, while Mrs Malcolmson's account refers to the Cunningsburgh district, partly in her own younger days about the year 1920, and partly in her parents' time. Our description applies also to the island of Whalsay, and it also agrees substantially with the description from Scousburgh already quoted on p. 65, with one from Unst given by J. M. E. Saxby in her *Shetland Traditional Lore* (287; 1932), and with a description reproduced from some earlier source in *Peace's Almanac and County Directory for 1903* (282). Our description does not apply to the district of Walls; there the oldest form of wedding now remembered is a 'day wedding', accounts of which can be found in J. T. Reid's *Art Rambles in Shetland* (273; 1869) and in the third volume of the *Shetland Folk Book* (294).

The reader may find it interesting to compare our description of a Shetland wedding, drawn from living memory, with the account of wedding customs drawn from various early English and Scottish sources given by Ellis in his edition of *Brand's Popular Antiquities* (268).

bride's side, and a married man from the bridegroom's side.[1] The guests gathered at the bride's house, at a time depending on the distance of the house from the church, for in the old days the bridal couple walked in procession to the church, often a distance of three miles or more. Generally the ceremony at the church was arranged to take place at about 3 o'clock. The men were in dark suits and the unmarried girls in white dresses—all the unmarried girls at the wedding were known as 'bridesmaidens', the bride's personal attendant being distinguished by the title 'best maid'.

Usually only the younger unmarried people took part in the procession to the church, while the older people stayed behind at the bride's home to prepare for the ensuing festivities. The procession was headed by a fiddler playing 'The Bride's March'—there were words to this which were sung by the company in the procession:

> Noo mun I lave fader and midder,
> Noo mun I lave sister and brither,
> Noo mun I lave kith and kin,
> And follow the back o' a fremd[2] man's son.

Following the fiddler at the head of the procession was a Gunner, and then in turn came the 'married folk', the best man and the bride, and the bridegroom and the best maid, followed in turn by the rest of the procession, arranged in couples in order of precedence, each bridesmaiden being partnered by a young man.

After the ceremony in the church, the procession reformed to the tune 'Woo'd and married an' a'':

> Woo'd and married an' a',
> Kiss'd and carried awa',
> An' is no the bride well off
> That's woo'd and married an' a'.

Then began the walk back to the bride's house; the fiddler was still in the lead, and after him came in turn the bridegroom and the bride, the best man and the best maid, and the 'married folk', and then the other couples as before. On the way home the Gunner fired shots 'to let the "hill-folk," i.e. the fairies, know that . . . they had better not try any of their cantrips'[3] (275). Sometimes extra Gunners accompanied the procession on the way home. They were usually each armed with a

---

[1] In North Roe the 'married folk' were known as the 'honest folk'. The latter term is also used in the accounts of Shetland weddings in *Peace's Almanac* and J. T. Reid's *Art Rambles in Shetland*; it was also used on the islands of Flotta and South Ronaldshay in Orkney (see p. 57).

[2] Strange, i.e. not related.   [3] Charms, spells.

blunderbuss which they filled with powder and paper wadding, and discharged whenever they felt inclined. Pieces of burning paper descended on the procession, to add to the general merriment: 'I mind o' us trying to keep the burning paper oot o' our hair' (152).

When the procession arrived back at the bride's home, the fiddler struck up the last of the three wedding tunes, 'The Bride's Welcome Home'. In the old days—that is, in our informants' parents' time—there now followed the ceremony of breaking the bride's scone. The bride's scone was a thin oatcake about eighteen inches in diameter; as the bride crossed the threshold of her parents' home on her return from the church, her mother took this scone and broke it into pieces over her head. A great scramble ensued among the bridesmaidens for the pieces, for it was popularly supposed that if a bridesmaiden slept with a piece of the bride's scone beneath her pillow, she would dream of the man she would marry (152). In Whalsay a substitute for this ceremony still took place within living memory; here the bride's scone was replaced by crumbled oatmeal cake, which was thrown over the bride by her mother on her return from the church, in the manner of confetti (188, 191).

After the breaking of the bride's scone, the company sat down to the wedding dinner. The number of guests here varied considerably; sometimes there were forty or fifty, sometimes two hundred or more. There was always plenty of stewed mutton, and sometimes a calf was killed to provide stewed veal. There was usually also a huge piece of boiled pork, served cold, and sometimes beef. 'I mind an old woman talking of her grandfather's wedding; there were five calves killed, besides mutton and pork.' There were also numerous 'flour scones', 'flour bannocks', 'flour broonies' [brownies], and 'oven broonies'. The 'oven broonies' were fruit cakes baked in the Dutch oven, while the 'flour broonies' were baked on a brand-iron, a flat steel plate on four short legs which was placed on the hearth-stone over a glowing peat which had stopped smoking (152).

The dinner was concluded with toasts, and then the tables were cleared and the dancing began. Sometimes, in places where the houses were set conveniently close together, the meal was prepared in one house and eaten in another, and the dancing took place in a third (152). On one occasion in Cunningsburgh some fifty years ago there were three weddings on three consecutive Thursdays, and a man who was related to two of the contracting parties and whose house was near those of the three brides took down the internal dividing walls in his house and allowed the dancing for each of the weddings to take place there.

Perhaps it should be added that, as in the houses in Orkney, the internal walls were of wood, and that they were probably held in place with wooden pegs rather than with nails! (154). The dancing at weddings also sometimes took place in a barn—in Shetland a barn is roughly of the same dimensions as one of the croft houses, but has, of course, no internal partitions.

During the course of the dancing, there would invariably be a visit from the Guisers. These were usually young men who had not been invited to the wedding, though sometimes they were members of the company who had suitably disguised themselves.

The costume of the Guisers was a strange one, and it would be hard to improve on the description given by J. T. Reid in his *Art Rambles in Shetland*:

'. . . in walks a tall, slender-looking man, called the "scuddler," his face closely veiled with a white cambric napkin, and on his head a cap made of straw, in shape like a sugar-loaf [i.e. conical], with three loops at the upper extremity, filled with ribbons of every conceivable hue, and hanging down so as nearly to cover the cap. He wears a white shirt, with a band of ribbons around each arm, and a bunch of ribbons on each shoulder, with a petticoat of long clean straw, called "gloy," which hangs loosely.'

The 'scuddler' was the leader of the Guisers. In Delting he carried a broom, and endeavoured to sweep everything in the room to the bride; on some occasions he even swept the dirt from outside the house in to her (152).

The remaining Guisers were known as 'skeklers'; they were dressed in a similar manner to the scuddler and were supposed to represent various characters. In some places they each danced a short solo as they entered (151), but in Walls (175) and Aith (181) they danced a Shetland Reel—this was known as the 'Guisards' Reel', and had a special tune of its own. After this, they joined in the general dancing for a while—always without speaking a word, lest they disclose their identity.

In the old days, when the wedding celebrations lasted for three days, the dancing on the first day of the wedding came to an end at about one o'clock in the morning, and the company then sat down to supper.

After supper there followed the ceremony of bedding the bride. The bridesmaidens took the bride into the bridal chamber, undressed her, and put her to bed, with much 'dancing about and kicking up a caper'. When the bride was safely ensconced in bed, all the women present at the wedding came to the bridal chamber to receive a piece of bridescake

F

from her, and then retired. The bridegroom was now brought in by some of the younger men and put to bed with his bride, and then all the men present at the wedding came in to 'hansel' the bride, that is, to give her a gift of money, receiving in return a piece of bridescake from the bride and a dram from the bridegroom (157, 192). The fiddler, throughout this whole ceremony, sat in a corner of the bridal chamber, 'playing a kin' o' a lilt' (192).

After the bedding of the bride, those of the company who lived nearby went off to their homes, while the remainder made themselves beds of oatsheaves in the barn 'and slept then and there in their wedding attire' (301). Next day, the festivities began again in the late afternoon, with dancing until midnight or so, and then on the Saturday the festivities began somewhat earlier and broke up in time for the guests to reach their homes before Sunday. On the second and third days of the wedding the refreshments were supplied by the guests, the women being responsible for the food and the men for the drink.

On Whalsay, three-day weddings last occurred just within living memory (197), but elsewhere they died out within our oldest informants' parents' time. They were followed by two-day weddings which were conducted on very similar lines, the festivities on the second day being usually brought to an end at about 9 p.m. In turn the two-day weddings have now given way to 'one-day weddings', where the dancing goes on right through the night. In Cunningsburgh, for instance, the last two-day wedding conducted on the old pattern took place about 1925 (157). In all districts, the bedding of the bride has been discontinued for some years now, but survived well within living memory.

The Auld Reel once played a special role in the ritual of a Shetland wedding. The most complete account of this comes from the island of Whalsay, where within living memory the ritual was still performed in its entirety—though there is now only one person on the island, an old lady of 89, who still remembers it (187).

According to the earliest memories of this old lady, the dancing on the first night of the wedding festivities began with a Shetland Reel. On Whalsay only one form of Shetland Reel is known, for three couples, and in the first Reel of the wedding the three couples were the bridegroom and bride, the best man and best maid, and the 'married folk'. This first Reel, which had no special name, was followed by other Shetland Reels, with the rest of the company taking the floor in turn, the fiddler being seated on 'a low stool on the resting couch [a long wooden settle] so that he was above the company'. As the evening progressed, an Auld Reel might be introduced just to give the dancers a rest from the vigorous setting of the Shetland Reel, but apart from the Auld Reel only Shetland Reels were danced.

At about 11 or 12 o'clock, when the first day of the wedding was drawing to an end, the 'Bride's Reels' began. These were a series of Auld Reels, in which all the womenfolk present danced in turn. The first of the Bride's Reels was danced by the bride and the best maid, the 'married woman' and the bride's mother, and two of the bride's closest female relatives (in Whalsay the Auld Reel was a dance for three couples). Thereafter the ladies took the floor in strict order of precedence, first the various female relatives of the bride and bridegroom, and then those female members of the company who were not related to either bride or bridegroom. And always it was just the Auld Reel: 'they grippit arms and keepit two and two thegither, and danced the figure 8 . . . they just keepit goin' on aroun''.

During the Bride's Reels, the men 'sweepit the bride' with straw brushes. These brushes consisted of bunches of oat-straw from which the grain had been removed—'gloy', in the local usage; the lower halves of the stems were bound together with a single ribbon, and the empty heads were tied together in twos and threes by separate ribbons which were left with long ends dangling. While the Bride's Reels took place, four or five men stood around the dancing-space waving these brushes over the dancers' heads, disarranging their hair and tickling their faces with the ends of the straw and the dangling ribbons. The bride, however, was supposed to remain untouched: 'they hadna' tae touch the bride'.

The Bride's Reels were followed by the Bridegroom's Reels, with the men taking the places of the ladies—one Auld Reel after another until all the man had danced. Here the girls took the straw brushes and 'sweepit the bridegroom', though again the bridegroom was the only man in the company who was not well and truly swept.

At the end of each of the Bride's Reels, the 'married woman' collected the 'fiddler's money' from the dancers. The bride and the other dancers in the first Reel usually gave a shilling, those in the next Reel gave a sixpence, and so on, descending to threepence from the last dancers of all. Some of the ladies excused themselves from the Bride's Reels, but these still paid their due. In the same way the 'married man' collected the 'fiddler's money' from the men at the end of each of the Bridegroom's Reels. This 'fiddler's money' was the only payment which the fiddler received in those days, but with a big company it was a more than sufficient reward.

When the final Bridegroom's Reel had been danced—and the whole series of Bride's Reels and Bridegroom's Reels may have lasted for nearly two hours—the company sat down to supper, and the first day of the wedding then concluded as usual with the bedding of the bride.

The full ritual of the Bride's and Bridegroom's Reels described above was probably last observed on Whalsay about the year 1890, and the history of these Reels subsequent to this date provides an interesting example of the devolution of a social custom.

The first change which took place was the introduction of the Shetland Reel into the Bride's and Bridegroom's Reels, and the virtual disappearance of the Auld Reel as a separate dance. The Bride's and Bridegroom's Reels still survived, but they no longer consisted exclusively of the Auld Reel; instead, for each of the Bride's Reels and each of the Bridegroom's Reels the fiddler played three or four tunes; he began with one or two tunes for the Shetland Reel, then changed to the tune of the Auld Reel, and then finally changed back to a Shetland Reel tune. While the first Reel tunes were played, the dancers performed the ordinary Whalsay three-couple Shetland Reel, then when the fiddler changed to the tune for the Auld Reel partners linked together and lilted through the figure 8 so long as the tune lasted. When the fiddler made his final change, the dancers quickly released hold of their partners and moved back into position for the Shetland Reel, and the dance then concluded as an ordinary Shetland Reel. Here, as in the earlier form of the custom, the dancers were still swept with the straw brushes, and the 'fiddler's money' was collected at the end of each Reel.

This form of the Bride's and Bridegroom's Reels is remembered by a fair number of the people on the island between the ages of 70 and 85, and it is interesting to note that several of these people regarded the inclusion of the Auld Reel in each separate Bride's or Bridegroom's Reel as an essential part of the ceremony, even though none of them was aware that the Bride's and Bridegroom's Reels once consisted exclusively of the Auld Reel. For example, a fiddler aged 76 who often played at weddings in the old days told us that one of the tunes for the Bride's and Bridegroom's Reels 'always had to be the Auld Reel' (192), and another man of similar age said 'the Bride's Reels werena' danced right without they danced the Auld Reel' (195).

The next change which took place was that the custom of asking the guests at the wedding to contribute the 'fiddler's money' fell into disuse, the fiddler now being paid a fixed fee by the bridegroom. When this occurred, there no longer seemed any point in everyone's taking part in one of the Bride's or Bridegroom's Reels, and in consequence all of these Reels except the first of the Bride's Reels and the first of the Bridegroom's Reels were discontinued. Soon, the Bridegroom's Reel too was discarded, and then only the Bride's Reel remained. One lady of 79 told us that at her own wedding on Whalsay the dancing on the first day concluded with just the Bride's Reel, which on this occasion consisted of only the Auld Reel, the dancers being herself, the best maid, the 'married woman', and three of her closest female relatives. In the course of the Bride's Reel the six dancers were swept with straw brushes, and she herself was actually touched by an over-enthusiastic sweeper. Here, her husband paid the fiddler a fee for his services (188).

The next development came with the discontinuing of the 'bedding of the bride'. The dancing now usually went on until the early morning, and there was no obvious point in the proceedings at which the Bride's Reel should take place, and accordingly it also was discarded. However, the name 'The Bride's Reel' still survived, for this name was transferred to the first dance of the wedding—the Shetland Reel which followed the wedding dinner—danced by the bridegroom and bride, the best man and best maid, and the 'married folk'. The custom of 'sweeping the bride' was also transferred to this first Reel, but soon disappeared from use (190).

The 'sweeping of the bride' is an extraordinary survival, for these Shetland sweepers, armed with their straw brushes, can be linked with kindred figures in ritual dance ceremonies throughout Europe, their purpose always being to sweep away evil spirits.

A ceremonial similar to that in Whalsay, involving the use of the Auld Reel, survived until recently in Cunningsburgh on the Mainland of Shetland.[1]

At weddings in Cunningsburgh, at the extreme reach of living memory, the dancing on the first day of the wedding concluded with two Auld Reels, which were known as the 'Bride's Reel' and the 'Men's Rant'. The first of these two Auld Reels, the Bride's Reel, came at about midnight; it was danced by the bride and the best maid, the 'married woman' and her (female) counterpart from the bridegroom's side, the bride's and bridegroom's mothers, and two of the bride's closest female

---

[1] Our information here is derived principally from two ladies in Cunningsburgh who had heard of the custom from people of their parents' generation (156–7).

We should add that we could find no trace of the ceremonial of the Bride's Reels and Bridegroom's Reels on either Burra Isle or Papa Stour. On Burra Isle, for as far back as living memory extends, the Bride's Reel has been the first dance of the wedding, an ordinary three-couple Shetland Reel performed by the bridegroom and bride, the best man and best maid, and the 'married folk'. On Papa Stour, even the oldest people knew nothing of the Bride's Reel, though they had heard of it.

relatives (in Cunningsburgh the Auld Reel was a dance for four couples). Immediately the Bride's Reel was over, the bride was put to bed, and then followed the Men's Rant. This was danced by the male counterparts of the ladies in the Bride's Reel, and immediately following it the bridegroom was put to bed by the men. Here the 'fiddler's money' was collected just before the Bride's Reel and the Men's Rant took place —the 'married man' simply went round the whole company with a hat. No one in Cunningsburgh has any recollections of 'sweeping the bride'.

In Cunningsburgh the Bride's Reel and the Men's Rant were probably last performed about the year 1885 (158). Thereafter, the Men's Rant dropped out of use, but the Bride's Reel survived by itself (now as the last dance of the wedding), probably until about 1897 (155). Then it too disappeared, and, as on Whalsay, the name 'The Bride's Reel' was transferred to the first dance after the wedding dinner, an ordinary three-couple Shetland Reel performed by the bridegroom and bride, the best man and best maid, and the 'married folk'.

Within living memory there has been only one Bride's Reel and only one Men's Rant in Cunningsburgh. However, two of our informants, one in Cunningsburgh (155) and the other in the neighbouring district of Sandwick (162), when talking to us about the Bride's Reel, began by following us in speaking of the Bride's Reel in the singular, and then in the course of the conversation unconsciously lapsed into speaking of the Bride's *Reels*, in the plural (although we had carefully refrained from mentioning the possibility that there may once have been more than one Bride's Reel). We asked them if they had any reason for speaking of the Bride's Reels in the plural, but they both said just that they had always used this term. It would appear, therefore, that the full ceremonial with a series of Bride's Reels and a series of Bridegroom's Reels was once known at Cunningsburgh, and possibly also at Sandwick.

CHAPTER V

Reel and Country Dance Steps

WITHIN the period covered by living memory, the steps used in Country Dances were relatively few, and all were fairly simple, calling for no particular skill in their performance. Most of the steps used in Country Dances were also used in Reels, and in addition there was a large number of steps which were peculiar to Reels.[1] These latter steps varied considerably in their complexity, and some were performed only by really expert dancers.

In this chapter we describe a number of Reel and Country Dance steps which we have learnt from various people, both young and old, in different parts of Scotland. We have not attempted to be exhaustive, and, in particular, we do not include any of the numerous Highland Fling steps which were used as setting steps in Reels. We also exclude Shetland steps since these are most conveniently dealt with in the chapter on Shetland Reels. With these exceptions, however, the steps described here do include all those which were most commonly and most widely used within living memory.

We have added notes on the various steps, giving such information about them as we possess, in particular, the names of the dancing-teachers who taught them. The fact that a step was included in the repertoire of a certain dancing-teacher tells us that that step was current throughout his territory in his day, and a list of the dancing-teachers who taught a particular step therefore indicates both the extent to which that step was used, and the region in which it was current. We give also references to old books or manuscripts in which descriptions of the steps can be found.

We should add here that readers who wish to obtain from this chapter some conception of the nature of these steps and of their use in social dancing, without actually learning to perform them, can obtain a good picture of the steps by simulating the appropriate movements with a pair of fingers.

[1] That is to say, so far as social dances were concerned; some Reel steps were also used in solo exhibition dances.

The style of performance of these steps was determined to a certain extent by the shoes worn by the dancers. We have already remarked that before 1914 light Highland dancing pumps were worn only by professional Highland dancers. In the more rural districts, the men as often as not wore their best outdoor shoes or boots for dancing, while elsewhere the standard footwear for men consisted of black patent leather dancing shoes. Ladies in both town and country wore the lightest shoes they could afford, always with a heel an inch or so high. Thus for men at least the normal footwear was relatively stiff and unyielding, while the ladies were affected to some extent by the heels on their shoes. In consequence, the men did not rise high on their toes, whilst ladies did not rise much higher on their toes than their heels already caused them to be. Moreover, there was no excessive pointing of the toes by either men or ladies.

THE BASIC POSITIONS

In the following, the *supporting foot* is the foot which bears the dancer's weight, whilst the other foot is called the *working foot*.[1]

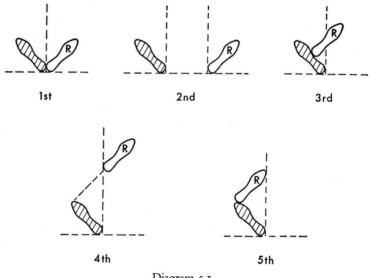

Diagram 5.1

In classical dancing there are five basic positions of the working foot;[2] these are shown in Diagram 5.1 in the case in which the working foot is

[1] Some of the weight can, of course, be taken on the working foot.
[2] These positions were first defined by Rameau, a French dancing-master, in 1725. There is some variation in the definition of 4th position among subsequent writers.

the right foot. In each position the working foot is at right angles to the supporting foot, and the two feet are equally inclined to the direction in which the dancer is facing.

There are also rear positions corresponding to 3rd, 4th, and 5th positions, in which the working foot is placed to the rear of the supporting foot; these rear positions are shown in Diagram 5.2, again in the case in which the working foot is the right foot.

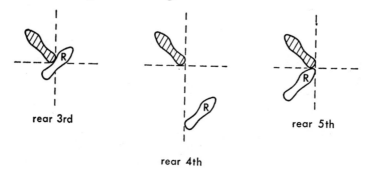

rear 3rd

rear 5th

rear 4th

Diagram 5.2

Many professional dancing-masters in Scotland made use of these positions in their teaching (even if they did not explicitly mention them by name) so that these classical positions alone do enable us to give a reasonable description of many of the steps which were in common use. They are, however, inadequate if we wish to be able to give exact descriptions of all the steps which were in use in Scotland within living memory, and we have therefore to define some further basic positions. In naming the additional positions which we require, we have simply added a qualifying word such as 'semi' or 'intermediate' to the name of the nearest classical position—we hope that by this method anyone who is familiar with the five classical positions will find it easy to remember the new basic positions. This is actually the method followed by the Scottish Official Board of Highland Dancing (242), and for the sake of standardization we have usually adopted the Official Board's terminology in those cases where our positions coincide with theirs.

In our choice of new basic positions, we have compromised between the desire for strict accuracy in our descriptions of steps and the necessity of avoiding a multiplicity of basic positions. In most cases the positions given in the steps described here are precisely those used by our informants. However, there are naturally a few cases where the positions used by our informants were not included in our basic positions, and in these cases we have simply used the basic positions nearest to our informants' actual positions.

We must emphasize too that we have introduced these further basic positions only to enable us to describe with reasonable accuracy the steps shown to us by our informants. We do not say, nor do we believe, that anyone who does not place his or her feet precisely in these basic positions is dancing incorrectly.

A *ground position* is one in which both feet are in contact with the ground. In the classical 1st, 3rd, and 5th positions,[1] the working foot is placed with the pads of the toes and the ball of the foot on the ground, and with the heel fairly close to the ground. In addition to this (classical) position, the working foot can also be *pointed* in a ground position on the toe, when only the tip of the big toe touches the ground, and it can also be placed on the *half-point*, when the pads of the first two or three toes are on the ground but the ball of the foot is not touching the ground, and on the *ball of the foot*, with the pads of the toes and the ball of the foot on the ground, and with the heel well raised.

In the various aerial positions, the working foot is off the ground. In a *very low aerial position* the toe of the working foot is about one inch off the ground, in a *low aerial position* it is in a horizontal line with the ankle of the supporting leg, and in a (normal) *aerial position* it is in a horizontal line with the centre of the calf of the supporting leg.

The *line of direction* is an imaginary line on the ground at right angles to the plane of the dancer's body, and passing from back to front. In the diagrams illustrating the basic positions, the line of direction is indicated by an arrow.

We write R for 'right' and L for 'left' when these words are used as adjectives; we write also RF and LF for 'right foot' and 'left foot' respectively.

In our descriptions of the basic positions we follow the classical convention in supposing that the supporting foot is inclined at an angle of 45° to the line of direction. This was the position taught by dancing-masters, but in ordinary social dancing there was a good deal of variation from this position, and many people danced with the supporting foot almost parallel to the line of direction.

The closed positions

A *closed position* is one in which the working foot is in contact with either the supporting foot or leg. As a matter of convenience we include also under this heading the various 5th aerial positions, although these

[1] At least so far as Scottish dancing is concerned.

are not strictly 'closed' in the sense defined above. The closed positions are then 1st position, the various 3rd and 5th positions, and the front and rear leg positions; the full descriptions of these are given in the following pages.

In a closed position, except where stated to the contrary, the feet are at right angles to each other and each is inclined to the line of direction at an angle of 45°. The heel of the supporting foot is fairly close to the ground.[1]

1st position. The two feet are placed as shown in Diagram 5.3, with heels together. The toes and balls of the feet are on the ground, and the heels are fairly close to the ground, both at the same level.

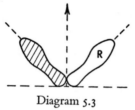

Diagram 5.3
1st position

3rd position. In this position the working foot is placed with the pads of the toes and the ball of the foot on the ground, and with the heel just touching the inner edge of the instep of the supporting foot[2] (Diagram 5.4).

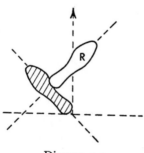

Diagram 5.4
RF in 3rd position

3rd very low aerial position. In this position the ball of the working foot rests against the inner edge of the instep of the supporting foot. The

[1] The actual height of the heel of the supporting foot from the ground varied considerably from dancer to dancer. It altered, too, according to the dancer's footwear.
[2] The instep is the *upper* surface of the foot between the toe joints and the ankle.

toe of the working foot is about one inch from the ground, and the sole of the working foot is at an angle of about 60° to the ground (Diagram 5.5).

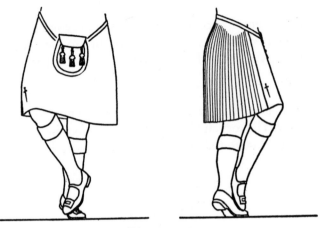

Diagram 5.5
RF in 3rd very low aerial position

Rear 3rd position. The working foot is placed with the inner edge of the instep touching the heel of the supporting foot, as shown in Diagram 5.6. The pads of the toes and the ball of the working foot are on the ground, and the heel is raised just off the ground.

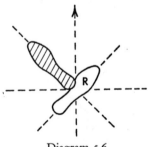

Diagram 5.6
RF in rear 3rd position

5th position. In 5th position, the working foot touches the big toe joint of the supporting foot. We use four different methods of placing the working foot in 5th position, and Diagram 5.7 shows these when the working foot is the RF.

(a) *RF in 5th position.* The RF is placed with the pads of the toes and the ball of the foot on the ground, and with the heel just touching the top of the big toe of the LF.

80

(b) *Ball of RF in 5th position.* The R heel is raised high off the ground and crossed right over the L toe.

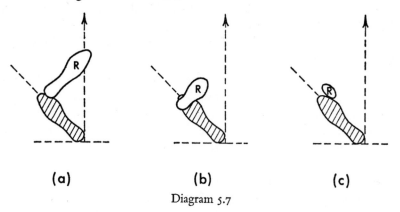

(a)   (b)   (c)

Diagram 5.7

(c) *RF on the half-point, or R toe pointed, in 5th position.* The RF is as nearly vertical as possible,[1] and the R knee points to the side. As usual, the LF is inclined at 45° to the line of direction, with the heel off the ground.

5th aerial positions. When the RF is in a 5th aerial position, the LF is inclined at 45° to the line of direction, with the heel off the ground, and the R toe is placed at the appropriate height vertically above the position in Diagram 5.7c, with the RF as nearly vertical as possible and with the R knee pointed to the side.

Rear 5th position. In this position the big toe of the working foot touches the supporting foot. We use three different methods of placing

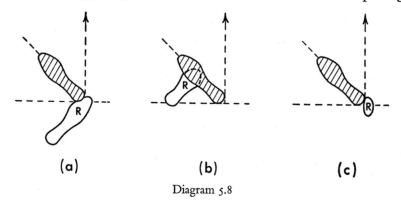

(a)   (b)   (c)

Diagram 5.8

[1] The position actually attained here depends on the stiffness of both the dancer's shoes and ankle-joints.

the working foot in rear 5th position, and Diagram 5.8 shows these when the working foot is the RF.

(a) *RF in rear 5th position.* The RF is placed with the pads of the toes and the ball of the foot on the ground, with the heel just off the ground, and with the top of the big toe just touching the edge of the L heel.

(b) *R toe closed under L instep in rear 5th position.* Both heels are well off the ground, and the R toe is right underneath the L instep.

(c) *R toe pointed in rear 5th position.* The RF is as nearly vertical as possible and the R knee points to the side. As usual, the LF is inclined at 45° to the line of direction, with the heel off the ground.

Front and rear leg positions. In the front leg position the working foot is placed with the outer edge of the sole against the shin of the supporting leg, with the sole of the foot vertical, and with the back of the heel just touching the bottom of the kneecap of the supporting leg (Diagram 5.9). In the rear leg position, the working foot is placed with

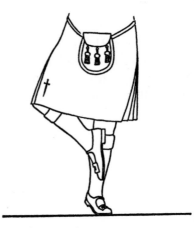

Diagram 5.9
RF in front leg position

the inner edge of the sole against the back of the calf of the supporting leg, with the sole of the foot again vertical, and with the heel at the same height from the ground as in the front leg position. In both positions the supporting foot is inclined at 45° to the line of direction, with the heel off the ground, and the knee of the working leg is pointed to the side.

We require also **low rear leg position** and **very low rear leg position.** In these, the working foot is placed against the back of the supporting leg as in the ordinary rear leg position, but with the toe of the working foot at the appropriate height off the ground.[1]

The open positions

An *open position* is one in which the working foot is not in contact with the supporting foot or leg. The open positions are the various 2nd and 4th positions and the crossed position.

In an open position, the supporting foot is inclined at 45° to the line of direction, with the heel off the ground. When the toe of the working foot is pointed in an open position, the knee of the working leg should be straight. When a step or spring is made on to the working foot in an open position, the knee of the working leg should be slightly relaxed.

2nd and 4th positions. The classical 2nd and 4th positions only enable us to describe movements of the working foot to the side, front, and rear. We require also further positions to enable us to describe movements of the working foot in other directions, and to these we give the

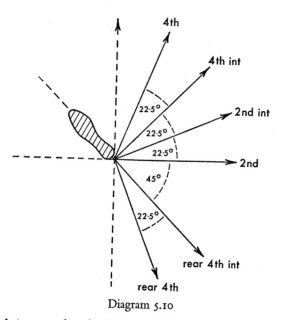

Diagram 5.10

names '2nd intermediate', '4th intermediate', and 'rear 4th intermediate'. These three new positions, and the classical 2nd, 4th, and rear 4th positions, are shown roughly by Diagram 5.10 in the case in which

[1] The rear leg positions are essentially rear 5th aerial positions. However, they occur so frequently in Scottish dancing that it seems worth while to give them a special name.

the working foot is the right foot. Here and later we abbreviate 'intermediate' to 'int.'

Not all of the various ground and aerial 2nd and 4th positions occur in the steps we have to describe, and we therefore restrict ourselves here to the precise definitions of those positions which we actually require.

(i) When the toe of the working foot is pointed in an open position, the working foot is, so far as possible, pointed in the appropriate direction shown in Diagram 5.10. An exception to this rule is 4th position, where the working foot is inclined at 45° to the line of direction. The actual positions of the working foot when the toe is pointed in 2nd, 4th int., and 4th positions are shown in Diagram 5.11 in the case in which the working foot is the right foot.

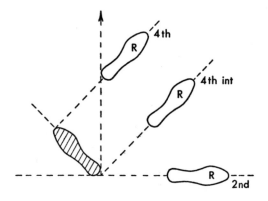

Diagram 5.11

(ii) When a step or a spring is made on to the working foot in an open position, the working foot is inclined at an angle of 45° to the line of direction. The positions of the RF when a step or spring is made on to it in 2nd, 4th int., 4th, and rear 4th positions are shown in Diagram 5.12. In the case of 2nd and 4th int. positions, the distance between the heels of the supporting foot and working foot is approximately one foot's length; the other two positions are determined as in the diagram.

(iii) We require also *semi-open positions*, in which the working foot is placed midway between 1st position and the corresponding full open positions. Diagram 5.13 shows the positions of the feet when a step or spring is made on the RF in semi 2nd and semi 4th positions. In each case the distance between the heels is approximately one half foot's-length.

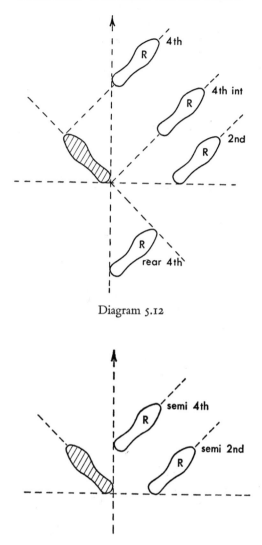

Diagram 5.12

Diagram 5.13

(iv) In the various 2nd and 4th *aerial* positions, the working foot is extended, at the appropriate height, in the directions shown in Diagram 5.10, the knee of the working leg being kept straight. In the 2nd, 2nd int., and 4th int. aerial positions, the working foot actually points in the directions shown in Diagram 5.10. In the 4th aerial position, the working foot is inclined at 45° to the line of direction, while in the rear 4th and rear 4th int. aerial positions, the toe of the working foot is turned out as far as possible. The relative positions of the feet in the various

G

aerial positions, as seen from above, are shown in Diagram 5.14, the working foot here being the right foot.

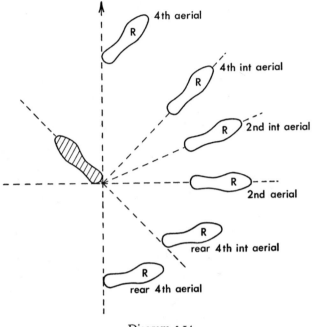

Diagram 5.14

(v) We require also a semi 4th very low aerial position. In this, the working foot is about one inch vertically above the semi 4th ground position (Diagram 5.13).

Crossed position. Diagram 5.15 shows the right foot placed in the crossed position. The feet are at right angles to each other and equally inclined to the line of direction, and both heels are close to the ground.

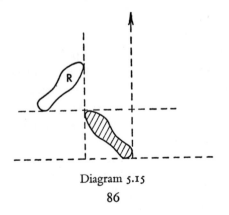

Diagram 5.15

COUNTING OF THE STEPS TO MUSIC

In our descriptions of steps, we describe the movements of the dancer's feet corresponding to the various beats of the music, the musical beats themselves being indicated by a system of counting. This counting of the beats is an important aid in the teaching of the steps—beginners tend to find it easier to perform movements to numbers than to perform them to the beats of a particular tune—so that the counting not only must correspond to the beats of the music, but must also be easy to say verbally. In this section we deal briefly with the different types of tunes used for Scottish dancing,[1] and with the method of counting the beats which we employ in each case.

On the mainland of Scotland, the Western Isles, and Orkney, Reels were almost invariably danced to strathspeys and reels. So far as we know, the only exception to this is a Reel from the island of Barra, Cath nan Coileach, which was danced to a jig. For Country Dances, on the other hand, there was much greater variety in the type of tune employed, and strathspeys, reels, jigs, Scotch measures, and schottisches were all in use.

Strathspeys and *schottisches* are both slow tunes in 4/4 time. They have a crotchet rhythm, that is to say that their essential musical rhythms are both of the form:

The difference between the two types of tune lies in the accenting of the beats and the way in which these beats are made up. In a strathspey, the four beats in each bar are almost evenly accented (there is, of course, a slightly stronger accent on the first beat of each bar), and many of the beats are made up of a semi-quaver and a dotted quaver. The following example shows the form of two typical bars of a strathspey.

In a schottische, the first and third beats in each bar are more heavily accented than the second and fourth, and most of the beats are made up

---

[1] For a more detailed discussion of these and other dance tunes, see (299).

of a dotted quaver and a semi-quaver. Thus a typical bar of a schottische is of the form:

A good example of a strathspey is 'The Marquis of Huntly's Highland Fling'; 'The Brig o' Perth' is a typical schottische.

In the steps performed to strathspeys and schottisches which are described here, the movements fall only on the four main beats of the music, and the counts '1, 2, 3, 4' which represent these beats (as indicated above) are therefore adequate for our descriptions of the steps.

Scotch measures and *reels* are both quick tunes in Common time, and nowadays both are usually written in 4/4 time.

A reel is a very smoothly flowing tune—good examples are 'The High Road to Linton', 'Mrs MacLeod of Raasay', and 'The De'il Among the Tailors'. The essential musical rhythm of a reel is a quaver rhythm, and the four beats in each bar are almost evenly accented (there is again, of course, a slightly stronger accent on the first beat). The rhythmic skeleton of a typical bar of a reel is thus as shown below, with the four beats on the notes marked 1, 2, 3, 4.

The musical beats of a reel are most naturally represented by the counts '1, 2, 3, 4' indicated above. This method of counting the beats, however, is not particularly well suited to the fairly numerous steps performed to reel tunes in which the movements fall on only the first and third beats of the bar, and in our descriptions of steps performed to reel tunes we use the more convenient counts '1 & 2 &' as shown below.

A Scotch measure is a much more 'bouncy' tune than a reel, typical examples being 'Petronella', 'Corn Rigs', and 'Flowers of Edinburgh'. A Scotch measure has a crotchet rhythm, with two main beats, and two weaker beats, in each bar, the rhythmic skeleton of a typical bar being as shown.

Here the four beats are most naturally represented by the counts '1 & 2 &', as indicated; the beats are of equal duration, but there is a strong accent on the beat '1', a medium accent on the beat '2', and weak accents on the two beats '&'.

Within living memory this type of tune does not appear to have been distinguished by any special name. The name 'Scotch measure' which we have adopted here is that which was commonly used for such tunes in the eighteenth and early nineteenth centuries.

For the majority of steps performed to reels and Scotch measures, the counts '1 & 2 &' given above are sufficient. In a few of the travelling steps, however, these counts do not adequately represent the timing of the movements. The particular steps concerned here begin with a preliminary movement at the end of the bar preceding that in which the main movements of the step take place, this preliminary movement being performed very slightly after the musical beat; the nearest approximation to the timing of these steps is that given by the counts '*a* 1 & 2 *a* 1 & 2 . . .' as shown below, and we therefore adopt this system of counting for these particular steps.

A *jig* is a quick tune in 6/8 time in which the melodic units are either a crotchet and a quaver or a triplet of quavers. Jigs are further subdivided into *single* or *double* jigs according as the first or the second of these melodic units predominates. Thus in a single jig the essential musical rhythm is

while in a double jig it is

In words, a single jig has the rhythm 'tum-ty tum-ty tum-ty tum-ty', while a double jig has the rhythm 'tumpity tumpity tumpity tumpity'. Typical examples of single jigs are 'Scottish Reform' and 'The New Rigged Ship', while 'The Irish Washerwoman' is a good example of a double jig.

The steps used in social dances to jig tunes all have the inherent rhythm of a single jig[1]—this does not prevent their performance to a double jig. Thus for such steps we have only to consider a system of counting which fits the single jig, and here we adopt the counts '1 and 2 and' as indicated below. There is a strong accent on the count '1', a medium accent on the count '2', and weak accents on the two counts 'and'.

1   and   2   and

It remains only to mention the tempos of these tunes. Within living memory, reels, Scotch measures, and jigs have all been played at a tempo of 60 to 64 bars per minute,[2] schottisches have been played at 40 bars per minute, and strathspeys at 40 to 42 bars per minute. These tempos apply equally to Reels and Country Dances.

The only one of these tempos which requires special comment is that of the strathspey. It is now a widely held belief that Country Dances to strathspey tunes were slow dignified dances, and the tempo adopted for these dances nowadays is sometimes even as low as 26 bars per minute. This funereal tempo used for strathspeys today appears to be entirely a modern development, and we have neither met nor heard of any dance musician practising before 1914 who played strathspeys for dancing at other than the brisk tempo given above. It is true that there were 'slow strathspeys', but within living memory such tunes have been solo pieces for the expert fiddler, and the only dance ever known to have been performed to them was the Strathspey Minuet, a Scottish form of the Minuet which was completely dead by 1850.

It is convenient to have a single term to describe those dances which are performed to reels, Scotch measures, or jigs, and in the sequel we shall refer to such dances as being 'in quick tempo'. We shall also refer to those dances which are performed to strathspeys or schottisches as being 'in strathspey tempo'.

[1] There are two exceptions to this, but we deal with these steps separately in Chapter XI.

[2] Shetland is exceptional here (see Chapter IX).

DESCRIPTIONS OF THE STEPS

The steps are divided into 'strathspey travelling steps', 'strathspey setting steps', 'quick travelling steps', and 'quick setting steps', the setting steps being danced more or less on the spot, usually by two dancers facing each other.

In our descriptions of steps we observe the following conventions.

(i) The dancer faces to the front unless otherwise instructed.

(ii) Throughout the steps the knees should be kept out, and the heels should not touch the ground unless instructions are given to the contrary.

(iii) The positions of the working foot are relative to the other foot (*and move with the dancer*).

(iv) We assume, except where instructions to the contrary are given, that all steps are begun from 1st position. (When the steps are used in actual dances, they will naturally be begun from various positions, but we leave the reader to make such changes as are required in each case.)

(v) The movements of each step are described under 'counts' corresponding to the musical beats. Where the step occupies one bar of music or less, we give only the appropriate counts; where it occupies more than one bar we usually give both the bar numbers and the counts. The bar numbers are printed in bold face type, and the counts corresponding to the musical beats in ordinary type (thus, for example, **2.** 3 denotes the count '3' in the second bar of the step).

If no significant movement in the step falls on a particular beat of the music, we simply make no mention of the count corresponding to that beat.

The dancer should finish the movements described under each count exactly on the musical beat corresponding to that count. Thus, for example, if the movement described against a particular count is 'hop on LF and point R toe in 2nd position', then the dancer's LF should reach the ground, and his R toe should reach 2nd position, exactly on the musical beat corresponding to that count. He must therefore begin the movement before the musical beat.

When the movement on a particular count brings the working foot into a ground position, then the foot should remain on the ground until it is time to begin the next movement.

(vi) When the instructions under a particular count say '*step* on the RF' (and similarly for the LF), then the RF reaches the ground exactly on the musical beat corresponding to that count. When the RF reaches the ground, the weight is at first more or less equally distributed between the two feet, and is then gradually transferred to the RF. (The transference of weight actually takes place after the musical beat, and should, if we were to proceed strictly in accordance with (v), be mentioned in the instructions under the succeeding count. However, we take this as implicit in the original instruction to 'step on the RF'.)

(vii) *Step to the right on the RF* means that the final position of the RF when the step is completed is directly to the right of its starting position. Similar meanings apply to *step to the left on the LF*, and *step forward* (on either foot). Note that the final position of the working foot here is not necessarily one of our basic positions.

(viii) When one foot is *closed* to another, the weight is taken on both feet.

(ix) *Hop on LF* means the action of rising off the ground and landing with the weight on the LF, and similarly for *hop on RF*. We shall generally[1] use the term 'hop' where the supporting foot is the same before and after the action. Except where stated to the contrary, there is no horizontal movement of the foot on which the hop is made.

(x) *Spring* means the action of rising off the ground and landing again, either on one foot, or on both feet. We shall generally use the term 'spring' either where the weight is transferred from one foot to the other during the action (when we say there is a spring on to the new supporting foot), or where the weight is equally distributed on both feet after the action is completed (when we say there is a spring on to both feet).

When a spring is made off both feet on to both feet, there is no horizontal movement of the body.

(xi) A *balance backward on to the RF* is begun with the RF in a front open aerial position. To perform the movement, bring the RF back to 5th position and spring lightly on to it. The spring off the LF is made just before the RF reaches 5th position (the two feet should actually touch each other), and after the spring the LF is extended backwards to some rear aerial position. Similarly, *balance forward on to the RF* is begun with the RF in a rear open aerial position. The RF is brought down into rear 5th position and just before it meets the ground there is a light spring off the LF on to it. After the spring, the LF is extended to some front aerial position. Similar remarks apply to *balance backward or forward on to the LF*.

---

[1] But not always; there are occasional exceptions at the beginnings of steps.

STRATHSPEY TRAVELLING STEPS

Among the various strathspey travelling steps which were in use within living memory, there were two which may be regarded as basic, and we begin with the descriptions of these; in each case we describe the movements performed with the right foot. Both steps occupy one bar of music, and the counting is the standard one for strathspeys and schottisches (p. 88).

Strathspey travelling step A

Count 1 Step forward on RF.
Count 2 Close LF to rear 3rd or rear 5th position.
Count 3 Step forward on RF.
Count 4 Hop on RF and take LF to 4th low aerial position. (The LF swings straight through from back to front in a leisurely easy movement, with no appreciable bend of either knee.)

We have found this step only in the Lowlands, the East and Central Highlands, and Orkney; we have never met it in the West Highlands and the Western Isles. The step was virtually the only step used in Country Dances in strathspey tempo. It was also commonly used in Reels, and at least four prominent teachers in the Lowlands and the adjacent Highlands, Peter Marshall of Kirkpatrick-Durham, John Aird of Stranraer,[1] 'Dancie' Reid of Newtyle, and James Neill of Forfar, taught it as the proper strathspey travelling step for these dances. In Orkney, where it was used in the old native Reels, it appears to have been the only strathspey travelling step known on the islands prior to the advent of mainland teachers such as Mr MacDougall (p. 55).

A variant of Step A, in which the 'swing through' of the left foot on count '4' is performed with a slight lift of the left knee, was taught by John Muir of Motherwell and his pupil, Professor Blackley of Lanark. The former taught it only for use in Reels, the latter for use both in Reels and in the Country Dance Glasgow Highlanders.

Strathspey travelling step B

Count 1 Step forward on RF.
Count 2 Close LF to rear 3rd or rear 5th position.
Count 3 Step forward on RF.

---

[1] John Aird had his headquarters in Stranraer and taught throughout Wigtownshire, probably from about 1880 until some time between 1918 and 1930. The other three dancing-teachers referred to here have already been mentioned in Chapter I.

Count 4 Hop on RF and bring LF to front leg position, with the L knee turned well out.

This was the usual strathspey travelling step in the Highlands and the Western Isles. It was also used in the Lowlands, but was much less common there than step A. Its use, in all districts, was almost entirely confined to Reels, and it was taught as the correct strathspey travelling step for these dances by both Highland and Lowland teachers, for instance, David Anderson in Dundee, J. Scott Skinner in the North-east, Mr MacDougall in the West Highlands, James McCulloch in southern Ayrshire,[1] Professor Buck in the Borders, and Mr D. G. MacLennan in Edinburgh. Professor Buck also taught this step as the correct step for use in Country Dances in strathspey tempo, but his pupils were surprisingly resistant on this point and reverted to step A as soon as they had ceased to attend his classes.

Before about 1900, step B was the normal strathspey travelling step used in the Scotch (Foursome) Reel by competitors at the Highland Games, although Games dancers, with their light shoes, would normally 'close' on count '2' by bringing the toe of the rear foot right underneath the instep of the front foot (39).

We have also met two steps which appear to be variants of step B. The first, step C below, is occasionally used in Reels and Country Dances at the big Highland Balls (83); step D was sometimes used by Games dancers about the year 1900 (31, 91), and it may well have been in use before this date.

Strathspey travelling step C
Counts 1–3 As in step B.
Count 4 Hop on RF and bring LF to 3rd very low aerial position.

Strathspey travelling step D
Count 1 Step forward on RF.
Count 2 Close L toe under R instep in rear 5th position.
Count 3 Step forward on RF.
Count 4 Hop on RF and pass LF through front leg position (with the L knee turned well out) and forward to 4th low aerial position.

[1] James McCulloch taught in the southern half of Ayrshire from about 1887 until 1937. He made his headquarters in Crosshill, and his territory covered roughly the region between Ballantrae, Barrhill, Dalmellington, Dalrymple, and Dunure. He died in 1941 at the age of 82.

It is interesting to compare the descriptions of these four steps A–D with the descriptions of Reel travelling steps given in the early nineteenth century by two dancing-masters, Francis Peacock of Aberdeen, and F. J. Lambert of Norwich. Peacock's description (204; 1805) is as follows.

'The common step for the *promenade*, or figure of the reel ... is done by advancing the right foot forward, the left following it behind: in advancing the same foot a second time, you hop upon it,[1] and one step is finished. You do the same motions after advancing the left foot, and so on alternately with each foot.'

Peacock says that the Gaelic name of this step is 'Cèum-siubhail', from 'Cèum, a step, and siubhail, to glide, to move, to go on with rapidity', and he implies that the step was in common use in the Highlands in his time.

The value of this description of Peacock's is considerably enhanced by the fact that he was an old man when he wrote it. He taught in Aberdeen from 1744 until his death in 1807 at the age of 84, so that his description probably refers to the period about 1750–1800. Moreover, as he remarks, his position in Aberdeen gave him a knowledge of the different steps used throughout the Highlands: 'Our Colleges draw hither, every year, a number of students from the Western Isles, as well as from the Highlands, and the greater part of them excell in [Reels] ...; some of them, indeed, in so superior a degree that I, myself, have thought them worthy of imitation'. In his book Peacock gives a number of Reel steps, and all of these have Gaelic names, a sign that they were current in the Highlands.

The second description, by Lambert (260; c. 1820),[2] is that of 'the step forward in four movements, which is used in forming the figure of the reel'. Lambert mentions this as 'the most useful' of the 'Scotch steps', his description being as follows.

'The first movement is made by walking forward with the right foot to the fourth position; the second movement by placing the left foot behind the right to the fifth position; the third is another walk with the right foot to the fourth position; and in the fourth movement the left foot is brought forward to the fourth position, at the same time making

[1] Unfortunately Peacock does not specify the movements of the left foot during the hop.
[2] Of Lambert, we know only that he practised in Norwich.

a hop upon the right foot; the left foot remains raised from the ground ready to make the same step.'[1]

Lambert's description is clearly that of our step A, and it is interesting to note that he describes the Lowland step A rather than one of the Highland steps B–D. It is probably also this same Lowland step to which Elizabeth Grant of Rothiemurchus (a Highlander herself) referred, when in 1810 she remarked rather disparagingly of 'the orthodox English regular four-in-a-bar style of evenly goose-stepping the Scotch reel' (279), for there is undoubtedly a similarity between the 'swing-through' of step A and the 'goose-step'.

We cannot identify Peacock's 'Cèum-siubhail' with the same certainty, for all four of our steps A–D fit his description. It seems likely, however, that the 'Cèum-siubhail' was similar to one of the Highland steps B–D rather than to the Lowland step A. We should add that Atkinson (226; 1900) identifies the 'Cèum-siubhail' as our step D, but gives no reasons for this identification.[2]

We know of no other description of step A in print, but step B is described in the ballroom guides of Anderson (220–3; c. 1886–1902), Smith (224; c. 1889), MacNeilage (227; c. 1900), and Orr Robertson (228; c. 1900). All these writers give it as a Reel step.

Before we leave steps of this general form, we must mention one such step which has been introduced within comparatively recent years. This is as follows.

Strathspey travelling step E

Count 1 Step forward on RF.

Count 2 On the actual count '2', close the L toe under the R instep in rear 5th position, and, as soon as the LF touches the ground, swiftly extend the RF to 4th int. low aerial position.

Count 3 Bring RF back from this position and spring on to it, at the same time taking LF to rear leg position, with the L knee turned well out (there is very little forward movement on the spring).

Count 4 Hop on RF and bring LF to front leg position, still with the L knee turned out.

---

[1] Neither Peacock nor Lambert state whether their steps were intended to be used with both strathspeys and reels, or with only one of these. In the absence of evidence to the contrary, we must assume that they were intended to be used with both.

[2] Atkinson actually refers to the step under the name 'Kemshóole'—this word is given by Peacock as a guide to the pronunciation of the Gaelic name.

This step is said to have been introduced about the year 1900 by the late James A. Gordon, a well-known Highland dancer (39). It is now very common among Games dancers, and has been adopted as the standard strathspey travelling step by the Scottish Official Board of Highland Dancing (242). It is also used occasionally at the big Highland Balls (83). The only dancing-teachers whom we know to have taught it for use in ordinary social dancing were James Muir of Motherwell and Joseph Wallace junior of Kilmarnock—the former taught it only for use in Reels, the latter for use both in Reels and in the Country Dance Glasgow Highlanders.

All the steps described so far are basically of the same form, namely 'step, close, step, hop'. There are also a few steps which may be described simply as 'step, hop, step, hop' or 'spring, hop, spring, hop', and we give one of these here.

Strathspey travelling step F

Count 1   Take RF forward to 4th low aerial position and spring lightly on to it (the RF comes back a little as the body comes forward). As the RF drops, the L knee bends so that the L toe comes just off the ground in its original position.

Count 2   Hop on RF and at the same time bring the LF straight forward just a little past the RF and then back into 3rd very low aerial position.

Counts 3, 4 With no perceptible pause of the LF in this position, take it forward to 4th low aerial position to perform counts 1 and 2 contrariwise.

When the step is repeated a number of times (as is usually the case), there is no perceptible pause of the RF in 3rd very low aerial position at the end of count '4' before it moves forward to 4th low aerial position for the next count '1'.

This step is used occasionally in both Reels and Country Dances at the big Highland Balls (83).

So far as we know, the only step of this type described in the literature is that given by Atkinson (226; 1900): 'Whenever you have occasion to use the *Kemshoole*, you may substitute a series of light springs from foot to foot (two to each bar), each spring being followed by a light hop, during which the disengaged foot is brought to the front'.

97

We must mention finally the strathspey travelling step used today in Country Dances and Reels by members of the R.S.C.D.S.[1] This appears to be an elaboration of step A made possible by the modern use of light heel-less dancing pumps for ordinary social dancing, and we have never met it among old people.

STRATHSPEY SETTING STEPS

Within living memory the strathspey setting steps most commonly used in Reels were those comprising the solo dance, the Highland Fling. All Highland Fling steps have the same musical length as the normal setting period in a Reel, i.e. eight bars of music, and they thus provide suitable and interesting Reel steps. Most dancing-teachers taught their pupils the Highland Fling as a solo dance, and at the same time taught them to use the individual steps of the dance as setting steps in Reels.

In addition to the steps from the Highland Fling, there were a number of strathspey setting steps which belonged properly to Reels. These steps, which were generally known as 'Strathspey steps', were quite different in character from the Highland Fling steps, in that they often incorporated a certain amount of sideways movement[2] and made much use of foot positions close to the ground.[3] Within living memory, these Strathspey steps were most often taught as 'ladies' steps', but there is ample evidence that they were once performed by both men and women.

The only other strathspey setting step which we know to have been performed in Reels is the 'Highland Schottische step'. This step, which has taken its name from its use in the Circle Dance, the Highland Schottische, is derived from an old Strathspey step; it seems to have been known in most districts, and was particularly common in the Borders and in Orkney.

Of the various Country Dances in strathspey tempo which we have met, the most widely distributed was Glasgow Highlanders. This dance actually incorporates a complete sixteen-bar sequence of the Foursome Reel, comprising an eight-bar period of setting followed by a 'reel of four', and the setting steps used in it were simply those appropriate to the Foursome Reel. In all the other Country Dances in strathspey tempo known to us, the only setting steps used were the 'Common Schottische step' and the 'Highland Schottische step', the former step being used

[1] For a precise description of this step, see Milligan (240).
[2] Most Highland Fling steps (though not all) were danced on the spot.
[3] The Strathspey steps were sometimes called 'side-steps', and sometimes 'low steps'.

whenever the period of setting occupied two bars, the latter when it occupied four bars.

In the following pages we give some examples of the 'Strathspey' steps, together with the two Schottische steps. The Highland Fling steps seem to belong more properly in a discussion of solo dances, and we therefore do not include them here.[1]

We begin with the Strathspey steps. Most of these steps are one bar or two bars in length, and in theory they can be combined in any way the dancer pleases to fill the normal eight-bar period of setting. In actual practice, however, each basic step was usually repeated with the right foot and left foot alternately throughout the eight bars of setting.

In each of the steps below we describe the movements performed with the right foot. The counting is the standard one for strathspeys and schottisches.

Strathspey step A

1. 1 Step on RF in 4th position.
   2 Hop on RF and bring LF to rear leg position.
   3 Step back on LF in its original position.
   4 Hop on LF and bring RF to front leg position.
2. 1 Step on RF in rear 5th position.
   2 Step to the left on LF.
   3 Step on RF in crossed position.
   4 Hop on RF and bring LF to rear leg position.

This step, or some slight variation of it, was fairly common, and was included among the Strathspey steps taught by several dancing-teachers.[2] The actual version given above, for instance, was common in Roxburghshire (61). Another version, using 4th int. position instead of 4th position on the count 1. 1, was taught by James Muir of Motherwell, while a third version, using 4th int. position on count 1. 1 and 4th int. low aerial position on counts 1. 4 and 2. 4, was taught by both James Muir and Joseph Wallace junior of Kilmarnock.

We have also met a fourth version in which the movements in bar 2 were replaced by the following:

[1] Descriptions of various Highland Fling steps can be found in the books of MacKenzie (232), Taylor (237), and MacLennan (239), and in the S.O.B.H.D. handbook (242).

[2] This Strathspey step was published by the R.S.C.D.S. (234) as a suggested setting step for the Country Dance Glasgow Highlanders, and it has now become so closely associated with this dance that it is today known as 'the Glasgow Highlanders step'.

2. 1 Step on RF in crossed position.
   2 Step to the left on LF.
   3 Close RF to 5th position.
   4 Hop on RF and raise LF to rear leg position.

This last version was one of several Strathspey steps taught on the island of South Uist about the year 1890 by John MacMillan, a native of the island who taught dancing in his spare time. John MacMillan was a pupil of Ewen MacLachlan, a teacher from Morar who taught on South Uist from about 1840 until his death in 1879. Mr MacMillan taught the Strathspey steps as 'ladies' steps', but Ewen MacLachlan is known to have taught them to both sexes.

A Strathspey step very similar to this last version is described in a Scottish manuscript of 1818 (203), and another very similar step is given by Atkinson (226).

In addition to the versions mentioned above, James Muir and Joseph Wallace junior also taught a version of the step in which a complete turn to the right is made on bar **2**. The movements here are:

2. 1 Step on RF in rear 5th position and begin to turn to the right, pivoting on the balls of both feet (Diagram 5.16 (a)).

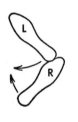

(a)

(b)

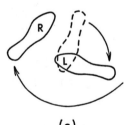

(c)

Diagram 5.16

   2 Continuing to pivot to the right, step on LF in the position shown in Diagram 5.16 (b).

3 Continuing to pivot to the right, step on RF in the position shown in Diagram 5.16 (c).

4 Hop on RF and bring LF to rear leg position or 4th int. low aerial position.

The turn should be completed on the first three counts.

Strathspey step B. We give under this heading two very similar 1-bar steps which were taught by John MacMillan in South Uist. The movements of the first are the same as those of the second bar of John Mac-Millan's version of step A, viz.

Count 1 Step on RF in crossed position.
Count 2 Step to the left on LF.
Count 3 Close RF to 5th position.
Count 4 Hop on RF and raise LF to rear leg position.

The movements of the second step are:

Count 1 Step on RF in rear 5th position.
Count 2 Step to the left on LF.
Count 3 Close RF to rear 5th position.
Count 4 Hop on RF and raise LF to 5th low aerial position.

This second step is an interesting survival, for it is almost identical to the 'single cèum-coisiche' described by Peacock in 1805 (204):

'You pass the right foot behind the left to the fifth position, making a gentle bound, or spring, with the left foot, to the second position; after passing the right foot again behind the left you make a hop upon it, extending the left toe.'

According to Peacock, the name of the step is derived from the Gaelic 'Cèum, a step, and Coiseachadh, to foot it, or ply the foot'. The term 'single' in Peacock's nomenclature merely indicates that the step occupies one bar of music.

Both of the steps above are described by Atkinson (226), subject only to small differences in the position of the free foot on count '4'.

Strathspey step C

1. 1 Hop on LF and point R toe in 5th position.
    2 Hop on LF and point R toe in 4th int. position.
    3 Hop on LF and point R toe in rear 5th position.
    4 Hop on LF and point R toe in 2nd position.

2. 1 Hop on LF and point R toe in 5th position.
   2 Hop on LF and point R toe in 4th int. position.
   3 Bring RF back and drop on it, at the same time raising LF to low rear leg position.
   4 Hop on RF and point L toe in 4th int. position.

We were shown this step by the late Miss Margaret Paterson, who taught dancing in Auchencairn, Kirkcudbrightshire, between the two World Wars. Miss Paterson learnt the step about 1895.

Strathspey step D. This step begins with the RF in 4th int. low aerial position.

1. 1 Balance backward on to the RF, taking LF to a loose low rear leg position (the LF should be about 4 inches from the R leg).
   2 Hop on RF and point LF in 4th int. low aerial position.
   3 Balance backward on to the LF, taking RF to a loose low rear leg position (as in count '1').
   4 Hop on LF and point RF in 4th int. low aerial position.
2. 1 Step on RF in 5th position.
   2 Step on LF in rear 4th position.
   3 Close RF to 5th position.
   4 Hop on RF and point LF in 4th int. low aerial position.

This was one of the Strathspey steps taught by John Muir of Motherwell.

The Common and Highland Schottische steps. These two steps derive their names from their occurrence in the Circle Dances, the Common Schottische and the Highland Schottische. Both steps were used in Country Dances in strathspey tempo, and the Highland Schottische step was also used in Reels.

The Common Schottische step

Count 1 Step to the right on RF.
Count 2 Close LF to rear 5th position.
Count 3 Step to the right on RF.
Count 4 Hop on RF and bring LF to low rear leg position.

The 'close' on count '2' was sometimes made in rear 3rd position, and rear leg position was sometimes used on count '4'.

Within living memory, this step was the most common setting step in Country Dances in strathspey tempo; it was used whenever the period of setting occupied 2 bars, and was then performed once with the right foot and once with the left.

The Highland Schottische step. There were a number of versions of this step in use before 1914, but within living memory the following was the most common.[1]

1. 1 Hop on LF and point R toe in 2nd position.
   2 Hop on LF and bring RF to rear leg position.
   3 Hop on LF and point R toe in 2nd position.
   4 Hop on LF and bring RF to front leg position.
2. 1 Step to the right on RF.
   2 Close LF to rear 5th position.
   3 Step to the right on RF.
   4 Hop on RF and bring LF to rear leg position.

In Country Dances this step was used whenever the period of setting occupied four bars, and was then performed once with the right foot and once with the left. In Reels (and in the Country Dance Glasgow Highlanders) it was usually performed with right and left feet alternately throughout the setting time.

The 'Highland Schottische step' given above occurs in most descriptions of the Highland Schottische after about 1875, but in descriptions of the dance prior to this date the movements on bar 1 of the step are of a different form. For example, in Willock's *Manual of Dancing* (213; 1865)[2] the commencing movements of the Highland Schottische, performed by the man with his left foot, are described as follows:

'The gentleman hops twice on the right foot, giving a beat in the fifth position in front, and one behind, with the left foot. He then passes to the left with the same step as that in the [Common Schottische] . . .'

A step which was apparently similar to this earlier Highland Schottische step was taught by James Neill of Forfar, both as a strathspey setting step for use in Reels and also for use in the Circle Dance the Highland Schottische. Here the movements on bar 1 of the step, which Mr Neill himself called 'beat before and beat behind', were as follows.

1. 1 Hop on LF and point R toe in semi 4th position (with the R knee bent so that the lower part of the leg is vertical).

---

[1] In the sequel, we use the term 'Highland Schottische step' to mean this particular version.

[2] The author of this ballroom guide, H. D. Willock, was a dancing-master in Glasgow.

2 Hop on LF and bring RF to front leg position.

3 Hop on LF and point R toe in rear 5th position.

4 Hop on LF and raise RF to rear leg position.

It is probable that these movements of Mr Neill's belong to an early version of the Highland Fling, for in a ballroom guide published about 1860 by members of the Lowe family (212) it is stated that the Highland Schottische 'commences with a portion of the first step of the Highland Fling as follows: The gentleman hops twice on the right foot, at same time giving a beat before, and one behind with the left'. It will be recalled that Mr Neill was a pupil of two members of the Lowe family.

QUICK TRAVELLING STEPS

The most widely used quick travelling steps were the *chassé* and the *hop-one-and-two*. Each of these steps occupies four counts of the music, but we actually describe them performed successively with right and left feet. For reels and Scotch measures the timing of the steps is most closely represented by the counts '*a* 1 & 2' given on p. 89, that is to say:

Both steps begin on the last count '*a*' of the bar preceding that in which the main movements of the step take place.

The chassé

Count *a*	Rise on the ball of LF and
Count 1	step forward on RF.
Count &	Close LF to rear 3rd position.
Count 2	Make a small step forward on RF.

Chassé RF

Counts *a*1	Step forward on LF, with a lilt on the RF as the LF passes it. The lilt takes place on the count '*a*' and the step forward is completed on the count '1'. (In the lilt the R instep bends so that the R heel is momentarily raised a little from its normal position and then lowered again, whilst the ball of the RF remains on the ground.)
Count &	Close RF to rear 3rd position.
Count 2	Make a small step forward on LF.

Chassé LF

Counts *a*1 Step forward on RF, etc.

The 'close' on the count '&' in each bar was also sometimes made in rear 5th position.

The hop-one-and-two. This differs from the chassé only in that the lilt is replaced by a definite hop and that the 'close' is normally in rear 5th position. The movements are:

Count *a*	Hop on LF and	
Count 1	step forward on RF.	Hop-one-and-two RF
Count &	Close LF to rear 5th position.	
Count 2	Make a small step forward on RF.	
Counts *a*1	Step forward on LF, hopping on the RF as the LF passes it. The hop takes place on the count '*a*', and the LF meets the ground on the step forward exactly on the count '1'. There is little or no forward movement of the RF during the hop.	Hop-one-and-two LF
Count &	Close RF to rear 5th position.	
Count 2	Make a small step forward on LF.	
Counts *a*1	Step forward on RF, hopping on the LF, etc.	

On the counts '*a* 1' the rear foot travels smoothly forward with the toe close to the ground, and arrives in the forward position just in time to make the step on the count '1'; the slight delay before the hop emphasizes the drive forward on this step. It must be stressed that there is no pause with the foot raised immediately prior to this step forward on '1'.

The 'close' on the count '&' in each bar was sometimes made by closing the toe of the rear foot right underneath the instep of the front foot—this was the usual position for a dancer wearing light shoes. The 'close' was also sometimes made in rear 3rd position, but this was less common than the use of rear 5th position.

In most parts of Scotland, the usual quick travelling step in Country Dances and the usual quick travelling step in Reels were one or the other of these two steps.

Most of the dancing-teachers who practised within living memory taught the chassé as *the* correct quick travelling step for use in Country Dances, and among the teachers who did so we may mention Mr William Adamson and his father in East Fife, David Anderson, James Neill, and 'Dancie' Reid in Angus and Perthshire, Mr MacDougall in the West Highlands, Joseph Wallace junior in Kilmarnock, Professor McQuiston in southern Ayrshire and Wigtownshire,[1] Professor Buck, Andrew Cochrane,[2] Mr Fletcher, and James Laidlaw in the Borders, Mr George Maxwell in East Lothian, and Mr D. G. MacLennan in Edinburgh. In contrast, we know of only five teachers who taught the hopone-and-two for use in Country Dances, namely Professor Blackley of Lanark, Mr Galbraith of Biggar,[3] James McCulloch of Crosshill, and Peter Marshall of Kirkpatrick-Durham and his pupil and partner, Thomas Shanks, and it is noteworthy that all five of these teachers practised in the south-west, in Lanarkshire, Ayrshire, Dumfriesshire, and Wigtownshire.

In Reels, the hop-one-and-two was much more frequently used than the chassé, particularly in the Highlands, the Western Isles, and Orkney. Neither step, however, was widely *taught* as a Reel step within living memory, for many dancing-teachers did not teach any Reels in which a quick travelling step of this type was required (see p. 153). Among the teachers who taught the hop-one-and-two as a Reel step were David Anderson, Mr MacDougall, and Mr D. G. MacLennan, and it is interest-to note that all three taught it only for use in Reels, and that they taught the chassé for use in Country Dances. We have heard of only three teachers who taught the chassé for use in Reels, namely James Neill of Forfar, Joseph Wallace junior of Kilmarnock, and Andrew Cochrane of West Gordon.

We have also encountered the following alternative form of the hopone-and-two which was sometimes used in Reels, usually only by good dancers. It was, for instance, used by David Anderson in exhibition work, and it was also taught by Mr MacDougall in Arisaig about the

[1] Professor McQuiston belonged to Ayrshire, and held regular classes in southern Ayrshire and Wigtownshire about the year 1900.
[2] Andrew Cochrane was a part-time teacher who held classes in the vicinity of his home at West Gordon in Berwickshire from about 1872 until some time after 1914. His repertoire included a number of uncommon Country Dances, such as Cuckoo's Nest, Bonnie Briest Knots, Merrily Dance the Quaker's Wife, and Mason's Apron. He was taught dancing by his uncle, George Cochrane, who was his predecessor as the local teacher in the Gordon district. George Cochrane died at some time between 1870 and 1880; Andrew Cochrane himself died in 1934 at the age of 82.
[3] Mr Galbraith of Biggar taught from about 1885 until about 1930, and had a regular round of classes in Biggar, Douglas, Muirkirk, Cumnock, and New Cumnock. He left home each Monday on his bicycle with his fiddle strapped to his back, and stayed one night in each of the last four places named, returning to Biggar each week-end.

year 1900; we have also met it in Lanark (81). Like the hop-one-and-two, the step occupies four counts of the music, and begins on the final count '*a*' of the bar preceding that in which the main actions of the step take place. We describe the step performed with right and left feet successively.

Count *a* Hop on LF and bring RF to front leg position.
Count 1 Step forward on RF.
Count & Close L toe under R instep in rear 5th position. } RF
Count 2 Make a small step forward on RF.

Count *a* Hop on RF and bring LF to front leg position, with
       the L knee turned well out.
Count 1 Step forward on LF.
Count & Close R toe under L instep in rear 5th position. } LF
Count 2 Make a small step forward on LF.
Count *a* Hop on LF, etc.

We must also mention here the *skip-change-of-step*. This step is used by members of the R.S.C.D.S. as a travelling step in Country Dances and Reels, and is said to have been collected from old people when the R.S.C.D.S. was first formed in 1923. Performed successively with the right and left feet, the skip-change-of-step is as follows.

Count *a* Hop on LF and swing the RF quickly forward to 4th
      low aerial position.
Count 1 Step forward on RF.
Count & Close LF to rear 3rd position. } RF
Count 2 Make a small step forward on RF.

Count *a* Hop on RF and swing the LF quickly forward to 4th
      low aerial position.
Count 1 Step forward on LF.
Count & Close RF to rear 3rd position. } LF
Count 2 Make a small step forward on LF.

The action of the 'swing-through' is much faster than that of the 'step forward' in the hop-one-and-two, and the foot which comes forward is here held in 4th low aerial position for a fraction of a second before the step forward is made on the count '1'.

The principal difference between the skip-change-of-step and the hop-one-and-two lies in the faster 'swing-through' and the 'hold' in the former, and we have on occasion found it difficult to ascertain from informants who had been taught steps of this type in the past whether they had in fact been taught the skip-change-of-step, the hop-one-and-two, or some intermediate step. However, the majority of the quick travelling steps of the 'hop, step, close, step' type which we have met have certainly been nearer to the hop-one-and-two than to the skip-change-of-step, and, in particular, we know quite definitely that in the step of this type taught by Professor Blackley, Mr Galbraith, James McCulloch, Peter Marshall, Thomas Shanks, and Mr D. G. MacLennan, there was no quick 'swing through' and 'hold' of the front foot.

We should add that the only name for a step of this type which we have heard used by old people is 'the hop-one-two-three'. In naming the step on p. 105, we have therefore simply used this name, altering it only to conform with our system of counting.

The descriptions of these various steps of the form 'hop, step, close, step' should be compared with the descriptions of Reel travelling steps given by Peacock and Lambert (p. 95). The discrepancy between our 'hop, step, close, step' and Peacock's and Lambert's 'step, close, step, hop' is more apparent than real, for Peacock's and Lambert's descriptions presumably give the movements beginning on the count '1', whereas we have described the movements beginning on the preliminary count 'a'. Both the hop-one-and-two and the skip-change-of-step are possible interpretations of Lambert's description, though the skip-change-of-step agrees more closely with this description than does the hop-one-and-two. All three of the steps described above fit Peacock's description of the 'cèum-siubhail', but the alternative form of the hop-one-and-two seems here to be the most likely candidate.

The antiquity of the chassé can be established more definitely, for there is a description of this step in a Scottish manuscript of 1818 (203)[1] which agrees almost exactly with that given above:

[1] This manuscript, entitled *Contre-Danses à Paris 1818*, is in the National Library of Scotland. The title is misleading, for the author was evidently an expert on dancing in Scotland, and the manuscript, which is written in English, is concerned primarily with Scottish practice. The manuscript is in the form of a small bound notebook, and contains descriptions of steps and figures used in Reels, Country Dances, and Quadrilles, together with the descriptions of a few Country Dances. The numbering of the pages is not consecutive, suggesting that the manuscript may consist of extracts from some larger manuscript or printed work, but no such larger work is known either in this country or in the Bibliothèque Nationale in Paris. The notebook was bought a few years ago in a Paris bookshop by a London book-dealer, and nothing is known of its origin.

'Chassé.

1 B[ar]   Right for.^{d} into Pos. IV before.

               Left forward behind it; (or rather with a spring into its place.)

               Right for.^{d} into Pos. IV before.

               Left up Parallel to right; rise on right toe as left passes.

2^d B[ar]   Left for.^{d} into Pos. IV before.

               Right up behind it; (or with a spring into its place as above.)

               Left for.^{d} into Pos. IV before.

               Right up parallel to left: rise on left toe as right passes.

3^d B[ar]   Right forward etc.'

The manuscript makes it clear that this 'chassé' was used in both Reels and Country Dances at the time when the manuscript was written.

A number of other descriptions of 'chassé' steps are given in various eighteenth-century books on dancing, but these steps are not of the same form as the chassé described here.

Travelling pas de Basque. This step approximates in rhythm to the pas de Basque (p. 110). The name is our own—we have never heard the step given a name.

The step occupies one bar of music, and we describe the movements performed with the right foot. The counting here is the standard one for reels and Scotch measures.

Count 1 With a slight spring off the LF, drop forward on to the RF.

Count & Close LF to RF, the weight remaining almost wholly on the RF (the position of the LF is variable, usually rear 3rd position, but with the feet almost parallel to each other).

Count 2 Make a very small step forward on the RF.

This step was used frequently in Country Dances and Reels in all parts of the country, and is still used at the big Highland balls. It was never taught by dancing-teachers, and was, indeed, generally regarded by them as 'bad dancing', but it is in fact a very safe and suitable step for use on a highly polished floor.

Galop step (Slip step). This is of quite different type from the preceding steps. Performed to the left it is as follows.

Count 1   Spring on to LF in 2nd position.

Count &   With a slight spring off the RF, close RF to 1st position.

Counts 2 & Repeat counts '1 &'.

The step can also be performed to the right, in the obvious way. The counting here is the standard one for reels and Scotch measures.

This step takes its name from its use in the Galopade, an early nineteenth century Circle Dance. Within living memory it was most often used in Country Dances, in a *galop* up or down the centre, where a couple took ordinary ballroom hold with each other[1] and moved sideways. The galop step was also very occasionally used in the Country Dance figure *hands round*, but more often this figure was performed with the chassé or the hop-one-and-two.

Pivot step. This step is used when two people swing each other, or when three or more people swing in a basket figure. If the direction of rotation is clockwise, the pivot step is performed by pushing oneself along with the left foot, the action being that of a child pushing a scooter. The left foot should do all the work, and the right foot remains directly beneath the body to support the weight. As the left foot pushes backwards, the body is moved forward, and the right foot moves with it. For tunes in Common time, the left foot pushes on the count '&', and the weight returns to the right foot on the count '1', then the left pushes on the next count '&', and the weight drops back on the right on the count '2'. If the direction of rotation is counter-clockwise, the roles of the left and right feet are interchanged.

In all these quick travelling steps we have given only the counting for reels and Scotch measures. For jigs, the counts '1 & 2 *a*' or '1 & 2 &' are replaced by the counts '1 and 2 and', as indicated on p. 90.

QUICK SETTING STEPS

The pas de Basque. This step was used throughout Scotland as the normal setting step in Country Dances in quick tempo, and indeed in most parts of Scotland it was within living memory the only setting step used in such dances. It was also widely used as a setting step in Reels.

There were basically two different versions of this step in common use, and we describe these in turn. In each case we describe the movements performed with the right foot and give the counting for reels and Scotch measures, which is here the standard '1 & 2 &'. For jigs these

[1] That is to say, the man holds the lady's right hand in his left hand and places his right arm round her waist, while she places her left hand on his right shoulder.

counts should be replaced by counts '1 and 2 and' as on p. 90. The step occupies one bar of music.

Pas de Basque, version I

Count 1   Step on RF in semi 2nd position. This step is normally taken from 5th position, and in this case the R toe moves in an arc of a circle (Diagram 5.17).

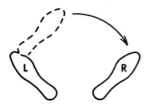

Diagram 5.17

Count &   Place LF in 5th position.

Count 2   Momentarily transfer the weight to the LF and beat with the ball of the RF in rear 5th position.

At the end of count '2', both feet should be on the ground, and this position is retained throughout the last count '&' of the bar.

Mr D. G. MacLennan has told us that he used to teach his pupils to place the ball of the LF in 5th position on the count '&', but the use of this position (which requires the dancer to be higher on the toes than does ordinary 5th position) was unusual. We have also met some people, though only a few, who used 3rd position on count '&' and rear 3rd position on count '2' in place of the front and rear 5th positions.

The step was never performed in a bouncy manner. Indeed, Mr Mac-Lennan has told us that when the step is danced correctly the dancer's shoulders should not move up or down at all.

Pas de Basque, version II.

Pas de Basque, version II. This differs from version I in that the front foot is extended after the beat behind on the count '2'. We assume in our description of this version that the dancer starts in the finishing position of the same step performed with the LF, i.e. with the weight on the LF and the RF in 4th int. very low aerial position.

Count 1   Bring RF back and drop on it, and carry LF round towards 5th position.

Count &   Place LF in 5th position.

Counts 2   Momentarily transfer the weight to the LF and on the count '2' beat with the ball of the RF in rear 5th position. Immediately following the beat, extend the LF to 4th int. very low aerial position so that it arrives there on the count '&'. (This extension of the LF is a leisurely easy movement, and should not be performed with a flick.)

Some dancers used front and rear 3rd positions in place of the two 5th positions on the counts '& 2'. The step was also sometimes performed with a slight sideways movement on count '1', and there were also varying degrees of extension.[1]

Before 1914, version I was by far the more common of these two versions, and was taught by most, and indeed probably all, professional dancing-teachers. Among the teachers whom we definitely know to have taught it were Mr William Adamson and his father in East Fife, David Anderson, James Neill, and 'Dancie' Reid in Angus and Perthshire, Ewan Clayton[2] and Mr Troop[3] in the North-east, D. G. Brown in Inverness,[4] Mr Bailey in the Glasgow region,[5] Professor Blackley and Mr Galbraith in Lanarkshire, Joseph Wallace junior in Kilmarnock, John Aird and James McCulloch in the South-west, Professor Buck, Andrew Cochrane, Mr Fletcher, and James Laidlaw in the Borders, Mr George Maxwell in East Lothian, and Mr D. G. MacLennan in Edinburgh.

On the other hand, before 1914 version II seems to have been used only by people who had never attended dancing classes, and even among such people it was not particularly common. We have never heard of any professional dancing-teacher who taught it prior to the First World War, and indeed to some of the old dancing-teachers it was definitely incorrect. Mr D. G. MacLennan, for instance, has said to us that this version is simply 'bad dancing', and when we demonstrated it

[1] Version II, with front and rear 3rd positions in place of the two 5th positions on the counts '& 2', is the version of the pas de Basque taught today by the R.S.C.D.S. for use in Country Dances.

[2] Ewan Clayton of Elgin was a well-known piper and Highland dancer. He was a stonemason by profession, and held dancing-classes in his spare time. He taught in the neighbourhood of Elgin, and we have also records of his classes from the Island of Flotta about 1905 and from Barra about 1910–14.

[3] Mr Troop taught dancing in Aberdeenshire about 1895.

[4] D. G. Brown combined the professions of dancing-master and tailor, as did his father before him. He was born about 1868 and taught dancing in Inverness and the surrounding districts from about 1890 until at least 1910.

[5] Professor Bailey taught round about Glasgow c. 1892–1900.

to 'Dancie' Reid's daughter, her scornful comment was that 'only people who had never learnt to dance did that step' (53).

Version II should not be confused with a version of the pas de Basque which was used by exhibition and competition dancers in Reels. This is as follows.

Pas de Basque, version III. This also has an extension of the front foot following the beat behind. We describe the step performed with the right foot, and assume that the dancer starts with the weight on the left foot and with the right foot in 2nd int. low aerial position (this is the finishing position of the same step performed with the left foot).

Count 1   Spring on to RF in semi 2nd position.

Count &   Place LF on the half-point in 5th position.

Counts 2 &   Momentarily transfer the weight to the LF and on the count '2' beat with the ball of the RF in rear 5th position. Immediately following the beat, extend the LF to 2nd int. low aerial position so that it arrives there on the count '&'. (This extension of the LF is made with more vigour than in version II, but again must not be performed with a flick.)

This version was performed more on the toes than either of the other two versions. The extension was also sometimes made either to 2nd low aerial position or to a position slightly in front of 2nd int. low aerial position.

Two teachers of Highland dancing in Kirkmichael in Perthshire, Miss Lilian and Miss Flora MacMillan, have told us that their father, Hugh MacMillan, taught them this version of the pas de Basque when they were children, and that he himself had used this version when he competed in the Games about 1902–4. This, however, is the earliest occurrence of this version which we have been able to trace.

Version III, with a slightly different rhythm, is used nowadays in the Sword Dance, Gille Callum, but this use seems to date back only to about 1910, and before that, the version of the pas de Basque used in Gille Callum was similar to version I, with no extension of the foot on the last count '&'. The introduction of version III to the Sword Dance seems to be due to Sydney Black and Robert Cuthbertson, two well-known Highland dancers (39).

The earliest description of the pas de Basque known to us is in the

Scottish manuscript *Contre-Danses à Paris 1818* quoted previously (203), and is as follows.

'B I Spring off right into Pos. II a little back
   ,,   Slide left into Pos. IV before
   ,,   Slide up right into Pos. V behind
   ,,   Rest one second.
Pos. III is often substituted for Pos. V in this step.'

In the manuscript the step is listed as one of the 'Quadrille Steps for Setting', but it is also specified as the setting step to be used in the Country Dance figure 'Change Sides and Set; back again and set'.

This version of the pas de Basque still survives in the ballet. It differs from both of our versions I and II in the use of 4th position on the second movement, but is similar to version I in that it finishes in a closed position. It would appear, therefore, that the evolutionary process has been from the manuscript version to version I by the substitution of 5th position for 4th position, and thence to version II by the addition of the extension.

Version I of the pas de Basque is given by Anderson (220–3), Smith (224), MacNeilage (227), Orr Robertson (228), MacKenzie (232), and MacLennan (239). Anderson does not use the name 'pas de Basque' but instead calls the step 'the Petronella step', probably in order that he can maintain his claim to give 'full tuition in the art of dancing without the use of French terms'. Smith also uses the name 'Petronella step', but in this he is simply copying Anderson, whom he quotes on every possible occasion.

So far as we know, the first writer to describe a pas de Basque with an extension is Atkinson (226; 1900), his description being as follows.

'Count one: Spring lightly to the right on to the R, immediately placing the L behind the R ankle.
   and: Smartly slip the L to the left, passing lightly on to it.
   two: As smartly displace the L with the R, at the same time extending L to second [low aerial?] position.'

We know of no other writer who gives a similar description of the pas de Basque, and we have not met this particular form of the step among our informants. It is possible, however, that this was a forerunner of the Games version III.

In the south-west of Scotland, the pas de Basque was frequently known as the 'balance-step'—this was, for instance, the name used by

Professor McQuiston and Peter Marshall in Dumfriesshire and Wigtownshire. John Aird of Stranraer called the step the 'single balance', the term 'single' being used to distinguish it from the following 'double' form of the step which he taught for use in Reels.

Double balance, or Double pas de Basque. This occupies two bars of music. Performed with the RF, the movements are as follows.

1. 1   Step on RF in semi 2nd position.

    &   Place LF in crossed position.

    2   Momentarily transfer the weight to the LF and beat with the ball of the RF on the spot.

    &   Place LF in a position about 3 inches to the left of 5th position.

2. 1   Momentarily transfer the weight to the LF and beat with the ball of the RF on the spot (the RF should not be closed up to the LF here, but should remain in the same position as at the end of count '1. 1').

    &   Place LF again in crossed position.

    2   Momentarily transfer the weight to the LF and beat with the ball of the RF on the spot.

As in version I of the pas de Basque, both feet should be on the ground at the end of count '2. 2' and should remain there throughout the last count '&' of bar 2.

When used as a Reel setting step, this 'double balance' was performed either with right and left feet alternately throughout the setting period, or in the following sequence:

1, 2   Pas de Basque (version I) with RF, LF.

3, 4   Double balance with RF.

5–8   Perform bars **1–4** contrariwise.

Reel steps in quick tempo. The remaining quick setting steps which are described here were used only in Reels,[1] and not in Country Dances.

Most Reel setting steps for use in quick tempo are half a bar, one bar, or two bars in length, and in theory they can be combined in any way the dancer pleases to fill the normal eight-bar period of setting.[2] In actual practice, however, only a few combinations occurred, and probably most often a single step was repeated with the right foot and left foot alternately throughout the eight bars of setting. For instance, the most

---

[1] That is to say, so far as social dancing was concerned. Some of them were used in solo exhibition dances.

[2] The period of setting in a Reel may exceptionally occupy 16 bars of music.

common combination in the Lowlands consisted of eight pas de Basque performed with the right and left feet alternately. Another favourite combination consisted of a two-bar setting step performed once with the right foot and once with the left, followed by two pas de Basque and either four points, four shuffles, or four highcuts. Of these last three steps, shuffles and highcuts are described later. With the four points, the last four bars of such a combination is:

5, 6 Pas de Basque with RF, LF.
7. 1 Spring on to RF and point L toe in 4th position.
    2 Bring LF back and spring on to it, at the same time pointing R toe in 4th position.
8 Bringing RF back, repeat bar **7**.

The counting here, and throughout this section, is the standard counting for reels, i.e. '1 & 2 &' (p. 88). When the steps are performed to jigs, the counts '1 & 2 &' are replaced by counts '1 and 2 and', as on p. 90.

Four of the steps described here (steps K, M, N, O) are half a bar in length. They were used either by themselves for the full 8-bar period, or for filling in an odd 2 or 4 bars in the period. Shuffles and highcuts (steps N, O) were usually used at the end of a setting period, and were not normally used in the same 8-bar period as 'four points'.

There are three 1-bar steps (steps A, F, G). These were always repeated with alternate feet for either 2, 4, 6, or 8 bars. With two exceptions, the remaining steps are 2 bars in length, and these were always repeated with alternate feet for 4, 6, or 8 bars. So far as we know, two different 2-bar steps were not used together in the same 8-bar period of setting. The two exceptions, steps R and S, are 8-bar steps.

Six of these steps (I, J, K, M, O, P) were first taught to us by our teachers, Pipe-Major David Taylor and Mr Jack McConachie, and we have since met them repeatedly among our informants. The remaining steps have all been collected from various informants.

Quick Reel step A (Spring, step, close). There were two versions of this step in use, both occupying one bar of music. As usual, we describe the movements performed with the RF.

Version I

Count 1   Spring on to both feet, with the RF in 5th position.
Count &   Make a small step to the right on RF.

Counts 2 &   Momentarily transfer the weight to the RF, and on the count '2' close the LF to rear 5th position. Immediately following the 'close', extend the RF to 2nd low aerial position so that it arrives there on the count '&'.

If these movements are followed by the same movements performed contrariwise, then the RF is brought back for the spring on count '1' of the second bar, so that there is no sideways motion of the body on this spring.

Version II

Count 1   Spring on to both feet, with the RF in 5th position.
Count &   Make a small step to the right on RF.
Count 2   Close LF to rear 5th position.

Here there is no extension. At the end of count '2', both feet should be on the ground, and this position is retained throughout the last count '&' of the bar.

Version II of this step was a fairly common Reel step, and was taught by a number of teachers, in particular James Neill of Forfar, James Mc-Culloch of Crosshill, and Joseph Wallace junior of Kilmarnock. It is also described, either by itself or as a part of other longer steps, in the books of Anderson (220–3), Smith (224), and MacKenzie (232). Version I was less common, and the only teacher whom we know to have taught it is Mr D. G. MacLennan. The name 'spring, step, close' is our own; we have never heard the step given a name by old people.

The 'spring, step, close' was at one time one of the basic quick tempo Reel setting steps. This can be inferred from the Scottish manuscript *Contre-Danses à Paris 1818* mentioned earlier (203), for of the eight 'Quick Reel Steps' described in this manuscript, no fewer than five contain a 'spring, step, close' movement similar to version I above.

The description of the movement given in the manuscript is actually couched in classical ballet terms:

'Assemble dessous w^t right (*or* Assemble with right behind) Glissade dessous to left.'[1]

Brief definitions of the terms 'assemble behind' and 'glissade' are given in the manuscript itself, and these agree with the more detailed definitions given by two contemporary writers, Lambert (260) and Strathy

[1] The manuscript also adds the information that the movement occupies one bar of music.

(208). Using the manuscript definitions of these terms, as amplified by Lambert and Strathy, we find that in our notation the manuscript movement is as follows. It commences on the last count '&' of the bar preceding that in which its main actions take place, and in order to exhibit as clearly as possible its similarity to version I above we describe it performed successively with right and left feet (the manuscript description quoted above is actually that of the movement performed with the left foot).

Begin with the weight on both feet, and with LF in 5th position. Then:

	&	Take the weight on the RF and slide the L toe into 2nd position, with the L knee turned well outwards.	Assemble dessous with left
1.	1	Spring lightly off the RF, bringing the LF back, and land on both feet, with the RF in 5th position.	
	&	Slide the RF to 2nd position.	Glissade dessous to right
	2	Close LF to rear 5th position.	
	&	Take the weight on the LF and slide the R toe into 2nd position, with the R knee turned well outwards.	Assemble dessous with right
2.	1	Spring lightly off the LF, bringing the RF back, and land on both feet, with the LF in 5th position.	
	&	Slide the LF to 2nd position.	Glissade dessous to left
	2	Close RF to rear 5th position.	

A comparison of the actions on the four counts '1 & 2 &' of bar 1 here with the actions in version I of the 'spring, step, close' shows how close is the similarity of these two steps to each other.

In addition to the five quick Reel setting steps in the manuscript which contain the movement

'Assemble dessous wᵗ right, glissade dessous to left,'

another two of the eight steps in the manuscript contain the very similar movement

'Assemble dessus with right. Glissade dessus to left.'

The 'dessus' here (in place of the 'dessous' above) means that rear 5th position is now used in place of 5th position, and vice versa.

A movement similar to the 'spring, step, close' is described by

Peacock (204) under the name 'Cèum Badenoch'. This is actually of the form 'step, close, spring', but since Peacock tells us that we may 'change, divide, add to, or *invert* the different steps' which he describes, we need not regard the difference in the order of the actions in the Cèum Badenoch and the 'spring, step, close' as significant. Peacock's description of the Cèum Badenoch is as follows.

'You make a gentle spring to one side with the right foot, immediately placing the left behind it; then do a single Entrechat, that is a cross *caper* or leap, changing the situation of the feet, by which the right foot will be behind.'

It is probable that the 'spring, step, close' was partially replaced by the pas de Basque when the latter came into favour in Scotland as a Reel setting step. The two steps are essentially similar,[1] and the pas de Basque, with its wider application to Quadrilles and Country Dances, as well as to Reels, would have had the stronger chance of survival.

There are several pieces of evidence which support the theory that the 'spring, step, close' was in this sense the predecessor of the pas de Basque. For instance, in the version of the solo dance Seann Triubhas taught by James Neill of Forfar, which goes back to at least 1850, the first step consists of six 'spring, step, close' steps followed by four points. On the other hand, in the version of this dance which was in common use about 1890, the first step consisted of six pas de Basque and four points or shuffles (39). Again, in the manuscript *Contre-Danses à Paris 1818* there is a quick Reel step of the form 'balance and spring, step, close'. We know of no subsequent record of such a step, but in David Anderson's ballroom guides (222–3) there is a 'balance and pas de Basque' to take its place (see Reel step J).

The unusual pas de Basque described by Atkinson in 1900 (p. 114) combines some of the features of both the 'spring, step, close' and the standard pas de Basque, and may be a transitional form.

Quick Reel step B (Triple spring side cut)

1. 1 Spring on to both feet, with the RF in 5th position.
   2 Spring on to both feet, with the RF in rear 5th position.
2. 1 Spring on to both feet, with the RF in 5th position. } 'Spring, step, close',
   & Make a small step to the right on RF. } version II,
   2 Close LF to rear 5th position. } with RF

[1] More precisely, the pas de Basque with the right foot is similar to the 'spring, step, close' with the left foot.

This step was taught by various teachers, including Mr William Adamson of East Fife, James Neill of Forfar, Joseph Wallace junior of Kilmarnock, and Peter Marshall of Kirkpatrick-Durham. It is also described in the books of Anderson (220–3) and MacKenzie (232). In the manuscript *Contre-Danses à Paris 1818* (203) there is a very similar step: 'Assemble dessous with right. Assemble dessous w^t left. Assemble dessous w^t right. Glissade dessous to left' (cf. Quick Reel step A; these instructions correspond to the 'triple spring side cut' performed with the *left* foot). The name 'triple spring side cut' is MacKenzie's; we have not heard it used by old people.

Quick Reel step C. Performed with the RF, this step is as follows.

1. 1 Spring on to both feet, with RF in 5th position.
     & Step on RF in the position shown in Diagram 5.18.
     2 Close LF to 5th position.

2.   Version II of the 'spring, step, close' with RF.

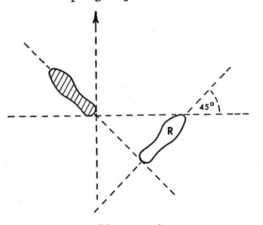

Diagram 5.18

This step was taught by Joseph Wallace junior of Kilmarnock. He taught it in the sequence:

1–6 Perform the step above with RF, LF, RF.
7, 8 Version II of the 'spring, step, close' with LF, RF.

Quick Reel step D. When the step is performed with the RF, the movements are:

1. 1 Spring on to both feet, with RF in 5th position.
     & Step on RF in the position shown in Diagram 5.18.

    2 Close LF to 5th position.

    & Step on RF in semi 4th position.

2. 1 Close LF to rear 5th position.

    & Step on RF in the position shown in Diagram 5.18.

    2 Close LF to 5th position.

This step also was taught by Joseph Wallace junior of Kilmarnock. He taught it in the same sequence as step C, ending with two 'spring, step, close' steps.

Quick Reel step E. Performed with the RF, this step is as follows. Begin with the RF in 2nd aerial position, with the foot held at 45° to the line of direction.

I. 1 Spring off the LF and bring the LF up to strike the R heel with the L heel, then drop back on the LF in its original position, leaving RF in 2nd aerial position, as at the beginning of the step.

    2 Repeat count '1'.

2.   Version II of the 'spring, step, close' with LF (? RF).

If these movements are followed by the same movements performed contrariwise, then version II of the 'spring, step, close' is replaced by version I, the extension here being made to 2nd aerial position, with the extended foot held at 45° to the line of direction.

This, too, was taught by Joseph Wallace junior of Kilmarnock, and here also he taught it in the same sequence as step C, ending with two 'spring, step, close' steps.

Quick Reel step F (Single balance). This step occupies one bar of music. When performed with the RF, it is begun with the weight on the LF and with the RF in 4th int. low aerial position. The movements are:

Count 1   Balance backward on to RF, taking LF to a loose low rear leg position (the LF should be about 4 inches from the R leg).

Count 2   Hop on RF and point LF in 4th int. low aerial position.

This step was taught by James Neill of Forfar. A very similar step, in which the balance backward is from 4th aerial position is given by Anderson (221–3) and MacKenzie (232). A step of this type also appears in the manuscript *Contre-Danses à Paris 1818* (203).

Quick Reel step G. This again occupies one bar of music. When performed with the RF, it is begun with the weight on the LF and with the RF in a loose low rear leg position (the RF should be about 4 inches from the L leg).

Count 1   Balance forward on to RF, extending LF to 4th int. low aerial position.

Count 2   Hop on RF and bring LF in with a circling movement to a loose low rear leg position (the LF should be about 4 inches from the R leg).

This step, which was taught by James Neill of Forfar, is simply a single balance performed in the reverse direction.

It is possible to combine this step with the single balance, e.g.

1–3   Single balance with RF, LF, RF.

4. 1   Balance backward on to LF, as in single balance with LF.

   2   Hop on LF and retain RF in a loose low rear leg position.

5–8   Step G with RF, LF, RF, LF.

Quick Reel step H (Double balance). When performed with the RF, this step is begun with the weight on the LF and with the RF in 4th aerial position. The movements are:

1. 1   Balance backward on to RF, taking LF to rear 4th aerial position.

   2   Balance forward on to LF, taking RF to 4th aerial position.

2. 1   Balance backward on to RF, taking LF to rear 4th aerial position.

   2 &   Hop on RF and brush LF forward past the calf of the R leg, then shake LF twice in 4th aerial position. The hop is made on the count '2', and the shake is completed on the count '&'.

This step was shown to us by Mr William Adamson, the East Fife teacher. Anderson (220–3), Atkinson (226), and MacKenzie (232) describe a step which differs from this only in that the double shake in bar 2 is replaced by a simple extension of the LF in 4th aerial position. The name 'double balance' is Mr Adamson's, and is also that used by Anderson (222–3) and MacKenzie.

Quick Reel step I (Balance and round the leg). When this step is performed with the RF, it is begun with the weight on the LF and with the RF in 4th int. aerial position.

1. 1 Balance backward on to RF, taking LF to rear 4th int. aerial position.

    2 Balance forward on to LF, taking RF to 4th int. aerial position.

2. 1 Bring RF back and spring on to it, taking LF to rear leg position.

    & Bring LF to front leg position.

    2 Hop on RF and extend LF to 4th int. aerial position.

This is probably a fairly recent development of the double balance (step H). The name is that used in the S.O.B.H.D. handbook (242).

Quick Reel step J (Pas de Basque and balance). The movements of the step performed with the RF are:

1. 1 Spring on to RF in semi 2nd position.

    & Bring LF to 5th position (either in the ordinary position, or on the ball, or on the half-point).

    2 & Momentarily transfer the weight to the LF and on the count '2' beat with the ball of the RF in rear 5th position. Immediately following the beat, extend the LF to 4th int. aerial position so that it arrives there on the count '&'.

2. 1 Balance backward on to LF, taking RF to rear 4th int. aerial position.

    2 Balance forward on to RF, taking LF to 4th int. aerial position.

This step was common everywhere. We have records of its use, for instance, from such widely separated places as Barra (131) and North Ronaldshay (149). It is described by some writers as a ladies' step, but it was in fact used by both sexes.

The pas de Basque and the balance were sometimes performed in the reverse order. A step of this 'balance and pas de Basque' type was taught by Mr William Adamson of East Fife, and by Dougal McKelvie, a part-time teacher on the Isle of Arran about the year 1900. A 'balance and pas de Basque' is also described by Anderson (222–3).

Quick Reel step K (Backstep with a hop). The basic movement of this step occupies two counts. Performed with the RF, it is as follows.

Count & Hop on LF and at the same time carry RF smartly round past the L ankle towards very low rear leg position.

Count 1 Step on RF in rear 5th position (either with the R toe just touching L heel, or with the R toe closed right underneath the L instep).

When the step is repeated with alternate feet, it is usual to begin with

123

the RF, and the first count '&' of the step occurs on the last beat of the bar preceding that in which the main actions of the step take place. The counting is thus as follows.

1. &
   1 } 'Backstep with a hop' with RF.

   & 2   'Backstep with a hop' with LF.

2. &
   1 } 'Backstep with a hop' with RF, etc.

When the step is repeated in this manner, it is necessary to move slightly forward on the hop on the counts '&' in order to counteract the slight backward movement on the counts '1' and '2'.

The 'backstep with a hop' was very widely distributed throughout the Highlands, Orkney, and Shetland. It is one of the earliest Reel steps to be recorded, for it is described by Francis Peacock in 1805 under the name 'minor cèum-coisiche' (204): 'You have only to place the right foot behind the left, sink and hop upon it, then do the same with the left foot behind the right' (the term "minor" in Peacock's nomenclature merely indicates that the step occupies half a bar of music). The step is also described as a general step for use in Reels by Atkinson (226).

The step is often referred to simply as 'the backstep'.

Quick Reel step L (Pas de Basque and backstep with a hop). Performed with the RF, the movements are:

1. 1   Step on RF in semi 2nd position.   ⎤ As in
   &   Place LF in 5th position.   ⎥ version I
   2   Momentarily transfer the weight to the LF and   ⎬ of the
        beat with the ball of the RF in rear 5th posi-   ⎥ pas de
        tion.   ⎦ Basque

2. &
   1 } 'Backstep with a hop' with LF.

   & 2   'Backstep with a hop' with RF.

Note that both feet remain on the ground on the last count '&' of bar **2.**

We have met this step only in Benbecula (119, 122).

Quick Reel step M (Shuffles). We describe first a shuffle performed with the LF. This is begun with the weight on the LF and with the RF in 4th int. low aerial position.

124

Count 1 Spring off the LF, and bring the RF back and drop on it, at the same time extending LF to 4th int. low aerial position.

Count & Brush LF in to 3rd position and immediately out again to 4th int. low aerial position (so that it arrives in the latter position on the actual count '&').

On the count '1', the LF reaches 4th int. low aerial position at exactly the same time as the RF meets the ground. Immediately following the count '1', the LF begins to move in towards 3rd position, meeting the ground on the way in at approximately semi 4th position. It then brushes along the ground until the sole of the foot meets the R instep, then brushes out again to 4th int. low aerial position, leaving the ground on the way out at approximately semi 4th position.

The starting position used above is the normal one, and the step, performed with alternate feet, is thus as follows.

1. 1 & Shuffle with LF.
    2 & Shuffle with RF.
2. 1 & Shuffle with LF, etc.

The shuffles step seems to have been fairly common as a Reel step, particularly in the West Highlands. Anderson (223) gives it as a step for the solo dance Seann Triubhas under the name 'single shuffles', and it is also in the S.O.B.H.D. handbook (242).

Quick Reel step N (Double shuffle). As in the case of the shuffle, we describe the step performed with the LF. It is then begun with the weight on the LF and with the RF in semi 4th very low aerial position.

Count 1 Spring off the LF, and bring the RF back and drop on it, at the same time extending LF to semi 4th very low aerial position and bringing it back in towards 3rd position.

Count & Brush LF in to 3rd position (with the ball of the foot on the floor) and out towards semi 4th very low aerial position, then back again into 3rd position, and out to semi 4th very low aerial position.

The starting position above is the normal one, and the step is performed with left and right feet alternately for as long as desired.

This step was taught by John Muir of Motherwell, who knew it by the name 'double shuffles'. In the Arisaig district about 1900 it was used by the better dancers as a substitute for the pas de Basque (31). It is described by MacKenzie (232) under the name 'shuffles', though only as a step for the Sword Dance. It is probably the same as the step called 'double shuffle', which was one of 'the three most favourite steps' in the Melrose district about 1805 (285).

Quick Reel step O (Highcuts). We describe first a single highcut performed with the RF; this occupies two counts.

Count 1   Spring on to LF on the spot, taking RF out towards 2nd aerial position and then back into rear leg position. (The LF should meet the ground on the count '1', and at the same instant the RF should reach rear leg position.)

Count &   Immediately on landing, take RF again out towards 2nd aerial position and then back into rear leg position (so that it arrives there on the actual count '&').

Throughout these two counts, the R knee should point to the side, and the movements of the RF should be in the plane of the body. So far as possible, the actual movements of the RF should be produced by moving the lower part of the R leg from the knee (and not by moving the leg as a whole from the hip joint). During the initial spring, there is usually a slight movement of the LF out to the left towards 2nd aerial position and back.

Highcuts are usually performed in a series of four, with left and right feet alternately (beginning with the *left* foot). This occupies two bars of music.

Highcutting seems to have been known in all districts of the mainland of Scotland and the Western Isles for as far back as living memory extends. In ordinary social dancing it was used only by the better dancers, though most dancing-teachers included it in their repertoires.

John Muir and his family knew the step as 'pigeon's wing' or 'winging'—this name is probably derived from the similarity of the step to the ballet step *jeté battu* or *jeté brisé*, which is sometimes known as 'les ailes de pigeon'.[1] A step called 'pigeon's wing' was another of 'the three most favourite steps' in the Melrose district about 1805 (285), but whether this was highcutting we cannot say.[2]

In spite of the striking nature of the highcutting step, there is no description of the step in print before 1900, when it appears for the first

[1] See, for example, Desrat's *Dictionnaire de la Danse* (278; 1895).

[2] Mr D. G. MacLennan has informed us that the name 'ailes de pigeon' was also sometimes given to the step 'side-cutting', which is used in the solo dances Seann Triubhas and The Sailor's Hornpipe. A description of this step can be found in Mr MacLennan's book (239).

time in MacNeilage's ballroom guide (227). It is possible, however, that the 'cutting double quick time' mentioned by MacTaggart in 1824 (p. 28) was a form of highcutting. The highcutting step is also described by several writers subsequent to MacNeilage, in particular Scott Skinner (229) and MacKenzie (232). It is always given as a step for men only.[1]

There is also a variant of the highcut known as the double highcut, which we first learnt from our teacher Mr Jack McConachie. This occupies one complete bar of music, and, performed with the right foot, is as follows.

Count 1   Spring on to LF on the spot, taking RF out towards 2nd aerial position and then back into rear leg position, as in ordinary highcut.

Count &   Immediately on landing, take RF again out towards 2nd aerial position and then back into *front* leg position.

Counts 2 &   Highcut with RF.

The double highcut is usually performed in the sequence 'highcut LF, highcut RF, double highcut LF', or the same contrariwise.

Double highcuts were almost certainly confined to exhibition dancers; they are described only by MacLennan (239).

There is another step which is very similar to highcutting. Performed with the RF, this is as follows.

Counts 1 & Spring on to LF on the spot, and beat the RF twice against the calf of the L leg in rear leg position. (The LF should meet the ground on the count '1', and at the same instant the RF makes the first of the two beats against the back of the L calf. The second beat is made on the count '&'.)

In contrast to the highcut, the beats here are made by swivelling the whole of the R leg from the hip, without any appreciable change in the angle of the R knee.

This step was taught by Peter Marshall of Kirkpatrick-Durham and his partner Thomas Shanks under the name 'double-hit'. We ourselves first learnt it from Pipe-Major David Taylor under the name 'ball-kick'.

It is worth while to note that highcuts, double highcuts, and double-hits can all be performed in hard shoes without damage to the supporting leg!

[1] MacNeilage states that the working foot should make three beats in rear leg position. All the other writers agree with our description.

Quick Reel step P. Performed with the RF, this is:

1. 1 & On the count '1', spring on to both feet, with the RF in 5th position. Immediately following the spring, the RF is extended to 2nd int. aerial position so that it reaches there on the count '&'.

   2 Hop on LF and shake the R leg in 2nd int. aerial position.

2. 1 Step on the RF in rear 5th position.

   & Make a small step to the left on LF.

   2 & Momentarily transfer the weight to the LF and on the count '2' close the RF to rear 5th position. Immediately following the 'close', extend the LF to 2nd int. low aerial position so that it arrives there on the count '&'.

If these movements are followed by the same movements performed contrariwise, then the LF is brought back for the spring on count '1' of the third bar, so that there is no sideways motion of the body on this spring.

The shake on count '1. 2' and the extension on count '2. &' can also be made in 2nd aerial and 2nd low aerial positions respectively.

This was a very common step, and was included in the repertoires of many dancing-teachers. It is also described by MacKenzie (232),[1] and a very similar step is given by Anderson (222-3).[2] MacKenzie calls the step 'the side cut', a name which also appears in Fordyce's poem *A Country Wedding* (258; 1818):

'The younkers are smirking to see her side-cutting.'

Quick Reel step Q. When this particular step is repeated with alternate feet, there are differences between the first and subsequent repeats, and accordingly we give the movements performed with the right and left feet successively. The step commences on a preliminary count '*a*' (see p. 89).

Begin with RF in 5th position.

   a Make a very small hop on LF, taking RF just off the ground.

1. 1 Beat lightly with the ball of the RF in 5th position.

   & Make a small step to the right on RF.

[1] MacKenzie uses the 2nd aerial positions on the counts '1. 2' and '2. &'.
[2] The S.O.B.H.D. handbook (242) describes a variant of this step incorporating an extra hop on the LF on the second count '&' of bar 1. We have not met this variant among old people, nor does it occur in any of the works on Scottish dancing published prior to the S.O.B.H.D. handbook.

	2	Close LF to rear 5th position.
	&	} Repeat the 'step, close' of counts '1. & 2' twice.
2.	1 & 2	
3.	1	Drop on RF in rear 5th position, and at the same time raise the LF to 5th low aerial position.
	&	Make a small step to the left on LF.
	2	Close RF to rear 5th position.
	&	} Repeat the 'step, close' of counts '3. & 2' twice.
4.	1 & 2	

Subsequent repeats begin as in bar **3**.

This step was taught in Arran about 1900 by Dougal McKelvie, a part-time teacher there. It was also known to a number of people of McKelvie's own generation in Arran, so that it presumably goes back to some dancing-teacher who taught in Arran before about 1880 (38). The step is very similar to one described by Peacock (204) under the name 'double cèum-coisiche'.

Quick Reel step R ('The Flying Shuffle and Parry Out'). This is an 8-bar step; begin with the weight on the LF and with the RF in rear 5th position.

1.	1	Hop on LF, and at the same time bring the RF closely round the LF and brush it into 5th position. (The R toe should be on the ground for the last two or three inches of the RF's movement.)
	&	Immediately the RF reaches 5th position, brush it out to 4th int. low aerial position so that it actually arrives in that position on the count '&'.
	2	Hop on LF, and brush the toe of the RF into 5th position.
	&	Immediately the RF reaches 5th position, brush it out to 4th int. low aerial position so that it actually arrives in that position on the count '&'.
2.	1	Bring RF back and spring on to it, and at the same time take the LF closely round the RF and brush it into 5th position (as in count '1. 1').
	& 2 &	Perform counts '& 2 &' of bar 1 contrariwise.
3–6		Repeat bars **1, 2** twice.
7.	1	Spring on to both feet, with RF in 5th position.
	2	Pivoting on the balls of both feet, make a half-turn to the left, finishing with RF in rear 5th position.
8		Repeat bar **7**, to finish facing in the original direction.

When the working foot brushes out and in again on the counts '& 2 &' of bars 1–6, it meets or leaves the ground in approximately semi 4th position.

This step was taught in Banffshire about the year 1890 by Adam Myron.[1] The first person who told us of 'the flying shuffle and parry out' had forgotten how to perform the step, and it was not until we actually saw the step performed that we realized the 'parry out' was a pirouette.

Quick Reel step S. This also is an 8-bar step. The movements are:

1.	1	With the weight on the L toe, place the RF in rear 5th position.
	&	Swivel the LF on the ball of the foot to the position shown in Diagram 5.19 (a), then lower the L heel to the ground and transfer the weight to it.
	2	Swivel the LF on the heel to the position shown in Diagram 5.19 (b), then lower the L toe to the ground and transfer the weight to it. At the same time, close the RF to rear 5th position as in Diagram 5.19 (b).

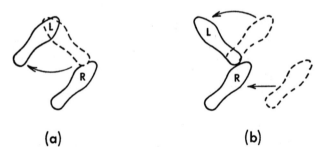

(a)   (b)

Diagram 5.19

2.	& 1 & 2 }	Repeat the movements of counts '& 2' of bar 1 twice.
3, 4		Perform bars 1, 2 contrariwise.
5.	1 & 2	Perform the movements of counts '1 & 2' of bar 1.

[1] Adam ('Dancie') Myron belonged to a family of dancing-masters who practised in the North-east. He himself normally had five or six series of classes running concurrently in different places, each on a different night of the week. His classes were held in farm barns, and each series lasted for three months, his fee for the quarter being 4s. 6d. He was a familiar figure in the Banffshire countryside sixty years ago, walking from the place where one class was held to the next, wearing a big Highland cloak, his fiddle tucked under his tippet in a 'poke'. He died at an advanced age about the year 1910.

6. 1 & 2   Perform the movements of counts '1 & 2' of bar **1** contrariwise.

7. 1   Spring on to both feet with RF in 5th position.

    2   Spring on to both feet with LF in 5th position.

8. 1 &   Hop twice on RF (on the counts '1, &'), at the same time carrying LF round in a circle towards rear 5th position (Diagram 5.20; the L knee is slightly bent, and the LF passes over 4th int. and 2nd positions, then being about 6 inches above the ground).

    2   Place LF in rear 5th position (so that the movement is finished with both feet on the ground).

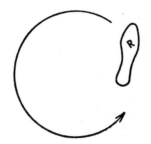

Diagram 5.20

The order of the two springs in bar **7** may possibly be incorrect.

This step was taught by John Muir of Motherwell. The movement used in bars **1** and **2** occurs in various solo step-dances, and is sometimes called the 'heel-roll'.

CHAPTER VI

The Threesome and Foursome Reels and the Reel of Tulloch

THE Reel, as a form of dance, can be traced back in Scotland to pre-Reformation days, but the early references give practically no details. The first such reference known to us occurs in Douglas's *Virgil*, Book 13, *c.* 1525 (243):[1]

> 'And gan do dowbill brangillys and gambatis,
> Dansys and rowndis traysing mony gatis
> Athir throu other *reland*, on thar gys:
> Thai fut it so that lang war to devys
> Thar hasty fair, thar revellyng and deray,
> Thar morysis and syk ryot, quhil neir day.'

The first mention of a 'Reel' which we can identify as at least similar to modern Reels is in 1710, when we find the 'Threesom Reel' described as a dance 'where three dance together'.[2] From 1710 onwards references to Reels are fairly frequent, but until 1776 the only specific form mentioned is a Reel for three persons. From 1776 onwards there are references also to Reels for four persons, the first being in Topham's description of dancing in Edinburgh (249; 1776). After about 1800 other Reels, involving five, six, or eight dancers, are mentioned in the literature, but these do not seem to have survived into the period covered by living memory, and we shall be concerned here only with Reels for three and four.

The first actual descriptions of a 'Reel of Three' and a 'Reel of Four' are given in Thomas Wilson's *An Analysis of Country Dancing* (257;1811), and other more or less contemporary descriptions occur in the Scottish

---

1 'Reilling' is also mentioned in the poem 'Peblis to the play', allegedly written by James I (1394–1437), but the earliest extant version of this poem is in the Maitland Folio MS., written *c.* 1580.

2 See under *Rele* in the glossary to Ruddiman's edition of Douglas's *Virgil* (246; 1710).

manuscript *Contre-Danses à Paris 1818* (203), in Barclay Dun's *Transla-tion of nine . . . Quadrilles . . .* (205; 1818), and in a later work by Thomas Wilson (261; 1821).[1] These various books give three different versions of a 'Threesome Reel' or 'Reel of three', all of which consist of setting steps danced on the spot, alternated with a travelling figure in the form of a figure 8 (Diagram 6.1 (a)). The differences from one version to another are relatively small and concern only such things as whether the dance begins with the travelling figure or with setting, and whether the dancers return to their own places, or interchange places, at the end of each repetition of the travelling figure. In the sequel, we use the name 'the Threesome Reel' to cover any dance which has the same basic

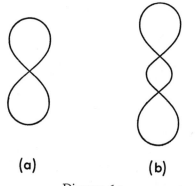

(a)   (b)

Diagram 6.1
Track of travelling figures in (a) the Threesome Reel, (b) the Foursome Reel

structure as these three versions, that is to say, which consists of setting steps danced on the spot, alternated with a travelling figure in the form of a figure 8.

Similar remarks apply to the Foursome Reel; all the versions of this dance described in the books mentioned above consist of setting steps, alternated with a travelling figure in the form of a figure 8 with an extra loop added (Diagram 6.1 (b)), and in the sequel we use the term 'the Foursome Reel' to cover any dance which has this same basic structure. We also use the terms 'reel of three' and 'reel of four' to mean the travelling figures of the Threesome and Foursome Reels, respectively.

There is no direct evidence to prove that the Reels for three mentioned in the literature between 1710 and 1811 were 'Threesome Reels' in the sense defined above, but there is considerable indirect evidence for this. It is probable that the Foursome Reel of the type described above also

---

[1] Thomas Wilson was a dancing-master in London from about 1800 to about 1850. Barclay Dun taught in Edinburgh from about 1798 to at least 1838.

goes back well into the eighteenth century, but the evidence here is less strong than in the case of the Threesome Reel.

The Threesome Reel began to die out during the first half of the nineteenth century and had virtually disappeared from use as a social dance by the beginning of the period covered by living memory. The Foursome Reel remained in use up to and after the First World War, but from about 1880 it was more often danced in combination with another dance, the Reel of Tulloch, than performed as a dance on its own.

The dance called the Reel of Tulloch, or, in Gaelic, Ruidhleadh Thulachain, seems to have been composed about the year 1800.[1] So far as we know, the first reference to it is on the occasion of a ball held by the Edinburgh Society of Highlanders in 1819, when four of the office-bearers of the Society opened the ball with the dance (259). The Reel of Tulloch also featured in the piping and dancing competitions organized by the Highland Society of Edinburgh—these competitions took place in Edinburgh annually from 1784 to 1826, and then triennially until 1844. The dance was first performed at these competitions in 1829, and was repeated in 1832, 1838, and 1844 (297).

A letter written by one of the dancers at the Edinburgh competitions in 1835 (297) throws some light on the origin of the Reel of Tulloch, for in this letter the dance is referred to as 'The Breadalbane Ball reel . . . mostly termed the reel of Tulloch'. This would seem to indicate that the Reel of Tulloch was originally a 'Society' dance which was developed at the Breadalbane Balls, just as the modern Eightsome Reel was developed at the Northern Meeting Balls and the Skye Balls.

The first printed description of the Reel of Tulloch is that in *The Ballroom Annual* (267; 1844), where the dance is given under the title 'The Duchess of Sutherland's New Highland Reel'. The identification of this 'New Highland Reel' with the Reel of Tulloch presents no difficulty, in spite of the different title, for this same description is given in Willock's *Manual of Dancing*, (213; 1865) and Wallace's *Excelsior Manual of Dancing* (217–18; c. 1872, 1881)[2] under the title 'Hullachan', an English rendering of the Gaelic 'Thulachain'. We may safely ignore the title in *The Ballroom Annual*, for several of the other dances described in this work have been assigned new aristocratic titles by the author.

---

[1] The *tune* 'The Reel of Tulloch' is in the MacFarlan MS. (c. 1740) in the National Library of Scotland.

[2] J. F. Wallace was a dancing-master in Glasgow. So far as we know he was not related to the family of dancing-teachers of this name in Kilmarnock.

The early version of the Reel of Tulloch described in *The Ballroom Annual* and the books of Willock and Wallace was performed by four dancers, presumably to the tune 'The Reel of Tulloch'. It somewhat resembled the Foursome Reel, and its most distinctive feature was the use of swinging with linked arms to replace a part of the usual setting. It may have been partly in strathspey tempo and partly in reel tempo, but we cannot be certain of this.

Between the years 1860 and 1875 the form of the Reel of Tulloch underwent considerable changes and several different versions were in current use, but by the beginning of the period covered by living memory there emerged a more or less standard version of the dance, which consisted simply of alternate setting and swinging. This standard version (which was still a dance for four) was usually performed only to the tune 'The Reel of Tulloch', and was now definitely in quick tempo throughout.

It was this standard version of the Reel of Tulloch which, from about 1880 onwards, was combined with the old Foursome Reel. Probably at first the dancers in a Foursome Reel simply substituted at will the figures of the Reel of Tulloch for those of the Foursome Reel whenever the musician chanced to play the tune 'The Reel of Tulloch'. Later, the combination became more formalized, in that it became the accepted custom that, if the musician played the tune 'The Reel of Tulloch' in the course of a Foursome Reel, then the dancers should break into the alternate setting and swinging of the Reel of Tulloch. This was, for instance, the case in Glen Roy from at least 1890 up to about 1910 (87–89), and was also the case at the Kilberry Balls from 1887 until 1914 (p. 41). The same situation existed also at Blair Atholl about the year 1896, where, in a Foursome Reel, 'you just did what the piper played. If he played the Reel of Tulloch, you did it. Sometimes a piper would play a strathspey, then a reel, then another strathspey, and then the Reel of Tulloch' (84).

In some parts of Scotland the combination of the Reel of Tulloch with the Foursome Reel became in the course of time completely formalized. In these parts each district included in its local repertoire one and only one combination, with a definite sequence of figures which was known to everyone. Where this was the case, it also usually happened that one or both of the original dances disappeared from general use as separate dances. For example, at Arisaig about 1900 the local repertoire included a particular combination of the Foursome Reel and the Reel of Tulloch, consisting of the Foursome Reel to strathspey tunes followed without pause by the Reel of Tulloch; it also included at this time the Foursome Reel as a separate dance, but not the Reel of Tulloch (31).

The particular combination accepted in any one district was usually taught by the local dancing-master in his classes, and in many cases it is probable that the dancing-master was himself the originator of that particular combination. Frequently, too, the disappearance of the separate dances from the local repertoire was due to his omitting them from the dances which he taught.

In most parts of the mainland of Scotland and the Western Isles, the Foursome Reel was, within living memory, known as the 'Scotch Reel'. Another name for the dance was the 'Highland Reel', but we have met this only in the districts around Lochcarron, Dunkeld, Alford, and Dufftown, and in Glen Urquhart and Strathglass. Gaelic speakers in Mull and Islay—people who were old in 1900—knew the dance as 'Ruidhleadh Ghaelach', but in other Gaelic-speaking areas which we have visited the dance was known—even to those who spoke only Gaelic—as the 'Scotch Reel'.

When the Foursome Reel was combined with the Reel of Tulloch, the name 'Scotch Reel' or 'Highland Reel'—whichever was locally current—was used not only for the original Foursome Reel but also for the combined dance. Further, in those places where the original Foursome Reel disappeared from general use as a separate dance, the name 'Scotch Reel' or 'Highland Reel' still survived as the name of the combination of the Foursome Reel with the Reel of Tulloch. In Arisaig, for example, about the year 1900 the name 'Scotch Reel' was used both for the Foursome Reel, which was there invariably danced to one or more strathspeys followed by one or more reels, and for the local combination consisting of the Foursome Reel to strathspey tunes followed by the Reel of Tulloch. To distinguish one from the other, the first was given the subsidiary title 'Strathspey and Reel', the second, 'Strathspey and Reel of Tulloch' (31). Similar subsidiary titles were not uncommon at about this period, and their existence has sometimes given rise to the erroneous belief that the 'Strathspey' and the 'Reel' were, like the Reel of Tulloch, distinct dances on their own.

It is interesting to trace the use of the name 'Scotch Reel' in the early records. The name seems first to have been applied to the Threesome Reel—for instance Sir John Gallini in his *Treatise on the art of dancing* (247; 1765) wrote that 'It is to the Highlanders of North Britain, that I am told we are indebted for a dance ... called the *Scotch Reel*, executed generally, and, I believe, always in *trio*, or by three'. Later, the name seems to have been used for both the Threesome and Foursome Reels;

in 1805, for instance, the Aberdeen dancing-master Francis Peacock begins his 'Observations on the Scotch Reel' with the remark that 'The fondness the Highlanders have for this quartett or trio (for it is either one or the other) is unbounded' (204). As the Threesome Reel disappeared from use, so the name 'Scotch Reel' was assigned to the Foursome Reel only—for example, Barclay Dun in 1818 describes the Foursome Reel under the name 'the Scotch Reel' without mentioning the existence of the Threesome Reel (205). The name 'Scotch Reel' is also used as the name of the Foursome Reel in some of the nineteenth-century ballroom guides, notably those of Wallace and Anderson.

The style in which these various Reels were performed, whether Foursome Reel, Reel of Tulloch, or combination of the two, was, within living memory, remarkably uniform throughout Scotland. One of the distinctive features of this style was the characteristic use of the arms. When setting, the men normally accompanied their steps with arm movements, sometimes raising one arm, sometimes both, just as the steps and their own taste demanded; when they did not have their arms raised, they placed them akimbo—this was the most characteristic position of all. In the reels of four the men usually either raised both arms or again placed them akimbo, and in the swinging in the Reel of Tulloch they usually raised the free arm. Ladies, both when setting, and in the reels of four, normally either had their arms akimbo, or (less commonly) held their skirts at the side.[1] They could, however, also raise their arms if they wished, and in the swinging in the Reel of Tulloch they frequently raised the free arm.

Another distinctive feature of the style in which Reels were danced—common to every district—was the snapping of finger and thumb. Both men and ladies 'crackit their fingers' in this way, and the men, particularly, would echo the beats of the music, 'knappin' their fingers aboon their heads'. This snapping of finger and thumb has now almost entirely disappeared, but it has left one legacy, for the Games dancer of today still holds the thumb against the middle finger, ready for the snap that is now never made.

Both this use of the arms and the finger-snapping were peculiar to Reels. In all the other dances in use within living memory, the dancers held their arms loosely by their sides (ladies held their skirts if they wished), and there was no snapping of fingers.

The men generally danced their setting steps in Reels with great vigour. The older ladies danced quietly, but younger girls would sometimes emulate the men.

[1] Remember that up to 1914 ladies' skirts were long.

There was everywhere much 'heuching' by the men. On the other hand, the attitude to 'heuching' on the part of ladies seems to have varied from one place to another. In many districts in the Highlands and the Western Isles, for example in Arisaig, Moidart, Skye, Mull, Benbecula, and South Uist, it was unusual (though not unknown) for ladies to 'heuch', yet in other districts, for example in parts of Aberdeenshire and in Barra, it was by no means unusual. Again, in many parts of the Lowlands, it was the accepted custom for ladies to 'heuch'.

The attitude of the dancing-masters to this use of arms, to the finger-snapping, and to 'heuching' shows the extent to which these things were accepted as a proper part of Reels. David Anderson of Dundee, for instance, allowed both men and ladies to snap their fingers and 'heuch' in his class. Further, he taught the men to raise their arms when appropriate, and otherwise to have them akimbo, and he taught ladies to have their arms akimbo or to hold their skirts. In the Borders, Professor Buck allowed both sexes to raise their arms and snap their fingers, but 'heuching' was forbidden in his classes. In Banffshire, Adam Myron allowed both sexes to raise their arms, but only men were permitted to snap their fingers. He discouraged 'heuching' in his classes, and sometimes forbad it. John Muir of Motherwell was another teacher who forbad 'heuching' in his classes, but he did permit the raising of arms in a Reel—'that was part of the dance' (46).

The actual positions of the arms which were normally used in Reels within living memory are roughly as shown in Diagram 6.2. The palms

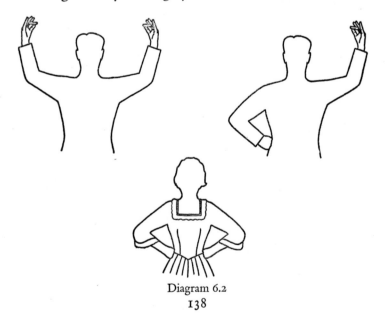

Diagram 6.2
138

of the raised hands are turned to the face, and the fingers are spread slightly apart, with the thumb touching the middle finger. When the arms are placed akimbo, the elbows point directly to the side; the hands may be placed on the waist either with the wrist bent and the back of the hand pressed against the waist, or with the wrist straight and only the backs of the fingers pressed against the waist.

We must emphasize here that the raised arm positions shown in Diagram 6.2 were those normally used in ordinary *social* dancing; in *competition* dancing, the arms were sometimes held in a more curved position, closer to the head. We were ourselves taught to hold our arms in the position shown in Diagram 6.3, with the hands directly above

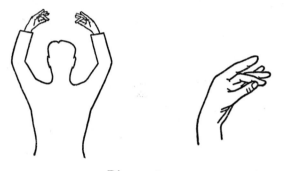

Diagram 6.3

the shoulders and the elbows at eye level. Here again, the palms of the raised hands are turned to the face, and the fingers are spread slightly apart, with the thumb touching the middle finger. This latter position is the one given in Mr D. G. MacLennan's *Highland . . . Dances* (239). It also agrees more closely than does that in Diagram 6.2 with the position recommended by David Anderson (223) for use in the Highland Fling: 'hold up the hand [with] . . . the arm bent and the hand right above the head (about 4 inches)'.

The raising of the arms is governed by a single rule, namely that when only one arm is raised, then that arm should be the one opposite to the working foot (more succinctly, 'opposite hand to foot'). When there is a rapid interchange of weight from one foot to the other (as in high-cutting), then naturally both arms are either raised or placed akimbo; and it need hardly be said that in ordinary social dancing each dancer pleased himself whether he raised his arms or not. It is probable that this raising of the arms was primarily an aid to balance, notwithstanding the many theories which ascribe the custom to an unexplained desire on the part of male dancers to imitate the shape of the antlers of a stag.

We turn now to the full descriptions of the various Reels mentioned above. We confine ourselves here to details of figures and steps, since the style of performance has already been discussed.

It seems desirable to include the Threesome Reel in this section, but we are unable to give a full description of this dance collected from living memory.[1] We therefore give the description of the dance as noted in various printed and manuscript sources. In the case of the other dances, our descriptions have all been collected from people who have actually performed the dances in question, and here we refer to printed and manuscript sources only as a matter of historical interest. We add also descriptions of two forms of the Reel of Tulloch involving more than four dancers, namely the Double Reel of Tulloch and the Reel of Tulloch in a Circle, together with the description of a dance of very similar form, the Everlasting Jig.

THE THREESOME REEL

This dance is performed by three people, any combination of the sexes being permissible. The dancers stand in a line, with the two at the ends of the line facing inwards, and with the centre dancer facing one of the others. We describe the dance performed by a man and two

Diagram 6.4

ladies;[2] in this case the man begins in the centre, the starting positions being those shown in Diagram 6.4.[3] The dancers should presumably be about 3 feet apart.

[1] We have never met anyone in Scotland who has actually danced the Threesome Reel as a social dance, although one of our informants remembered having seen the dance several times in his youth, at Tomnahurich Bridge near Inverness, about the year 1895 (12). We have also collected a version of the dance which David Anderson used for exhibition purposes, but this version differed somewhat from that which was used in social dancing.

[2] The description which follows is that given by Atkinson (226; 1900); we have added only the instructions which specify the particular ladies to whom the man should set. Other descriptions of this version, less complete, are given by Wilson (257; 1811), and in the manuscript Contre-Danses à Paris 1818 (203).

[3] We recall that we use circles to denote men, and squares for ladies.

Music Bars	Description of the Figures
1–8	The three dancers dance a reel of three. The man and 1st lady begin this by passing each other, and at the end the man faces 2nd lady (further details of this reel of three are given below).
9–16	All three dance setting steps on the spot. The man sets to 2nd lady, but chooses setting steps in which he rotates, so that he can 'give attention to both ladies while ostensibly setting to one'.
17–24	They again dance a reel of three. The man and 2nd lady begin this by passing each other, and at the end the man faces 1st lady.
25–32	They all dance setting steps on the spot, the man setting to 1st lady and choosing his steps as before.

This sequence of 32 bars is repeated ad lib. The dance terminates either with a final repetition of this 32-bar sequence, or with a final 16-bar sequence consisting of the movements described under bars 1–16 above.

In the 'reel of three', which forms the travelling figure of this Reel, the dancers follow each other round a 'figure 8', each passing between the other two on going through the centre position. The two people who are facing initially may begin the reel by passing each other with either shoulder. If, for instance, the two people who are facing initially are the man and 1st lady (as in the reel of three in bars 1–8 above), and if they begin by passing each other with the right shoulder, then the ensuing movements of the three dancers are as shown in the

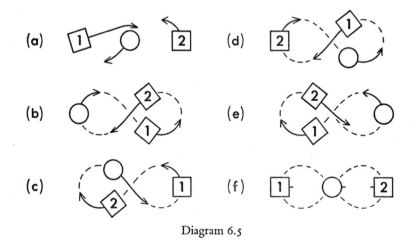

Diagram 6.5

successive illustrations of Diagram 6.5.[1] Each dancer returns to his or her original place at the end of the reel of three, and the phrasing should be such that the figure flows evenly throughout the music allotted to it.

If the two dancers who are facing initially begin the reel of three by passing each other with left shoulders (Diagram 6.6 (a)), then the dancers describe the figure 8 in the reverse direction to that above (Diagram 6.6 (b)).[2, 3]

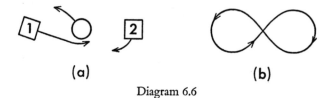

(a)   (b)

Diagram 6.6

Atkinson states that the reels of three in the Threesome Reel were normally 'right shoulder' reels, although 'left shoulder' reels were permissible. On the other hand, Wilson specifies 'left shoulder' reels only.[4] In any one Reel, the reels of three would probably be all 'right shoulder' or all 'left shoulder'.

There is also an alternative version of the Threesome Reel in which the dancers come into the centre place in turn. Here in each reel of three the centre dancer and one of the outer dancers repeat a half loop of the figure 8 in order to change places. This version is given in the manuscript *Contre-Danses à Paris 1818*, and also by Wilson (261; 1821).

According to Atkinson, the Threesome Reel was in his time performed to a selection of strathspeys followed without pause by a selection of reels. In earlier times, other combinations of music were also used; for example, about the year 1815 the dance could be performed to a combination of strathspeys, reels, and jigs (206). Originally, the Threesome Reel was probably performed to reel tunes only, for strathspeys do not seem to have come into general use for Reels until some time during the first half of the eighteenth century (297).

The setting and travelling steps used in the Threesome Reel were almost certainly the same as those used in other Reels.

[1] In the sequel we shall describe such a reel of three as a 'right shoulder' reel of three.
[2] Such a reel of three will in future be described as a 'left shoulder' reel of three.
[3] We have described the reel of three in detail to avoid any possible confusion, and so that we can simplify some of the later descriptions; we do not, however, recommend that the reel of three be taught in separate stages corresponding to the successive positions in Diagram 6.5.
[4] The manuscript *Contre-Danses à Paris 1818* does not specify the directions of the reels of three.

THE FOURSOME REEL

This dance is performed by two couples.[1] To begin, the dancers stand in line, with the two ladies at the ends and the two men in the centre, and all face their partners. If space permits, the men should be about 2 ft 6 in. from each other and about 4 ft 6 in. from their partners (Diagram 6.7).

Diagram 6.7

The dance consists of the repetition of the following 16-bar sequence.

Music Bars	Description of the Figures
1–8	All four dancers perform a reel of four; the ladies finish this in their own places, and the men finish in each other's places (further details of this reel of four are given below).
9–16	All set on the spot, using any appropriate Reel setting steps.

On each repetition of this sequence, the men exchange places with each other in the reel of four, whilst the ladies always return to their own places. Thus the men set to the opposite ladies during the first 8-bar setting period (i.e. 1st man sets to 2nd lady, 2nd man to 1st lady), then to their own partners during the second setting period, and so on alternately.

Within living memory the dance was usually performed to a selection of strathspeys followed without pause by a selection of reels; a typical set of tunes for the dance consisted of 64 bars of strathspeys plus 64 bars of reels, so that the dancers performed the basic sequence of reeling and setting four times to strathspey tunes and four times to reels.[2] Other combinations of strathspeys and reels were also used; for example, at the Kilberry Balls the dance was sometimes performed to a reel only, and sometimes to a reel followed by a strathspey—'whatever the piper chose to play' (p. 41). Again, at Blair Atholl about the year 1896 'you just did what the piper played' (84). As we have already mentioned in

---

[1] It was also sometimes danced by four men. For example, at the Atholl Highlanders' Balls held at Blair Castle before 1914 there was always one Foursome Reel during the evening, known as 'the Rams' Reel', in which only the men of the Atholl Highlanders Regiment danced (84). [Cf. *Ram-reel* in Jamieson's *Dictionary* (264; 1825): 'a dance by men only'.]

[2] David Anderson, in describing the Foursome Reel, says that 'The Reel can be danced as long as desired, but four times of the Strathspey and Reel Time are quite sufficient' (220; *c.* 1886).

Chapter V, strathspeys were played at a tempo of 40–42 bars per minute, and reels at 60–64 bars per minute.

In the Foursome Reel, as in all other Reels, the dancers were free to choose whatever setting steps they pleased, and it was quite usual to find all four dancers performing different steps at the same time. With strathspey tunes, the most common setting steps were the steps of the solo dance, the Highland Fling; the 'Strathspey steps' (pp. 99–102) were also used fairly frequently, as was also the Highland Schottische step (p. 103). With reel tunes, all the quick setting steps described in Chapter V were used in one district or another.

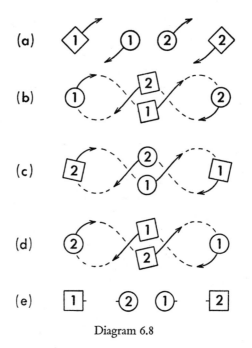

(a)

(b)

(c)

(d)

(e)

Diagram 6.8

In the reel of four, which forms the travelling figure in this Reel, the dancers follow each other round a track in the shape of a figure 8 with an extra loop added. The dancers begin the reel of four by passing the person facing them with right shoulders (Diagram 6.8 (a)), and their positions at the ends of the second, fourth, sixth and eighth bars of the figure are shown in Diagram 6.8 (b–e) (the rule is 'pass with right shoulders at the ends and with left shoulders in the middle'). The ladies end the reel of four in their original places whilst the men end in each other's places. Within living memory, the usual name for this figure was 'the figure 8', and when one danced it, one 'cut the figure 8'.

In the Lowlands, the most common travelling step used with strath-spey tunes in the Foursome Reel was Strathspey travelling step A (p. 93), and in the Highlands it was Strathspey travelling step B (p. 93). All the other Strathspey travelling steps C–F (pp. 94–7) were also used in the Foursome Reel, although the steps D and E were more or less restricted to Games dancers. With reel tunes, the usual travelling step was the hop-one-and-two (p. 105), but the chassé (p. 104) and the travelling pas de Basque (p. 109) were also used. In all of these steps, the dancer begins with the right foot.

In dancing the reel of four, dancers of the opposite sex should 'give shoulders' to each other, that is to say that when two dancers of the opposite sex approach each other preparatory to passing, they advance their nearer shoulders. Two dancers of the same sex, on the other hand, advance their opposite shoulders, thus passing almost face to face. This 'giving of shoulders', which was a feature of the Foursome Reel in the old days, is most strongly marked in the part of the Reel performed to strathspey tunes.

With the Strathspey travelling steps of the form 'step, close, step, hop' (i.e. steps A–E, pp. 93–6), there is in the reel of four an associated turn of the dancer's body which more or less automatically achieves the giving of the appropriate shoulders. The dancer leads with the right shoulder on the first 'step forward on RF' (count '1. 1'), the shoulders being almost parallel to the direction of travel. On the succeeding 'close LF to RF' and 'step forward on RF' (counts '1. 2, 3') the dancer swings the right shoulder slowly back, then on the 'hop on RF' (count '1. 4') swings the left shoulder slightly forward, ready to lead with it on the next 'step forward on LF' (count '2. 1'). These movements are continued throughout the reel of four, the lead with the right shoulder always being much more strongly marked than that with the left. If the dancer's arms are raised or akimbo (or, in the case of a lady, holding her skirts), they naturally turn with the shoulders, giving emphasis to the turn. A similar turn of the body is associated with the quick travelling steps, the hop-one-and-two and the chassé, but there it is less strongly marked.

There is an alternative starting position for the dance, in which partners stand beside each other. Each lady is on her partner's right, and the couples face each other at a distance of about 6 ft (Diagram 6.9 (a)). Here the ladies begin the reel of four by passing each other with the left shoulder; the men stand still for the first two bars of the music, then on the third bar they come into the reel of four by passing first the opposite lady with the right shoulder, then each other with the left (Diagram

6.9 (b)). From this point on the dance proceeds as before; the dancers finish the reel of four in line, as in Diagram 6.8 (e), then set to each other, then reel again, and so on.

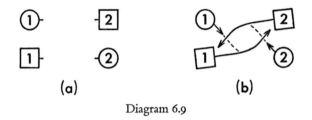

(a)   (b)

Diagram 6.9

The 'side-by-side' starting position shown in Diagram 6.9 (a) was, within living memory, very much more common in ordinary social dancing than was the 'in-line' position shown in Diagram 6.7. On the other hand, the 'in-line' position appears to be the earlier of the two, and for this reason we have preferred to give it first. In Games dancing, the 'in-line' position was (and still is) used almost exclusively.

In the Highlands and the Western Isles the Foursome Reel as described here (with either starting position) remained in general use up to and after 1914.[1] In the Lowlands, on the other hand, the dance was rather uncommon within the period covered by living memory, for there it had been largely supplanted by the combination with the Reel of Tulloch. Of the dancing-teachers who practised in the Lowlands since about 1890, only a few seem to have taught the Foursome Reel as a separate dance—among those who did so were John Muir of Motherwell and his son James, David Anderson of Dundee, and (on the borders of the Highlands) James Neill of Forfar. John and James Muir and David Anderson actually taught the Foursome Reel both as a separate dance and in combination with the Reel of Tulloch, but James Neill seems to have taught the Foursome Reel and the Reel of Tulloch only as separate dances.

It is of interest to compare the description of the Foursome Reel given here with those given in various printed and manuscript sources. The descriptions of the dance given in the Lowes' Ball-Conductor (211; c. 1830)[2] and in all subsequent Scottish ballroom guides coincide exactly

---

[1] But see also the remarks concerning the old West Highland circular Reel on p. 156.
[2] This was a joint work written by Messrs J., R., J., and J. S. Lowe, four members of a family of dancing-teachers whose activities appear to have covered most of Scotland. The first author, Joseph Lowe, taught in Edinburgh in the winter and in Inverness in the summer, the second author, R. Lowe, taught in Glasgow from October to March, in Montrose from April to June, and in Brechin from July to September, the third

with that given above. The *Ball-Conductor* gives both starting positions, and is actually the first source of any kind to give the 'side-by-side' position. All the later guides give the 'in-line' position, but not all give the 'side-by-side' position.

Of the descriptions prior to 1830, that of Barclay Dun (205; 1818) is incomplete and gives only the starting position ('in-line', as in Diagram 6.7) and the initial movements of the dancers in the reel of four. So far as it goes, this description agrees with ours. On the other hand, the description given by Thomas Wilson in his *Analysis of Country Dancing* (257; 1811), which is the earliest description of any, differs from ours to a certain extent. In Wilson's version, the starting position is in line, but with the *ladies* in the centre, and further, the dancers begin the reel of four by passing with left shoulders and finish it always in their own places. In a later work (261; 1821) Wilson repeats this description, but adds a footnote to say that a 'right shoulder' reel of four is also permissible.

We note finally two variants of the Foursome Reel. The first of these was danced up to about 1910 in Bonchester, Chesters, Oxnam, and Crailing in Roxburghshire, and in Westruther and West Gordon in Berwickshire. Here the dancers began in line, facing their partners, with the *ladies* in the centre. The first part of the dance was performed to strathspey tunes, and consisted of alternate reeling and setting, the dancers returning to their own places at the end of each reel of four. The second part was performed to reel tunes, and here the dancers performed the reel of four as before, but, instead of setting to their partners, they swung each other with ordinary ballroom hold (in the clockwise direction only), using the pivot step (p. 110). In West Gordon this version was almost certainly included in the lessons of the local teacher, Andrew Cochrane (23–24, 60).

The second variant was mentioned to us in a letter by Archibald Campbell of Kilberry: 'A certain school of thought used to declare that [in the part of the Foursome Reel performed to reel tunes] . . . the figure of 8 should be abandoned [because of the difficulty of completing it in eight bars] and the dancers should follow each other round . . . in an oval. I don't know where this came from, but I have seen it done on a platform. In a crowded ballroom it is impossible, though I have seen its

---

author, John Lowe, taught in Perth from November to April, in Arbroath from May to June, and in Elgin from July to September, while the fourth, J. S. Lowe, taught in Dundee from December to April, and in Fife during the summer. They may be said, therefore, to speak with authority!

advocates try to do it, and get hopelessly tied up. It was never done at Kilberry. Indeed, an old piper at Kilberry used to play an extra two bars in his reel in order to allow dancers to get round [the "figure 8"] in time ... to start the setting in the proper position.'

This same oval (elliptical) figure is given by Atkinson as an alternative to the reel of four ('figure 8') in that part of the Foursome Reel performed to reel tunes. An oval figure of this form is also mentioned in the manuscript *Contre-Danses à Paris 1818*, with the comment that 'it was introduced from England two or three years ago under the name of "fashionable", most probably because in England this reel [i.e. the Foursome Reel] was never properly understood or valued'.

THE REEL OF TULLOCH

We confine ourselves here to the more or less standard version of the dance which was current subsequent to about 1880. The following version, which is that taught by James Neill of Forfar from about 1890 onwards (and possibly earlier) contains the essentials of this standard Reel of Tulloch.

The dance is performed by two couples. To begin, the dancers stand beside their partners, each lady on her partner's right, facing the opposite couple and about 6 ft from them, as in Diagram 6.9 (a).

The dance consists of alternate setting and swinging. Immediately after the start of the dance, the dancers form a line of four, and in the course of the setting and swinging each dancer progresses steadily along this line, one place at a time. On reaching an end position, the dancers stand still for 16 bars of the music, then begin to progress back along the line. The progression is continued, forward and back, and then forward again, until all have regained their original places.

In most parts of Scotland the dance was performed to the tune 'The Reel of Tulloch', but in Roxburghshire and Berwickshire, where it was often known as the 'Hullachan Jig', it was performed to the tune 'The Irish Washerwoman' or some similar double jig. In either case the tempo was about 60–64 bars per minute.

Music Bars	Description of the Figures
1–8	The two ladies come into the centre and set to each other. While the ladies are setting, the men move into line with them, forming a line of four (Diagram 6.10 (a)).
9–16	The two ladies swing each other, first with the right arm

(4 bars), then with the left (4 bars), and finish facing the opposite men (Diagram 6.10 (b)).

17–24   All set, the 1st man to 2nd lady, the 2nd man to the 1st lady.

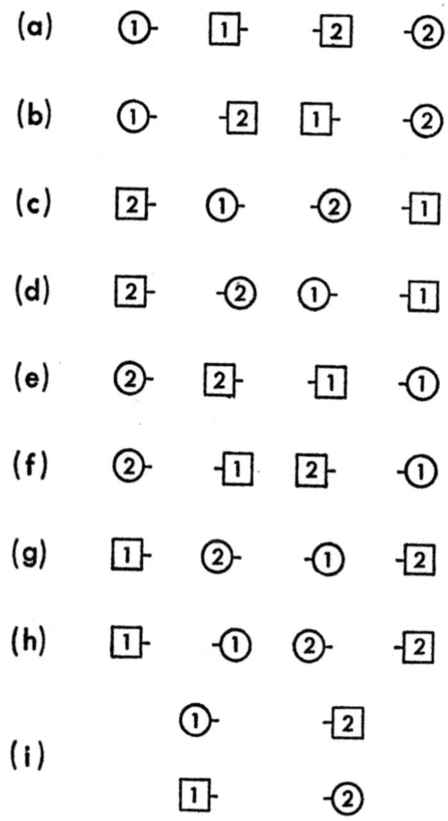

(a)   ①-   [1]-   -[2]   -②

(b)   ①-   -[2]   [1]-   -②

(c)   [2]-   ①-   -②   -[1]

(d)   [2]-   -②   ①-   -[1]

(e)   ②-   [2]-   -[1]   -①

(f)   ②-   -[1]   [2]-   -①

(g)   [1]-   ②-   -①   -[2]

(h)   [1]-   -①   ②-   -[2]

(i)   ①-   -[2]

      [1]-   -②

Diagram 6.10

25–32   The 1st man and 2nd lady swing each other, first with the right arm (4 bars), then with the left (4 bars). At the same time, the 2nd man and 1st lady do likewise. Finish with the two men in the centre facing each other (Diagram 6.10 (c)).

33–48   The two men set to each other for 8 bars, then swing each other, first with the right arm, then with the left, finishing facing their partners (Diagram 6.10 (d)).

49–64   All set to partners for 8 bars, then swing partners, first with the right arm, then with the left, and finish with the two ladies in the centre facing each other (Diagram 6.10 (e)).

L

65–128 The alternate setting and swinging is repeated, first by the ladies alone in the centre, then by all, dancing with opposite partners (Diagram 6.10 (f)), then by the men alone in the centre (Diagram 6.10 (g)), then finally by all, dancing with partners (Diagram 6.10 (h)). At the end of the final swing, the couples turn into their original places (Diagram 6.10 (i)).

During the 8-bar setting periods, the dancers use any quick Reel setting step they please, putting in as many different steps as possible in the course of the dance. The swinging is performed with the pivot step (p. 110); to swing with the right arm, the two dancers concerned bend their right arms at the elbow, making an angle of almost 90°, and each cups his or her right hand behind the other's arm, just above the elbow (the thumb of the cupped hand should be placed alongside the fingers; on no account should one grip the other person's arm between fingers and thumb). Swinging with the left arms is performed similarly. In each case the free arm is normally held in the raised position.

There is an alternative hold for the swinging, known as the 'Hulla-chan hold'. To swing with the right arms, the two dancers concerned link right arms, and each passes the left hand behind the back to grasp the other person's right hand; at the same time each dancer brings the left shoulder slightly forward, so that the body is inclined towards the other person. The 'Hullachan hold' with the left arms is similar. In the original form of the Reel of Tulloch, this 'Hullachan hold' was used by both men and ladies, but within living memory it has been used principally when two ladies swing each other.

There is also a special method of making the change of direction in the middle of the swing; this is invariably used by Games dancers, but is (and was) also used in social dancing. In this, the two dancers concerned swing with the right arms for 3 bars (6 pivot steps, counting[1] '1 & 2 & 3 & 4 & 5 & 6'), making one and a half turns. They then perform either two points or two highcuts (pp. 116, 126) with RF, LF (counts '7, 8'), making approximately a quarter turn to the right on the spot on the second count (count '8'). They then take left arms and swing for 4 bars (8 pivot steps, counting '1 & 2 & 3 & ... 7 & 8'), making two complete turns. The change of direction should take place when the dancers are directly in the line of four (Diagram 6.11).

An alternative method of making the change of direction in the swing

---

[1] The counting is that for a reel.

was taught by Mr William Adamson and his father in East Fife. Here the two dancers concerned swing with linked right arms for 2 bars (4 pivot steps), making one complete turn and ending in their original places. They then set to each other with two pas de Basque, RF, LF, and then swing with linked left arms for 4 bars (8 pivot steps), making one and a half turns to change places. In each turn, the free arm is raised.

COUNT '7'

COUNT '8'

Diagram 6.11

In some places, particularly in the Borders, the swinging was often performed with ordinary ballroom hold, and in one direction only, namely clockwise. At Kilberry 'there was little linking of arms except by those who wished to be genteel'. Two dancers of the opposite sex used ordinary ballroom hold (this was known locally as 'presenting') while two men used the 'bear-hug', clasping each other round the waist, 'almost as if about to wrestle' (107).

The dance is also sometimes begun from an 'in-line' position. In one version which we have met, the ladies stand in the centre facing each other, with their partners behind them in the outer positions. In another version, the men stand facing their partners, as in Diagram 6.7. In the first version the ladies begin the dance by setting to each other while the men stand still, and in the second the dancers all begin together by setting to partners. Both versions consist of alternate setting and swinging, and each dancer progresses along the line of four in an exactly similar manner to that described in the previous version.

COMBINATIONS OF THE FOURSOME REEL AND REEL OF TULLOCH

We give here some of the particular combinations which we have met. Most of these were taught by prominent dancing-teachers, and were current at least in the districts which these teachers served. These several versions illustrate very well the manner in which a well-known dance can vary from one district to another.

In each version, the part belonging to the Foursome Reel forms the first part of the dance, and is performed either to strathspeys followed by one or more reel tunes, or to strathspeys only. The Reel of Tulloch forms the conclusion of the dance, and is performed to the tune 'The Reel of Tulloch'.

Version I. Start either in line, as in Diagram 6.7, or side-by-side, as in Diagram 6.9 (a). Reel and set three times (or any odd number of times) to strathspey tunes and once to a reel, ending by setting to partners. Begin the Reel of Tulloch by swinging partners, and thereafter set and swing with the usual progression. The Reel of Tulloch may be allowed to run until the dancers have regained their original places, or it may be ended after 64 bars, when partners are dancing together in the other couple's place.

We were taught this version by our teachers, Pipe-Major David Taylor and Mr Jack McConachie. It was also the version taught by Mr D. G. MacLennan and several other Highland dancers of his generation, and was frequently danced at the Games.

Version II. Start in line as in Diagram 6.7, reel and set four times to strathspey tunes, then reel, set, and reel again to a reel tune, finishing by facing partners. Begin the Reel of Tulloch by swinging partners.

This version was taught by Professor Blackley of Lanark.

Version III. Start side-by-side as in Diagram 6.9 (a), and reel and set several times to strathspey tunes. The music then changes to 'The Reel of Tulloch', and the ladies step into the centre and set and swing, while the men move to the outer positions; thereafter the Reel of Tulloch follows with the usual progression.

This is the 'Strathspey and Reel of Tulloch' which was current in Arisaig about 1900 (31).

Version IV. Start in line, with the *ladies* in the centre and the men on the outside, all facing partners. Reel and set four times to strathspey tunes, all returning to *original* places after each reel of four. Begin the Reel of Tulloch by swinging partners. Preferably end the Reel of Tulloch after 64 bars, when partners are dancing together, in the other couple's place.

This unusual version was taught in the South-west by Peter Marshall and his pupil and partner, Thomas Shanks (cf. the version of the Foursome Reel from the Borders given on p. 147).

It will be noted that in versions III and IV there is no reel of four in quick tempo, so that these versions do not require a quick travelling step of the form of the hop-one-and-two or chassé. Other versions with this same feature were taught by a number of teachers, in particular 'Dancie' Reid of Newtyle and Professor Buck.

THE DOUBLE REEL OF TULLOCH

This dance is simply an arrangement of two separate sets of the Reel of Tulloch in the form of a cross. In order to make the arrangement possible, the two sets perform the dance 16 bars out of phase with each other, that is to say that the two pairs of one set of four dancers are setting and swinging at the same time as the central pair of the other set, and vice versa. A possible starting position is shown in Diagram 6.12; here

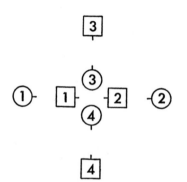

Diagram 6.12

the two sets consist of 1st and 2nd couples, and 3rd and 4th couples respectively. The 1st and 2nd ladies set and swing in the centre, while 3rd and 4th couples do the same on the outside, then the 1st lady and 2nd man, and the 2nd lady and 1st man, set and swing on the outside, while the 3rd and 4th ladies set and swing in the centre, and so on.[1]

We have heard of this dance only in Lochaber (96) and at Ardgour (95). In Lochaber, where it was performed some sixty years ago, the dance seems to have been largely a matter of the informal combination of two sets of dancers—if there was sufficient space available on the floor when the Reel of Tulloch was announced, then two sets of dancers could, if so inclined, combine their sets to form a cross. The order in which the sets began had to be arranged, but this was probably just

[1] It is also possible, but less satisfactory, for the two sets to perform the dance eight bars out of phase. This form of the dance is described by Atkinson (226; 1900).

done at the time, and the ending of the dance was probably adjusted likewise. The same seems to have been true at Ardgour, where the dance was performed about 1920.

THE ROUND ABOUT HULLACHAN, OR REEL OF TULLOCH IN A CIRCLE

Here the dancers form one large circle round the room, with the men and ladies placed alternately. The ladies all face in one direction round the circle, the men in the other, so that each man is facing a lady. All now set to and swing the person facing them, exactly as in the ordinary Reel of Tulloch, then pass on to the next person round the circle and repeat the setting and swinging, then pass on to the next, and so on. In this way the dancers move round the circle, one place at a time, setting and swinging each person they meet.

This dance was most common in Roxburghshire and Berwickshire. In these districts it was known as the 'Round About Hullachan', and was usually danced to 'The Irish Washerwoman' or some similar double jig; the swinging was normally performed in the clockwise direction only, using ordinary ballroom hold, and the usual setting step was the pas de Basque. The dance was sometimes included by Professor Buck in his classes, and it was almost certainly taught by Andrew Cochrane of West Gordon. The dance was also known in East Lothian under the name 'Reel of Tulloch in a Circle', and was there included in the repertoire of the local teacher, Mr Maxwell. It was also known on the island of Barra about the year 1910 (and possibly earlier) under the name 'Lady Glenorchy's Reel' (130).

THE EVERLASTING JIG, OR IRISH JIG

This dance was popular up to about 1914 on the Argyllshire coast and on the adjacent islands.

One version of the dance, which we recorded in Lochdonhead in Mull (117), is the same as the 'Reel of Tulloch in a Circle', except that the dancers are here placed in couples anywhere in the room and change partners in a completely haphazard manner. In this particular version, the couples swing in the clockwise direction only, using ordinary ballroom hold. A similar version was known at Benderloch in Argyllshire, but there the dance was used as a form of elimination dance: 'You faced your partner and stepped like in a Reel, and clinked partners, but just as you were about to arm your partner someone else turned her for you, and you were out' (108).

At Kilberry the dance seems to have lost the swinging. There, 'the Everlasting Jig . . . was really a sort of romp. Partners would stand up and jig opposite each other until someone cut in between them. The man or woman displaced had to go off and cut in between another pair. This frolic continued for as long as the piper chose to play' (107).

It is interesting to compare the Everlasting Jig with the dance 'America' which Samuel Johnson and James Boswell saw at Armadale in Skye in 1773, on their tour to the Hebrides (290): 'We had . . . in the evening a great dance. We made out five country squares without sitting down: and then we performed with much alacrity a dance which I suppose the emigration from Skye has occasioned. They call it 'America'. A brisk reel is played. The first couple begin, and each sets to one—then each to another—then as they set to the next couple, the second and third couples are setting; and so it goes on till all are set a-going, setting and wheeling round each other, while each is making the tour of all in the dance. It shows how emigration catches till all are set afloat. . . .'

The reference here to 'wheeling round each other' is particularly interesting, since this indicates that dances involving setting and swinging were known in the Highlands before the first recorded appearance of the Reel of Tulloch.

CHAPTER VII

Some lesser-known Reels from the Main-land of Scotland and the Western Isles

THE OLD WEST HIGHLAND CIRCULAR REEL

THIS is a dance for two couples with the usual Reel structure, the travelling figure here being a simple circle.

We have met this dance only in the extreme West Highlands and the Western Isles, in the districts of Moidart, Morar, and Arisaig, and the islands of Eigg, Skye, Barra, South Uist, and Benbecula. It was known by various names; in Barra one of our informants (130) had heard it spoken of as 'Seann Ruidhleadh Muchairt na Cailleachan', the 'old roundabout Reel of the old women', while at Torrin in Skye it was sometimes known as 'Ruidhleadh Mòr', the 'big Reel' (112). Most often, however, it was known as a form of 'Scotch Reel', for instance as 'the old style Scotch Reel' (Moidart, 36; Morar, 94; Eigg, 114), or the 'old-fashioned way' of dancing the Scotch Reel (Moidart, 98).

At one time in the districts mentioned, the circular Reel seems to have been the Reel in general use, while the ordinary Foursome Reel, with its 'figure 8', was not danced at all. When we visited Eigg, Skye, South Uist, and Benbecula in 1953–6, there were still a number of old people in these islands who could recall the days when the common Reel in use there was the circular Reel, and the Foursome Reel was unknown. In Eigg, for instance, the old circular Reel was in general use up to about 1893, and the Foursome Reel was not danced there before this date (114–15). Again, in South Uist about the year 1885 'all Scotch Reels had circles and not figures of eight' (124), while at Torrin in Skye, up to as late as 1900 'the only way in which people did the Scotch Reel' was with the circle figure (112). In the other places mentioned, Moidart, Morar, Arisaig, and Barra, the old circular Reel was understood to have been the 'original' Reel for four danced there, but the actual date when it began to be replaced by the Foursome Reel is outside living memory.

156

What is significant here is the fact that in the Western Isles at the beginning of the period covered by living memory the 'figure 8' was completely absent. Had the circle and the 'figure 8' both been in use, it might have been the case that the circle was simply a modified form of the oval figure in the Foursome Reel which was introduced to Scotland from England about 1815 (p. 148). However, since the 'figure 8' was at one time completely absent, we must conclude that the original Reel in the Western Isles, and presumably also in the West Highlands, was the circular Reel, and that the Foursome Reel, with its 'figure 8', belongs properly to the Eastern Highlands and the Lowlands.

In all the districts mentioned, the old circular Reel has not been danced since about 1900, or even earlier. Its place was taken by the Foursome Reel—in effect, the 'figure 8' was simply substituted for the circle figure.

The following description of the circular Reel was given to us by a number of informants in the various places mentioned above (134).

To begin the circular Reel, the dancers stand beside their partners, each lady on her partner's right, facing the other couple and about 6 ft from them (Diagram 7.1).

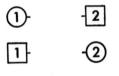

Diagram 7.1

The dance is performed to one or more strathspeys followed without pause by one or more reels.

Music Bars	Description of the Figures
1–8	All follow each other round in a circle (without giving hands). The ladies begin by passing across in front of their partners (Diagram 7.2 (a)); the men stand still for the first two bars, then on the third bar they join in the circle a quarter of the circumference behind their partners. All four then dance round, equally spaced round the circle (Diagram 7.2 (b) shows their positions at the end of bar 4), and finish in a line of four facing partners (Diagram 7.2 (c); the men depart from the circular track on bars 7, 8).

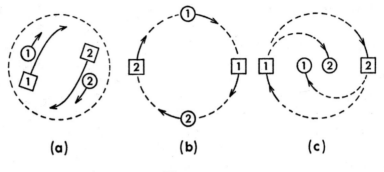

Diagram 7.2

9–16   All set to partners with Reel setting steps appropriate to the music.

17–24   The four dancers again dance round in a circle, all now start-ing together. The ladies move off directly to their left, while the men dance out to the left and join in the circle a quarter of the circumference behind their partners (Diagram 7.3 (a)). The ladies dance a complete circle, while the men depart from the circle on the last two bars of the phrase, so that all finish in the places shown in Diagram 7.2 (c). The approximate tracks of 1st and 2nd men throughout the whole 8 bars are shown in Diagram 7.3 (b) and 7.3 (c), respectively.

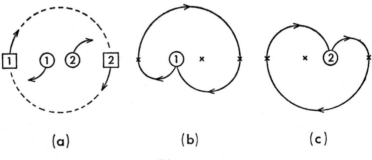

Diagram 7.3

25–32   All set to partners with Reel setting steps appropriate to the music.

33–   Repeat the movements of bars 17–32 as often as desired.

In South Uist (124, 127), and probably elsewhere, the dance was sometimes combined with the Reel of Tulloch, just as was the ordinary

Foursome Reel; in this case the Reel of Tulloch followed without pause at the end of the circular Reel.

The strathspey travelling step used in the circular Reel was the usual Highland step, Strathspey travelling step B (p. 93), while the quick travelling step was either the hop-one-and-two (p. 105) or the travelling pas de Basque (p. 109). The setting was performed with any Reel setting step appropriate to the music, and the style of performance was exactly similar to that of the ordinary Foursome Reel (pp. 137–9).

It is possible that the 'in-line' position to which the dancers return after each circle is a late addition to the dance, for it would seem to be much more natural for the dancers to remain in the circle when setting, turning only to face their partners. A form of the dance in which the dancers remained in the circle would obviously have been well suited to the old-fashioned 'black house', with the fire placed in the centre of the floor—the dancers could then simply have circled the fire.

RUIDHLEADH MÒR (The big Reel)

When we visited Torrin in Skye in 1954, we found that the name 'Ruidhleadh Mòr' was commonly used there for the old circular Reel for four, and when we remarked to one of our informants, Mr Charles Mathieson, that the name seemed inappropriate, we were referred to an older friend of his, Mr Neil MacKinnon (111), for the explanation. We later visited Mr MacKinnon, and from him we learnt that originally the name had belonged to another dance, essentially a version of the old circular Reel for as many dancers as please, which died out in the district about 1895. Mr MacKinnon had seen this dance once, at a wedding in Torrin at about that date. On that occasion, the twenty or so people present formed one big ring round the room. When the music began— the dance was performed to reel tunes throughout—the dancers moved round clockwise in a circle, one behind the other (without joining hands), then stopped and danced ordinary Reel setting steps, then danced round in the circle again, and so on. So far as Mr MacKinnon knew, this particular wedding was the last occasion when the dance was performed at Torrin.

THE EIGHT MEN OF MOIDART

On July 23rd, 1745, Prince Charles Edward landed on the shores of Moidart to begin the '45 Rising. Today the spot where he stepped ashore is marked by seven huge oak trees, 'The Seven Men of Moidart'.

Tradition still current in Moidart has it that on that occasion there were seven fishermen 'hooking for bait' on the shore, and their delight on seeing their Prince was so great that they danced with joy on the sands. The dance which they performed was a dance for eight, and in place of the eighth person they stuck one of their spades into the sand; afterwards, their dance—whatever it was—became known as 'The Eight Men of Moidart' (100).[1]

Within living memory, there were two different dances of this name in Moidart. We were told of the existence of one of these dances by Mr Donald Cameron, the post-master at Acharacle, when we were on a short visit to Moidart in 1954. On that occasion we were unable to obtain full details of this dance, but on a further visit in 1956 in company with Dr Rhodes we were able to recover it more or less completely. This later visit also brought to light the second 'The Eight Men of Moidart', which we found in Glenuig.

We describe the latter dance first, since it is unquestionably the older of the two.

The Eight Men of Moidart from Glenuig

We obtained the details of this dance from Mr Angus MacPherson and his sister Mrs Ann MacDonald (36), who learnt it in their own home when they were young.

So far as Mr MacPherson and Mrs MacDonald know, the dance has not been performed in Glenuig since about 1900, and for some time before that date it was performed only in their own home—it had already died out in the ordinary social dances in the glen. At that time Mr MacPherson and his sister lived at Smearisary, the remotest part of Glenuig. They were two of a large family of children, and in the winter evenings they used to dance with their brothers and sisters in the kitchen of their croft, while their parents sang puirt-a-beul for them. Their father and an old friend of his taught them various dances, and among these was 'The Eight Men of Moidart'. With so many in the family, they had no need to draw friends in from outside to dance with them, and thus knowledge of the dance eventually became confined to their family alone.[2]

The Glenuig dance is a Reel for eight and is composed of two of the old West Highland circular Reels, with the two circles flattened to ovals

[1] Two somewhat different versions of this tradition are given by the late Calum MacLean in his book *The Highlands* (302).

[2] A delightful description of the tiny community of Glenuig has been given by Calum MacLean in his book (302). Mr MacLean refers to Mr MacPherson as a noted story-teller, and tells also how he collected two waulking songs from Mrs MacDonald.

and interlaced with each other. It is thus a form of double circular Reel, and indeed Mr MacPherson told us that it was sometimes called the 'Double Reel'.[1] The dance could easily date back to 1745 or earlier, and it might well have been danced on the sands of Moidart on that celebrated July day.

The dancers stand in two lines, as shown in Diagram 7.4, each dancer facing the opposite line. There should be a distance of about 2 ft 6 in. between two adjacent dancers in the same line, and the two lines should be about 6 ft apart.

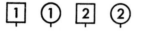

Diagram 7.4

The dance is performed to one or more strathspeys played at the usual tempo of 40–42 bars per minute.

To begin, the 1st and 3rd couples, and the 2nd and 4th couples, dance interlacing ovals, the men following their partners. In the following description we letter the places as follows

A   B   C   D

H   G   F   E

Music Bars	Description of the Figures
1, 2	1st and 3rd ladies change places, passing each other with right shoulders. Starting at the same time, but allowing the other two ladies to cross first, 2nd and 4th ladies change places, also passing each other with right shoulders. During these two bars, the men stand still.
3, 4	1st man dances across to place E, while 3rd man dances across to place A. Starting at the same time, but allowing the other two men to cross first, 2nd man dances across to place G, while 4th man dances across to place C (both

---

[1] Mr MacPherson was actually familiar with the circular Reel for four described earlier in this chapter.

pairs passing by the right). Meanwhile 1st lady moves to F, 2nd lady to H, 3rd lady to B, and 4th lady to D (Diagram 7.5).

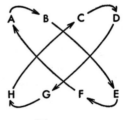

Diagram 7.5

5, 6   1st and 3rd ladies cross back to own places, again passing with right shoulders. Then the 2nd and 4th ladies cross back to own places, also passing with right shoulders. Meanwhile 1st man moves to F, 2nd man to H, 3rd man to B, and 4th man to D (Diagram 7.5).

7, 8   1st and 3rd men, and then 2nd and 4th men, cross back to the positions shown in Diagram 7.6, each pair passing by the right. Meanwhile the ladies turn about so that all finish facing partners (Diagram 7.6).

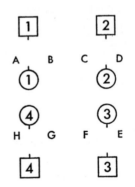

Diagram 7.6

(We have divided this sequence of 8 bars into 2-bar phrases only for ease of description, and the positions given at the end of each 2-bar phrase must be regarded as approximate only. The actual dance should flow evenly, with no noticeable pauses.)

9–16   All set to partners with strathspey setting steps.

17–24   The interlacing ovals are repeated, all now starting at the same time, and moving initially in the directions shown in Diagram 7.7. The order in which the dancers cross in the middle is the same as in bars 1–8, and all finish facing partners as in Diagram 7.6.

25–32 All set to partners with strathspey setting steps.

33– Repeat the sequence of bars 17–32 as often as desired.

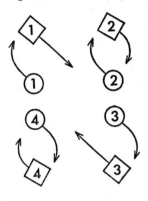

Diagram 7.7

The dance can be concluded by 1st and 4th couples, and 2nd and 3rd couples, each dancing a Reel of Tulloch (pp. 148–50), beginning in the positions shown in Diagram 7.6.

The strathspey travelling step which Mr MacPherson and his sister were taught to use in the ovals was the usual Highland step, Strathspey travelling step B (p. 93). For setting, they used either a Highland Fling step or the Highland Schottische step. The style of performance was similar to that in the ordinary Foursome Reel (pp. 137–9).

After Mr MacPherson and his sister had shown us this dance, we visited most of the older people in Glenuig in search of further information. We found that a number of people had heard of the dance, but no one other than Mr MacPherson and his sister had ever seen it performed.

One lady, Mrs Flora MacDonald (34), recalled her father talking of what he had been told by his own father, who died about 1890. In Mrs MacDonald's grandfather's day—so her father said—the only social dances in use in Glenuig were the Scotch Reel, the Reel of Tulloch, the Highland Schottische, and The Eight Men of Moidart. Country Dances, the Quadrilles, and the Lancers were first brought into Glenuig about the year 1875, when the glen was visited by an itinerant dancing-teacher called Frazer.[1] In her grandfather's time, The Eight Men of Moidart was danced regularly; her father had seen it danced, but had never taken part in it.

[1] Mr Angus MacPherson's father attended Mr Frazer's dancing classes.

The Eight Men of Moidart from Mingarry

This second 'Eight Men of Moidart' is the one which we heard of in 1954. It belongs to the neighbourhood of Mingarry in Moidart, and was last performed there about 1932, when it was revived for a short period through the efforts of two local people, Miss Ann MacDonald and her brother Ronald, who remembered the dance from their youth. At this time there was a Country Dance group at Salen, Loch Sunart, and among the dances performed by this group was the Country Dance 'The Eight Men of Moidart', which the members of the group had learnt from one of the R.S.C.D.S. *Country Dance Books*.[1] Miss Mac-Donald saw this Country Dance performed by the Salen group, and this inspired her to revive 'The Eight Men of Moidart' which she had learnt at Mingarry in her younger days. Aided by her brother, she taught the version which she remembered to a small group of friends gathered in her home for the purpose, and these people performed the dance once at Acharacle and two or three times at Mingarry. It did not become popular, however, and again fell into disuse.

Miss MacDonald told the late Dr Fergusson of Salen that she learnt the dance at the Christmas parties which Lord Howard of Glossop held at Mingarry for the tenants on his local estate (106). This would presumably have been about 1885, for Miss MacDonald died in 1944 aged a little over 80, and we know that Lord Howard ceased to hold his Christmas parties at Mingarry about 1886. The dance itself is rather similar to the modern Eightsome Reel, and is almost certainly of nineteenth-century date.

We had the greatest difficulty in recovering this dance, and have had to piece the description together from information from a number of sources (35, 99–105). The following description gives a correct general picture of the dance, and we have noted at the end those points where there is some uncertainty.

The dance is performed by four couples, to any reel tune. The dancers stand in square formation, facing their partners (Diagram 7.8).

Music Bars	*Description of the Figures*
1–16	All dance a 'grand chain' round to places, giving right hands to partners to begin (i.e. the ladies move round the set clockwise, the men counter-clockwise, passing each other

[1] The R.S.C.D.S. dance is taken from a collection of Country Dances published in England *c*. 1754, and we know of no evidence that it was ever performed in Scotland prior to its publication by the R.S.C.D.S.

with alternate right and left shoulders and giving alternate right and left hands on passing). When partners meet
halfway round the chain, and again at the end of the
chain, the men bow and the ladies curtsy, taking two full
bars for this on each occasion (bars 7, 8 and 15, 16).

17–24   The 1st lady goes into the centre and curtsies to her partner,
who bows in return (bars 17, 18). They then set to each
other (bars 19, 20), and then swing, first with the right
arm (bars 21, 22) and then with the left (bars 23, 24),
finishing in original places.

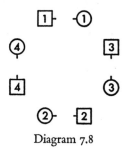

Diagram 7.8

25–32   All join hands in a ring and dance round to the left and back.
33–40   The 1st lady goes into the centre and curtsies to the 2nd man,
who bows in return (bars 33, 34). They then set to each
other (bars 35, 36) and then swing, first with the right
arm (bars 37, 38) and then with the left (bars 39, 40),
finishing in original places.

41–48   All join hands in a ring and dance round to the left and back.
49–80   The sequence of bars 33–48 is repeated twice more, the 1st
lady dancing first with the 3rd man, and then with the 4th
man.

81–88   The 1st man and the 2nd lady set to each other in the centre
(bars 81, 82), swing each other once round with the right
arm (bars 83, 84), set again (bars 85, 86), and swing each
other with the left arm to finish back to back in the
centre, facing partners.

89–96   The 1st man and 1st lady, and the 2nd man and 2nd lady,
set to each other, swing with the right arm, set again, and
swing with the left arm.

97–104   The 1st and 2nd couples dance a reel of four up and down
the dance, the 1st lady and 2nd man beginning the reel by
passing each other in the middle with left shoulders. All
finish in original places in the square.

During bars 81–104 the 3rd and 4th couples stand still.

105–128　The 3rd and 4th couples now perform the sequence of bars 81–104 across the set, the 3rd man and the 4th lady beginning. The 1st and 2nd couples stand still.

129–136　All join hands in a ring and dance round to the left and back.

137–144　All dance a 'grand cross' twice round (i.e. the men give left hands in the centre and place their right arms round their partners' waists, and all dance twice round counter-clockwise). Finish in original places.

Except where noted, the dancers set with the pas de Basque (always beginning with the right foot). For the 'grand chain', circles, reels of four, and the 'grand cross', either the hop-one-and-two or the chassé can be used. The swings are performed with either of these steps or the pivot step, and the arm-hold is the same as that used in the Reel of Tulloch (p. 150).

The bow used by the men was peculiar to this dance, and was quite unlike the standard bow performed at the beginning of other dances. Here the men placed the right foot behind the left foot (in a loose rear 5th position) and bent the left knee slightly as they bowed.

We are not quite certain of the sequence in bars 81–128, and it is possible that the dance may end as follows:

Bars 81–88　The 1st and 2nd couples dance a reel of four, finishing in a line up and down the set with the men back to back in the centre facing their partners.

Bars 89–96　The 1st man and 1st lady, and also the 2nd man and 2nd lady, set to each other, swing with the right arm once round, set again, and swing with the left arm to finish in their original places in the square.

During bars 81–96 the 3rd and 4th couples stand still.

Bars 97–112　The 3rd and 4th couples perform the sequence of bars 81–96 across the set, while the 1st and 2nd couples stand still.

Bars 113–128　As described in bars 129–144 above.

There is also some doubt whether the 1st lady joins in the ring after turning each man (bars 25–32, 41–48, etc.), and it is possible that she should stay in the centre and dance quick Reel setting steps while the others dance round her.

CATH NAN COILEACH (The Combat of the Cocks)

We learnt this dance and the one which follows, Ruidhleadh nan Coileach Dubha, in 1953 from an old piper on the island of Barra, Neil MacNeil (131). Both dances have affinities with the old circular Reel.

When Mr MacNeil was a boy—he was 88 when we first met him in 1953—these two dances were performed all over the island at gatherings in the croft houses. They were also among the dances taught in a dancing-school held at Castlebay about the year 1881 by a teacher called Ronald Morrison, better known as 'Ronald-the-dancing-master'.[1] Mr MacNeil himself left Barra about 1886 and lived on the mainland for some years, and he never saw the dances subsequently. It is probable that they fell into disuse shortly after he left Barra, for we could find no one else on Barra who remembered them.

Dances called 'Cath nan Coileach' and 'Ruidhleadh nan Coileach Dubha' are mentioned in Alexander Carmichael's *Carmina Gadelica* (280; 1900), though unfortunately Carmichael gives no description of them. Before we visited the Isles in 1953 we compiled from such books as this a list of the names of 'forgotten' Gaelic dances, and it was our mention of the names on our list to Mr MacNeil that brought back to his memory these two particular dances. Our visit to him in 1953 came some sixty-seven years after he last saw Cath nan Coileach and Ruidhleadh nan Coileach Dubha performed, yet he was able to recall not only the figures of these dances but also the appropriate music and phrasing. And on another visit which we made to him a year later he repeated the same descriptions exactly.

These two dances were the first we collected. Our discovery of them proved to us that dances last done sixty years previously could still be recovered from the memories of old people, and it was this proof which encouraged us to continue our search for old dances elsewhere in Scotland.

According to Mr MacNeil, the dance Cath nan Coileach is intended to represent the bickering of fighting-cocks and the manner in which they circle round one another preparatory to actual combat.

The dance is performed by two couples, to the pipe jig 'Bochd liath nan gobhar' ('The shaggy grey buck', p. 169).[2] The dancers stand in the

---

[1] Ronald Morrison died about 1916 at the age of 80 or so. He came from South Uist, and was a pupil of the Morar dancing-master Ewen MacLachlan who practised in South Uist from about 1840 to 1879.

[2] Mr MacNeil knew this tune by the title 'Cath nan Coileach'.

form of a cross, opposite to their partners, with whom they join crossed hands (Diagram 7.9). They retain this 'cross' formation throughout the dance.

Diagram 7.9

The dance consists of the repetition of a 64-bar sequence. For the first 32 bars of this sequence the music is played at a tempo of about 60 bars per minute, and for the second 32 bars it is played at a tempo of about 75–80 bars per minute. The music then returns to the slower tempo for the first 32 bars of the next repetition of the 64-bar sequence, then goes back to the faster tempo for the second 32 bars, and so on.

Music Bars   *Description of the Figures*

1–16   All four (with crossed hands joined) dance an appropriate quick Reel setting step on the spot.

17–32   All dance round in a clockwise direction (not necessarily finishing in original places).

[The music now quickens to the faster tempo.]

33–48   All four (still with crossed hands joined) dance the 'backstep with a hop' (p. 123) on the spot.

49–64   The dancers spin round as fast as they can in a clockwise direction, using the pivot step (again not necessarily finishing in original places).

[The music now returns to the slower tempo.]

65–   Repeat this sequence as often as desired.

Mr MacNeil's description of the figures and the phrasing of the dance was absolutely precise.[1] He was, however, unable to dance the steps for us, and we therefore had to show him various steps and ask him which were most like those used in the dance in his young days. In this way we discovered that the pas de Basque and the Quick Reel steps J and P were all used for the setting in bars 1–16, that 'something like' the hop-one-and-two was used in bars 17–32, and that the pivot step was used in

[1] We questioned Mr MacNeil particularly on the 16-bar phrases, but he was completely adamant on this, both on our visits in 1953 and again in 1954. When we have performed the dance in public we have found it preferable to reduce these 16-bar phrases to 8 bars in length.

BOCHD LIATH NAN GOBHAR

RUIDHLEADH NAN COILEACH DUBHA

bars 49–64. In the case of the 'backstep with a hop' used in bars 33–48, Mr MacNeil described this step accurately enough for us to recognize it, and our identification of the step was confirmed when we performed it for him.

RUIDHLEADH NAN COILEACH DUBHA
(The Reel of the Blackcocks) FROM BARRA

This is the second of the dances which we learnt in 1953 from Neil MacNeil.

The dance is performed by two couples, to the reel tune 'Ruidhleadh nan Coileach Dubha' (p. 169) played at normal reel tempo. To begin, the dancers stand beside their partners, each lady on her partner's right, facing the other couple and about 5 ft from them (Diagram 7.10).

Diagram 7.10

Music Bars	Description of the Figures
1–8	The 1st man and 1st lady go down on one knee, while the 2nd couple set to them with quick Reel setting steps.
9–16	The 2nd couple now kneel, while the 1st couple rise and set with quick Reel setting steps.
17–24	The 2nd couple rise, and all join hands in a ring and dance two or three times round clockwise, finishing in original places.
25–	Repeat the sequence of bars 1–24 as often as desired.

The steps used here were the same as those used in bars 1–32 of Cath nan Coileach; there was no difference between the men's steps and the ladies' steps. The men used arm movements ('opposite hand to foot') or kept their arms akimbo, just as they pleased, while ladies had arms akimbo. Both men and ladies 'heuched' and snapped their fingers.

There is a Gaelic dance-song to the tune 'Ruidhleadh nan Coileach Dubha',[1] the first verse of which is as follows.

[1] See, for example, MacDonald, *Puirt-a-beul* (281). This dance-song was known to Mr MacNeil.

> Ruidhleadh nan coileach dubha
> 's dannsaidh na tunnagan,
> Ruidhleadh nan coileach dubha
> Air a' bhruthaich shiòs ud.

or in English

> Reeled the blackcocks
> And danced the ducks,
> Reeled the blackcocks
> On the banks up there.

A number of the older Gaelic dances contained a certain amount of miming, and we believe that this miming was largely determined by the words of the appropriate dance-song. The dance Ruidhleadh nan Coileach Dubha is a case in point—here the kneeling couple represent the ducks, while the dancing couple are the blackcocks.[1]

LONG BHARRACH (The Barra Ship)

When we visited the Isles in 1953, we had on our list of 'forgotten' Gaelic dances the name 'Long' (the ship), which is mentioned by Mr D. G. MacLennan in his book (239) as the name of an old Hebridean dance. On our visit that year we were able to find only one person in the Isles who had any memories of a dance with a name like this, Miss Rachel MacLeod of Castlebay, Barra (129), who had heard from her mother and grandmother of a dance called 'Long Bharrach' (The Barra Ship). Unfortunately, all that Miss MacLeod knew of this dance was that it had been performed by some fishermen from Barra at a wedding in North Uist about the year 1865.

On our visit in 1953, we asked Neil MacNeil about both 'Long' and 'Long Bharrach', but neither name stirred his memory. However, when we saw Mr MacNeil again in 1954, we found that 'Long Bharrach' had partly come back to him since our previous visit. The dance was still performed in his young days, and was another of the dances taught by Ronald Morrison in his dancing classes at Castlebay. It was performed to a reel tune peculiar to the dance and seven people took part in it. Six of the dancers stood in a ring, forming the 'outline' of the ship, and the seventh, a man, stood in the centre of the ring to represent the mast. The centre man danced with each of the other dancers in turn —and we know no more than this, for this is all that Neil MacNeil could remember.

[1] For other examples of miming associated with the use of dance-songs, see (295–6).

RUIDHLEADH NAN COILEACH DUBHA
(The Reel of the Blackcocks) FROM SOUTH UIST

This dance was collected by Dr Rhodes in 1956 from Mrs Margaret MacAskill of South Boisdale, South Uist, who was then aged 80 (125). In Mrs MacAskill's young days, the dance was performed at gatherings in the crofts in Smerclett, at the southern end of South Uist. Like the Barra dance of the same name, it is a very compact dance, well suited to the small croft houses.

The dance is performed by two couples, to the reel tune 'Ruidhleadh nan Coileach Dubha' (p. 169) played at normal reel tempo. To begin, the dancers stand beside their partners, each lady on her partner's right, facing the opposite couple and about 5 ft from them, as in Diagram 7.10 on p. 170. We adopt here the usage suggested by this diagram and refer to 1st man and 2nd lady, and similarly 1st lady and 2nd man, as 'opposites'.

Music Bars	Description of the Figures
1–4	All change places with opposites, passing with the right shoulder.
5–8	All set to opposites across the dance, using any quick Reel setting step.
9–16	All take hold with opposites, each person having the right hand on the other's waist and the left hand on the other's shoulder, and swing with the pivot step in the clockwise direction for 4 bars, then reverse the hold (i.e. place left hand on waist, right hand on shoulder), and swing in the opposite direction for 4 bars. All finish in the opposite couple's place, with each lady on her partner's left.
17–20	The two ladies change places and then the two men do the same, each pair passing with the right shoulders.
21–24	All set to partners.
25–32	All swing partners, first in the clockwise direction and then counter-clockwise, as above, finishing in original places.
33–36	The two ladies change places and then the two men do the same, each pair passing with the right shoulders.
37–40	All set to opposites across the dance.
41–48	All swing opposites, finishing in the opposite couple's place, with each lady on her partner's left.

49–   Repeat the sequence 'change places, set, and swing' as often as desired, setting and swinging alternately with partners and with opposites.[1]

THE THREESOME (OR HANKIES) REEL

This dance was common as a social dance in the Border counties (Roxburghshire, Selkirkshire, Peeblesshire, and Berwickshire) up to about 1920. It was also common in the Alford district of Aberdeenshire and the Dufftown district of Banffshire up to at least 1905. In the Borders it was definitely not included in the repertoires of the various local teachers, nor was it taught by any of the teachers who practised within living memory round Alford and Dufftown.

The dance is performed by a man and two ladies, to any strathspey. The music is played at the usual tempo for strathspeys, i.e. 40–42 bars per minute.

To begin, the dancers stand in a line with the man in the centre, all facing at right angles to the line (Diagram 7.11 (a)). In each hand the man has a handkerchief held by one corner, and the two ladies each take one of the handkerchiefs by the opposite corner. The ladies are numbered as in Diagram 7.11 (a), the 1st lady being on the man's right.

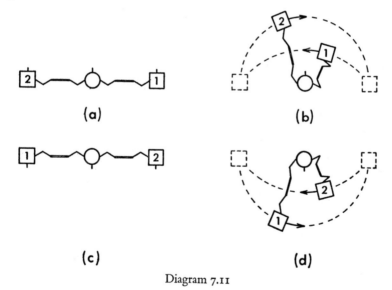

(a)   (b)

(c)   (d)

Diagram 7.11

[1] Mrs MacAskill was uncertain about the manner in which the repeats are performed. It is possible that at the end of bar 48 each lady should be on her partner's right. It is also possible that after bar 32, bars 1–32 should be repeated as often as desired.

The Border version of the dance is as follows (16, 61[1]).

Music Bars	Description of the Figures
1–8	All three dancers set, using the Highland Schottische step.
9–10	Using the Strathspey travelling step A (p. 93), the two ladies dance round in front of the man to change places with each other, the 1st lady passing under the arch made by the man and the 2nd lady. Meanwhile the man dances on the spot (step RF, LF, RF, hop on RF, step LF, RF, LF, hop on LF), making a half turn to his left under his own left arm (Diagram 7.11 (b)). The two ladies finish in each other's place, and all face in the opposite direction to that in which they faced originally (Diagram 7.11 (c)).
11–12	Still using the Strathspey travelling step A, the two ladies again dance round in front of the man to change places with each other, the 2nd lady now passing under the arch made by the man and the 1st lady. Meanwhile the man dances on the spot (as before), making a half turn to his right under his own right arm (Diagram 7.11 (d)). All finish in original places (Diagram 7.11 (a)).
13–16	Repeat bars 9–12 (so that the ladies make two complete circles round the man in bars 9–16).
17–	Repeat the sequence of bars 1–16 as often as desired.

The version which was performed in the Alford and Dufftown districts differed from this only in that the 1st lady passed under the arch made by the man and the 2nd lady *each* time the two ladies exchanged places.[2] The Highland Schottische step was still used for the setting, but the Highland Strathspey travelling step B was used in place of the Lowland step A (85).

We must emphasize that wherever we have met this dance as a social dance it was performed to strathspeys only, and there was no part in reel tempo. We have, however, met an exhibition version of this dance which does have a part in reel tempo. This exhibition version was taught to children by two teachers of Highland dancing in Kirkmichael in Perthshire, Miss Lilian and Miss Flora MacMillan. They learnt the

[1] We give here only our principal sources for the figures; we obtained confirmation of these figures from a number of other people in the Borders.

[2] The arches figure in bars 9–16 was sometimes performed in this manner in the Borders, but the alternate 'under and over' was there more common.

dance from their father, Hugh MacMillan, who died in 1946 at the age of 80. The same version also seems to have been taught by 'Dancie' Reid of Newtyle, and it is possible that he learnt it from Hugh Mac-Millan. For about the last twenty years this exhibition version has been performed regularly at the Kirkmichael Games.

In this exhibition version the dancers stand as in the version above (Diagram 7.11 (a)) but in place of handkerchiefs they use tartan ribbons fitted with swivelling rings. The figures, which are slightly different from those above, are as follows. The first 48 bars are performed to a strathspey, the second 48 bars to a reel, the tempos being as usual (p. 90).

1–4	The two ladies change places as in bars 9, 10 of the version above, but all use the Strathspey travelling step E in place of step A. All finish as in Diagram 7.11 (c).
5–8	Repeat bars 1–4 to places.
9–16	All set with any Highland Fling step which does not involve a turn (the same step for all three).
17–48	Repeat bars 1–16 twice, with different Highland Fling steps.

[The music now changes to a reel.]

49–96	Repeat bars 1–16 three times, using the hop-one-and-two for the circling figure, and any suitable quick Reel step for the setting.

It should be noted that in this version the ladies take 4 bars to exchange places, so that in the 8-bar travelling figure of the dance they make only one complete circle round the man. Moreover, the same lady passes under the arch each time.

It is possible that this exhibition version was also used as a social dance, but we have not met it as such.[1]

THE REEL OF SIX FROM LAUDERDALE

This dance was known variously as the Reel of Six, the Sixsome Reel, and the Six Reel,[2] and within living memory seems to have been performed only in and around the town of Lauder and the village of Oxton in upper Lauderdale. In the town of Lauder itself the dance began to fall

[1] The exhibition version above, with handkerchiefs in place of the tartan ribbons, is given in the R.S.C.D.S. *Country Dance Books*. According to a footnote, this R.S.C.D.S. version was collected in Perthshire and Angus, the area covered by 'Dancie' Reid.

[2] An arranged version has been published in the R.S.C.D.S. *Country Dance Books* under the name 'The Oxton Reel' (see p. 181).

out of use about 1900, and after this date it was only occasionally performed at the ordinary dances there, though it remained a regular part
of the programmes at the annual Volunteers' Ball in the town up to
about 1908 (70–72). In the village of Oxton it survived a little longer,
for there it was performed regularly at the village dances until about
1910. It should be added, however, that at this period dances were
rather rare events in Oxton, and there were usually only two a year.
These two dances were held in the schoolroom, which was the only
'hall' available, and both were rather big affairs called 'Social meetings'
—'people got dressed up for them' (18, 26). The dance was also performed at kirns on the bigger farms and the estates in the district, Boon,[1]
Addinston, Blythe, Spottiswoode, and possibly also Legerwood (see the
map below). It was probably danced also at Westruther, but was not
known at either West Gordon or Earlston. Within living memory it
has not been taught by any of the dancing-teachers who held classes in
the district, and nothing is known of how it first came to be performed
there.

At Oxton the dance was regarded just as an ordinary social dance, but
elsewhere in the district it was considered as 'rather special'. At the kirns
at Spottiswoode, the owner of the estate, Lady John Scott,[2] used to ask
for the dance to be performed for her. The Spottiswoode kirns came to
an end about 1896, but up to that date they had been one of the great
local events. All the tenants and farm-workers on the estate were invited,
together with the neighbouring farmers and all the local tradesmen who
had done work for the estate; the invitations covered their families also,
and the ages of those present ranged from six upwards. Lady John Scott
usually had a house-party to coincide with the event, and the members
of the house-party would come down to the kirn for the first part of the
evening, Lady John Scott herself being carried down in her sedan chair,
accompanied by a piper who afterwards played for some of the dancing
at the kirn (71, 74). It is possible that the encouragement which Lady
John Scott gave to the performance of the dance at her kirns was a
material factor in ensuring its survival; she was deeply interested in the
older way of life of the countryside around her home, and many 'old

[1] There is a brief description of the kirns at Boon (though no mention of the Reel of
Six) in R. Shirra Gibb's *A Farmer's Fifty Years in Lauderdale* (286). Dr Gibb farmed
Boon from 1872 to 1922, and his book provides a good picture of life in Lauderdale
during this period. During his tenancy of the farm he held some forty-six kirns there,
and the Reel of Six was performed regularly at these up to about 1903, or even later
(68).

[2] Lady John Scott (1810–1900) is perhaps best known today as the composer of
'Annie Laurie'.

customs lingered under her protecting care long after they had disappeared everywhere else' (283).

Any study of the Lauderdale Reel of Six is complicated by the fact
that within living memory there were two substantially different versions of the dance in use. One of these versions was performed mainly in
and around Oxton and the other mainly in and around Lauder, but there

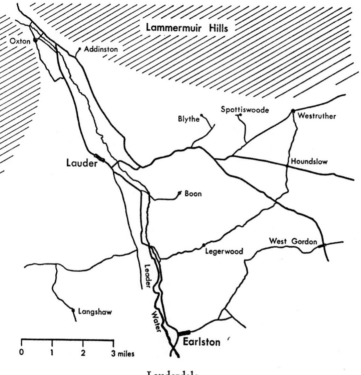

Lauderdale

were also occasions when the Oxton version was performed in the
Lauder district, and vice versa, for Lauder and Oxton are only four
miles apart, and the two communities naturally intermingled on social
occasions. At the village dances at Oxton it was always the Oxton version which was performed, even if—as generally happened—there were
Lauder people present. Again, at the Volunteers' Balls in Lauder there
would usually be a contingent of Volunteers from Oxton present, but
on these occasions they formed their own one or two sets, while the
Lauder people did likewise, and then the two versions were performed
side by side. We give both versions here, and we begin with that from
Oxton.

The Reel of Six, Oxton version

This version of the dance is performed by any number of sets of three couples. Each set is in longways formation, and the sets are arranged so that the dancers stand in two long lines down the hall, with the men in one line and the ladies in the other, each man being opposite his partner. At Oxton, in the old days, there were usually six or seven three-couple sets on the floor, arranged in this manner (Diagram 7.12).

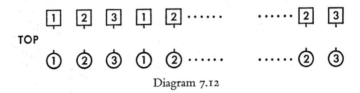

Diagram 7.12

The dance is performed throughout to the strathspey 'Cameron's got his wife again', played at a tempo of 40 bars per minute. It contains six different 'figures', the last three of which are performed twice in succession. In each figure the dancers begin with a travelling movement, at the end of which they return to their own places; they then turn partners once round with right hands, and then set to partners with a Strathspey setting step. In the first three figures the dance belies its name, for here the various three-couple sets combine to form one long set from the top to the bottom of the room, and all the dancers dance together; it is only in the last three figures that the dance justifies the name Reel of Six, in that here the dancers keep to their own three-couple sets.

The musical lengths of the first three figures depend on the number of dancers taking part. The exact phrasing is decided by the couple at the top of the room, who simply begin the next figure—at an appropriate point of the music—whenever they feel that the other dancers are in a position to do so. The last three figures are fixed in length, each occupying 24 bars (or, with the repetition, 48 bars).

For the travelling movements and the turns, the Lowland Strathspey travelling step A was invariably used; in the setting, the normal steps were either Highland Fling steps or the Highland Schottische step. The style of performance was similar to that of other Reels.

Figure I

The top man and top lady cast off (i.e. the top man makes a three-quarter turn to his left, the lady a three-quarter turn to her right) and dance down behind their own lines to the bottom of the room. The other dancers follow them, all coming up to the top of the room before turning off and dancing down (Diagram 7.13). All meet partners at the bottom, give right hands to each other, and lead up the centre to places. On regaining places, all turn partners once round with right hands, and then set to partners with a Strathspey setting step. As far as possible the turn should be begun halfway through an 8-bar phrase of the music, and the setting should be begun at the start of the next 8-bar phrase.

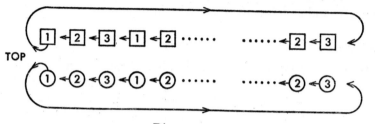

Diagram 7.13

When everyone is ready, and when the top couple has set for at least 8 bars, the top couple begin the next figure.

Figure II

All face the top, and join crossed hands in front with partners (i.e. the man takes his partner's right hand in his right hand, and her left hand in his left hand, their hands being held breast high, about 6 inches in front of them, with the man's right arm over the lady's left). The top couple turn off to their left and dance down behind the men's line, and the other couples follow them, all coming up to the top of the room before turning off and dancing down. As the top couple on their way down pass the tail of the procession of couples on their way up, the top couple lead across to the far side of the room, and then continue on their way to the bottom, where they turn to their right to lead up the centre (the couples thus trace out a figure '8', as shown in Diagram 7.14; the tail of the procession on the way down crosses over in the centre just in time to allow the top couple to pass by on their way up). On regaining places, all turn partners and set as in Figure I.

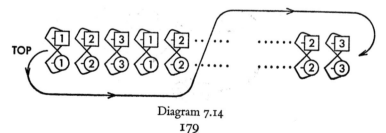

Diagram 7.14

Figure III

The couples repeat Figure II, except that partners now join crossed hands
behind their backs.

From this point onwards the dancers keep to their original sets of
three couples, and we therefore give the instructions now for only one
three-couple set. The remaining figures, IV–VI, are phrased strictly to
the music, and each is performed twice in succession.

Music Bars	Figure IV
1–12	The 1st couple face each other, the 2nd couple face down, and the 3rd couple face up, and all dance a 'grand chain', beginning by giving right hands to the person facing them, as shown in Diagram 7.15. All finish in original places.
13–16	All turn partners once round with right hands.
17–24	All set to partners with a Strathspey setting step.

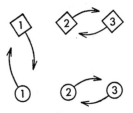

Diagram 7.15

Music Bars	Figure V
1–12	The top lady faces down and her partner crosses over to come behind her, placing his hands on her waist. At the same time the 3rd man crosses over to come behind his partner, and the 2nd lady crosses over to come in front of hers, both couples facing up, and both men placing their hands on their partners' waists (Diagram 7.16). From

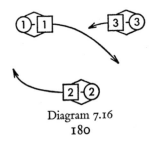

Diagram 7.16

these positions the three couples now dance a reel of three, each couple moving as a single unit, with the man guiding his partner by means of the hold on her waist. The 1st and 2nd couples begin the reel by passing each other with right shoulders, and all return to their own places at the end.

13–24   All turn partners once round with right hands, and set to partners with a Strathspey setting step.

Music Bars   *Figure VI*

1–12   All join hands in a ring, facing inwards, and dance round to the left for 6 bars, then return to the right to places.

13–24   All turn partners once round with right hands, and set to partners with a Strathspey setting step.

This version of the Reel of Six was described to us by Mrs Helen Sutherland (18) and Mr Alexander Scott (26), both of whom performed the dance regularly in their younger days in Oxton, about 1895–1905. Mrs Sutherland did not remember the repetition of the last three figures, but in all other respects her description and Mr Scott's were identical. We also obtained confirmation of the first three figures from Mr Scott's sister (19).

An arrangement of this version for six couples has been published in the R.S.C.D.S. *Country Dance Books*. This arrangement was based on information collected from Mrs Sutherland about 1925–6 by the late I. C. B. Jamieson, who at that time was the factor on an estate at Langshaw, between Lauderdale and Gala Water. Jamieson had either heard of or seen a performance of the dance at one of the Volunteers' Balls in Lauder in the early years of this century, and was anxious to recover it. On one occasion he was present at a meeting of the Langshaw Women's Rural Institute when the members of the Oxton Institute were there on a visit, and he asked if anyone could remember the dance. He was immediately directed to Mrs Sutherland, and at his request she taught the dance to a group of twelve people from Oxton, from whose performance he noted it. Subsequently Mrs Sutherland's group performed the dance at one or two concerts in Oxton, and also at the Border Musical Festival at Galasheils. To mark the fact that the dance had been recovered in Oxton, Jamieson renamed it 'The Oxton Reel', and it is published under this title (18).

It should be noted that neither Mr Scott nor his sister took any part in the revival of the dance organized by Jamieson and Mrs Sutherland.

Mr Scott himself has seen the revived version only once, at a concert in Oxton, while his sister has not seen the dance since about 1910. Their information is therefore completely independent of that of Mrs Sutherland.

The Reel of Six, Lauder version

This version differs from the Oxton version in that the dancers keep to their own three-couple sets throughout the dance (so that the name 'Reel of Six' is here much more appropriate); there are also considerable differences in the individual figures of the two versions.

There are again six figures in the dance, and the appropriate tune is 'Cameron's got his wife again', played at the same tempo as before. The steps and style of performance are as in the Oxton version.

To begin, the dancers stand in an oval formation, facing partners, as shown in Diagram 7.17, with 1st and 3rd men about 6 ft from their partners, and with 2nd man and 2nd lady about 8 ft apart.

TOP

Diagram 7.17

Music Bars	Figure I
1–8	All set to partners with a Strathspey setting step.
9–12	All turn partners once round with right hands.
13–16	1st couple, with right hands joined, lead down the centre into bottom place, while the other couples move up one place.
17–48	Repeat the sequence of bars 1–16 twice, first with 2nd couple leading down the centre, then with 3rd couple leading down, so that all finish in original places.

Music Bars	Figure II
1–8	All set to partners with a Strathspey setting step.
9–12	All turn partners once round with right hands.

13–16   The three ladies stand still, while the three men change places, 1st and 2nd men moving down one place, and the 3rd man coming up to top place (the 3rd man passes in front of 2nd man and behind 1st man, as shown in Diagram 7.18 (a)).

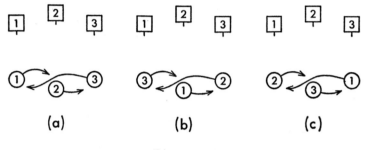

(a)   (b)   (c)

Diagram 7.18

17–24   All set with a Strathspey setting step, 1st man to 2nd lady, 2nd man to 3rd lady, and 3rd man to 1st lady.

25–28   These same three pairs turn once round with right hands.

29–32   The three ladies stand still, while the three men again change places, the 1st man now going to 3rd place, the 2nd man to 1st place, and the 3rd man to 2nd place, the 2nd man passing in front of 1st man and behind 3rd man (Diagram 7.18 (b)).

33–40   All set with a Strathspey setting step, 1st man to 3rd lady, 2nd man to 1st lady, and 3rd man to 2nd lady.

41–44   These same three pairs turn once round with right hands.

45–48   The three ladies stand still, while the three men return to their original places, the 1st man passing in front of 3rd man and behind 2nd man (Diagram 7.18 (c)).

Music Bars   *Figure III*

1–8   All set to partners with a Strathspey setting step.

9–12   All turn partners once round with right hands, finishing in a line up the centre of the set, all facing the top, the men being behind their partners with their hands on partners' shoulders.

13–24   (The chase.) The top lady, followed by the others, turns off to her left and dances down outside the men's side of the set, turning at the bottom to lead up the centre (Diagram 7.19). All finish in original places.

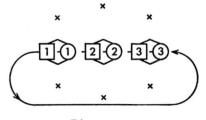

Diagram 7.19

Music Bars	Figure IV

1–8   All set to partners with a Strathspey setting step.

9–12 All turn partners once round with right hands, finishing in the centre of the set, the 1st couple facing down, the 2nd and 3rd couples facing up, the men being behind their partners, with their hands on partners' waists.

13–24 From these positions the three couples now dance a reel of three, each couple moving as a single unit, with the man guiding his partner by means of the hold on her waist. The 1st and 2nd couples begin the reel by passing each other with right shoulders (Diagram 7.20), and all finish in two parallel lines, about 6 ft apart.

Diagram 7.20

Music Bars	Figure V

1–8   All set to partners with a Strathspey setting step.

9–12 All turn partners once round with right hands.

13–16 The 1st couple, with right hands joined, dance down the centre for two steps (bars 13, 14), then dance back up to places, again with two steps (bars 15, 16).

17–24 All set to partners with a Strathspey setting step.

25–28 All turn partners once round with right hands.

29–32   The 3rd couple, with right hands joined, dance up the centre for two steps, then return down the centre to places in the same way.

33–40   All set to partners with a Strathspey setting step.

41–44   All turn partners once round with right hands.

45–48   The 2nd man dances down the centre for two steps, then returns to his place up the centre in the same way, while 2nd lady dances up the centre for two steps and back down again.

Music Bars	Figure VI

1–8   All set to partners with a Strathspey setting step.

9–12   All turn partners with right hands. The 1st and 3rd couples turn once round and finish on their own sides, the 1st couple facing each other, and the 3rd couple facing up. The 2nd couple turn one and a half times to finish on the opposite sides, facing down.

13–24   All dance a 'grand chain', beginning by giving right hands to the person facing them. Finish with 1st and 3rd couples in their own places, and with 2nd man and 2nd lady in each other's places.

We first heard of this version of the Reel of Six in 1954 from Mr James Inglis of Denholm (16), who saw it at a Volunteers' Ball in Lauder about 1906. The description above was given to us by Mr David Watson (71), who performed the dance frequently in his youth. We had some difficulty in disentangling the Lauder version from the Oxton version, for Mr Watson has done both, but the only real uncertainty in our description lies in the exact sequence of changes in Figure II. Mr Watson was certain that in this figure each man danced with all the ladies, and he was also sure of the first change of position in bars 1–16, but he was uncertain of the exact nature of the succeeding changes. Mr Watson also thought that what we have described here as Figure III was not really a figure on its own, but formed the conclusion of Figure II; if this is so, then there is a figure missing from the dance.

The only other person we could find in Lauder who had any recollections of the figures of the dance was Mr John Wilkinson (73), who learnt the dance from his mother when he was a child—he and his brothers and sisters often danced it in their own home in the winter evenings. Of the complete dance, Mr Wilkinson could remember only what we have described here as Figures II and III; his memory of the first change of position (Figure II, bars 1–16) was quite definite, but unfortunately he too was uncertain of the exact nature of the succeeding changes; his description of the 'chase' (the term was his mother's) was similar to that of Mr Watson, except that the 1st lady led round to the right instead of to the left.

The 'oval' formation at the beginning of the dance was given to us by both Mr Watson and Mr Wilkinson, but we are not certain for how much of the dance this formation is retained. Mr Wilkinson was certain that the dancers were still in the oval formation in the figure containing the changes of position, but Mr Watson thought that the dancers went into two parallel lines at the end of Figure I. This oval formation is somewhat mysterious, for it does not seem to serve any useful purpose, and it is possible that a figure has at some time been lost from the beginning of the dance.

We should add here that one other person in Lauder, Mr Will Shaw (70), confirmed that in the Lauder version the dancers kept to their own three-couple sets throughout the dance, but was unable to remember any of the figures.

We have little doubt that the Lauder version is closer to the original form of this dance than is the Oxton version. The joining of the three-couple sets into one long set in the first three figures of the Oxton version is almost certainly an addition to the dance, for it is quite inappropriate to the name 'Reel of Six'. There is some similarity between these first three figures of the Oxton version and two dances known in the North of England, the Durham Reel, from the town of Durham, and Turn off Six, from upper Wharfedale, and it is possible that there has been some intermixing here of two different dance-forms.

CHAPTER VIII

Some Orkney Reels

OF the various dances which were performed in Orkney within living memory there were four Reels which were peculiar to that region, namely the Sixsome Reel, the Eightsome Reel from the Mainland and Rousay, the Eightsome or 'Axum' Reel from North Ronaldshay, and a Reel for six called Hands Across from the Mainland district of Dounby.[1]

The Sixsome Reels and the two Eightsome Reels are all true Reels, consisting of setting steps danced on the spot, alternated with a travelling figure (which depends on the particular Reel in question). Orkney has a terminology for the two basic parts of a Reel which is shared only by Shetland, the dancers being said to be 'dancing' when they set to each other, and to be 'running the reel', or, more simply, 'reeling', when they perform the travelling figure. Thus in the Orkney terminology all three of these Reels consist of alternate 'dancing' and 'reeling', beginning either with 'dancing' or with 'reeling' according to the particular Reel concerned.

The fourth dance, Hands Across, is of an unusual form; it consists of the repetition of a 32-bar sequence comprising three 8-bar travelling figures and an 8-bar period of setting.

THE SIXSOME REEL

This dance was probably once known throughout Orkney, for we have noted its occurrence in all the districts of Orkney of which we have records, that is to say the Mainland districts of Birsay, Dounby, Harray, and Stenness, and the islands of Rousay, Burray, Flotta, South Ronaldshay, and North Ronaldshay. On South Ronaldshay the dance has been occasionally performed at weddings in comparatively recent years. On Flotta it fell out of use about 1912, but was revived for a short period

---

[1] Descriptions of these dances were first published by one of the authors in a series of articles in the *Orkney Herald* (298).

about 1920 before it finally disappeared, and on North Ronaldshay it was similarly revived about 1925. In the other places named it was last performed about 1905.

The dance is performed by three couples who stand initially in two lines, with the men in one line and their partners opposite to them in the other. Partners should be about 4 ft 6 in. apart, and the distance between adjacent couples should be about 3 ft.

The dance consists of the repetition of a 16-bar sequence comprising a reel of three performed by the three couples acting as single units, followed by setting on the spot. There were slight variations from one district to another in the manner in which the reel of three was performed, and we describe first a version of the dance which we obtained from Flotta (143, 145). Here the numbering of the couples is as shown in Diagram 8.1, and the basic 16-bar sequence is as follows.

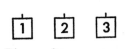

TOP

Diagram 8.1

Music Bars	Description of the Figures
1–8	The three couples dance a reel of three, each couple moving as a single unit, with the lady leading and the man following immediately behind her. To begin the reel of three, the 2nd lady turns her back on her partner and dances up round behind the 1st lady, her partner following her (Diagram 8.2). At the same time the 1st and 3rd ladies

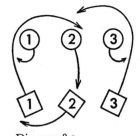

TOP

Diagram 8.2

dance across and round behind their partners as shown in Diagram 8.2, their partners meanwhile taking a step forward and turning to enter the reel of three behind them.

188

The couples complete the reel of three and return to the positions shown in Diagram 8.1, the 1st and 3rd men passing their partners by the left and right shoulders respectively to regain their places at the end of the reel.

9–16   All set to partners with suitable Reel setting steps.

On Flotta the reel of three in bars 1–8 of the basic sequence was also sometimes begun by the 1st and 3rd ladies passing inside their partners, as shown in Diagram 8.3 (141). On South Ronaldshay and North

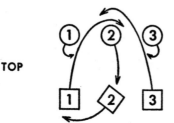

Diagram 8.3

Ronaldshay this latter method of starting the reel of three was the normal one, but in these places the position of the top of the set was the reverse of that in Flotta, and the directions in which the dancers moved initially were as shown in Diagram 8.4. On South Ronaldshay the dancers returned to their own positions at the end of each reel of three (140), but on North Ronaldshay there was some sort of progression (149).

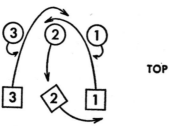

Diagram 8.4

In all districts the basic sequence was first performed several times to one or more strathspey tunes and then several times to one or more reel tunes. The number of repetitions of the basic sequence was arbitrary except on Flotta, where the basic sequence was always performed three times to strathspeys and three times to reels (this fixed number of repetitions of the basic sequence is unusual in a Reel, but most of the older people on Flotta confirmed it).

189

In all the districts where we know the dance to have been performed, the travelling step in strathspey tempo was Strathspey travelling step A, and in reel tempo it was either the travelling pas de Basque or (less commonly) the hop-one-and-two. The commonest setting step in strathspey tempo was the Highland Schottische step, but Highland Fling steps were also used fairly frequently; in reel tempo the commonest setting step was the pas de Basque (Version I). Ladies normally held their skirts out to the side when setting, but could also raise their arms if they wished; men normally had their arms raised or akimbo. In most districts both men and ladies 'heuched' and cracked finger and thumb, but on Flotta neither of these was common.

On Flotta and South Ronaldshay the Sixsome Reel was used at weddings as the 'Bride's Reel'. This was the first dance at a wedding, and the three couples who took part, in order from top to bottom of the set, were the bridegroom and bride, the best man and best maid, and the 'honest folk'. The dance was performed once through with the dancers in these positions and the fiddler then paused for a few seconds. During this pause the top man (the bridegroom) moved round the back of the other two men to the bottom of the set, and the other two men moved up, and the dance was then repeated with the men in these new positions. A further pause, and a further change in the same manner, brought the honest man up to the top place to face the bride, and the dance was then repeated once more (21, 140–4).[1]

It is interesting to note that a very similar form of 'Bride's Reel' was danced in parts of Shetland (287; 1932; probably from Unst). The dance was a three-couple Shetland Reel with a progression in the travelling figure: 'The bride dances the first "turn"[2] with the bridegroom. Then they "run" through the figure 8 and she "sets" to the married man. After dancing with him and a "run" thereafter, she sets to the best man. Finally, she returns to her own man. Meanwhile he has been dancing with the "mairéd womman" and the best maid. That is called the Bride's Reel.'

THE EIGHTSOME REEL FROM THE MAINLAND AND ROUSAY

In this Reel, as in the Sixsome Reel, the dancers form two parallel lines, with the men in one line and their partners opposite to them in the other.

[1] On Flotta the ladies sometimes changed places instead of the men.
[2] A 'turn' is a part of the tune (see p. 200).

The dance consists of the repetition of a 16-bar sequence comprising a reel of four performed by the four couples acting as single units, followed by setting on the spot; this sequence is first performed several times to one or more strathspey tunes, and then several times to one or more reel tunes. Here, however, we have been unable to obtain precise information on the manner in which the reel of four is performed.

We met this Reel only in Birsay and Stenness on the Mainland of Orkney and on the island of Rousay. On Rousay it was last performed about 1910, having been used very infrequently for some years previously (147–8), while in Birsay and Stenness it fell out of use about 1885–90 (135–6). On Rousay it was known as either the 'Eightsome Reel' or the 'Eight-couple-Reel', the term 'couple' here presumably referring to the fact that the dancers 'run the reel' in couples.

THE 'AXUM' REEL FROM NORTH RONALDSHAY

We learnt this dance from Mr and Mrs Roy Scott of North Ronaldshay, now living on the Mainland of Orkney (149).[1] Mr Scott learnt the dance from his father, and he and his wife have helped greatly in keeping it alive in North Ronaldshay, where it is still performed at weddings.

Four couples take part in the dance. They stand initially as shown in Diagram 8.5, with the four ladies at the corners of a rectangle about 8 ft by 6 ft.

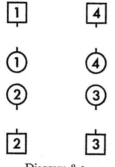

Diagram 8.5

The first part of the dance is performed to any strathspey tune, played at the usual tempo of 40–42 bars per minute.

Music Bars	Description of the Figures
1–8	All 'dance', i.e. set to partners with suitable setting steps.

[1] There is an inaccurate description of this dance in one of the R.S.C.D.S. *Country Dance Books*.

9–16   All 'run the reel'. In this reel, the pattern of which is shown
in the accompanying diagrams, all the dancers follow the
same track, all moving in the same direction. The 1st
couple finishes in the 3rd couple's place, the 2nd couple
in the 4th couple's place, and vice versa.

The dancers begin the reel by passing partners with left
shoulders, the direction in which each begins to move
being shown in Diagram 8.6 (the 2nd and 4th men diverge
slightly from the standard track at the beginning of the
reel, regaining it behind their partners).

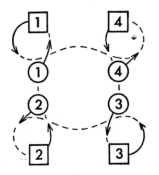

Diagram 8.6

At the end of the second bar of the reel, the ladies are
halfway along the sides, and the men halfway round the
loops (Diagram 8.7).

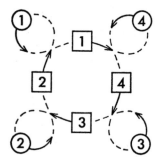

Diagram 8.7

During the third bar of the reel each lady moves on to a
loop. The man who is already on that loop takes small
steps so that he stays on the loop, passing round the lady

192

left shoulder to left shoulder. The positions of the dancers at the end of this third bar are shown in Diagram 8.8.

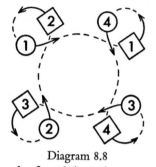

Diagram 8.8

During the fourth bar, the men leave the loops, passing behind the ladies, and at the end of the bar the men are halfway along the sides, and the ladies halfway round the loops (Diagram 8.9).

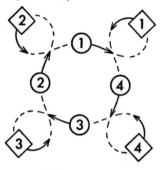

Diagram 8.9

In the fifth bar, each man moves on to a loop. His part-ner is already on that loop, and she takes small steps so that she stays on the loop, passing round her partner left shoulder to left shoulder.

In the sixth bar, the ladies leave the loops, passing behind

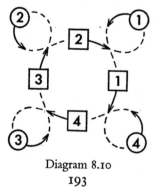

Diagram 8.10

their partners, and at the end of the bar the ladies are half-way along the sides, and the men halfway round the loops (Diagram 8.10).

During the seventh bar of the reel, the ladies move on to the next loop, the positions at the end of this bar being as shown in Diagram 8.11.

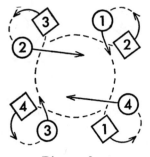

Diagram 8.11

During the eighth bar, the dancers move in the directions of the arrows shown in Diagram 8.11, to finish facing partners as shown in Diagram 8.12 (the 2nd and 4th men have to diverge slightly from the standard track, but the other dancers remain on it. The 1st man passes to his place in front of 2nd man, and the 3rd man in front of 4th man).

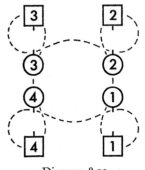

Diagram 8.12

17–24   All 'dance', i.e. set to partners with suitable setting steps.
25–32   All repeat the reel figure of bars 9–16, finishing in original places as in Diagram 8.5.

This sequence of 32 bars is repeated—still to a strathspey tune—as often as desired. Then in the course of one of the reel figures one of the dancers or one of the onlookers calls 'run it oot'. The fiddler thereupon gradually speeds up the music until it is approximately at reel tempo (60–64 bars per minute), still keeping to the same strathspey tune as in the last reel figure prior to the call of 'run it oot'. During this part of the dance, the dancers keep moving continuously round the figure of the reel, making about four complete circuits, and taking 16 bars of music to a circuit. The phrasing in this second part is similar to that in the reel figures in the first part, except that the dancers keep the figure flowing evenly throughout, and do not attempt to form into two lines at the end of each 8-bar phrase (bars 11–14 of the first part are typical of the movements in the second part; bars 9–10 and 15–16 are not). There is no setting in this second part of the dance.

In Mr Scott's father's earliest days, the principal setting step used in the first part of the dance was the Highland Schottische step, and this remains the most popular setting step for the dance at weddings on North Ronaldshay today. However, after Mr Mackenzie taught dancing on the island about 1882 (see p. 56), Highland Fling steps have also been used. The travelling step for the first part of the dance is Strathspey travelling step A (p. 93); in the second part this step changes imperceptibly into the hop-one-and-two as the music quickens.

Mr Scott told us that in his younger days ladies usually held their skirts out to the sides when setting, and men normally had their hands either by their sides or on their waists; it was rather rare to see men raise their arms. In the reel figures, both men and ladies normally had their hands by their sides.

The following remarks concerning the reel figure may be helpful. It will be noticed that each dancer, when going round a loop, passes by the left two people of the opposite sex. The dominant impression of the reel obtained by an onlooker should be the periodic grouping of the dancers at the corners, and the dancers should therefore keep as close as possible to each other when describing the same loop. It is also necessary to use shorter steps on the loops than on the intervening portions of the path.

To learn the reel in the first instance, we suggest that the track be drawn in chalk on the floor, the portions between the loops being drawn as straight lines. The emphasis should be put on the fact that each dancer passes two others by the left at each corner. The exact phrasing is largely governed by this, and should not be unduly stressed. The actual dance should flow evenly, and the positions shown in the diagrams should be taken as a guide, but not as a rule.

It is perhaps not obvious that the 'Axum' Reel is essentially a combination of two Foursome Reels arranged at right angles to each other. This is made clearer if we deform the starting positions of the four couples in the 'Axum' Reel into the form of a cross, as shown in Diagram 8.13 (a). If the eight dancers now start to perform on their own

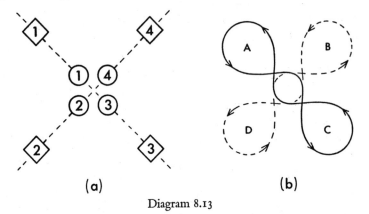

(a)   (b)

Diagram 8.13

line of the cross the standard 'figure 8' of the Foursome Reel, in the reverse of the usual direction (i.e. they give *left* shoulders to partners to begin), and if as soon as they come on to the central loop of their own reel they pass directly to the left-hand outer loop of the other reel (i.e. a dancer leaving the outer loop A in Diagram 8.13 (b) passes directly to the loop B, one leaving loop B passes directly to loop C, and so on), and if they proceed from reel to reel in this manner, then the figure which they describe is that of the 'Axum' Reel, with the corner loops somewhat enlarged (Diagram 8.14). Moreover, if in describing the loops the

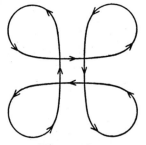

Diagram 8.14

dancers preserve as far as possible the normal phrasing of the Foursome Reel, then we obtain precisely the correct phrasing of the figure of the 'Axum' Reel, with the ladies being halfway round the loops at the end of the fourth bar of the figure (cf. Diagram 8.9).

The 'Axum' Reel played a particular role in weddings in North Ronaldshay. It was performed as the last dance of the evening, just before the newly married couple retired. The newly married couple stood in the centre of the room, back to back, with their arms linked, and the 'Axum' Reel was performed round them. Then at some point while the dancers were 'running it oot', the fiddler suddenly stopped playing, and the bride and bridegroom had to attempt to unlink their arms and turn and kiss each other before any of the four girls in the dance could kiss the bridegroom, or any of the four men could kiss the bride.

The dance was also sometimes performed twice in succession in this manner, the first time being performed by eight girls who had to try to kiss the bridegroom before his bride could do so, and the second time by eight men who had to try to kiss the bride before the bridegroom could do so.

This use of the 'Axum' Reel may be a relic of a ceremonial similar to that of the Bride's and Bridegroom's Reels in Shetland (see p. 71), and it is possible that the continuous reeling in the second part of the 'Axum' Reel is derived from a dance of the same type as the Shetland Auld Reel, rather than from the normal 'quick-time' of a Scottish Reel.

HANDS ACROSS

We have met this dance only in the Dounby district of the Mainland of Orkney, where it was popular about 1895. For a number of years it fell into disuse, but after the 1914–18 War it was revived again, and was danced quite frequently at Dounby until about 1923. One of our informants had danced it about 1895, the others knew it only from the revival (137–8).

TOP

Diagram 8.15

Three couples take part in the dance, and initially they stand facing partners as shown in Diagram 8.15. Partners should be about 4 ft 6 in. apart, and the distance between adjacent couples should be about 3 ft.

The dance is performed to any reel tune.

Music Bars	*Description of the Figures*
1–8	All give right hands across to the diagonally opposite person ('shaking hands' grasp) and dance round clockwise (bars 1–4), then turn about (turning to the right), give left hands across, and return to places (bars 5–8).
9–16	All join hands in a ring and dance round clockwise for four bars, and then back in the opposite direction to places. (The dancers turn round at the beginning of the fourth bar, and for the rest of this bar dance backwards, ready to return at the beginning of the fifth bar. In this figure the arms should be bent to keep the ring small and compact.)
17–24	1st man and 2nd lady, 2nd man and 1st lady, and 3rd man and 3rd lady now face each other, link right arms, and pass each other as shown in Diagram 8.16 (they do not turn), and then proceed round the set in that direction, linking left and right arms alternately, until all are back in original places. (The set should be kept very compact here, and the dancers should swing straight from one arm to the next.)

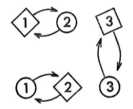

Diagram 8.16

| 25–32 | All set to partners with quick Reel setting steps. |
| 33– | Repeat this 32-bar sequence as often as desired. |

The travelling step used in bars 1–24 was the travelling pas de Basque. The most common setting step was the pas de Basque (Version I).

CHAPTER IX

Some Reels from Shetland

I T is difficult to convey in a written description of a dance the degree of enjoyment which can be obtained from the actual performance of the figures, and this is particularly so in the case of the Shetland Reels. At first glance these Reels appear to be a succession of relatively simple figures performed with equally simple steps, but in fact the fitting of the figures to the music can require considerable skill, while the steps used give a vigour and a drive to the dances which is seldom found elsewhere.

SHETLAND REELS

'Shetland Reels' exist in a variety of forms—we have met one for two couples, three for three couples, and two for four couples. All these Reels consist of setting steps danced on the spot, alternated with a travelling figure, the latter depending on the particular Reel in question; in the two-couple Reel the travelling figure is a simple 'four-hands across', in the three-couple Reels it is a 'reel of three', danced with each couple acting as a single unit, and in the four-couple Reels it is a 'reel of four', again danced with each couple acting as a single unit.

Shetland has the same terminology as Orkney for the different parts of a Reel, i.e. the dancers are said to be 'dancing' when they set to each other, and to be 'running the reel', or, more simply, to be 'reeling', when they perform the travelling figure. Thus a Shetland Reel consists of alternate 'dancing' and 'reeling', beginning either with 'dancing' or with 'reeling' according to the particular Reel in question.

The two-couple Reel seems to belong only to the West Side of the Mainland of Shetland. In Walls it had no special name—it was simply one of the two local forms of 'the Shetland Reel', the other form being for three couples. The particular one of these two forms which was danced in Walls on any given occasion depended mainly on the number of people who wished to take part. If only two couples wished to dance, then the two-couple form was used, and similarly with three couples;

four couples would form two two-couple sets; and five couples would split into a two-couple set and a three-couple set.

In the districts of Easter and Wester Skeld the two-couple Reel was known as the 'Four-man's Reel' or 'Fourpenny Reel'. In these districts two other Shetland Reels were also known, one for three couples, known as the 'Six-man's Reel' or 'Sixpenny Reel', and the other for four couples, known as the 'Eight-man's Reel' or 'Eightpenny Reel'. Here the term 'Shetland Reel' seems usually to have meant the three-couple form.

The four-couple Reels were rather uncommon, and outside the Skeld district we have noted them only from Sandwick, Cunningsburgh, and Burra Isle. On the other hand, a three-couple Reel of one form or another seems to have been known in every district in Shetland.

In the two-couple Reel, the dancers stand initially at the corners of a square, with the two men side by side, facing their partners, and about 4 ft from them. In the three-couple and four-couple Reels the dancers form two lines, about 4 ft apart; partners are directly opposite each other, one in each line, and the distance between adjacent couples is about 2 ft 6 in.

When these Reels were performed in a croft, the end of the room where the hearth was situated was normally regarded as the 'top', and the dancers had their backs to the 'sides' of the room. The fiddler usually sat beside the fire—on whichever side he pleased—and on Whalsay (192) and in certain parts of the Mainland (150) there was a convention among older people (that is, people born about 1860) that the top man in each set had his back to the fiddler. However, since about 1900 there does not seem to have been any particular rule to determine whether the top man should be on the right or left when the set is viewed from the top of the room, and either alternative seems to have been permissible. The couple marked No. 1 in the various diagrams which follow may therefore, unless otherwise stated, be at either the top or the bottom of the room.

All the Shetland Reels given here are performed to any reel or Scotch measure. The different parts of a tune are known in Shetland as the 'turns' or 'turnings' of the tune, and most of the tunes which were used for Shetland Reels within living memory have two 'turns'. These two 'turns' were usually labelled as the 'dancing turn' and the 'reeling turn', or vice versa, according to whether the local versions of the dances began with 'dancing' or 'reeling'.

On the Mainland, all the various Shetland Reels began with 'dancing', and there the fiddler normally passed from one tune to another at the end of some repetition of the 'reeling turn' of the first tune. In some districts it was usual for the fiddler to insert a second repeat of the final 'reeling turn' of the first tune before breaking into the next tune, and the dancers thereupon repeated the reel. In Esha Ness, some of the older people greeted the change of tune with a shout of 'dar she wasters'[1] (150). Such a 'double reel' needed no explicit warning from the fiddler or the master of ceremonies, for the Shetlanders' awareness of the music was (and still is) of an unusually high order.

'Double reels' sometimes also occurred at other points in the dance, for in the course of the reel one of the dancers might call for a 'double reel', and then the fiddler would simply repeat the 'reeling turn' while the dancers 'ran the reel' twice over (168).

The tempo of the music for a Shetland Reel varied considerably from one fiddler to another. Among the many fiddlers whom we met, it will suffice to give four examples, namely John Irvine of Whalsay, aged 76, who played at a tempo of 62 bars per minute, Fraser Hughson of Aith, aged 77,[2] who played at a tempo of 51 bars per minute, Peter Fraser of Finnigarth (West Walls), aged 75, who played at a tempo of 53 bars per minute, and Thomas Moar of Wester Skeld, aged 76, who played at about 40 bars per minute.

We pass now to the detailed descriptions of these various Shetland Reels, postponing until later the discussion of style of performance and steps.

The two-couple Shetland Reel

We collected this Reel in Walls, West Walls, Easter Skeld, and Wester Skeld (199). It is still danced occasionally in the Walls and West Walls districts, but has not been performed for many years in Easter and Wester Skeld.

The four dancers stand as shown in Diagram 9.1.

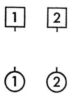

Diagram 9.1

[1] 'There she westers.'
[2] Mr Hughson was actually brought up on Papa Stour, and learnt to play the fiddle there.

Music Bars	*Description of the Figures*
1–8	All 'dance', i.e. set to partners.
9–16	All give right hands across to the diagonally opposite person ('shaking hands' grasp) and dance round clockwise (bars 9–12), then turn about (turning to the right), give left hands across, and return to places (bars 13–16).
17–	Repeat this 16-bar sequence as often as desired.

We are not certain how far round the dancers should go in the 'four hands across' figure. One lady in Wester Skeld (165) was adamant that they should go twice round in one direction and twice round in the other, but it is probable that in general this was a matter of the dancers' ages and inclination.

Two three-couple Shetland Reels

Two very similar three-couple Reels were danced within living memory on the Mainland of Shetland and on most of the other islands. These two Reels differ principally in the positions in which the dancers begin and subsequently 'dance'; in one Reel the dancers stand in two parallel lines, with all the men in one line and their partners opposite to them in the other (Diagram 9.2 (a)); in the second Reel the dancers again stand in two parallel lines, but here the men and ladies are placed alternately in each line (Diagram 9.2 (b)).

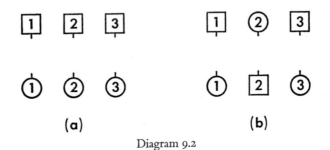

(a)   (b)

Diagram 9.2

The older of these two three-couple Reels is probably that in which the men are in one line and the ladies in the other (Diagram 9.2 (a)), and we begin with the description of this.

Music Bars	*Description of the Figures*
1–8	All 'dance' (i.e. set to partners) in the positions shown in Diagram 9.2 (a).

9–16　The three couples dance a reel of three, each couple moving as a single unit, with the lady leading and the man following immediately behind her. To begin the reel of three the 2nd lady crosses over and passes her partner by the left shoulder, turning ('sunwise') to her right round the 1st man, and, as she does so, her partner takes a step forward and turns to close in behind her (Diagram 9.3). At the same time the 1st and 3rd ladies turn their backs on their partners and move as shown in Diagram 9.3, their partners following behind them. The couples complete the reel of three and return to the places shown in Diagram 9.2 (a), the 2nd man passing his own partner by the right shoulder at the end of the reel to regain his own place.

17–　Repeat this 16-bar sequence as often as desired.

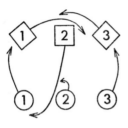

Diagram 9.3

It is also permissible for the 2nd lady to begin the reel by passing her partner with the right shoulder and turning round the 3rd man. The initial movements of the six dancers are then as shown in Diagram 9.4.

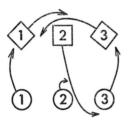

Diagram 9.4

The second of these two Reels, where the dancers start as shown in Diagram 9.2 (b), differs from this first Reel only in the manner in which the dancers run the reel. Here the three ladies turn their backs on their partners and move either as in Diagram 9.5 (a) or as in Diagram 9.5 (b). The men follow their partners through the reel, and all return to the positions in Diagram 9.2 (b).

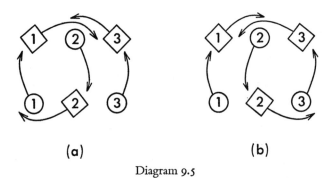

(a)   (b)

Diagram 9.5

Just before the end of the reel in this second Reel, each lady passes through her partner's place, and in some districts it was customary for the ladies to turn at this point to face their partners (turning the shorter way about) and dance backward across the set into their own places.

The first of these two three-couple Reels was, up to about 1910, the only three-couple Reel danced in Walls, West Walls, Wester Skeld, Burra Isle, and Papa Stour (200), and we also know it to have been danced at some time in Aith, Hillswick, North Roe, Bressay, and Yell. In Walls, West Walls, and Burra Isle, and possibly elsewhere, it has been superseded by the second Reel, but it is still danced on Papa Stour. The second Reel seems to have been current for as far back as living memory extends in the Sandwick and Cunningsburgh districts of the Mainland (155, 161), but in some of the other parts of Shetland it is of relatively recent introduction.[1]

The three-couple Shetland Reel from Whalsay

This Reel has been danced on Whalsay for as far back as living memory extends, and is still performed there at weddings. The description given below was noted from an actual performance of the dance in the house of Mr John Irvine, a noted Whalsay fiddler (192), and was confirmed by most of the older people on the island.

The dancers stand initially in two lines, with the men and ladies placed alternately in each line. When the dance was performed in the

[1] We were first shown the second Reel above by Mr Pat Shuldham-Shaw of London, who has published a description of it in the *Journal of the English Folk Dance and Song Society* (292). A description of this same form is also given by Mr D. G. MacLennan in his book (239).

croft houses in the old days, the top of the set was next to the fire, the fiddler sat on one side of the room near the fire, and the top man had his back to the fiddler (192). A typical arrangement is shown in Diagram 9.6.

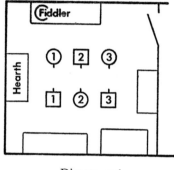

Diagram 9.6

Music Bars	*Description of the Figures*
1–8	All 'run the reel', i.e. the three couples dance a reel of three, each couple moving as a single unit, with the lady leading and the man following immediately behind her. To begin the reel of three, the ladies turn their backs on their partners, the 2nd lady moves up towards the top of the room round the back of the 1st man (i.e. towards the fiddler), and the other two ladies move accordingly, the men simply following behind their partners (Diagram 9.7).

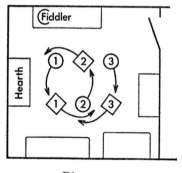

Diagram 9.7

After a complete reel of three (figure 8) the 3rd couple returns to the bottom place, while the 1st and 2nd couples dance a further half loop to interchange places (i.e. the top couple comes into the centre place and the

205

centre couple into the top place). Just before the end of the reel, each lady passes through the position where her partner finishes the reel, and, as she does so, she turns to face him (turning the shorter way about) and dances backward across the set into her own place.

9–16   All 'dance', i.e. set to partners.

17–   Repeat this 16-bar sequence as often as desired. With each repetition of the sequence the 1st and 2nd couples interchange places, while the 3rd couple returns to the bottom place each time.

In Whalsay certain tunes for the Reel (for instance, 'Soldier's Joy' and 'The De'il among the Tailors') had 'double dancing time'—these were tunes which consisted of three parts (or 'turnings') so that they were 24 bars in length. When one of these tunes was played, the dancers simply set to partners, i.e. 'danced', for double the normal length of music; no explicit warning was necessary, for in the old days the islanders were thoroughly familiar with the tunes in use, and danced appropriately.

The two top couples in this Whalsay Reel were always known on the island as 'the fore-oars', while the bottom couple were said to be 'in the hole'. In general the more expert dancers tended to dance as 'the fore-oars' (they then had to change places every time they ran the reel), while the less able dancers took the easier bottom positions 'in the hole'.

The terms 'fore-oars' and 'hole' are derived from the old Shetland six-oared fishing boats, the sixearns, which fell into disuse during the period from about 1880 to 1920. A typical boat of this type was divided into seven compartments by the thwartship benches, and the 'hole', or 'shott-hole', was the compartment furthest aft. The hole was occupied by the helmsman when the boat was under sail, but was empty when the boat was proceeding under oars, for a sixearn carried only a crew of six, and all six rowed (293).

The crew of a sixearn usually consisted of four men and two 'fee'd boys'. The four men owned the boat between them, and shared the proceeds from the fish caught on all but one of the thirty-three strings of lines which the boat carried. The fee'd boys were essentially apprentices; they were paid a fee for the summer's work, and in addition received the proceeds from the fish caught on the one remaining string of lines. When the crew had to row, the four experienced men took the forward oars, the 'fore-oars', and the apprentices took the two oars nearest the 'hole'—precisely the same distribution of ability as was usual in the Whalsay Reel (192).

Another Whalsay dance which bears traces of the days of the old sixearns is The Drunken Skipper. This is a variant of the Whalsay three-couple Reel which was performed by men only. Usually someone called for it towards the end of an evening's dancing, and at a wedding it was sometimes incorporated in the Bridegroom's Reels.

The tune for the dance is 'The Drunken Skipper', a reel tune with a 'dancing turn' of unusual form. The dance is performed by six men, who probably represent the crew of a sixearn. They form up as for the Whalsay three-couple Reel, three of the men taking the ladies' places, and 'run the reel', exactly as described above, to the 'reeling turn' of the tune. When the music changes to the 'dancing turn', the men commence to 'dance' as usual, but as the 'dancing turn' progresses they all begin to stagger about as if drunk. After about the sixth bar of the 'dancing turn' the tune slows down very considerably, and the men's apparent drunkenness increases until they all collapse on the floor. The fiddler then strikes the strings of his fiddle two or three times with the bow as a signal for the men to rise, and as they come to their feet he breaks into the 'reeling turn'. The dancers then repeat the whole procedure as often as they please.

The dance was probably somewhat rough, for the dancers tried to fall on top of each other as they collapsed on the floor, and everyone naturally tried to be the topmost of all. In the old days two repetitions of the complete sequence were usually sufficient, and the dance normally concluded as an ordinary three-couple Reel. The dance was last performed on Whalsay about 1930, and its use there extends as far back as living memory will take us (187, 192, 197).

The 'Eight-man's Reel' or 'Eightpenny Reel' from Skeld

This is a four-couple Reel which we met in the district of Skeld. It was last performed there about 1910 (165-6).

To begin the 'Eight-man's Reel', the four couples form two parallel lines, with all the men in one line and their partners opposite them in the other. The dance consists of alternate 'dancing' and 'reeling', beginning with 'dancing', and the 'reel' here is a reel of four (i.e. a figure 8 with an extra loop) performed by the four couples acting as single units, with the men following immediately behind their partners. We are not completely certain of the manner in which the reel is run, but from the information we obtained it seems very probable that the dancers should begin the reel as shown in Diagram 9.8.

The tempo of the music for this Reel was probably rather slower than that for the other Shetland Reels (166).

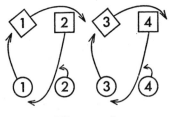

Diagram 9.8

A four-couple Reel with the same starting positions as the 'Eight-man's Reel' was also danced on Burra Isle many years ago (177).

The four-couple Shetland Reel from Sandwick and Cunningsburgh

In this Reel the dancers again form two parallel lines, but with the men and ladies placed alternately in each line. As in the Skeld 'Eight-man's Reel', the dance consists of alternate 'dancing' and 'reeling', and the 'reel' was again a reel of four performed by the four couples acting as single units. Here, however, we have no definite information on the manner in which the reel is begun.

This Reel was performed in Sandwick up to about thirty years ago, but was never very common there (161). It was also performed occasionally in Cunningsburgh (159).

The style in which Reels were danced in Shetland

Although in the old days in Shetland there was relatively little social intercourse between one crofting community and another, there does seem to have been a fairly standard 'Shetland style' in the dancing of Reels. Perhaps the most characteristic feature of all, common to every district, was the use of three quick stamps with alternate feet to terminate the reel (the stamps actually occur on the counts '1 & 2' of the last bar of the 'reeling turn'). These three stamps also formed a part of some of the more common setting steps.

Since the dancing space in the croft kitchens was very restricted, and since there were usually six or more people dancing at a time, the steps employed tended to be compact, with few of the open positions so common on the mainland of Scotland. There was an old Shetland saying that one should 'dance tight, tight and peerie-wise[1] wi' your feet' (151), and this aptly sums up the style.

[1] 'Smallwise.'

In the old days the men danced their setting steps with great vigour, accompanying them with loud 'heuchs' and a crack of finger and thumb; some of the men, snapping two fingers on each hand, could almost keep note for note with the music.

The ladies danced much more quietly than the men, and in particular they never 'heuched' or snapped their fingers. In the old days their long skirts tended to hide their feet, and they danced appropriately: 'there wasna' sae much o' a step in it; it was mair their body . . . they were lilting on their heels, and it was the action o' the body which made the dance. You couldna' see their feet' (192).

In Lunnasting, Esha Ness, and Hillswick it was usual for partners to join both hands when setting to each other, holding their hands at the level of the tops of their heads with their arms straight, thus forming a double arch (150–1). In Papa Stour about 1900, partners usually joined right hands when they set to each other (182). Elsewhere in the districts which we visited, partners did not usually join hands when setting. Men had their hands both raised, or both on their waists, or both by their sides. Ladies sometimes held their hands on their waists, with palms upward and thumbs to the front, but more often they had their hands by their sides. In the days of long frocks ladies sometimes held their skirts out to the side, but usually they 'let them go'. In the 'reel' it was usual everywhere for both men and ladies to have their hands by their sides, though in the days of long frocks ladies sometimes held their skirts with one hand to ensure that they did not trip over them.

The travelling steps in use were very varied. The chassé, the travelling pas de Basque, a 'step-hop', and a lilting walk were probably about equally common. The hop-one-and-two was also used, but was not particularly common. About 1900 the older ladies often used the chassé —'they seemed to have a gliding motion'. On Whalsay the men's 'lilting walk' was almost a springy run, with the feet lifted up behind, and with the arms swinging in opposition to the feet, the elbows well bent. And always there were the three quick stamps to end the reel.

In Whalsay about the year 1900, the older ladies used to 'doock' (duck) in the course of the reel—this was one of the ways in which their dancing was 'mair their body'. The 'doockin'' was actually a form of quick curtsy made by bending the knees slightly, with the body kept erect. It was usually performed about halfway round the reel, and again at the end: 'they doockit when about half round, and when they backed into their places. They didna' gae far doon at a'' (189, 191–2, 196). 'Doockin'' was also performed on the Mainland of Shetland, but we do not know whether it was ever the normal practice there.

In a three-couple Reel, the dancers often inserted extra spins in the course of the reel, usually at the 'corners' of the figure 8 (i.e. at the points marked with a cross in Diagram 9.9 (a)). To make such an extra

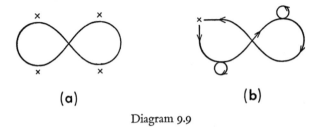

(a)   (b)

Diagram 9.9

spin, the dancers simply turned about more or less on the spot (usually turning away from the figure 8), and then continued with the reel. Usually a dancer would not have time to insert more than one or two such extra spins in the course of any one reel; a typical track with two extra spins is shown in Diagram 9.9 (b). Both men and ladies performed these extra spins, but ladies probably did them more frequently than men.

Even when extra spins were inserted, the reel was never allowed to extend into the 'dancing turn' of the music. Some of the old fiddlers were very strict on this point and would stop playing if the dancers were not back in their places ready to 'dance' at the beginning of the 'dancing turn' of the tune. For instance, William Hutchison, a fiddler who lived many years ago on Whalsay, would 'just knock off playing and ask "could you no reel a peerie grain faster?"' (192). Other fiddlers were more kind-hearted, and would insert an extra two or four bars of music in the 'reeling turn' to enable the dancers to complete their reel in time with the music. Usually, however, such measures were not necessary, for Shetlanders paid very close attention to the music to which they danced.

Setting steps for Shetland Reels

The foot positions used in Shetland dancing are all very natural ones, with the feet almost parallel to each other. The classical positions of dancing defined in Chapter V are not particularly appropriate here, and we therefore give names, A, B, C, D, to four new positions which occur in the steps which follow. All four are ground positions, and they are illustrated in Diagram 9.10 in the case in which the RF is the working foot. In position B, the heels should be about 9 inches apart, and in all four the heels are only just off the ground.

In addition to these four new positions we also make use of a few of the basic positions defined in Chapter V.

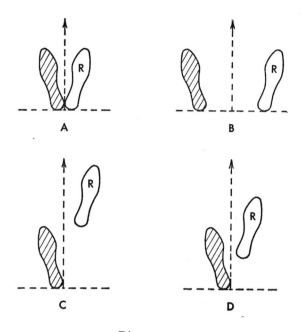

Diagram 9.10

Except where stated, the counting used here is the standard one for reels and Scotch measures given in Chapter V.

Most of the setting steps used in Shetland Reels within living memory seem to have been peculiar to Shetland and we have met only two steps which are known elsewhere, namely the 'backstep with a hop' and the pas de Basque.

The 'backstep with a hop' (p. 123) was known everywhere in Shetland as the 'backstep'. It was by far the most common setting step for men, and was also occasionally danced by ladies ('it depended on the music. When there was good music, we [ladies] might do the backstep'). Usually the step was performed with alternate feet, either for the whole of the 'dancing turn', or for all except the last bar, when three quick stamps were substituted. It also occurred as a part of the following step, which is essentially a combination of the 'backstep with a hop' and the characteristic three stamps.

This combined step begins on a preliminary count '&':

&	⎤	'Backstep with a hop' with RF, LF, RF, making
1. 1 & 2 &	⎬	the last step on the RF (on the count '**2.** 1') a
2. 1	⎦	heavy one.
&		Beat with LF in 5th position.
2		Beat with RF in rear 5th position.
&	⎫	
3. 1 & 2 &, **4.** 1 & 2	⎬	Perform the movements above contrariwise.
4. &, 5–8		Repeat these movements from the beginning.

This combination was a common setting step for men, but was rarely danced by ladies.

The pas de Basque has been known in Shetland as far back as living memory extends, but seems to have been more common as a ladies' step than as a men's step. It was normally danced with the feet almost parallel to each other, and the usual form of the step was version I, described on p. 111.

Up to about 1920 many ladies used to perform the pas de Basque with a turn of the body, at the same time holding their skirts out to the side. The movements in this 'turning pas de Basque' are approximately as follows. Start in position A, as shown in the dotted positions in Diagram 9.11 (a).

1. 1 Step on the RF in the position shown in Diagram 9.11 (a), moving the foot in an arc of a circle. At the same time, turn the body to the right so that it faces in the direction of the large arrow in this diagram.

    & 2 Close the LF to the RF as shown in Diagram 9.11 (a), moving the foot in an arc of a circle (count '&'), and then beat with the ball of the RF on the spot (count '2'). Throughout these two counts the body remains facing in the direction of the large arrow in Diagram 9.11 (a).

2. 1 Step on the LF in the position shown in Diagram 9.11 (b), moving the foot in an arc of a circle. At the same time, turn the body to the left so that it faces in the direction of the large arrow in this diagram.

    & 2 Close the RF to the LF as shown in Diagram 9.11 (b), moving the foot in an arc of a circle (count '&'), and then beat with the ball of the LF on the spot (count '2'). Throughout these two counts the body remains facing in the direction of the large arrow in Diagram 9.11 (b).

3–8 Repeat these movements twice, starting from the final positions in Diagram 9.11 (b), then repeat bar **1** once, and finish with three quick stamps, LF, RF, LF, facing the front.

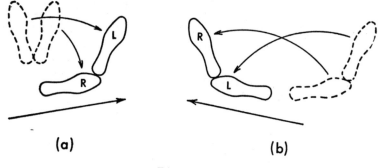

(a) (b)

Diagram 9.11

Sometimes the dancers in a three-couple Reel performed this 'turning pas de Basque' with hands joined in their two lines. On the first bar of the 'dancing turn', the dancer at one end of each line turns to the right (beginning the step with the RF), the next person turns to the left (beginning the step with the LF, as in bar **2** above), and the third turns to the right (again beginning with the RF). They then continue turning from side to side, so that the centre dancer in each line turns first to face the person on one side, then the person on the other. As the dancers turn, so they swing their hands backward and forward, two adjacent dancers swinging their nearer hands backward and their other hand forward as they turn to face each other. Typical positions at the ends of successive bars of music are shown in Diagram 9.12.

(a) Positions at end of bar **1** (say)   (b) Positions at end of bar **2**

Diagram 9.12

This combination of the 'turning pas de Basque' with the hand-swinging was the normal practice on Foula (186). It was also performed on the North Mainland (150–1), and in Delting was sometimes known as 'gracing the dance' (151).

P

There are a number of ladies' steps which incorporate 'three stamps', and we give next two examples of these (in one of these examples the 'three stamps' may possibly be derived from the three beats of the pas de Basque rather than from the characteristic ending of the 'reeling turn'). Each of our examples is a 2-bar step, and we describe the movements performed with the RF. In an actual Reel these steps would normally be repeated with alternate feet throughout the 'dancing turn' of the tune.

The first example comes from Burra Isle (179). It will be seen that in this step the 'three stamps' (on counts '2. 1 & 2') actually form a pas de Basque.

1.	1	With a lilt on the LF (but no hop), place the R heel about 9 inches to the right of the L toe.
	2	Again with a lilt on the LF (but no hop), point the R toe in 4th position.
2.	1	Step on the RF in semi 2nd position.
	&	Step on the LF in 3rd position.
	2	Beat with the RF in rear 3rd position.

The second of these ladies' steps is from the Out Skerries (151).

1.	1	Drop on the RF in rear 3rd position, at the same time taking the LF to 4th int. low aerial position.
	2	Drop on the LF in 4th int. position, at the same time raising the RF just off the ground.
2.	1 & 2	Beat with RF, LF, RF in these positions.

In Whalsay the most common ladies' step up to about 1910 was a form of sidestep, often incorporating a 'doockin'' motion (191, 196, 198). This step was also common at one time in Yell, and it may well be a member of an older generation of steps which were current in Shetland prior to the period covered by living memory.

The step consists of a series of simple movements, which we here call 'sidesteps', performed first to one side, then to the other, then back in the first direction, and so on. The changes of direction need not occur at any regular division of the 'dancing turn', and can occur as often as the dancer pleases. In an actual Reel the 'sidesteps' were usually performed in an arc of a circle centred on the dancer's partner, but for the sake of simplicity we describe them as if they are made in a straight line in the sideways direction.

The step is begun with a small spring which takes place very slightly after the musical count '&', and the nearest approximation to the timing of the step is that given by the counts 'a1a2a1a2...' as shown below (cf. p. 89). The basic sidestep occurs on the counts 'a1' or the counts 'a2', the movements performed to the right being as follows (we describe the movements against the counts 'a1'):

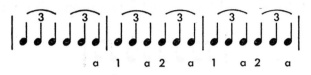

Count *a*   Starting in position B (Diagram 9.10), make a very small spring off both feet and land on the *LF* about 5 inches to the right of its previous position.

Count 1   Put the RF down about 5 inches to the right of its previous position (so that the feet are again in position B).

To begin the step from position A there is an initial movement:

Count *a*   Make a small hop on the LF on the spot and lift the RF just off the ground.

Count **1.** 1 Put the RF down in position B.

Then follows a series of 'sidesteps' to the right, followed by a 'change' movement:

Count *a*   From position B make a very small spring off both feet and land on the RF, more or less on the spot.

Count 1   (or '2', according to the position of the 'change' movement in the music). Put the LF down in position B.

Following this 'change' movement there is a series of 'sidesteps' to the left, then another 'change' movement (the reverse of that above), then another series of 'sidesteps' to the right, and so on.

The 'doock' in this step is a quick curtsy inserted just before each change of direction and is made by bending the knees on the last 'side-step' of each series.

Of all the Shetland Reel steps, the most complicated is the 'Whalsay shuffle', or 'Whalsay scruffle'. As its name implies, this step belongs to the island of Whalsay,[1] where it was the principal (and sometimes the only) setting step used by men. People in other parts of Shetland regarded it as a characteristic Whalsay step, and most Whalsay men took pride in being able to dance it well.

---

[1] And possibly also to the Out Skerries.

The 'Whalsay shuffle' is essentially a double shuffle performed with the shuffling foot well in front of the supporting foot. The counts '1 & 2 &' which we have used hitherto are not adequate for the description of this step, since here movements occur on the notes not denoted by the counts, and we therefore use the fuller system of counting '1 an & a 2 an & a' (pronounced 'one an and a two an and a') given below.

1 an & a 2 an & a

The basic movement in the 'Whalsay shuffle', which we here call a 'double shuffle', occupies either the counts '1 an & a' or the counts '2 an & a', and, performed with the RF, is as follows.

Start with the LF in position D, with the weight on the RF. Throughout the step keep the balls of both feet in contact with the ground, with the heels raised a little.

Count 1   (or '2', according to the position of the 'double shuffle' in relation to the music). Slide the LF back in and transfer the weight to it, and at the same time push the RF along the ground on to position C, so that the two feet reach their final positions simultaneously, exactly on the count. Just before the RF begins to move, there is a slight flexing of the R instep (effectively there is a spring off the RF, except that the ball of the RF never leaves the ground).

Count an   With no pause of the foot in position C, brush the RF back into position D.

Count &   With no pause of the foot in this position, push the RF along the ground out again to position C.

Count a   Again with no pause in position C, begin to brush the RF in towards position A so that on the actual count 'a' the foot is passing approximately through position D.

The movements of the 'double shuffle' with the LF are simply those above performed contrariwise, and the whole 8-bar step is as follows (193, 198).

1. 1 an & a 'Double shuffle' with RF.
     2 an & a 'Double shuffle' with LF.
2–8   Repeat bar **1** seven times.

The 'double shuffle' can also be varied with a 'single shuffle'. This 'single shuffle' occupies either the counts '1 &' or the counts '2 &', and is as follows (again we describe the movements performed with the RF).

Start with the LF in position D, with the weight on the RF.

Count 1   (or '2', according to the position of the 'single shuffle' in relation to the music). Perform the actions of count '1' of the 'double shuffle'.

Count &   Perform the actions of count '1' of the 'double shuffle' contrariwise, starting with the RF in position C.

A typical sequence involving both the 'double shuffle' and the 'single shuffle' is as follows.

1. 1 an & a 'Double shuffle' with the RF.
    2 an & a 'Double shuffle' with the LF.
2. 1 &   'Single shuffle' with the RF.
    2 an & a 'Double shuffle' with the RF, starting with the LF in position C.
3, 4   Perform bars 1, 2 contrariwise.
5–8   Repeat bars 1–4.

The 'Whalsay shuffle' has been danced on Whalsay for as far back as living memory extends. It was never performed by ladies, but there was a less energetic shuffle step which ladies did sometimes use. This was roughly as follows (190–1).

Start in position A.

1. 1   Step on LF.
    an & a 2 With the weight on the LF, brush the RF out to position D (count 'an'), in again a little (count '&'), then out again to position D (count 'a'), and then back again into position A (count '2'). The weight is transferred to the RF on the final count '2'.

    an & a ⎫
2. 1   ⎬ Perform the movements of counts 'an & a 2' contrariwise.
            ⎭
    an & a 2 Repeat the movements of counts '1. an & a 2', etc.

(The difference between this and the men's step lies primarily in the fact that there is here no 'spring' to change feet at the end of each 'double shuffle'.) On bars 1, 2 the dancer moves a short distance to her right, then on bars 3–6 she moves back to her place and out to her left, and then on bars 7, 8 she returns to her original place. Like the Whalsay sidestep, this step was usually performed in an arc of a circle centred on the dancer's partner.

A SELECTION OF SHETLAND REEL TUNES

We present here some good examples of Shetland reel tunes. The first six of these were collected by Mr Tommy Anderson of Lerwick, who has very kindly made his recordings available to us. The version of 'Ahunt the decks o' Voe' is an old family version of Mr Anderson's. 'Pit hame da borrowed claes' ('Put home the borrowed clothes'), 'Jeannie shock da bairn' ('Jeannie choke the bairn'), and 'Oot b'aist da Vong' ('Out by east the Vong') are three famous Vidlin reels, and were collected from Mr Henry Thomson of Vidlin, now living in Ollaberry. The title of 'Willafjord' commemorates the days when Shetlanders were engaged in the Greenland whaling, and this version of the tune was collected from Mr Bobbie Peterson, Breiwick, Tingwall. 'Donald Blue' was collected by Mr Anderson from Mr Fraser Hughson of Aith, and the last of the tunes, 'Lucky, can ye link ony?', was collected by F. R. and T. F. from Mr James Scollay of Burravoe, Yell.

AHUNT THE DECKS O'VOE

PIT HAME DA BORROWED CLAES

JEANNIE SHOCK DA BAIRN

OOT B'AIST DA VONG

SOME REELS FROM SHETLAND

WILLAFJORD

DONALD BLUE

LUCKY, CAN YOU LINK ONY?

THE AULD REEL

The characteristic feature of the Auld Reel is that the dancers reel continuously, without setting. In the Whalsay and Cunningsburgh versions, and also in a dance of similar nature performed in Westerwick, partners dance side by side, with linked arms or some similar hold. In the Walls and Papa Stour versions, the men follow their partners, exactly as in the three-couple Shetland Reel.

The Auld Reel from Whalsay

This version is danced by three couples, to a tune peculiar to Whalsay, known there as 'The Auld Reel' (p. 228). Partners dance side by side, the lady on the man's right, with nearer arms round each other's waists. In the old days they sometimes joined outer hands (holding the joined hands out in front of them at shoulder level, with elbows slightly bent), but most people seem to have kept the outer hand free.

To begin the Reel, the dancers move initially in the directions shown in Diagram 9.13. Thereafter they dance a continuously repeated reel of

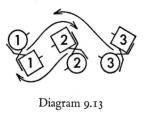

Diagram 9.13

221

three, using a walking step with a very pronounced lilt (two steps to each bar of music).[1]

The Auld Reel as a dance by itself has probably not been danced on Whalsay since about 1900, and we found only two people (187–8) who remembered it as such. All our other sources for this dance (190–2, 194–5) remember it only as a part of a composite dance incorporating both the Auld Reel and the (Whalsay) Shetland Reel. For this composite dance the fiddler first played one or two ordinary Shetland Reel tunes, then changed to the tune of the Auld Reel, and then finally changed back to a Shetland Reel tune. The dancers performed the ordinary Whalsay Shetland Reel while the first Reel tunes were played, then, when the fiddler played 'The Auld Reel', partners linked together and 'liltit through the reel' so long as the tune lasted. When 'The Auld Reel' tune ended, the dancers quickly released hold of their partners and moved back into position for a Shetland Reel (probably taking the place nearest to them), and the dance then concluded as an ordinary Shetland Reel. This composite dance died out on Whalsay at some time between 1920 and 1930.

When the Auld Reel was used in the Bride's Reels and the Bridegroom's Reels on Whalsay, it was performed exactly as in the course of an ordinary social dance, except that the dancers were either all ladies or all men. On such occasions the dancers usually kept their outer hands free, for 'you had to keep awa' the strae brush' (187).

The Auld Reel from Cunningsburgh

This version of the Auld Reel is performed by four couples, and consists of a continuously repeated reel of four, with each couple moving as a single unit.

The couples stand at the corners of a square of side about 6 ft, facing into the square. Partners stand beside each other, the lady on the man's right, facing at an angle of about 90° to each other. They place nearer arms round each other's waists and join outer hands, holding the joined hands out in front of them at shoulder level, with elbows slightly bent (Diagram 9.14 (a)). Partners may also dance side by side, with nearer arms round each other's waists and with the other hand free.

The four couples dance a continuously repeated reel of four, starting the first reel of four in the 'side-by-side' position (p. 145). To begin the first reel of four, the 1st and 2nd couples pass each other with the left shoulders, then the 1st couple pass the 3rd couple with the right

---

[1] It is probably also permissible for the two couples who are facing initially to begin the Reel by passing each other with the left shoulders.

shoulders while the 2nd couple pass the 4th couple with the right shoulders. The 3rd and 4th couples stand still for the first one or two bars (or possibly dance on the spot), then enter the reel of four by passing each other with left shoulders. Thereafter the couples follow the usual track, as shown in Diagram 9.14 (b).

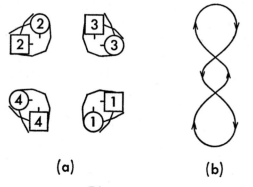

(a)   (b)

Diagram 9.14

At any point on the centre loop (or thereabouts), the couples can insert extra spins at will. To perform such a spin, a couple simply rotate on the spot, the two partners still remaining in the same position relative to each other. When a couple moving round the reel find the path blocked by a rotating couple, the moving couple simply dance back along their tracks a little (still facing in the forward direction) until the way is clear, and then move forward again.

The travelling step for the Auld Reel in Cunningsburgh was a repeated hop; the dancers hop on the one foot for as long as they can—maybe for two complete reels—then change to the other foot; as far as possible partners change feet simultaneously.

There is no tune called 'The Auld Reel' known in Cunningsburgh today, and within living memory the dance has been performed to such tunes as 'Ahunt the decks o' Voe' (p. 218) and 'Napoleon's March to Moscow'. The former, for instance, would be played at a tempo of approximately 48 bars per minute, with two hops to each bar of music.

The preceding account of the Auld Reel was obtained from Mrs Margaret Smith of Aith, Cunningsburgh (159), who danced it frequently as an ordinary social dance in her young days, about 1900–10. Mrs Smith last performed the dance at a wedding in Cunningsburgh in 1946.

Another lady, Mrs Robina Christie (153), who danced the Auld Reel at various weddings in Cunningsburgh up to about 1903, confirmed the continuous reel of four and the hopping step, and told us that the local term for the latter was 'heckling'. She also confirmed both the 'holds' given by Mrs Smith, and said that the dancers could also link nearer arms: 'they hooked arms and danced round a figure 8'.

The version of the Auld Reel which was performed by the bride and her attendants as the Bride's Reel was revived about 1928 by members of the Cunningsburgh Women's Rural Institute. They were taught the dance by Miss Joan Laurenson of Cunningsburgh, who had performed the dance in her younger days. When Miss Laurenson taught the dance to the members of the W.R.I., she suggested that, since the extra spins which the couples introduce into the reel of four tend to obscure the pattern of the dance to an onlooker, it would be preferable for demonstration purposes for the couples to spin in some prescribed order. After some experiment, the members evolved such a regularized form of the dance, which they have since performed (under the name 'The Bride's Reel') on a number of occasions (157), and we ourselves were given a very fine demonstration of it on our visit to Shetland, with the dancers dressed in the costume of the period 1860–1900.[1]

In 1943 Miss Laurenson told the Rev. A. Barclay Wilson, the Minister of Cunningsburgh Church, that the tune for the Auld Reel when it was performed by the bride and her attendants as the Bride's Reel was 'Da Black an' da Broon'—Mr Wilson noted the tune from her singing (160).

We should add that we actually met Miss Laurenson when we visited Shetland in 1959—she was then 86—but her memories of the Bride's Reel were not clear, and she could remember only that the Bride's Reel and the Auld Reel were the same dance, and that the Bride's Reel was the last dance at a wedding.

The Auld Reel from Walls

This version was known locally in the Walls district either as 'The Auld Reel of Finnigarth' or 'The Muckle Reel of Finnigarth'. It is performed by three couples, to a tune called 'The Muckle Reel of Finnigarth' (see the *Shetland Folk Book*, Vol. II).

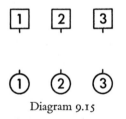

Diagram 9.15

[1] Neither Mrs Margaret Smith nor Mrs Christie took part in this revival—Mrs Smith has seen the revived version only once, and Mrs Christie has not seen it at all. The account of the dance which we obtained from Mrs Smith and Mrs Christie is therefore independent of the revival.

The dancers stand in two lines, with the men in one line and their partners opposite them in the other. The spacing of the set is similar to that in a three-couple Shetland Reel (Diagram 9.15).

To begin the Reel, the centre lady crosses over and passes her partner by the right shoulder, turning to her left round the 3rd man, and as she does so, her partner takes a step forward and turns to close in behind her. At the same time the top and bottom ladies turn their backs on their partners and move as shown in Diagram 9.16 (a), their partners follow-

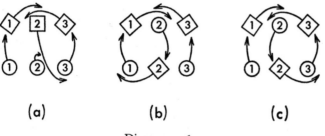

(a)   (b)   (c)

Diagram 9.16

ing immediately behind them. The couples then dance a continuous series of reels of three, each couple moving as a single unit, with the men following immediately behind their partners. As the centre couple pass through the centre position at the end of the first reel of three, they turn to their *right* to begin the next reel of three (Diagram 9.16 (b)), the top and bottom couples altering their paths accordingly (the 1st couple have to turn rather sharply to their right in order to pass the 3rd couple by the left). At the end of the second reel of three, the centre couple turn to their left again (Diagram 9.16 (c)), and so on alternately.

The tune, which contains seven 'turnings', is played twice through for the dance, beginning at a tempo of 54 bars per minute. This tempo is maintained until the end of the fifth turning of the repeat of the tune, and then during the last two turnings the tempo is gradually increased to the normal tempo for a Shetland Reel. At the end of the repeat of the tune the dancers should be in their original places, and the fiddler then breaks into 'The Back Reel' (see the *Shetland Folk Book*, Vol. II), when the dancers perform an ordinary three-couple Shetland Reel. The step for the Auld Reel proper is a walking step with a pronounced lilt, two steps to each bar of music. The transition from the Auld Reel to the Back Reel is marked by three stamps on the last bar of the Auld Reel tune.

In the Auld Reel proper, the dancers do not mark the end of each successive reel in any way; they simply move smoothly into the next reel, the men remaining behind their partners. They do not re-form in the original two lines until the beginning of the ensuing Shetland Reel. The track of the 1st and 3rd couples in the Auld Reel proper is actually a repeated figure 8, in the direction shown in Diagram 9.17 (a), although the order in which the two couples pass through the centre varies from one repetition to the next. After the first half of the first reel of three, the centre couple dance a double-looped figure 8, as shown in Diagram 9.17 (b). The dancers do not insert any extra spins in the course of the reels.

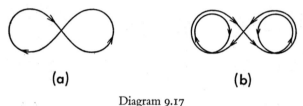

(a)   (b)

Diagram 9.17

It is probably also permissible for the centre lady to begin the first reel by passing her partner with the left shoulder and turning to her right round the 1st couple. In any case, the centre couple begin each successive reel by turning in alternate directions.

This version of the Auld Reel comes from the Walls district, and has been largely kept alive by a family of noted fiddlers of the name of Fraser, who owned the croft of Finnigarth in West Walls. The district round Finnigarth is very remote and for many years the Frasers of Finnigarth were the principal fiddlers in the district. Their house was the chief dancing-place of the local community, and the Auld Reel was kept up in the gatherings there. The dance was also known in Walls itself, and there it was performed fairly regularly up to about 1910. It was revived a few years ago by a group of people from Walls, both from their own memories of the dance and from the memories of older people.

In the old days the dance was performed on any sort of occasion 'just as a kind of light dance'. It would normally be performed several times during an evening's dancing, though usually in the later part of the evening when the dancers were beginning to tire.

The description of the dance above was given to us by Mr Peter Fraser, the present owner of Finnigarth and himself a noted fiddler (175), and also by two of the leading participants in the recent revival, Mrs Barbara Cheyne (169) and Miss Mary Smith (173). We also obtained confirmatory information from two of the older people in West Walls (174, 176).

We should add that the tune as now played is highly irregular in its construction. It seems certain that part of it has been lost, for we were told by several people in the Walls district that it originally had more than seven turnings.

A dance of somewhat similar form to the Auld Reel of Finnigarth was danced up to about the year 1905 at Westerwick, a very remote group of crofts beside a rocky bay in the West Side of Shetland. In this dance, the dancers reeled continuously, arm-in-arm with their partners. They did not 'dance' (i.e. set), but 'just keepit on until they came to some turning. Then they slippit and went some other way'. Our informant, Mrs Thomas Moar (166), who was brought up in Westerwick, could not remember the name of the dance. Her husband had seen a similar dance (possibly without the change of direction) in his young days in Wester Skeld. He also could not remember the name of the dance, but it may have been the 'Muckle Reel' which a lady of 75 told us was danced in Wester Skeld 'before her time' (165).

The Auld Reel from Papa Stour

This version, for three couples, comes from the island of Papa Stour, where it was known as either 'The Auld Reel' or 'The Muckle Reel'. It was performed to several tunes, all bearing the name 'The Auld Reel' or 'The Muckle Reel' (p. 229).

There is some confusion regarding the actual figures of the dance, and we received several contradictory accounts. It seems probable, however, that about 1895 the dance consisted of a continuously repeated reel of three, each couple moving as a single unit, with the men following behind their partners (181, 183).

TUNES FOR THE AULD REELS

All the tunes which are specifically for the Shetland Auld Reels are highly irregular in their structure, and it seems very likely that they are of considerable antiquity. With the exception of the version of the 'Auld Reel of Finnigarth' given in the *Shetland Folk Book* (p. 224), we give here all the Auld Reel tunes known. All were collected by Mr Tommy Anderson of Lerwick.

THE AULD REEL OF WHALSAY

As played by Mr John Irvine of Whalsay. Tempo: 56 bars per minute.

A FRAGMENT OF A MUCKLE REEL FROM WALLS

As played by Miss Jean Pole of Walls. Tempo: 54 bars per minute.

HREE TUNES FOR THE AULD REEL OF PAPA STOUR

I) As played by Mr George Peterson of Papa Stour.

our times; B twice; C twice; D twice; E four times; back to A again; 21 seconds for the
nplete tune.

II) As played by Mr George Peterson.

three times; B once; C three times; D four times; back to A again; 14 seconds for the
nplete tune.

III) As played by Mr Fraser Hughson of Aith.

twice; B three times; C twice; D three times; E three times; F once; lead into A again; 21
conds for the complete tune.

CHAPTER X

Some Country Dances

IN this chapter we describe a few of the many Country Dances which were performed in Scotland within living memory. Our aim here is to illustrate the general development of the Country Dance in Scotland, and we have selected the dances which we describe with this in mind.

Country Dances—that is to say dances of the longways progressive type—were first brought into Scotland from England, about the year 1700, when Scottish society was first beginning to free itself from the austerity of the early Presbyterian Church. At this period, and indeed right up to the middle of the nineteenth century, a Country Dance consisted of a tune and a particular sequence of figures performed to that tune, and the name of the dance was that of the tune. A number of more or less standard Country Dance figures were known, such as 'hands round', 'hands across', and 'right and left', and in each dance the sequence of figures was constructed largely from these standard figures. The first Country Dances to be performed in Scotland doubtless made use of English tunes, but Scottish tunes were employed from at least 1704, and from about 1730 onwards most of the Country Dances performed in Scotland were set to Scottish tunes.

There were also Scottish contributions to the figures, but to a much smaller extent. The first Country Dance figure which seems to have originated in Scotland is the figure 'set and turn corners', which appeared about 1720. A more definitely Scottish contribution is the combination of this figure with reels of three in the sequence 'set and turn corners and reels of three with corners'.[1] This particular combination, which was almost certainly inspired by the Scottish Threesome Reel, attained considerable popularity in Scotland, and was used in over two-fifths of the Country Dances known to have been performed in Scotland before 1775. However, these two figures appear to be the total of Scottish contributions to the Country Dance up to about 1775,

[1] This combination is described in detail on pp. 246–7.

and the remaining figures in the Country Dances performed in Scotland before this date follow the English pattern.

Between about 1775 and 1830 there were introduced a number of new Country Dance figures which incorporated ideas from the Cotillion, the Quadrilles, and the Waltz, and as a result of these introductions Country Dances now tended to lose their distinctive English (and, to a lesser extent, Scottish) national characteristics and to acquire instead the more international flavour of the contemporary polite ballroom. This 'ballroom' development of the Country Dance continued in Scotland right up to the beginning of the twentieth century, but in England Country Dances began to disappear from the polite ballrooms about 1830, and by 1850 only one or two Country Dances remained in use in English society. Thus the development of the Country Dance subsequent to about 1830 is almost entirely a Scottish development, although in fact there is little of this development which is national in character.

Up to about 1775, Country Dances were in Scotland almost entirely confined to the upper classes, and from at least 1720 onwards their tempo was very slow, to accord with the elaborate dress of the period. The vast hooped skirts worn by ladies of fashion, which were first introduced about 1715, particularly necessitated a relatively slow tempo, and so far as we can tell there was no distinction between reels and strathspeys when these tunes were used for Country Dances, both types of tune being played at approximately 30 bars per minute. After about 1775–80 the hooped skirt fell into disuse except for great State occasions, and with the return to a less elaborate form of dress the tempo of Country Dances increased considerably. There was now a clear distinction between reels and strathspeys when these tunes were played for Country Dances, and it is during this later period, from about 1775 to about 1830, that Country Dances in strathspey tempo first emerge as a distinct type. The increased tempo also made Country Dances more acceptable to the ordinary people of Scotland, and by the beginning of the nineteenth century Country Dances had spread throughout most of the Lowlands, among all classes of society. However, their spread into other regions of Scotland was much less rapid, and essentially Country Dances must be regarded as Lowland dances.

In a Country Dance, in the sense in which we have understood the term in this book, the dancers stand initially in two lines down the room, with the men in one line and their partners opposite them in the other, the men having the top of the room on their left. A set consists of a number of adjacent couples, and in each set the couples are numbered from the top (Diagram 10.1.)[1]

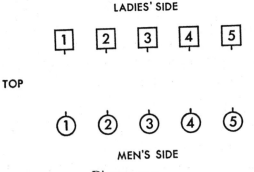

LADIES' SIDE

TOP

MEN'S SIDE

Diagram 10.1

A typical Country Dance consists of the repetition of a certain sequence of figures involving two or three adjacent couples. In the case where the basic sequence involves two couples, the first couple begin the dance by performing the sequence with the second couple, and at the end of the sequence the two couples have exchanged places with each other. The first couple (starting from second place) now repeat the sequence with the third couple, and end in third place, then repeat the sequence with the fourth couple, and so on, moving one place down the set with each repetition of the sequence. The second couple commence the dance (from top place) with the third couple as soon as the latter are disengaged, and in turn each new top couple commences as soon as there is a disengaged couple immediately below them. In this way each couple progresses down the set, and this progression continues until all have regained their original places. A similar progression applies in the case where the basic sequence involves three couples, the couples again progressing one place down the set with each repetition of the sequence.

In the eighteenth and early nineteenth centuries the sets for Country Dances usually consisted of ten or twelve couples, and in one or two places in the Borders (16, 69) and Angus (6) such 'long' sets were still in use at the beginning of the period covered by living memory. In most places, however, relatively short sets have been used for as far back as living memory extends; thus in Angus and Perthshire the number of couples in a set was usually five, in the West Highlands it was anything from four to seven, and elsewhere in Scotland it was almost invariably

---

[1] If in the course of the dance a man and his partner cross over to each other's side, we shall say that they are then 'improper'.

four. Exceptionally, in East Lothian, the number of couples in a set was sometimes as low as three, but this was only for a 'heavy' dance—one which was especially vigorous—where the basic sequence involved only two couples.[1]

The spacing of the set naturally varied with the amount of room available, but in general the two lines of dancers would be about 6–7 ft apart, and the distance between adjacent couples would be about 3 ft.

In the urban ballrooms the style of performance of Country Dances was sedate, but in the country districts—and particularly at the kirns—it was more vigorous (though less so than that of Reels). There was everywhere a certain amount of 'heuching' by the men, but most teachers discouraged this. It was rare for hands to be raised, and there was no finger-snapping. Men normally held their hands by their sides, though a few teachers (in particular, Mr William Adamson and his father in East Fife) taught men to place their hands on their waists. Ladies either held their hands by their sides or, alternatively, held their frocks.

Country Dance Steps

The principal steps for Country Dances have already been dealt with in Chapter V, but for convenience we summarize here the main points concerning these steps.

The common quick travelling steps in Country Dances were the chassé, hop-one-and-two and travelling pas de Basque (pp. 104, 109). Dancing-teachers in certain parts of Lanarkshire, Ayrshire, and Dumfriesshire taught the hop-one-and-two as the correct step for most travelling figures, but elsewhere dancing-teachers invariably taught the chassé for this purpose. The pivot step (p. 110) was normally used for swinging, and the galop step (or slip-step, p. 109) was also used in one or two particular figures. The quick setting step, except in a few dances where a special 'set and turn step' was used, or where the dancers substituted special 'treepling' steps, was invariably the pas de Basque (p. 110).

The normal Strathspey travelling step in Country Dances was the Lowland step A (p. 93). A few dancing-teachers taught the Highland step B (p. 93), but outside their classes this step was rarely, if ever, used for Country Dances. The usual setting steps in strathspey tempo were the Common and Highland Schottische steps (p. 102), the former being

[1] The facts in this chapter have in the main been given to us and been confirmed by so many people that it would be impossible to acknowledge them all; we therefore list our sources only where the information concerned has been obtained from relatively few people.

used where the period of setting occupied two bars, the latter where it occupied four bars.

The special 'set and turn step' mentioned above is a step from the Quadrilles which was taught by Mr William Adamson and his father in East Fife for use in two particular Country Dances, the Quadrille Country Dance and Royal Albert (see pp. 252, 253). This step can be performed in either Common time or 6/8 time, and occupies four bars of music, the movements being:

1. 1 Step on RF in 2nd position.
     2 Close LF to rear 5th position.
2. 1 Step on RF in 2nd position.
     2 Close LF to 5th position.
3, 4 Perform bars **1, 2** contrariwise.

Here the heels should be just off the ground, and in 5th position the heel of the front foot is placed against the toe of the rear foot.

Country Dance Figures

We make particular mention here of a few of the figures which occur in the dances described later in the chapter.

The Pousette. This figure, which is performed by two couples starting from adjacent positions, is one of the principal figures used to achieve the progression down the set. It occurs only in dances in quick tempo, and occupies eight bars of music.

In the form of the pousette used in Scotland within living memory, the two couples essentially just waltz round each other. The dancers take ordinary ballroom hold or some similar hold with their partners and use a simple waltz-type step, and the two couples move round each other in a counter-clockwise direction to exchange places, each couple at the same time rotating on its own axis in a clockwise direction, making two or more complete turns in the performance of the figure (Diagram 10.2). The two men then place their partners in position on the ladies' side, and fall back to their own side with one or two pas de Basque while their partners dance pas de Basque on the spot.[1]

Usually the two couples just passed directly into each other's place, as in Diagram 10.2, but sometimes they circled round each other one and a half times; in neither case were the turns made in a precise manner.

[1] This pousette, together with the step given here, is described in detail by Orr Robertson (228).

The pousette is also sometimes performed with one of the two couples starting improper; here the relevant couple simply insert an extra half turn in the figure.

TOP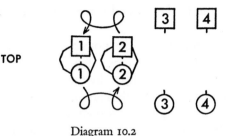

Diagram 10.2

The step used in the 'turning' part of the pousette is roughly as follows; we describe the movements performed with the RF and give the counting for tunes in Common time (for 6/8 tunes the counts 'I & 2' below should be replaced by the counts 'I and 2'):

Count I   Step on RF.
Count &   Close LF to 1st position.
Count 2   Make a small step on the RF.

Here the steps on the counts 'I' and '2' are taken in the directions appropriate to the turning movement of the dancer, and are made on the ball of the foot, with both heels just off the ground. The men normally begin the pousette with the LF and their partners with the RF. There is no spring in the step, and the whole effect of the pousette is that of a smooth, almost lazy, circling motion.

This form of pousette was taught as the correct form of the figure by all the professional dancing-teachers who practised in Scotland within living memory, except for two or three teachers in the North-east who substituted swinging in place of the pousette. The hold used by the dancing-teachers in the pousette was ordinary ballroom hold, but two other holds were in occasional use outside the teachers' classes. One of these holds was a simple two-hand hold, the man taking his partner's right hand in his left and her left hand in his right. This two-hand hold was used by a few of the older people in parts of East Lothian (43, 45) and in Liddisdale (15) about the year 1900, but does not seem to have been used elsewhere within living memory. With the other hold, picturesquely described as 'the Cumberland wrestling style' (16), the man places his hands round his partner's waist, and interlaces his fingers behind her back, while she rests her hands on his shoulders. We have records of the use of this hold in the pousette from the Borders, Angus,

Perthshire, the Argyllshire coast, Lanarkshire, and Ayrshire, and in all these regions it was quite common up to about 1900. Within living memory it was usually regarded as 'an awfu' country thing—ploughmen used to come to dances and catch the girls round the waist like that'.

In the Borders the step in the pousette was sometimes varied to a 'polka step' of the form 'step, close, step, hop', with the free foot lifted just off the ground on the hop. In these regions (and also in East Lothian) the pousette was usually known as 'the polka off' or 'polka it off', but in fact the polka step was used only when the music was particularly suited to it, and otherwise the waltz-type step was used.

After about 1914 the circling movement of the two couples in the pousette was frequently replaced by swinging on the spot—in the Border terminology 'polka it off' was replaced by 'birl it off'. Since the couples did not progress in the swinging, this change produced minor changes in the figures of those dances where pousette occurred—most often the figure 'down the centre and back to the top' was replaced by 'down the centre and back to second place'. This swinging seems to have originated in the North-east, and it was actually taught there by one or two teachers well before 1900, in particular by a Mr Lilly, who taught in parts of Kincardineshire about 1890, and by Mr Troop, who taught round Aberdeen about 1895.

There is a certain similarity between the waltz-type pousette step described above and version I of the pas de Basque (p. 111), and this similarity has led to an occasional use of the word 'pousetting' in place of the word 'setting'—we have met this use in places as widely separated as Kirkmichael in Perthshire, Fort William, and Stranraer. 'Professor' Bailey, who taught in the Glasgow region about 1892–1900, actually taught the pas de Basque under the name 'the pousette step', so that, for instance, in the 'diamond' figure of Petronella the dancers 'pousetted round about'.

The pousette has a long history, for a figure of this basic form, in which two adjacent couples move round each other, occurs in English Country Dances from at least 1700 onwards. Up to about 1790 this Country Dance figure had no particular name, but after this latter date it became known by the name 'pousette', which seems to have been originally the name of a very similar figure used in the Cotillion.

The Country Dance pousette of about 1800 was a simple movement in which the two men took their partners by both hands and pushed or pulled them out of the line of the set and then back into line again so that the two couples moved round each other in a counter-clockwise direction, either exchanging places or returning to their own places. Following the introduction of the Waltz to Britain in the early years of the nineteenth century, the 'sauteuse' Waltz step was introduced into the pousette, and the forward and backward motion of the original figure was replaced by the circling motion of the Waltz. This change, which took place in Scotland at some time before 1818 (203), was no doubt facilitated by the fact that the original hold used for the Waltz in Britain was a two-hand hold, the same as that used in the original pousette. After about 1820 other 'ballroom holds' came into fashion for the Waltz, and some of these were naturally transferred to the pousette, eventually superseding the two-hand hold. In particular, two of these new 'ballroom holds' which came into use at this period were the 'half support', which is the present-day ballroom hold, and the 'entire support', which is the 'Cumberland wrestling style' hold (211). Thus the two 'ballroom holds' used in the pousette within living memory are both derived from the early Waltz, while the two-hand hold is a relic both of the original pousette and of the original Waltz.

A return to the two-hand hold has been made in the pousette used today by members of the R.S.C.D.S. This particular form of pousette was developed during the early days of the Society, and is apparently a modification of a pousette invented about 1925 by Mr John Duthie (65), who played a prominent part in the Country Dance revival in the Border counties. Mr Duthie's original pousette is described in the book *A Complete Guide to Scottish Country Dancing* (238), of which he is co-author.

Right and left. Within living memory the name 'right and left' was given to three quite distinct Country Dance figures. These three figures were not usually regarded as interchangeable, and in any given district each dance containing a 'right and left' was performed with a particular one of the three figures. Only two of these three forms of right and left occur in the dances described in this chapter, but for the sake of completeness we give all three forms here. Each is danced by two couples and occupies eight bars of music; versions I and III occur in both quick and slow tempos, but (so far as we know) version II occurs only in quick tempo.

Version I. This version, which is a chain for four, is normally begun with the two couples in their own places. All face partners, and dance a 'chain' round the rectangle shown in Diagram 10.3, i.e. the 1st man and 2nd lady move round the rectangle clockwise, the 1st lady and 2nd man counter-clockwise, passing each other with alternate right and left shoulders and giving alternate right and left hands on passing. The dancers take two bars for each side of the rectangle, and at each corner

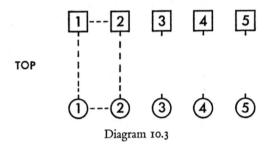

TOP

Diagram 10.3

(including the last) they turn in the shortest direction (i.e. a quarter of a turn).

Version II. In this version one of the two couples taking part usually begins the figure improper, and here we describe it with the 1st couple doing so. In this case the 1st and 2nd ladies begin by changing places while the men stand still (bars 1, 2; Diagram 10.4), then the 1st and 2nd

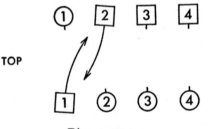

TOP

Diagram 10.4

men change places while the two ladies stand still (bars 3, 4), then the two ladies cross back (bars 5, 6), and then the two men cross back (bars 7, 8). In each crossing the two dancers concerned pass each other with the right shoulders and without giving hands.

With other starting positions the figure is similar, the basic pattern being 'one diagonal pair change places, then the other, then the first pair cross back, then the second'.

Version III. This version is usually begun with one couple facing the other across the set, the men having their partners on their right (Diagram 10.5 (a)). In the first half of the figure (bars 1–4) each couple crosses over to the place of the opposite couple, the lady passing between

238

the opposite man and lady, while the man passes outside the opposite lady (Diagram 10.5 (a)). The lady goes directly to the other lady's place while her partner passes behind her to the man's place, and as they reach the opposite side both turn to the left to face back across the set, keeping more or less shoulder to shoulder so that they wheel into the other couple's place together (the track of the 1st couple in this part of the figure is shown in Diagram 10.5 (b)). This completes the first half of the

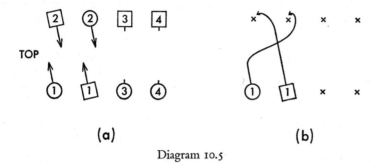

TOP

(a)   (b)

Diagram 10.5

figure, and the second half is a repetition of the first half, taking the two couples back to their starting positions.

Version I is the oldest of these three figures, and is found in Country Dances from at least 1700 onwards. It was becoming obsolete by the beginning of the nineteenth century, and occurs in very few of the Country Dances known to have been performed in Scotland within living memory.

Version II may possibly be derived from a Cotillion figure. As a Country Dance figure it first appears in Matthew Welch's *Variety of English Country Dances ... the figures ... explained* (248; 1767);[1] it is also given, with minor variations, in several early nineteenth-century books. It was fairly common in the Country Dances performed in Scotland within living memory, and in most districts it was the form of 'right and left' used in Circassian Circle.

Version III belongs properly to the Quadrilles, but it found its way into Country Dances about 1850. It is given as a Quadrilles figure by Wallace in his *Excelsior Manual of Dancing* (217; *c.* 1872), and as a Country Dance figure by Orr Robertson (228; *c.* 1900). It was used in particular in the Country Dances Glasgow Highlanders and Queen's Welcome, and in the Square Dance La Russe. In some places it was also used in Circassian Circle.

[1] In Welch's figure, one of the pairs pass with the left shoulders instead of both with the right.

In East Lothian, the usual form of 'right and left' employed in Country Dances was version II, and there this version was universally known as 'cut the figure 8', a somewhat confusing terminology since the same phrase was also used to describe the reel of four in the Scotch (Foursome) Reel. We have also heard the phrase 'cut the figure 8', and also the phrase 'through the Foursome Reel', applied to the form of the 'right and left' (our version I) which occurs in the Angus Country Dance Jacky Tar (6, 54). This apparent confusion between the 'right and left' and the figure of the Foursome Reel may possibly derive from some early form of Reel in which a figure similar to the 'right and left' was used, and it is perhaps significant in this connection that Dr Rhodes has discovered in Cape Breton Island a Reel with a crossing figure similar to version II of the 'right and left' (see Appendix, p. 278).

Ladies' Chain. This is one of the figures which the Country Dance borrowed from the Quadrilles, and its presence in a dance is a sure indication of a nineteenth-century date. It occurs only in dances in quick tempo, and occupies eight bars of music. It is performed by two couples, and is usually begun with one couple facing the other across the set, the men having their partners on their right (for example, 1st and 2nd couples in Diagram 10.6 (a)).

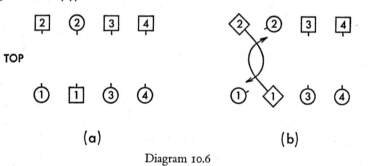

(a)   (b)

Diagram 10.6

To perform the figure, the two ladies give right hands to each other, cross over, and turn the opposite man with the left hand, then cross back, again giving right hands to each other, and turn their own partners with the left hand, finishing in their original places. The correct step for the figure is either the chassé or the hop-one-and-two, and the ladies take two bars to cross over, two bars to turn the opposite man, two bars to cross back, and two bars for the final turn with partners; while the ladies are crossing back to their partners, the men dance more or less on the spot.

When the ladies give right hands to each other in crossing over, they are essentially performing a half turn (Diagram 10.6 (b)), and it is helpful if they give some weight to each other when they take hands.

In the Borders a turn under the arms was frequently incorporated into the turns of the ladies' chain, this being done in one of two ways. In one method (13, 61), each man turns under his own arm while the lady

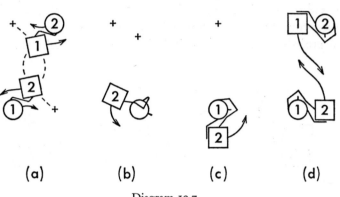

(a)   (b)   (c)   (d)

Diagram 10.7

dances round him; thus when the lady gives her left hand to the opposite man, he immediately makes a quarter turn to his right and passes the lady's hand (held in his left hand) over his head as she dances round him, so that he turns under his own left arm (Diagram 10.7 (a), (b)). As she draws level with him in his new position (Diagram 10.7 (c)), he places his right arm round her waist and helps her round to complete the turn (Diagram 10.7 (d)). She then crosses back (giving right hand as usual to the opposite lady) and turns in the same way with her own partner.

In the second method (13, 28), the man turns the lady under her own arm, while he does not turn at all. When the lady gives him her left

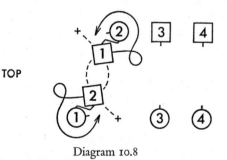

TOP

Diagram 10.8

hand (in his left), he immediately turns her once round to her right under her own left arm. She then dances round behind him, and as she

241

does so he passes her left hand from his left hand to his right behind his back, then he leads her round beside him with her left hand in his right (Diagram 10.8). With this method the man remains facing in the same direction throughout; in a crowded room, he would normally move forward a little to allow the lady to pass behind him, but otherwise need not move from the spot.

In the Borders, neither of these two methods of performing the ladies' chain had any special name, and indeed they appear at first sight to be mere impromptu embellishments. In fact, however, the second method —and probably the first also—is derived from the eighteenth-century

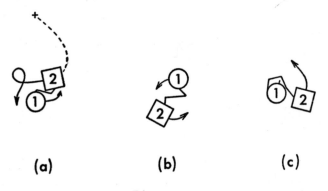

(a)   (b)   (c)

Diagram 10.9

figure 'allemande'. We first realized the origin of these turns when we were shown a 'ladies' chain with allemande' by a dancing-teacher in the north of England, Mr Roland Cowper, third generation of his family to follow the profession of dancing-teacher. In Mr Cowper's figure, which had been passed down in his family, the man steps forward as he takes the lady's left hand in his, and begins to turn to his left to keep looking towards her as he turns her once round to her right under her own left arm (Diagram 10.9 (a)). He then continues turning to his left as she dances round him, so that he is always looking towards her (Diagram 10.9 (b)), and they complete the turn side by side (Diagram 10.9 (c)).

Mr Cowper also told us that the 'allemande' could be used in a similar manner in the figure 'right and left' (Version III above); here the partners take right hands as they reach the opposite side, and the man turns the lady once round to her left under her own right arm while he dances round her in a clockwise direction, so that they finish side by side with the lady on the man's right. Mr Cowper also told us of a further form of 'allemande', a 'slow allemande', occupying four bars of music, in which the partners take right hands and face each other, and the man turns his partner once round to her left under her own right arm. He stands still on the spot, and she takes four slow gliding steps for the turn.

All these various 'allemande' figures are derived ultimately from the Allemande, a dance of German origin. 'Allemande' figures came into the Country Dance about 1767, and probably came via the Cotillion. Welch (248; 1767) gives a diagram to illustrate the Country Dance allemande, and this shows that the figure was performed by two dancers who interlace their arms in some way and make one complete turn round each other, beginning and ending in the same place. Other descriptions given in early nineteenth-century books vary considerably, but all agree that the allemande was a figure performed by one couple who start and finish the figure in the same place. In addition, however, from at least 1805 onwards there were allemande figures involving two or more couples. Thus a collection of Country Dances taught by a dancing-master at Blantyre Farm in 1805 (202) contains, in addition to a simple 'Allaman' and an 'Allaman backward', also an 'Allaman 6', an 'Allaman six round', and an 'Allaman 2 couples', though unfortunately the manuscript gives no description of these figures.

We have been unable to find anyone among our sources in Scotland who can remember a Country Dance figure for two or more couples known as 'allemande', so that we are unable to throw any further light on the subject from information derived from living memory. One elderly man (82) whom we met in Strath Bran in 1956 told us that he had performed a dance called Soldier's Joy incorporating an 'allemande 3 couples' on LochTayside about 1885, but unfortunately he could not remember how the allemande, or even the remainder of the dance, was performed.[1]

Basket figures. There are two of these figures, the swing in a basket of three, and the swing in a basket of four. The swing for four originated in the Quadrilles, and was first introduced into Country Dances about 1850, there giving rise in turn to the swing for three. Both figures occur only in dances in quick tempo, and each occupies eight bars of music.

The swing in a basket of three is performed by a man and two ladies who form a compact ring, all facing inwards, with each person's arms round the others' waists. In this position they swing round to their left with the pivot step, performing three or four complete revolutions in the eight bars.

[1] Two different 'allemandes' for two couples have been published by the R.S.C.D.S. (234), the first having been superseded by the second.

The swing in a basket of four is performed by two couples. The dancers again form a compact ring, facing inwards, with the two men opposite each other, and the men take hold of each other's wrists behind the ladies' backs while the ladies lean against the men's arms and hook their own arms over the men's (Diagram 10.10).[1] In this position the four dancers swing round to their left with the pivot step, again making three or four complete revolutions in the eight bars.

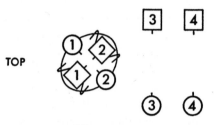

Diagram 10.10

The basket for four can be dangerous if the men lift the ladies off the ground so that the ladies' feet fly outwards, and there is no doubt that there was a good deal of horseplay of this type in the kirns when the Country Dance was declining after the 1914–18 war. However, if the men keep their hands at the level of the ladies' waists, and if the ladies lean well backwards, then the 'basket' can be rotated as fast as the dancers please without the ladies' feet leaving the ground.

The basket figures for three and four were particularly popular in East Lothian, and there they were known as 'swing three' and 'swing four'.

Descriptions of the Dances

In the descriptions of the dances which follow, we describe only the basic sequence of figures performed by the 1st couple dancing with the 2nd or 2nd and 3rd couples.

DUKE OF PERTH (BROWN'S REEL)
PEASE STRAE
KEEP THE COUNTRY, BONNY LASSIE

We remarked at the beginning of this chapter that in the eighteenth and early nineteenth centuries a Country Dance consisted of a tune and a particular set of figures performed to that tune, and the name of the

[1] Alternatively (but less preferably), the ladies can rest their hands on the men's shoulders.

dance was that of the tune. Often the same tune was used with two or more different sets of figures, and these counted as different dances; often, too, the same figures occurred set to different tunes, and these again counted as different dances. The dances which we are considering here come into this latter category, since all have the same figures, but each uses the tune of the appropriate title.

Of the three dances, Duke of Perth or Brown's Reel was the most widely known, and was very popular throughout Angus, Perthshire, and East Fife. Within living memory the name Brown's Reel has been simply an alternative name for the dance, and either under this title or as Duke of Perth the dance was always performed to the tune 'Duke of Perth'.[1] On the other hand, it seems likely that Brown's Reel was once a distinct dance on its own, with the same figures as Duke of Perth but having a tune of its own entitled 'Brown's Reel', and the missing tune may well be the 'Brown's Reel' which appears in a manuscript collection of music written by Peter Hardie, a fiddler of Tullymet who was born about 1775 (225). It is possible also that the 'Brown' who figures in the title was one of the Browns of Kincardine in Strathspey, a noted family of fiddlers who are credited with being the originators of strathspeys (252).

Duke of Perth or Brown's Reel was included in the repertoires of all the dancing-teachers whom we know to have practised in Angus, Perthshire, and East Fife, and it was also taught by several teachers who held classes in Inverness-shire and Argyllshire.

Pease Strae was confined to the South-west, to Lanarkshire, Ayrshire, Arran, and Galloway. It was particularly popular in Lanarkshire and Ayrshire, and was included in the repertoires of all the dancing-teachers in these two counties.

Keep the Country, Bonny Lassie was the most uncommon of the three dances, and we have met it only in the upper parts of Ettrick, where it was included in the repertoire of James Laidlaw.

The following figures are those of Duke of Perth or Brown's Reel as taught by various teachers in Angus, Perthshire, and East Fife, including, for example, James Neill, 'Dancie' Reid, David Anderson, and Mr William Adamson and his father Alexander Adamson. They are also the figures of Pease Strae as taught by Professor Blackley of Lanark and Joseph Wallace junior of Kilmarnock, and are also the figures, except for some doubt in the last figure, of Keep the Country, Bonny Lassie as taught by James Laidlaw.

[1] The tune 'Duke of Perth' is properly a reel, but for this dance it is always played at half speed, so that it has the rhythm of a Scotch measure.

Music Bars	*Description of the Figures*
1–8	The 1st couple turn with linked right arms and cast off one place (i.e. the 1st man passes down behind the 2nd man while the 1st lady passes down behind the 2nd lady), then meet in the centre below 2nd couple, and turn with linked left arms.
9–16	Coming straight from this turn, the 1st man now turns the 3rd lady with linked right arms whilst the 1st lady turns the 2nd man in the same way (bars 9, 10), then the 1st couple turn each other for three-quarters of a turn with linked left arms (bars 11, 12), then the 1st man turns the 2nd lady and the 1st lady turns the 3rd man, each with right arms linked (bars 13, 14). The 1st couple then turn each other with linked left arms, either for a quarter turn or for one and a quarter turns, to finish back to back in the centre, the 1st man facing 3rd lady, the 1st lady facing 2nd man (bars 15, 16).
17–20	The 1st man and lady set to 3rd lady and 2nd man, respectively (bars 17, 18), and turn them with linked right arms, finishing back to back in the centre, the 1st man facing 2nd lady, the 1st lady facing 3rd man (bars 19, 20).
21–24	The 1st man and lady set to 2nd lady and 3rd man, respectively (bars 21, 22), and turn them with linked right arms (bars 23, 24).
25–32	The 1st man now dances a reel of three with 2nd and 3rd ladies, beginning the reel by giving left shoulders to 3rd lady, while at the same time the 1st lady dances a reel of three with 2nd and 3rd men, beginning the reel by giving left shoulders to 2nd man. The 1st couple end the reels in 2nd place improper, then meet in the centre and link right arms to begin the first turn of the repetition of the sequence.

The travelling step used for Duke of Perth or Brown's Reel in Perthshire, Angus, and East Fife, and for Keep the Country, Bonnie Lassie in Ettrick, was usually the chassé, and for Pease Strae in the South-west it was usually the hop-one-and-two. In all three dances the setting was invariably performed with pas de Basque. Teachers seem to have differed in their opinions concerning the 'quarter turn or one and a quarter turns' in bars 15, 16; for example, James Neill, 'Dancie' Reid, and Mr Adamson taught the quarter turn here, while David Anderson and Professor Blackley taught the one and a quarter turns. The use of linked arms for all the turns, however, was universal.

The figures in bars 9–16 and 17–24 appear in the early printed collections of Country Dances under the names 'swing corners' and 'set and turn corners' respectively. If the 1st couple is dancing with the 2nd and 3rd couples, the 1st man's *first corner* is the 3rd lady, and his *second corner* is the 2nd lady, while the 1st lady's *first corner* is the 2nd man, and her *second corner* is the 3rd man (so that the two first corners, and similarly the two second corners, are diagonally opposite to each other). Thus 'swing corners' is simply 'turn first corner, then partner, then second corner, then partner', while 'set and turn corners' is 'set to and turn first corners, then set to and turn second corners'.[1] The term 'set and turn corners' was still in common use within living memory, but we have not heard the term 'swing corners' used by any of our informants.

The earliest of the three dances to appear in print is Keep the Country, Bonny Lassie, which was first published in Boag's *Collection of Favourite Reels and Strathspeys* (253; c. 1797). The version given by Boag differs in the last figure from the version above, and hands are used for the turns instead of linked arms:

'First Cu Swing the Right hand and cast off one Cu: Swing the Left hand round Swing the Corners and your Partner each time Set Corners and turn lead outsides.'

The next printed description of the figures is in *The Ballroom* (210), a ballroom guide published in 1827 by Monsieur J. P. Boulogne, a French teacher of dancing who practised in Glasgow. Boulogne gives two titles for the dance, Duke of Perth and Keep the Country, Bonny Lassie, and his description of the figures is as follows.

'1. The first couple turn by the right hand and pass one couple, they turn left hands, the lady turns the second gentleman, and the gentleman the third lady; the first couple turn again with the left hand, the gentleman the second lady, and the lady the third gentleman, they turn half round.   16 [Bars]
'2. Set at the corners and turn,   8 [Bars]
'3. The reel of three.   8 [Bars].'

This version, under the same two titles, is reprinted in a late edition of the Lowes' ballroom guide (212; c. 1860), and it also appears, under the

[1] We should add that the method of performing the turns in 'set and turn corners' with linked arms was not in general used in other dances in which the figure occurred.

single title Duke of Perth, in the ballroom guides of Willock (213; 1865), Allan (214–16; *c.* 1870–90), and Wallace (217–19; *c.* 1872–1900). The same instructions are also repeated by David Anderson (220–3; *c.* 1886–1902), but he gives them under the alternative names Duke of Perth and Brown's Reel. In all these descriptions the turns in bars 1–16 are made with a hand-hold and the final turn of the swing corners in bars 15, 16 is only 'half round', i.e. a quarter turn; it is not until 1897, in J. N. MacLeod's *Pocket Companion to the Ball-Room* (225; 1897), that we find a printed description which gives the arm hold and the one and a quarter turns. On the other hand, there is an early description of Duke of Perth in the manuscript collection of dances taught at Blantyre Farm in 1805 (202), and this gives the longer turn, nearly a hundred years before its first appearance in print:

'Hook right hand with partner—turn round—throw off a couple. Hook with partner with left turn round downmost Ladies with right partner with left upmost Lady with right partner with left twice round. Sett cross pr reels.'[1]

The sequence 'set and turn corners and reels of three with corners' which forms the last half of Duke of Perth is undoubtedly a Scottish contribution to the Country Dance, and it occurs in a high proportion of the Country Dances performed in Scotland during the eighteenth century. After 1800 the sequence tended to fall out of use, but a few dances containing it remained very popular until 1914 and even later. However, in spite of this continuing popularity, no *new* dance containing this sequence was published after 1835, so that not only is the presence of this sequence in a dance an indication that the dance is Scottish, but it is also an indication that the dance was composed before 1835.

JACKY TAR

Three different Country Dances of this name were performed in Scotland within living memory, one in Angus, one in Perthshire, and one in East Lothian. We give here the Angus dance, which is the most interesting of the three (6, 54). It illustrates the use of material from the

---

[1] It is interesting to compare this manuscript description with one which we took down from Mr Peter Crerar of Ballachraggan, Strath Bran (82): 'Cleek pairtners, cleek corners, cleek pairtners twice round, set corners and reel of three.'

Mr Crerar was M.C. at dances at Amulree for thirty years or more, and he used to call out this description at the beginning of Duke of Perth to remind the dancers of the figures. He himself learnt the dance from a teacher called MacPherson on Loch Tayside about 1885.

Quadrilles in Country Dances, for it contains a four-bar set, and a four-bar turn performed with ballroom hold and the pivot step, which are derived from the 'set and turn' used in the Quadrilles. On the other hand, the remaining figures of the dance, version I of the 'right and left' and 'hands across', are two of the oldest Country Dance figures.

The Angus Jacky Tar, like the other two dances of this name, is performed to the well-known tune 'Jacky Tar'. The dancers form up as usual for a Country Dance, and just before the music starts the 1st man and lady exchange places.

Music Bars	*Description of the Figures*
1–8	The 1st and 2nd couples dance version I of the right and left *down* the set, i.e. 1st man begins by giving right hand to 2nd lady, and 1st lady the same to 2nd man. The 1st man and lady end in each other's place, and the 1st man joins right hands with 2nd lady, the 1st lady does the same with 2nd man, and all face partners across the set (Diagram 10.11).

TOP

Diagram 10.11

9–12	In this position, 1st and 2nd couples set to partners with four pas de Basque.
13–16	1st and 2nd couples swing partners with ballroom hold and the pivot step, ending with the 1st couple improper.
17–24	1st and 2nd couples dance 'four hands across and back', i.e. they all give right hands across to the diagonally opposite person ('shaking hands' grasp) and dance round clockwise (bars 17–20), then turn about to the right, take left hands, and return to places, the 1st couple still improper, the 2nd couple on their own sides.
25–28	The 1st and 2nd couples join right hands with partners and set with four pas de Basque, the 1st couple facing down and the 2nd couple facing up.

29–32   1st man and 2nd lady, and similarly 1st lady and 2nd man, swing with ballroom hold and the pivot step. The 2nd couple finish in 1st place, while the 1st couple finish in 2nd place improper, facing the 3rd couple.

The usual progression then continues, and at the bottom the 1st couple cross to their own sides. The normal travelling step for the 'right and left' and 'four hands across' was the chassé.

This version of Jacky Tar was common throughout Angus up to about 1910. It was taught by James Neill of Forfar, and it was known also to 'Dancie' Reid of Newtyle, though the latter did not teach it much. It was also taught by William Robertson in the Brechin district, and the following description of it was published by him in his little ballroom guide *The Pupils' Aid to the Memory and Guide to the Ball-room Dances* (231; *c*. 1905).

'When standing the same as for a contra dance the first lady and gentleman change places, then the first and second couples, commencing with opposite partners, give right and left hands round to places. Take hold of opposite partner's hand, balance, then turn own partner. Right hand across, eight steps round, give left hand across, and eight steps back. Balance with your own partner, then turn opposite one.'

Here the 'balance' step may have been either the pas de Basque or a step similar to Mr Adamson's 'set and turn step' described on p. 234.

This is the only printed description of the dance known to us other than that in the R.S.C.D.S. *Country Dance Books*, where the dance is renamed Come Ashore Jolly Tar.[1]

THE RIFLEMAN

This dance was restricted to the Border counties, where it was still in regular use as late as 1926. It was taught by Professor Buck at all his classes in the Borders, and was also taught by James Laidlaw in Ettrick and by Andrew Cochrane in the Gordon district. In this dance the influence of the Quadrilles is very strong indeed, for the dance incorporates the whole of the first figure of the First Set of Quadrilles.

The dance is in quick tempo, and is performed either to the tune of the same name (see *The Border Dance Book* (235–6)), or to 'The White Cockade', the description being as follows (13, 28, 61, 63).

---

[1] The tune normally used in Angus for Jacky Tar consists of only the second and third parts of the tune given in the *Country Dance Books*.

Music Bars   *Description of the Figures*

1–8   The 1st couple cross over, passing with right shoulders and without giving hands, and dance down behind the opposite lines. They return to the top, still behind the opposite lines, take arms with the second person on that side, and make a quarter turn into the centre (Diagram 10.12 (a)). All four finish facing down the set, arm in arm (Diagram 10.12 (b)).

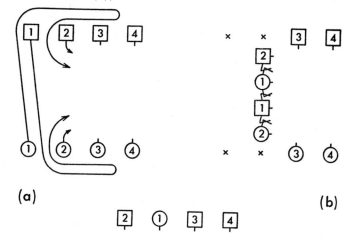

(a)   (b)

(c)

Diagram 10.12

9–16   All four go down the centre arm in arm (bars 9–12), then release arms and turn about (the 1st man and 2nd lady turning towards each other, the other pair the same), then take arms again and lead up the centre. As the line of four approaches the top, the 2nd man and lady come into the centre in advance of the 1st couple, and all finish in the positions shown in Diagram 10.12 (c).

Now follows 'first figure of Quadrilles', i.e.

17–24   The 1st and 2nd couples dance 'right and left', version II, ending in the positions shown in Diagram 10.12 (c).

25–28   The 1st and 2nd couples set on the sides, the 1st man setting to 2nd lady, the 1st lady to 2nd man.

29–32   The 1st man and 2nd lady, and the 1st lady and 2nd man, swing with ballroom hold and the pivot step, ending as in Diagram 10.12 (c).

33–40   The 1st and 2nd couples dance 'ladies' chain' across the set, the ladies crossing over to turn their own partners first, and then the other man.

41–48   1st and 2nd couples either pousette right round so that the 1st couple ends in 2nd place, or 'birl it off', i.e. swing on the spot with ballroom hold and the pivot step.

Both of the allemande-type turns described on p. 241 were frequently inserted into the 'ladies' chain' in this dance. The travelling step used in bars 1–24 and 33–40 was usually either the chassé or the hop-one-and two; the former was used by all three of the Border teachers mentioned above.

So far as we know, the full form of this dance does not appear in any printed or manuscript source. An abbreviated form is given in *The Border Dance Book* (235–6).

QUADRILLE COUNTRY DANCE

We have met this dance in the Kilmarnock district of Ayrshire, where it was taught by Joseph Wallace junior, and in East Fife, where it was taught by Mr William Adamson and his father. It again shows the influence of Quadrilles, for it contains both the 'ladies' chain' and the Quadrilles 'set and turn'.

We give below the version of the dance taught by Mr Adamson, which uses the 'set and turn step' described on p. 234. It is performed to 'The Girl I Left Behind Me' or any similar tune.

Music Bars   *Description of the Figures*

1–8   The 1st man leads the 2nd lady down the centre and back, with right hands joined. As they return up the centre, the 2nd man moves into top place, and the dancing pair cross over to finish in the positions shown in Diagram 10.13, facing their partners.

9–12   1st and 2nd couples set to partners with the 'set and turn step'.

13–16   1st and 2nd couples swing partners with ballroom hold and

the pivot step, ending in the positions shown in Diagram
10.13, but facing across the set.

17–24   1st and 2nd couples dance 'ladies' chain'. As the four
dancers complete the last turn with their partners, they
take ballroom hold and

25–32   pousette, 1st couple ending in 2nd place.

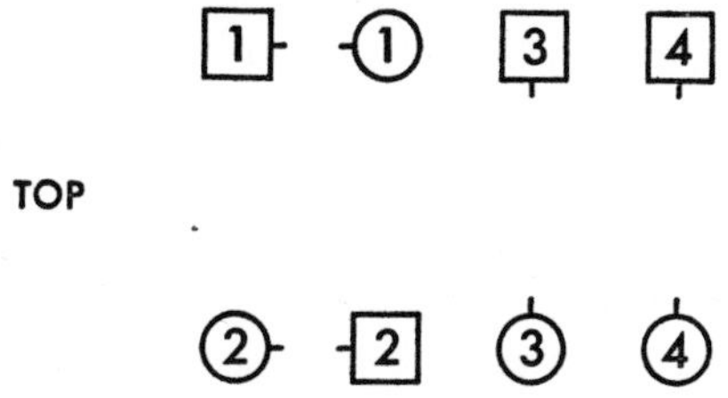

TOP

Diagram 10.13

The travelling step used by Mr Adamson in bars 1–8 and 17–24 was the
chassé. He also frequently taught the dance with a reel of four in place of
the 'ladies' chain', the reel being begun from the side-by-side position
(p. 145).

The Quadrille Country Dance was first published in a late edition of
the Lowes' ballroom guide (212; *c.* 1860), the description given there
being as follows.

'First gentleman takes the second lady down the centre and up, leaving
her beside her partner, while he joins his own. Two top couples set and
turn partners. Ladies chain across. Top couples pousette.'

The dance was also reprinted in the ballroom guides of Wallace (217–
219; *c.* 1872–1900) and Anderson (220–3; *c.* 1886–1902). All the printed
descriptions agree with Mr Adamson's version, but, as in the case of the
Lowes' description, give no details.

ROYAL ALBERT

As its name implies, this is a nineteenth-century dance, and it shows very
strongly the influence of the nineteenth-century ballroom on Country
Dances. It was taught by Mr William Adamson and his father in East
Fife, by Mr Maxwell in East Lothian, and by Joseph Wallace junior in
Kilmarnock; it was particularly popular in East Lothian, where it was
performed up to about 1920 or even later, and it was also performed
regularly at the Marine Gardens at Portobello on the outskirts of
Edinburgh about 1910–14.

We give first the version of the dance taught by Mr Adamson and his father in East Fife. This is performed to any good 6/8 jig, the instructions being as follows.

Music Bars	*Description of the Figures*
1–8	The 1st man and 1st and 2nd ladies swing in a basket of three.
9–16	All three go down the centre arm in arm, the 1st man in the middle with his partner on his left. They release arms at the bottom, turn about (the ladies turning towards the man, the man turning to his left), take arms again, and lead up to the positions shown in Diagram 10.13, the 2nd man moving to top place as they come up the centre.
17–40	1st and 2nd couples set to and turn partners and then dance a 'ladies' chain' and pousette, exactly as in bars 9–32 of the Quadrille Country Dance (using the 'set and turn step' for setting to partners).

The travelling step used by Mr Adamson in bars 9–16 and 25–32 was the chassé.

In East Lothian there were three or more different versions of this dance in use, the furthest from Mr Adamson's version being the following, which comes from the Gullane district (76, 78–79). Here the favourite tunes were 'The Rose Tree', 'The Bottom of the Punchbowl', and 'The Lass of Patie's Mill' (79).

Music Bars	*Description of the Figures*
1–8	The 1st man and 1st and 2nd ladies swing in a basket of three.
9–16	All three go down the centre arm in arm, the 1st man in the middle with his partner on his left. Without releasing arms, they return up the centre *backwards*, and when they reach the top (still facing down the set) the 2nd man comes into the centre to face them.
17–24	The 1st and 2nd couples dance either a 'right and left', version II, or a 'ladies' chain', in the latter case using ballroom hold and the pivot step for the turns.
25–32	1st and 2nd couples swing in a basket of four ('swing four'), each man having his partner on his left. At the conclusion of this basket, the 2nd couple finish in 1st place, while the 1st man retains his left arm round his partner's waist and swings her round to the right to pick up the 3rd lady for the repeat of the sequence.

In this version the travelling figures were performed with any of the appropriate quick travelling steps.

So far as we know, Royal Albert does not appear in any printed collection, and the only description of the dance known to us is in a manuscript notebook of dances written about 1867 by a dancing-master in Dundalk in Ireland for one of his pupils, Miss Kate Hughes (272):

'Top gent swing the two top ladies (8 [bars]); arm in arm down the centre and up (8); set and turn partners (8); right and lefts (8); set and turn partners (8); ladies chain (8): pousette.'

All the Scottish versions of this dance are simply shortened forms of this manuscript version, with in some cases 'swing four' in place of the pousette. It seems likely that this version in Miss Hughes's notebook is close to the original, and its abnormal length no doubt contributed to the diversity of the various versions which survived within living memory, for presumably different dancing-teachers, in shortening the dance to a more normal length, omitted different figures.

It will have been observed that in the two dances given in this chapter in which the dancers go down the centre and back in a line of three or four, the dancers link arms, in contrast to the current practice, where the dancers take hands. Within living memory the use of linked arms in this figure—for example, in the two dances given here and in such dances as Meg Merrilees, Glasgow Highlanders, and Queen Victoria—was universal, and an examination of the nineteenth-century Scottish ballroom guides shows that the use of linked arms here has been the standard practice in Scotland since about 1830. Before 1830, the figure 'down the centre and back in a line of three or four' was not particularly common, but where it occurred it seems to have been performed with a hand-hold. The change from the hand-hold to the linked arms in this figure, which took place between 1818 and 1830, is symptomatic of the trend away from the extreme formality of the eighteenth-century ballroom, for the proffered arm belongs to the modern world, while the offered hand belongs to the age of courtly dancing.

MERRY LADS OF GLASGOW

The Merry Lads of Glasgow was one of the dances taught about 1900–1910 by the East Lothian teacher Mr Maxwell. It was performed at the East Lothian kirns until about 1930, and in one or two places it survived almost up to the Second World War. It is in quick tempo, and was invariably performed to the tune 'Buffalo Girls', which was known in East Lothian as the tune of a bothy ballad entitled 'Whar'll bonny Annie lie'. So far as we know the dance does not appear in any printed source.

The following description comes from the districts of Pencaitland (17), Haddington (42), Gullane (78), and Dirleton (79).

Music Bars	Description of the Figures
1–8	The 1st couple 'swing in the centre', i.e. they take ballroom hold and swing with the pivot step.
9–16	The 1st couple take right hands and dance down the centre. The 2nd couple follow them down, also with right hands joined, and form an arch at the bottom. The 1st couple, still with right hands joined, dance underneath the arch and up to the top, where they cross over to end in 1st place improper, while the 2nd couple return to their own places.
17–24	The 1st and 2nd couples dance 'right and left', version II, the ladies crossing first.
25–32	The 1st and 2nd couples swing in a basket of four ('swing four'), each man having his partner on his right. The 1st couple finish in 2nd place and the man retains his right arm round his partner's waist and continues to swing her as in bars 1–8, while the 2nd couple cross to their own sides and finish in 1st place.

The 'down the centre and back' was performed either with the chassé or with the galop step, the dancers facing partners in the latter case.

In Pencaitland this dance was normally performed with only three couples in a set, because 'it was an awfu' heavy dance'.

THE HAUGHS O' CROMDALE

This is one of the relatively small group of Country Dances which are in strathspey tempo. It provides a further illustration of the use in the Country Dance of figures derived from other dance-forms, for it incorporates the movements of the Circle Dance the Highland Schottische. This fact also enables us to date the dance with reasonable accuracy, for it must have been composed after the introduction of the Highland Schottische, i.e. after about 1855.

The Haughs o' Cromdale was popular in the Dalbeattie district of Kirkcudbrightshire before 1914, and the following description was given to us by the late Miss Margaret Paterson of Auchencairn, who both performed and played for the dance in her younger days. In the Dalbeattie district the dance was always performed to a schottische such as 'Kafoozalum', 'Orange and Blue', or 'Wha's a' the steer, kimmer', played at a brisk tempo of about 42 bars per minute (52). A version of the dance has been published in the R.S.C.D.S. *Country Dance Books*, and so far as we know this is the only occurrence of the dance in any printed source.

Music Bars	Description of the Figures
1, 2	The 1st man and 2nd lady give right hands to each other and dance round in a clockwise direction, making a half turn.
3–8	The 1st man and 2nd lady retain right hands, and the 1st lady and 2nd man join in to form 'four hands across', giving right hands to each other. All four dancers dance round in a clockwise direction for two bars (bars 3, 4), then turn about (to the right), take left hands, and return to the places shown in Diagram 10.14 (a) (bars 5–8).
9–16	The 1st and 2nd couples take ordinary ballroom hold and dance the Highland Schottische round each other in a counter-clockwise direction (Diagram 10.14 (b)), ending with the 1st couple in 2nd place.

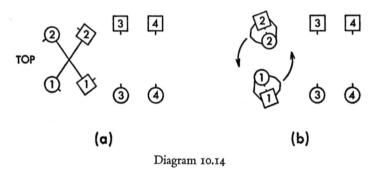

(a) (b)

Diagram 10.14

The Highland Schottische used in bars 9–16 was one of the standard forms of the dance, the men's steps being:

Bars 9–12	Highland Schottische step with LF, RF.
Bar 13, Count 1	Step to the side on LF.
Count 2	Hop on LF and raise RF to rear leg position.
Counts 3, 4	Perform counts '1, 2' contrariwise.
Bars 14–16	Repeat bar 13 three times.

The ladies' steps were the same movements performed contrariwise. In bars 9–12 the Highland Schottische steps were performed more or less in the line of the dance, and in bars 13–16 the two couples danced round each other, each couple at the same time rotating on its own axis in a clockwise direction.

For the 'hands across' in bars 1–8 the Lowland Strathspey travelling step A (p. 93) was used.

It is perhaps not generally recognized that, among the Country Dances which survived in Scotland within living memory, dances in strathspey tempo are relatively uncommon. Of the ninety or so Country Dances which have been collected in Scotland from living memory, only fifteen are partly or wholly in strathspey tempo, namely Glasgow Highlanders, The Perth Medley from the Perth Hunt Balls, The Haughs o' Cromdale above, The Braes of Tulliemet from Selkirkshire, Bonnie Briest Knots, Duchess of Gordon, The Shepherd's Crook, and Loch Erichtside from Roxburghshire and West Berwickshire, The Jimp Waist, The Braes of Busby, The Duchess of Atholl's Slipper, Dalkeith's Strathspey, and Earl of Home from unspecified parts of the Borders, Orange and Blue from East Lothian, and Peggy's Love from Morayshire.[1]

The dance Glasgow Highlanders should strictly be excluded here, for it is essentially a combination of a Country Dance with the Foursome Reel, and originally only the Foursome Reel part of the dance was performed in strathspey tempo. The Perth Medley is also only partly in strathspey tempo, and we exclude it too from further consideration. This leaves only thirteen Country Dances wholly in strathspey tempo, out of a total of approximately ninety dances.

These thirteen dances in strathspey tempo have the common feature that within living memory they were performed only in very restricted parts of the country. Moreover, within living memory most of them survived only at the kirns and country weddings in these districts, and were not performed in the polite ballrooms. Indeed, from the evidence

[1] We have excluded here two dances, Glasgow Flourish and The Lovers' Knot, which are given in the R.S.C.D.S. *Country Dance Books* as in strathspey tempo. Glasgow Flourish (properly 'Let Glasgow Flourish', the motto of the City of Glasgow) is a doubtful case, for it is listed in David Anderson's ballroom guides (220–3) as in 'hornpipe time'. The Lovers' Knot is also a very doubtful case; the figures of this dance were collected by the late I. C. B. Jamieson from an old shepherd who had danced it in Ettrick in his youth, and according to Jamieson's informant the dance could be performed to either a reel or a strathspey (288). It seems likely, however, that the proper tune for the dance was a reel, for we have been told by a niece of the Ettrick teacher James Laidlaw that Mr Laidlaw taught the dance to a reel tune (28).

available from living memory Country Dances in strathspey tempo appear to have been rare in the nineteenth-century ballroom, and this impression is substantiated by an examination of the printed collections of Country Dances published in Scotland between 1800 and 1914, for among the 200 or so dances in these collections only two are definitely in strathspey tempo,[1] namely Madge Wildfire's Strathspey and Jeanie Dean's Strathspey, both in Sutherland's collection of 1820 (207).[2] It seems likely, therefore, that the Country Dance in strathspey tempo is a dance-form which belongs principally to the late eighteenth century rather than to the nineteenth century.

[1] We have again excluded Glasgow Highlanders, which is in the ballroom guides of Anderson (220–3), Mozart Allan (216) and Orr Robertson (228).

[2] In addition there are two doubtful cases—the reason for the uncertainty here lies in the absence of music in the pocket ballroom guides.

CHAPTER XI

The Art of Treepling

THE art of 'treepling' in social dances—the art of beating out the rhythm of the music with the feet—is one of the lesser-known features of Scottish dancing that has now almost entirely disappeared. So far as we know, treepling steps were performed by men only, and were usually confined to Country Dances, though they were also occasionally used in Reels.

The art survived longest in East Lothian, where it was still practised at the farm kirns as late as 1914—one of our informants, a lady in the Gullane district, recalled being at a number of dances in stone-floored barns 'with the men's tacketty boots rattling away' (78). Another of our East Lothian informants (45) told us that her father, a fiddler and spare-time dancing-teacher, who died in 1908 at the age of 67, was an expert at 'treepling' in Country Dances, and since he presumably learnt this art in his younger days, it would seem that the custom of treepling in Country Dances goes back in East Lothian to at least 1860.

Treepling was also performed in Roxburghshire and West Berwickshire. In Roxburghshire Mr George Young told us that his father, who died in 1938 at the age of 76, was able to treeple, and that around Jedburgh treepling was not uncommon among people of his father's generation. His father could even 'treeple it' in the Country Dance figure pousette (61). In West Berwickshire, Andrew Cochrane of West Gordon used to give 'a course of treepling' to particularly able pupils. Andrew Cochrane himself performed treepling steps only in exhibition step-dances, but his pupils frequently inserted them in Country Dances, and also in the Hullachan Jig (23).

Although treepling seems to have been relatively uncommon within living memory, there are some indications that it was quite prevalent among country people in the period preceding that covered by living memory. We may mention here in particular a passage from the Lowes' *Ball-Conductor* (211; *c.* 1830) where the writers remark that '. . . there is more of a Gentleman's breeding observed in conducting his partner down a [Country] dance . . . than some seem to be aware of, and it would be well if some Gentlemen would give a little more attention to their partner's mode of stepping, and not drag them along as if by force, whilst they themselves are *capering, rattling, or shuffling*[1] their feet in the rudest manner. Such barbarism must be disgusting to every person accustomed to more cultivated conduct, and cannot please any but such as are equally rude with those who are guilty of it'. From this passage we may reasonably infer that 'capering, rattling, or shuffling' was by no means uncommon among the 'ruder' or less 'cultivated' sections of the community, and 'rattling, or shuffling' is a fairly accurate description of treepling.

The finest exponent of treepling whom we have met is Mr Andrew Grierson, son of the East Lothian fiddler and dancing-master mentioned above (77). Mr Grierson had both setting and travelling steps, and he could, for instance, treeple throughout the 'diamond' figure of Petronella. He could also use his travelling steps for such figures as the 'down the centre and back' in Petronella and the 'chasing' figure in Flowers of Edinburgh.

Mr Grierson's steps are based on the movement known to step-dancers as the 'treble' (see, for example, 220–3). This treble movement is performed in Common time and occupies either the counts 'an & a 1' or the counts 'an & a 2', the system of counting here being that used in Chapter IX, i.e.

an & a   1 an & a 2 an & a

Performed with the RF, the treble is as follows.

Counts an &   Make a double beat with the ball of the RF in semi 4th position.

Count a   Bring RF back to 5th position and momentarily transfer the weight to it.

Count 1   (or '2', according to the position of the treble in relation to the music). Beat with the ball of the LF in rear 5th position, transferring the weight to it on the beat.

The double beat here is made with a forward and backward movement, the ground being struck with the ball of the foot. On the forward stroke (on the count 'an'), the foot remains roughly parallel to the

---

[1] The italics are in the original.

ground throughout the movement, and essentially is just bounced off the ground in a forward direction (Diagram 11.1 (a)); the second beat is then made by pulling the foot backward and at the same time pulling the toe down so that the ball of the foot strikes the ground (Diagram 11.1 (b)). After the second beat (which takes place exactly on the count '&'), the foot continues to move back towards 5th position in preparation for the third beat of the treble on the count 'a'.

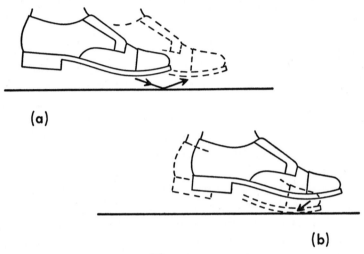

(a)

(b)

Diagram 11.1

For setting, and for the 'diamond' figure of Petronella,[1] Mr Grierson used a step which he termed a 'double' (actually a form of 'double treble'; see, for example, 220–3); this begins on a preliminary count '&', and, starting with the RF, is as follows.

[1] The 'diamond' figure of Petronella is performed by 1st couple dancing from their own places, and is usually performed with the pas de Basque. The two dancers turn into the centre, making three-quarters of a turn to their right so that they face each other up and down the set, the man being below his partner (bars 1, 2); they then set to each other in these positions (bars 3, 4), then turn to each other's place, again making three-quarters of a turn to their right (bars 5, 6), and again set to each other (bars 7, 8). The 1st couple are now improper, and they return to their own places by continuing the alternate turning and setting (bars 9–16), so that in the complete figure each traces out the pattern of a diamond. This 'diamond' figure forms the first 16 bars of Petronella, the remaining figures being 'lst couple down the centre and back (bars 17–24), and 1st and 2nd couples pousette (bars 25–32)'.

The dance Petronella seems to have enjoyed remarkable popularity throughout the last three-quarters of the nineteenth century, for it appears in every ballroom guide published in Scotland from 1823 to 1914 (e.g. 209–25, 228–33), and it was also included in the repertoire of all the dancing-teachers whom we know to have practised in Scotland within living memory.

&	Bring the RF in from 4th low aerial position towards 1st position, making a beat on the ground with the ball of the RF as it passes through semi 4th position.
1. 1	Step on RF in 1st position and transfer weight to it.
an & a 2	Treble with LF.
an & a **2.** 1 }	Treble with LF.
an & a 2	Treble with LF.

Here the beat on the preliminary count '&' is made in exactly the same manner as the backward beat in the treble. Mr Grierson also used a modified form of this step, which we shall call a 'modified double', in which the single beat on the preliminary count '&' is replaced by a double beat, made as in the treble, on preliminary counts '& a'.

The treepling movements used by Mr Grierson for the 'diamond' figure of Petronella are then as follows (to simplify the writing of our description here we treat the final counts '& a' of bars 2, 4, 6, etc., as preliminary counts preceding bars 3, 5, 7, etc.).

& **1, 2**	Perform the double with the RF, moving to the first point of the diamond, making three-quarters of a turn to the right.
& a **3, 4**	Perform the modified double with the LF in the centre of the set, facing partner.
& a **5, 6**	Perform the modified double with the RF, turning into partner's place.
& a **7, 8**	Set to partner, using the modified double with the LF, etc.

Note that there is no movement on the second count 'an' in each of bars 2, 4, 6, etc.

Mr Grierson had two travelling steps, rather similar in form.

Step A

& **1.** 1 an & a 2 }	As in the 'double', *starting with the LF.*
&	Spring on to RF in semi 4th position, raising the LF to a low loose rear leg position.
2. 1	Drop on LF in rear 5th position, and at the same time raise RF to a low 5th aerial position.
an & a 2	Treble with RF.

263

&—   Repeat the spring, drop, and treble (always with the same foot) as often as desired.

Here the main forward movement occurs on the springs, but some forward movement may also be made in the trebles.

Step B

1. &
   1 an & a 2 } As in the 'double', *starting with the LF.*

   an   Beat with the ball of the RF slightly in front of 5th position.

   &   Beat with the ball of the LF in rear 5th position.

   a   Beat with the ball of the RF slightly in front of 5th position.

2. 1   Beat with the ball of the LF in rear 5th position.

   an & a 2   Treble with RF.

   an—   Repeat the four alternate beats and treble (always on the same feet) as often as desired.

Here the main forward movement occurs on the four alternate beats.

Although the term 'treepling' is presumably derived from the name of the treble movement described above,[1] some of the treepling steps used within living memory do not contain the treble movement. For example, the principal treepling step taught by Andrew Cochrane of West Gordon does not employ the treble, but instead makes use of the movement known to step-dancers as the 'flatter' (see, for example, 220–3). This flatter movement, as taught by Andrew Cochrane, is performed to a double jig, and occupies either the counts '1 and a' or the counts '2 and a', the system of counting here being that shown below.

1 and a   2 and a

Performed with the RF, the flatter is as follows.

Count 1   (or '2', according to the position of the flatter in relation to the music). With a small spring, spring on to the LF in 1st position, landing with a heavy beat on the ball of the foot.

[1] Cf. the description of a country dancing school *c.* 1824 given by MacTaggart (p. 28), where a step, to 'trible Bob Major', is mentioned.

Counts and a   Make a double beat with the ball of the RF in semi 4th position, the beats being made with a forward and backward action as in the treble.

The flatter movement was usually performed either with alternate feet, or twice with one foot, then twice with the other, and so on (22, 23).[1] In the Hullachan Jig, for example (see p. 148), the flatter was often performed with alternate feet throughout the 8-bar setting period (23).

Another treepling step not containing the treble was shown to us by Mr David Kirkcaldy of Gullane (78), who learnt it from other dancers in the Dunbar district of East Lothian about 1908. Mr Kirkcaldy's step was used for setting in Country Dances in place of the pas de Basque, and was performed to any tune with a quaver motion, such as a reel or a double jig. When performed to a double jig, it occupies one bar of music; it begins with the feet together, more or less parallel to each other, and (with the system of counting given above) is as follows.

Count 1   Step on the spot on the ball of the LF and transfer the weight to this foot.
Count and   Step on the spot on the ball of the RF and transfer the weight to this foot.
Count a   Step on the spot on the ball of the LF and transfer the weight to this foot.
Count 2   With the weight still on the LF, beat with the R heel on the spot.
Count and   Step on the spot on the ball of the RF and transfer the weight to this foot.
Count a   With the weight still on the RF, beat with the L heel on the spot.

Throughout the step, the feet are kept close to the ground, and move as little as possible from their original positions. Each heel-beat is made simply by flicking the toe up and the heel down, and the step which follows a heel-beat is made simply by flicking the toe down again. The six movements of the step can be repeated as often as desired (the step is not repeated with the opposite foot).

When the step is performed to a reel, it is fitted to a 4-bar phrase. The six movements above are repeated four times, one movement to each successive quaver (this occupies three bars of music), and the 4-bar phrase is completed with two stamps, with LF and RF, on the counts '1' and '2' of the fourth bar.

[1] The resulting steps here are the steps known to step-dancers as the 'single flatter' and 'double flatter' respectively (see 220–3).

We mention finally that in the Angus Country Dance Jacky Tar (see p. 248) many of the men used to set with a 'Jacky Tar' step, which consisted of a succession of trebling movements. This was common among people of our informant's parents' generation—'lots of folk could do it' (54).

Dancing in Cape Breton Island, Nova Scotia

by F. RHODES

CAPE BRETON ISLAND lies off the north-eastern end of the Nova Scotian peninsula, and extends about 85 miles from east to west and about 105 miles from north to south. Until the middle of the eighteenth century the settlers on the island were mainly French, the nearest British settlements being on the mainland of Nova Scotia and on Prince Edward Island. Then in 1758 British forces captured and destroyed the French fortress at Louisburg on the south-east of the island, and the ruined town became the centre of a small British community. The British settlements on the mainland of Nova Scotia increased steadily, and after 1769 so did those on Prince Edward Island. However, no corresponding development took place on Cape Breton Island until after 1784, when the island was separated administratively from Nova Scotia and placed under its own Governor, who chose Sydney, in the east of the island, as his capital. Immigration now began in earnest, and between 1784 and about 1800 immigrants came from all over the British Isles to settle the eastern half of the island. In the next two decades large numbers of people sailed from the Scottish Highlands and the Western Isles to open up the west coast of the island and the country round Grand Narrows. Most of these early immigrants crossed the Atlantic during the summer months when sailing conditions were at their best, and thus arrived too late to start farming before the short Nova Scotian summer was over. Many of them therefore stayed with already established immigrants until the next spring, when they could begin the task of clearing the trees from new 200-acre lots to make their own farms. In the middle of the nineteenth century there was another burst of immigration when the mineral resources of the island began to be developed; this time, however, the immigrants were mainly Irish labourers and miners from England and Wales (19).[1]

[1] The bracketed numbers in the appendix refer to the list of informants and bibliography for the appendix.

267

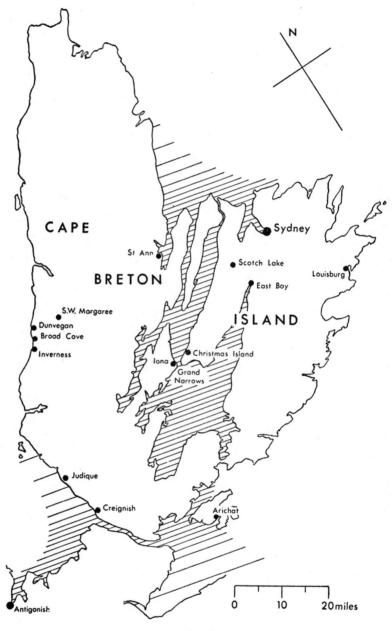

Cape Breton Island, Nova Scotia

The Highlanders who settled in Cape Breton Island at the beginning of the nineteenth century handed down to their children many memories of their life in Scotland and of their early days on the island, and many of these traditional memories were recorded in the 1920's. Such records show that even in the very beginning the settlers did not allow the hardness of their lives to prevent them from following the recreations of their forefathers, and dancing seems to have played just as big a part in their social life as it did in Scotland. The *History of Inverness County*, a book which records the details of those who settled the west coast of Cape Breton Island, contains for example the following account of one family (19).

'MacMillans (The Dancers)

'Allan MacMillan was born in Lochaber, Scotland. About the year 1817 he came to America, landing at Pictou and spending his first winter in the new world with relatives at the Gulf shore of Antigonish.[1] In 1820 he came to Rear Little Judique in the county of Inverness where he took 200 acres of land.

'On the eve of his departure he was married by Fr William Fraser (afterwards Bishop of Arichat) to Catherine Rankin of Lochaber. She was a Catholic and he a Protestant. He remained in the Protestant faith until his last illness, when he became a Catholic, and received the last rites of the Church at the hands of Reverend Alexander MacDonell of Judique. He was a celebrated dancer, and after coming to this country, kept a dancing class in both the settlements of Judique and Creignish. He had four of a family, namely: John, Donald, Ann, Sarah.'

From the same source we learn of Lauchlin MacDougall, who emigrated with his four grown-up sons from Moidart. Like the MacMillans, the MacDougall family spent the first winter in Antigonish; then in 1808 Lauchlin settled three of his sons, Alexander, Duncan, and Archibald, side by side on the last 600 acres at Broad Cove Banks, and his fourth son, Hugh, on another site at Dunvegan. It is recorded that Archibald had a son Lauchlin, 'This Lauchlin was a particularly cheerful and pleasant man, with an immense fund of the old Scottish legends', while Duncan had a son John who was 'a man of great industry and good judgment, a famous dancer, and withal a kind and genial host'.

In Cape Breton Island, as in the Scottish Highlands and the Western Isles, a good deal of dancing took place in the people's houses. The early Scottish settlers built for themselves quite large frame houses with three

[1] Pictou and Antigonish are both on the north shore of the Nova Scotian mainland.

269

or four good-sized rooms on the ground floor, and thus had much more space in their homes for dancing than in their old croft houses in Scotland. The only alternative places for indoor dancing in the early days were barns and schoolrooms, for public halls were not built until the early years of this century—the first in Inverness County was built about 1900. Among the younger people outdoor dancing was also common, the wooden bridges being particularly popular as dancing-places; also, in the summer, whole districts would organize 'picnics', when large open-air dance floors would be built out in the forests for a day or two of merrymaking.

The dances taken to Cape Breton Island by the Scottish settlers seem to have consisted only of 'four-handed Reels', 'eight-handed Reels', a group of solo dances, and a few of the old Gaelic dance-games.

Most of the various forms of four-handed Reel[1] danced in Cape Breton Island have close affinities with the old West Highland circular Reel described in Chapter VII—they consist of setting steps danced on the spot alternated with a simple circling figure, the setting steps being performed with the dancers either in a straight line or in a square formation. I also met one form of the four-handed Reel in which the dancers swung each other instead of setting and in which the travelling figure was performed by the diagonal pairs changing places. This last form, which is very similar to the South Uist version of Ruidhleadh nan Coileach Dubha, was described to me by the oldest of my informants, Mrs Jack MacDonald of Scotch Lake (she was over 100 at the time when I visited her, and she put aside the painting of her garden shed in order to dance for me). Another of my informants, Mrs Archie Kennedy of Dunvegan, had actually performed a dance called Ruidhleadh nan Coileach Dubha to her mother's canntaireachd as a very young child, and although Mrs Kennedy could not remember this dance in full detail, her memories of it fitted Mrs MacDonald's form of the four-handed Reel. It seems very likely, therefore, that Mrs MacDonald's four-handed Reel was in fact Ruidhleadh nan Coileach Dubha.

Up to about 1939, the Scottish Foursome Reel, with its 'figure 8', was known only to those people on Cape Breton Island who had travelled outside the island, and I could find no evidence that it was ever danced at the ordinary dances among the descendants of the old Scottish settlers. The situation in Cape Breton Island thus provides strong evidence that about the period 1800–20 the Foursome Reel, with its 'figure 8', was not used in the West Highlands and the Western Isles (and indeed in more central regions of the Highlands such as Lochaber),

[1] Descriptions of these various forms are given on pp. 276–9.

and that the common Reel for four in these districts at that time was circular in pattern. We thus have confirmation of the evidence in this direction gathered by Dr and Mrs Flett and myself from living memory in Scotland.

In addition to its 'English' name, the Cape Breton Island four-handed Reel also had two Gaelic names, 'Ruidhleadh Cheathrar' ('Foursome Reel') and 'Ruidhleadh Bheag' ('small Reel').[1] The latter of these two names distinguished the four-handed Reel from the eight-handed 'big' Reel, 'Ruidhleadh Mòr'. The old Ruidhleadh Mòr was the dance which earned the title 'the wild eight', and was a very bois-terous form of the Reel of Tulloch in a Circle described on p. 154 (4, 6, 12, 14). At some time in the middle of the nineteenth century the 'wild eight' fell into disfavour with the priests, and this led, apparently on the instructions of the bishop of the time, to a temporary ban on all social dancing—in some parishes the priests even went so far as to collect and destroy all the fiddles. The 'wild eight' in its original form does not seem to have survived the priests' ban, but the eight-handed Reels which were danced after the ban lapsed combined the alternate setting and swinging of the 'wild eight' with quieter circle figures. These more recent eight-handed Reels were not fixed in form but varied from one district to another, and also varied according to the inclination of the dancers. Moreover, for as far back as living memory extends—from at least 1880—it has been quite common for these eight-handed Reels to divide into two four-handed Reels near the end, just as in Scotland the modern Eightsome Reel has, since at least 1894, often divided into two Foursome Reels.[2]

The solo dances brought to Cape Breton Island from Scotland were taught by a number of men on the island. In Broad Cove, Ronald Kennedy told me of the dancing classes which his father had held in that district up to about 1900. Ronald was not himself taught by his father, but as a young boy watched him teaching others the Fling, the Swords, Seann Triubhas, Flowers of Edinburgh, Jacky Tar, Duke of Fife, and The Girl I Left Behind Me, each of these being a solo dance with twelve steps. Ronald Kennedy's father had been taught by his own father, John Kennedy, who emigrated from Canna in 1790, going first to Prince Edward Island, and then moving a few years later to Broad Cove, where he commenced the dancing classes which were continued by his son.

[1] In the Canadian census of 1941 there were approximately 10,000 people in Cape Breton Island who listed Gaelic as their mother tongue.

[2] A typical eight-handed Reel of this more recent form is described on p. 279.

A little further north, in South West Margaree, one family has preserved some of the solo dances taught to an earlier generation by Donald
Beaton, an itinerant tailor. The dances handed down from Donald
Beaton were the seven noted above, and also Tullochgorm, Irish
Washerwoman, and Princess Royal, all ten of these dances again having
originally twelve steps (1). As with the Kennedys, dancing seems to
have stayed in the Beaton family too, for subsequent to Donald Beaton
a schoolteacher Angus Beaton held dancing classes in the town of
Inverness and on the bridge at South West Margaree (3). Again, in
Creignish, where Allan MacMillan 'the dancer' held one of his dancing
classes in the early 1820's, dancing classes continued to be held up to
about 1900, and there were also classes in solo dancing in Iona and
Christmas Island (10, 14).

The majority of the steps used in the various solo dances which survived among the Scottish communities on Cape Breton Island are very
uniform in style, and employ a form of stepping in which the dancer
marks the rhythm of the music with toe and heel beats and brushing
movements, the feet being kept close to the ground throughout.[1]
Although this form of stepping is unlike that seen at modern Scottish
Highland Games, there is no doubt that the Cape Breton Island solo
dances originated in Scotland, and indeed some of these dances can be
shown on internal evidence alone to be related to solo dances which can
still be found in the Scottish Highlands and the Outer Isles. This same
form of stepping was also very largely used in the setting periods of the
Cape Breton Island four-handed and eight-handed Reels. In the Reels,
however, the steps were much less regular in construction than in the
solo dances, and each individual step consisted of a number of very short
sequences of movements of a more or less standard nature, these
sequences being joined together as the dancer pleased in order to match
as far as possible the notes of the music. The style of stepping used in the
Cape Breton Island Reels is thus in close accord with the style seen by
Colonel Thornton in the Scottish Highlands in 1804,[2] where the dancers

'all shuffle in such a manner as to make the noise of their feet keep
exact time'.

When the solo dances taught by the dancing-teachers began to be
forgotten, extemporized stepping of a form similar to that used in the
Cape Breton Island Reels came to be used in place of the solo dances in

[1] This form of stepping was employed even in the Fling and Seann Truibhas, but
not in the Swords.
[2] See p. 30.

exhibitions and competitions, so that until very recent years the dancing on these occasions was quite dissimilar in style to that seen on similar occasions within living memory in Scotland. This discrepancy in style was not widely appreciated in Cape Breton Island until in 1939 the Gaelic College at St Ann started teaching modern Highland Games dancing together with some of the Country Dances published by the Royal Scottish Country Dance Society and some of the dances collected by Mrs Mary Isdale MacNab of Vancouver. Since then many people in Cape Breton Island have doubted the Scottish origin of the stepping, and either have considered it to be an importation from Virginia or have attributed it to the French settlers from Louisburg or later non-Scottish immigrants. While all these factors may have had some influence on the present-day style, it is certain that the roots of the step-dancing lie in the solo dances and Reel steps which were brought from Scotland early in the nineteenth century.

The step-dancing, whether of a formal nature as embodied in the solo dances, or of an extempore nature as used in the Reels, was always a source of competition between the men. One of the popular tests of skill was 'Smàladh na Coinnle', the 'smooring of the candle', in which a lighted candle was placed on the floor and the dancer was required to flick off the top of the wick with his feet whilst dancing, without extinguishing the flame (16). In an alternative form of this test, the dancers were required to snuff the candle between their heels while dancing (6). Again, at the end of an evening's dancing the two best dancers were often made to 'dance it out', taking it in turn to dance as many complete steps as possible on a block of wood 18 inches high and 12 inches in diameter (10).

Of the old Gaelic dance-games which the immigrants brought with them from Scotland I could find only vague memories.[1] The centenarian, Mrs MacDonald of Scotch Lake (5), was the only person I met who had heard of Marbadh na Béiste Duibhe (The Killing of the Otter), Tri Criodhan Caorach (Three Sheep's Trotters), and Cailleach an Dùdain (The Old Woman of the Milldust), which last she thought to be just 'a plain jigging twasome'. But several people knew of Dannsa na Tunnag (The Duck's Dance), both as a children's game and as a dance for adults; and one 93-year-old lady danced a bit of it for me (15). Another dance of which I found some memories was Dannsaidh na Biodaig (The Dirk Dance); one version of this was performed over a dirk stuck in the ground with the point upwards (5, 10), while in

[1] For descriptions of a number of these old dance-games recorded in Scotland, see (21).

another version the dirk was sometimes flourished and sometimes danced over on the ground (2).

Between 1890 and 1900 a number of Square Dances—Quadrilles, Lancers, Saratoga Lancers, and the Caledonians—invaded the island. These new dances were danced with waltz and polka steps, and with a sedate walking step. Moreover, they had to be danced properly—when there was dancing in the houses the young people practised in a back room until they were proficient enough to join in the sets in the front room. At first the older people continued to dance the old Reels in their own homes, but when the first public halls were built in the different townships between 1900 and 1920 most social dancing was transferred to these, and thereafter the programmes consisted mainly of square sets. For the dances in the public halls at this time the couples paid for their admission to the hall, and also paid an additional charge for each set in which they took part. Within more recent years the full repertoire of the square sets has gradually been lost until now each district has its own single-figure Quadrille which is danced with little regard for footwork or phrasing. In the village halls nowadays, this 'square dancing' alternates with 'round dancing', this latter term being used to describe a couple dance derived from the Waltz, the Polka, and the couple dances of the 1920's, danced to boisterous Canadian-Scottish tunes. Only in a few halls in the largest towns will returned wanderers dance Waltzes, Quicksteps, Slow Foxtrots, or jive.

It will be noticed that the step-dancing classes closed down soon after the square sets were introduced—the step-dancing was no longer required for use in the fashionable social dances. Now only a few people occasionally step-dance in the square dances, the stepping is passed on in very few families, and one of the best young dancers whom I saw had picked up his steps from the television.

In addition to the various square sets, there was also a number of two-couple dances used within comparatively recent years in Cape Breton Island which consisted of selections from the 'head couple' figures of the Quadrilles. These dances, which were usually known by the generic title 'The French Four', were derived either from the square sets or from the Parisian Quadrilles, a form of Quadrilles for two couples.[1] The various four-handed Reels are sometimes referred to as 'the Scotch Four' to distinguish them from the French Fours, but both types of dance are

[1] The Parisian Quadrilles consisted of the 'head couple' figures of the First Set of Quadrilles. They were first introduced in England and Scotland, as a separate dance for two couples only, about the middle of the nineteenth century, and are described in the ballroom guides published by the Glasgow teachers Willock and Wallace.

referred to by different people as 'the Single Eight'. The situation is not made any clearer when one comes across versions of the French Four containing figures similar to the version of the four-handed Reel which involves swinging. However, there is no evidence to suggest any origin for the two-couple dances other than Scotland or the Quadrilles, and each collected two-couple dance fits naturally into one or other of these two categories.

It is significant that Country Dances were completely unknown among the Scottish communities in Cape Breton Island until their introduction by the St Ann College in 1939, for this indicates that such dances were not danced by the ordinary people in the Highlands and the Outer Isles about the period when the main Scottish immigration to Cape Breton Island took place. This is in agreement with the evidence gathered from living memory in Scotland that Country Dances were first introduced among the ordinary people of these regions about 1850.

In the old days in Cape Breton Island, the big occasions for dancing other than the summer picnics in the forest were the 'milling frolics', when neighbours gathered together to 'waulk' the new cloth, and the weddings. No one whom I met remembered the full set of dances of an old Highland wedding, but many remembered that the dancing began with 'Ruidhleadh nan Caraid' ('The married couple's Reel'), a four-handed Reel danced by the bride and bridegroom with the bridesmaid and best man. This was followed by a second four-handed Reel danced by a set of relations of the bride and bridegroom, and after this everyone danced. Just one man (6) mentioned that later in the evening the bride and bridegroom danced another four-handed Reel, to the tune 'The Bedding of the Bride', and that from this Reel the bride was stolen away.[1] As in Scotland, with the change in the fashion of dancing the wedding Reel became in some places just a set of Quadrilles; but it is through the Ruidhleadh nan Caraid that the four-handed Reel is best remembered. The dancing at the wedding did not end with the end of the reception, for on their way home the guests 'danced away each cross-roads' before parting to go on their separate ways (10). A custom similar to this survived within living memory in South Uist, for there the bridal party, as they walked from the church to the reception, danced a Scotch Reel at each cross-roads on their way, 'to dance away the cross' (17).

[1] Cf. p. 47.

Descriptions of the Dances

I give now descriptions of the Cape Breton Island four-handed and eight-handed Reels, and I begin with the details of the figures, leaving until later the question of steps. I must add a warning here against too rigid an adherence to my descriptions, for within living memory the forms of the Cape Breton Island dances were much less clearly defined than was normal in Scotland, and the dancers varied the figures with much greater freedom.

THE FOUR-HANDED REEL

(I) *Circular forms*. The forms of the four-handed Reel which I consider under this heading are all true Reels, with alternating phrases of circling and setting; all display also the characteristic change of rhythm, for in each case they are begun to a strathspey and in the course of the dance the music changes to quick tempo. For the part in quick tempo the music usually consisted of one or more reel tunes, but Scotch measures and jigs were also played occasionally. The normal tempo for strathspeys was 44 to 48 bars per minute; for tunes in quick tempo the usual tempo at the beginning of the period covered by living memory was about 52 bars per minute, but in more recent years it has been 60 bars per minute.

In all the four-handed Reels the two couples begin in square formation. In the case of the circular forms of the dance my informants were almost equally divided between those who described a dance which remained in square formation throughout, and those who described one in which the dancers moved into line. I describe the latter first (18).

In this form the two couples stand opposite each other, with the ladies on the right of their partners, as in Diagram 1 (a). Throughout this section I follow the usage suggested by this diagram and refer to 1st man and 2nd lady, and similarly 1st lady and 2nd man, as 'opposites'.

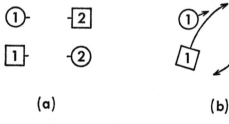

(a)   (b)

Diagram 1

Music Bars	*Description of the Figures*
1–8	All dance round clockwise in a circle, without giving hands; the ladies begin by passing to their left in front of their partners, and each man joins in the circle behind his partner (Diagram 1 (b)). All end in a line, with the ladies in their original places and the men back to back in the middle facing their opposites. (This circle figure is the same as that in the old West Highland circular Reel described on p. 157, except that there the men finish facing their own partners.)
9–16	All set to opposites.
17–24	All again dance round in a circle, the ladies moving off to their left and each man following his opposite. The ladies return to their own places, and the men finish facing their own partners. (The movement is again similar to that in the old West Highland circular Reel.)
25–32	All set to partners.

This 32-bar sequence is performed first in strathspey tempo and then in quick tempo; some of my informants said that it should be performed twice in strathspey tempo and then two or three times in quick tempo, while others told me that the number of repetitions varied from one occasion to another. The setting periods were also sometimes doubled in length, and this depended entirely on the fiddler; the circling figure was invariably performed to one part of the tune and the setting to another, and if the fiddler chose to repeat the setting part of the tune, then the dancers simply continued to set until the end of that part. In any case, whatever the phrasing, the ladies always return to their places at the end of each circle figure, while the men set alternately to their opposites and their partners.

The form of the four-handed Reel in which the square formation is preserved throughout has a number of variants. In the simplest of these the ladies stand on the left of their partners and the dancers alternately circle clockwise and set to their partners (2, 10).[1] In another variant the setting alternates with a travelling figure consisting of a circle clockwise round to places followed by another circle round to places with right hands joined in the centre. The dancers move slowly round the circle taking eight bars for each complete circle, while the lengths of the setting periods depend as before on the fiddler. There were generally four lots of setting in strathspey tempo and four in quick tempo (8).

[1] Cf. Ruidhleadh Mòr, p. 159.

In a third variant the couples face each other as in Diagram 1 (a), and the ladies begin by moving across to their left in front of their partners, who follow the ladies round the circle, exactly as in Diagram 1 (b). So far the movement is that of the old West Highland circular Reel, but in this case the circle stops when the ladies reach their own places and each man is in the place diagonally opposite to his own. This circling figure, which occupies eight bars, is followed by eight bars of setting to opposites (i.e. 1st man to 2nd lady, 1st lady to 2nd man), and then the circling figure is repeated to bring the men back to their own places, where they set to their partners. This whole sequence occupies thirty-two bars, and is performed twice in strathspey tempo and twice in quick tempo (3, 7).

I am inclined to believe that the square form of the four-handed Reel is older than the in-line form, and that the latter arose through two sets of the four-handed Reel being danced side by side in the eight-handed Reel, and there being flattened out to give the dancers more space.

(II) 'Crossing' forms. In some forms of the four-handed Reel a 'crossing' figure is substituted for the circle (5, 12, 13). Starting with the two couples facing each other as in Diagram 1 (a), the two ladies cross to each other's place, passing each other with right shoulders. The two men then cross to each other's place, passing with right shoulders, then the ladies cross back, then the men do likewise, each pair again passing with right shoulders. The movements are continuous, the tracks of the dancers being two crossing ovals (Diagram 2).

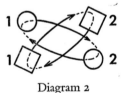

Diagram 2

It seems extremely probable that this 'crossing' figure is a development from the circle; it will be noticed that in Diagrams 1 (b) and 2 the initial tracks of the two ladies are roughly the same.

(III) A form involving crossing and swinging. This is the form given to me by the centenarian, Mrs MacDonald of Scotch Lake (5), and is probably the same as the dance Ruidhleadh nan Coileach Dubha which another of my informants (2) had danced as a young child (see p. 270). It should be compared with the South Uist version of Ruidhleadh nan Coileach Dubha described on p. 172.

In this form of the four-handed Reel, the two couples face each other as in Diagram 1 (a), with the ladies on their partners' right. The dance is in quick tempo only, and is performed to any reel tune.

Music Bars	Description of the Figures
1–8	The two couples dance the crossing figure as described under (II).
9–16	Partners swing each other, each having right hand on the other's waist and left hand on the other's right arm. The step here is either the pivot step or a walking step.
17–18	Set to partners while changing the hold to the opposite side (i.e. left hand on waist, right hand on arm).
19–24	Partners swing in opposite direction.

This sequence is repeated several times. The men might swing opposites alternately with partners or might swing partners each time.

I am not completely certain of the phrasing of the swinging. In the 'square dancing' nowadays Cape Breton Islanders swing for as long as they feel inclined, and this seems to have been true in the latter days of this dance also.

THE EIGHT-HANDED REEL

The eight-handed Reel is in quick tempo, and is performed to either reels or Scotch measures. The sequence and the phrasing of the dance are not fixed, and here I only give a typical sequence and indicate reasonable phrasing (13). The four couples start as in Diagram 3, with the ladies on

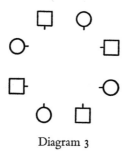

Diagram 3

their partners' right. As in the four-handed Reel the dancers mark the rhythm of the music with their feet throughout the dance.

279

Music Bars	*Description of the Figures*
16	All join hands in a ring and circle to the left and back again.
8	All swing partners.
16	All dance a 'grand chain' round to places, giving right hands to partners to begin (i.e. the ladies move round the set clockwise, the men counter-clockwise, passing each other with right and left shoulders alternately and giving right and left hands alternately on passing).
8	All swing partners.
8	Ladies stay in their places while the men set to and swing the next lady on their right.
16	The men set to and swing the next two ladies round the square.
8	The men return to their partners (who are still in their original places) and set to and swing them.

(In the preceding thirty-two bars the ladies also set to the men.)

16	All dance a 'grand chain' as before.
8	The men join hands in a ring and circle to the left round to places, while the ladies step on the spot outside the men's ring.
8	The ladies join hands in a ring and circle to the left round to places, while the men step on the spot outside the ladies' ring.
8	The men dance right hands across, i.e. they join right hands in the centre and circle round to places, while the ladies step on the spot.
8	The ladies dance right hands across while the men step on the spot.
64	Two four-handed Reels danced side by side, adjacent couples dancing together. Any form of the four-handed Reel might be used.
64	Set and pass chain, i.e. all set to partners for eight bars, then pass each other and set to the next person, then pass again and set to the next person, and so on, taking eight bars for each pass and set. Continue in this way round the square, partners meeting again halfway round, and then back again in their places.

Setting steps for the four-handed and eight-handed Reels

The setting steps used in the four-handed and eight-handed Reels are mostly low on the ground, and are built up from a number of basic movements which are adapted to any quick or slow Common time tune.[1] Ordinary hard-soled shoes are worn for dancing, and the feet are kept almost parallel throughout most of the steps; the body is held upright, the arms hang loosely by the sides, and there is almost no vertical movement of the body. The same steps are used by both men and ladies.

The reader who is accustomed to Scottish dancing will need first to develop the art of beating out a rhythm with the toes and heels without ever having both feet off the ground. The four examples of one-bar phrases given below will help him to do so; they are used in various combinations to take up and maintain the rhythm of the dance when the dancer is not inclined to use more elaborate steps.[2] The counts are given for reels (p. 88), and the movements are described for the right foot only.

Phrase A. Start with both feet on the ground.

Count 1   Rock forward to take the weight on the balls of both feet, then on the count beat the L heel on the ground, immediately lifting the ball of the LF just off the ground.

Count &   Rock back on to R heel, immediately lifting the ball of the RF just off the ground.

Count 2   Rock forward on to the ball of the LF, lifting L heel.

Count &   Rock forward on to the ball of the RF, lifting R heel.

Each count is marked with a distinct beat of the foot.

Phrase B. Start with the weight on the LF and with the RF just off the ground.

Count 1   Place the ball of the RF on the ground.

Count &   Drop on to the flat of the RF, making a beat with the R heel, and at the same time lift the LF just off the ground.

Count 2   Place the ball of the LF on the ground.

Count &   Drop on to the flat of the LF, making a beat with the L heel, and at the same time lift the RF just off the ground.

Again each count is marked with a beat. The feet are lifted only just enough for the dancer to be able to make a beat when they are put down again.

---

[1] The steps can also be adapted to jigs.
[2] These phrases occurred in various examples of stepping demonstrated to me by one or more of my informants.

Phrase C. Start with the weight on the ball of the LF and keep it there throughout.

Count 1   Beat the L heel on the ground.
Count &   Beat the ball of the RF in 1st position.
Count 2   Beat the L heel on the ground.
Count &   Beat the R heel in 5th position.

The beats with the L heel are made by rocking the L foot, keeping the ball of the foot on the ground. The L knee is bent to lift the L heel—there is no vertical movement of the hip.

When the dancer needs to spring to change feet, or to hop as in the following phrase, the emphasis is placed on the beat on landing, and the vertical movement is kept to a minimum.

Phrase D

Count 1   Hop on LF.
Count &   Brush RF forward, making a beat with the ball or heel of the RF as the foot moves forward.
Count 2   Hop on LF.
Count &   Brush RF backward, making a beat with the ball of the RF as the foot moves backward.

Here the hops can be replaced by rocking heel-beats as in phrase C—the choice depends only on the lift of the music and the energy of the dancer. The brush forward may be in any direction, straight forward, diagonally outwards, or crossed in front of the hopping foot.

Phrase D can also be danced alternately on right and left feet, the first count then being a spring from one foot to the other. In this case the emphasis is placed on the first count in each bar, and the rhythm is similar to that of the pas de Basque.

More complicated steps are built upon the following movement. I here call it the 'treble' because of its similarity to the treble found in Scotland (see p. 261)—none of my informants had a special name for it. With the system of counting used in Chapters IX and XI, i.e.

& a   1 an & a   2 an & a

this treble movement occupies four successive counts, beginning on any

one of the subsidiary counts 'an'. Using, for instance, the counts 'an &
a 2', we have:

Treble with RF. Start with the weight on the LF.

Count an	Beat R heel in 3rd position.
Counts & a	Beat twice with the ball of the RF in 3rd position, momentarily transferring the weight to the RF after the second beat.
Count 2	Beat with the ball of the LF in rear 3rd position, transferring the weight to it on the beat.

The two beats on the counts '& a' are made simply by tapping the ball
of the foot on the floor; there is no forward and backward action as in
the Scottish treble.

The treble is often preceded by a movement which in Scotland has the
name 'catch in' (see, for example, 20); again my informants in Cape
Breton Island had no special name for it. The catch in is normally performed on the counts '& a 1', and is as follows.

Catch in with the LF

Count &	Hop on RF and lift LF to semi 4th very low aerial position.
Count a	Brush the LF in towards 1st position, making a beat with the ball of the foot on the way in.
Count 1	Beat the LF in 1st position, transferring the weight to it on the beat.

Two common combinations of the catch in and treble are as follows.
Catch in with LF and treble with RF[1] (counts '& a **1**. 1 an & a 2'), *then
catch in with RF and treble with LF* (counts '& a **2**. 1 an & a 2').

Catch in with LF and treble three times with RF[2] (counts '& a **1**. 1' for the
catch in and counts '**1**. an & a 2'; '**1**. an & a **2**. 1'; and '**2**. an & a 2' for
the three trebles).

The three successive beats on the one foot which occur in the treble
are also used in the following movement (essentially successive trebles
on alternate feet).

1. 1	Step on the LF in 1st position.
an	Beat with R heel in 3rd position.
& a	Beat twice with the ball of the RF in 3rd position.

[1] This corresponds to the Scottish 'single treble' (see, for example 20).
[2] This corresponds to the Scottish 'double treble' (see, for example 20). Compare
also the 'double' described on p. 262.

2	Step on the RF in 1st position.
an	Beat with L heel in 3rd position.
& a	Beat twice with the ball of the LF in 3rd position.

The catch in is also combined with double beats as follows.

Count 1 an & Catch in with LF as described above.
Count a   Beat R toe against L heel.
Count 2   Beat ball of RF on ground.

Alternatively the two counts 'a 2' may both be marked by beating the ball of the RF on the ground.

In all these combinations all the counts '1' and '2' should be emphasized.

It will be noticed that in phrases A–D only the counts '1 & 2 &' are used, while in the steps constructed from the treble and catch in the full eight counts '1 an & a 2 an & a' are used. In general, the dancers endeavour to combine movements of the two types, i.e. those with counts '1 & 2 &' and those with counts '1 an & a 2 an & a', in order to follow the tune quite closely.

Such 'beating' steps as these formed by far the greatest majority of the Reel steps used in Cape Breton Island within living memory. In particular, the treble and catch in were known to all my informants, and in the old days their use in the stepping seems to have been universal. In addition to such 'beating' steps, there were also a few steps of the more conventional Scottish type, for example, the 'backstep with a hop' (p. 123), and also steps similar to the Strathspey step B and the Quick Reel step Q described in Chapter V.

Travelling steps for the four-handed and eight-handed Reels

In travelling steps, as in the setting steps, the counts of the music are marked by beats. The walk, on counts '1' and '2' of a bar in reel time, becomes a 'brush' walk:

Count 1 Step forward on RF.
Count & Brush LF forward through 1st position.
Count 2 Step forward on LF.
Count & Brush RF forward through 1st position.

This may be alternated with the chassé:

Count 1 Step forward on RF.

Count & Close LF to rear 3rd position (recall that the feet are almost
            parallel).
Count 2 Step forward on RF.

The chassé in turn has extra beats inserted either by brushing the LF
forward on the last count '&' of the bar or by bringing the LF forward
with the three 'heel, toe, toe' beats of the treble on the last counts 'an
& a' of the bar. In the latter case all the eight counts of the bar may then
be marked by doubling up the first beats of the chassé, giving altogether:

I. 1   Step forward on RF.
   an &   Close LF to rear 3rd position with two beats.
   a 2   Brush RF forward and step on it.
   an   Brush L heel forward through 1st position.
   & a   Brush LF forward making two beats with the ball of the foot
          on the way forward, ready to step on the LF on the count
          '1' of the next bar.

Some dancers also used rather more springy steps, such as the travelling
pas de Basque described on p. 109.

Informants and References

We give here the names of our principal informants for the material given in this book, together with the year(s) when we visited them. We have also indicated by the initials F.R. those informants visited either by Dr Rhodes or by Dr Rhodes and T.M.F. together.

As some indication of the ages of our informants—and this is highly relevant to the material in the text—we mention that of the various informants listed below, fifteen were born before 1870, seventy-one between 1871 and 1880, ninety-six between 1881 and 1890, and thirty-eight between 1891 and 1900.

(i) Information about the following dancing-teachers has been obtained from the informants listed below.

ALEXANDER ADAMSON (1859–1939, E. Fife)
>   From his son (2) and also
>   (1) Miss Christina MacNaughton, Strathmiglo, Fife, 1956. Attended three sessions of Mr Adamson's classes c. 1905, 1913.

WILLIAM ADAMSON (E. Fife)
>   (2) Personal visits, Kingskettle, Fife, 1956, 1958, 1960.

JOHN AIRD (c. 1850–1925, Wigtownshire)
>   (3) Mr William Leith, Stranraer, Wigtownshire, 1959. Attended Mr Aird's classes c. 1906.

DAVID ANDERSON (c. 1850–1911, Dundee)
>   (4) Mrs C. F. Stewart, Broughty Ferry, Angus, 1954. Daughter of David Anderson, assisted him in his classes.
>   (5) Mrs Martha Dingwall, Dundee, 1960. Well-known Highland dancer, danced from c. 1895 until c. 1911 in an exhibition group organized by David Anderson.
>   (6) Mr James Ritchie, Kirkmichael, Perthshire, 1956, 1958. Attended Mr Anderson's classes c. 1904.

PROFESSOR BAILEY (c. 1855–?, Glasgow region)
>   (7) Miss Helen and Miss Jean Muirhead, Burnside, Glasgow, 1958. The former attended Professor Bailey's classes in Cambuslang c. 1892, the latter in Millerston c. 1898.

PROFESSOR BLACKLEY (1859–1941, Lanark)
>   (8) Miss Marion Blackley, F.B.A.T.D., Lanark, 1958, and correspondence. Daughter of Professor Blackley. Miss Blackley and her

sister assisted Professor Blackley in his classes, and took over his business on his death.

(9) Mr Abe Brown, Douglas, Lanarkshire, 1958. Attended Professor Blackley's classes for two sessions at Carmichael c. 1905.

(10) Mr William Marshall, Glespin, Lanarkshire, 1958. Attended Professor Blackley's classes at Craufordjohn c. 1904.

D. G. BROWN (c. 1868–?, Inverness)

(11) Mr Alexander Cumming, Lewiston, Inverness-shire, 1960. Attended three sessions of Mr Brown's classes in Inverness c. 1895.

(12) Mr Ewen Ferguson, Appin, Argyllshire, 1956. Attended Mr Brown's classes at Tomnahurich Bridge, Inverness-shire, c. 1891.

PROFESSOR R. F. BUCK (c. 1855–1954?, Borders)

(13) Mr Robert Anderson, Shiringscleuch, Ettrick, 1958. A fiddler and a dancer,[1] attended Mr Buck's classes at Ettrickbridge End c. 1919.

(14) Mrs George Cairns, Langholm, Dumfriesshire, 1958. Mr Buck used to lodge in her parents' house at Lilliesleaf on his circuit round Hawick, Lilliesleaf, and Selkirk, and Mrs Cairns attended his classes at Lilliesleaf on a number of occasions between 1897 and 1909.

(15) Mr Douglas, Jedburgh, Roxburghshire, 1954. A fiddler and a dancer; brought up in Liddisdale and attended Mr Buck's classes there c. 1897.

(16) Mr James Inglis, Denholm, Roxburghshire, 1954, 1958. A very keen dancer, with a wide knowledge of dancing in the Borders. Attended four or more sessions of Mr Buck's classes at different places in the Borders c. 1904–10.

(17) Mr John McCulloch, Pencaitland, E. Lothian, 1955. Attended Mr Buck's classes in Wigtownshire and in Pencaitland; was one of the M.C.'s at a weekly dance club in Pencaitland c. 1910–14.

(18) Mrs Helen Sutherland, Cameron Park, Edinburgh, 1958, 1960, and correspondence. Born and brought up at Oxton in Berwickshire, attended one session of Mr Buck's classes c. 1900, and also two sessions of Mr Fletcher's classes c. 1892 and 1894. Mrs Sutherland was the late I. C. B. Jamieson's source for the Reel of Six (p. 181), and the Country Dance Loch Erichtside.

(19) Mr and Mrs John Wilkinson, Stow, Midlothian, 1960. Both attended Mr Buck's classes at Oxton c. 1901, and Mrs Wilkinson also attended Mr Fletcher's classes at Oxton c. 1894.

EWAN CLAYTON (c. 1860–1935, Highlands and Islands)

(20) Miss Winnie Smith, Castlebay, Barra, 1954. A grand-niece of Mr Clayton. He stayed at her home regularly, and she had lessons from him c. 1910–14.

---

[1] Many fiddlers were non-dancers.

(21) Mr and Mrs Malcolm Ross, Flotta, Orkney, 1955. Attended Mr Clayton's classes on Flotta *c.* 1905.

ANDREW COCHRANE (1852–1934, W. Berwickshire)

(22) Mrs A. Bell, Jedburgh, Roxburghshire, 1960. Daughter of Andrew Cochrane, attended a number of his classes and balls *c.* 1896–1910.

(23) Mr Alex Lothian, High Cross, near Lauder, Berwickshire, 1960. A fiddler and a dancer, attended Mr Cochrane's classes at Houndslow *c.* 1902.

(24) Mr John Ramage, Westruther, Berwickshire, 1960. Attended Mr Cochrane's classes at Houndslow *c.* 1902.

ROLAND COWPER (Whitehaven, England)

(25) Personal visit, 1960. Mr Cowper's father and grand-uncle were dancing-masters in Workington and York.

MR FLETCHER (*c.* 1850–?, W. Berwickshire)

(26) Mr Alexander Scott, Carfraemill, Oxton, Berwickshire, 1959, 1960. Attended one session of Mr Fletcher's classes at Oxton *c.* 1892, and also those of a Mr Macbain *c.* 1890; was M.C. at local dances for a number of years.

Also from Mrs Helen Sutherland (18).

MR W. GALBRAITH (*c.* 1875–?, Lanarkshire and Ayrshire)

(27) Mr Robert Boa, Biggar, Lanarkshire, 1958. Attended Mr Galbraith's classes in Biggar in 1911.

JAMES LAIDLAW (*c.* 1840–95, Ettrick)

(28) Mrs Grace Scott, Selkirk, 1958. Mr Laidlaw was Mrs Scott's uncle, and lived with her family at the farm of Potburn in upper Ettrick.

Also from Mr Robert Anderson (13), whose father and aunt attended Mr Laidlaw's classes in Ettrick.

MR LILLY (?, Kincardineshire)

(29) Mr Milne, Ellon, Aberdeenshire, 1955. Attended Mr Lilly's classes at Auchenblae, Kincardineshire, *c.* 1886.

JAMES MCCULLOCH (1859–1941, S. Ayrshire)

(30) Mr William McCulloch, Kilmarnock, and Mrs McMath, Lendalfoot, Ayrshire, 1959 (at Ballantrae). Son and daughter of Mr McCulloch. Mr William McCulloch assisted in his father's classes.

MR MACDOUGALL (*c.* 1850–1920?, West Highlands and Islands)

(31) Mr Lachlan Gillies, Arisaig, Inverness-shire, 1954, and correspondence. A fiddler and a dancer, well known as a judge of Highland dancing at Highland Games. Attended Mr MacDougall's classes in Arisaig for several sessions *c.* 1900–4.

(32) Mr Sandy Gillies, Glenuig, Inverness-shire, 1956 (with F.R.). Attended two sessions of Mr MacDougall's classes in Glenuig *c.* 1898–9.

(33) Miss Louttit, St Margaret's Hope, S. Ronaldshay, Orkney, 1955. Attended Mr MacDougall's classes in St Margaret's Hope *c.* 1895.

(34) Mrs Flora MacDonald, Glenuig, Inverness-shire, 1956 (with F.R.). Attended Mr MacDougall's classes in Glenuig *c.* 1898.

(35) Mrs Hugh MacDonald, Langal, Moidart, 1954. Attended Mr MacDougall's classes at Mingarry in Moidart *c.* 1900.

(36) Mrs Ann MacDonald and Mr Angus MacPherson, Glenuig, Inverness-shire, 1956 (with F.R.). Sister and brother, both noted sources of old lore (see (302)). Mr MacPherson attended Mr MacDougall's classes in Glenuig *c.* 1899. Both learnt also from their own parents.

(37) Mr Duncan Murchison, Achintraid, Lochcarron, Wester Ross, 1954. Attended Mr MacDougall's classes at Tornapress, near Lochcarron, *c.* 1903.

DOUGAL MCKELVIE (*c.* 1855–?, Lamlash, Arran)

(38) Mr Buie, Birkenhead, Cheshire, 1956. Brought up in Lamlash, attended Mr McKelvie's classes every year from 1899 to about 1905.

DONALD G. MACLENNAN (Edinburgh)

(39) Personal visits, Edinburgh, 1956, 1958, 1959, 1960, and correspondence.

JOHN MACMILLAN (?, S. Uist)

(40) Mr Peter MacKay, Kilaulay, S. Uist, 1953. Attended Mr Mac-Millan's classes *c.* 1890.

MISS LILIAN and MISS FLORA MACMILLAN (Kirkmichael, Perthshire)

(41) Personal visits, Kirkmichael, 1956, 1958.

PROFESSOR MCQUISTON (?, S. Ayrshire and Wigtownshire)

PETER MARSHALL (*c.* 1860–1925, Dumfriesshire and Wigtownshire)

From Mr Thomas Shanks (56).

GEORGE S. MAXWELL (*c.* 1860–?, E. Lothian)

(42) Mr and Mrs William Cowan, Haddington, E. Lothian, 1958. Mrs Cowan attended Mr Maxwell's classes at Athelstaneford *c.* 1898. Mr Cowan is a fiddler, and played at dances and kirns round Haddington.

(43) Miss Christina Cumming, Athelstaneford, E. Lothian, 1958. Attended Mr Maxwell's children's classes in Athelstaneford every year from 1896 to 1902.

(44) Mr Thomas Gilhooly, Haddington, E. Lothian, 1955. Attended Mr Maxwell's classes in Haddington from about 1905 to 1910.

(45) Mrs E. H. Wood, Athelstaneford, E. Lothian, 1958. Attended Mr Maxwell's classes in Athelstaneford every year from 1896 to *c.* 1903. Mrs Wood's father was also a part-time dancing-teacher in Athelstaneford.

JOHN (PADDY) MUIR (*c.* 1837–1900, Motherwell and adjacent districts)

(46) Mrs Jessie Dyson, Glasgow, 1959. Daughter of John Muir, assisted him in his classes from *c.* 1895, and on his death continued his business in partnership with her brother and sister.

Also from Mr Muir's grandson, Mr Jack Muir (47).

JAMES D. MUIR (1870–1942, Motherwell and adjacent districts)

(47) Mr Jack Muir, Motherwell, Lanarkshire, 1959. Son of James Muir, still carries on his father's business as a dancing-teacher. Prominent member of the Scottish Official Board of Highland Dancing.

ADAM MYRON (*c.* 1830–1910, Banffshire)

(48) Mr Charles Milne, Dufftown, Banffshire, 1955. Grand-nephew of Mr Myron, a fiddler and a dancer. When Mr Myron was teaching in Mr Milne's neighbourhood, he used to ask Mr Milne to come and play for his classes, and in this way Mr Milne attended several sessions of Mr Myron's classes during the period from about 1890 to 1905.

(49) Mr and Mrs Duncan, Corsemaul, Glass, Aberdeenshire, 1955. Attended Mr Myron's classes *c.* 1891.

(50) Mr James Kellas, Bridgend, Cabrach, Banffshire, 1955. Attended Mr Myron's classes in the Cabrach from about 1895 to 1898.

JAMES NEILL (1834–1920, Angus and Perthshire)

(51) Mrs Griselda MacFarlane, Forfar, Angus, 1959 (with F.R.), and correspondence. Daughter of Mr Neill, assisted him in his classes in and around Forfar from about 1900.

Also from Mrs Will Cameron (54).

MISS MARGARET PATERSON (1877–1959, Auchencairn, Kirkcudbrightshire)

(52) Personal visit, Auchencairn, 1953, and correspondence. Miss Paterson taught dancing in Auchencairn from about 1920 to 1939, and for a good many years prior to 1920 was pianist in a dance band which played in Dalbeattie and the surrounding district. She was an early contributor to the R.S.C.D.S. *Country Dance Books.*

'DANCIE' REID (*c.* 1871–1942, Angus and Perthshire)

(53) Mrs Betsy Storrier, Kirriemuir, Angus, 1958, 1959. Daughter of Mr Reid, did a good deal of demonstrating for him from about 1910 onwards, and also played in his orchestra.

(54) Mr and Mrs Will Cameron, Kirriemuir, Angus, 1958, 1959. Mrs Cameron had lessons first from James Neill about 1915, and then from Mr Reid. Mr Cameron attended Mr Reid's classes in the Glamis district *c.* 1903. Mr Cameron was at one time a member of the 'Angus Occasionals', a band containing many distinguished Scottish dance-musicians. He also at one time had a band of his own.

(55) Mr Adam Rennie, Coupar Angus, 1956. Mr Rennie, who died in 1960, was well known as a band-leader and fiddler. He first

attended Mr Reid's classes in 1909, at the age of 12, and later assisted Mr Reid by playing for his classes; in all, he attended eight sessions of Mr Reid's classes.

THOMAS SHANKS (Wigtownshire)

(56) Personal visit, Dunragit, Wigtownshire, 1959. Mr Shanks attended two sessions of Professor McQuiston's classes, one as a boy *c.* 1900, and the second a few years later after he had left school. He then attended several sessions of Peter Marshall's classes, and about 1907 began to assist the latter in his classes. Later, Mr Shanks worked in partnership with Peter Marshall, and then, shortly before 1914, held classes on his own account.

J. SCOTT SKINNER (1843–1927, the North-east)

(57) Mr David Grant, Alford, Aberdeenshire, 1955. See p. 24.

MR TROOP (?, Aberdeen district)

(58) Mr Moncur, Culter, Aberdeenshire, 1955. Mr Troop used to hold his classes for the Newhills district in Mr Moncur's father's barn (earthern-floored, oil-lit), and Mr Moncur attended the classes for several sessions about 1895.

JOSEPH WALLACE, SENIOR (*c.* 1830–1900, Kilmarnock district)
JOSEPH WALLACE, JUNIOR (1856–1932, Kilmarnock district)

(59) Miss Elizabeth Wallace, F.B.A.T.D., Kilmarnock, 1959 and correspondence. Daughter of Joseph Wallace junior, granddaughter of Joseph Wallace senior, Miss Wallace assisted her father in his classes, and carried on his business on his death. Member of the Scottish Official Board of Highland Dancing.

(ii) Informants on the mainland of Scotland and the Western Isles not listed under (i).

Roxburghshire

(60) Mr John Wood, Crailing, Roxburghshire, 1960. A fiddler, played for dances round Jedburgh from 1907 onwards.

(61) Mr and Mrs George Young, Jedburgh, 1953, 1958.

Selkirkshire

(62) Miss Brydon and Mrs Elliot, Dundas Cottage, Ettrick, and Miss M. Brydon, Shank End, Ettrick, 1958. Miss M. Brydon attended Mr Buck's classes at Yarrow School *c.* 1902.

(63) Miss Davidson, Gilmanscleuch Cottage, Ettrick, 1958.

(64) Mr George Nichol, Selkirk, 1958 (in Ettrick). Worked in Ettrick as a shepherd from *c.* 1900.

(65) Mr John M. Duthie, Galashiels, 1958, 1960. Brought up at Birsay in Orkney, later moved to Lauder and then to Galashiels, where he played a leading part in the Country Dance revival. Co-author of the *Complete Guide to Scottish Country Dancing*.

(66) Mrs I. C. B. Jamieson, Clovenfords, Selkirkshire, 1953, 1958, and correspondence. Information from her husband.

Berwickshire

(67) Mr William Aitchison, Lauder, 1958, 1960. A fiddler, played at many of the dances and kirns in Lauderdale from about 1900 onwards.

(68) Mr Gordon S. Gibb, The Roan, Lauder, 1960. Son of Dr Shirra Gibb, who farmed Boon in Lauderdale from 1872 to 1922 (see p. 176 n.).

(69) Mr William Lothian, Lauder, 1960. Elder brother of Mr Alex Lothian (23).

(70) Mr William Shaw, Lauder, 1958, 1959 (with F.R.), 1960. Attended many of the kirns in the district from *c.* 1893 onwards.

(71) Mr David Watson, Lauder, 1960. As the son of one of the local tradesmen, Mr Watson attended most of the kirns in the district from an early age.

(72) Mr James Watson, Lauder, 1958, 1960. Brother of Mr David Watson above, in his young days a member of a local dance band.

(73) Mr John Wilkinson, Lauder, 1960.

(74) Mrs Mary Fergie, Westruther, Berwickshire, 1960. Attended the kirns at Spottiswoode from about 1886 to 1892 (see p. 176).

(75) Mrs Margaret Kerr, Longformacus, Berwickshire, 1960.

East Lothian

(76) Mr and Mrs Henry Barry, Longniddrie, E. Lothian, 1958.

(77) Mr Andrew Grierson, Daviot, Inverness-shire, 1959 (with F.R.). Originally from Athelstaneford, brother of Mrs E. H. Wood (45), taught to dance by his father.

(78) Mr and Mrs David Kirkcaldy, Gullane, E. Lothian, 1958 (with F.R.). Keen dancers who attended many kirns in the Gullane district from about 1912 onwards. Mr Kirkcaldy was born in Fife, and attended Alexander Adamson's classes at Ceres *c.* 1908.

(79) Mr Thomas Wood, Dirleton, E. Lothian, 1958. A fiddler, played at many of the local dances from about 1905 onwards.

Lanarkshire

(80) Mrs Jenny Cook, Douglas, Lanarkshire, 1958.

(81) Mr William Lawson, Lanark, 1958. A step-dancer and stage-dancer, held dancing classes in Lanark in his spare time.

Perthshire

(82) Mr Peter Crerar, Ballachraggan, Strath Bran, Perthshire, 1956. See p. 248 n.

(83) Mr and Mrs A. G. Reid, Balnakilly, Strath Ardle, Mr and Mrs F. K. Balfour, Kindrogan, Strath Ardle, Mr and Mrs D. Liddell and Mr H. Liddell, Ellangowan, Pitlochry, and Mr G. Dolby,

Wood End of Kindrogan, Strath Ardle, 1958. At Mr and Mrs Reid's invitation the above people gathered together one evening at Balnakilly to show us the dances performed within recent years at some of the big Highland Balls.

(84) Mr Stewart, Kirkmichael, Perthshire, 1956. Originally from Blair Atholl.

Aberdeenshire

(85) Mr William Baird, Culter, Aberdeenshire, 1955. Brought up in the Glen of Cushnie, near Alford, attended three sets of classes held there by various teachers between 1890 and 1900.

(86) Mr Forbes, Keig, Aberdeenshire, 1955.

Glen Spean and Glen Roy, Inverness-shire

(87) Mr Jock Kennedy, Achluachrach, Glen Spean, 1960. A fiddler and a dancer, brought up at Brae Roy at the head of Glen Roy and lived there until his retirement a few years ago. Attended dancing classes held at Brae Roy by a Mr Marshall *c.* 1890. Mr Marshall had been holding classes previously at Roy Bridge, and Mr Kennedy's father persuaded him to come up to Brae Roy—he stayed with the Kennedys and taught in the school-room every week-night for six weeks, ending his session with a ball. Mr Kennedy's family home at Brae Roy was the ceilidh house of the neighbourhood.

(88) Mr and Mrs Donald MacDonald (The Scout), Bohuntine, Glen Roy, 1960. Both attended classes held at Roy Bridge *c.* 1894 by a Mr James Burns, who taught in the Lochaber district, *c.* 1890–1910. Mrs MacDonald was brought up with her uncle in Bohuntine, and her childhood home was the ceilidh house of the neighbourhood.

(89) Mr James MacDonald, Bohenie, Glen Roy, 1960. A fiddler, piper, and dancer, attended Mr Burns's classes at Roy Bridge *c.* 1898 (see above).

(90) Mr John MacDonald (The Bard), Highbridge, Spean Bridge, 1960. Attended three sessions of Mr Burns's classes at Spean Bridge *c.* 1900, and before that attended classes held at Inverlair by a Mr MacPhail, a ploughman there who taught dancing in his spare time, and also classes held near Highbridge by a Mr Forbes, a Rannoch man who was competing at the various Highland Games in the district. Mr MacDonald is a noted source of old lore (see (302)), and his home at Highbridge was (and still is) the ceilidh house of the district.

Glen Urquhart and Strath Glass, Inverness-shire

(91) Mr Andrew Fraser, Balbeg, Glen Urquhart, 1960. Attended classes in Glen Urquhart *c.* 1886, and also later in Inverness; was a

Games dancer in his younger days, and continued to give exhibitions of Highland solo dancing up to the age of 70 (see also (302)).

(92) Miss C. Gordon, Miss Catherine Gordon, Mrs Treasurer, and Mr Peter Gordon, Milton, Glen Urquhart, 1960. Miss C. Gordon attended the same classes in Glen Urquhart as Mr Andrew Fraser above; Miss Catherine Gordon attended classes in Drumnadrochit c. 1905.

(93) Mr Alexander Montgomery, Strath Glass, 1960. A concertina player, played for dancing in Strath Glass from about 1907 onwards.

Morar, Inverness-shire

(94) Mr Ronald MacLean, Camusdarroch, Morar, 1956 (with F.R.).

Moidart, Inverness-shire and Acharacle and Salen, Loch Sunart, Argyllshire

(95) Mrs E. Creoll, Samalaman House, Glenuig, Moidart, 1956 (with F.R.).

(96) Mr Hugh MacDonald, Banavie, Fort William, 1956 (F.R.). Originally from Smearisary, Glenuig, has spent some time in Lochaber.

(97) Mrs MacLellan, Eilean Shona, Moidart, 1956 (with F.R. and Father Joseph Campbell of Mingarry).

(98) Mr Angus Livingstone, Dalilea, Moidart, 1954.

(99) Mr James Buchan, Paisley, 1956. Originally from Moidart.

(100) Mr Donald MacDonald, Fort William, 1954, 1956 (with F.R.). Originally from Moidart, nephew of Miss Ann MacDonald of Mingarry (see p. 164).

(101) Mr John (Blain) MacDonald, Cliff, Moidart, 1956.

(102) Mr and Mrs Angus MacIsaac, Banavie, Fort William, 1956 (with F.R.). Mrs MacIsaac comes from Mingarry in Moidart, Mr MacIsaac from Glenuig.

(103) Mr William Harrison, Acharacle, 1956 (F.R.).

(104) Miss Joan MacInnes, Acharacle, 1956.

(105) Mr and Mrs Gordon Menzies, Salen, Loch Sunart, 1956.

(106) Mrs M. H. Fergusson, Blairhoyle, Port of Mentieth, correspondence.

Argyllshire coast

(107) Archibald Campbell of Kilberry, Earls Court, London, 1959, and correspondence. Well known as a leading authority on piping matters.

(108) Mr Duncan Cowan, Ledaig, Benderloch, 1956.

(109) Mrs MacLucas, Ledaig, Benderloch, 1956.

(110) Mr Duncan Morrison, Ledaig, Benderloch, 1956.

Skye, Eigg, and Mull

(111) Mr Neil MacKinnon, Torrin, Skye, 1954.

(112) Mr Charles Mathieson, Torrin, Skye, 1954. A fiddler and a dancer.
(113) Mr Duncan MacPherson, Upper Breakish, Skye, 1954. A piper, often played for dancing.
(114) Mr Neil MacDonald, Cliadale, Eigg, 1953.
(115) Mrs Flora MacLellan, Cliadale, Eigg, 1953.
(116) Mr and Mrs Donald Black and Miss Flora Black, Lochbuie, Mull, 1957. Miss Flora Black attended the dancing classes held in Lochbuie *c.* 1900 by Mr Dudgeon (p. 40).
(117) Mr Dugald MacArthur, Lochdonhead, Mull, 1957. Attended dancing classes held at Lochdonhead *c.* 1904 by a Mr McCallum, a part-time teacher who taught mainly on the Argyllshire coast south of Oban.

Outer Hebrides

(118) Captain A. M. Kennedy, Wallasey, Cheshire, 1959. Originally from the Lochs district of Lewis.
(119) Mr Angus John MacLellan, Hacklett, Benbecula, 1953 (J.F., T.F.), 1955 (F.R.). A noted source of old tales and old customs.
(120) Mr John MacLellan, Crieff, Perthshire, 1956. Elder brother of Mr Angus John MacLellan above. Originally from Benbecula, and attended dancing classes held on Benbecula by a S. Uist man *c.* 1891. Mr MacLellan's wife came from Eriskay, and he has spent some time on that island.
(121) Mr Angus MacMillan, Griminish, Benbecula, 1953. The most noted of all Gaelic story-tellers.
(122) Mr Roderick MacPherson, Liniclett, Benbecula, 1953 (J.F., T.F.), 1955 (F.R.).
(123) Mrs Monk, Creagorry, Benbecula, 1953 (J.F., T.F.), 1955 (F.R.).
(124) Mrs Campbell, Garryheillie, Daliburgh, S. Uist, 1955 (F.R.). Originally from Loch Eynort, S. Uist.
(125) Mrs Margaret MacAskill, South Boisdale, S. Uist, 1956 (F.R.). Brought up at Smerclett, S. Uist.
(126) Mr John MacLeod, Eochar, S. Uist, 1953 (in Glasgow).
(127) Mrs Kate Morrison, Greybridge, Daliburgh, S. Uist, 1955 (F.R. with Rev. Mgr MacKellaig), 1956 (F.R.).
(128) Mr John MacIsaac, Eriskay, 1955 (F.R., via Dr Alasdair MacLean of Daliburgh, S. Uist).
(129) Miss Rachel MacLeod, Castlebay, Barra, 1953.
(130) Mr Farquhar MacNeil, Eoligarry, Barra, 1953, 1954 (in Jedburgh). Much information from his father and grandfather.
(131) Mr Neil MacNeil, Craigston, Barra, 1953, 1954. Our first source.
Also (132) See Nos. 36, 37, 88, 92, 93, 111, 113, 115, 119, 121.
(133) See Nos. 97, 102, 124, 127, 128, 130.
(134) See Nos. 36, 94, 112, 115, 123, 124, 127.

(iii) Informants in Orkney not listed under (i) and (ii). All visited in 1955.

Mainland
    (135) Mrs Corrigall, Dounby. Brought up at Kirbuster on the Mainland.
    (136) Mrs James Garson, Dounby. Information from her father, a noted fiddler from the Stenness district who died in 1947 at the age of 90.
    (137) Mr and Mrs John Findlater, Breckan, Dounby.
    (138) Mr and Mrs Tom Harvey, Banks, Dounby.

Burray
    (139) Mr Eric Sutherland, Lowerhouse.

South Ronaldshay
    (140) Mr and Mrs John Budge, Gammons. Mr Budge is noted as a fiddler.

Flotta
    (141) Mr and Mrs David Flett, The Dam.
    (142) Mrs Margaret Mowat, Bowcot.
    (143) Mr and Mrs Robert Rosie, Saraquoy.
    (144) Mr David Sutherland, The Smiddy.
    (145) Mr Fred Sutherland, Windbreak.

Rousay
    (146) Mrs Clouston, Wasbister.
    (147) Mr and Mrs Craigie, Breck, Sourin.
    (148) Mr Tom Gibson, Broland, Sourin.

North Ronaldshay
    (149) Mr and Mrs Roy Scott, Rendall, Evie, Mainland. Mr Scott belongs to N. Ronaldshay.

(iv) Informants in Shetland. All visited in 1959, by one or both of T.F. and F.R.

Mainland, general
    (150) Mr Tommy Anderson, Lerwick. From Esha Ness, a very fine fiddler, has collected fiddle tunes in Shetland for the Shetland Folk Society and the School of Scottish Studies of the University of Edinburgh.
    (151) Mr and Mrs John H. Johnson, Selly Oak, Birmingham. From Hillswick. Mr Johnson collected information on dancing in Shetland for the Shetland Folk-Lore Society *c.* 1930.
    (152) Mrs Catherine Laurenson, Lerwick. Belongs to N. Delting, has much information on old customs from her parents and other people of her parents' generation.

Mainland, Cunningsburgh district
    (153) Mrs Robina Christie, Skibhoull, Cunningsburgh.
    (154) Mrs Ann Halcrow, Quee, Cunningsburgh.

(155) Miss Barbara Halcrow, Punstow, Cunningsburgh.

(156) Miss Agnes Johnson, Ligg, Cunningsburgh.

(157) Mrs Laura Malcolmson, Westlea, Cunningsburgh.

(158) Mrs Elizabeth Smith, Aithsetter, Cunningsburgh.

(159) Mrs Margaret Smith, Aith, Cunningsburgh.

(160) The Rev. A. Barclay Wilson, Howden Court, Tiverton, Devon (late Minister of Cunningsburgh, visited at Torryburn).

Mainland, Sandwick district

(161) Mrs Margaret Smith and Miss Margaret Smith, Hill Cottage, Sandsayre Wick, Sandwick.

(162) Mr Thomas Thomson, Swinister, Sandwick.

Mainland, Wester and Easter Skeld districts

(163) Miss Jessie Cheyne, Creull, Wester Skeld.

(164) Miss Kate Hay, The Hill, Wester Skeld.

(165) Mrs James Isbister, Easter Skeld. Originally from Wester Skeld.

(166) Mr and Mrs Thomas Moar, Northouse, Wester Skeld. Mr Moar belongs to Wester Skeld, was a fiddler in his younger days; Mrs Moar comes from Westerwick.

(167) Mrs Robert Ridland, Parkside, Wester Skeld. Information from her mother, who was born in 1854.

(168) Miss Margaret Tulloch, South Houses, Easter Skeld.

Mainland, Walls and West Walls districts

(169) Mrs Barbara Cheyne, Elvister, Walls.

(170) Mr John Fraser, Reawick. Born and brought up in W. Walls, moved to Burrastow, Walls, in 1888, and then to Reawick in 1905.

(171) Mr Peter Henry, Lerwick. Originally from Walls.

(172) Miss Jean Pole, Walls. A fiddler, and a very keen dancer in her younger days.

(173) Miss Mary Smith, Elvister, Walls. Her father was a noted fiddler, her mother was one of the Frasers of Finnigarth, a family of noted fiddlers.

(174) Mr John Fraser, Kinkwell, W. Walls.

(175) Mr Peter Fraser, Lerwick. Present owner of Finnigarth in W. Walls, a fiddler, and descendant of fiddlers.

(176) Mr Thomas Fraser, Crabs, Scarpigarth, W. Walls. A fiddler in his younger days.

Burra Isle

(177) Mrs Elizabeth Pottinger, Branchiclate, Hamnavoe. Born in Oxna, and whilst living there danced in Hamnavoe. Moved to Hamnavoe in 1905.

(178) Mrs Margaret Pottinger, Beach, Hamnavoe. Came from Yell to Hamnavoe *c.* 1900.

(179) Mrs David Williamson, Bridge End.

(180) Mr John Williamson, The Croe.

Papa Stour

(181, 182, 183) Mr Fraser Hughson, Valleyfield, Aith, Mainland; Mr Thomas Hughson, Leapark, Weisdale, Mainland; Mr William Hughson, Weisdale, Mainland. Three brothers, all noted fiddlers, born and brought up on Papa Stour, moved to the Mainland in 1898.

(184) Mrs Mary Jamieson, Biggins, Papa Stour.

(185) Mr Alex Johnston, Hurdiback, Papa Stour. Leader of the Papa Stour Sword Dance team, author of a booklet on the Papa Stour Sword Dance.

Foula

(186) Mrs M. C. S. Holbourn and Mr L. A. Holbourn, Penkaet Castle, Pencaitland, E. Lothian, 1955. Mrs Holbourn's husband, the late Professor I. B. S. Holbourn, was Laird of Foula, and Mr L. A. Holbourn and his brothers are the present owners of the island.

Whalsay

(187) Mrs Janet Bruce, Sandshoull, Isbister.

(188) Mrs Flora Hutchison, Easthouse, Fladdabister, Mainland. Born and brought up in Fladdabister, moved to Whalsay in 1899, and was married there.

(189) Mr and Mrs James Hutchison, New Town.

(190) Mr and Mrs John Hutchison, Creads, Brough.

(191) Mrs Margaret Hutchison, Creadie Knowe.

(192) Mr John Irvine, Saltness. A noted fiddler, and a very good source of old lore.

(193) Mr Magnus Irvine, Saltness, and Mr William Irvine, Symbister. Sons of Mr John Irvine above.

(194) Mr Irvine and Mrs George Polson, Marister. Brother and sister of Mr John Irvine above.

(195) Mr and Mrs Andrew Moar, East Burns.

(196) Miss Elizabeth Nicolson, Symbister.

(197) Captain Robert Simpson, Symbister.

(198) Mr and Mrs Robert Williamson, Symbister, and Mr and Mrs William Williamson, Marister.

Also (199) See Nos. 163, 165, 168, 170–1, 174–5.

(200) See Nos. 164, 166, 170, 172, 174–5, 177, 180, 181, 184–5.

(B) BIBLIOGRAPHY: SCOTTISH WORKS ON DANCING

(This list contains only those books actually referred to in the text)

Works in manuscript

(201) Laing MS. 564a, Edinburgh University Library, *c.* 1745–70. (This is a small leather-bound notebook, signed Alex^r Bowman, containing the instructions, without music, for 122 Country Dances. In the R.S.C.D.S. collections and in Dr Thurston's *Scotland's Dances* the notebook is referred to as the Bowman MS.)

(202) 'A list of Country Dances according to Mr William Seymour from Kilbride, which he teached at Blantyre farm,' 1805. (We have seen only a copy of the original of this manuscript, in the Atholl Collection in the Sandeman Public Library, Perth; we do not know where the original is to be found. According to this copy, the manuscript contains instructions, without music, for thirty-seven Country Dances, three Eightsome Reels, and a version of the Bumpkin.)

(203) *Contre-Danses à Paris 1818*, MS. 3860, National Library of Scotland. (For a description of the manuscript see the footnote on p. 108.)

Printed works

(204) F. Peacock, *Sketches relative to the history and theory but more especially to the practice and art of dancing*, Aberdeen, 1805.

(205) Barclay Dun, *Translation of nine of the most fashionable Quadrilles, consisting of fifty French country dances as performed in England and Scotland*, Edinburgh, 1818.

(206) *The Companion to the Reticule*, Edinburgh (?), *c.* 1820. (This is principally a collection of dance music, but contains a few notes on dancing in Scotland before 1815.)

(207) John Sutherland, *The Heart of Midlothian, A Reel, The Laird of Dumbiedike's Favorite and Madge Wildfire's Strathspey and Reel, To which are added two favorite dances for 1820*, Edinburgh, *c.* 1820.

(208) Alexander Strathy, *Elements of the Art of Dancing, with a description of the principal figures in the Quadrille*, Edinburgh, 1822. (This book is largely an unacknowledged translation of J. H. Gourdoux, *Principes et Notions Élémentaires sur l'art de la danse pour la ville*, Paris, 1811.)

(209) J. Thomson, *A Guide to the Ball-Room*, Glasgow, 1823.

(210) J. P. Boulogne, *The ballroom, or the juvenile pupil's assistant*, Glasgow, 1827.

(211) J., R., J., and J. S. Lowe, *Lowe's Ball-Conductor and Assembly Guide*, 3rd edition, Edinburgh, *c.* 1830. Also (212) a further edition, much revised, *c.* 1860. (Our information about the further edition is derived from an incomplete copy in our possession.)

(213) H. D. Willock, *Manual of Dancing*, Glasgow, 1865.

(214) W. E. Allan, *New Reference Guide to the Ball-Room*, Glasgow, *c.* 1870. Also (215) a revised edition, *c.* 1880. Also (216) a further edition, again revised, published by Messrs. Mozart Allan under the title *Reference Guide to the Ball-Room*, Glasgow, *c.* 1890.

(217) J. F. Wallace, *The Excelsior Manual of Dancing*, Glasgow, *c.* 1872. Also (218) a pocket edition, published under the title *People's Edition of the Excelsior Manual of Dancing*, Glasgow, *c.* 1881. Also (219) a revised edition of the *People's Edition*, *c.* 1900.

(220) David Anderson, *D. Anderson's Ball-Room Guide, with full tuition in the art of dancing without the use of French terms*, Dundee, *c.* 1886. Revised editions (221, 222) *c.* 1891 and *c.* 1894. Also (223) *The Universal Ball-Room and Solo-Dance Guide*, Dundee, *c.* 1899, a revised and much enlarged version of the *Ball-Room Guide*. Also further editions of *The Universal . . . Guide*, with slight revisions, *c.* 1900 and *c.* 1902.

(224) William Smith, *Complete Guide to the Ballroom*, Inverness, *c.* 1889.

(225) John N. MacLeod, *Pocket Companion to the Ball-Room*, Kirkcaldy, 1897.

(226) J. Grahamsley Atkinson, *Scottish National Dances*, Edinburgh, 1900.

(227) Graham MacNeilage, *How to Dance the Eightsome Reel*, Alloa, *c.* 1900.

(228) James Orr Robertson, *Country Dancing*, in *Kerr's Collection of Reels and Strathspeys . . .*, Glasgow, *c.* 1900.

(229) J. Scott Skinner, *The People's Ball Room Guide*, Dundee, *c.* 1905.

(230) A. Cosmo Mitchell, *A Guide to Ball Room Dancing*, Aberdeen, *c.* 1905.

(231) William Robertson, *The Pupils' Aid to the Memory and Guide to the Ball-room Dances*, 6th edition, Brechin (?), *c.* 1905.

(232) Donald R. MacKenzie, *The National Dances of Scotland*, Glasgow, 1910.

(233) Aeneas MacKay, *Mackay's Ballroom Guide*, Stirling, *c.* 1912.

(234) Scottish Country Dance Society (later the Royal Scottish Country Dance Society), *The Scottish Country Dance Book, Books 1–21*, Glasgow, 1924–61. (Books 1–13, 18, and 21 contain some seventy dances collected from living memory.)

(235) Scottish Country Dance Club, *The Border Dance Book*, London, 1930. (The original edition of this book contains six dances, Jessie's Favourite, The Cuckoo's Nest, The Laddies o' Dunse, The Mason's Apron, Merrily Danced the Quaker's Wife, and The Rifleman. A new edition, containing these dances together with a further six, was published as *The First Border Book of Scottish Country Dances*, London, 1931, and a further twelve dances were published in *The Second Border Book of . . . Dances*, London, 1932.

Later, twenty-one of these dances, together with La Russe and Glasgow Highlanders, were published in a single volume (236) *The Border Dance Book, Scottish Country Dances. Compiled by Elizabeth MacLachlan*, Edinburgh, n.d. All the dances in these books were contributed by the late I. C. B. Jamieson.)

(237) G. Douglas Taylor, *Some Traditional Scottish Dances*, London, 1929.

(238) A. Anderson and J. Duthie, *Complete Guide to Scottish Country Dancing*, Edinburgh, c. 1930.

(239) D. G. MacLennan, *Highland and Traditional Scottish Dances*, Edinburgh, 1950.

(240) Jean C. Milligan, *Won't you join the dance*, London, 1951.

(241) H. A. Thurston, *Scotland's Dances*, London, 1954.

(242) The Scottish Official Board of Highland Dancing, *Highland Dancing*, Edinburgh, 1955.

(C) BIBLIOGRAPHY: GENERAL WORKS

(243) Gavin Douglas, The Aeneid of Virgil, translated into Scottish verse, MS. in Trinity College, Cambridge, c. 1525, printed in *The Aeneid of Virgil Translated into Scottish Verse by Gavin Douglas, Bishop of Dunkeld* (Bannatyne Club), Edinburgh, 1839.

(244) John Playford, *The Dancing Master*, 7th edition, London, 1686. Also (245) the 17th edition, London, 1721.

(246) *Virgils Aeneis, translated into Scottish verse by ... G. Douglas, ... A new edition ... To which is added a large Glossary ...* [by T. Ruddiman], Edinburgh, 1710.

(247) Giovanni Gallini (Sir John Gallini), *A treatise on the art of dancing*, London, 1765.

(248) Matthew Welch, *Variety of English Country Dances for the present year ... showing ... the Right and Left, etc., ...*, London, 1767.

(249) Edward Topham, *Letters from Edinburgh written in the years 1774 and 1775*, Edinburgh, 1776.

(250, 251) James Johnson, *The Scots Musical Museum*, Edinburgh, Vol. 2, 1788, Vol. 3, 1790.

(252) Thomas Newte, *Prospects and Observations, on a tour in England and Scotland*, London, 1791.

(253) *A Collection of Favourite Reels and Strathspeys ... Printed for and Sold by W. Boag*, London, c. 1797.

(254) James Currie, *The Life of Robert Burns ... with ... observations on the Scotish Peasantry*, Liverpool, 1800.

(255) MS. collection of music belonging to Peter Hardie, fiddler, of Tullymet (born 1775). (The manuscript is in the Atholl Collection in the Sandeman Public Library, Perth.)

(256) Col. Thomas Thornton, *A Sporting Tour through the Highlands of Scotland*, London, 1804.

(257) Thomas Wilson, *An Analysis of Country Dancing*, 2nd edition, London, 1811. (The first edition, published in 1808, is a much smaller work, and does not contain the descriptions of the Three-some and Foursome Reels given in the second edition.)

(258) Alexander Fordyce, *A Country Wedding . . .*, Lanark, 1818.

(259) *Caledonian Mercury*, Edinburgh, March 27th, 1819.

(260) F. J. Lambert, *Treatise on Dancing*, Norwich, *c.* 1820.

(261) Thomas Wilson, *The Complete System of English Country Dancing*, London, 1821.

(262) William Grant Stewart, *The Popular Superstitions and the Festive Amusements of the Highlanders*, Edinburgh, 1822.

(263) John MacTaggart, *The Scottish Gallovidian Encyclopedia*, Glasgow, 1824.

(264) John Jamieson, *An Etymological Dictionary of the Scottish Language* (supplementary volumes), Edinburgh, 1825.

(265) John Brockett, *A Glossary of North Country Words*, Newcastle, 1829.

(266) James Logan, *The Scottish Gael*, Vol. 1, London, 1831.

(267) *The Ballroom Annual*, London, 1844. (An abbreviated version of this work, possibly brought up to date by the inclusion of certain new dances, was published under the title *The Art of Dancing*, London, n.d., and in this form seems to have had a fairly wide circulation in Scotland.)

(268) James Brand, *Observations on the Popular Antiquities of Great Britain*, revised by Sir Henry Ellis, various editions, 3 vols., London.

(269) Robert Chambers (ed.), *The Life and Works of Robert Burns*, Vol. 1, Edinburgh, 1851.

(270) Gleniffer, 'Bab in the Bowster', *Notes and Queries*, 3 (1851), p. 45.

(271) 'Shetland Marriages', *Chambers Journal*, 12 (1859), pp. 383–4.

(272) Manuscript collection of dances written for Miss Kate Hughes by Aseh Thompson, dancing-master, of Dundalk, Ireland, 1867.

(273) J. T. Reid, *Art Rambles in Shetland*, Edinburgh, 1869.

(274) Charles Cowan, *Reminiscences*, privately printed, 1878.

(275) 'Recollections of a Shetland Wedding in the year 1837. By a Bridegroom's Man', *The Orkney and Shetland Guide, Directory and Almanac for 1891* [ed. James Anderson], Kirkwall, 1890.

(276) Sir Aeneas MacKintosh of MacKintosh, *Notes Descriptive and Historical Principally relating to the Parish of Moy in Strathdearn and the Town and Neighbourhood of Inverness*, privately printed, 1892. (The original was written *c.* 1783–4.)

(277) R. O. Heslop, *Northumberland Words*, Vol. 1, London, 1892.

(278) G. Desrat, *Dictionnaire de la Danse*, Paris, 1895.

(279) Elizabeth Grant, *Memoirs of a Highland Lady, 1797–1827*, London, 1898.

(280) Alexander Carmichael, *Carmina Gadelica*, Vol. 1, Edinburgh, 1900.

(281) Keith N. MacDonald, *Puirt-a-beul*, Glasgow, 1901.

(282) *Peace's Almanac and County Directory for 1903*, Kirkwall, 1902.

(283) Margaret Warrender (ed.), *Lady John Scott, Songs and Verses*, 2nd edition, Edinburgh, 1911.

(284) John Firth, *Reminiscences of an Orkney Parish*, Stromness, 1922 Also published in parts in the *Old-Lore Miscellany* of the Viking Club from 1910 onwards.

(285) Susan Sibbald, *The Memoirs of Susan Sibbald (1783–1812)*, London, 1926.

(286) Robert Shirra Gibb, *A Farmer's Fifty Years in Lauderdale*, Edinburgh, 1927.

(287) J. M. E. Saxby, *Shetland Traditional Lore*, Edinburgh, 1932.

(288) Scottish Country Dance Society, *Bulletin*, No. 2 (October 1932).

(289) Ion C. B. Jamieson, Manuscript notes on dancing in the Borders, *c.* 1932.

(290) James Boswell, *Boswell's Journal of a Tour to the Hebrides with Samuel Johnson, Ll.D. Now first published from the original MS.*, London, 1936.

(291) Sir Compton MacKenzie, *Whisky Galore*, London, 1947.

(292) P. Shuldham-Shaw, 'Folk Music and Dance in Shetland', *Journal of the English Folk Dance and Song Society*, 6 (1948–51), pp. 74–80.

(293) A. Halcrow, *The Sail Fishermen of Shetland*, Lerwick, 1950.

(294) Shetland Folk Society, *Shetland Folk Book*, 3 vols., Lerwick, 1947, 1951, 1957.

(295) J. F. and T. M. Flett, 'Some Hebridean Folk Dances', *Journal of the English Folk Dance and Song Society*, 7 (1952–5), pp. 112–27, 182–4.

(296) J. F. and T. M. Flett, 'Dramatic Jigs in Scotland', *Folk-Lore*, 67 (1956), pp. 84–96.

(297) J. F. and T. M. Flett, 'Some Early Highland Dancing Competitions', *Aberdeen University Review*, 36 (1956), pp. 345–58.

(298) T. M. Flett, 'Some Notes on Dancing in Orkney, Parts I–VI', *Orkney Herald*, Aug. 7, Sept. 4, 11, 18, Oct. 2, 9, 1956.

(299) 'Analytical Notes—Rhythm', *The Folk Dancer*, 2 (1955–6), pp. 87–88, 111–16, 135–9; 3 (1956–7), pp. 163–4.

(300) Programme of a dance held by the Kirkwall St Magnus Football and Athletic Club in 1884, *Orkney Herald*, October 4, 1955.

(301) Ursula Venables, *Life in Shetland. A World Apart*, Edinburgh, 1956.

(302) Calum I. MacLean, *The Highlands*, London, 1959.
(303) P. J. S. Richardson, *The Social Dances of the Nineteenth Century in England*, London, 1960.

(D) LIST OF INFORMANTS AND REFERENCES FOR THE APPENDIX

The following informants in Cape Breton Island were all visited in 1957.

(1) Mr John Gillis and Miss Margaret Gillis, Gillisdale, S.W. Margaree. Father and daughter; Mr Gillis's grandfather came from Morar.
(2) Mr and Mrs Archie Kennedy, Dunvegan. Mr Kennedy is the son of Mr Ranold Kennedy below; Mrs Kennedy's great-grandparents came from Moidart.
(3) Mr Ronald Kennedy, Broad Cove. His grandfather came from Canna (see p. 271).
(4) The Rev. Father McCormick, East Bay. His grandparents came from S. Uist.
(5) Mrs Mary Sarah MacDonald, Scotch Lake. A centenarian; her grandmother came from Barra.
(6) The Rev. Father Stanley MacDonald, Big Pond. His grandparents came from Kinlochmoidart.
(7) Mr Dan E. MacDonald, Iona.
(8) Mrs MacDougal, East Bay.
(9) Mr Neil R. MacIsaac, Big Pond.
(10) Mr Hugh F. MacKenzie, Sydney. Brought up at Christmas Island; his family came from Barra.
(11) Mrs Christina MacLellan, Inverness.
(12) Mr Frank MacNeil, Big Pond. His grandfather came from Barra.
(13) Mr James C. MacNeil, Gillis Point, Iona.
(14) Mr Steve R. MacNeil, Iona.
(15) Mrs MacTigue, Inverness.
(16) Mr Peter Glen Moriston, Sydney.
(17) Mrs Donald Walker, Daliburgh, S. Uist, Scotland, 1956.
(18) See Nos. 2, 3, 6, 7, 9, 11.
(19) J. L. MacDougall, *History of Inverness County, Nova Scotia*. privately printed, 1922.
(20) See main bibliography, Nos. 220–3.
(21) See main bibliography, No. 295.

Index

Titles of dances are in italics; definite and indefinite articles are not used as catch-words.

Places in the Mainland of Scotland are listed under counties; the various Western Isles are listed under Western Isles.

A

Aberdeenshire, general, 14, 27, 42, 64, 112, 138, 236; Aberdeen, 26, 95; Alford, 8, 45, 136, 173–4

Adamson, Alexander, 8, 105, 112, 151, 233, 234, 245, 252, 253, 254, 286

Adamson, William, 8–14, 17, 19, 20, 105, 112, 120, 122, 123, 151, 233, 234, 245, 246, 250, 252, 253, 254, 286

Aird, John, 93, 112, 115, 286

Alewife and Her Barrels, 29

Allan, Mozart, 248, 259

Allemande, 240–3, 252

America, 155

Anderson, David, 8, 18, 22, 26, 27, 94, 96, 105, 106, 112, 114, 117, 119, 120, 121, 122, 123, 125, 127, 137, 138, 139, 140, 142, 146, 245, 246, 248, 253, 286

Angus, 14, 232, 235, 240, 245, 248–50, 266; *see also* Anderson, David; Neill, James; Reid, 'Dancie'

Argyllshire, general, 49, 154, 236, 245; Ardgour, 153, 154; Benderloch, 5, 39, 154; Dalmally, 30; Kilberry, 40–2, 43, 135, 143, 148, 151, 155

Arran, 123, 129, 245

Atkinson, W. Grahamsley, 26, 96, 97, 100, 101, 114, 119, 122, 124, 140, 142, 148, 153

Auld Reel, 62, 63, 70–4, 221–9

Axum Reel, 56, 191–7

Ayrshire, 28, 35, 233, 236, 245; *see also* Blackley, Prof.; Galbraith, Mr; McCulloch, James; McQuiston, Prof.; Wallace, Joseph, Sen.; Wallace, Joseph, Jun.

B

Babbity Bowster, 2, 14, 40–5, 47, 50, 52, 53, 57, 58

Backstep with a hop, 123, 211, 284

Bailey, Mr, 112, 236, 286

Balance step, *see* Pas de Basque

Ballroom etiquette, 12, 17, 19, 25, 32, 50

Banffshire, general, 14, 27, 64, 130, 138; Dufftown, 45, 136, 173–4

Barn Dance, see Pas de Quatre

Basic positions, 76–86

Basket figures, 243–4, 254, 256

Beaton, Donald, 272

Bedding the Bride, 47, 69–70, 73, 74, 275

Belile's March, 29

Berwickshire, general, 36, 46, 147,

**basketball
concepts and
techniques**

Basketball
Concepts and Techniques

by **Bob Cousy**

and Frank G. Power, Jr.

72 - 385

Allyn and Bacon, Inc., Boston *Celtics*

To Those Who Wait: Eunice and Missy;
Ticia and Marie; Leslie, Wayne, and Gerry

FRANK, SR.
This Book's Inspiration

contents

KEY FOR DIAGRAMS

A, B, C, D, E   Offensive players

X_1, X_2, X_3, X_4, X_5 Defensive players

O_1, O_2, O_3, O_4, O_5 Offensive players in drills

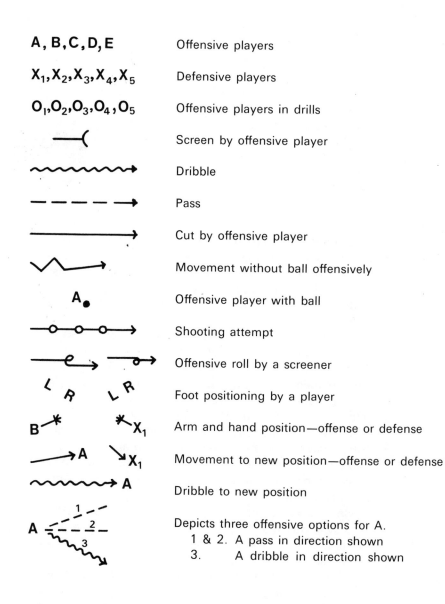

Screen by offensive player

Dribble

Pass

Cut by offensive player

Movement without ball offensively

Offensive player with ball

Shooting attempt

Offensive roll by a screener

Foot positioning by a player

Arm and hand position—offense or defense

Movement to new position—offense or defense

Dribble to new position

Depicts three offensive options for A.
    1 & 2. A pass in direction shown
    3.   A dribble in direction shown

foreword

No two men are more qualified to write a book on coaching basketball than Bob Cousy and Frank Power. Bob's life has been basketball, and probably no other name in the history of the sport has been so closely identified with it. Frank was both freshman coach and chief scout during Bob's six years at Boston College.

Cousy, who was an All-American college basketball player at Holy Cross, moved on to the National Basketball Association to become a legend with the Boston Celtics, leading them to six NBA Championships. In 1962, after retiring as an active player, Bob took over the coaching reins of Boston College. He put the school on the basketball map by carefully, systematically, and quickly building teams that ranked among the best in the nation. His teams had a phenomenal six-year record of 117 won and 38 lost (over 75 percent), and received five successive National Tournament bids.

On leaving Boston College at the end of the 1969 season, Bob was much sought after by many of the professional teams in the NBA. In the spring of 1969, he signed a contract with the Cincinnati Royals.

I have had the privilege of knowing and working with Bob Cousy for a great many years, including thirteen years as his coach with the Boston Celtics. During his great years with the Celtics, he was known as "Mr. Basketball," and in my opinion no player in the history of the game has ever been more deserving of such a title, nor carried it with more dignity and grace.

Bob Cousy is a highly intelligent man, and since his

early playing days he has been a keen observer and analyst of the game of basketball. In my judgment, he has as much knowledge and savvy stored up inside him about the game of basketball as any living person today. Bob was the spark plug and field general for the fast-break style of basketball played by the Boston Celtics, and he successfully continued this aggressive, exciting style during his coaching years at Boston College.

Frank Power is currently the Headmaster of Charlestown (Mass.) High School. His fame as a coach of high school football, basketball, and baseball is surpassed only by his stature in the academic field.

Frank began his basketball coaching career in the U.S. Navy in 1944. He has coached basketball in high school and prep school and at both freshman and varsity college levels. His overall twenty-five year record is 422 wins against 99 loses. Since 1953 (except for the 1963 season when he was interim varsity coach at B.C. until Bob ended his pro career), he has been the freshman basketball coach at Boston College. His record over the past five seasons has been an astounding 90 wins and 10 losses. Widely known as an erudite instructor and brilliant technician of basketball, he, therefore, is a natural collaborator for Cousy. Having worked closely with Bob for so many years, Frank is intimately familiar with, and in complete accord with the Bob Cousy brand of basketball. Together, they have written a definitive and highly informative book on the techniques of playing and coaching basketball. It should rank among the classic books on the game.

Arnold "Red" Auerbach

preface

In this book the authors have attempted to accomplish several objectives. Primarily, we wanted to present coaches and players with a sound, in-depth study of basketball from its basic elements through the complexities of team organization and the strategems of the game. We also endeavored to provide many varied offensive and defensive alignments suited to specific personnel for use within the framework of their experience. By assimilating into their teaching most of the proven techniques outlined, coaches can improve their team's capabilities.

This book is sectioned into five parts for easier reference. The major thrust of the book is necessarily focused on Parts Two and Three, Offense and Defense. Part One discusses essential coaching attributes and the overall operational aspects of the game. Part Four details the principles of complete game organization. Part Five covers statistics and conditioning.

We are deeply indebted to Buddy LeRoux, currently the Boston Red Sox trainer and for many years the outstanding trainer of many Boston Celtic Championship Basketball Teams, for contributing Chapter 13 on Conditioning and Training.

Chapter 4 is extremely valuable to both player and coach. We cannot stress too emphatically the significance of mastering the techniques presented in this chapter. The Cousy adaptation of the fast break is meticulously developed in toto from its elementary stages to its most advanced level. Also thoroughly presented is the Stack Set Offense as devised by Cousy and executed by his five National Tournament Teams.

Drills for perfecting the various techniques are presented next to the discussions of those techniques. In the appendix is a complete annotated Bibliography, as well as actual game scouting reports, practice schedules, and a game plan.

The authors wish to extend their appreciation to all the athletes in the photographs. Sincere thanks are extended especially to Miss Rowena Dores and to the others from Allyn and Bacon, Inc. without whose cooperation this book could not have become a reality. We are grateful to Fritz Massman (B. C. trainer) and Bill Mokray for technical assistance, "Lefty" Nelson, of Wilson Sporting Goods Company, for the use of necessary equipment; and the staff photographers of *Sub Turri*, Roger Pellisier, Joe Britt, Bill Gigliotti, Kevin Carney and Mark Killenbeck. Finally, our deep gratitude to Ken Gorman for his photographic patience and excellence.

part one
introduction

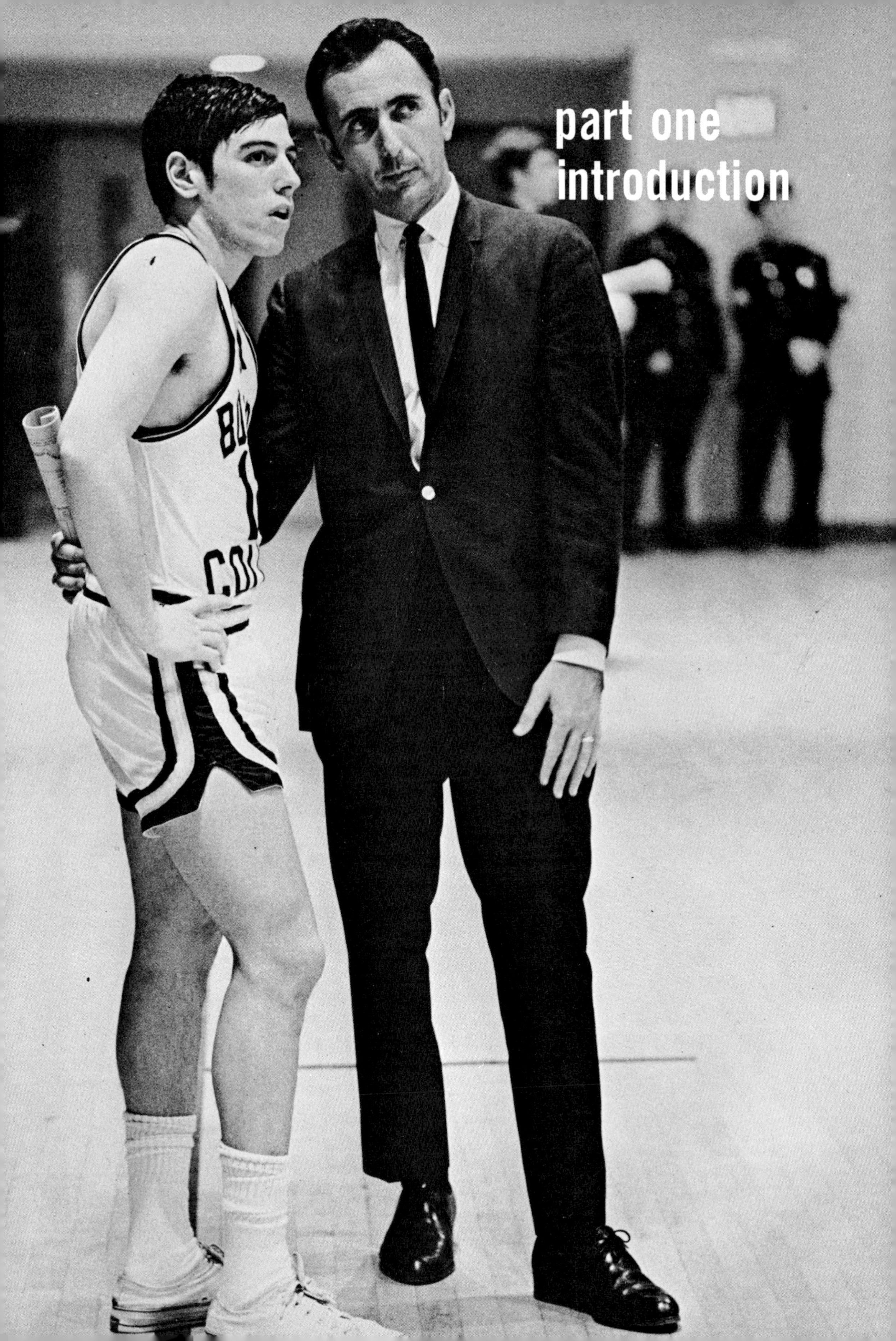

1

the
coach

A basketball coach is at once a teacher, a leader, a psychologist, a public relations liaison agent, and a professional man. In these capacities, he has an obligation to basketball and sports in general, to his players, to his fellow coaches, to the opposing participants and game officials, to the school or organization he represents, to the press and other news media, and to the community.

characteristics of a good coach

The coach is a prime influence on his players during their formative years; therefore, he should be an educated, cultured gentleman with high ideals and firm principles. He must be dignified, serious, businesslike, and even-tempered. He must have understanding, patience, and a personality that inspires confidence in those around him. He must be sincere in his relationships with his players—firm, without being stubborn. He must discipline himself, his players, and his staff within the framework of his moral philosophy. The coach does not necessarily have to have been an outstanding basketball player. However, he should be mentally attuned to the game, and he must be adaptable. Many great coaches were poor players, and many great players make poor coaches.

A coach seeking a job at a certain level should be aware of the duties involved. At the high school or college level he must have a common sense approach to basketball, keeping it in its proper perspective within the overall institutional administrative policy. At these levels, especially the former, teaching duties may come before coaching, which is merely one facet of the educational process of his players. The basic requirements for a coach are that he be a good teacher, both in the classroom and on the basketball court, and that he have unlimited knowledge of basketball. He must be able to organize his time, he must have patience and fortitude, and he must have a great desire to improve the techniques of his students.

In any school, a pleasant, friendly attitude by the coach can go a long way in helping his relationship with the student body, as well as his players' relationship with the other students. He should be available to students for consultations in his office at specified times. He must also get to know the rest of the faculty and the administrators. They will have a far better understanding of his problems if they are on friendly terms.

A good coach does not enter the coaching profession merely to earn a living. Coaching demands all of your time and interest almost twelve months a year—usually without

4

regard for social and family obligations. It is impossible to be a clock watcher and still function effectively as a coach. If you are not completely dedicated to the team, the players will know it. One of the authors heard his captain comment that the reason he knew the team had the coach's complete interest was that the coach never took long-distance phone calls while practice was going on.

Dedication comes easily to most coaches for a very selfish reason—their ego. Granted we love the game and enjoy teaching it to the youngsters, but the important motive is that the discipline and organization, as well as the success of the team, is a direct reflection on the coach.

The coach's reward is basically intrinsic: he can take pleasure in the travel involved, the meeting of different people, and the loyalty and friendship of the players, the administration and—perhaps most important—his peers. The financial gain is normally secondary.

The team looks to the coach for organization and leadership, and his ability in these areas is reflected by his players on and off the court. He must have sound judgment and the courage and ability to exercise his judgment when the situation warrants it. Many times a coach has the knowledge required but hesitates to act. This weakness will carry over and lead to a similar weakness among his players. A coach should always follow the instincts of his experience and knowledge when the occasion calls for a snap decision. Failure to do so always leads to the second guess and self-recrimination.

The coach must conduct himself ethically, using all practical means to win every contest. He must play every game within the rules and within the spirit of the game, accepting success with humility and failure with grace and restraint. He should never bring discredit on his profession or sport through inexcusable utterances or deeds. Since he is generally the school's most prominent representative, he should follow adminstrative policy carefully, remembering that his school and community are being judged by his actions.

Every coach should develop his own philosophy concerning basketball, based on his knowledge of the game, and his observations. In determining his game plan, he should make use of the observations that he has made and all objective material available, such as statistical reports that may be taken during games or scrimmage sessions. His first step is to select the type of offense and defense he wishes his players to use during the season. Then he must break the offense and defense down into fundamental procedures, designing drills for his players. He must convince them that the offense he has selected is one that will help the team win against their opponents.

the coach's basketball philosophy

5

planning the game

The coach must make practice as enjoyable as possible. When practice or playing becomes loathsome, monotonous, or too serious, players lose the proper mental attitude —that of always wanting more—and both the players and the coach suffer. When teaching the fundamentals, the coach must stress perfection. They should be so well learned that they become instinctive in a game situation. The squad should be encouraged to ask questions regarding the fundamentals, and the coach and his assistants should give help before and after practice. Weak fundamentalists will become weak basketball players.

The coach must teach his players to control the pace of a game. If an opposing team wishes to run against them, his players should be capable of slowing down the game. If an opponent uses a controlled type of defense, the coach's team must be able to speed it up.

Balance is one of the prime requisites in a team offensive philosophy. Basketball is a team effort: good shooters should take the most shots, and good rebounders should be in position when these shots are taken.

The coach must always think of putting the proper players in each position. The best ball handler should handle the ball most of the time. He is the team quarterback. His duties involve getting the ball to the good shooter when he is in position to shoot and seeing that the good shooter does not get the ball in a poor shooting position if he is the type who insists on taking the shot whenever he gets the ball. He should also be certain that the good rebounders are in position. Having the ball in the hands of the right player will definitely cut down the margin of error for the team offensively. Players should be made aware of what good aggressive defense will do. While aggressive playing may cause them to make more mistakes, it may also give them more scoring opportunities and the victory. The coach should allow players to take advantage of their individual skills and use their initiative, making sure that it conforms to the overall team effort.

psychological approach to the players

The coach should realize that players learn by example, and he should not expect anything from his players that he himself is not capable of giving in his leadership. He must live his philosophy of life, and inculcate leadership qualities and a winning attitude in his players.

Each hour, each day, each week during the season presents a new psychological problem. The coach must maintain a good team spirit as well as a team with good spirits. He should have his players on edge at all times. They should be up for each game. The coach must decide whether to use a psychological approach with the team in a pregame pep talk or whether such a talk would be more effective at half time. He must get the most from each of the players and he must be aware of the players who need the most understanding. He should also take psychological advantage of lineup changes. He should be cautious in his disciplinary measures and should be aware of team reactions to punitive action.

The coach must occasionally deal with unfortunate happenings during the year, and he should stay on top of any situation that might cause team friction. At the first sign of difficulty, the principals should be called in to talk it out. Any grievances can usually be settled if they are not allowed to fester.

The following are suggestions to the coach:

Hustling is one of the prime prerequisites for an aggressive team. Players should hustle from one place to another, hustle when called by a coach, and hustle entering and leaving the court. They should never sit or sprawl on a court. If they are all listening to an explanation or watching a demonstration they could rest on one knee, with an arm on the other knee.

For preseason practice, a coach should never select a starting team. He should change personnel constantly; otherwise he will discourage reserves by making them feel unnecessary. By matching his best players against each other in the preseason, he increases their individual ability and effectiveness. Interchanging personnel constantly gives potential starters the feeling of the reserves in competition, and conversely, it allows first-line reserves to coordinate their abilities to the better players during the development of basic offensive and defensive patterns in the preseason practices. The late installation of a starting team makes preseason practice much more competitive and allows simulation of actual game conditions.

A coach's criticism should always be constructive. A suggestion made to one player applies to all. Praise a player who makes an outstanding play or a suggestion and puts it into practice correctly. Whenever possible, emphasize the importance of the unglamorous defense and rebounding maneuvers that normally get little attention in the press.

A player should understand that criticism is like money —you should worry about the lack of it. The players a coach criticizes are usually the ones he uses. The boys should realize that they should not blame others for their own shortcomings, and that they will learn most from their own mistakes. They shouldn't run away from their problems, but face them and try to overcome them.

Imagination and visualization are two important elements not only in the coaching of the game, but in dealing with the players' personalities. The coach should be able to project future situations off the court as well as on it. He

7

should be able to make decisions based on sound reasoning, judgment and imagination.

Injuries should be reported to the coach or the trainer immediately. No injury is so slight it can be completely ignored. Ignoring them sometimes sidelines the players.

staff

the coach's relationships

A formal staff includes a coach and one, two, or more assistants whose philosophy of basketball coincides with that of the head coach. Assistants must have teaching ability, and they must be energetic and eager to teach. It is the duty of the head coach to create a livable atmosphere for the entire coaching staff. If an assistant is to do a good job, he has to feel that he is a part of the organization and that he is important to the success of the team. He should have a voice in the planning of the team's offensive and defensive systems, and he should be consulted concerning the personnel and the placement of personnel. If the assistants do not feel that their advice is looked for or heeded, they will not be effective in their jobs. A head coach should either accept the advice of an assistant or tell him why he feels the suggestion is not feasible. He should use the pronoun "we" rather than "I" and compliment the assistants in front of a squad.

important

The assistant should be willing to listen to and consider the ideas and techniques of his fellow coaches, accepting or rejecting what the others use. He must be able to use what he sees within the framework of the head coach's pattern, and he must be able to reject what would take more time or energy than he has at his disposal.

Basketball is played on many levels. It is played in biddy basketball by the nine-to-twelve-year-old group, in junior high school by the twelve-to-fourteen year olds, in high school by boys fifteen through eighteen, in college by boys eighteen to twenty-two, and by organized amateurs, semi-professionals and professionals. Organized squads are formed by YMCA's, boys' clubs, and settlement houses, and there are organized city and town leagues, teams from adult clubs, and semiprofessional leagues. Each team has a coach, but some of the coaches act as managers only. Many of the teams do not have time for much organized practice; therefore, the coach may not have a formal staff. However, he can discuss the game informally with a group of interested close friends or fellow coaches.

players

The coach's relationship with his players is one of the most important aspects of the coaching situation. He should have individual conferences with each squad member before, during, and after the season to discuss health, studies, outside problems, the player's contributions to the

8

team, and at high school level, selection of a college.

Players appreciate an interest in their health. A preseason physical examination is a prerequisite for a player. During preseason time the coach should be concerned with individual training and conditioning, and during the season, he should see that the player takes care of himself when he has a cold, avoids a cold whenever possible, and takes proper care of his feet and legs. Colds and injuries to the feet and legs are major causes of lost practice time. A good relationship with the trainer is important. Each new player should be introduced to him.

The player is in school to learn. A conference with the coach will help him see basketball and education in their proper perspective. The coach should encourage him to value knowledge and apply himself to his studies.

Many times players have outside problems, perhaps involving their family or a girl friend. The outward signs are lack of attention, tiredness at practice, no hustle, and preoccupation. A coach should try to draw the troubled boy out. If he feels the boy's problem is serious, he may seek information from others.

An individual preseason conference should emphasize the coach's philosophy of basketball. It should cover the player's ability, his goals, his ambitions, his weaknesses, his relationship with teammates, his leadership ability, his reliability, his life objectives, and so forth. Topics for discussion during the season include the player's approach to the game, his basketball progress to date, and the current season. With underclassmen, in post-season conference, the coach should discuss weaknesses they should be working on in the off-season, contributions and shortcomings of the season just passed, and next year's objectives. Post-season conferences with seniors can include advice on the selection of a college in the case of a high school student or discussion of post-college plans with college students. These conferences will go a long way towards building a rapport with the players, establishing the coach as a leader and as a friendly advisor.

The selection of a college is one of the most important topics at the high school level. The coach should evaluate the boy's ability to play basketball, giving his opinion of how good the boy is capable of becoming and what his correct level of competition will be. If the boy's ability is not great, he should be told that he will have to work harder in order to make a college team. Throughout the conference, the coach should emphasize that basketball is but a means to an end. If a boy is a great player, but a weak student, his choice of colleges will be limited. If he is a great player and a good student, many colleges will be open to him, and the level of basketball competition at each school could be a factor in his choice.

9

The coach should realize that each player is an individual. His personality, his mental ability and his basketball ability should be evaluated as separate entities which blend to create an individual. In many cases, background studies help the player evaluation. Information is available from school records, an inventory card by the coach, an autobiography by the college public relations department, and talks with parents and friends. The more the coach understands the player, the easier it is to coach him.

The coach should be friendly with his players, but he must be certain that they maintain the proper respect towards the entire coaching staff. He should be firm without being dictatorial; friendly without being a pal. He should be fair, not ruthless or unyielding in his attitudes. As a teacher, he must impart his knowledge to the players and try to get the most out of them. He must be concerned with their welfare and their moral character.

In theory, it is necessary to treat everyone the same when dealing with a small, close-knit group. However, in practice, that is not possible. A coach must understand his players completely. Some boys need additional stimulus to prepare for competition; others need to be toned down so that they won't get too tight and be unable to relax.

Even at the lower levels, whether he is coaching on a formal or informal basis, the coach should insist on a basic team discipline both on and off the court. (Off-the-court conduct is a true test of whether or not athletics builds character.) At these levels he should allow all of the youngsters to participate as much as possible, and he should try to keep the players abreast of the current trends in the game. Most important, he should teach them respect and fair play. He should be aware of the low level of competition at which he is teaching the game, because at that level the players are generally unsophisticated and unskilled, and they require a great deal of understanding.

The coach should publish and enforce his rules of discipline similar to those listed in our basketball outline (see Appendix A), and he should rigidly adhere to scheduled practice times and meetings.

other coaches

The coach's relationship with other coaches should always be on a professional level. Each opposing coach should be treated with dignity. If a coach fails to show proper respect for an opposing coach, evidence of his behavior should be delivered to the proper authorities, not to the press.

basketball officials

The coach must be aware of his responsibilities to the basketball officials. These men must have complete knowledge of the rules, be in good physical and mental condition, be able to react quickly, and have good judgment. The coach must support them and teach the players to give them the respect they deserve. The exchange of ideas between coaches and officials at rules and interpretation meetings is an important part of the coach-official relationship. The coach should also have officials work preseason practice and explain new rules and changes to the squad and the coaching staff. Besides improving the squad's knowledge of the game, this official participation will make the players appreciate the officials' position during the game. At games, officials should have a private dressing room, and the coach should not meet with them before the game unless the opposing coach is present.

It is unethical to criticize an official publicly. The coach must never make an uncomplimentary remark or suggestion to excite the players and fans. If anything has to be said, it should be said to the appointing authority by mail.

his profession

The coach also has a responsibility to his profession. He should talk with other coaches, observe their techniques, exchange ideas with them, attend clinics, and read current literature in the field. He should experiment with old and new ideas to test their validity and their reliability.

news media

A coach's relationship with the press, radio and TV media should be honest at all times. He should never give misleading information. When in doubt, the rule should be either have no comment or give the actual facts to the press.

At most levels the coach should select the proper offense for the material at hand. If necessary, he can adjust and change annually, but that is not recommended. He must do everything possible to extract the most out of what he has. That is the criterion of a good coach. It is not possible to succeed if a coach is using a shuffle or free-lance offense when perhaps a two-three offense is called for. At the upper levels of competition it is possible to fit the material to the coach's offensive philosophy. However, adaptability is essential.

In many cases, the opposition can make a coach change his basic defense to compensate for mismatches in size and speed. Here again it is imperative that the coach adapt the type of defense that he is using to the type of material that he has on hand. It is impossible at most levels to stay with the same basic philosophy offensively and defensively season after season.

the coach's basic approach to the game

11

choosing the team

Squads vary in size from twelve to fifteen players. They should never be larger than fifteen, nor smaller than twelve unless there is a B team or Junior Varsity team from which the coach can borrow for daily practice. A twelve-man squad is best. This number can be broken down into two squads for intersquad practice scrimmages, and it allows inclusion of one or two specialists who can be used under certain conditions.

Nothing is more difficult for a coach than determining which of the candidates for the basketball team should be accepted. Cutting the number of candidates to a workable group and selecting a team from this group involves sound judgment, good knowledge of the game, and insight into each candidate.

factors involved

Many factors go into the selecting of a squad. At the high-school level many candidates will have little experience. The basic physical factors that should be sought are coordination, speed and quickness (both vertical and lateral speed and quickness), balance, aggressiveness, reflexes, good hands, and height. (By height, we mean playing height, not the actual height. A boy six foot two inches may play at the height of six foot four, or a boy who is six foot six may play at six foot three, depending on his jumping ability, his timing, his reflexes, his quickness, and his coordination.) Other desirable characteristics are the ability to learn, desire, good mental attributes, enthusiasm, sound emotional background, and competitive instinct. A coach should not overlook a tall awkward boy if he has good hands, aggressiveness, and jumping ability.

Speed can be evaluated by having the boys run races. Coordination is determined by observing the smoothness of their movements. Desire and aggressiveness, or hustle, are very easy to see when the boys are working one-on-one or two-on-two, or when they are working in a team situation. One of the most important factors is balance. Many boys who are quick and have good speed do not have good body balance or control. They are apt to get themselves into trouble with the ball, bump into other players, change direction slowly, and make aggressive fouls.

Determination

At the high-school level, a squad can be selected in many ways, depending upon the number of candidates. The pre-practice physical education classes can be used as a basis of selection, and the coach can seek the help of a physical education instructor if he is not one himself. Class tournaments, intramurals, and game practice sessions can be of value. While the final selection of a team belongs with the varsity coach alone, he should not leave all of the evaluative factors to his own judgment. Each candidate should be discussed with other qualified observers who are watching

12

the workout. He should also make statistical and analytical charts comparing the attributes of each boy.

In high school, the first game is usually three weeks after the first practice session. This time factor sometimes shortens the evaluative process.

There are two ways to announce cuts. The first method is to post a list on a bulletin board. The second method is to talk to each boy being cut, pointing out his weaknesses and his strong points and telling him that if he can overcome the weaknesses and improve the strong points, he will have a chance to be selected the following year.

Several boys with outstanding ability will stand out immediately. After that, the selection becomes tougher. If a group of eighty tries out for a team, the coach can cut the number substantially by observing the boys in fundamental passing drills and dribbling drills. He should evaluate them on a merit scale, perhaps using 3 for excellent, 2 for above average, 1 for average, and 0 for poor or below average. The coach will know what boys are available from the previous year, so he can know how many of the new group he will have to work with. A word of caution at this time. It is best to announce to the squad that you are not infallible. If any rejected candidate feels that he is better than a player who has been retained, he should be encouraged to discuss his feelings with the coach in private.

The coach should be on the lookout for boys with ability in one area as well as those with all-round good abilities. For example, a boy with exceptional speed and very quick hands might be valuable to the team as an outstanding defensive player even though he is not a good shooter or a good ball handler.

good speed & hands could be good D player

When boys are very close in ability, moral, emotional, and academic factors must be used to help choose the players. The coach should always be on the alert for players who may cause friction. All players on a team must be compatible so that they can work together for their common objective. Boys who are difficult to get along with or who show emotional, mental, or social instability will make poor squad members.

varsity captain

Two individuals, the varsity captain and the senior manager, are extremely important to the coach's relations with the squad. There are two methods for selecting the senior, or varsity, captain. The first method is by election. All squad members or those members who have varsity letters meet after the close of the season under the supervision of the varsity manager or the coach and elect a captain for next year by means of a ballot. By the second method, the coach appoints a captain for each game during the season. At the close of the season the squad has a meeting and elects a player the team captain for the past season. We prefer the first method.

Prior to an election of a captain, the coach discusses with the players the qualities required in a captain. He must be an extremely stable person mentally, morally, and emotionally. He should get along well with all players on the team, and must have their confidence at all times. He should be a calm and confident leader on and off the court. He should be alert, with great competitive zeal that is a positive influence on his teammates. He does not necessarily have to be the best basketball player on the team, but he has to be a leader in basketball, in the classroom, and on the campus. The captain is a liaison between the coach and the squad, and if he takes his responsibilities seriously, his contribution can be immeasurable.

senior manager

The senior manager should also be a valuable asset. A good manager can take over some of the coach's duties, especially at the high school level. The selection of a manager should be the coach's prerogative, but before making his decision he should consult with his staff, the outgoing senior manager, an equipment man, and a trainer (if one is available). The senior manager helps plan trips, makes many essential arrangements, and on the college level, handles the financial matters. Many of his duties are indispensable. At a high-school level, for example, the senior manager must make sure that his other managers can keep score or run the clocks. Three of four managers should be at each practice session. They see to it that the gym lights are turned on, that the basketballs and practice shirts are available, and that any mechanical aids that may be used on the court, in the rims, or around the court are in working condition. On game night, six to eight managers are necessary. They should be able to record statistics efficiently, and one manager should take game notes from the coach, sitting next to him on the bench.

good idea

Most managers should start at a freshman or sophomore level in high school. The authors have had success with freshman squad members who played freshman college basketball but did not make the varsity squad. They became extremely efficient team managers, for they knew the organization and wished to be part of the team. Perhaps that is one of the most important characteristics to look for when selecting a manager: he must wish to be part of the group. Whether he is a basketball player or not is immaterial; compatibility and the amount of work he does is important.

The ideal competitive situation would be to have four managers at a freshman level, cut the number to three in the sophomore year (basing the choice on the work the boys have done during the preceding year), cut to two in the junior year, and select one varsity manager for senior year.

14

2

team organization and practice sessions

The modern coach must organize each phase of the basketball year to obtain optimum results. This period is divided into three areas.

1. Pre-practice—the period extending from the start of the school year to the date of the first permissible formal practice.

2. Preseason practice—the period from the first permissible formal practice day to the day of the first regularly scheduled game.

3. In-season practice—the period from the first regularly scheduled game to the last game (regularly scheduled or tournament). Planning must include consideration of unavoidable practice breaks for Christmas holidays and midyear exams.

Methodic planning for each area is required for a well-coordinated basketball program. Complete preparation for preseason and in-season practice sessions is imperative.

pre-practice organization

In pre-practice, (September–October), the coaching staff should meet formally every day, or at least several times a week. On the college level, the meetings should start at least at the beginning of the official school year. On the high school level, they should start at least six weeks before the official start of practice. All of the planning for the preseason should be done at these meetings. Other coaches (naturally not those of opponents) who are interested in discussion and an exchange of ideas can sit in on the meetings, which should be intense brainstorming sessions, with magnetic board, projector, screen, movies, diagram material, etc., on hand.

The time of the first allowable preseason practice in relation to the time of the first game is the most important single consideration. On the junior high school and high school levels, the State Principals' Association usually determines when practice can start. Some states do not allow basketball practice to start until the close of the football season. Other states allow practice to begin in the middle of November, still others allow it on the first of November, and some have no restrictions. The limit on the number of games played is also determined by the State Principals' Association. Twenty games (exclusive of tournaments) is the limit at a high school level in most states, and no more than two games a week may be scheduled. Three to five weeks of practice at most are usually available to the high school coach before his first game.

In colleges, the National Collegiate Athletic Association decides on the number of games—26 (exclusive of post-season tournaments), including outside scrimmages and regularly scheduled games. Practice cannot begin until October 15, and a game cannot be scheduled until December 1.

On a school-year calendar, the coach should mark the first day of practice, the first game, and the home games to be played during the season. He should mark the away games in a different color. (Travel plans and practice away from home must be taken into consideration in an overall master plan.) Next, he should write in the schedule for scouting opponents and the name of the man (either a member of the coaching staff or an expert who knows the team) who will scout. Games to be scouted should be listed in a third color. The days when practice will not be held should be X'd out.

Practice goals must be decided during the formal coaches' meetings, and a checklist should be made. The coach should also make a master preseason schedule, listing what he hopes to accomplish on offense and defense before the first game, then work within this program of operation to make up weekly and daily schedules and to determine the fundamental drills he wishes to incorporate. He should develop and use daily drills. The master plan should include the amount of time planned for each activity, and after practice starts the coach should keep a written record of time actually spent for each in the daily sessions and in the weekly sessions.

When the outline of the preseason practice schedule is complete, the coaching staff should determine the quickest method of selecting the team. The most important single task for a coach is to screen the candidates until he has a group that is a workable size and then make a team of the individuals in the group. The coaches know which squad members are returning. They also know what the abilities of other players who are trying out have been. But they should remember that youngsters with initiative who were rejected the previous year may have practiced during the off-season and become more coordinated and physically mature so that they may become valuable squad members. This is especially true of some tall high school boys who were not squad members previously because of lack of coordination.

Next, the coach must select the proper offensive and defensive alignments for the personnel available and condition the players. Prepractice conditioning must be super-

H. COACH
O. Director
D. Director
Trainer
2 or 4 Scouts
2 Talent Finders
1 Public Relations

17

vised by the captain or captains and the team manager, as the coach is not allowed to participate before an established date.

The coaches should review the previous season analytically, discussing the high and the low points during the season, and determining why they were high points or low points. If movies of the previous year's games are available they should be reviewed. Any areas of uncertainty on the players' part or of good team work should be marked on the film. Later, these areas can be shown to the players as points for improvement or duplication. Previous postgame reports should be analyzed, and current comments should be added by the coach.

The coaches should discuss the individual and group fundamental skills they hope to develop and determine what offense and defense will be used. They may have to change or adapt their original plans, depending on the type of material that the squad has. In that case, however, most coaches put in variations or options of what they have previously taught.

The coaches should decide whether practice sessions will be open to visitors or limited to players, managers and coach. Open practice sessions make for goodwill and added school interest in the team. Coaches should plan an occasional open practice session, perhaps during routine drills or fundamentals sessions or during full scrimmages, when the likelihood of criticism of players is minimal. Open practice sessions when the team is being selected indicates a democratic attitude by the coach.

I like closed practices!

As a general practice, however, closed sessions are perhaps best for players and coach. Many youngsters feel that a coach who is critical in front of their friends is downgrading them. Also, some coaches neglect to criticize objectively in deference to players' feelings in open practice sessions. This attitude, while understandable, is bad for correct team functioning. Closed sessions should be indicated by notices posted on doors to the gym, and the sessions should be policed by managers.

When school starts in the Fall, the captain and manager should be in charge of all returning players and new players who wish to work out until the formal practice begins. The captain and manager should insist that players follow the conditioning regulations prescribed by the coach. Group running, calisthenics, and weight lifting are good not only for the physical condition of the squad but also for squad spirit and cohesiveness. Playing two-on-two or three-on-three in free gymnasium time will also be helpful if the players do so within the framework of the drills that the coach has outlined in previous years. However, players must not form cliques in these informal sessions. All players must enjoy them so that the whole team will benefit.

18

Preseason is the most important time of the year for coaches; therefore, efficient master planning and good use of the time are imperative. Efficient preseason planning can result in a winning team. The coach should arrange the schedule so that each player may participate daily in all functions. He should use effective teaching methods in practice, and he must allocate enough time for salient requirements. He must also analyze all practice sessions.

The time allotted to practice sessions must be determined by the amount of time a coach has from the first practice session to the first scheduled game. Even experienced coaches should make a written weekly time chart and a daily schedule and duplicate them so that all coaches and managers have a copy; otherwise they will always leave something uncovered. The daily plan naturally should be broken down into the practice outline, and it should be checked against the master plan. Many coaches, too, have a tendency to practice too long early in the season. A practice session should be only as long as players can work at their optimum physical ability. It should rarely be more than two hours long. First, players cannot absorb information after working for two hours; second, players will put less effort into the practice in order to conserve energy for the finish; and third, the players have time limitations since they have other obligations. When an item has been covered during a preseason practice session, it should be checked off on the list of objectives.

organizing practice

There are many training problems in basketball, and all areas must be covered. Therefore, it is important to record the time spent in each area: conditioning, lectures, training rules, rules discussion, chalk talks, movies, staff meetings, regular drills, and pregame drills.

Practice for the entire season should be generally outlined before the squad reports so that coaches and players can schedule their time. The coach and his staff should make up the weekly preseason practice schedules in advance. Weekly practice schedules during the season are determined by travel schedules, scouting reports, and the squad's physical condition.

Making out a practice schedule before and during the season is tedious. Usually you should make a practice schedule no more than one week in advance—and sometimes a schedule must be revised during the week, occasionally on the day of practice. A sound practice schedule makes best possible use of the practice time.

Daily practice plans should be charted and posted so that players can report to specified areas for specific drills without delay.

Appendix B is a sample of the authors' weekly preseason

practice schedule with objectives. Samples of daily practice schedules evolved from the weekly objectives are in Appendix C. At the college level, preseason weekly practices cover six weeks. Each week must be outlined objectively, and each of the six weeks' objectives must be listed. Daily schedules list the number of minutes allowed to each drill and to each area and the type of work expected each day. The weekly objectives are kept on a master schedule plan so that the coaches can tell at a glance what has been accomplished and what has yet to be done. These are all kept within the framework of an overall master plan.

player selection

On the opening day of practice, the coach should give a get-acquainted talk to the entire group, both former squad members and new candidates, outlining what will be expected of them during the entire season. Formulating plans at this time will take care of any differences of opinion among squad members. A coach should attempt to keep players' morale high. Everyone must feel that it is possible for him to contribute something during the season.

The boys must have a desire to play the game. An aggressive team is always a dangerous team. The boys should be willing to pay the price for the opportunity to play. They should report in good physical condition and practice diligently so that they improve every day. The team's success is based on unity and selflessness. Loyalty to the school, the coaches, and the teammates is expected at all times.

Practice should be businesslike. The basketball court is a workshop, not a social hall. All players are expected to work towards maximum possible improvement. They either improve daily or they regress; therefore, practice must be designed to bring out the best in every player.

In many high schools, it is important to select the varsity squad in as short a time as is reasonable. To save time, returing varsity players may help screen new candidates, and the coach can screen potential players during physical education periods. The first practice session usually is devoted to a discussion of the rules of the game and the regulations that the team must follow. Then, as quickly as possible, the coach should reduce his squad to about twenty-five players. It is almost impossible to do any effective group work with a larger squad.

When sizing up candidates in early preseason practice, the coach should remember that players want to show to their best advantage in order to make the team or to make the starting five. If blisters or ankle turns occur, players normally are reluctant to tell the coach for fear he may feel they are malingering or their chances for making the team may be hurt.

The coach should never do on the court what can be

done off the court. He should never work with only one or two players during the team practice time. Individualized instruction should be given before or after daily practice.

Too much explanation is bad. Basketball players learn mainly by doing and understanding why they are doing, not by listening.

teaching techniques

The coach should not over-teach in the early preseason practice sessions or make them so strenuous that players lose their ability to retain what is being taught. Players can and should work when physically tired, but they can't learn when they are tired, so coaches should not introduce new material at that time.

The most significant point to stress at all times is the importance of possession of the ball. The player should be told never to pass to a voice. He should also be warned that bad shots are detrimental to the team, and that short passes are safer from interception than long passes. After an incorrect or extraneous maneuver, the coach should always ask the players, "why?" replacing them in scrimmage momentarily, if necessary, for brief individual conferences. Coaches should do this frequently during practice scrimmages, because the players should know the reason for everything they do on the court. A coach should criticize softly and encourage loudly, informing the team often that practice makes playing habits permanent. Players who are practicing bad habits should be corrected immediately. Even in a drill on passing, the coach should correct a player who makes a poor or improper cut, briefly explaining the proper technique. The coach should strive constantly for mental anticipation, instinctive reaction, and intelligent aggressiveness on the part of all players. These intangibles make a good player a great one.

After determining the best offensive and defensive patterns for the material at hand, the coach should be positive in their installation. He should help players develop confidence in these patterns and in the coach by patiently implementing the offense and defense selected. First, a strategy should be explained and diagramed. Second, the players should walk through the various parts of the offense or defense, run through it at half speed, then do it full speed, with no opponents. Third, the strategy should be implemented full speed with defenders. At this stage, the defenders usually are junior varsity or freshmen who are the weakest players. This enables the team to practice their strategy successfully, thus developing a positive attitude as to their ability. The coach thereby negates any doubts the players may have. He should use as a motto, "Better learn a little a lot, than a lot a little."

Coaches should take advantage of individual abilities,

without letting individual abilities take over to the disadvantage of the team. They should also allow for free-lance patterns that won't hurt the team. The style of play that a coach incorporates offensively should blend with the material at hand and be based on good offensive floor balance and movement, proper execution of play patterns, and good timing.

the coach's daily duties

For all daily practice sessions, the coach should arrive on the court dressed for practice at least a half hour before the beginning of practice. He should review the day's schedule to familiarize himself with the routine of the practice. The manager or assistant manager should check the time allotted for each part of the practice session and inform the coach when the time is up for each drill. The coach should be sure that the necessary materials are available. These include basketballs, scrimmage shirts, training aids, extra shoelaces, tape, and towels to be used for obstacles in drill. (We prefer to use towels as obstacles rather than chairs or other players. Chairs are bulky, and stationary players are not taking part in the drills. Managers can carry an armful of towels and place them in the proper spot easily and quickly.)

Before practice begins, the coach can give individual attention to players, discussing shortcomings observed in the previous practice session, praising good playing, or working with one or two players. In early preseason, before cutting the squad down to workable size, a coach should give time to new candidates for on-the-spot evaluation, making players who are in the questionable category feel that he has given them sufficient time. This attitude and attention by the coach makes the selection process much less painful for both the coach and the candidates who are dropped.

The coach should be sure that the players begin before practice workouts as soon as they arrive.

He should make certain that all players are on time and that the practice starts at the prescribed time. The organized practice time, in which the timing by the manager is all-important, should begin with a whistle.

Key to Preseason Practice ←

drilling

Drilling is the secret of good performance at critical times in a ball game. It is essential for game pressure. Early preseason practice should stress conditioning and fundamentals, for the team must be in excellent condition before the first game. A player, preferably a captain, should lead the conditioning drills, which should be executed at top speed and at intervals to maintain full interest. Complete coordination of eye, mind, and muscles should be taught, first slowly, then increasing in tempo to full speed. Players must be warmed up before strenuous work begins.

The importance of carefully conceived and skillfully organized and executed drills cannot be overemphasized. The players should devote about 20 percent of the time to shooting and foul shooting, and drills should incorporate the ingredients of the team's planned defenses and offenses. However, do not drill initiative and motivation out of a good basketball player. The best players can drill themselves to perfection.

Drills for fundamentals, simulating game conditions whenever possible, should be organized early in the preseason, when they are most important. An experienced coach will know what drills will be best for his team, both for teaching his offense and defense, and for conditioning his players; a new coach must decide what drills to use and how long to spend on them. Drills should be simple and competitive, and they should cover as many techniques as possible. They also should be selective. Don't use too many drills or too complicated a drill, and don't use a drill just because somebody else has used it.

Drills are good only when they are completely assimilated by the squad. The coach must give the reason for each operation and explain the correct method of every technique. First, an explanation gives the players confidence; second, it shows them that there is a reason and an explanation for everything. The coach should analyze any mistakes that the players are making and compliment those players who are doing the drills well.

Drills allow for concentrated practice in specific areas. Preseason conditioning drills must be utilitarian, therefore whenever possible, they should include fundamental techniques. Early in the year, many necessary conditioning drills use running without involving the ball or defensive techniques.

Drills serve as a change of pace in the daily practice routine. They are excellent for before practice or pregame warm-up.

They should be simple, of short duration, and interesting. A variety of drills keeps players interested in seeking perfection in fundamentals, preventing boredom and complacency. Too little time on drills, leaving the desire for more, is much more effective than too much time in drills. When they become drudgery and there is a lack of enthusiasm and desire, incorrect habits and improper techniques will be formed. Drills should be spirited, evoking constant chatter and desire for perfection.

Drills should be readily applicable to the team's offensive and defensive pattern. In fact, coaches should devise their own drills. Too many of today's drills have been adapted from ones that were handed down from coaches of generations ago. The adaptable, inventive coach is general-ly the successful coach.

There are three steps to learning. First, the student must be interested and ready to learn. A competent coach who has the full attention of a receptive student can teach him the proper fundamentals of the game, stressing the ac-quisition of accuracy before speed. The second step is prac-tice. Once the player understands the techniques involved he practices willingly for hours on end. The final step is the examination—in the case of basketball, the actual playing of the game itself.

Proper teaching techniques should be used in drills. The coach should first demonstrate, explaining the mechanics of the drill and how it is essential to team play and the over-all team philosophy. He should use simple, concise lan-guage and consistent terminology, defining each new term. The players should then practice the drill slowly until they have mastered the movements and understand the drill's purpose. The coach should correct and criticize. Finally, the coach should quicken the pace of the drill to full speed to teach correct fundamental techniques under game tempo, correcting individual mistakes.

To properly inculcate basic team concepts early in the preseason, skeleton teams should be used offensively and defensively. These concepts are broken down and practiced in drills involving two-on-two and three-on-three groupings. Much of the offense and defense to be used in the season should be broken down into drills. Man-to-man attack and defense, zone attack and defense, pressure attack and de-fense, and combination attack and defense must be skele-tonized if they are to used. Coaches should also discuss how they want jump balls to be handled. Drills should be repetitive so that proper reaction becomes instinctive. Players should not have to think about what they are going to do.

Every drill must demand perfect or near perfect perform-ance from every player. Coaches must be constantly ob-servant and highly critical, making corrections immediately. They must overcome a tendency to ignore or overlook slight irregularities or imperfections in a player's form or habits. Coaches should remember that practicing something incor-rectly is just as habit forming as practicing something cor-rectly. Perhaps the most important motto for drills is prac-tice makes permanent.

Competitive drills hold players' interest, and the use of rewards for winners and penalties for the losers creates in-centive and enthusiasm. Winners could be given a pair of sweat socks, and losers could be made to run laps, or do extra wind sprints.

Most drills should be performed under as much pressure as possible. The more game conditions are simulated in practice, the more beneficial the drills are.

24

All drills should have short, definitive names so that players know exactly what to do as soon as the name is called. Through drills, teams develop unity. Players become accustomed to the movements, attitudes, habits and idiosyncrasies of teammates.

New drills can be explained during a brief practice break one day then incorporated into the practice for the next day. Drills should be scheduled so that a physically strenuous drill is followed by one that is easier. Several small groups working all players strenuously are more beneficial than one large group where several players are not working. The coach should plan to use all his players in drill activities every day in early season. At the end of a hard practice, the coaches should incorporate a drill that the players enjoy. This implementation will leave the players in a good frame of mind, anticipating the following day's practice.

The selected drills found in this book are some of those used to advantage by the authors. Hundreds of other excellent drills are available to the discerning coach.

selecting and evaluating players

Early preseason scrimmaging should be done in order to help select the squad. At this time, coaches should plan scrimmage teams for balance, with good players scattered evenly among the teams used. Daily evaluations of each scrimmage should be made. Many coaches today tend to drill too much and scrimmage too little. The right amount of scrimmage for a team depends on the experience and physical and psychological condition of the players.

After the squad is selected in the early season, scrimmage sessions should involve five-man teams of varying ability. In selecting squads for early preseason scrimmage practice, allow designated players of equal ability to pick the other members of their teams. Use a different selection order each round until each designated player has made four choices. A manager should record the selections and give the list to the coaches. Vary selectors as often as possible. Allowing the players to select their teams enables the coach to see how the players rate each other. He also gains insight into personality clashes or cliques within the squad. If there are three teams, they should scrimmage for approximately five to eight minutes, with the winning team staying on. With four teams, play a round robin tournament, winners playing winners, losers playing losers. This procedure should be followed until each player has run approximately twenty minutes of full-court scrimmage. These scrimmage practice sessions should be interrupted for criticism and analysis when necesssary, using the double whistle procedure outlined in our team offense drill section.

We feel that teammate evaluation sheets should be used. Filling these out takes approximately five minutes during a practice session. They should be issued to the squad with-

25

out warning. Be certain that a manager has an adequate supply of sharpened pencils on hand.

Following is an outline of the factors to be evaluated:

I. Positive
   A. Three players who always take good shots
   B. Three best shooters
   C. Three best rebounders
   D. Three best drivers
   E. Three best passers
   F. Three best defensive players
   G. Three best team players offensively
   H. Three best team players defensively
   I. Three best hustlers
   J. Three quickest players
   K. Three players with best straightaway speed
   L. Four players you most like to play with
   (Naturally, the evaluator cannot include himself in any of these categories.)

II. Negative
   A. Three players who habitually take bad shots
   B. Three poorest shooters
   C. Three poorest rebounders
   D. Three poorest drivers
   E. Three poorest passers
   F. Three poorest defenders
   G. Three poorest team players offensively
   H. Three poorest team players defensively
   I. Three poorest hustlers
   J. Three players who are least quick
   K. Three players with least speed
   L. Four players you least like to play with

The coaches should collect the unsigned evaluation sheets, transfer the information to a master sheet and destroy the individual sheets. It is best to destroy them with the manager present, so that he can assure the squad that the sheets are not kept. The coach and assistant coaches should also fill out evaluation sheets, keeping the results confidential. The coaches should then assess the player-evaluation results against their own evaluations. Many times it will be obvious to the coaches that there are possible discrepancies or inadequacies in their own thinking. Also, personality clashes or conflicts may be festering, so evaluations by the involved players should not be taken seriously in the master evaluation. However, for harmonious team relationship the coach should try to resolve any conflicts. A good coach should be able to meet any contingency, and flexibility is an asset. Therefore, coaches should be prepared to learn from these evaluations. The use of teammate evaluation sheets and player selection of teams for early season scrimmage contributes a great deal

26

[Handwritten marginal note:] I think this would be very beneficial, since they should SCRIMMAGE + DRILL BEFORE PRE-SEASON + SHOULD KNOW THE PLAYERS. YOUR PLAYERS SHOULD HAVE GOOD MINDS

toward development of team spirit and understanding of the squad.

A self-evaluation sheet is also important to players. This sheet should cover the intangibles as well as the qualities that coaches can observe. The qualities that we feel should be included are basketball instinct, attention, ability to follow the coach's instructions, alertness, aggressiveness, coordination, relative speed, team defensive abilities, individual defensive abilities, team offensive abilites, and individual offensive ability.

Ratings of 4 for excellent, 3 for good, 2 for fair and 1 for poor should be given. Many times a coach will find that players are downgrading themselves. Other players may have an exaggerated opinion of themselves. Through individual talks, the coach may be able to help the players evaluate themselves realistically. Self-evaluation sheets should be destroyed after they have served their purpose.

scrimmaging in early season

Scrimmaging is important all during the season. While we do not scrimmage much during the first week, we allow candidates of dubious ability to scrimmage full court, as often as feasible, with some of the better players so that they will feel they were given every opportunity to become a member of the squad. Coaches should remember that scrimmaging is ten teaching situations at once; by scrimmaging, players learn to react under game conditions. All scrimmages must be properly officiated. During early preseason scrimmages clocks must be available, as well as all the statistical sheets that are used in scheduled games. The assistant coaches should record positive and negative factors during a scrimmage so that constructive changes can be made in the practices that follow. The head coach should be on the court, using the double whistle technique to stop practice when something is fundamentally wrong. All aspects of each scrimmage should be charted and recorded so that individual player analysis is complete. All preseason scrimmage statistics should be recorded on a master copy for dissemination and use with the squad. Shooting percentages, foul shooting percentages, and all of the various aspects of statistical information should be available to the squad as the result of these scrimmages.

If there are enough players for four balanced five-man teams, run a tournament type of competitive scrimmage allowing two teams to play approximately eight minutes, then the next two to play for eight minutes. The winners then play for first and second place and the losers play for third and fourth place. This brings an element of competition into the practice, motivating the players to play well in the early season to reach a visible goal. Scrimmaging in early season enables the players to work under the pressure they will be under in actual games. This type of scrimmaging should not take place until the team has learned the necessary offensive and defensive fundamentals.

These early scrimmages should be handled by officials. An experienced basketball official should be present at the first early scrimmage to explain the rule changes and the rule emphasis for the forthcoming season.

Tells exactly what has to be Done + Drilled on in preseason — Read several times, this is Good.

At the close of each practice session, there should be a post-practice coaches' meeting, twenty minutes to one half hour long. At this meeting the coaches should analyze the practice session and decide if it accomplished what they planned. The coaches should also analyze each player's basketball progress, attentiveness, and attitude. Each player should be rated on a 4-excellent, 3-good, 2-fair, 1-poor scale. A record of this analysis should be kept. Then at the end of the second week the coaches can discuss any apparent weaknesses with the players in a before practice session. It is imperative that the coaches cover the following areas thoroughly so that the players are completely prepared by the first game: Offensively, fast-break basic pattern against man-to-man and zone defenses, pressing defenses and combination defenses; jump ball situations at all three areas—the offensive and defensive ends and the center circle—when control is probable and when control is doubtful; out-of-bounds plays, both from the side and under the basket, first for possession of the ball and second for a basket; a free-throw alignment for a possible fast break; semi-freeze and stall situations; a one-shot play for late in the game; the rebounding fundamentals for the individual and the team; and last minute and late game situations when behind, with the score tied, and when ahead.

Defensively, team defense in a man-to-man situation; the methods of stopping the fast break at the defensive backboard, cutting off the outlet or delaying the break; zone defense (aggressive, loose or pressing); pressure defenses; the defensive rebounding pattern for both individual and team; last minute situations and late game situations when behind, with the score tied, or when ahead.

The pregame warm-up drills to be used for a 20-minute period should be properly practiced so players know what to do when they come on the court before a game. Naturally the team must be well-conditioned for the first game. The coach must explain all details, even those which seem minor—for instance, how a substitute should enter a game (he should report to the scorer's table and wait there until an official beckons him onto the court) or signals that can be used from the bench to change the team's offense or defense. These areas must be completely covered in preseason practice and then checked off the preseason master plan. Even after an item is checked it should be reviewed

28

constantly. Many times coaches feel that players will get enough shooting before daily practice, but this is not necessarily true; therefore, shooting drills should take up approximately 20 percent of the total preseason practice time. The coach should put the number of minutes actually spent in each area of practice on his master sheet weekly, and this should be totaled each preseason week so that none of the fundamentals are left uncovered. The coach must control the offense and defense used by the scrimmaging teams in preseason practice sessions. For example, in a 15-minute scrimmage, Team A may use the stack offense for the first eight minutes and a two-one-two offense for seven minutes. Team B may use man-to-man loose defense for the first five minutes, a two-three zone for the next five minutes, and a press defense for the last five minutes. Similar assignments are made for A on defense and B on offense.

A manager should keep an offense pattern chart for such scrimmages, noting the number of possessions, the number of shots, and the baskets scored for each team from the offense used. For example:

Team A
1. Stack offense   33 possessions   31 shots   14 baskets
2. 2-1-2 offense   24 possessions   17 shots   6 baskets
3. Fast-break   17 possessions   16 shots   10 baskets

These statistics indicate the effectiveness of the offenses and defenses used when assessed against the offensive-defensive time allotments.

in-season practice sessions

Once the regular season has started, practice time should be shortened. As most teams play two games a week, two or three days prior to a game the on-court practice session should be approximately an hour and three quarters long. Game plans should be part of the practice session on the days preceding most games.

On pre-game days, sessions should be limited to an hour and a half or less. Before practice the coach might review a scouting report with the squad. If games fall on consecutive days, usually the complete scouting report for the second game should not be given until after the game with the first scouted opponent has been completed. A partial report may be presented on the second opponent, however, if a strategy requires on-court practice for implementation against the second opponent. Looking ahead, beyond any —DAMN RIGHT game, is bad. After reviewing a scouting report in a session before the practice, the coach should go over it on the floor, with the junior varsity, a freshman group, or the lower men in the squad simulating the opponents. The coach should also review post-game analyses with the as-

29

sembled squad for glaring errors and mistakes. At this time, he should praise the positive aspects of the game just completed, if possible injecting some humor into the meeting.

Coaches should include remedial and developmental fundamental skill drills in practice sessions to correct obvious weaknesses that have been noted in games. Again, they should use a time schedule and follow it. The amount of time spent in each aspect should be recorded and summarized on a master sheet.

The scrimmage time for reserves should be all important on the day after a game has been played. If possible, all reserves who have had little playing time should be given a full thirty- to thirty-five-minute scrimmage session, because they must be kept in the best possible condition. If they are not in condition, the overall team ability will suffer. The coach should keep a record of each practice session, which can be consulted and analyzed both during and after the season.

training devices

Coaches should take advantage of all training aids and mechanical devices available within their means. The most practical training aids have been devised by imaginative coaches on a limited budget.

Essential low cost or free items include a full-year school calendar, bulletin boards, blackboards, clipboards, adhesive tape (a strip, marked at intervals, is used on the edges of backboards for jumping drills, and a strip can be put around the ball to check proper rotation while shooting), towels (for floor markers or obstacles), players' notebooks, no-bounce or weighted basketballs, rim inserts that make the basket circumference smaller (to improve shooting), portable magnetic boards, and mechanical rebound devices.

If a school has an audiovisual department, instant TV replay equipment, overhead projectors, and tape recorders may be available. Where the budget allows, game movies should be taken. For years, we have used an observer-to-bench telephone system during games to take advantage of a higher, better viewing position.

30

part two
the offense

3

individual-player offense

This chapter describes the essential techniques for successfully executing the various offensive tasks performed by individual members of a modern basketball team: shooting, passing, dribbling, and footwork. Consistent, however, with our view that each player should be allowed as much latitude as possible in perfecting his own most effective style, we have emphasized, in our detailed descriptions of proved techniques, the underlying principles that make a given technique work. Although any technique seems mechanical at first, even unnatural, hours of practicing it, together with a thorough understanding of the principles involved, should lead to each player's evolving the variations that best realize his own natural potential.

fundamental principles

shooting

In basketball, the objective of offense is accurate shooting—to throw the ball through the basket defended by the opponent. All basketball players recognize this, of course, and most practice their shooting year round; but, since most of his practice is not in the presence of a coach, each player should become his own severest critic, which means he must have a clear understanding of the principles affecting the success or failure of every shot.

This does not mean that there is no room for experimentation. In basketball, as in golf, baseball, or boxing, there is considerable latitude for the participant to develop a style of his own. In fact, this kind of experimentation, rather than a slavish imitation of a player whose strengths and weaknesses may be entirely different, should be encouraged. This does mean, however, that there are fundamental principles underlying the success of every great player, regardless of stylistic variation, and that these principles must be mastered and constantly practiced by every serious shooter.

Therefore, before examining the specific techniques associated with the various kinds of shots an accomplished basketball player is expected to have in his repertory, we have presented in some detail those fundamental principles that we believe are at work in every scoring shot from every basketball floor. For convenience, these have been divided into two categories: (1) Mental, comprising concentration, confidence, and the ability to relax; and (2) Physical, comprising sighting, body balance, force, timing, coordination, and follow-through.

1. **Mental Principles.** There is probably no arguing the fact that the game of basketball is to a great degree mental;

at no time is psychological conditioning more critical than when shooting. Knowing when to shoot and being able to do so effectively under pressure are, ultimately, what distinguishes the great shooter from the passable. Fortunately, although it is sometimes ignored, one's ability to improve the mental aspects of his shooting is often far less limited than his ability to improve the physical aspects. Regardless of how much he practices or how well he conditions himself physically, only a modest amount of improvement is possible regarding a basic disadvantage in speed, reflexes, strength, or height; however, the history of basketball, like that of other sports, affords many examples of players who were able to achieve greatness despite relatively mediocre physical talent. Usually, such successes are attributed to determination, which is really too general a term. We believe the determined player will find *concentration, confidence,* and the *ability to relax,* to be the essential mental principles that, when mastered, will take him at least halfway toward becoming a great shooter.

Concentration. *Concentration* might be called mental discipline. It is the fixing of attention on the job at hand and is an ability characteristic of every great athlete. Through continuous practice, good shooters develop their concentration to the extent that they are oblivious to every distraction—in fact, they frequently become more accurate when under pressure than when not—whether the distraction is a clutch situation or an opponent's waving, shouting, or even fouling. To develop a high order of concentration, the shooter should practice under conditions as near as possible to those of an actual contest and should discipline himself to be constantly critical of every aspect of his technique. At first, this will require a conscious effort, but in time it will become as reflexive as ''feeling'' the ball.

Ability to relax. The *ability to relax* is closely related to concentration. It is a cliché that great clutch players have ice water in their veins, but we are convinced that the seemingly superhuman coolness that some players have under pressure is nothing more than a kind of practiced absentmindedness regarding everything but the immediate task. Watch a great foul shooter as he reaches the foul line and begins the ritual of adjusting his feet and bouncing the ball—nearly always a set number of times. As his eyes open wide in sighting the basket, his trance-like concentration is so intense, there is little wonder that he is undisturbed by the crowd or game pressures. In fact, a smart defensive player, realizing this, will try to break the shooter's concentration, either by engaging him in conversation or by saying something intended to upset him. Again, the best counter is an absentminded, or single-minded, preoccupation with the task at hand.

Confidence. Every shot must be made with *confidence* —a gut certainty that the ball will drop through the basket without touching the rim. Confidence, however, is not probability. In truth, the two are at odds. Although a good shooter never takes a shot that he is not confident he will make, he often misses; therefore, the probability of his making any given shot is somewhat less than the 100 percent that his confidence leads him to expect. Clearly, then, when we say, "Don't shoot when in doubt," we have something different in mind than we do when we say, "Don't take a low-percentage shot except in desperate circumstances." In fact, a player may be confident of making a low-percentage shot and not at all confident of making what should be for him a high-percentage shot. There is no problem in the first instance, since the shooter simply makes a rational decision not to shoot unless the situation is dire, in which case confidence is appropriate—even essential. The second instance, however, is a problem, since high-percentage shots should neither be wasted nor passed up.

There are several reasons why a player might lack confidence when confronted with a shooting opportunity having a good statistical probability of success: he may be off balance; he may have had his confidence shaken by a string of misses; he may be overly tense or tired; or he may have a lapse in concentration. None of these are mutually exclusive; in fact, one often contributes to the other.

Probably every player experiences "off nights" when nothing works, but an equally familiar phenomenon is that of a player's returning to peak form in the second half after a miserable first half. This ability to make a mental recovery is like the ability some players have of recovering in mid-air after an off-balance take-off: each is the mark of a superbly trained athlete.

Good Point

2. Physical Principles. Shooting a ball and connecting with the target involves six factors. These are (1) *sighting*, or locating, a target whose position relative to the attacker is to some extent constantly changing; (2) maintaining a *body balance* that allows a coordinate effort of leg, trunk, and arm muscles; (3) *generating the force*; (4) *timing* the attack so that each event in its development occurs at the right instant in the sequence; (5) *coordinating hand and eye* to effect a desired trajectory; (6) effecting *follow-through* and recovery. The following is a brief discussion of each of the problems as they pertain to shooting baskets. With few modifications, however, they would apply to any game in which muscles are used to strike or throw at a target.

6 points to shooting well

Sighting, or locating the target. The difference between *sighting* and *aiming* is that in aiming, a device (for

This sighting is VERY important

36

example, a gun) is visually aligned with a target; thus, visual attention is equally divided between the pointer and the target. In sighting, however, the eyes are used merely to locate, or fix, the target in space, and the computing of an intercept trajectory is left for the brain to do automatically.

The brain's ability to determine a trajectory to a known location can be demonstrated by closing the eyes and touching either the nose or an ear lobe with a forefinger. To convince yourself of this ability, for a visually fixed target, focus your eyes on a nearby object, and without aiming, point your finger at the object. Notice that there is a strong tendency for your attention to shift from the object to your finger and that considerable concentration is required in order to remain focused on the object. (Notice, too, that when concentrating on the object your eyes open quite wide.) The reason that it is so important for the eyes to remain focused on the target is that they, too, are a kind of computer, continuously updating a three-dimensional fix on whatever is being held in focus. Naturally, the smaller the area focused upon, the smaller the fix, and the greater the potential accuracy.

Sighting for a shot.

This brings us to the problem facing a basketball player of having as his *real* target not a concrete object, but an open area inside the rim of the basket. Since his eyes cannot focus on empty space, the best he can do is to select a sighting point as nearly on line with the intended trajectory and as near the real target as possible. When making a bank shot, the shooter solves the problem by focusing on a spot related to the painted rectangle above the basket. For all other shots, however, he must decide upon a sighting point somewhere on the rim. Personal preference determines whether the point selected is on the front or the back rim, but he should decide upon one or the other and stick with that sighting point for all similar shots. Also, remembering that the eye computes distance by comparing texture, converging lines, etc., against past experience, the basketball player intent upon improving the accuracy of his shooting should determine, for the longest shot that he would normally attempt, the smallest number of rim cords upon which he can focus his eyes. Then, for every shot, he should fix upon the same number of cords, while conscious that he wishes to "drop" the ball either just beyond (front rim) or just before (back rim) the point sighted. *The sighting point must be held in constant and clear focus from the moment the shot is begun to the completion of follow-through.*

Body balance. When properly balanced, a shooter can coordinate the efforts of each muscle to produce a net force in the direction of the basket. Although the degree of balance may vary, from the near perfect stance of a two-hand set shot to the "last-effort" recovery of an aggressive drive-in, the shooter's ability to control the trajectory of the ball is directly dependent upon his ability to control the acceleration forces generated by his own body; it is doubtful whether a shot ever succeeds unless, at the moment of release, the shooter has enough control to complete a smooth, continuous follow-through. Some players have such exceptional body control they can shoot successfully from positions that would be awkward and unmanageable for another player. Each player must develop his ability to judge whether or not he is in a position to initiate a shot and complete a follow-through that will leave him poised for a possible rebound.

Generating the force. From physics, we know that when several forces act upon an object the effect is the same as that of a single force equal to the vectorial sum of the force components; that is, the more horses pulling in the same direction, the greater the horsepower. To a weightlifter, this means that it is possible to synchronize the efforts of leg, back, shoulder, and arm muscles to lift a considerably heavier weight above the head (as in a *jerk*)

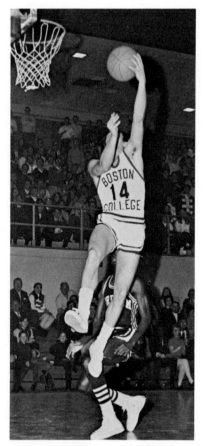

Recovery of balance on drive-in shot.

38

than is possible with the arms alone (as in a *press*). To a basketball player, it means that the force that he can impart to the ball ranges from that required for a long *two-hand set shot* to that required for a *tip-in* a few inches from the basket. Thus, beginning at the ball, each of the following adds to the total force imparted: (1) a forward, supple action of the wrist and fingers; (2) a sudden extension of the arm, snapping the shoulder and elbow; and (3) a sharp, knee-locking thrust with the legs, while (4) rising to balls of the feet. Since the force imparted by a muscle under strain is difficult to control, best results are obtained when all muscles can be brought into a smooth, coordinated effort that is well within individual limitations. In a jump shot, obviously, much of the energy generated is converted to altitude, from which the remaining force required to reach the basket must be provided by the arms, wrists, and fingers.

Timing, or rhythm. The *timing* of a shot begins with getting the correct foot down for takeoff (jump shot) and ends with follow-through and recovery. In a set shot, perfect timing results in a smooth, continuous thrust, from the floor upward, developing a peak force at the fingertips the instant before, and sustained through, fingertip release. In a jump shot, body momentum decreases rapidly to zero, and the shot must be timed so that fingertip release occurs at the highest point of the jump, when the only forces imparted to the ball are those of the arm, fingers, and wrist. When this is done perfectly, an illusion is created of the shooter's "hanging" momentarily in space while he gets the shot away. Any nonsynchronized acceleration, however, of the body or its members (for example, jerking the head) will directly affect the trajectory of the ball.

Hand-eye coordination and fingertip control. All forces imparted to the ball by the shooter should pass through the fingertips. This allows the fingers to make fine trajectory adjustments at release and provides a "soft" natural backspin. (By stating that the optimum trajectory is that which results in the ball's entering the basket at the highest possible angle commensurate with the lowest possible velocity, we shall have said all that can be said dogmatically about trajectory. Many good shooters use a low trajectory, for it allows somewhat better control of velocity and accuracy. However, the ball "sees" a smaller rim opening and is easier to block using a low trajectory. The disadvantages of a high trajectory are the increased velocity and decreased accuracy, despite the larger apparent target. The best rule is to follow the natural inclination to "just drop the ball over the rim." Combined with a natural backspin, a medium, or optimum, trajectory results in the "soft touch" kind of shot that, even if slightly off target, will

39

either drop in or hang on the rim for an easy tip-in.)

In the section on sighting, we alluded to the exceptional directional sensitivity of the forefinger. Combined with a supple, sure wrist action, this dexterity, or "feel," becomes the ultimate factor in determining shooting accuracy. In adjusting his hands preparatory to shooting, the shooter should space his fingers comfortably to hold the ball firmly in his fingertips and on the heels of both hands—the palms held slightly clear and the three middle fingers aligned perpendicular to the seams. Players should practice their "feel" until this adjustment becomes a reflexive procedure as soon as they receive the ball.

Follow-through. Throughout the act of shooting, as in any sport involving hand-eye coordination, the brain continues to compute the precise amount and direction of the force needed to reach the target (the basket). Although these computations continue automatically, in what computer people call *real time,* there is, nevertheless, sufficient lag to make compensations impossible for any abrupt accelerations at, or just before, the instant of release. Success, then, depends upon constant sighting and a smooth, continuous build-up of a propelling force that reaches its peak at the instant the ball leaves the fingertips, which means that a follow-through period in which the forces generated are allowed to diminish is an *essential* part of the shooting sequence.

fundamental techniques for specific shots

Before describing the specific techniques associated with the various shots that a player might have in his offensive repertory, the authors again emphasize the importance of improvisation to the particular style of each player. Basketball is a game that has changed drastically in recent years, largely as a result of the innovations of individual players whose experimenting with accepted techniques led to the development and recognition of revolutionary new techniques. For example, dunks, behind-the-back passes, jump shots, shot-blocking, and even one-hand set shots were all, at one time, considered ineffectual showboating. What accounts for their present respectability is utilitarianism, the criterion against which every technique or individual refinement must be considered. As every innovator knows, however, success in experimenting proceeds after mastering the basics.

The Basic Shots. Virtually every shot required can be adapted from a mastery of six basic techniques: (1) two-hand underhand, (2) one-hand underhand, (3) two-hand set, (4) one-hand set, (5) jump, and (6) hook. Although specific adjustments are necessary for various ranges and purposes, for example, free throws, drive-ins, tip-ins, lay-

40

ups, pivots, turn-arounds, and step-aways, the "basic six" will provide the nucleus of a repertory for exploiting any situation.

Priority, however, should be given to mastering the shots that are likely to be most useful to a given player for a given position. For example, there would be little advantage in a seven-foot center's practicing two-hand set shots from 30 feet out, or a six-foot guard's practicing close-in pivots. As a rule, centers should perfect a versatile repertory of close-in (within 12 feet of the basket), right- and left-hand hooks, jumps, turn-around jumps, and overhead sets, adapting this repertory to the various pivots, lay-ups, tip-ins, etc. Forwards, on the other hand, should spend considerable time practicing medium range (13 to 20 feet) jumps, drives, sets, and hooks, particularly from the sides, and proportionately less time practicing the close-in pivots and long-range sets. The essential shots for a guard are the long-range (beyond 20 feet) sets, medium-range jumps, and a variety of overhand and underhand shots for quick drive-ins and lay-ups.

1. Two-hand underhand. Although most frequently used as a free throw, the *two-hand underhand* is also adaptable to certain drive-in situations; for example, the two-hand underhand lay-up described later on.

Except for the position of the hands, the *set position* for an underhand shot is essentially the same as that for any set shot. The feet are spaced approximately the width of the shoulders (the toes pointed toward the basket), either on line or slightly staggered (as always, latitude is allowed for personal preference). The knees are flexed, and the weight is concentrated evenly on the balls of the feet, the heels lightly touching the floor. The shoulders are squared, and the head is erect, the eyes focused on the sighting point. The ball is held in the fingertips, close to the body and below the waist, with one hand on either side of the ball, fingers pointed downward and thumbs pointed at the basket. The palms are off the ball, and the fingers are spread comfortably wide. The elbows are relaxed and slightly flexed.

With a preliminary swing (free throw), the arms are brought forward to chest level, the knees straightening. In the same rhythm, the shooter reassumes the starting position and starts the ball forward and up as the knees straighten and lock. At full extension, when the arms are parallel to the floor, the ball is released with an upward flip of wrists and fingers, imparting a natural backspin. The back is straight at all times. The weight comes up on the toes, as the heels rise from the floor. The arms follow through, with the palms reaching toward the basket and the thumbs pointing inward.

2. One-hand underhand. Except in theory, the *one-hand underhand* is probably never used from a set position. The usefulness of this shot, however, as adapted to such special-purpose shots as underhand lay-ups and pivots, will compensate generously for time spent in mastering it. Its advantage is the additional reach possible when only one arm is extended toward the basket.

From an initial position similar to that of the two-hand underhand, the shooter reaches toward the basket with one hand under the ball, allowing the off hand to fall away. With his shooting arm fully extended and his eyes focused on the sighting spot, the shooter "lifts" the ball toward either the basket or a spot on the backboard by raising his arm and adding a soft flick of his wrist and fingers. Follow-through is with the palm upward and the arm bending slightly at the elbow. Executed as described, the shot will carry with a minimum forward rotation. Any side rotation of the hand position at release, however, culminating in a follow-through with the hand edgewise and the wrist cocked upward, will impart a sidespin, or "English," that must be compensated for when sighting.

3. Two-hand set shot. The *two-hand set* shot may be taken from the chest position or from an overhead position. *Chest position.* Although not widely used in modern basketball, the two-hand set from the chest position has one

Two-hand set shot.   Two-hand overhead set shot.

advantage in that it has the longest accurate range. It is not, however, readily adaptable to the fast-break offense used by many teams.

In the set position, the feet are spaced and aligned for balance and comfort. Each player should determine the foot position that gives him the most confidence and then use that position for all similar shots. The important thing is that the shooter feel relaxed and mobile. The weight is on the balls of the feet, with the heels resting lightly on the floor; both knees are flexed; and the upper body is bent forward slightly from the waist, with the back straight. With the fingers spread wide, the thumbs and little fingers on the same line, and the thumbs close together in the rear, the ball is held comfortably in the fingertips of both hands, about a foot in front of the body and just below chin level. The elbows are held fairly close to the body, the head is stationary and erect, and the eyes are fixed on the sighting point.

Execution is a simultaneous thrust with arms and legs—rising from the heels and locking the knees and elbows—and a flick with the wrists and fingers in the direction of the basket, imparting a soft backspin to the ball. Follow-through is a continuation of the inward and downward rotation of the thumbs, leaving the hands declined slightly at the wrists, the palms turned outward. Eye concentration throughout is essential.

Overhead position. A variation of the two-hand set shot is the *two-hand overhead set.* Although its range is somewhat less, this is an excellent shot for a corner man, since it forces the defender to raise up from a good defensive crouch and move in closer to the shooter. The set position is also a basic passing position for feeding the pivot, as well as an excellent stance from which to fake and drive to the basket. The shooting technique is the same as in that of the conventional two-hand set, except the ball is held above the forehead instead of at the chest, and the hands are positioned somewhat lower on the ball.

4. One-hand set shot. The *one-hand set* retains much of the balance, range, and accuracy of the *two-hand set* while realizing a substantial increase in speed and flexibility. Because its techniques are essentially the same as those for all nonhooking, one-hand overhead shots, including the jump shot, it should be the basic shot in the repertory of every player.

As with the two-hand set, the position of the feet is a matter of personal choice, although most players prefer the foot under the shooting hand to be slightly forward. The level that the ball is carried when in the set position also varies with the player, one preferring to shoot from the chest, another from the shoulder. As a rule, however, the higher the ball is carried in the set position, the closer the shooter can be to a defender and still get the shot away.

One-hand set shot.

The starting point also affects the range—the higher the ball the shorter the range. The position of the shooting hand is on the low-back side of the ball, the fingers spread comfortably wide, with the palm facing the basket and held clear of the ball by the fingertips and the heel of the hand. The position of the off hand is on the low-forward side, palm away from the basket. The function of the off hand is to provide additional balance and control: the off hand falls away the instant before release, and the impetus to the ball is transmitted solely by the shooting hand. Otherwise, shot execution is the same as for a two-hand set: as the shooter rises to his toes and thrusts with his legs, he simultaneously thrusts his shooting arm to full extension, his hand and fingers flexing downward smoothly at the wrist in order to impart a soft backspin as the ball is released.

A variation of the one-hand set from the shoulder or chest position is the one-hand set from the hip. In this instance, the ball is started at hip level from the shooting side and is brought up for a release directly above the shooter's line of sight. (A release from the shoulder or chest position is slightly to one side of the line of sight.) In a crouch, as though to dribble, and holding the ball in both hands, the shooter steps forward with the foot *opposite* his shooting hand, at the same time that he starts the ball up and toward the basket. Revolving his hands so that his shooting hand is hindmost, he times the thrust off his *opposite* foot to occur simultaneously with the extension of his shooting hand. Release and follow-through are the same as for all one-hand shots.

Running one-hand set (two-count stop). The running one-hand set shot is useful at long ranges when shooting off a dribble or after receiving a pass. It is essentially the same as the one-hand set from the hip. Using a two count, the shooter (1) starts the ball up to above his shoulder as the foot under his shooting hand strikes the floor, and (2) as the *opposite* foot strikes the floor, he thrusts upward with the knee of the shooting-hand foot (to change momentum) and extends his shooting hand toward the basket for an *opposite-foot* release. Follow-through with the hand and eyes is the same as for a stationary one-hand set.

Running one-hand set (one-count stop). A variation of the one-hand running set shot with a two-count stop is the same shot with a one-count stop and off the *strong foot.* Its advantage is its effectiveness against a defender positioned to guard a shot off the *opposite* foot. For the one-count stop, the dribbler stops and braces, in one count, on his strong (shooting-hand side) foot, lifting the opposite knee high to slow his momentum, and, at the one count, shoots off his strong foot. Surprise is the key element. This shot should be practiced and added to the shooter's repertory only after having mastered other set-shot techniques.

Running one-hand set shot with left foot takeoff.

Running one-hand set shot showing right foot takeoff.

5. The jump shot. The *jump shot* is one of the most effective offensive weapons. Although it is possible to become a good, even great, offensive player without it, there is no other shot that puts quite so much pressure on a defense. When preceded by a fake, a fast, accurate jump shot is virtually impossible to block. The fake, in fact, is an essential element in the jump shot's effectiveness. To guard against the jump, the defender (unless he has a considerable height advantage) must be able to synchronize his own jump perfectly with that of the shooter—a task made extremely difficult by even the simplest fake.

If movement is toward basket, from the shoulders up, shot execution is essentially the same as for a one-hand set shot; therefore, once the techniques of set shooting have been perfected, it should prove relatively easy to expand one's shooting arsenal to include a versatile assortment of jump shots for any reasonable range. Since the propelling force must be supplied almost solely by the arm, wrist, and fingers, usefulness is limited primarily to the short to medium ranges, although some jump shooters are consistently successful as far out as 26 feet.

Take-off can be either from a stationary position, facing any direction, or from a position on the move after dribbling, pivoting, or receiving a pass. Although highly individualized, takeoff from a stationary position is generally from both feet; when moving, it is usually from the foot opposite the shooting hand. Similarly, the position of the legs once the shooter is in the air is determined by what feels comfortable and natural: there are great shooters who tuck their legs, others who leave them extended and spread, others extended and together. Also, depending upon balance, distance from the basket, and defensive pressure, the jump can be either straight up, inclined toward the basket, or falling away. In all instances, however, the objective is to arrive at a near-stationary, balanced shooting position, above the floor and facing the basket, with the shooting arm cocked and poised to shoot. When perfectly timed, the effect is an illusion of the shooter's hanging in mid-air for the instant required to get the shot away. When the jump is improperly timed or poorly executed, the result is an awkward, off-balance shot having very little chance of entering the basket. Regardless of individual style, the following techniques are essentially the same for all jump shots, whether stationary or moving.

As he begins his crouch the shooter carries the ball in both hands to a *preliminary position* near the shoulder of his shooting side. If the player is moving, the crouch occurs on count two of a two-count stop (*see Running one-hand set shot*) and is initiated by the foot opposite the shooting hand; if he is stationary, the crouch is with both legs, the weight evenly distributed on the balls of both feet. The

Jump shot at takeoff.

46

Jump shot techniques.

elbows are held slightly forward and under the ball, and the hands are positioned with the off-hand leading and the shooting hand trailing, the fingers spread comfortably as for a one-hand set shot. While sighting the target and as the legs unflex at the start of the jump, the shooter raises the ball with both hands to a *shooting position* slightly forward and either straight above or above and to the shooting side of his head. (Taller players tend to prefer a more overhead position than do shorter players.) Approaching the apex of the jump, with the elbow of his shooting arm pointed at the basket, the shooter cocks the wrist of his shooting hand so that the palm faces up and forward and his off-hand rides high and in front. Considerable concentration is necessary in order to ensure continuous sighting as the shooter's hands and forearms cross his line of vision. Reaching the apex of the jump, he uncocks the forearm and wrist of his shooting hand in a quick, supple motion, allowing his off-hand to fall away, and imparts with his fingertips a soft, natural backspin to the ball. Follow-through is completed with the shooting arm fully extended and the hand and fingers declined at the wrist as though to dip inside the basket.

47

Hook shot.

6. Hooks. The *hook* is an extremely versatile and effective shot in the close-in to medium ranges. Centers and forwards in particular should begin early in their careers to master its techniques, both with the left and the right hand.

The hook shot can be executed after a dribble to either side, it can follow receiving a pass-in and pivoting, or it can follow an offensive rebound and a pivot. In each instance, the shot is taken off the foot opposite the shooting hand. As described here, the hook is initiated from a back-to-the-basket pivot.

For a right-hand hook, the shooter pivots to the left, pushing off his right foot and turning his body and head to pick up the sighting point while his right hand, palm up, extends out parallel to the floor. Taking off from his left foot, he completes a continuous, sweeping overhead arc toward the basket. As in every shot in basketball, success depends upon effective sighting, a soft wrist, fingertip control, and a smooth continuous follow-through. A correctly executed follow-through will leave the shooter facing the basket and in good position for a rebound.

Adaptations and Variations. After a player has mastered the fundamental techniques of set, jump, and hook shooting

48

from various distances within his own optimum-percentage area, he should then begin to elaborate upon these techniques by incorporating the specialized fakes, pivots, turns, etc., that apply to the play situations most often developing from his team position. Informal practice to perfect close-in shots with either hand will significantly add to a player's value as an offensive threat.

Correct hook shot follow-through.

Lay-ups. A *lay-up* shot is used in the following situations: (1) a player receives a pass, close-in, while cutting toward the basket; (2) a player dribbles past defenders and under the basket.

Approaching from the right, the shooter grasps the ball strongly in both hands as his right foot hits the floor. Keeping his body between the ball and the defender, coming down hard on his left foot, and thrusting sharply upward with his right knee (as in a *high jump*), he carries the ball in both hands, as high as possible, with the right hand behind the ball, wrist cocked and facing the basket, and the left hand in front, wrist away from the basket (as for a one-hand set or jump shot). At the top of the high jump, with both arms above his head (erect, with eyes fixed on a spot above and to the right of the basket), he allows his left hand to fall away as his right arm, wrist, and fingers extend to "place" the ball against the sighting point in a motion similar to that of trying to grasp the basket rim from a running start without the ball. (The backboard should be used for lay-ups approached from the side.) Follow-through is completed, and the shooter alights with hips down, knees bent, and body-weight low, ready to move immediately into position for a rebound or to go on defense. (When approaching the basket from the left, the left hand should be used, and all direction considerations are reversed.)

Start of right-hand lay-up.

A modified lay-up shot, preferred by many players because of better control of the ball and a softer "touch" when laying it against the backboard, is done with the hand positions reversed. The approach and take-off are the same as before, but the ball is carried with the right hand in front, palm facing slightly upward (as for a one-hand underhand shot); as the left hand falls away, the right arm is extended and the ball is laid up by a soft flick of the wrist and fingers.

Little or no spin, or "English," should be used for either shot, since the "softness" depends upon a minimum of wrist and finger action. Therefore, the shooter must select a sighting point from which the ball should touch-off and fall, with very little momentum, into the basket.

Left-hand lay-up with hand under.

Lay-up with hand behind.

Special purpose lay-ups. Although one of the two variations described above should be used in most lay-up situations, the exceptionally talented player may find that two additional lay-up shots will significantly increase his scoring opportunities: the *floating two-hand underhand lay-up* and the *driving one-hand underhand lay-up*.

The two-hand underhand lay-up can be used by a hard-driving guard coming down the lane in front of a closely defended basket. Instead of the high jump of the conventional lay-up, a broad jump is begun toward the basket, from 6 to 9 feet out, with a take-off from either foot. After take-off (the feet may be tucked under the thighs), the shooter "floats" toward the basket, the ball held between both hands. (See two-hand underhand shots.) Release is timed for the apex of the jump and is effected by extending both arms forward and flipping the ball up with wrists and fingers.

The driving one-hand underhand lay-up is useful either for a miscalculated take-off too far from the basket or as a calculated tactic to counter pressure from a defender in position to block a conventional overhead shot. Again, the shot is made from a broad jump, but in this instance the take-off foot is the same as for a conventional lay-up—left foot for right-hand shot, right foot for left-hand shot. The

Two-hand underhand lay-up.   Two-hand underhand lay-up.

ball is initially held in both hands, the body between it and the defender. After take-off, however, the hand nearer the defender falls away and the shot is accomplished by a reaching motion—the arm extended forward at shoulder level, the shooting hand under the ball, and the wrist and fingers used to flick the ball toward a sighting spot on the backboard, slightly above and to the shooter's side of the basket. (See One-hand underhand shots.) Some rotation of the wrist may be required in order to impart a slight carrying spin.

Floating one-hand lay-up with left hand under ball.

Under-the-basket shots. Frequently, a player cutting under the basket finds himself with the ball, too close in for any form of a lay-up. In this situation, he has two alternatives for a high-percentage shot: the first is either a *semi-hook* or a *short-hook,* taken from the approach side of the basket; the second is a *layback,* or *reverse lay-up,* taken from the side opposite the approach.

Semi-hook and short hook. Take-off for both the semi-hook and the short hook is from the foot opposite the shooting hand, with the ball held high and in both hands. In the semi-hook, however, as the shooter rises from the floor he turns to face the basket, allowing his off hand to fall away and hooking overhead and toward the basket with his shooting arm, the elbow and wrist inclined in a shallow arch. For a short hook, the shooter does not turn toward the basket. Instead, he gets the ball away by a full overhead hook, with the arm relaxed and extended, and a soft flick of the wrist and fingers.

Semi-hook shot.   Short-hook shot.

Layback, or reverse lay-up. The layback, or reverse lay-up, is initiated from the opposite side from which the basket is approached. Actually, approach can be either from a side or from the rear, utilizing the four-foot area between the backboard and the end line. Take-off is from the foot opposite the strong hand. With the head tilted backward to see the sighting point, the ball is carried upward in both hands. At full extension, the off hand falls away and the shooting hand rotates inward toward the little finger. The ball is released by a soft flick of wrist and fingers. This is a difficult shot to master, and the ambidextrous shooter might consider the advantage of using his weak hand, instead, for an almost conventional lay-up.

Reverse lay-ups.

Drive-in hook. A very important weapon in the repertory of smaller backcourt players is a *drive-in hook shot* to be used when a taller defender switches to block a direct drive to the basket. While still in motion, the shooter begins with the same take-off as for a conventional lay-up, but when the ball is level with his shoulders, it is extended out, held in the shooting hand, away from the defender. A high-trajectory shot is then effected by an overhead hook with the arm fully extended.

Drive-in hook using right hand.

Drive-in hook using left hand.

Close-in jump shot. Following a quick stop and fake, a *close-in jump shot* can often be executed before the defender can react. Moving from his weak to his strong side, the attacker stops, fakes, and takes off from his strong foot. Turning in mid-air toward the basket, he shoots quickly with one hand at the apex of his jump. The attacker uses the same technique when moving from his strong side, except a slight fall away may be necessary in turning toward the basket.

Close-in pivot shots. Most close-in scoring opportunities come either to the medium- or low-pivot man or to a forward when his back is toward the basket. Therefore, players in these positions must master the following: *right-* and *left-hand hooks; turn-arounds; step-in pivots; underhand pivots; step-aways;* and *jump turns.*

Hooks. Properly executed, a close-in, back-to-the-basket hook shot is almost impossible to block. Because of the three-second time restriction in the foul-lane area, however, speed in getting the shot away is essential. Ideally, the pass-in should be received shoulder height, with the feet in position for a pivot in either direction. However, should pass reception require establishing one foot as the pivot, by taking a step in the direction of the pass, then the step should be taken with the foot nearest the basket. Upon receiving the ball, the shooter should execute a head and shoulder fake while bringing the ball to shoulder level. (Obviously, the shooter must be capable of shooting with either hand if a fake is to be convincing.) Depending upon opportunity and ability, the shooter follows his fake with a quick pivot either obliquely toward, parallel to, or away from the end line. For shot execution see page 48.

Turn-arounds. The *turn-around* is a simple pivot shot to master. Its successful execution requires that a step, pivot, take-off, and shot be effected in one continuous motion. The ball is received with both hands, with the weight evenly distributed on both feet in order that a turn may be made in either direction. For a right-hand shot, a head-shoulder fake to the right is quickly followed by a step to the left with the left, or non-pivot, foot; a simultaneous pivot to face the basket; an upward thrust with the right knee; and a left-foot take-off. During the execution of the turn, the ball is brought with both hands up to a shooting position above the head. Shot execution is as described for a jump shot (page 46).

Step to end line preliminary to short hook.

Left-hand hook. Preliminary fake to left, then step with right foot.

Left-hand hook shot. Step away from basket.

57

Step-in pivot. From a close-in pivot position, it is sometimes possible to take advantage of a defensive lapse by following a fake with a pivot directly toward the basket. If he sees that the defender is moving in the direction of the fake, the pivot man, synchronizing his movements with the defender's lapse, can drop his non-pivot foot straight back, pivot quickly toward the basket, and trap the defender behind him. The object is to maneuver into the position of a fulcrum around which the pivot is executed. The shot can be either a hook, a turn-around, an underhand pivot, or a lay-up.

Underhand pivot shot.

Step-in pivot.

Underhand pivot. When a pivot man is in a close-in, back-to-the-basket position and feels pressure from a defender behind him, he can fake to the side of the pressure, execute a *step-in pivot* in the opposite direction, and shoot under the defender's arm with an underhand, upward motion. The ball is released toward the basket with a lifting rotation of the forearm and wrist of the shooting hand, imparting a soft carrying spin. Sighting must take into account both the spin and the lower arc. Rhythm and follow-through are essential.

Step-away. The *step-away shot* is useful when the back-to-the-basket pivot player has the ball but is not closely

58

guarded because of a lapse by the pivot defender; for instance, when the defender reacts to a pivot fake by moving away from the shooter and toward the basket. The shot is executed by stepping away from the basket with the non-pivot foot, pivoting on this foot to face the basket, and simultaneously thrusting upward with the other knee for a rear-foot take-off, using a one-hand shot to the basket. Since this shot is easily blocked by a close defender, the fake, pivot, and shot must be perfectly timed.

Step-away pivot shot.

Jump-turn. Many pivot players consider the *jump-turn shot* to be their best back-to-the-basket offensive weapon. Its success is largely due to its simplicity and to the effectiveness of an easily executed fake. In making the shot, the back-to-the-basket pivot brings the ball up to the shooting position while simultaneously executing a straight-up jump-turn to face the basket, timing the one-hand release for the apex of the jump. The fake is accomplished by a quick straightening of the knees and upward motion that simulates the beginning of a take-off, making it impossible for the defender to synchronize his jump with that of the shooter.

59

Tip-in. The *tip-in* is not just a lucky slap at the ball, and should be practiced as a regular shot in the repertory of any tall player. An offensive rebounder should be ready to make a *tip-in shot* of any rebound in his area and within five feet of the basket.

Facing the basket, with knees flexed, hands up, and elbows shoulder high, the tip-in shooter times his take-off to make fingertip contact just as he is reaching the top of his jump. With the fingers spread and the wrist flexible, the shooting hand first controls the ball and then flicks it upward with a soft trajectory to the basket. Even if control is not possible, some kind of contact, such as a slap, should be made with the ball. Sighting, fingertip control, and follow-through are the same as for any one-hand shot. (Although some players prefer to go up for the ball with both hands in order to be in better position for a rebound should a tip-in prove not feasible, most players can jump quicker and higher with only one hand up, which is the recommended technique whenever a tip-in opportunity is likely.)

Tip-in shot.

The free throw. Free-throw shooting should be a regular part of every practice session and should take place under as near game conditions as possible. Every player must determine his best-percentage medium- or long-range shot and use that shot for all free throws. (To be proficient, a shooter should make at least 75 percent of his free throws in practice.) If, however, a player is not particularly proficient in any one medium- or long-range shot, he should be taught to master the two-hand underhand shot for free throws. (Although the jump shot is used for free throws by many outstanding players who feel more confident with it than with any other shot, the shooter must take special care not to step on the foul line and thus nullify

60

Two-hand-under foul shot.

a successful throw.) The following fundamentals should be practiced until they become second nature for any free throw, regardless of style:

1. Dry hands and fingers before entering the free-throw circle; shake the arms, wrists, and fingers to relieve any tenseness.

2. Before accepting the ball from the official, look to both sides and behind to check opponents' offensive alignment and teammates' positions.

3. Receive the ball from the official before positioning yourself at the free-throw line.

4. Move up to the line, and set feet in the exact position that you always use for free throws.

5. Spin the ball in your hands to acquire proper feel; bounce the ball on the floor a few times to relax your arms and body and to accentuate feel.

6. After assuming final hand placement, inhale and exhale slowly.

7. Shoot.

The free throw should become as mechanical and reflexive as possible. Therefore, preliminary actions and foot positions should be the same for every shot.

shooting drills

Most drills in basketball, except for preseason conditioning or fundamental drills, should include shooting as the finish of the drill. A good shooter sights properly, has good body balance prior to the release, and releases the ball quickly. He has good arm and body movement throughout the shot, with the hand and fingers of his shooting hand following through toward the target and his head stationary. He imparts a good backspin on the ball by shooting with the wrist and fingertips. His palm never touches the ball. In all shooting drills, the shooting side should be changed frequently.

Diag. 3-1, BASIC LAY-UP DRILL

The squad breaks evenly with eight players on each side. The first two players in the left-hand line each have a ball. X_1 dribbles in, and X_9, in the right-hand line, starts in at the same time. X_1 leads X_9 to the basket with a bounce pass. X_9 receives the pass, goes up in good lay-up form, and takes the shot with his right hand. X_1 rebounds. X_9 continues on to the left side of the court. X_1 passes to X_9, who dribbles outside up the sideline until he may pass clearly to X_3. X_1 goes to the right line.

The drill continues, with X_2 dribbling in and passing to X_{10}, and so on. Change sides frequently so that players shoot from both sides and the middle. This drill should be used daily at all levels, as a primary warm-up drill and a primary lay-up shooting drill. It can also be used as a pregame warm-up drill. Coaches should watch that the player takes the lay-up in correct form. He should use a 1-2 step rhythm prior to the shot, take off on the foot opposite the hand he is shooting with (left foot for a right hand shot), step up to the basket with his other foot, pumping the knee up, high jump up in the air rather than broad jumping toward the basket, and take the ball up with both hands. He should look through the back of the right hand, releasing the left hand just as he is ready to give the ball a slight flick with the right wrist and the right fingers (imparting no spin to the ball), and alight in good position to rebound.

The shooter may also use the alternate method of laying up with the palm of the shooting hand facing the shooter, again protecting the ball with two hands. The eyes should be up on the target at all times.

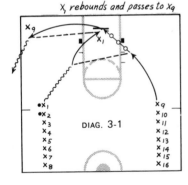

X_1 rebounds and passes to x_9

DIAG. 3-1

Diag. 3-2, LAY-UP DRILL, DEFENSIVE PRESSURE

The alignment is the same as it is in Diag. 3-1, but in this drill the passer will give defensive pressure to the shooter so that the shooter becomes accustomed to laying the ball up or jump shooting under game conditions with a defensive player moving toward him. It is a good pre-game warm-up drill.

X_1 again dribbles the ball in and passes to X_9, who starts cutting *after* X_1 starts dribbling. The pass should go directly across the foul lane to X_9. As X_9 goes up for his lay-up attempt, X_1 gives him defensive pressure. X_1 doesn't necessarily try to block the shot, but he should make X_9 protect the ball without preventing him from shooting. X_9 rebounds his shot, dribbles (outside) up the left side, passing to X_3. Players should alternate sides.

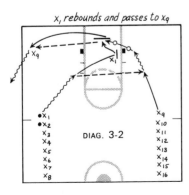

X_1 rebounds and passes to x_9

DIAG. 3-2

Diag. 3-3, INTERMEDIATE JUMP SHOT DRILL, DEFENSIVE PRESSURE

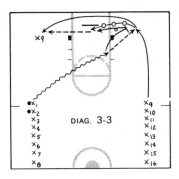

DIAG. 3-3

The players align themselves as in Diag. 3-2. X_1 dribbles in to the foul-circle area. X_9 cuts toward the baseline to about 15 feet from the basket. X_1 passes to X_9 and follows his pass, exerting defensive pressure on X_9 by attempting to deflect the shot or harass X_9 by jumping up in front of him. X_9 may shoot or he may fake a shot to draw a reaction from X_1, then shoot. Both X_1 and X_9 rebound the shot, X_1 attempting to retain good defensive rebound position and X_9 looking for the tip-in if the shot is missed. X_9, either on a pass out from X_1 or by dribbling out himself, passes to X_3, next in line on the feeder side. X_2 and X_{10} continue the drill when X_1 and X_9 are clear of the basket area. Players should shoot from many intermediate (12 to 18 feet from the basket) areas, with shooter and defender both rebounding. Shooters should always follow in on their own shots as they best know the area of deflection on missed shots. Defenders rebound to improve their box out skills. Players should exchange sides after each shot.

Diag. 3-4, SHOOTING DRILL, TWENTY-ONE

DIAG. 3-4

This competitive, fun drill is one of the oldest basic shooting drills. It is beneficial at every level of basketball and should be used frequently—preseason, during the regular season, and at any postseason practice. Since it involves constant movement, it is a good conditioning drill.

Two players stand on each side of the basket, at least 18 feet from the basket. X_1 and X_2 play against X_3 and X_4. Both X_1 and X_3 have a ball. X_1 shoots, follows his shot, and passes out to X_2. X_3 shoots, rebounds his own shot, and passes back to X_4. Each player in turn shoots and rebounds his shot. One point is scored for a successful shot. The first team to score 21 outside shots wins. Usually, teams have to lead by two points to win the game.

A penalty may be prescribed for the losers. One of the penalties that we enjoy using is to place the losing players across the court, bent over with their backs to the winning team. The winners get two shots with a ball at the buttocks of the losers.

Diag. 3-5, JUMP SHOT AND FOLLOW DRILL

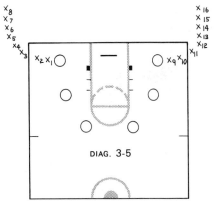

DIAG. 3-5

The squad is broken into two or three teams. Usually, small men are pitted against big men for spirited competition. Players may also be divided according to position, so that forwards, centers, and guards are in separate groups, or the first team may shoot against the second team and against the third team. The players jump shoot, follow their shots, and pass back to the next players in their line. All players must shoot from one of three spots on either side of the basket (see diagram). Usually, the teams play until one team scores 15, and again the losers may have to pay some type of penalty.

Diag. 3-6, PASS-PICK-POP DRILL

This is similar to some drills that we use for setting screens and for cutting. It is a good pregame warm-up drill. Players form four lines, two on each side of the court. Four players stand at the foul line extended near each sideline, and four players stand even with the hash marks at the foul lanes extended. The first two players in the lines at the hash marks each have basketballs. X_5, in the left

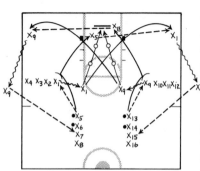

DIAG. 3-6

DIAG. 3-7

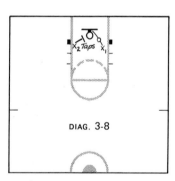

DIAG. 3-8

line, passes to X_1 and picks for him. X_1 dribbles once or twice and takes a jump shot—pass, pick, pop. X_5 rebounds the ball and passes it to X_1, who clears to the other side of the court. X_1 passes to X_{15}. The players switch to the opposite line after each shot. X_{13} passes to X_9 and picks for him. X_9 takes a pop shot from the foul line extended. X_{13} rebounds and passes to X_9, who clears to the side and passes to X_7.

Diag. 3-7, LOB PASS AND SHOT DRILL

The lob pass shot may be made in two situations. The first is indicated by *A* in the diagram. A defensive player (X_1) is between the center and the guard to the left. G_1 practices lobbing the ball to the center, G_1, who takes a shot. This is a good drill for teaching players the timing necessary when they must lob a pass to a teammate who is being overplayed in a low or medium pivot position. The second situation is indicated by *B* on the diagram. C_2, the pivot man, is low on the weak side. He is being played by X_2. As C_2 starts high, and X_2 attempts to beat him to the high post position, C_2 reverses direction and goes to the basket to receive a lob pass from G_2 and shoot. This drill should be practiced both in preseason and during the season.

Diag. 3-8, OFFENSIVE TIP DRILL

This drill is executed by players in pairs to perfect their timing in tipping the ball when it rebounds off the backboard or rim. Each player must tip from the left side of the basket, from the right side of the basket, and from the front of the basket for accuracy. One player taps the ball from one side so it will hit the backboard or rim and go over the basket. His partner, on the other side, will tip the ball for a score. The player should tap the ball against the backboard one, two, or three times before tapping it over, varying the number so that his partner must time his spring each time. The players should exchange positions frequently.

Coaches should look for a good one-hand tip and proper fundamental techniques. The player should hold both hands about shoulder height, and as he starts up for the ball his arms and hands should go straight up with the elbows in an almost square position. The palm of the tipping hand should be facing the ball and the fingers should be well spread. The player should tip the ball just as he is reaching the peak of his jump. The ball is actually cradled in the tipper's fingers and the tipping motion is a continuation of the jumping motion with the tipping fingers controlling the ball for an infinitesimal amount of time, as though the player is actually taking a shot. As he "catches," cradles, or cups the ball in the tipping fingers a flick of the fingers and wrist of the hand should be enough to propel the ball accurately. Cupping is necessary for complete control.

We work this drill very close into the basket so that players may tip balls which have a good chance of going in. Any ball that is more than five feet from the basket should never be tipped; it should be caught in both hands. For tipping, both hands should be up. If the player misjudges the rebound, there is a chance that the off hand will have at least partial control of the ball. Having both hands up also eliminates the possibility of fouling with the non-tipping hand.

Diag. 3-9, OFFENSIVE TIPPING DRILL VARIATION

Place towels (or chairs) in front of the tipper at the three stations, left of basket, right of basket, and in front of basket. Be certain the tipper stays behind the towel until he is ready to tip the ball. The same fundamental techniques are used in this drill as in Drill 8, so when the first player tips the ball, it will rebound in the direction of his partner. The towels are on the court so that the players will have to maneuver around them before tipping. The player who is tipping should not move until the ball has been released by his teammate, then he should fake in one direction and come back in the opposite direction, as though avoiding a defensive box-out.

DIAG. 3-9

passing

Passing is the foundation for all scoring plays; its importance is second only to shooting. Left alone, however, most players would spend a great deal of their time perfecting their shooting technique, and little on their passing. Therefore, during formal practice, coaches must balance the training by reversing the emphasis.

fundamental principles

Many of the principles and techniques of shooting apply equally to passing, and the reader would do well to review the beginning of this chapter before proceeding: just as a shooter does not take a shot he is not confident of making, a passer does not attempt a pass unless he feels certain that it will be completed.

The fundamental requirements of every basketball pass are that it be, in precisely the right proportions, *accurate, well-timed, quick, deceptive,* and *relevant.* Although an excellent shooter may make only 50 percent of his attempts, a good passer must approach 100 percent effectiveness. To do so, he must develop certain of his perceptive abilities to the point that they become an instinctive awareness —even when he does not have the ball.

1. **Court Awareness.** The accomplished passer must be constantly aware of the positions and the relative physical and mental capabilities of every player on the court. This includes each player's speed, ball-handling ability, aggressiveness (both on offense and defense), reaction to fakes, rebounding ability, and shooting ability.

2. **Peripheral Vision.** Since it is neither possible nor desirable that the passer always look directly at each potential receiver and each defender, he must develop his peripheral vision to the point that he can see everything that takes place within 90 degrees on either side of the direction he is facing. This means that with practice he will be able to encompass a 360 degree field of vision by simply turning his head 90 degrees right and left.

3. **Anticipation.** The accomplished passer knows the best opening and how a play might develop, even before he has

the ball. Anticipating the movements both of receivers and defenders, he can react with a well-timed pass that arrives at his receiver's best reception zone at the optimum moment for offensive advantage.

4. Judgment. This is the perceptive attribute of knowing when a fake is or is not necessary; whether to use a lob, bounce, or straight pass; what receiver is in the best offensive position; who not to pass to because of poor position, exceptionally strong defender, etc; what the maxim, "not too fast, not too slow, not too high, not too low," means for a given receiver; and, finally, how to make each pass relevant to the objective of scoring.

Obviously, judgment is not unrelated to the other attributes of perception. Where court awareness, peripheral vision, and anticipation provide the passer with a four-dimensional frame of reference in which to operate, the ultimate measure of his judgment and his excellence as a passer is his ability to pull all factors together and execute, within his own limitations, an accurate and meaningful pass, with just the right amount of deception and quickness.

basic passes

This section contains descriptions of the more conventional passes that a player will have an opportunity to use. It should be remembered, however, that any pass is a good one that meets the criteria of accuracy, timing, quickness, deception, and relevance. Although a poor passer will usually improve his effectiveness by staying with the simpler passes, a gifted passer should not feel limited by arbitrary or standard techniques, but should use whatever methods are at his disposal for successfully completing the play. Of course, each passer must remember not only his own passing limitations, but also the reception limitations of each team member. A player may be a valuable member of the team because of his rebounding, shooting, or defensive abilities, yet be unable to handle certain kinds of passes. It is the passer's responsibility to throw him a pass that he *can* handle.

Other considerations of judgment are the inherent advantages and disadvantages of lob passes and bounce passes. Since both of these are slower than a pass thrown parallel to the floor, they should be used only when there is a compelling reason for doing so. A lob pass, for example, might be used with good advantage to throw over a defender to a pivot man going into the basket; to lead a fast-breaking cutter; to throw an easy-to-handle pass over a defensive man to a teammate coming into a high pivot; to exploit a distinct height advantage under the offensive basket; or to complete an out-of-bounds play. A bounce pass, on the other hand, can be used to get the ball past

Lob pass to cutter.

tall or high-hand-guarding defenders, to penetrate a zone, or to exploit any situation in which a side, carrying, or reverse spin can be used with advantage.

Although almost any pass can be completed from a jump, it is best to attempt such a pass only in rare instances —for example, when it is impossible to complete a jump shot or when double-teamed by a pressing or zone defense.

Two-Hand Chest Pass. This pass is used from any position on the court, primarily for short, fast passing of distances up to twenty feet. The basic foot and body position is the same as that for a two-hand set shot from the chest. Feet are spread comfortably, knees flexed, body bent slightly forward from the waist, and the ball held comfortably, chest high, in both hands. Fingers are widespread. The pass is executed by stepping in the direction of the receiver, preferably with the foot closest to the receiver, and coordinating this movement with a full extension of the arms and a quick snap of the wrist and fingers, the weight shifting forward to the extended foot. If the receiver is closely guarded, the target should be a hand held in the clear, away from the defender; otherwise, the target should be the receiver's chest. Often this pass can be used to fake a two-hand chest shot that becomes a lob pass over the head of the defenders. A natural, easy-to-handle backspin is imparted at fingertip release.

Two-hand chest pass.

Two-Hand Bounce Pass. Except for the release, the two-hand bounce pass is the same as a regular two-hand chest pass. Depending upon the circumstance, the ball can be released with either a top spin, a backspin, or little or no spin. Normally, the ball should strike the floor two-thirds of the way to the receiver and bounce high enough to be caught at the waist. *The ball should always strike the floor closer to the receiver than to the passer.*

Top spin. Top spin is used to give a bounce greater distance. Initially, the ball is held as for a two-hand set except that the wrists are cocked upward just before execution. From a deeper crouch and off a more exaggerated forward step than for a regular two-hand pass, both arms are fully extended down and away, and as the stepping foot hits the floor, the ball is released by a powerful, forward and downward flip of the wrists, forcing the ball out over the index fingers. Follow-through is with the thumbs pointing in the direction of the pass, and the fingers pointing downward.

The top-spin pass should strike the floor somewhat farther from the receiver than would a no-spin pass. Because it tends to ''take-off,'' the top spin is the most difficult of the bounce passes to handle.

Backspin. Backspin is used when the passer wishes to blunt the rebound, as when leading a cutter or making a sharp, quick pass that bounces close to a pivot player. Execution is the same as for a top spin except that the wrists and fingers flick inward and down and the arms do not fully extend. Last contact is with the thumbs, and follow-through is with both hands and forearms rotated inward, palms facing outward, and thumbs downward.

The backspin pass should strike the floor somewhat closer than normally to the receiver. Because it tends to

Two-hand bounce with back spin.

"come up," it is the easiest bounce pass to handle when the receiver is moving into the pass.

Normal or little spin. The normal bounce pass, with little or no spin, is a change-of-pace pass that can be used by a guard or forward for feeding a pivot man, for passing through a zone, for out-of-bounds plays, or for passing off at the end of a fast break. Execution is similar to a two-hand chest pass except that the step in the direction of the pass is slightly larger and the body crouch is more exaggerated. The arms and hands move forward and downward, with a natural, quick flick of the wrists and fingers.

It is also possible to impart a left- or right-carry action in order to pass around a defender to a teammate. For a left carry, the hands are rotated sharply counterclockwise at release, causing the ball to veer to the left after striking the floor. For a right carry, the hands are rotated clockwise. Through practice and experimentation, each player will be able to anticipate the correct amount of carry for a variety of situations.

Two-Hand Pass from Over the Shoulder. Stance and the initial position of the hands are similar to the chest pass. To begin a shoulder pass, however, the ball is brought back over the left or right shoulder, both hands remaining in their relative positions but with the outside hand lower and more to rear, the palm more under the ball, and the fingers pointing up. The inside hand rides forward and up. The pass is executed by stepping in the direction of the receiver, with the foot opposite the ball, and extending the arms with a quick inward flick of the wrists and fingers.

Although not a notably efficient pass, the initial two-hand-over-the-shoulder position frequently occurs when the ball is being protected from a defender and allows the passer to take advantage of a quick opening. Possible

Two-hand over-shoulder pass.

Two-hand bounce with no spin.

variations are bounce passes, one-hand passes (allowing the inside hand to fall away as for a one-hand set shot), or an over-the-shoulder drop to a man either standing or cutting behind the passer. Since a one-hand pass from this position is usually more effective than the two-hand pass, it should be used when there is an alternative.

Two-Hand Overhead Pass. The two-hand overhead is one of the most effective passes that a player can master. It can be used from all parts of the court, although it is most commonly used by forwards passing either into the pivot or into a guard cutting to the basket. It is especially useful to players when feeding the pivot, when closely guarded, or when initiating a fast break after a defensive rebound.

Stance and hand position are the same as for a two-hand overhead set shot. The ball is held on each side and toward the back with widespread fingers, the thumbs pointed toward each other. From a position directly overhead, arms partially extended, the pass is initiated by a quick, short step in the direction of the receiver, rising on the toes and shifting the weight onto the forward foot as the ball is released by extending the arms and flicking the wrists and fingers downward. The target area for this pass should never be lower than shoulder level, as the downward force makes lower passes difficult to handle. The follow-through rotates the thumbs inward and downward. Very little body movement is required.

Because execution is so similar to an overhead set shot, a lob pass from this position can be extremely deceptive. Forwards in particular should master the shoot, fake, and drive options.

Two-Hand Underhand Pass from the Hip. This pass has a number of variations and can be made from either hip. It is

Two-hand underhand pass from hip.

Two-hand overhead pass.

primarily used for short, soft, easily handled passing in close areas and is generally handled at waist level or a little lower.

From a crouched position, weight evenly distributed on both feet, and the head forward, the player passes from either the right or the left hip, with the opposite foot forward. Hand position is similar to a two-hand underhand shot to the basket: fingers are spread wide and pointing downward; thumbs are pointed toward each other. The inside hand is close to the hip; the outside upper arm is parallel to the floor, with the elbow pointing rearward, and the lower arm is parallel to the body. If passing for distance (twelve feet maximum), the passer releases the ball with a short step off the opposite foot, a full extension of both arms, and an under-and-forward flick with the wrists and fingers. Follow-through leaves the fingers and arms fully extended and the thumbs pointed upward and slightly outward.

On lateral, guard-to-guard crosses or longitudinal, forward-to-guard exchanges, this pass is executed by stepping

Hand-off, leaving ball.

Hand-off squeeze pass.

with the foot nearest the defender and the basket, raising the ball slightly, and squeezing it out of the hands so that it pops up about six to eight inches to be easily handled by the receiver. A shovel-pass variation is used by pivot men to flip the ball to cutters, from the front or from either side, as a short pass or a close hand-off. Another variation is a two-hand, backward underhand pass, either to a stationary teammate behind the passer or to a guard cutting outside. This is effected by flipping the wrists and fingers backward and upward, allowing the hands to follow through. For any backward pass, however, the passer must first turn his head in order to make certain of the receiver's position.

Because of the frequency with which they occur and because of the natural tendency to let attention relax, close passes must be rigorously emphasized during formal practice. Coaches must constantly stress the importance of such fundamentals as timing and the height and softness of the exchange. To avoid fumbles and interceptions, the passer must lay the ball up waist high so that it hangs, hands off, for the receiver to catch easily without danger of colliding with the passer's hands, feet, or body.

one-hand passes

As a rule, one-hand passes can be used for longer distances than two-hand passes, but a one-hand pass is somewhat more difficult to control and often requires more time to execute; for example, a baseball pass or a hook pass. Within twenty-five feet, therefore, a two-hand pass is generally more appropriate, although the ruling factor is opportunity, which may require a one-hand pass at any distance.

The techniques described below are for right-hand passes; the techniques for the left hand are simply the mirror image of those for the right.

One-Hand Baseball Pass. The one-hand baseball pass can be used as a long pass from any position on the court and is often used to inbound the ball quickly after a score or to initiate a fast break.

From a well-balanced stance, feet spread, weight evenly distributed, the player brings the ball with both hands (fingertip control) to a point above the right shoulder and just behind the right ear. In this passing position, the right hand is behind the ball, a little to the outside, with the fingers pointing upward and the palm toward the target; the left hand is on the front side and helps guide the ball into position. Facing the right sideline and with both feet on a line to the target, the passer reaches back with the ball, his weight shifting onto his rear foot, and releases the pass by stepping forward on the opposite foot and throwing the ball with a quick snap of the elbow, wrist, and fingers. At reach-back, the left hand moves off the ball, and at shoulder level it moves in the direction of the pass. At release, the weight shifts to the opposite foot, and follow-through is completed with an inward and downward rotation of forearm and wrist, arm extended and thumb pointed at the floor. Body weight pivots around the front foot so that the passer ends up facing the receiver, his toes pointing in the direction of the pass. It is important that the follow-through of fingers be an exaggerated rotation inward toward the thumb. Should the wrist rotate outward, in the direction of the little finger, the ball will have a tendency to curve and will have a hard-to-handle spin.

Although some passers can impart a backspin in order to throw the ball over the heads of defenders and hold up the bounce to lead a break-away man, it is an extremely difficult pass to control, and should not be attempted by the average passer, who will usually be more effective with a moving, two-hand chest pass.

Hook Pass. The hook pass is used as follows: to initiate a fast break when defensive pressure from one side negates the use of a baseball pass; to feed the pivot when defensive pressure negates the use of a two-hand overhead pass; and by a pivot man, to pass off to a cutter. The techniques are essentially the same as those for a hook shot and can be executed either with or without a jump.

Baseball pass.

Hook pass.

One-hand underhand pass.

The pass is made with the hand farthest from the defender. Stepping away with his outside foot and protecting the ball with his inside elbow and arm, the passer releases the ball with an arm-extended hook and a flick of the wrist and fingers, taking care neither to impart more force than is absolutely necessary nor to propel the ball on a downward trajectory. For greater quickness, the pass can be made with the passing arm not fully extended, but compensated by more wrist and finger action. Follow-through is the same as for a hook shot.

One-Hand Underhand Pass. This pass is used when the passer is moving at great speed in one direction and a cutter is breaking toward him from the opposite direction. It is a very difficult pass to control, and should only be attempted by good passers when no other alternative is practicable.

Off the front foot, left or right, the pass is released underhand with a stiff wrist and the passing arm fully extended, the impetus coming from the snap of the elbow, the fingertips providing direction and control.

One-Hand Cross-Body Pass. This pass is similar to the baseball pass. It is used for shorter distances when quickness is

74

essential. From a baseball passing position, the ball is released with a quick extension of the arm across the body and with a powerful snap of the elbow and wrist. The thumb and fingers rotate inward, toward the body, with the thumb pointing at the feet during follow-through.

One-Hand Push Pass (after a lateral fake). The one-hand push pass to one side, after faking a two-hand chest pass in the opposite direction, can be used either to feed a cutter or a pivot man or as a safety pass when a defensive man must be moved away from the passing lane. It can be either a straight pass or a bounce pass and is essentially the same as a two-hand pass, except one hand is used only to help control the ball, the impetus being supplied solely by the hand and arm on the side from which the pass is released. As the defender moves with the fake, the pass is released to the opposite side by a full extension of the arm and a brisk snap of the wrist and fingers and a balance step in the direction of the pass; follow-through is with the arm and hand only—parallel to the floor for a straight pass, declined slightly toward the target spot for a bounce pass.

One-Hand Bounce Pass. This is an excellent pass to use off a dribble when a long, quick, and accurate pass to a cutter is needed. The passing motion is similar to a baseball pass except that the release is made off a dribble and the arm is not drawn back. As the ball comes off the floor on the last dribble, it is caught and controlled by the passing (dribbling) hand. In one long passing motion, the passer extends his arm with the ball and releases (as the opposite foot strikes the floor) with a strong elbow, wrist, and finger action. Follow-through will be determined by the spin imparted. (See Two-Hand Chest Pass.) The pass should be timed to bounce up to the waist of the cutter in full stride.

One-hand cross-body pass.

One-hand side-bounce pass.

When thrown hard enough to reach a receiver even though it is partially deflected, the bounce pass should reach its target. It requires a longer windup and, consequently, more time to execute. Therefore, it should be used with discretion. Normally it is most effective against a tall defender.

One-Hand Behind-the-Back Pass. This pass should never be used except as a short flip pass to a teammate coming behind for a screen or when it is the only pass possible to a free cutter—as at the end of a two-on-one break. It can be either a straight pass or a bounce pass.

The passer either turns his head slightly or uses peripheral vision to pick up the receiver. Cupping the ball in his passing hand, inclined at a right angle to his forearm, the passer carries the ball behind his back and releases with a back-hand flip of his wrist: his fingers point at the receiver, and his body pivots on the right foot (right-hand pass) away from the path of the pass.

One-Hand Tap Pass. This pass is used to deflect a ball in flight to a teammate who is in a better position to control it and possibly score. The pass is effected by a supple action of the wrist and fingers and is essentially the same as a tip-in shot. When two hands can be used, somewhat better control is possible.

passing and ball-handling drills

The most important drills in preseason practice are those involving passing, ball handling, and reception of the pass. The coach must review the fundamentals of good passing with the players. All passes made in drills must be 100 percent accurate and must have 100 percent chance of reception. Any time a player in a drill makes a poor pass or makes a pass in which reception is not clean, the coach should correct the passer or the receiver. All passes should be as hard as possible, and passing should be crisp and sharp at all times. A player receiving the pass should see the ball from the passer's hands into his own hands, just as the passer should see the man he is passing to before he makes the pass. When a pass results in poor reception or loss of ball, the passer is usually at fault.

Diag. 3-10, TWO-LINE FUNDAMENTAL PASS DRILL

Designed for beginning basketball players, this drill should be used at early preseason practice at all levels to reemphasize the basic type of passes and the necessity for good fundamental technique in passing and receiving. It is one of the finest fundamental passing drills available.

Players form two groups of eight, with one group in each half of the court. Each group forms two lines, one on each side of the court. The two lines face each other approximately fifteen feet apart, with a distance of six feet between each player in each line.

X_1, the first player with the ball, uses a two-hand chest pass to

Behind-the-back pass.

X_2 (1). As he releases the ball, he follows his pass to his right, between X_2 and X_4. As soon as X_2 receives the pass, he makes a short pass back to X_1 (2), who is moving towards him going between him and X_4. This pass travels between six and eight feet. As he comes into position between X_2 and X_4, X_1 hands off or gives a short flip pass to X_4 (3). Meanwhile, X_2 crosses and takes X_1's initial position. X_4 uses a chest pass to X_3 (4) and follows his pass to his left, going down the line. As he comes forward, X_3 returns the pass to X_4 (5), approximately six feet away, and assumes the initial position of X_4. X_4 hands off to X_5 (6). X_5 throws a chest pass to X_6 and follows the pass to the right going down towards the end of the line. X_6 returns the pass to X_5 and crosses to X_5's initial position. X_5 hands off to X_8. X_8, at the end of the line, begins the drill again, going in the opposite direction. He makes a two-hand chest pass to X_7, follows the pass, receives a short, six-foot return pass, then hands off to X_6, and the procedure continues. The drill moves up and down the line, and when the ball gets back to X_1, he can change the type of pass, as instructed by a coach.

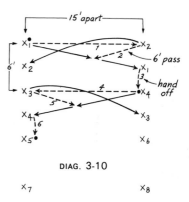

DIAG. 3-10

This is a fairly difficult drill to install with the players, but once they understand the movement, they learn to make and receive all types of passes standing still, on the move, and handing off. They can use a two-hand chest pass, two-hand overhead pass, two-hand bounce pass, hook pass, baseball pass and all short passes and hand-offs. The fifteen-foot distance between lines can be extended by having each player take one step backwards.

This is one of the finest fundamental passing drills available to any coach. It would be well worthwhile for any coach to incorporate it in his practice, especially at the lower levels of basketball where techniques are not as well grounded and players are not as well co-ordinated as they are at the senior high school and college level.

Diag. 3-11, BULL IN THE RING DRILL

This is one of the oldest and best passing and defending drills. Six players form around the free-throw circle, evenly spaced, and take a step back. One player, the bull in the ring, stands in the middle of the circle, facing the outside player who has the ball. The player with the ball, using any type of pass, passes sharply and accurately to any player around the circle except the two players adjacent to him. By faking, deception, or fake passes he tries to bypass the man in the middle. The bull attempts to touch the ball using defensive fakes and trying to determine where the pass will be thrown. When he touches the ball, he changes places with the passer. As passing skill develops, the coach may put a player in the ring for making a bad pass, even though it wasn't touched. This is a fun drill for the players. Many times they will try to get a certain player to be the bull by passing to him constantly, and they keep him in the ring as long as possible.

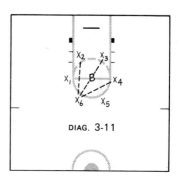

DIAG. 3-11

Diag. 3-12, TWO-MAN, TWO-BALL DRILL

X_1 and X_2 each have basketballs. They pass to each other as quickly as possible, making the passes extremely accurate. This drill calls for good ball handling, since a player must get rid of one ball quickly so that he can receive the other ball. The ball should be passed on different planes. One player may bounce the ball while the other uses a chest pass, or one player may use an over-the-head type of pass while the other uses a chest pass or a bounce pass.

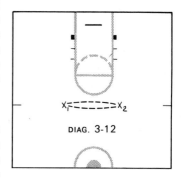

DIAG. 3-12

77

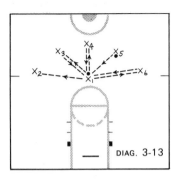

DIAG. 3-13

We recommend this drill for early season work to sharpen the reflexes of the players and to increase their passing accuracy.

Diag. 3-13, TWO-BALL PASSING DRILL

X_1, at the point, faces five players. He has a ball, and one of the other players has a ball. He passes to any one of the five players while the other man with the ball passes to him. His object is to keep passing accurately while receiving passes from the other players. The man at the point must be extremely quick and alert, have good reflexes, and make accurate passes. As long as he can make good passes he stays at the point. When he makes a bad pass, another player takes his place. The drill should continue until all players have been at the point.

Diag. 3-14, THREE-LINE PASS-AND-GO-BEHIND DRILL

This drill may be used full court or half court. Its purpose is to improve the players' ability to pass and receive accurately and sharply as they move up and down the court. Three lines form at one end of the court. Player 6 passes to his left to Player 1, who has moved onto the court. Player 6 goes behind Player 1, who immediately passes to Player 11 and goes behind Player 11. Player 11 passes back to Player 6, the man who initiated the drill. The players continue to pass and go behind the receiver down to the far end of the court, then they turn and come back. Players must pass quickly and accurately, never letting the ball touch the floor. If the ball touches the court, the three players should repeat the drill. This is an excellent pregame half-court warm-up drill.

DIAG. 3-14

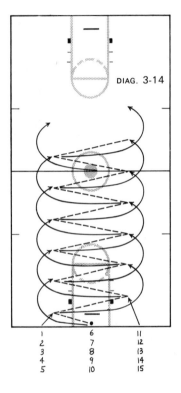

1	6	11
2	7	12
3	8	13
4	9	14
5	10	15

Diag. 3-15, REBOUNDER, OUTLET PASS DRILL

This drill teaches rebounders to make accurate two-hand-overhead, one-hand-overhead, hook, and baseball passes to the outlet men. A coach stands in the outer half of the free-throw circle and shoots. One rebounder stands on each side of the basket. The rebounder on one side rebounds the ball and passes it quickly to the outlet man on that side, who returns the ball to the coach. The outlet man should move from one position to the other so that the rebounder has to pick up his position before releasing the ball.

After they have rebounded two or three times, the rebounders go to the back of the rebounding line, and the drill continues. Outlet men and rebound men should exchange positions during this drill, which should be used for three to five minutes daily in preseason practice. The outlet men normally should be guards who will be getting outlet passes. The rebounders should be centers and forwards who would be in position to catch the ball and make the outlet pass.

Diag. 3-16, LONG PASS DRILL

The players line up in pairs at one corner of the court. A coach stands at mid-court on each side of the court. The inside player, in this diagram X_2, starts dribbling, and X_1 sprints hard. X_2 dribbles up to a position from which he feels he can safely pass the ball over the outstretched hands of the coach, using a two-hand chest pass. The coach does not try to stop the pass every time; only occasionally.

DIAG. 3-15

78

The pass should be made so that X_1 can receive it in full stride and lay it in the basket without a dribble. X_2 should sprint to the basket, tap the rebound to X_1, and continue on up the other side of the court. X_1 dribbles after X_2 and makes a two-hand chest pass to him over the other coach. X_2 then goes in for a lay-up shot. X_1 sprints, obtains the rebound, and passes to the next pair in line. When the players come back they should exchange positions.

This very strenuous, continuous drill is one of the important fundamental drills in teaching fast-break basketball. It should also be used as a conditioner.

In this drill, it is possible to use the two-hand overhead pass (a very difficult and slow pass to make at a long distance); however, we recommend using only the two-hand chest pass or occasionally, the one-hand baseball pass. At first, the players will get discouraged because they will not pass accurately, but as they get confidence in their ability to make the pass, favorable results will accrue from using this drill.

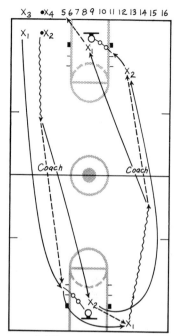

DIAG. 3-16

Diag. 3-17, TWO-LINE, FULL-COURT, PASS DRILL

The players are divided into two groups. Each group is divided into two lines with four men to a line. Each group has a ball. Two players, the first in each line, pass the ball back and forth, running as hard as they can to the far end line. When they get there, they pivot and come back, using the same passes, and then hand the ball off to the next two in line. The ball should not be held for any length of time, and no bounce passes should be used.

A variation of this drill is to have the players pass and receive the ball with their far hands. In this way they have to pass and receive the ball up and down the court using one hand. However, if the pass must be grasped in two hands, the return pass should be made with two hands. It is very difficult to maintain possession of the ball with only one hand, but it will give the players a good feeling for catching bad passes. The premium is placed on accuracy and correct passing techniques.

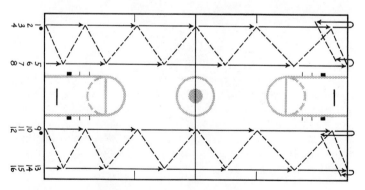

DIAG. 3-17

Dribbling is an integral part of basketball offense. Along with passing and shooting, it is one of three methods used to advance the ball. It is the only method for moving with the ball. Inexperienced players, however, tend to waste their dribble by bouncing the ball purposelessly as soon as they obtain possession. By doing so, they lose their mobil-

dribbling

ity, thus one third of their offensive potential. A player who has not used his dribble is "alive" (mobile). A player who has used his dribble is "dead" (immobile).

There are four uses to which dribbling is purposeful:

1. To penetrate a defense in order to gain a scoring opportunity

2. To protect the ball when pressured defensively

3. To move the ball into offensive territory, when the defense is in a good protective position or when the offense is re-forming after initial penetration is unsuccessful

4. To protect the ball in the closing moments of a game

fundamental principles

The three most important principles of dribbling are *posture, ball control,* and *field of vision.*

1. Posture. The basic body position for dribbling is as follows: The knees are flexed, hips lowered slightly, and the weight balanced and flowing forward onto the back of the front foot; the upper torso is bent forward at the waist, and the head and shoulders are held erect for balance and

Basic dribble posture.

control; the free hand is available for protection if necessary. Different types of dribbling call for varying degrees of crouch, but body control must be such as to keep open the options of a dribbler in motion: to shoot, pass, change direction, or stop.

2. Ball Control. The ball is controlled by the fingers, with the wrist, elbow, and arm coordinating to regulate the height and speed of the bounce and to cause the desired lateral and longitudinal displacement. With the palm cupped and never contacting the ball, the fingers are spread comfortably, and the dribble is initiated by a supple wrist action that tosses the ball lightly floorward. As the ball rebounds, it is caught for an infinitesimal moment in the inverted cup formed by the fingers, the wrist yielding to absorb the upward force, and is again tapped to the floor. The cycle is repeated as many times as the dribbler wishes so long as his wrist is kept facing the floor and there is no perceptible stopping of the ball.

No player is a proficient dribbler until he can perform equally well with either hand.

3. Field of Vision. Peripheral vision is as important to the dribbler as it is to the passer. With his head held erect and facing to the front, the dribbler's field of view should encompass everything forward of an imaginary line drawn through his shoulders and extended to the court perimeter. Although he should never consciously look at the ball, it is continuously within his vision, as are all the players, officials, court markings, and the basket.

With practice, a player's peripheral vision can be improved until he can take in, at a glance, everything within a 180 degree arc; by swiveling his head 90 degrees right and left, he can get a picture of the entire court in less time than it takes to complete one dribble. This ability is especially valuable to key playmakers. Coaches can demonstrate the method by having a player face away from a lamp placed approximately ten feet to his rear and then having him turn his head quickly 90 degrees right and left. Normal peripheral vision should enable him to see the lamp from either side without turning his shoulders.

basic forms of dribbling

High (Speed) Dribble. When speed is essential and defensive pressure allows, the high, or speed, dribble should be used; for example, when driving to the basket, when leading a fast break, or when bringing the ball into offensive territory without opposition. The body is almost erect, with only a very slight forward crouch for balance, as the dribbler moves in a full stride limited only by his ability to control the ball. For a proficient dribbler, this limit should be very near his top running speed. The dribbling arm is almost at full extension, pushing the ball forward and slightly to the dribbling side. The height of the balance is above the waist and below the shoulders, varying with the individual player, but must be such as to allow maximum running speed. The ball is continually tossed floorward with a pumping motion.

Low (Protective) Dribble. The low dribble is used when it is necessary to protect the ball from a defender; for instance, when closely guarded in a drive to the basket; when clearing the ball from a crowded area, without the possibility of a pass; or when protectively dribbling in position in order to remain "alive" while waiting for offensive balance after an unsuccessful play attempt. The dribble is approximately knee high; the body is in an extreme crouch; and, on the dribbling side, the upper arm and elbow are held close in. The ball is controlled by the usual method.

Against extreme defensive pressure, the dribbling height can be farther lowered, and the body positioned completely between the defender and the ball. In this situation, the dribbler continuously pivots around the foot closest to the defender and combines head and body feints to upset the defender's timing. The free arm is used for balance and protection; the head is erect; the eyes are alert; and the elbow of the dribbling arm is held close to the side.

Change-of-Pace Dribble. The change-of-pace dribble is used to fake the defender into relaxing his guard during an apparent routine dribble. It is an excellent driving maneuver when using a screen or when driving in for a basket against a defender in good position. The change of pace is effected

High dribble-drive.

High-speed dribble.

by changing the dribbling speed. For example, a change from slow to fast can be used after deceiving a guard into expecting a routine move. A change from fast, to slow, to fast can be used, dribbling fast into the basket; slowing to deceive a close defender into expecting a stop, change of direction, or cross-over; and then suddenly continuing with the original move to the basket.

Low protective dribble.

Protective dribble against a defender.

methods of changing direction and hands while dribbling

1. **Simple Change of Direction.** When a defender is retreating and not too close (four to five feet away), but on the dribbling-hand side, the dribbler should change hands, using a minimum of body turn. Execution is simply pushing the ball across for the opposite hand to pick up the dribble as the foot on the original dribbling-hand side con-

tacts the floor. Little change of direction is necessary, since the dribbler is now between the ball and the defender.

2. Cross-over. This method should be used when a more evasive tactic than a simple change of direction is called for. As the foot on the dribbling side contacts the floor, a hard push-off is initiated toward the opposite foot, the dribbling hand lowering slightly to the outside of the ball and angling it across the body for the opposite hand to pick up the dribble. If the defender is close, extreme caution must be used to prevent him from intercepting or deflecting the ball. The maneuver is completed with a long cross-over step by the foot on the original side of dribble. The change of direction must be emphatic, with an exchange of dribbling hands, in order to throw the defender off pace and to protect the ball as he recovers.

Change-of-direction dribble.

Cross-over dribble.

Protective pivot dribble. Notice that the dribbler's head is up.

3. Reverse (Pivot) Dribble. This maneuver is very effective during a one-on-one drive to the basket when the defender has good position on the ball side. It is also useful in a congested area when trying to protect the ball and outmaneuver the defensive guard. Less foot action is required

84

in the latter instance, and the feet may be kept closer together to afford greater body protection for the ball. The
procedure is reversed when starting from a left-hand
dribble.

As the right foot contacts the floor, the dribble action is
moved back to a position outside the right heel. A stride
step is taken with the left foot while the ball is bounced progressively to the left and behind the right foot. Executing a
pivot on the left foot and turning his back to the defender,
the dribbler picks up the dribble with his left hand. A push
off the right foot increases the pivoting speed. At all times,
the dribbler's body must be kept between the ball and the
defender.

Lateral pivot dribble for ball protection.

85

4. Behind-the-Back Dribble. For the exceptional ball handler, this maneuver is safer than the cross-over and quicker than the reverse, with the same end result. With his right hand, the dribbler bounces the ball even with his left foot

Pivot dribble to basket.

as his right leg comes forward in stride. As his right foot contacts the floor and his left leg is moving forward and out of the way, the dribbler adroitly angles the ball behind his back, causing the ball to bounce up under his left hand, which picks up the dribble.

dribbling drills

Dribbling drills should attempt to teach all phases of the dribble, including the low or control dribble in which the player has to maintain good body position with respect to the defensive player. Therefore, some drills should include control dribble type of movement for use when a defender is guarding the dribbler, but is not making a serious effort to take the ball away. When defenders are used, the coach should be certain that the dribbler's knees are bent, his body is in a fairly-well crouched position with his back straight and his head up, and his body is between the defender and the ball. For the control dribble, the ball should not come up too high, and the player should have his head up at all times to see the whole court. The dribbler should be ready to use his body to protect the ball if the defender moves in with his hands or obstructs the dribbler's path.

Other drills should include the high, or speed, dribble, used primarily when there is no defensive opposition or when the dribbler is in front of a defender and is driving hard towards the basket. For this dribble, the dribbler is in an upright position. He should control his dribble, keeping it a little above his waist in the chest area and pushing the ball farther out so that at each bounce the dribbler runs into the ball. He should maintain a maximum speed while he is dribbling.

The cross-over dribble, change-of-pace dribble, and the pivot dribble should also be included in dribbling drills, as well as a tactic in which the dribbler comes to a stop with good balance, pivots, and hands off to another player.

In the early part of the season, competitive drills are the best type to use.

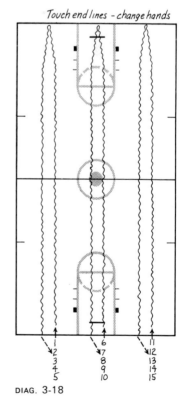

Touch end lines – change hands

Diag. 3-18, FULL-LENGTH DRIBBLE DRILL

The squad is broken up into three teams with an even number of players on each team. The first player in each line starts on a command from the coach, using a one-hand speed dribble as fast as he can until he touches the end line at the opposite end of the court. At the end line, he pivots and returns the full length of the court, dribbling with the other hand. When he touches the end line at the starting point, he passes to the next player in line. Coaches should caution their players not to receive or pass the ball until the dribbler has touched the line, and the next player in line should not start before the ball crosses the end line. This is an excellent drill to use when a competitive drill is needed to renew player enthusiasm.

DIAG. 3-18

87

Change dribbling hand at each obstacle

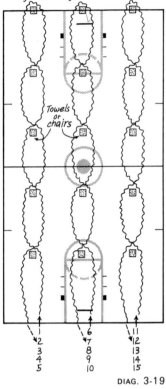

Towels or chairs

1	6	11
2	7	12
3	8	13
4	9	14
5	10	15

DIAG. 3-19

DIAG. 3-20

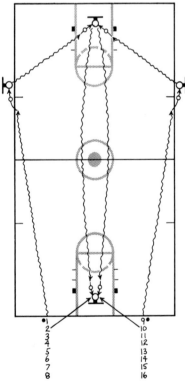

1	9
2	10
3	11
4	12
5	13
6	14
7	15
8	16

Diag. 3-19, OBSTACLE DRIBBLE DRILL

The squad forms three groups of equal ability. Approximately five obstacles should be put on the court for each group. We prefer to use towels because they are easy to place and to pick up. The managers can put the towels in position quickly. The players dribble from one end to the other, changing hands as they go by each obstacle. They use the right hand through the first obstacle on the left, then cross-over dribble to change the ball to the left hand to pass the obstacle on the right. They dribble around the obstacle at the far end of the court and return, still changing hands as they go around the towels on the court. When the players touch the starting line, they hand off to the next players in line.

The coaches should stand at the cross-over spots and check technique. Players must keep their heads up. When they cross the ball over, they should move it close to the body as the foot on the side they are crossing from comes forward. (If a player is dribbling from right to left, the ball should be moved over as the right foot comes down and bounced up as the left foot comes forward.) This drill can be used whenever competition is essential to the players. It is a fun drill that breaks the monotony of daily practice, and it is especially useful to teach correct fundamental dribbling early in the year.

Diag. 3-20, FULL-LENGTH LAY-UP AND DRIBBLE DRILL

The squad forms two teams. The first man in each line dribbles to a side basket, lays the ball into the basket, retrieves the ball and dribbles to the basket at the far end of the court, lays the ball in and retrieves it, then dribbles back to the starting end and makes a lay-up shot. The next man in line rebounds the ball from the near basket and repeats the drill. This is an enthusiasm-evoking type of drill that boosts morale while it teaches the speed dribble. Coaches should be constantly alert for players with their heads down or players not controlling the ball properly. They should also check the players' form when they go in to make the lay-up shot.

Diag. 3-21, FULL-LENGTH DRIBBLE PIVOT DRILL

The squad forms three teams, and the manager puts out approximately five obstacles (towels or chairs) for each group. Players 1, 6, and 11 dribble hard up to the first obstacles, come to a stop at the right of the obstacles (still dribbling), pivot on their left feet, change the balls from their right hands to their left hands, go around the obstacles to the left, and continue to dribble with their left hands. At the next obstacles they stop, pivot on their right feet, go around the obstacles to the right, and continue to the third set of obstacles. Again they pivot on their left feet and change hands, maintaining the dribble at all times. The players continue to the far end, go around the last obstacle, then return, pivoting at each obstacle. After they touch the end line, they hand off to the next player in line.

Early in practice, this drill will indicate those who have difficulty with their dribbling and pivoting. It is especially beneficial for those who are not good dribblers, because it teaches good ball control. Players enjoy this competitive drill, so it should be used frequently in early season.

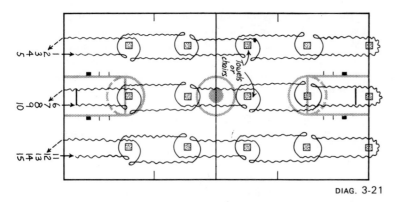

DIAG. 3-21

Diag. 3-22, HEADS-UP DRILL

This is an excellent dribbling drill to use with beginners to teach them to keep their heads up and to improve their peripheral vision so that they can observe an open man down court at all times. It is one of our favorite drills. The players line up under a basket behind one end line. The first player in line, with his head up, dribbles hard towards the coach, who is halfway between the near foul circle and the mid-court circle, facing the far basket. At the far end of the court are three players facing the dribbler—one near the left sideline, one at the head of the far foul circle and one near the right sideline, approximately in a straight line across the court. As the dribbler goes by the coach, the coach points to the player he wishes the dribbler to pass to, alternating the players. If he points to his left, the receiver on that side (X_1 in the diagram) reaches towards the dribbler. The dribbler immediately passes to that player and cuts towards him. He receives a hand-off pass, continues dribbling to the basket, and lays the ball in. He retrieves his own rebound and dribbles back up either side of the court on the outside. When he gets beyond the near foul line, he passes to the next player in line without a ball. The second player, who starts when the preceding dribbler passes, dribbles by the coach and passes to the man designated by the coach. The coach should raise his hands straight over his head when he wants the player at the head of the circle to get the ball; if he pointed straight ahead, he might be blocked off by the dribbler. The coach should indicate the receiver as soon as the dribbler goes by him and cannot see where the coach is pointing. Many players will anticipate the coach's signal and pass to the wrong man.

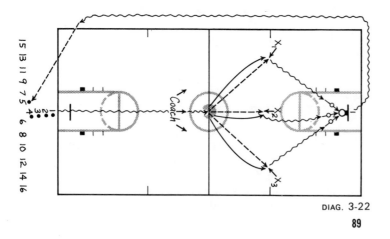

DIAG. 3-22

The players enjoy the passing and the movement of this drill. It is rapid, with players dribbling with their heads up at full speed, looking with peripheral vision at the whole front-court area.

The coach should use this drill for four or five minutes, changing the receivers frequently so that one man doesn't stay too long in one of the pass receiving positions. Use four or five balls.

Diag. 3-23, DRIBBLE, PIVOT, PASS DRILL

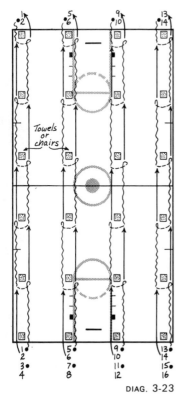

DIAG. 3-23

Four players stand at the left sideline, four just to the left of the foul lane, four just to the right of the foul lane, and four at the right sideline. The first and third players in line have basketballs. Obstacles are put in the court for each group.

This is a dribble pair drill in which the players learn to stop, pivot on the inside foot (the foot nearest the towel), and pass off to a player trailing. The trailer must time his movement so that the dribbler has time to conclude his fundamental moves before the pass off. The receiver then dribbles hard to the next obstacle, pivots, and passes back to the first player, who is trailing. The players must dribble under control, using the hand on the outside of the obstacle they are moving to. Each member of a pair dribbles on opposite sides of the obstacles. As they go down the court, the first man must make a good jump stride stop at the obstacle, landing with the pivot foot (the foot nearest the obstacle) in back of or parallel with the other foot. As he pivots, the man behind him takes a hand-off pass and then dribbles hard to the next obstacle, using the outside hand. Going down the court, one player will dribble with his right hand, stop, pivot on his left foot, and hand off. The second player will dribble with his left hand, stop, pivot on his right foot, and hand off.

Four pairs go at once. When the pairs reach the far end, they wait for the other groups to complete their drill. To go back, the men reverse their positions.

This is a teaching drill that should be used frequently in pre-season practice. The players learn to dribble with each hand, to pivot on either foot, and hand off in both directions.

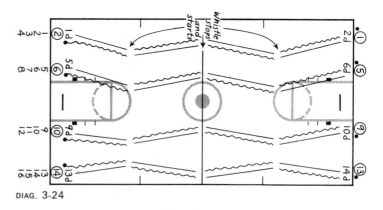

DIAG. 3-24

Diag. 3-24, CHANGE-OF-PACE DRIBBLE DRILL WITH A DEFENDER

The players form four lines as in Drill 23, the first player acting as defender and the second player dribbling. The dribbler dribbles under control with the defender maintaining position on him. The

90

dribbler does not attempt to dribble by the defender, he merely protects the ball. When the whistle blows, the dribbler stops, maintaining his protective dribble, then he changes hands and dribbles until the next whistle. The coach should whistle three or four times in the course of dribbling from one end of the court to the other, stopping the players at the head of the near circle, at mid-court, at the head of the far circle, and at the far end line. Each time, the dribbler should change hands and direction. At the far end of the court the defender and the dribbler exchange responsibilities.

This drill teaches the player to dribble under control and to be able to stop and maintain a dribble, and it teaches the defender to get back into position if he has lost position on the dribbler. Coaches should watch for good body position and a good, low, control dribble from the dribbler and a good boxer's shuffle by the defender. If the defender can stop the dribbler, the dribbler must stop under control, maintaining his dribble if possible, and then move with his dribble when the whistle stops and starts the others.

Diag. 3-25, DRIBBLE FAKES AND DRIVE DRILL

This is an individual drill in which the squad is broken up into three or four groups stationed near the hash marks. Each group should have two balls. Each player must dribble, fake, stop, reverse, change direction, change pace, and finally drive into the basket and lay the ball in, making certain that no player from the other side is driving in as he makes his movement. The players may use any fakes, drives, or dribbles they wish and they may start anywhere on the court. Forwards usually start from a corner, faking to the baseline or to the middle, reverse dribbling, then driving in to the middle or along the baseline. Centers may start from the foul-line area or from a pivot area, using fakes and dribbling in. Players should change sides of the court frequently so that they are not driving from the same position all the time.

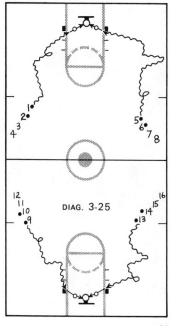

DIAG. 3-25

This section comprises those additional skills that the individual player must command on offense. Included in this category are *starting, stopping, turning and pivoting, faking or feinting, jumping, cutting, pass receiving, and moving without the ball.*

starting

At the start of a dribble, the pivot foot cannot leave the floor until the ball leaves the hand. For shooting or passing, the pivot foot can leave the floor, but it cannot be returned before the ball is released.

footwork and miscellaneous offensive skills

The player on offense, as on defense, must always be balanced for a step in any direction. In the normal offensive stance, the feet are spaced approximately the width of the shoulders; the hips, knees, and ankles are comfortably flexed in a semi-crouch; the weight is forward on the balls of the feet, the heels slightly off the floor; and the head is erect and centered. The start is initiated by shifting the weight to the stepping foot and pushing off with a strong thrust of the trailing foot. Without the ball, the upper arms are at the sides, close to the body, with the elbows pointing downward. The forearms are parallel to the floor, and the hands are above the waist and ready for receiving a pass.

stopping

Basketball players must learn to stop quickly with perfect balance. In addition, a player having ball possession must stop within the limits specified by the rules. When the ball is caught while both feet are off the floor, and the player lands on both feet simultaneously, the rules are the same as for receiving a pass while standing: either foot may be used as the pivot. When the ball is caught while one foot is on the floor (*one count*), that foot becomes the pivot

Defender stops after wheel-and-guard. Dribbler stops, maintaining dribble.

foot, and the other foot becomes the stepping foot (*two count*). There is no pivot foot when the ball is caught on one foot and the player jumps and lands on both feet simultaneously.

Of the two methods of stopping with the ball, the *two-foot jump stop* and the *stride stop*, we have found the latter to be more natural and easier to teach. When stopping in stride, the player, running in a slight crouch, lowers his hips as his pivot foot contacts the floor (*one count*), flexing his pivot-foot knee until it almost touches the floor as the stepping foot makes contact (*two count*). The stepping foot strides longer than normally, the entire foot slapping the floor in order to gain maximum traction. Instantly, the forward leg thrusts back to regain body balance. The ball must be protected by holding it in both hands, with the body between it and the defender.

For those who can master it, the two-foot jump stop has the advantage of allowing either foot to be used as the pivot. There is danger of the body weight being too far forward, however, resulting in an extra step and a travelling violation. This stop is performed by catching the ball while both feet are in the air, landing with both feet parallel, body weight very low, and the entire bottom surface of the shoes in contact with the floor.

Two-foot parallel stop.

Stride stop.

turning and pivoting

For our definition, a *turn* can be considered any change in the direction that a player is facing, with or without the ball, whether moving or stationary. Cross-overs and simple changes of direction are examples of turns when moving with the ball; jump turns, pivots, and facing movements, in the last instance without particular regard to foot position, are examples of turns when stationary. Of the last category, only pivots and jump turns with an aerial release are legal when having ball possession. Without ball possession, the only requirement of a turn is that proper balance and offensive poise be maintained; with possession, care must be taken to observe the rules governing the pivot foot. (See Starting and Stopping.)

A *pivot* is a legal maneuver for changing, without dribbling, the direction that a player is facing when in possession of the ball. The *pivot foot* is as defined under *Starting* and *Stopping*. Using the ball of his pivot foot as a swivel point, a player is free to rotate his body so long as he does not permit his pivot foot to move from its position or to break contact with the floor. The force of rotation is supplied by the outside, or *stepping,* foot, which the ball handler is permitted to move in an arc around the pivot foot

94

Rear pivot.

as freely as he chooses—either left or right, forward or backward.

Pivoting is one of the most fundamental movements in basketball. It is most often used following a stop after dribbling or receiving a pass, and, within the compass of a player's pivoting range, it is an effective means of moving vigorously with the ball for any offensive advantage, such as gaining a better position for shooting or passing or for protecting the ball from an aggressive defender.

There are three basic pivots: the rear pivot, the front pivot, and the reverse pivot.

1. Rear Pivot. When forced by a defender to stop near a sideline, a dribbler must quickly reorient his body in order to protect the ball and to face into the court for a pass-off. Since the sideline and the defender prevent a forward movement, a rear pivot is called for. Using the foot away from the sideline as his pivot foot, the ball handler crouches, moves the ball with both hands to a position behind his hip and away from the defender, and thrusts hard with his stepping foot (nearest the sideline), rotating his body backward around the pivot foot until he has a view of midcourt or is able to pass-off to a teammate.

To maintain proper balance, the stepping foot remains close to the floor during the pivot, and the weight alternates smoothly between the pivot and stepping foot. Between pivots, with his back to the defender, the man with the ball may reach outward with it to avoid being tied up. For the actual pivot, however, pulling the ball close to his body, elbows wide, both protects the ball from a defender and minimizes the rotational arm of inertia to be overcome.

2. Front Pivot. When a man with the ball is not being pressed and has stopped while facing a sideline or away from the basket, he can shift his weight to his pivot foot and swing his stepping foot forward and around, pivoting to face the desired direction. Upon completing the pivot, the player resumes a two-foot balance and carries the ball from its pivot position, close to his chest, to a position suitable for passing, shooting, or protecting.

From the high-post position when either foot is eligible for the pivot, most players prefer to initiate the front pivot by swinging the leg closest to the sideline and pivoting on the other foot. After receiving a pass, the high-post player pulls the ball in to a position in front of his pivot hip, drops his opposite shoulder, crouches slightly, pivots 180 degrees, and initiates a shot, pass, or drive.

3. Reverse Pivot. The reverse pivot differs from the pivots above in that it is executed on the balls of both feet simultaneously. Following a stride stop, his body still in a crouch and his weight forward, the player pulls the ball to his waist, rises to the balls of both feet, thrusts his weight back, and pivots 180 degrees toward the trailing foot. Completing the pivot, still on the balls of both feet, the player then takes a full step in the new direction with the original forward foot. During the course of this maneuver, body weight, which is kept low throughout, moves from the forward foot to the trailing foot and back to the forward foot as it steps out in the new direction.

Reverse pivot. Stride stop.

Reverse pivot. Pivot on balls of both feet.

Reverse pivot. Full step away from defender.

97

This pivot is frequently used to protect the ball from a defender directly in front of a player stopping while facing the basket. Except that it is much more vigorous, the movement is similar to a military *face to the rear while marching*.

faking or feinting

As used here, *faking* and *feinting* are near-synonymous terms for movements intended to confuse or mislead a defender so as to upset his timing or balance or to rob him of a positional advantage. Faking with ball possession, for example, can be used to obtain passing or shooting room or to open a passing or driving lane. Faking without possession can be used to keep a defender away from a play situation or to free a teammate for a pass or shot. The accomplished player has an assortment of deceptive moves for every play situation.

Ball Fakes. A short, quick movement of the ball in one direction, followed quickly and in the same motion by a pass, pivot, shot, or dribble in another direction, is an extremely effective and simple means of gaining an advantage over a defender. The diversionary movement should be such as to allow the intended action to follow, not drawing back but as a sudden redirection. For example, a forward

Head fake by pivot.

Ball fake by pivot.

may fake a two-hand chest pass to a guard and, from full arm extension, execute a two-hand bounce pass under the arms of the defender and into the pivot.

Foot Fakes. All change-of-pace and change-of-direction maneuvers, with or without the ball, are preceded by a foot or leg fake. Since a step transfers some weight to the extended foot, however, a faking step must be short enough to allow an immediate thrust back onto the other foot as it steps off in the intended direction. For dribble fakes, the feinting movement of the non-pivot foot must be slight and without a transfer of weight, since the pivot foot is not permitted to leave the floor until the ball leaves the dribbling hand, and the step off in the intended direction must be with the non-pivot foot.

Other foot fakes are as follows: (1) a quick step forward and back, followed by either a set shot or a fake set shot and a drive to the basket; (2) a quick bending of the knees to fake a jump shot, followed by a drive to the basket (if the defender jumps) or a continuation of the jump shot (if the defender does not jump).

Head-and-Shoulder Fakes. Many pivot men use quick head-and-shoulder fakes in one direction and move in the opposite direction for a shot. Success depends upon sharp, concise movements for momentary deception without compromising balance. Head-and-shoulder fakes are also used before a change of direction cut, a reverse cut from a stationary position, and most dribble fakes.

Eye Fakes. Many good defensive players watch the eyes of their opponents. An alert player on offense can turn this against a defender by the use of misleading or deceptive eye movements. The most effective eye fakes are those using peripheral vision to conceal the true path of a pass, whether the faking is by the passer or the receiver.

Arm-and-Hand Fakes. The best example of an arm-and-hand fake on offense is the pass receiver's keeping his arms at his side, watching the ball with his peripheral vision, and raising his hands at the last instant to catch the pass over the head of a defender. The opposite technique, faking a catch, can be used to draw a defender out of position.

Combinations. Most faking maneuvers are in reality, combinations of deceptive movements using the ball, eyes, head, shoulders, arms, hands, legs, and feet. Basketball is a game of advantage, and the intelligent player, with or without the ball, is constantly working to place the defender at a disadvantage by using whatever combination of fakes and feints necessary to disguise the offense. Purposeless or irrelevant faking, however, works only to the disadvantage of the player himself, causing misplays, needless turn-overs, and early tiring.

Combination fake by pivot —head, shoulders, arms and ball.

99

special faking techniques

The following are faking techniques for specialized situations when in scoring areas with the ball. Each should be mastered for use when facing the basket, when facing away from the basket, and after recovering an offensive rebound.

Up and Under. Upon receiving a pass, the player brings the ball up quickly to the shooting position for a set shot. If the defender moves in and up to defend against the shot, the player steps long toward the basket, pushing off his pivot foot but making certain to release the ball for the dribble before the pivot foot leaves the floor. The initial step must be directly into the basket, to either side of the defender, preferably to the side of an uplifted or stepping foot. Driving by a defender's uplifted foot puts him at a disadvantage, since regaining position will require that he first return the foot to the floor and then push off the opposite foot for a move that is defensively relevant.

In the pivot area, the *up-and-under* move calls for faking an above-the-head pivot shot and executing a step-in under-

Up-and-under fake.

100

hand shot under the upstretched hands of the defender. A similar move can be used by a player after making an offensive rebound with a defensive rebounder between him and the basket: a quick, upward head-and-shoulder fake from a crouched position, *with the ball well protected* forces the defender up; the shooter then steps in under the defender and lunges to the basket, holding the ball in both hands until laying it up.

Rocker Step. The *rocker-step* drive is similar to the up-and-under movement. After receiving a pass, the player steps toward the basket as though to drive. As the defender retreats protectively (if the defender does not retreat, the driver should continue into the basket), the player draws back his stepping foot, straightens upright, and brings the ball up as though to shoot. Should the defender advance, the player thrusts his stepping foot toward the basket and dribbles by the defender. Some players bring the stepping foot back behind the pivot foot after the first fake. The most effective rocker movement, however, is with little or no drawback of the foot: a quick back-straightening motion, followed by a second, short extending of the out-thrust foot, quickens the move without losing any of the faking effectiveness.

Rocker step.

jumping

A player's ability to jump can be improved by practicing technique and by daily exercise. Drills such as jumping up and touching the rim several times a day provide the player with both the means and the incentive for improving. If he cannot jump and touch the rim from a standing position, he should jump to touch either the net or the backboard, striving for higher jumps at each practice. Other means of improving are stretching exercises and skipping rope.

In addition to jump shooting, which has been discussed, there are two situations in which jumping is fundamental: (1) jump balls and (2) rebounding.

1. Jump Balls. The jump-ball situation occurs several times during a game and, because of held balls, can involve any member of a team. The importance of gaining possession in these situations is obvious; each player, therefore, must be thoroughly familiar with the techniques for gaining maximum height, timing the official's toss, tapping the ball, and legally impeding a taller opponent.

Obtaining maximum height. For a center jump, the player positions the foot of his strong side so that it just touches the smaller, two-foot circle. His opposite foot is on an imaginary line extended out from the center of the circle and is spaced approximately the width of his shoulders. (For jump balls in the free-throw zone, the two-foot circle must be approximated.) Preparing for the jump, he flexes his knees; raises his forearms to where they are inclined slightly upward, his upper arms pointed downward and comfortably close to his body; and concentrates his eyes on the ball in the official's hand. As the official starts the ball upward, the near foot takes a short step inward, the far foot following in rhythm to a comfortably close position, and the hips are thrust downward to a coiled, crouched position, the leg muscles tensed and the weight balanced evenly on the balls of both feet. As the leg muscles uncoil, starting the upward thrust, the arms are swung up in vigorous coordination and the near arm and shoulder extend up to maximum jumping height. Just before the apex, the far arm and shoulder are forced down to increase the height of the near hand. The legs are straight. The jumper lands on the balls of his feet, his body in a semi-crouch and his arms out from his sides for balance.

Although some players use, successfully, such unorthodox technique as extending the far arm rather than the near arm for the tap, there are definite mechanical advantages in the orthodox method described here. Coaches would do well, however, to use discretion when tampering with success.

Timing the jump with the toss. The rules are that the

ball cannot be tapped until it has reached the apex of the toss. Although officials are instructed to toss the ball higher than either player can jump, each official tends to toss the ball up somewhat differently—some high, some low; others at an angle, either right, left, close, or away. As well as he is able, the player should consider all of these factors when timing his jump.

Compensating for observed inequities in the official's toss-up and concentrating on the ball, the jumper moves closer, starting his body in motion as the tossing hand starts to move. The spring upward is timed so that the feet leave the floor just after the official releases the ball—the player's upward velocity being faster than that of the ball. The ball is tapped at the exact coincidence of maximum height for jump and toss.

Tapping the ball. The ball diameter is slightly more than nine inches; the average hand length is slightly more than seven inches: controlling the tap by striking the ball on its lower hemisphere with the tips of the three middle fingers has the effect of adding from six to eight inches to a jumper's height. At contact, the force of the tap is dampened slightly by the give in the evenly spaced fingers. The trajectory of the ball should be a shallow arc, the direction supplied by the rotating of the wrist and palm of the tapping hand, just before contact, to face the intended recovery area. Usually, the teammate who is the strongest rebounder is stationed in front of the tapper, since that is the area to which the tap is most easily directed. Should that area be defended by taller or stronger opponents, an alternate area must be predetermined.

Legally impeding a taller jumping opponent. When opposed by a taller or better jumper, a player may use several legal tactics in an attempt to either upset his opponent's timing or hinder or deflect his tap. The first is to take an early jump in order to draw a poorly timed or early jump from the opponent. A second is to crowd into the mid-court line or foul line, close to the opponent, and attempt to affect his timing and balance without fouling. For example, the strategy here might be to disrupt the opponent by leaning into him before the toss and then stepping back quickly just as the ball is released. A third tactic is for the shorter jumper to use the hand-away jump technique and, in attempting to tap the ball, to follow-through causing incidental contact with the opponent's hand (while on the ball) and resulting in a shortened or deflected tap having a better possibility of reception by a teammate of the jumper at a disadvantage.

2. Offensive Rebounding. Defensive rebounding is discussed in chapter six, "Individual Player Defense." Although there is some overlapping, the techniques and starting positions for offensive and defensive rebounding are essentially different.

Rebounding technique. The two most important principles of rebounding technique are balance and timing. To maintain his balance in the congested area under the basket, the player must establish a wide, strong base in which to operate. His feet should be spaced as widely as comfort will allow. His knees are slightly bent, his hips lowered, and his body braced. His elbows are held wide at shoulder level, his upper arms parallel to the floor, and his forearms and hands are held high and parallel to his body. His fingers are widespread, his palms facing the basket. His body should be balanced slightly forward, with the weight on the balls of his feet.

In rebounding, the timing of the jump is even more critical than its height. The factors governing timing are the height and direction of the rebound, which, in turn, are determined by such factors as shot trajectory and distance; whether the ball hits the backboard or rim; their resiliency; and the amount of spin on the ball. Considering each of these factors when timing his jump, the rebounder springs into the ball, attempting either a tip-in, a tap-off, or a two-hand retrieval. Should he elect to retrieve the ball, he should do so at the highest point of his jump, with his legs and elbows spread wide and his buttocks extended rearward for maximum protection. Turning the ball over while he is still in the air, so that one hand is below and one above, the offensive rebounder lands with feet and elbows

Offensive rebounding. Teammate of shooter getting good rebound position.

104

wide, hips low, and buttocks extended. (A taller rebounder might elect to come down more upright, with the ball held high, in order to effect more quickly either a second shot or a pass-off.) Bringing the ball strongly to his chest, the rebounder avoids a held ball by quick fakes and pivots, if necessary, in combination with a drive, shot, or pass-off. He should not make the mistake of shooting hurriedly or off balance, but should treat the rebound as he would the retrieval of a loose ball: if a shot opportunity presents itself, it should be taken immediately; otherwise the ball should be cleared to back-court, and the play pattern resumed.

Offensive rebound tactics. Many coaches spend a great amount of time teaching defensive rebounding but little on the offensive phase. Since few teams make as many as half of their shots, however, the probability of losing the ball upon shooting can become greater than that of scoring a basket. Obviously, rebounding on offense can not be left to hustle and chance, but must be given the same emphasis as is rebounding on defense.

Although the defense generally has the inside position, the offense has several means by which it can neutralize this positional advantage. First, knowing when a teammate is likely to shoot, the player on offense can gain a split-second advantage in maneuvering time and thus prevent his being blocked out for the rebound. The defender cannot look for rebounding positions until the shot is released, since turning too soon makes him susceptible to a fake and cut to the basket; however, teammates of the shooter should know his shooting habits well enough to move instinctively into a favorable position as soon as a play begins to develop that is likely to produce a shot. Second, teammates of the shooter should have a better feel for how his shots typically behave when coming off the rim or backboard: the rebounds of missed shots attempted by a given player tend to follow a definite pattern, depending upon spin, use of backboard, trajectory, etc; teammates, as well as the shooter himself, should be alert to these characteristics and adjust for them when moving into position.

A third means of neutralizing a defender's advantage of inside position is to crowd him with body pressure in order to affect his timing and balance. Should the offensive rebounder detect the defender's leaning back when crowded, he can maintain or increase the pressure and then suddenly slide around causing the opponent to lose his balance.

Effective use of body, leg, shoulder, and elbow pressure can upset an opponent's mental poise as well as his physical poise. The congested rebounding area is the scene of much allowable or overlooked body contact. So long as he does not use his hands or jump over a positioned defender, an aggressive and combative rebounder can do much to make up for whatever disadvantage he may have in height or initial position.

The rebounder on offense also has the advantage of not having to strive always for two-hand control. This allows him to seek a closer position to the basket, from which he can attempt a tip-in. Even if the tip is unsuccessful, he or a teammate will get a second opportunity to either recover the ball, tip it for a score, or bat it to one of, generally, two offensive guards standing outside the top of the free-throw circle, ready either to retreat on defense or to retrieve a ball batted over his head. Success under the offensive boards often depends upon the offensive team's ability to keep the ball in play until either a score is made or a team member gains possession. After each jump, a rebounder on offense should land on the balls of his feet, his hips low, and his arms and hands high, ready for a second, third, fourth, or fifth effort if necessary. Extra determination is in itself an advantage.

Often the play pattern will cause a defender to leave his man while a shot is being attempted by another player. For example, a back-court shot from the opposite side may cause a defender guarding a forward away from the ball to drop off toward the free-throw area in order to help his teammates in defense. The freed offensive forward should then be able to move into a good rebound position without being blocked off the backboards. Even if he is unable to get inside the guard, he should at least manage a side-by-side situation. If the pivot man can also gain a positional advantage in such instances, which he should do easily when his defender plays him in front, the offensive team will be in an excellent position to control its own rebound.

cutting

Cutting to the basket is a tactic to elude a guard when a teammate has the ball. Cutting successfully requires the use, either individually or in combination, of such maneuvers as change of direction, change of pace, pivots, fakes, stops, starts, and turns (see applicable sections in this chapter). Many players, unfortunately, know neither when nor how to cut. They simply run at top speed, hoping to outdistance the defender.

Although speed is the greatest natural asset a basketball player can have, without finesse it is wasted: when the cutter uses sheer speed, without deception, the defensive guard can adjust for it and neutralize its effectiveness. Timing his movements with the position of the ball, however, the cutter can use whatever methods necessary to gain a step advantage, at which time he can open his stride and attempt to outrun his adversary. Approaching the basket, the cutter should raise a hand as a target and

Back-door cut.

shout to catch the passer's attention (only if the cutter is open). Should the cutter be unable to gain a step, he may still gain the advantage by stopping suddenly and facing the passer.

Cuts should always be either in a straight line or in a series of straight lines (broken line), and each fake, feint, change of direction, or change of pace must be quick and sharp. A curved or rounded path allows the defender to cut inside and regain position.

It may be necessary to use many preliminary cuts before loosening a defense sufficiently for a scoring attempt. Often, the passer cannot complete a play to the cutter because of a shift by the defense, poor timing on the part of the cutter, or loss of ball control by the passer. Therefore, if the cutter does not receive the pass, he should not

107

become discouraged or disgusted but should continue to move.

Although any cut is effective that loosens the defense, purposeless movement is tiring and can interfere with offensive patterns. Good cutting opportunities occur in situations such as when a defender turns his head and momentarily loses sight of the man he is guarding, allowing the man to cut behind him.

Often, two cutters will start their movement simultaneously: the player cutting off the ball, using the passer as a screen, is primary; the player starting farthest from the ball is secondary. In this instance, the secondary cutter must watch in the direction of the primary cutter and pull off if there is danger of interference. Should the secondary cutter and not the primary get clear, however, the secondary continues to the basket and shouts to draw the passer's attention. A "cut off the ball" is a cut initiated when a player finds himself and his defender on the outside of a teammate in possession of the ball. Unless the teammate is in a pivot position and maneuvering for a shot, the player without possession can use him as a screen to "wipe off" the defender and cut for the basket.

Cutting is also purposeful when a player finds himself and his guard so close to a teammate in possession there is danger that the guard will be able to double-up on the teammate and force a held ball. In this instance, the purpose of cutting is to relieve the pressure on the ball.

A "back-door" cut can be used when a player without possession is being overplayed by his guard, between him and the ball. The cut is initiated with a good feint toward the ball, followed by a change of direction—pushing off hard on the foot opposite the direction of the cut.

One of the best times to cut is immediately after passing, when the defender tends either to relax, his man having relinquished possession, or to concentrate on intercepting the pass. Either defensive error will open the way for a cut, a quick return pass, and a good scoring opportunity.

When an offensive player discovers early in the game that the man guarding him is weak in defending a particular movement, he should use discretion in exploiting his discovery in order that the opposing coach does not immediately replace the man. By using the move sparingly, while probing for other weaknesses, the cutter will ensure that the play will be available should the need arise for a high-percentage shot late in the game.

pass receiving

The way a pass is caught is determined by such factors as the flight path and velocity of the ball, the movement of the receiver, the proximity of defensive players, and the kind of offensive move to be made with the ball after it is received. There are, however, certain fundamental techniques that apply equally to the receiving of any pass. The first of these is "seeing" the ball into the hands. Fumbles, when not caused by the passer, are inevitably the result of the receiver's taking his eye off the ball before it is securely in his hands. The alert player on offense has the ball in constant vision, even though it may be his peripheral vision, whenever his proximity to a teammate having possession is such that a pass between them is likely or possible. Once the ball is in the air, the receiver continues to track it with his peripheral or direct vision until the instant before reception, at which time he must begin to focus directly on the ball and continue doing so until he has positive, two-hand control. Only then does he divert his attention to the task of dribbling, passing, or shooting.

The principles of hand-eye coordination were discussed at some length in the section on shooting, at the beginning of this chapter. The same principles apply to catching a pass that apply to shooting, though the techniques are reversed. Instead of sighting a stationary target and coordinating the hands to impart an intercept trajectory to a ball, as in shooting, pass receiving requires the tracking of a moving target and coordinating the hands to do the actual intercepting. In addition, however, catching the ball requires that the kinetic energy associated with its flight be quickly and completely absorbed by the fingers, wrists, and arms of the receiver. With practice, this can be accomplished with near-perfect consistency by focusing the eyes on the surface of the ball as it nears, while consciously anticipating the objective of grabbing and holding it. As a consequence, the hands should move instinctively at the right instant to grasp the ball firmly in the fingertips, spaced comfortably to absorb the spin, the wrists and arms recoiling naturally to absorb the momentum.

Whenever possible, a pass should be caught in both hands, the receiver stepping toward the ball. When the situation demands a one-hand catch, the off-hand must be immediately brought up to assist in protection and control. A retreating catch should occur only as the result of a bad pass.

The mental attributes of a pass receiver are alertness for the unexpected pass, relaxed confidence in the sureness of his hands, and disciplined eye concentration.

Receiving Straight Passes. When catching a straight pass in an outside area and with no defensive pressure, the receiver, his eyes on the ball, steps toward the passer with either foot, extending both hands chest high in front of his body, his palms facing each other with fingers wide-spread. The ball is caught in the fingertips, and the arms recoil naturally toward the chest. When catching a straight pass in an outside area and with defensive pressure, the receiver steps back with one foot to the side of the defender, blocking him from the ball, extends an arm to the side of the step, and makes a one-hand catch. The fingers of the catching hand are widespread and slightly cupped; the hand and arm yield with the ball, cushioning the force of the pass; and the body turns slightly toward the catching hand as the other hand is brought up quickly for control, grasping the ball firmly in the fingertips of both hands.

Receiving a straight pass while moving away from the passer can be accomplished with either one or both hands, although both hands should be used whenever possible.

A one-hand reception is usually made when cutting at full stride with the defender in pursuit. In this situation, the hand away from the defender is held up as a target, and the off-hand comes up for control after the one-hand catch. The timing of passer and receiver should be such that, without breaking stride or lowering the ball, the receiver can follow through for a shot. Should it be necessary to pull the ball in before releasing the shot, the defender may be able to flick the ball out of the receiver's grasp.

Receiving a Pass in the Pivot Area. Receiving a pass in the pivot area requires either that the receiver be moving strongly toward the ball or that he catch the ball with the hand away from the defender. If the pivot man is sure of the defender's position, he may hold up a hand to the opposite side as a target for the passer; otherwise, the passer must himself decide where to put the ball so that it is best received and protected. The techniques for catching the ball are the same as described for receiving a pass in an open area—the fingers widespread, the wrists and forearms recoiling naturally to absorb the force. Pivot men, however, must practice at great length their ability to handle, when under defensive pressure, the various straight, lob, and bounce passes used to feed a pivot. Since bounce passes tend to be low and with a spin, they should always be caught with both hands, the palms facing each other, and the spin absorbed by supple, widespread fingertips. The pivot player must learn to catch lob passes with either hand or both hands and shoot or pass in one motion. A quick pass back to the first passer often produces a score when his defender drops off with the pass-in.

Receiving a Hand-off, or Flip Pass. Players on offense must be able to receive a hand-off perfectly when moving at top speed. They must be especially alert when crossing in a congested area with a teammate in possession, since the hand-off is often preceded by a fake and may be hurried by defensive pressure.

Normally, the hand-off, or flip pass, is with little or no spin, and the ball is received, waist high, by a deft, two-hand grab, the receiver immediately following through with a pass, dribble, or shot. In the pivot area, however, the

110

receiver must be alert for either an over-the-shoulder drop pass, a quick bounce pass, or a simple hand-off that may be poorly timed and hurriedly executed.

individual offense without the ball

The ability of a player to function within the framework of the offense when he does not have the ball is no less important than his ability to pass, shoot, and dribble. Just as his responsibility with ball possession is to either score or to move the ball into a position of offensive advantage, his responsibility without possession is to move in such a way as to advance the offense either by getting open to receive a pass or by drawing the defense away from the ball or a play. Although meaningless movement must be avoided, continual evasive maneuvers consisting of stops, starts, and feints in order to free oneself for a pass, even if unsuccessful, puts pressure on the defender and keeps him from double-teaming the man with the ball. Since, however, an unplanned move is not only useless, but may interfere with the play action, each player without possession must maneuver intelligently, coordinating his moves with the actions of the player having possession.

In a planned attack, the man with the ball determines the pattern within which the other offensive players regulate their movements. An example of this is the situation in which the team is in a two-three alignment, with a guard dribbling toward the right corner man; the pivot man is in the right, medium pivot area. When the guard passes to the right corner and follows his pass toward the corner man's defender, it signals the four other players on offense that the guard intends either to set a screen for the corner man or to attempt a change-of-pace or change-of-direction cut to the basket for a return pass. Therefore, the forward receiving the pass should be prepared either to return a pass to the cutter, to take advantage of the screening maneuver, or, if his defender reacts to a fake, to drive along the end line to the basket. The pivot man should move away from the area, using fakes and pivots to draw his defender's attention away from the point of attack. Should the pivot defender remain in the area, however, the pivot man must immediately assume a favorable offensive position, either at the free-throw line or in the low-pivot area on the ball side.

The uninvolved guard should start toward the corner on the opposite side, as if to screen for the opposite-side forward. The move is timed to cause the guard's defender to turn his attention away from the play. The guard may fake the move-in, however, and then abruptly pull back toward the side of the ball, close enough either to be a safety release for the man in possession, should the play attempt be shut off, or to be in good position to retreat quickly on defense should there be an interception or a lost rebound after a missed shot.

The movements of the far-side forward complement those of the far-side guard; he may either fake an interchange with the guard or feint toward the foul line as if to receive a pass in the middle. Since he is the key rebounder on the side away from the ball, his movements have the dual function of drawing the attention of his defender away from the point of attack and placing himself in the best rebound position, as determined by the rebound position assumed by the pivot man: one of the two should be under the basket, on the side away from the shot; the other, in the free-throw lane about ten feet in front of the basket.

The play of the two or three team members not involved in the principal action is the most difficult of individual-player offensive techniques to teach. Much depends upon the intelligence and self-discipline of the player himself, since he must not only synchronize his actions with the other uninvolved team members, in decoying defenders away from the play, but he must also be alert to a sudden change in the play's development that should call for his own direct involvement. The following are some of the moves available to a player without the ball in carrying out his responsibilities on offense:

1. A cut to the ball or basket, at the proper time and without interfering with the play action

2. A screen for a teammate, whether with or away from the ball

3. Properly timing a cut off of a teammate's screen, whether the teammate does or does not have possession

4. Maneuvers that will result in best rebound position when a teammate shoots

5. Feints and faking maneuvers that exploit the weaknesses of an individual defender, decoying him to the team's advantage and distracting his attention from the point of attack

6. A quick defensive retreat should the opponents gain possession

7. A move into position for an outlet pass should a teammate have to relinquish possession because of defensive pressure

8. Individually assigned moves for special situations (jump balls, out of bounds, free throws)

9. Countermoves should the defensive team change its tactics; for example, a change from a man-to-man to a press or a zone defense.

The player on offense should bear constantly in mind that even when he does not have the ball his every move has an impact, either negative or positive, on the success or failure of a scoring attempt. Attuning his thinking to that of his teammates and being aware of the offensive and defensive capabilities of every man on the floor, the accom-

112

plished player is involved, directly or indirectly, in the score of every basket.

footwork drills

Diag. 3-26, REVERSE CUT DRILL

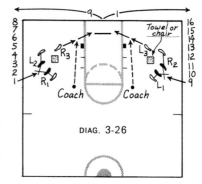

DIAG. 3-26

Two eight man lines are formed at either side of the court. The first players on each line step on the court. A folded towel (or a chair) is in the court, approximately 14 feet from the end line and 8 to 10 feet from the foul line. The players face the basket at a 45-degree angle, and a coach stands at either side at the foul line extended or just behind it with a ball. The player on the left makes a short movement toward the coach with the right foot, maintaining good body balance. Then, with the weight over his right foot, he pushes off, taking a short step with his left foot, avoiding the obstacle, and a long stride with the right foot, driving hard to the basket without the ball. The coach leads him with a bounce pass or a two-hand chest pass, and the player continues in, making a lay-up.

The player on the right uses the same techniques, mirroring the process. He fakes towards the coach with a short movement of his left foot, takes a short step towards the basket with the right foot, then a long stride with the left foot.

The coaches must alternate their passes, timing them so that only one player at a time goes into the basket for the shot. A manager underneath the basket retrieves the balls and passes them back to the coaches.

After the players shoot, they exchange lines so that they will practice both a reverse cut to the left and a reverse cut to the right. This maneuver is extremely important whenever a player is being overplayed.

A player may be used instead of the coach to give the player practice in passing to a moving target, and the number of groups may vary. Instead of two groups of eight there could be four groups of four, using both ends of the court.

This drill, which should not be run more than five minutes at a time, should be used frequently during the preseason. The coaches should look for good footwork, a good pass, good pass reception, and good lay-up form.

Diag. 3-27, FAKE REVERSE AND INSIDE CUT DRILL

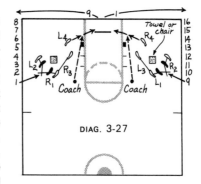

DIAG. 3-27

This tactic is used as a countermove to the reverse cut. Again we place a towel (or chair) in the same relative position on the court as in Drill 26, and the players make basically the same initial movement. Each fakes in good balance, turns slightly towards the ball at a 45-degree angle from the basket, and takes a short step toward the ball with his near foot. A player on the left would take the short step with his right foot, then transfer his weight slightly to the left foot to move a defender, and push off that foot. He would then take a long stride with his right foot and a long stride with his left foot, turning towards the coach or the player who is passing the ball. Receiving a bounce pass or a chest pass that leads him into the basket, he takes a lay-up shot. A manager retrieves the ball and passes it back to the coach, and the players change lines.

The mirror technique is used on the opposite side, with the player starting on his left foot. This movement may be a foot slide of six or eight inches, or there may be no foot movement at all depending on the balance and ability of the player.

At lower levels, footwork drills involving change of direction, change of pace, and turning toward the ball to receive a pass while running full speed should be devised and incorporated in early preseason work.

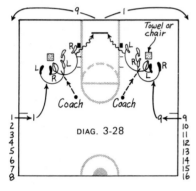

DIAG. 3-28

Diag. 3-28, STOP, PIVOT, GO DRILL

A towel (or chair) is placed 12 feet from the foul lane at the second lane marker. The players form two lines, one on either side of the court. A coach-passer is at the top of the key to that side. The first player in each line drives hard towards the towel (or chair), comes to a complete stop, then executes a rear pivot back towards the coach, pivoting on the inside foot, pushing off and swinging the non-pivot foot toward the basket, facing the coach. At the pivot, the coach or a teammate passes to him. The player takes a full stride with the pivot foot, dribbles into the basket, if necessary, and lays the ball in. After his shot, the player changes lines. The manager retrieves the ball and passes it back to the coach.

For footwork drills, players can be broken up into smaller groups, using players as passers, to utilize both ends of the court. No more than two of these drills should be used each day, and they should not be run for more than 3 to 5 minutes a day. They should be run at a fast pace, as the players are alternatively moving fast during the drill and then resting while moving back into position. A great improvement of individual footwork, maneuverability, and body balance will be evident after the continued use of these drills in preseason practice.

coordinating individual offensive techniques into play patterns

An efficient basketball team must coordinate the movement of five individuals into a pattern of play in which all contribute effectively and intelligently to the team effort. Most successful basketball plays involve only two or three offensive players in the play structure, with the remaining teammates maneuvering and decoying opponents away from the point of attack.

If a team can outnumber their opponents at the offensive end (one offensive player unopposed, two offensive players against one opponent, three offensive players against two opponents, etc.), it will be successful in scoring a basket most of the time. These opportunities, however, are not always available. The best offensive patterns when an outnumbering advantage is unobtainable are two offense against two defense and three offense against three defense. All offensive players must become so well versed in these play patterns that their movement is intuitive and reflexive to counter various defensive measures. When more than three offensive players are involved in one pattern, the timing, movement, and ball handling become complex, and the chance for errors increases. As the number of players involved increases, the greater the chances for defensive double-teaming, deflections, or interceptions.

Two-man patterns involve guard with guard, guard with forward, and forward with center. Three-man patterns involve guards and forward; guard, forward, and center; or guards and center. All players should be versatile enough to maneuver from more than one position or section of the court, and they must recognize the pattern potential in all areas in order that they may involve themselves, if conditions warrant, or move away with decoying maneuvers to lure their guard from the attacking area.

A great deal of practice time must be given to two-on-two and three-on-three situations, using a limited court area. Game conditions can be simulated best by using no more than half of the front court.

Most play patterns include a screen, which is a legal maneuver by an offensive player who, without causing contact, delays or prevents an opponent from reaching a desired floor position. The following plays are the only ones that do not require a screen.

Pass-and-Cut. The pass-and-cut, or "give-and-go," is a basic offensive play in which a player simply passes (gives) to a teammate and cuts (goes) to the basket, attempting to break free of his guard and expecting a return pass from his teammate. If the defender moves with the first pass or turns his head, the ensuing cut should be fast and straight. However, a fake, feint, change of direction, or change of pace may be necessary in order to draw a reaction from the guard. When they see the pass-and-cut maneuver initiated, other offensive players must decoy their guards away from the basket area and passing lane. If free to receive a pass, the cutter should raise his hand nearest the basket as a passing signal and target. The pass can be either a straight pass, a bounce pass, or a lob pass, as the situation warrants.

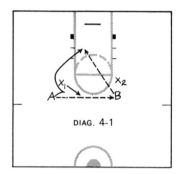

DIAG. 4-1

Diag. 4-1, PASS-AND-CUT, OR GIVE-AND-GO
A passes to B, faking in B's direction to move his own defender, X_1. As X_1 moves towards B, A pushes off his right foot around X_1, cutting directly to the basket. B returns the pass.

Change of Direction. A change of direction (reverse, "backdoor") cut is used when one guard brings the ball toward the other guard or the forward on his side of the floor when they are closely guarded. As the guard dribbles toward the forward, the man guarding the forward on the left side of the floor will be overplaying him on the ball side to prevent an easy ball exchange. As the guard approaches, the forward will step with his right foot toward the dribbler, decoying the defender toward the ball with him. As the right foot contacts the floor, with the body weight on this foot, the forward pushes hard off this foot and quickly turns toward the basket, shifting the weight and stepping with a short step on the left foot, crossing with the right foot in full stride to the basket. The body weight is low to facilitate a quick start on the direction change. The dribbler should fake a pass as the right foot of the forward hits the floor to lure the defender into overplaying. Usually, a bounce pass or high lead pass to the outstretched left hand is used.

DIAG. 4-2

Diag. 4-2, CHANGE OF DIRECTION, OR REVERSE CUT
A has the ball; B is on the left sideline. B steps towards A with his right foot. As his foot is coming down, A fakes the pass. X_1 moves out. B pushes off the right foot, takes a short step with his left foot, crosses long with the right foot and receives a pass behind X_1 from A.

117

DIAG. 4-3

DIAG. 4-4

DIAG. 4-5

Diag. 4-3, CHANGE OF DIRECTION, INSIDE CUT

B fakes towards the basket, stepping with his left foot and drawing X_1's attention. B pushes off the left foot, takes a short step with the right foot and a long step with the left foot, cutting inside X_1, and receives a pass from A.

Dummy. The "dummy" play is a deceptive, nonfake reception of a pass when a cutter or a stationary offensive player near the basket is closely guarded by a defender who is face-guarding or has lost sight of the ball in order to concentrate on his man. The passer should pass the ball over the head of the defender using either a straight two-hand pass or a lob pass. The receiver must be relaxed and unconcerned, as though he is out of the play. He must make no movement that will alert the defender. As a concentrating defender may be intent on the eyes of the receiver, the "dummy" must pick up the flight of the ball *without eye movement*, using peripheral vision. When the ball is almost on the defender, the receiver reaches up quickly and catches the ball at the last instant. This maneuver is excellent in out-of-bounds situations.

Diag. 4-4, DUMMY PLAY

B is being guarded by X_1. B is in a low-pivot position facing A. X_1 cannot see the ball, since he is looking directly at B with his arms extended or up. B must dummy X_1 into thinking that he is not going to receive the ball. He must remain expressionless, making no movements and not looking directly at the ball. A passes to B as the ball passes over X_1's head, and B must move his arms quickly to catch the ball and shoot in one motion.

Diag. 4-5, DUMMY PLAY FROM OUT-OF-BOUNDS

This is an excellent out-of-bounds play for a big man who is guarded by a smaller opponent.

Making a V to Obtain the Ball. This movement may be a fake towards the basket and a push off the far foot back towards the ball in order to receive a pass, or it may be a fake towards the ball and a quick push towards the basket to receive the pass (Diag. 4.6[1]).

DIAG. 4-6

118

Receiving an Inside Hand-off. Play situations can be determined by the man guarding the potential pass receiver. If the guard allows for passage between the offensive man and the defensive man, the passer should nod as he passes to indicate that he wishes the ball back (Diag. 4.6[2]). If the guard closes, the offense can use an inside screen. All players should be alert to good cuts by teammates towards the basket or towards good shooting areas when their defensive opponents are in poor position with respect to the ball. Any time an offensive player can cut inside his defender and receive a pass within 15 feet of the basket, he is in excellent shooting area and should be given the ball. This play may be made at the strong side (guard to forward (Diag. 4.7[1]) or forward to guard (Diag. 4.7[2]), or it may be made to a forward on the weak side when the ball is in possession of a guard on the opposite side, if the keyhole area is open.

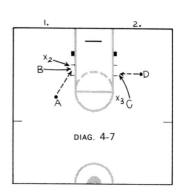

DIAG. 4-7

Screens are involved in all other play patterns. A screen can be set as close to an opponent as desired, short of contact, so long as the screening player is in the normal field of vision of the opponent and the opponent can avoid contact. Outside the field of vision, a screener must be far enough away from the opponent to allow him a normal step. Screens can be stationary or moving, with or without the ball, inside a defender (between the defender and the basket), outside a defender (between the defender and the offensive teammate that he is guarding), or to either side of a defender. It is important that all players know how to screen and how to cut or dribble off a screen, because when offensive balance and defensive balance are equal, screening is the best way to obtain an offensive advantage. The primary function of a screen is to free the cutter or dribbler for a good shooting opportunity. The secondary purpose is to beat a switching maneuver by defense by taking advantage of inside position resulting from the exchange in defensive responsibility.

plays involving a screen

DIAG. 4-8

Inside Screen. When the defender is close to the offensive player being screened for, the screener should be inside the defender, closer to the basket.

Diag. 4-8, INSIDE SCREEN

A has passed to B and has moved into position between B's guard, X_1, and the basket. He is setting an inside screen for B.

Diag. 4-9, INSIDE HAND-OFF

A has passed to B. He moves between B and X_2 (B's defender), receives an inside hand-off, and dribbles in to the basket. A must always signal the intent for an inside handoff, perhaps by nodding his head as he passes the ball to B.

DIAG. 4-9

Outside Screen. When the defender is loose, the screener should be outside the defender, between the defender and the teammate he is guarding.

DIAG. 4-10

Diag. 4-10, OUTSIDE SCREEN
A passes to B. Since X_2, B's guard, has dropped back, playing B loosely, A screens outside X_2 between him and B.

Diag. 4-11, OUTSIDE HAND-OFF
A has passed to B and has cut behind him. A receives a hand-off pass outside B. (A hand-off is the normal procedure whenever an offensive player passes to a teammate and cuts behind him.) A may dribble in to the basket or shoot a set shot.

DIAG. 4-11

Lateral Screen. When the defender is guarding an offensive player in such a way that lateral screening, or side screening, may open the offensive player for a jump shot, a set shot, or a drive or cut to the basket, the screener stops on either side of the teammate's guard. An advantage to the lateral screen is that it comes in the field of vision of the defender, so it can be set very close to him with a widespread foot base, making it very difficult for him to avoid being screened legally.

Back Screen. When an offensive player moves behind a stationary teammate who has the ball, or dribbles behind a teammate, a back screen is being set up. Both defenders will be inside, closer to the basket than the offensive men.

Rear Screen. When a forward or pivot player moves from a position out of the visual field of a defender behind that opponent, he sets up a rear screen. It is an inside screen that is set by a player moving from a close-to-the-basket position to the rear of the opponent. An excellent rear screen maneuver is to have the pivot player break from his position toward the ball posessor, who passes to him. The pass is usually high, so the pivot man jumps and catches it in the air. He must be well in front of his guard as he moves into the ball from directly behind the passer's defender. As the pivot player contacts the floor, he pivots toward the basket, holding the ball over his head. The passer-in cuts off the pivot man, to either side, running his guard into the rear screen. The pivot man passes to the cutter if no switch is made or dribbles in for an easy lay-up himself if his defender switches to the cutter.

Double Screen. A double screen is set when two offensive players stop in a shoulder-to-shoulder position, parallel to, perpendicular to, or oblique to, the end line, anywhere within shooting distance of the basket. Many set offensive patterns use a double-screen maneuver to obtain good jump shooting and cutting opportunities.

120

If an offensive player is not facing the basket when he sets an inside, double, or lateral screen, either stationary or moving, he must know the techniques of the offensive roll, a pivoting maneuver used by a screener after the teammate he screened for cuts off the screen. The screener pivots on the left foot, rolling right, when the cutter goes to the right and on the right foot, rolling left, when the cutter has cut to the left. The pivoting foot should slide imperceptibly toward the screened opponent for body balance and to initiate and facilitate the rolling action. This foot movement should be simultaneous with the cutting action of the teammate screened for. The push is off the non-pivot foot, with the arm and shoulder on that side swinging hard in the direction of the pivot to speed up the turning action. This foot steps directly toward the basket before contacting the floor. Body balance must be maintained through a low center of gravity while in motion, therefore the knees are flexed and the hips lowered to effect proper weight control. The screener must anticipate defensive pressure during this maneuver and counteract its force by keeping the body balance centered above the foot spead, using the opponent's force to accentuate his into-the-basket movement to beat the switch. When a lateral screen is made facing the end line, the pivot is made on the inside foot (right foot on the left side, left foot on the right side), rolling into the basket as the cutter comes off the screen, with the screener looking for a return pass if the defense switches or for inside rebounding position if the cutter shoots. The offensive roll allows the screener to pivot and face towards his original position and the ball to receive a pass for a jump shot if both defenders concentrate on the cutter or to become a trailer if the cutter is moving into the basket with the ball. The roll also prevents a blocking foul on the screener if the cutter's guard is moving backward toward the screener without room to avoid contact.

offensive roll

If possible, players should adhere to the principles that apply to player movement when a cutter or dribbler is screened for.

When an inside or lateral screen is made, the cutter or dribbler should always move off the screener toward the direction from which the screen came. If a guard on the left screens for a forward on that side, the guard moving from the outside toward the end line, the forward should cut behind the screener to the outside. When a rear screen or a double screen is set, the cutter or dribbler may cut to either side of the screen. The screener determines the type of screen he will position for; the cutter or dribbler must cut closely off the screen, timing his movement so that the defender is in fact impeded by the screen.

screening principles

121

The position of the defensive opponent guarding the player being screened for dictates the screening maneuver. When the defender is close, the screener may pass to the teammate if possible, or dribble in and set an inside screen or a lateral screen. The inside screen should be used whenever practicable, preferably with the screener facing the basket. While the screen can be set with the screener facing any direction, facing toward the basket allows the greatest visual field for the screener, and it allows quick movement toward the basket without pivoting.

When the defender is playing loose (three to four feet or more away) an outside screen should be used. As a shot over the screen is the first offensive option in this situation, the player being screened for must be within his accurate shooting range. Should the defender close in on the player being screened for as the screener is moving into position, the screener must change to an inside or lateral screen. He may also go behind this teammate and set a back screen for himself, if this position is within his accurate set-shooting range.

Whenever a screen is set for an offensive player, he must cut off the screen, unless defensive adjustments make a different maneuver more practical. For example, if a forward has received a pass from the guard on his side, who follows the pass to set an inside screen, and the forward's defender shifts toward the screen to neutralize its effectiveness, the defender leaves the end line open for a drive. The forward does not cut off the screen, because the defensive adjustment gives the forward a better percentage offensive maneuver.

In all cases where the man being screened for does not have the ball, a cut must be made. If the screener has the ball, the cut will relieve defensive pressure at the point of attack. If the ball is not in the possession of either the screener or the cutter, the cut will open a congested area and perhaps clear this area for an optional offensive play.

Any time a defender picks up his man in the back court or near the mid-court line, and the ball is closer to the offensive basket than this defender and the offensive player he is guarding, the player in possession should dribble into a position between the defensive man and the basket. The guarded teammate should move slowly up-court, delaying his forward progress until the dribbler is in position. Then he should cut as close off the dribbler as possible, so that the defensive guard cannot slide through. The dribbler must maintain his dribble, because he will be able to drive into the basket if his guard switches. If there is no switch, the dribbler can pass to the free cutter. All other offensive teammates must move their defenders away from the direct cutting, passing, or dribbling lane to the basket.

122

This principle (cutting off the ball whenever the ball's position is between any offensive player's guard and the basket) applies at all times except when a low or medium pivot is in possession and maneuvering for a close-in shot. When an inside screener has the ball and a defensive switch to the cutter takes place, the screener is open for a shot, or if dribbling, he may drive.

Diag. 4-12, CUTTING OFF THE BALL, OR A RUN-AROUND

A dribbles directly in line between B's defender (X_2) and the basket. B moves X_2 into A and cuts close off A towards the basket, receiving a pass if open.

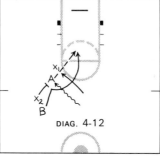

DIAG. 4-12

When the player cutting off an inside screen is in possession and a defensive switch is made, the screener, if facing the basket, should step toward the basket with the foot opposite the side the cutter comes over. If his back is to the basket, he should use the offensive roll. The player in possession should pass to the screener as soon as the defensive switch maneuver takes place. At that instant, the passing lane is widest, because the switching defender is intent on stopping the dribbler, and the screened defender has not had time to readjust his defensive position inside to protect against the screener. The best pass to use in this situation is a quick bounce pass, although a lead two-hand pass (chest or overhead) or lob pass can be utilized also.

Diag. 4-13, PASSING TO THE SCREENER ON A SWITCH

A has passed to B and screened inside B's defender, X_2. B dribbles off the screen to his right, the direction from which the screen came. X_1, A's guard, switches to B as B dribble drives for the basket. At X_1's switch, B passes immediately to A. It is important that the ball be passed as the switch is made, since that is when the opening is the widest and both defenders are generally intent on the driver.

DIAG. 4-13

When a screen is set, the player using it must follow proper cutting procedure. He must determine where the best screening spot will be and maneuver effectively, using fakes and feints if necessary, to gain time and position before moving off the screen. The cutter may, for example, take his defender below the screen and change direction, coming back hard toward the screen, running as close to

DIAG. 4-14

the screener as possible to prevent the defender from sliding between the offensive players.

Diag. 4-14, SCREENING AWAY FROM THE BALL POSITION

C at the head and to the right of the key has the ball. A has set an inside screen for B. B cuts tightly off A's screen. If there is no switch B is free underneath for a basket. If X_1 switches, B should go straight across the foul lane and A should make an offensive roll to the basket. C would pass to A on the offensive roll.

Diag. 4-15, TAKING ADVANTAGE OF A SWITCH

B, the tall forward, has set a lateral screen for A, the guard. A dribbles off B's lateral screen. X_2 switches to pick up A, the dangerous offensive player. B, uses an offensive roll into the basket. He now has the smaller defender, X_1, guarding him. He assumes a pivot position, taking advantage of the usual mismatch in size, and anticipates a pass from A. The option here will be to allow A to go one-on-one with the bigger defender, X_2, outmaneuvering this defender while B draws X_1 away.

DIAG. 4-15

When two offensive players cut off a teammate in any pivot position, the player who passes into the pivot man is always the first cutter, with the second cutter timing his movement off the first cutter, moving in the direction the first cutter comes from to set the moving screen. The first cutter can stop to set a stationary screen for the second cutter, hesitating long enough to free the teammate, then continue with his cut if open, fall back for defensive protection, or assume rebound position if a shot is taken. Defensive realignment determines the offensive techniques.

All players should anticipate defensive switching maneuvers and take advantage of the offensive benefits that can result. When a guard and forward or center combine in a two-on-two offensive pattern, and a defensive switch is made, a big defender will usually be guarding the smaller offensive player while the smaller defender guards the taller offensive man. The smaller offensive player should pass into the pivot area, to a taller teammate who has a shorter opponent. The taller offensive player in the pivot area should also realize that his shorter teammate will probably have quicker maneuvering ability than his taller defender and be

Guard dribbles off for-   *Guard's close dribble*
ward's lateral screen.   *necessitates switch.*

Forward uses offensive roll, taking smaller defender in close to basket.

Guard passes in to take advantage of mismatch (note two-hand overhead pass).

125

ready to clear the pivot area if no play is made into the pivot mismatch (short defender guarding taller offensive player). The better play in this mismatch situation is usually to make the play into the pivot area, because if the taller offensive player has position, an excellent scoring possibility is present with the probability of a three-point play resulting.

two-on-two play pattern techniques

The most common play patterns in two-on-two situations are guard and guard plays, guard and forward plays, guard and center plays, and forward and center plays. The techniques are similar in the guard-to-guard and guard-to-forward combinations, but in the latter, as in the guard or forward to center combination, the probability exists that a switch will result in a short man defending a taller offensive man, and vice versa.

outside-screen or back-screen plays

This is one of the most important two-on-two maneuvers in basketball. The outside-screen or back-screen play maneuvers are utilized when two offensive players, the farthest out in possession of the ball, are one behind the other farther from the basket than their defenders.

These screening positions are most common when guards cross laterally, the guard closer to the basket hands off to the other guard crossing behind him, and both stop and turn to face the basket, or when a guard passes to the forward on his side of the court who is being played loose and follows his pass to set up behind a stationary outside screen. The guard can also dribble in and hand-off to the forward who is behind him. The player in possession after the pass should always remain "alive" and be within his accurate set-shot range. If neither defender forces over the screen, the player in possession takes a set shot. If one defender moves toward the ball over one side of the stationary screen, the man in possession should drive to the opposite side, and the screener should step toward the basket, stepping first with the foot closest to the defender who is moving toward the handler, keeping the defender behind him while breaking to the basket. (This first step with the correct foot is all important. If the far foot steps first, a quick-reacting defensive player may regain good defensive position on the screener.) The dribbler should continue to the basket or to a good shooting position unless the other defender attacks him. If that happens, he should pass immediately to the screener. The best passing lane opens as soon as the second defender moves into his path to play him, as that defender has now committed himself, and the screener, who has position on the first defender, is moving into the basket. Both offensive players should be alert for

126

Two-on-two outside screen.

Two-on-two outside screen. Screener's guard steps to ball. Screener steps to basket with foot on that side (right).

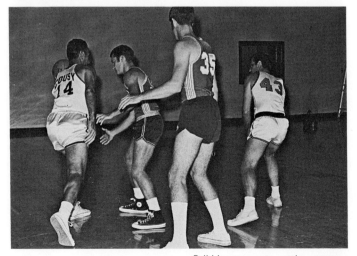

Dribbler passes to cutting screener.

defensive switches that result in mismatches in size if the defenders regain good defensive positions.

The forward's approximate position should be between twelve and fifteen feet from the end line and between six and nine feet from the sideline when he receives the pass-in from the guard on his side. This general location can be approximated quickly by establishing the catching position at two or three steps from the sideline tangent to the front half of the free-throw circle. Correct positioning is important, because the forward must be able to drive either left or right. If placement is too close to the end line, there may not be enough room to drive in that direction. If the defensive man guarding the forward moves in to a close-guarding position, the guard can adjust his position while moving in, using an inside screen or going behind the forward to set up a back screen for himself. The forward uses a hand-off pass or flip pass to the guard behind him and the same offensive procedure described above is followed, reversing the positions. The guard-to-forward play pattern is one of the basic two-on-two plays in basketball, and must be practiced at length by all players so that it can be executed rapidly and precisely before defensive assistance can be deployed by the opponents and so that correct movement becomes instinctive.

Diag. 4-16, OUTSIDE SCREEN PLAY MANEUVER

(This is also applicable if A goes behind B setting a back screen with B handing the ball to A.) A passes to B. X_2 is playing B loosely, providing an opportunity for an outside screen. A sets the outside screen, facing the basket. The defenders, X_1 and X_2, are side by side guarding A and B. The options: (1) B may set shoot over A's outside screen if the screen is set within B's percentage shooting range. (2) If X_2 moves around A on the baseline side, B drives opposite, to his right. As X_2 comes around, A will step towards the basket with his left foot, pinning X_2 behind him. Then he will step with his right foot as B is dribbling. If X_1 picks up B on his movement right, B passes immediately to A who is inside X_2. (3) If X_1 moves around A on the outside, B will start his dribble to the left. A will step towards the basket with his right foot, to keep X_1 behind him, and then step with the left, expecting a pass from B. (4) B may make a jump shot if the defensive pickup of X_1 or X_2 is slow. (5) B may drive into the basket if he is free.

DIAG. 4-16

lateral screens

Lateral screens are used in guard and guard, guard and forward, forward and center, and guard and high pivot center situations when an outside screen or inside screen is not expedient, or when a lateral screen will open a teammate for a good close in or medium jump shot opportunity. A lateral screen is set with the screener's body perpendicular to that of the opponent being screened.

Guard-to-Guard. In the guard-to-guard play, the man with the ball may hand off to his teammate crossing behind him and set a lateral screen, or a player can set a lateral screen for the dribbler as the dribbler crosses behind him. In either

No. 43 sets lateral screen.

Dribble off lateral screen.

case, the screener can stop close to the defender, because the defender can see the screening movement.

When the man with the ball hands off and sets a lateral screen, he should stop and use an offensive roll immediately after the teammate moves by him, stepping imperceptibly towrad the second opponent in the direction of the end line with the foot nearest the end line, and pivoting on that foot away from the opponent he has screened to avoid his causing any contact and to obtain and hold an inside advantage on this opponent if there is a defensive switch. His non-pivot foot steps directly toward the basket. He should continue toward the basket quickly with the inside hand up

Lateral screener slides right foot and rolls on switch.

Pass to screener after his offensive roll.

as a target for a pass if defense exchanges assignments. If a defensive switch occurs, the best passing lane opens immediately after the defensive exchange is made.

Diag. 4-17, LATERAL SCREEN, GUARD FOR GUARD

A has passed to B, then moved into position setting a lateral screen on guard X_2, B's defender. (The L and R in the diagram are the positions of the left and right feet of screener A.) B, on receiving the ball, dribbles hard to his left off the screen. Just as B begins his movement, A slides his left foot imperceptibly towards the left corner. It is a very slight adjustment. As he makes this slide, X_2, moving to stay with B, bumps into A, causing him to pivot on this left foot. A then takes a long 180 degree arc swing with his right foot so that he faces directly towards the basket. (The second L and R indicate the position of A's feet at the end of this offensive roll.) He is now in front of X_2. B makes a return pass to A if X_1 switches. The arrows at the right of this diagram show A's direction and X_2's direction. They indicate that the lateral screen is set with A's body perpendicular to the direction of X_2's body.

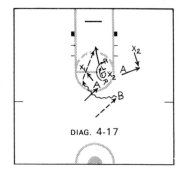

DIAG. 4-17

Guard-to-Forward. The guard-to-forward lateral screen is an excellent method of forcing a defensive switch that will put a smaller defender on the taller forward, who can take advantage of pivot maneuvers in close to the basket. The guard may pass in and screen for the forward or he may dribble in and use a hand-off or flip pass to the forward, who cuts behind him. If the forward has the ball, he may pass back to the guard and come out of the corner position to lateral screen for the guard. A dribble out and lateral screen utilizing the hand-off or flip pass to the guard may also be used.

When the guard lateral screens for the forward, the guard is generally facing the end line. As the forward cuts behind him, the guard should step slightly toward the end-line with his inside foot and pivot, or pivot immediately without the step, depending on which alternative is most likely to keep the forward's defender behind him in case of a switch. The pivot is on the inside foot, the outside foot and leg turning through a greater than 180 degree arc before contacting the floor, facing the body toward the opposite sideline and into the basket. Quick movement toward the basket following this pivot turn is essential, the shielding of the defender through the pivot maneuver and the resultant pressure of the defender in atempting to regain defensive positions will accentuate this starting speed. If a defensive switch is made, and a good shooting opportunity is not available to guard or forward during the play pattern, the guard should quickly back out to the forward's original position to receive a pass out from the forward, who now has the smaller defender guarding him. Either a fake and drive maneuver by the guard, with the forward clearing the area, or a return pass to the forward in good

131

pivot position should be attempted. Teammates of these offensive players must recognize the play potential at the attack point and steer their opponents accordingly.

Diag. 4-18, LATERAL SCREEN, GUARD FOR FORWARD

B is in the forward position; A is a guard. A has set a lateral screen for B. (The L and R indicate the position of A's feet.) B dribbles off, anticipating a switch by X_1, A's defender. A, as B starts his movement, slides his right foot imperceptibly towards the left corner as X_2 moves to guard B. X_2 bumps A. A's left foot now makes a 180 degree arc, he pivots on right foot, and ends up with the position L and R facing the basket. (The arrow indicates A's new direction after the offensive roll.) B passes to A on the switch. The arrows to the upper left indicate A's facing position is perpendicular to X_2's position.

Diag. 4-19, LATERAL SCREEN, FORWARD FOR GUARD

The forward, B, has passed to Guard A and set a lateral screen for A. (The L and R indicate the foot position of B.) As A starts his dribble to the left, tightly off the screen so that X_1 can't slide through, B slides the left foot slightly forward towards the foul lane. As X_1 moves to stay with A, he bumps B. B makes a 180 degree arc swing, pivoting on the left foot and swinging the right foot and leg. He is now facing the basket. As A comes off the screen, X_2, B's defender, switches; therefore, A passes to B, who moved inside X_1 on the offensive roll. The arrows at upper left indicate the perpendicular body positions of B and X_1.

Forward-to-Center. Many times a pass in to the pivot man from the forward and a protective return pass to the forward necessitated by defensive pressure in the pivot area leaves the forward fairly deep in the corner. A pass out to the guard may be impractical because his defender is overplaying at an intercepting angle and the guard's reverse or "back-door" cut doesn't open him for a pass. A rear screen by the pivot man is impractical as the forward is too close to the end line. In this or similar situations, the pivot man should take a lateral screening position on the outside of the forward's defensive opponent, permitting the forward to drive to the middle or into the outer free-throw area. The pivot will be facing into the near corner when he lateral screens. As the forward drives off the screen, the pivot man should pivot on the foot nearer the basket and raise the hand nearer the basket as a target for the forward in case a defensive switch is made. This is excellent territory for a quick lob pass to the center, or possibly a bounce pass if there is no congestion in the area.

Diag. 4-20, LATERAL SCREEN, CENTER FOR FORWARD

The center cannot use a rear screen in this case, because B has only one direction in which to drive. C is facing into the left corner of the court (R and L indicate his foot position). B drives towards the middle, outside C. As B starts his movement, C slides the right foot slightly towards the corner and X_2 bumps C, accentuating his pivot movement on the right foot so that the left foot swings 180 degrees. (The L and R facing the basket with the arrow indicates C's new foot placement.) As X_3, C's defender, switches, B passes in to C. Arrows at lower left indicate perpendicular body facings of C and X_2.

DIAG. 4-20

Guard-to-Center. The guard-to-center lateral screen opportunity usually appears when the center is in a high-pivot position and the guard has received a pass out from the forward on his side. The screening area for the center is to the side-center, left or right, between an imaginary extension of the free-throw line and the top of the free-throw circle. As the guard receives the outlet pass from the forward, the center positions himself close on the side of the guard's defender. The guard drives off the screen into the free-throw line area. If no switch is made, the guard can take the fifteen-foot jump shot or he can drive into the basket for a lay-up, but he should anticipate either forward's defender stepping into his dribbling path. If that occurs, the pass-off should be made to the side the pressure comes from, because if either forward's defender moves into the free-throw line in anticipation of the driving move, that forward should be moving into the open under-the-basket area expecting the pass-off from the guard. If a switch is made, the guard should make a short lob pass to the center, who should have pivoted into the free-throw lane toward the basket. The center should expect the high lob pass, because on the switch he is picked up by a much shorter opponent whose stature negates a bounce pass. The passer must see a clear passing lane, however, as there is the likelihood of a defender guarding a forward moving into the area.

133

In all lateral screening situations the screener must know how to execute the offensive roll for full advantage in case of a defensive switch. The screener can never be premature in this pivot roll technique, as moving too soon will allow the defender to fight over the top of the screen and nullify its effectiveness. If the lateral position is held too long, the opponent being screened can regain position and destroy the inside position advantage the screener should secure.

When a lateral screen is used with a third offensive teammate in possession of the ball, the cutter should take a switching defensive player away from the point of attack if he is not clear in order to open a passing lane and allow the screener to receive a pass from the teammate in possession. Many times the switching defender picking up the offensive player cutting off the screen will anticipate a pass-in to the screener after the switch, therefore the cutter should maneuver to attract the complete attention of his guard. If the guard leaves him, the cutter must position himself quickly for the best offensive advantage, as he will be free for a shot.

Diag. 4-21, LATERAL SCREEN WITH THE BALL AWAY FROM THE SCREENING AREA

B screens for D. A has ball. The defenders, X_2 and X_4, are concentrating on the cutter, D. B has passed to A, then moved in to set a lateral screen for D. B's initial position was low near X_4. D cuts to the right off the screen. (He always cuts in the direction from which the screen came.) X_2 switches and moves with D on his cut. X_4 also moves with D. B pivots slightly on the left foot, swings the right foot 180 degrees back towards the ball. B's new position is facing the ball (left and right foot movement shown). A passes to B. B, on a roll back towards the ball, gets the ball for a short jump shot.

DIAG. 4-21

inside screen and rear screen

All set offensive play patterns use the inside screen as a basic technique in attempting to provide open shooting opportunities. The inside screen and rear screen are the best methods of impeding the defense for a cutter in order to gain an advantage when a third offensive player has the ball. They are also excellent screens for out-of-bounds plays.

134

In setting the inside screen, the screener must take a position that will place him in the direct line between the defender being screened and the basket. The screen can be either stationary or moving, with the ball at the screening area, or away from it. The onus is on the screener to position himself so that the cutter, using deploying or delaying fakes and feints, can cut close to the screen quickly, preventing his defender from remaining in good defensive position. Proper timing of the cut, considering the status

Inside screen. Player with ball dribbles.

Switch on inside screen (note open passing lane).

135

and position of the ball and the location of the screen, is the responsibility of the cutter. If a switch is made defensively, the cutter must continue along his path to open the passing lane into the screener, who has the inside path to the basket since the screened defender is behind him.

Diag. 4-22, REAR SCREEN

C, in a medium pivot position, has moved up quickly from behind X_1, A's defender. A passes to C. C catches the ball in the air, lands, and pivots immediately to face the basket. He must not be too close to X_1 so that he can act as a rear screen out of X_1's sight. A moves X_1 into C, then cuts to the basket. C passes to A. If there is a switch, C does not pass to A, and C is open for a shot or a one-bounce drive into the basket.

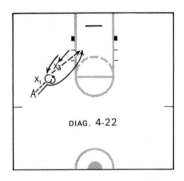

DIAG. 4-22

When a player has set an inside screen from fifteen to twenty feet out from the basket and away from the ball, he should execute an offensive roll toward the ball position after the cutter has gone by. The defenders of both the screener and the cutter are usually intent on minimizing the effectiveness of the cutter, and they underestimate the potential of the screener. Using the roll, the screener can maneuver himself into excellent medium-range shooting territory and usually be free for a shot without extreme defensive pressure.

When executing an inside or rear screen the screener should face the basket whenever possible, because if defense switches, the screened opponent will bump the screener toward the basket in his effort to regain defensive position as the cutter goes by. The dribbler can use a change-of-pace dribble to advantage when setting an inside screen against a switching defensive team by maintaining his dribble, hesitating, anticipating a switch or movement by his defender to delay the cutter when the cutter uses the screen, and quickly resuming a fast driving dribble into the basket to outmaneuver his defender.

When using an inside or rear screen, the screener must be careful to allow room for a normal step by the opponent being screened. Since these screens are set out of the visual field of the screened defender, the responsibility for ensuing contact rests with the screener. As the screener

136

must be cautious in positioning for the inside screen, the cutter must maneuver his defender into the screen. If the defender is playing close, the cutter should take his man below or even with the screen, using change-of-pace or change-of-direction maneuvers to position the defender so that the cutter can cut hard and tight off the screen. If the defender is playing loose, the cutter should back the man into the screen by moving directly toward it and using head and shoulder fakes to disguise his final movement off the screen.

Drive off a screen.

The most common type of three-on-three play in basketball is "splitting the post" or "scissoring-off-the-post." It utilizes an inside screen and a rear screen and involves the high pivot man and both guards or a medium pivot man and the forward and guard on the ball side.

The high pivot man moves into a position in the outer half of the free-throw circle. As he reaches position, the ball is passed in from either guard. The pivot man is facing mid-court, his back to the basket, with a well-balanced foot spread. He must be extremely protective of the ball as there will be much congestion in the area. The passer-in cuts first, hesitating slightly then following his pass, from left to right or right to left, cutting close off the pivot man. The second guard cuts closely behind the moving first cutter in the opposite direction, timing his cut so that his defender is impeded in the crossing maneuver.

three-on-three play pattern techniques

Diag. 4-23, SCISSOR MOVEMENT, BASIC

Involves two guards, A and B, and the center. A passes to C, the pivot man, and cuts to the right. B fakes a step, then cuts to the left. The passer is always the first cutter, going to the outside of the pivot. The other cutter cuts behind the first cutter in a scissor movement.

Diag. 4-24, SCISSOR MOVEMENT USED WITH SHOT OVER DOUBLE SCREEN

C receives a pass from B, who moves in his original scissor movement to the outside of his pass. A fakes and completes the scissor. X_1, A's defender, slides back behind B and C to negate the effectiveness of A's cut. A stops, receives a pass from C, and shoots an 18-foot jump shot over the double screen set by B and C.

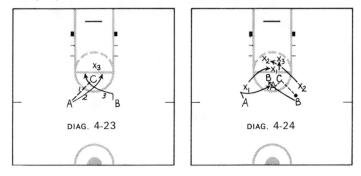

DIAG. 4-23   DIAG. 4-24

The pivot man must quickly assess the defensive reactions to determine whether the first cutter or second cutter will be in the more advantageous scoring position. He must also be aware of his own defender's reaction. After handing off to either guard, the pivot man should step toward the basket with the foot to the side he handed off on and move in quickly toward the basket. This step opens his body position toward the ball side, allowing for a quick return pass (generally a high lob pass) if his defender switches to the cutter and bringing him into good rebounding position in case the man in possession shoots.

138

Defensive tactics used to upset this scissoring action can be neutralized easily by using optional "splitting the post" maneuvers. Some defensive pivot players will overplay to the side where the play initiated, expecting the second cutter, who will come this way, to receive the pass. The post defender can step in and draw the offensive charge. The pivot man should observe this defensive shift, using a slight head turn and peripheral vision. A good fake hand-off and a step to the basket with the foot opposite the post defender's position, a pivot and a one-bounce dribble will free the pivot man for a lay-up. The pivot man may also take a medium turn-around one-hand shot.

Diag. 4-25, SCISSOR MOVEMENT-PIVOT TECHNIQUE

B has passed to C and started his cut. The pivot man, C, observes his defender, X_3, move to the right in anticipation of B's cut. A delays his cut on seeing the defensive deployment. C pivots on the right foot and steps back with a long left stride. C may (1) dribble to the basket or (2) take a jump shot.

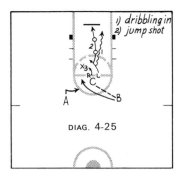

DIAG. 4-25

Many guard defenders in a split-the-post attack drop back to about a step in front of the pivot and automatically switch on the crossing guards. To negate this defensive tactic, the second cutter can change direction immediately after starting his cut behind his teammate and both cutters can go through on the same side as the first cutter, or the first cutter can stop in front of a defender on the same side that he passed in from instead of crossing, and the second guard can stop behind the pivot and guard double screen for a medium range shot.

Diag. 4-26, SCISSOR MOVEMENT WHEN DEFENDERS ANTICIPATE THE SCISSOR AND SWITCH PREMATURELY

B passes to C and cuts. A starts his cut behind B. He observes that X_2 has stopped following B and that his own guard, X_1, will pick up B. A changes direction immediately and cuts to the same side of the pivot as B.

The splitting-the-post maneuver can also be used by a medium pivot and the forward and guard on the ball side. Usually the forward makes the pass in to the pivot and cuts first, with the guard timing his cut behind the forward.

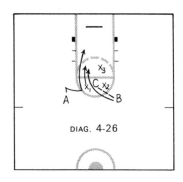

DIAG. 4-26

Many good shooting opportunities open up in this maneuver. If the forward receives the hand-off pass as the first cutter, he is in excellent range for a short fake-and-jump-shot. The guard, cutting behind the forward, is also in good short jump-shooting range if the defense drops back, and the guard can also continue into the basket for a lay-up if the defense is screened. The pivot man should step to the basket and open to the side of the hand-off as he will have inside position if his defender switches. Many shooting opportunities for step-away one handers, hook shots, or turn-around jump shots, may be available to the pivot player. It is important that the two offensive teammates not involved in these play patterns lure their defenders away from the point of attack and retreat so that they give good defensive balance if the ball is intercepted or possession is lost in the rebounding action.

Diag. 4-27, SCISSOR MOVEMENT USING THE CENTER, FORWARD, AND GUARD

(1) Forward, B, passes into pivot, C. (2) B cuts to the outside of his pass. (3) A, the guard, fakes and cuts off B's movement.

DIAG. 4-27

three out-two in screening maneuvers

Many excellent medium-range shooting opportunities can be obtained from a three out-two in pattern when three players coordinate their movements using inside screens. It is especially effective in obtaining the good medium range jump-shot for an outstanding shooter. Any of the five players can be set up for this shot. To set up the left corner man, the left outside man passes to the outside middle man and follows the pass setting an inside screen. The middle man dribbles close off the screen to the left, causing his defender to slide through between the screener and the screener's defender. The left corner man, alerted for and anticipating the movement, starts away from the screening area toward the basket. The middle man, dribbling with the ball, inside (or lateral) screens close to the left end of the free-throw lane or closer to the basket if possible. The left corner man, who has changed direction, comes back hard behind the screen for a medium-range

140

shot. (If the middle man cuts free off the first screen, the left corner man can continue on under the basket to open the left side for the driver.)

Diag. 4-28. THREE MAN SCREEN WEAVE (MEDIUM JUMP SHOT FOR A GOOD SHOOTER)

A, in possession of the ball, passes to B, then moves across the lane to set an inside screen for B. B dribbles off the inside screen. A moves away, deploying X_1 away from the ball area with him. D fakes to the baseline and cuts back behind B's dribble screen. This is now an outside screen. D gets a hand-back or drop-back pass from B and shoots a jumper over the screen. A passes to B and screens inside. B dribbles off A, D fakes away and comes off B's screen on X_3, and shoots.

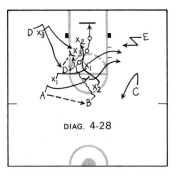

DIAG. 4-28

This maneuver can be used to set up a shot for any offensive player (except a pivot man) from any offensive alignment. We call the maneuver "Get One For." It obtains a medium jumper after a fast three man weave.

In this weave, or figure eight, a player sets up a shot for a designated teammate. The passer or dribbler who initiates the movement should be adjacent to the player to be set up. He passes or hands off to a player on his right to "get one for" a designated teammate to his left and vice-versa. After his pass, he screens for the receiver, who passes to or dribbles and hands off to the teammate the team wishes to "get one for." This potential shooter receives the ball and shoots over his passer's screen. This type of tight, cutting, screening weave is applicable to any type of offense.

Diag. 4-29, "GET ONE FOR" WEAVE FROM A TWO-THREE OFFENSIVE ALIGNMENT

In this offense we are getting one for A, the left forward. B starts the movement by passing or dribbling away from A. C fakes, changes direction, receives a hand-off and a screen from B, and continues laterally toward the left corner. A fakes to the baseline, comes behind C's dribble move, and receives a hand-off pass. He takes one or two bounces and shoots if the defensive deployment permits.

DIAG. 4-29

Diag. 4-30, "GET ONE FOR" WEAVE FROM THE TANDEM ALIGNMENT

In this offense, A is at the point, B and C are at the right lane, and D and E are at the left lane. While we only need three men, we are using the other two players on the court to show offensive balance and deployment. We are getting one for D. A dribbles to the right side, and C comes behind him. A hands-off and holds the screen, and C dribbles across the lane. D comes behind E and C and receives the ball. He dribbles and takes an intermediate jump shot at the basket. The timing of D's initial move is crucial. (This weave can also be implemented using passing only.)

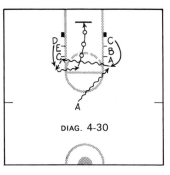

DIAG. 4-30

141

two out-three in screening maneuvers

A series of inside and rear screens can be set from a two out-three in offensive pattern without the ball. The guards can control the ball in the backcourt, and as it is passed to the right, the low or medium pivot man can use a rear screen for the right forward who cuts to the basket. If the defense does not switch, the forward may be open for a shot; if they do switch, the pivot will be inside his defender for a shot. If nothing materializes, the right forward continues to his left and screens to the inside for the left forward, the pivot man moving to a position in the right corner. The ball passes from the right guard outside to the left guard. The left forward cuts off the right forward's screen into the basket, and the right forward rolls, anticipating a pass if the defense switches. If no good shooting opening appears, the left forward continues to the right to screen for the pivot man stationed in this area, as the ball is passed from left guard to right guard. The movement can continue indefinitely as long as the guards can retain positive control of the ball in good passing position.

double screens

The double screen is incorporated into many set offenses, both as primary plays and as optional maneuvers after the initial pattern is executed. A double screen is set by two offensive men standing shoulder to shoulder within shooting range, facing the basket or facing away from it. A third offensive player attempts to run his defender into this block. Usually the cut off a double screen can be to either side, going toward the basket for a close-in shot or away from the basket for a medium-range shot. If the defense switches, one of the players setting the double screen may be open. The open screener should employ the offensive roll technique or step toward the basket, whichever is applicable. Because of the proximity of three offensive players and their defenders, many times two defenders can guard the three offensive players momentarily if one defender is screened. As the play involves at least four offensive players —the cutter, the two screeners, and the passer—proper timing is difficult. When properly timed, however, double screens offer a variety of options that result in excellent scoring opportunities. This type of screen is especially effective in setting up good medium-range shots for an outstanding shooter who is not a good ball handler.

The offensive roll is an integral part of maneuvers involving a double screen, for many double screens are set with the screeners facing away from the basket. When a defensive switch is made, the screener whose opponent switches must roll to the basket to take full advantage of his position inside the screened defender.

142

Diag. 4-31, DOUBLE SCREEN, GUARD AND CENTER FOR THE FORWARD ON A CUT TO THE BASKET

A passes to B. A moves in as though to get a return pass and sets a double screen next to the low pivot, C. D fakes to the baseline and cuts around A and C's double screen into the foul lane area for a pass from B. X_4 is screened by the double screen of C and A.

Diag. 4-32, DOUBLE SCREEN, FORWARD AND CENTER ON A CUT AWAY FROM THE BASKET

C, the low pivot, and D, the forward, set a double screen low along the left foul lane. E, the right forward, cuts to the baseline side and comes behind the double screen, cutting away from the basket. He receives a pass from A for a short jump shot behind C and D's double screen.

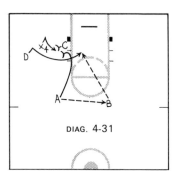

DIAG. 4-31

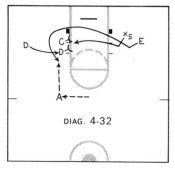

DIAG. 4-32

In practice sessions, the coach must emphasize the individual offensive tactics that precede and follow the screening maneuver: passing, cutting, opening to receive a pass, faking, pivoting, and rebounding. The ability of all players to recognize and execute basic play patterns quickly, utilizing the correct fundamental techniques of offensive basketball, is the cornerstone to success in competition. The proper mental approach has to be an integral part of all individual and team effort. Some players are better shooters than others, some better passers, some better rebounders, some stronger, some more aggressive, but all must be unselfish. Selflessness must be the predominant characteristic in all players to guarantee team success. No one player —not even a super-star—can carry a team without the co-ordinated mental and physical endeavors of his teammates.

Knowing when to shoot requires a completely disciplined attitude on the part of every player. A player should shoot whenever he has confidence that the shot he is taking will score; when defense cannot block the shot; when there is no open teammate in a better percentage area; and when teammates are in position to rebound (except on a close-in or lay-up shot). Game factors may alter these determinants. All players must recognize the strengths and shortcomings of themselves and their teammates. They should play to the strong points of their teammates and to the weak points of their opponents.

incorporating fundamental techniques into screening patterns

In the execution of all play patterns, offensive players must constantly be aware of defensive deployment as well as their teammates' positions. The ability to generate and take advantage of defensive commitment is the prime essential in the success of any offensive play pattern.

guard with guard

Two guards must work together on the following techniques: advancing the ball against pressure; screening for each other off the high post; reading the intent of a guard who passes and moves away; setting up a defender to properly time a cut off a guard's screen; moving their opponent away from the attack point; returning to that area as a safety outlet at the proper time; dropping back as a possible defender in case possession is lost; getting open to receive a pass in the most advantageous attacking area, properly timing the movement with the status and position of the other guard; and coordinating their movements so that they function as a smooth working unit, complementing each other at all times.

guards with forward

Guards must work with forwards in properly timing the forward's pass reception by gauging defensive deployment, the forward's feinting maneuvers, the guard's deceptive fakes, and the use of the correct pass to correct spot. Guards must always move after a pass is made. The guard must recognize when all forwards will change direction (reverse) and execute the play using deception, timing, and the proper pass (usually a bounce or lob pass). The guard must coordinate his screening maneuvers with the forward's. Both must recognize the defensive positions that dictate the type of screen to employ, and react to defensive commitment by taking maximum offensive advantage of the play situation.

guard with center

Guards should work with centers under pressure. A guard should pass to the center, who has come out from under the basket after using evasive action against a defender to receive a pass, generally in the high pivot. They must both learn proper timing, with the center jumping into the high pass or stepping forward with body crouched and balanced for bounce pass. Multiple types of passes and passing postures must be utilized, with the passer maintaining positive attacking control of the ball until the proper passing moment.

Guards and centers should practice the rear screen turnaround play. (Center breaks toward guard's defender, receives high pass in air, turns around after reception. Guard,

144

cutting tight, runs his defender into the center. Both utilize options determined by defensive tactics.)

Guards and centers must perfect the placement and timing on the lob pass execution, used when an aggressive defender maintains a fronting position on the center as he attempts to obtain a high-pivot position. Some guards can pass off the backboard in this situation, but that procedure is not generally recommended.

Guards should practice passing to the center in the medium pivot area, as some occasions demand that the guard make the pass-in. (The forward pass-in to this area is preferable in most play situations.)

The guard and center must coordinate their movements in setting a double screen for a guard or a forward.

Centers must practice with all guards to recognize backcourt shooting opportunities so that rebound position can be established before the defenders can out-position them.

forward with forward or center

Forwards must team with other forwards and centers to coordinate movement and timing in passing into the medium- or low-pivot areas when the most advantageous position is taken by a teammate. (Players passing into pivot areas must pass to the hand of the pivot man away from his defender. This is the safest pass as it is farthest from the defender. It also indicates the defender's position to the pivot man and forces the pivot man to move into the pass.)

Forwards must perfect the lob pass to the center, used when defense overplays in front as the center attempts to obtain low- or medium-pivot position. (This pass is extremely effective, but it is also dangerous, due to the possibility of the far forward's defender sagging deep into the free-throw lane. If this sag is too far in, the possibility of a cross-court pass to the far forward exists.)

Forwards and centers should practice the rear screen turn-around play outlined for guards and centers. They must also practice getting open for the diverse shots that are available close in to the basket, utilizing individual feints and fakes, a teammate's screen, or an unwary defender's screen of his teammate to obtain a quick advantage before shooting.

Forwards must work with centers on movements when the ball is in the pivot area, cutting, screening, reversing direction, pivoting, and rolling to get free for a shooting opportunity. Pass execution and reception must be emphasized because of congestion in the area.

Forwards must be alert for guards cutting free from the weak side. They must be ready to decoy their defenders away from the play area, and they must watch for shooting opportunities that open for teammates in order to get an advantage in starting for rebound position. If they are removed from the rebound area, or if the rebound bounces away from their position, they must be ready for instant transition from offense to defense. They must be alert to opportunities for double screening plays for the guards or the other forward and for good screening position for a guard, especially away from the ball.

Forwards and centers must be constantly aware that they are functioning in a tight, limited area, and that control and possession of the ball is imperative. They must assess the defensive positions, the play possibilities, the proximity to sideline or end line, their ball-handling shortcomings (if any), the degree of passing difficulty to a teammate in an advantageous position, and his weaknesses (if any) in pass reception, and they must always be prepared for the unexpected defensive maneuver. They must be aware of the best safety release area for an outlet pass at all times.

All play patterns diagramed in this chapter *must* be incorporated into the drilling procedures at all levels for maximum team offense efficiency. These drills will inculcate teammates with instinctive knowledge of each others probable movement in any play situation.

Diag. 4-33, OFFENSE, DEFENSE, OPTION

This drill is designed to teach good one-on-one offensive moves for O_1, who has the ball, as well as good individual defense. X_1 is a defensive player. P, the option man, is an offensive player who may only pass or screen; he cannot shoot. Three men work the drill, interchanging as O_1, X_1, and P. This drill challenges the player on defense, because he has no assistance. It teaches the offensive player how to cut off or drive over a screen and how to fake towards the screen to move the man in and then go by him. If O_1 is in trouble, he can always pass back to P. P may be any place except the area within 15 feet of the basket. If he were in that area, serving as a blind screen, he would take X_1 out of the play and give O_1 a very simple unopposed shot.

This drill should be used at four or five baskets at a time, with each coach taking charge of two or three of the baskets. This is an excellent individual offensive and defensive drill that makes all players work hard on offense and on defense and gives them a rest when they are the option man.

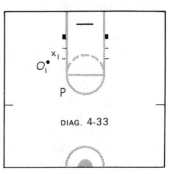

DIAG. 4-33

Diag. 4-34, OFFENSIVE DRILL, TWO-ON-TWO

On the left side of the court, O_1 and O_2 are on offense and X_1 and X_2 are on defense. On the right side, O_3 and O_4 are on offense and X_3 and X_4 are on defense. The coach generally stands at the foul line as the players work first one side and then the other. In this drill, players practice all the basic two-on-two plays that we have outlined previously. The coach will comment on the players and criticize the players, stressing offensive movement. The first pass should be made to O_2 or O_4 so that they may start to work on the offensive functions of the plays. The coaches will tell the players what to do and walk through any play situations for which they have not made the correct instinctive move.

This is an excellent drill for teaching players how to beat switches and how to set each other up for a good shot. The players should interchange on offense and defense and on the sides of the court.

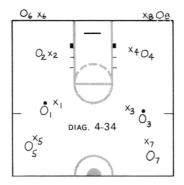

DIAG. 4-34

team offense

The successful offensive basketball team must coordinate the movement of five individuals into various patterns of play so that all contribute effectively and intelligently to the team effort. There are as many successful offenses as there are successful coaches.

The primary function of an offense is to obtain a high percentage shot from the basic play pattern and secondary variations while maintaining adequate rebound coverage and taking proper defensive measures. Those involved in the primary aspect must attack the defense to immobilize it, while the remaining men use deploying tactics to concentrate their opponents' attention away from the focal point of attack, at the same time remembering the place where they can carry out their team functions—rebound responsibility, defensive balance, secondary shooting, and so forth.

Many different approaches to offense may be used. Each should be well devised and skillfully executed, based on unified movement by players with properly ingrained individual fundamental techniques.

selecting an offense

The coach chooses the offense to be used by his team, basing his decision on his own knowledgeability but primarily on his players' abilities. He should adapt the good parts of any system to his own philosophy. Teams should strive for maximum efficiency within the framework of the total abilities of the players involved. The coach must make use of the many talents on the team and take measures to protect players who lack talent in certain areas. Good ball handlers should handle the ball most of the time, and good cutters should be exploited. The good rebounders should be in position to rebound, and the good shooters should be constantly screened for by knowledgeable teammates.

Seldom do all players on a starting team possess similar abilities. Therefore, the coach should use the positive attributes of all in his offensive planning, blending these talents into the team pattern. He should assign individual duties that best utilize the personal abilities of each player. The types of shots each player takes should be determined by his basic shooting ability. Perfection of the offense comes from constant practice of correct techniques, first in small groups of two or three, then in team groups using drills incorporating various aspects of the team offense. The speed, timing, and deception of movement are the important factors in the effectiveness of the offense. All offenses should be adaptable for use against the three types of defenses—man-to-man, zone, and combination.

A coach should be learning constantly—reading books and magazines on basketball, attending clinics, and swapping ideas with other coaches—integrating into his own offense any new tactics that are suitable for his personnel. Offenses are seldom entirely new. Chances are that one used ten years from now will be an adaptation of something that was in common usage five years ago.

The coach should know his material before installing a system. If he is new and doesn't know his material, his preseason practice will be essential in determining the system. The success of a system is due to the personnel more than the coach. If it is the wrong system, regardless of the coach's ability, it cannot succeed. For example, if a coach has slow players, they cannot fast break effectively; if he has tall, uncoordinated players, he cannot use a four- or five-man weave type of offense effectively.

As a rule, coaches should not change their offense in midstream. When change is essential, they should adapt from the existing structure so that the change will not be too radical.

While coaches should try to have the best combination of personnel as quickly as possible, they should not be too hasty in their selection. It's best to keep players on their toes and unsure of their position for a while so as to obtain maximum potential from each man. The best teams have set starting combinations; therefore, coaches should practice their five best players together as a unit as soon as their superior ability is evident. The more compatible the players are off the court the better they will function on the court. Through bull sessions, they will obtain a better understanding of their individual characteristics.

personnel

Necessary changes must be made decisively. The team will probably know before the coach that changes should be made. Coaches normally need two or three replacements at most—in the center position, in the forward position, and in the guard position. If there are only two replacements, the change might be to a forward-center combination or guard-forward combination. Starters may be moved to new positions, but it is not advisable.

Replacements must have as much practice time and game time as possible so that they coordinate their movements with those of the starters. Coaches should never wait until pressure-situations to insert a first-line sub.

There are two types of offense—free-lance and control. In a free-lance type of offense, players make their own patterns, depending on the defensive deployment and the

type of offense

ability of the opponents. Free-lance is not as free or uncontrolled as the term implies, because all two-on-two and three-on-three plays should be drilled completely. Control basketball is a system in which a team maintains control of the ball until one player is in an unguarded high-percentage area. Any basic system can be used to implement a control-type of basketball.

There are several basic offensive systems that teams may use in attempting to obtain high-percentage shots. All must fall into one of the following classifications, based on the position of the offensive players in relation to the basket and to the defensive players guarding them.

1. Five Offensive Players Outside. If five offensive players are eighteen to twenty feet from the basket, all defensive players are closer to the basket than the closest offensive player is. Offenses that begin from this structure are a three-two (wide) and a five-man weave.

2. Four Offensive Players Outside and One Inside. The four offensive players are farther out than the four opponents and one player is nearer the basket. Normally this is a four-man weave system or a single pivot type of offense in which the corner men are approximately eighteen or nineteen feet from the basket.

3. Three Offensive Players Outside and Two Inside. Three offenses start from this structure. (1) A double pivot places the two larger men in closer to the basket than the other three. A three-two offense may have three front men moving while the two inside men are stationary in close to the basket. (2) A one-three-one offense uses a tandem pivot, one high, one low. (3) An overload offense overloads one side of the court, passing the ball to the side that has only one player and having a teammate who was away from the ball cut off a post man towards the ball.

4. Two Offensive Players Outside and Three Inside. This is a standard two-three offense in which the forwards are within eighteen feet of the basket.

5. One Offensive Player Outside and Four Inside. The authors use this as a primary offense. Designated the stack offense, it has four players in close to the basket.

physical makeup

The type of offense to be used is determined by the physical makeup of the team. Each team fits into one of the following categories.

Five Tall Men. This type of team should not use the fast break unless more than two players are fast, and one is an exceptional ball handler. The team should use a definite set offense, shooting over screens. If they have one good ball handler, we would recommend the stack offense. If they have two good ball handlers, they could use a two-three offense, with the low men screening for each other and watching for the easy inside shot.

Four Big Men and One Small Man. Assuming that the small man has good or better than average speed and ball handling ability, this team should attempt to use the fast break with the small man as the middle man. Their set offense can be a two-three if one of the taller men can handle the ball. It could also be a stack offense or an unorthodox offense devised by the coach, taking advantage of overall team size and using low double screens for the bigger players.

Three Big Men and Two Small Men. This is normally the ideal type of basketball team. It can use the fast break or it can use a set two-three offense in which the three big men stay in close for the offensive rebounds.

Two Big Men and Three Small Men. We recommend the fast break for this team, possibly using a three-two offense with the two big men as a double pivot, side by side or in tandem. They could also use a one-three-one set offense.

One Big Man and Four Small Men. This team could use a controlled fast break. A good set offense for them is a four-man weave, using the one big man as a moving pivot. They can also use a one-three-one offense with the big man as the high pivot and the next tallest man as an inside man moving towards the corners. Another good offense for them is a three-two with flash pivots (men moving into the pivot area quickly and moving out as plays develop).

Five Small Men. In high school, the five men would be six feet or under; in college they would be six feet three inches or under. This team's offense should incorporate aggressive defensive tactics as an offensive weapon, depending on their speed and ball handling ability to penetrate towards the basket as quickly as possible. They can use a three-two moving offense or a five man weave offense. The players should only take good high percentage shots from within the eighteen to twenty foot area.

balance and protection

All players must be deployed to provide balance and protection to the offense. At least one player (preferably one and one-half players) should play defense in every offensive pattern to protect against offensive mistakes.

The offense must keep the floor balanced with continuous designed movement, meanwhile, never allowing the defense time to regroup or think. Of course, players must maintain team organization always knowing their position with relation to teammates. One man must always be moving to or away from each offensive station. Such positioning is essential for good offensive rebounding opportunities. Offensive rebounding positions must be organized within the framework of the team structure on each pattern. The team must be balanced so that it can use both inside and outside scoring threats. Movement by a screener is important, as an alert screener may be able to take a quick shot unopposed if he is left open momentarily while his defender concentrates on the cutter.

Coaches must determine the type of pivot they wish to use. If the defense is playing in a zone-structure, the offense must pressure it. A high pivot forces the defense to concentrate on this area. However if the high pivot man is uncoordinated and not quick, the defense may easily block him out on the rebound. Players must be situated to spread the defense as much as possible to allow more space for offensive maneuvering. It is possible to have an overloaded offense with four men on one side of the court, but it limits the direction of movement.

Primary receivers who are close to the man with the ball must not be so close that one defender can play two or that two defenders can double-team the ball. A primary receiver must use offensive faking and footwork to clear himself to receive the pass. He must be cognizant at all times of his location on the court with respect to the deep corners, the hash marks, the sidelines and the mid-court line, as these are restrictive barriers. Timing is an intricate and essential ingredient in floor balance, for players must know when they should move toward the ball and when they should move away from it.

Primarily, a team's offensive movements are determined by the opposing defenders' movements. Good offense requires overall balance—offensive balance in the area of the basket for shooting and rebounding, defensive balance in case of a mistake or misplay, strong-side movement on the side of the ball, and weak-side movement away from the ball. Players should understand and be aware of the movement of teammates in every situation. They must be able to move with the ball and without the ball. Moving without the ball is necessary because a man guarding a standstill offensive player can guard others at the same time. Of course, players must always move with a purpose.

components of a team offense

The following eight factors are essential for every team offense.

1. It must be synchronized. All players must understand their part in relation to the movements of the others. All players must understand the movement required of each of the five offensive positions.

2. It must have a smooth transition from one phase of offense to another, coordinating ball and player movement.

3. There must be three offensive rebounders, one player who is half offensive rebounder and half on defense, and one player moving back to play defense at all times.

154

4. It must have continuity, moving efficiently from the fast break, or penetrating aspect, to the pattern aspect.

5. It must be uncomplicated.

6. Each aspect should be easy to learn.

7. The coach should resist a natural tendency to adopt additional patterns.

8. Players must have patience in obtaining the good shot.

offensive philosophy and principles

There are two types of offensive attacks: the aggressive, fast, penetrating type and the slowdown, or ball-control, type. In each type, offensive pressure should constantly be exerted upon the opposing defense. Using an aggressive offense, the team should get the ball upcourt as quickly as possible, taking the good percentage shot when it appears. This offense weakens the opponents' offensive rebounding structure, as they are thinking in terms of retreat on defense and a slowdown offense that is more susceptible to aggressive defensive pressure. In the second type of offense, the team slows down the attack or changes the tempo of the game. This offense is essential when a team is out-personneled, when the opponents are an excellent running team, when leading late in the game, and when the opponents' defensive posture is set. You cannot attack a set defense with a fast, penetrating attack. Quick percentage shots after quick penetration improves the offensive rebound recovery chances, as the defense is moving and is not in good blocking-out position or in good team position for getting the rebound.

Teams that use a penetrating attack are generally in the superb condition so essential for late game strength in close ball games. Their object is to score by the most direct method. Attacking aggressively and with pressure each time upsets opponents. Such attack eliminates unnecessary ball handling and offensive movement. It develops individual and team aggressiveness, allows for the frequent use of substitutes, keeps the players alert, and confuses and disorganizes the defense. It increases the defensive rebounding strength of the attacked fast-break team. All offensive players have the opportunity to score if they are hustling, so the penetrating attack is enjoyable for the team to play and for the spectators to watch. With this attack, it is possible to employ sneak-away tactics with one man sneaking when the opponent shoots.

Coaches must be aware of the negative aspects of the penetrating offense and make sure their players do not take foolish chances. They should teach the men the value of ball possession. Teams that penetrate aggressively are sometimes prone to excessive fouling, and they get themselves into forcing situations. Players may expend their energy needlessly. Sometimes players break too soon, or they break when the defenders are set defensively, thus making for a poor type of attack.

For best results a team should use the fast break and an aggressive ball penetration offense combined with a set-play theory of attack. If it is to be a well-balanced team offensively, it must be able to play fast and slow.

In the attack, a team must always be able to function against man-to-man, zone, press, and combination defenses and be able to play control basketball, using stalls and freezes. (Control pattern does not necessarily mean slow movement. It implies the proper execution of fundamentals to ensure the efficiency of a given pattern.) The team must also be able to implement last second plays, jump-ball plays, and all offensive out-of-bounds plays with maximum efficiency.

For the following reasons, teams should strive for short jump shots rather than penetration all the way to the basket. First, the defense places bigger men near the basket so that they can block shots of small men penetrating too deeply. Second, the short jump is a maximum efficiency shot, as players are better shooters today than in the past. Third, according to the offensive charge rule, the man driving to the basket is responsible for contact when a defender moves into his path.

The following factors are *musts* for an effective offense. The players must believe that the coach has selected the best possible offense for the existing situation. Each player must know his own strengths and weaknesses and the strengths and weaknesses of his teammates. Players must be selfless, subjugating their individual wills to the best interest of the team. The ''we won'' ''we lost'' attitude is important.

All offensive players must move during play patterns. Timing is essential, and it is only accomplished through long hours of work together. Patience is another important ingredient. Offensive patterns must be practiced in fundamental drills with and without opposition, starting with one man against one for basic individual techniques, then progressing to two-on-two, three-on-three, four-on-four and finally five-on-five. The basic play combinations were discussed in Chapter 4.

In the team effort every man is important. Therefore, the coach must praise those who are in secondary roles, decoying men away from the focal point of attack. The coach should give the players a critique on the offensive opportunities they missed, telling them if they passed up a good shot; if they took a bad shot; if they missed a cutting teammate, or if they did not decoy their men away from the focal point of attack.

Players should get the ball in play quickly if the ball is out-of-bounds after a basket, especially against pressing teams. They should look for quick penetration against a man-to-man press by using fakes and reverses or side-line screens. Intelligent aggressiveness should be a basic attack philosophy. Quick upcourt movement forces situations that may not have been there at the time of the change in possession. Aggressive attack may cause mistakes, but they will be counteracted by the opportunities opened.

In the attack philosophy, the middle man should know the position of offensive and defensive men before the ball is centered. He should know which men are breaking down-court on his team and which opponents are moving into position to protect against them. If the outlets are cut off when the ball is rebounded defensively, it is possible to pass up the middle to a teammate who may then pass to the middle man. This strategy puts the middle man in front of the man who was overplaying him to the ball at the defensive end.

When the ball is moving upcourt quickly, it should be passed only to men moving towards the basket. Men who are cutting away from the basket towards the baseline or the sidelines are not usually in good penetrating offensive position and should not be given the ball upcourt unless they may easily take an unopposed good percentage shot.

In offensive planning, the following important principles must be adhered to.

1. All players must take the high percentage shot. This is perhaps the most important single offensive principle. The shot should be a lay-up if possible or a medium jumper within the player's good shooting range, and it should never be forced or hurried. Teammates must be in rebounding position unless the shot is a lay-up or within six feet of the basket. The shooter must be in better shooting position than any of his teammates.

With proper ball movement and proper player movement, a player never has to be told when he has the shot. If a player is coming off the screen unopposed and the ball is passed to him within the good shooting area, we say the shot has come to him. If the man cutting off the screen continues his movement on a switch, the screener is open, and the ball is passed to the screener without defensive opposition and within the eighteen-foot area, the shot has come to him.

2. All offenses must be based on the margin-of-error theory. The ball should always be in the hands of the player

important offensive considerations

157

most unlikely to make a mistake at that juncture; for instance, the same middle man should have the ball whenever the offense attempts a fast-break. When the team is using a set-pattern the best ball handler should have the ball until the pattern moves into offensive shooting position. Then he should give the ball to a teammate who has the ability to make a good shot or pass. Normally, guards make longer passes; centers and forwards, shorter passes.

We want our ball-handler to have maneuvering room at all times without being double-teamed; therefore we use the ''stack offense,'' in which one player controls the ball until the shooters and rebounders deploy into advantageous offensive position. This play usually necessitates only one pass for a good shot—or at most, two. If you do not obtain the shot you are looking for within this framework, return the ball to the best ball-handler, who will then proceed to a different play within the structure of the stack offense.

3. The best defense is possession of the ball, and to obtain the maximum efficiency from possession, all team members must be completely aware of its value. The loss of the ball offensively without a shot is the most serious failure in team basketball. It is essential that a team obtain a good shot every time it has the ball.

Many teams talk about a shooting percentage, which is based on the number of shots made divided by the number of shots taken. If a team takes sixty shots and makes thirty shots, it has a shooting percentage of fifty percent. However, the true norm is not the shooting percentage but the possession percentage. That is based on the number of times a team has possession of the ball divided into the number of points a team has scored, taking into consideration the number of times the team loses a ball by a bad pass, a tie-up for a held-ball, or an offensive foul.

4. Players should know how to play without the ball, and when to come to the ball from either the ball side or the weak side. They must also know how to come to the ball—by V'ing in, V'ing out, changing pace, or changing direction. They should take advantage of every opening, being careful never to clog the pivot area. All players must see the ball, know the offensive keys for their team, and understand their teammates' reactions. If a player has screened with his back to the basket or the ball, he should use an offensive roll to open to the ball. Correct timing is imperative. The coach should make the players aware of the weaknesses in the offensive set system so that they can guard against mistakes.

5. Each player should know his own shooting ability and the position from which he makes the highest percentage of shots. In addition, he must know the shooting abili-

ties and ball-handling abilities of his teammates, making certain that they receive the ball where they can take advantage of their positive attributes and do not receive it where their weaknesses will hurt the team effort. If players know when they have a shot and when they do not, they will lessen the number of bad shots.

A player expecting to receive a pass must decoy his defender away so that when he gets the ball he is not under pressure and he does not have to force or hurry the shot. The game plan should include special plays for good spot shooters, and the coach should correct those who pass up good shots. The coach should control the type of shot taken by each player. Many times great shooters take a high percentage of the shots.

6. Players must see the total offensive picture: both the offensive deployment of their teammates and the defensive alignment of the opponents. Except for a low-pivot man with the ball, players should be facing the basket and the greater part of the playing court area when they receive the ball. Therefore, there should be no pass to a man moving away from the basket unless it is necessary for possession and protection. The player who receives a ball when he is not facing the basket should immediately front pivot.

7. The offense must control the defensive alignment. This is both a team function and an individual function. Each player must control his own defensive man, maneuvering him so that he can anticipate the defender's moves and deploy him away from the point of attack or take advantage of a defensive weakness to obtain an offensive advantage. A basic offensive principle is that the defender tells an offensive player what he should do—to control a defender, the offensive man must know how the defender is playing. If the defense is playing zone, each offensive player must attempt to control the man in whose area he is located, keeping the defender occupied with offensive movement. If an opponent guarding man-to-man is a good defensive player, it is best to keep him away from the ball as much as possible by deploying to the weak side or by cutting off teammates away from the ball.

8. Teams should eliminate mistakes and never force a play. The elimination of mistakes means complete protection of the ball at all times. Players should never take unnecessary chances when they have possession of the ball, nor should they force a pass or shot. However, many players tend to do this, for several reasons. First, they accept the challenge of a good opponent. Second, they want the first offensive move to result in a good shot. (In most offensive movement this is not possible, and players should not force the shot if it does not appear with the first pass.) Third, they try to rectify an error by making an immediate good

159

offensive play. (People who make bad passes are inclined to follow the ball in an effort to retrieve it. Rather than following the ball, they should retreat.) Fourth, a player may make a bad defensive error that gives his opponent an easy basket then try to rectify it immediately by making a basket himself with a forced or hurried shot.

Normally, the best method of overcoming a bad play is intelligent reaction. For example, if an opponent intercepts the ball and is breaking for the basket, the player should get back in good defensive position immediately. Even if the opponents score, if the erring player follows the ball and inbounds it immediately, there may be a chance to get the basket back quickly, as the opponents may have weakened their defensive structure by a fast aggressive rush at the basket to take advantage of the mistake.

9. The offense must be flexible, changing structure repeatedly during the offensive thrusts. It should be able to adjust to any style of defense instantaneously, incorporating elements of individual or dual free-lance possibilities.

10. The offense should have good timing; continuous movement must be coordinated. Opportunities for scoring maneuvers at the ball and away from the ball must be staggered. To make sure that he will be at the right place at the right time, a player should use stops, starts, changes of pace, and changes of direction. Timing requires accurate steps in definite direction from each player, especially by those at the focal point of attack.

11. The offense must be able to adapt to any defense. For example, a smaller team may work one-on-one on bigger men, a faster team opposing a slower team may speed up the game, a larger team should work to its big men, and every team should play to opponents who are weak defensively if there are any. If there is a good offensive opponent, concentrate his attention defensively in hopes that it will affect his offensive ability or discourage him defensively. Essentially, all offensive players are forwards working for the best possible shot and best scoring opportunity, and all five defenders are guards, protecting the basket against the scoring thrusts of the opponents. Within the team offensive structure the importance of transition from the defensive to the offensive posture is extremely important. The calling of the word *ball* indicates, that a team has the ball and that members should go quickly to the best offensive position.

A number of offensive systems are adaptable for teams, and the plays that can be devised within each structure are unlimited. The coach should build his own offense rather than copy another's, expending a great deal of time in its development. He must have confidence in it, yet know its limitations. The players must be able to visualize it and understand it completely.

Each pattern should entail options of men moving to the basket at various times, with one player (not necessarily the same player each time) in defensive posture ready to go back if the ball is lost. For best offensive results, players should normally move at moderate speed, varying the speed up or down. This is essential for body control and for setting up the defender. The offense must be able to reverse the direction of the ball, moving it from one side of the court to the other rapidly, and in a concerted movement, in order to keep defenses honest to prevent double-teaming by the opponents. The coach must keep the players in a set-pattern moving, because it is harder for defense to guard an opponent in motion.

Team set patterns must have definitive cutting movement—weak-side cutting, baseline cutting, lateral cutting and cuts out front for defensive protection and for the outside set shot. Only one cutter should move to the basket at a time. If two cutters are cutting to the basket from opposite directions, the least advantageous cutter should stop or deploy. Normally, the first cutter is given preference. However, if the second cutter is moving in from a position away from the ball and he is open, the first cutter should give way to him.

Teams should not congest the keyhole area, as they place too many hands around the ball in a confined area, and the pivot player may be tied up with the ball. The coach should plan combinations that strengthen the offense, using free-lance or instinctive patterns for two or three players. He should utilize all his offensive threats but concentrate on the two or three best players, if possible. He should take advantage of team offensive ability so that all players may have scoring opportunities. This prevents double-teaming on the best scorers, and it is good for team morale.

The coach and the team must determine the defensive point of attack and the opponent's defensive philosophy in order to better attack this defense. They should find the defensive weaknesses and move the offense into patterns that will take advantage of it.

The coach should be certain that offensive rebounding coverage is adequate and defined in all patterns. The team must be prepared for all defensive possibilities.

the set-pattern after the opponents' defensive alignment is set

Both audible and visual signals can be used by players to regulate the type of play to be used. An audible signal is usually the calling of the name or number of the alignment

signals

or pattern. Some teams name their plays for colleges or great players.

A visual key can be (1) an arm or finger signal to designate the number of a certain play; (2) ball movement or ball location; and (3) player movement. Normally, the player with the ball determines offensive movement. If he passes and moves in a certain direction, it is a signal; players must be aware of the initiating offensive moves so as to obtain good timing in all plays.

methods of determining the opponent's defense

The ability to determine whether an opposing team is in a man-to-man, zone, or combination alignment, is extremely important. Definite probing offensive movement must be made in order to predetermine the types of offensive thrusts that must be made against the defense. The first movement is a diagonal cut through the defense by an offensive guard as the ball is moving upcourt. If his opponent does not go through with him, it is a zone, matchup, or combination defense. Second is a vertical cut in which a player passes and cuts directly to the basket. Again, if his opponent does not go through with him, the defense is probably a zone or combination. The third movement may be a lateral cut to further check the opponent's defense. It is possible to incorporate all three movements into one play to recognize the opponent's defense quickly. Determining the defense is important, as the basic principle of attack is different for each type. Some defenses will follow the man through initially to deceive the offensive team. However, after two or three passes, the true defense should be obvious.

the fast break

The fast break is the ultimate offensive weapon. It affords maximum penetration on many occasions and penetration to within a 15-foot radius of the basket on all occasions. In a three-on-two or a four-on-three situation the tactic often results in a lay-up shot. Even if the defense responds quickly enough to get back into position, the fast-breaking unit is still within a fifteen- or sixteen-foot radius of the basket, so the player, with one pass or one pivot, can set up either a wing man or the middle man or take advantage of a jump-shooting opportunity.

Running a fast break combats the numerous changes in defense that one sees today on the college level and even, occasionally, on the high school level. Such changes can be very confusing, regardless of how well the team or individual is coached or drilled. Few high school or college teams have players who can adjust quickly enough to a different defense on three or four occasions and who know immediately what offense to employ. They might, even though it is extreme, call for time out to get instructions from the coach. This is not a practical solution. It is better to get downfloor quickly to eliminate the necessity of worrying about what particular defense the opposing team has changed to.

Running an effective fast break puts extreme pressure on the opponents, affecting their offensive tempo and causing the coach to have to adjust his defenses. The break may force the defenders to play a slow and deliberate style of basketball that will affect their own game adversely. Through a fear of being caught upfloor, rebounders may drop off the offensive backboard too soon, to the advantage of the fast-breaking team. Conversely, they may stay too long, in an effort to slow down a break. Another positive psychological factor is that running the fast break effectively invariably leads to better defense on the part of the fast-breaking team. A successful break stimulates the players' aggressive defensive play, so that they come up with many more loose balls, violations, and aggressive rebounds.

If a team is known for its fast break, the opponent (unless he feels he has a decided advantage and does not have to change strategy before the game) will do everything possible to get the team to play a slowdown or deliberate game rather than the other way around, so the fast-break team attempts to get the opponent to accelerate his attack as much as possible. If the fast break is being run properly—if the defensive board is being controlled and the men are getting downfloor quickly the majority of times—it will make the opponents play more of a running game—eventually a wide-open game.

The classic fast break—middle man with ball, lanes filled, trailer and safety men in position.

Kids shoot well today, In order to capitalize on this talent, the offense should get downfloor more quickly than the defense. If the best ball handler gets downcourt quickly, before the defense sets up, with a minimum of ball-handling, he can achieve with one pass and a fifteen-foot jump shot or a lay-up shot what it would take three, four, five, or more passes to achieve in any kind of pattern situation.

Another important advantage of the fast break is that it makes every player a potential scorer. The mediocre scorer, who would get no more than half a dozen scoring opportunities a game when running patterns, can pick up two, three, or four easy baskets a game if he hustles on a fast break.

Lastly, the fast break adds to the game, making it more colorful, interesting, and fast-moving—the kind of game spectators prefer.

drilling

The fast-break options must be practiced repeatedly so that the players react instinctively and the middle man knows the characteristics of his teammates—their speed, shooting ability, mobility, psychological reaction to the fast break, etc.

The following drill is particularly effective. One freshman or weaker varsity team comes down the floor with the ball and takes a shot. (This team remains on the floor throughout the drill.) When the opposing varsity team gets the ball, it immediately starts a fast break. The coach has two or three fast-break units alternating as the attacking team. This attacking unit must retreat defensively to beyond mid-court when they lose the ball. They are then replaced by another attacking unit, and the drill is repeated.

This drill serves many purposes. Initially, the weaker team practices working out of a stationary offensive pattern. The members of the team that is on defense initially, besides getting defensive practice, prepare themselves mentally for the instant transition to offense necessary for the fast break. They become defensively aggressive and alert so that they can get the ball more quickly and force the opposing team into mistakes or violations. They rebound more aggressively, positioning the men properly for the fast break. This drill also serves as a conditioning drill, as it can be repeated over and over, shuttling as many as twenty men into it.

positions for the fast break

When used selectively, the fast break takes advantage of varying skills of all players on the team. The men should be in the positions in which they function to the utmost of their abilities. The best ball handler, best dribbler, quickest man is in the middle position. The lanemen—the shooters—have the most speed and know how to penetrate on a movement to the basket. Normally, the guard who makes the pass to the middle man (or the other guard who is defensively stationed in the front-court area) is in the best position to fill the second lane. The opposite forward is usually the man who fills the third lane. In order to have a successful fast break, these men have to get into their positions as quickly as possible, taking the shortest path downfloor. Instant transition from a defensive posture to an offensive posture is essential. The fourth man down the floor fills the trailer position. The fifth man is the first defender back downfloor. The option is almost not to take the fast break if the situation doesn't develop this way. The margin of error must be cut down to the nth degree. It does no good to run three successful breaks out of five if the other two result in loss of the ball through a violation.

This system allows all the men more freedom to freelance at the end of the fast break, capitalizing on individual initiative, and makes it a bit more fun for the players, instead of putting them in a completely patterned, disciplined situation. We feel that we strike a happy medium, offensively, in that if the fast-break opportunity shows itself, the players are able to take it and exercise their initiative. If it does not show itself they continue in a disciplined pattern.

In order to run an effective fast break, a team has to exert extreme and aggressive defensive pressure—getting into position quickly, forcing the opponents to violation, stealing the ball, etc. The fast break allows for the close-in baskets—the lay-up baskets—cheap baskets compared to the ones that require a lot of work in a pattern.

starting the fast break

There are several ways to start the fast break. To implement a fast offense, possibly the most important thing is to get everyone on a team thinking fast break in the sense of an instantaneous transition from defense to offense. A pressure man-to-man defense lends itself to the starting of an immediate fast break, because all the men are in ready position, on their toes, playing aggressive defense. This makes the mental, as well as the physical, transition to the necessary positions easier. Every man must be thinking fast break at all times. The man must be prepared to give the signal as soon as he gets possession of the ball. Most teams probably use the vocal signal "ball" to indicate to four of the men, who possibly do not see the ball, that one of their teammates has it and they should get into position.

Most of the time, the fast break begins by the rebound being taken off the defensive board, and its success depends on how quickly the rebound can be cleared out. To execute a successful fast break it is necessary to have good positioning on the defensive backboard. The men have to be certain of their responsibilities.

Before the game, the forwards should be told whether they are to go to the board strong to acquire the rebound, box and hold the man off the board without going for the rebound, or box and then go to the basket. The primary rebounder, perhaps the center, should also have explicit instructions. The chances are that he would be given the responsibility of making an attempt at the rebound almost every time, rather than boxing out his own man, assuming that he has the inside position and the quickness to get to the board before his defender.

The two outside men should also be given alternatives, depending on who they are guarding and what the men are doing. If one of the guards is guarding a good backcourt rebounder who is in the habit of going to the basket, the coach may want the guard to box him out before clearing to the outlet area. Alternatively, he may allow the man to break to his basket to be ready for a long pass, knowing that the big men on his own team are closer to the basket and probably will get the rebound most of the time. The coach may prefer a third alternative—having the guards position themselves on a seventeen- or eighteen-foot radius of the basket. If the ball is tapped out, they have a good opportunity to gain control of the ball, because they are inside the opponent's small men and quicker than their big men. The middle man should be told to get to the side of the floor that the rebound will probably come off to.

When the defensive rebound is acquired, it is important for the rebounder to signal as quickly as possible so the other four men know he has possession of the ball. He must guard against making the signal before he has possession. If he anticipates possession and hollers "ball," four men abandon their rebounding and defensive responsibilities and start downfloor, while the offensive rebounder gets the ball or keeps it in play.

Of course, there is a split second to be gained on the fast break if players can react as soon as they are certain that a man on their team will get possession of the ball. Such knowledge comes with timing and getting accustomed to each other—knowing, for instance, who the primary rebounder is. If the best rebounder is going up clearly for a rebound with no aggressive pressure on his back, this might allow a wing man or even a guard to start down on the break. However, it is important that they do not leave too soon.

Ideally, the rebounder should release the ball to the outlet before he has even hit the ground. However, this may be too advanced for boys on a college level and certainly at a high school level. Once the rebounder has the ball, he must try to pivot to his outside, on the same side the rebound came off on, in order to make the outlet pass. Assuming that he'll be one of the bigger men, he should raise the ball over his head as quickly as possible to eliminate the possibility of a guard stealing or deflecting it. He doesn't necessarily look for the middle man. He looks for the man he can clear the ball to, because this move is the one that starts a successful fast break.

Whenever possible, the middle man should receive the outlet pass. The middle man and the primary rebounder must establish such a rapport they will be able to anticipate each other's reactions without an actual signal, thus increasing the speed and effectiveness of the fast break. If the middle man does not have to box out when the ball goes up, he should try to position himself on the side where the rebound comes off, get out to the side where he is clear of pressure, and make his position known by vocal signals or hand signals. If he can do this and receive the outlet pass, he can assume the middle position immediately, saving a little time and the necessity for an additional pass. If the outlet pass comes to a guard the coach does not want in the middle, that guard will have to make a second pass to the opposite guard designated to be in the middle.

The longer the rebounder holds the ball the less chance the break has of being successful, or even starting. If he is getting a sense of pressure on the outside, it might be necessary for him to take one dribble to clear himself. He should never dribble unless it is an extreme situation. If the ball is stolen here, close to the dribbler's own basket, it usually results in an easy two points for the opponent. He should protect the ball rather than dribble. If it is necessary, however, the player can protect the ball along the baseline

Rebounder, still in air, looks for outlet pass to start fast break.

side, take one dribble, and clear himself of the pressure. If he is being overplayed to that side to the point where a dribble will not do the job, he may pivot to the middle, still trying to make his outlet pass to the same side as the rebound came off. (We do not, except in rare instances, advocate clearing the ball up the middle of the floor, because the retreating defensive men usually position themselves up the middle.)

The pass must be made aggressively; it should not be a lob pass, since that pass gives the defense time to move in to steal or deflect it. When the player turns outside or inside to get the ball to the outlet man on the same side, he must be aware of the defensive alignment. If the outlet man is under excessive pressure, the player with the ball may reverse his position in a back door move. The outlet man must be prepared to adjust to this maneuver.

The primary responsibility of the player is to start the fast break without throwing the ball away. If he is going to sacrifice safety for the sake of starting the break a little more quickly, he is better off not starting the break.

The fast break can also be started from interceptions of one kind or another and from violations. In the case of a violation, the official handles the ball, which may slow down the start of the break. However, there is still an advantage to be gained if a violation is called. The new offensive team may get over to the sidelines or jump on the ball so that they can get it into the hands of the official, get it back as quickly as possible, and take advantage of the fast break before the defense sets up. Knowing that the official must handle the ball, the opponents may not get back on the defense as quickly as they should.

Another way to start a fast break is from an out-of-bounds play. After a basket, the coach may assign the closest man or specific men to take the ball out-of-bounds as quickly as possible. Occasionally a coach will prefer not to have certain men take the ball out-of-bounds at any time.

Middle man penetrating under control, moving defense to their right to feed his right wing man. Both wings are wide in full stride, turned to ball.

After a foul shot is a fourth time to start a fast break. Certain teams are primarily geared to develop a play, and there is an advantage to be gained in starting it off a foul shot rather than off a basket, since the men can be positioned advantageously on a foul shot.

A fast break can also start from a fumbled ball, a bad pass, a loose ball, an interception, a jump-ball and a missed or made free-throw.

passes used

The length of the pass and the type of pass that will be used to clear the rebound to the outlet man will depend on the defensive pressure on the rebounder and the middle man. If the pressure on a rebounder is negligible, he can use either the two-hand-over-the-head snap pass or the one-hand baseball pass. The first is the safest, quickest pass. It is the most common pass in a fast-break situation, since the guards or the outlet men are usually no more than fifteen to eighteen feet away from the rebounder at the time of the rebound. As the player gets the rebound, the ball is almost always over his head, since his arms are completely extended. As he comes down, he just has to pivot and release the ball.

Opportunity to use the baseball pass does not present itself often. There are relatively few players who throw that pass accurately, but when a player does have good control of it he can throw the ball harder and farther, and the farther he can throw it the quicker he can start the fast break. He can throw to an outlet man downcourt, perhaps at the half-court line. If the passer must rely on a two-hand overhead pass, the outlet man would normally have to retreat and come much closer.

To make the baseball pass, the player has to get the ball in position and wind up. While he is winding up two things happen: (1) the man closest to him has an opportunity to adjust and perhaps deflect the pass and (2) the time it takes him to get the arm back enables the defensive men to get in defensive position on him and on the receiver. The rebound is valueless if the pass to the outlet man is not a good pass. If the outlet man is under pressure, the pass must be on the outside shoulder away from the pressure. If he is not under pressure, it should be a lead pass that will get the outlet man started in the direction downfloor that he must take in order to start the fast break a bit more quickly. If he has to come back for the pass, or if he has to stand momentarily and wait for the pass to get to him, it will delay the play.

moving downfloor

There are conflicting theories on the best way to handle a fast break. Some coaches believe that the ball can move downfloor more quickly if it is passed back and forth from the center to the lanes. Advocates of this technique feel that, in a standard three-on-two fast-break situation, it is more difficult for the two defense men to adjust their position if the ball is moving quickly from middle to lane than if it is moving down the middle. However, the ball must be passed back and forth to men running at top speed, and the lane men are very often big men who are not as agile as the middle men and tend to be a little more clumsy with the ball. They would have to make two or three perfect passes to the inside, leading the man and being careful of the defense.

We advocate that the middle man keep the ball. When he gets the ball in the center position and starts downfloor he maintains possession of the ball (in theory) all the way to the opposite foul line and makes the play. The ball is in the hands of the best ball handler, who can advance it downfloor as quickly as if it were being passed back and forth. No time is lost in starting the break as a result of this. However, if seconds were lost, it would be preferable to pay that penalty rather than running in a helter-skelter fashion or taking the increased possibility of throwing the ball away.

The middle position is the most critical position on the fast break, since the middle man develops the play, brings the ball downfloor, and decides what has to be done with it when it gets into the penetrating area. The lanemen simply have to get downfloor as quickly as they can in the most advantageous positions, depending on the defensive deployment. The wing men must get downfloor to the basket as quickly as possible, not waiting for the ball. If the middle man is going to release the ball early, it is his responsibilty to make sure that the ball gets to them. They should get a step or two in front of their defensive man or

Rebounder finding middle man in center court.

lag a bit behind, so that they will be open for a pass. The trailer man must also beat his man down the floor. The fifth man down floor will be several seconds behind the play. If a shot is taken and missed by either the wing or the trailer, he may be in an excellent position to knife through the middle and make a rebounding shot. If the opponents have regained possession of the ball, he must realize that he is the first man that must get back on defense and do so as quickly as possible. By placing men— not merely allowing the closest man to take the middle position—you cut down the margin of error, since you always have the ball in the hands of the best ball-handler.

Once the middle man gets the ball in a center position, he maintains control of the ball with a dribble all the way down the floor until he gets into penetrating area, at which time he must decide what he should do with it—whether to continue on to the basket or whether to throw to the lane man. The pass he makes must, in theory, lead directly to the score. If he passes to either of the lane positions or to a trailer position, he must try to make the play so that the man who receives the ball does not have to put the ball to the floor before the shot is taken. If a big man is in the lane position or in the trailer position, giving him the ball a bit too early and forcing him to take even one dribble increases the margin of error. The entire thinking on the fast break should be geared to cutting down errors or the opportunity for errors whenever possible.

Players must get the ball to the middle man behind the mid-court line as quickly as possible. If the middle man is the man who receives the outlet pass, he simply dribbles into the middle taking the pass to the middle of the court, depending on his defensive pressure. If he is not the man who receives the outlet, he must come to the ball, as

Middle man moves defender to his left, opening his left wing man.

171

quickly as possible, determined by where the defense is stationed. If there is a defensive man between him and the ball he has to move laterally toward the other guard, who has received the outlet pass, staying between the guard and the ball so there is no question of an interception. If there is no defensive pressure and the defensive men are getting back downcourt quickly, he can move in a more diagonal path downcourt. Thus he can receive the secondary pass or the pass into the middle so that it always leads him into a position where he doesn't have to be concerned about defensive pressure or anyone stealing the ball. He is the one, once the first outlet pass has been made, who is going to make or break the fast break.

An alert middle man must be aware of who the lane men are, who his trailer man is, if possible, and what the defensive deployment in front of him is in order to be able to develop the play properly. As he approaches the head of the offensve key and the beginning of penetrating area, he must be under complete control, thinking about how he is going to develop the break, how he is going to move the defense, and what lane he is going to go to with the pass. If a slower defensive man has taken a position against him in a three-on-two situation and is attempting to delay the advancement of the ball, the middle man can usually get around him very quickly. If they are matched off or the opponent is quicker, the middle man should release the ball to one of the wing men, even at a half-court position, thus developing a two-on-one situation by taking himself more or less out of the play rather than delaying the continuation of the fast break.

He should also consider getting the ball up a bit earlier if the wing man who is the best shooter has a step or two on his defender, and if a lay-up situation can develop before he reaches the foul-line area. The middle man's tactic when he reaches the foul line will depend on the defensive align-

Middle man tactic. In three-on-two he moves defense to his left.

172

ment and adjustment. He may stop his dribble completely and pass to either wing. Alternatively, he may simply stop his progress at the line, maintaining his dribble, and concentrate his attention on either wing, so that the defensive men fall back on the wings. He can then continue to the basket. He must be concerned with finishing off the break with perfect execution—going to the correct lane man or the trailer, depending on how he has moved the defense, and making the pass that leads directly to the score. If he has moved the defense properly and done his faking, he can make the pass so that the lane man or the trailer simply finishes his movement with a step up to the basket in lay-up fashion. (He must try to give the ball to the wing man who is the stronger driver, preferably a forward, since he would be taller than the guard.)

middle man's tactics

There are a number of alternatives open to the middle man when he reaches a position within a radius of about fifteen feet from the basket. In unbalanced situations, he may, depending on the defensive adjustment, continue to the basket himself for a shot, pass to his right wing or his left wing in the classic three-on-two situation, or execute a trailer play if the trailer man (usually a big man) is in position. If the defense is balanced off, he again has the option of trying to effect the shot by passing to either wing and screening for the opposite wing, or taking the ball in himself to either wing and simply setting a lateral screen for a short jumper over the screen.

In theory, if an overbalanced situation is present at the end of the court the middle man, a wing man, or the trailer should be able to make a driving lay-up; the latter two without dribbling. Actually, this result will depend on two factors:

He passes to right wing.

Middle man tactic continued.

Split of defenders when they fall off to wing men.

Fake to right wing.

As defender falls back, middle man has shot at foul line.

Ball is in penetrating area.

Back defender does not move with pass to right wing.

Right wing has short jumper (middle man now open at foul line).

Fast break trailer play, flip pass.

176

1. The middle man's timing in moving the defense and releasing the ball must be such that the receiver never has to dribble.

2. Once the receiver (a wing man) gets the ball, he must continue directly to the basket. If the low defensive man on that side picks him up, he may have to pass back to the middle man, who must remain at the foul line for this purpose. If the wing man drives for a basket himself, in spite of the guard, he may make a three-point play.

When the overbalance situation is not present, the middle man must immediately take alternative steps to effect a shot, without slowing down the fast-break momentum. He should go into the three-on-three or the two-on-two situation, either screening for a teammate or passing to one wing and screening for the opposite wing. The third alternative, the trailer play, is normally initiated by one of the two forwards or the center who is not involved in the initial fast break. He beats his man down the floor, alerting the middle man to his presence by calling out "right" or "left," indicating the side to which he is coming. This is an excellent alternative to exercise if your middle man is mobile. The middle man moves the defense to one side so that the trailer can come through. If the ball is given to the trailer at the proper time, it is almost impossible for the defense to adjust back in time to stop him. A three-point play will probably result.

Trailer play. Pivot and two-hand underhand pass.

If the middle man cannot make the play himself when he hears the trailer's call, he may pass to the opposite wing man and clear to the other side; in theory, opening up the middle. The wing man must then pass to the trailer. The problem with this alternative is that it necessitates two passes, raising the margin of error. We would prefer that the middle man keep the ball, knife off to his right or left as he reaches the middle, hopefully drawing the defensive man with him, and pass off to the trailer. The pass would be either a backward flip as he veers to the side without turning to look at the trailer, or a two hand underhand pass after he pivots quickly and protectively back to the middle.

Coaches differ in their beliefs on what the wing men should do if they reach the basket area and have not received a pass from the middle man. Some coaches have the men go completely under the basket; others have them step aside. We advocate, buttonhooking and coming back to the ball, in case the middle man has been delayed or prevented from making the pass. However, if the trailer is following the wing man in, the wing man should not buttonhook back. He must continue under the basket to the opposite side in order to lure his guard along with him, leaving the lane wide open for the trailer. If the guard does not go with him, this wing man will be free under. The opposite wing man must be mentally alert for this alternative and decoy his defender. If the defender retreats, the opposite wing man may stop quickly, opening himself for a short jumper.

The middle man may have to waste some time around the middle area if one wing is a little behind the other. He should use lateral movement and a lot of movement towards the basket to make the defense think he is going into the basket himself, so that the pass to the wing will be more effective.

He should also attempt to pass whenever possible with the outside hand. If the passer is right handed and he wishes to go to his left lane, he is going to be passing across the defender if he uses his right hand. To cut down the chances of a deflection or an interception, he should strengthen his other hand. If he doesn't have the power in his left hand to make this play, he must use a two-handed pass and step towards the receiver, keeping his body between the defender and the ball. When the middle man gets in the fifteen foot area, the best pass to use ninety percent of the time is the bounce pass, because an aggressive bounce pass is almost impossible to intercept; even if it is deflected, it can get through the hands of a deflector and still reach its target. If the wing man cannot take the shot himself, he should pass back to the middle man, not to the opposite wing. The wing man may seem to be clear, but his defender has only about eight to ten feet to get back into position to deflect or intercept the ball.

two-on-one and five-on-four situations

We have explained the principles of the classic three-on-two and trailer (four-on-three) situations that develop most of the time in a fast break. Most of these principles apply in a two-on-one situation. It is obviously a more simplified situation. The two offensive men must keep spread as much as much as possible in the front court while moving in to the basket. We do not advocate passing the ball back and forth. If the ball is in the hands of a guard, he should drive into the basket, looking for the lay-up shot and forcing the

Trailer following right wing man.

Right wing man takes defender through.

Trailer open right. If defender stays, right wing man opens under.

179

lone defender to jump to try to block the anticipated shot. He must be sure to dribble all the way into the basket. If he stops prematurely, he will not force the defender to commit himself, and that commitment is essential. If the driver feels he has the advantage when the defender jumps, he can attempt the lay-up. If not, he can drop the ball back down to the remaining man.

The five-on-four situation is really a trailer situation in that the fifth man must hang on the periphery of the action, possibly fifteen or so feet from the basket on the side away from the trailer, where he can receive a pass if his defensive

Three-on-three. No fast break advantage.

Middle man dribble-screens for left wing.

Left wing cuts off middle man for jump shot or drive.

man switches to the trailer. If he draws his defensive man with him, the trailer man will be clear for a pass. Depending on the reaction of the defensive man, the middle man can pass to the trailer or the fourth man.

falling back on a pattern offense

The following three-on-three situation was developed in case a fast break does not show or the third defensive man gets back in position. Use a simple pass-and-pick away movement by the middle man. It's purpose is to free the opposite wing man for a short jump shot with an option of

Three-on-three. Middle man passes left.

Middle man screens right.

Left wing passes to cutter.

a pass to the screener, depending on the defensive adjustment. But even if the break reaches the penetration and the defense has evened off in a two-on-two or three-on-three or four-on-four situation, the offense should carry it one step further and look for the short fifteen-foot jump shot rather than kicking it back out and starting a set pattern all over again. This action takes advantage of the fact that the offensive players have gotten downfloor first, before the defense has completely set.

No team can depend on a fast break exclusively, so it must have a pattern it can fall back into, whether it is two-one-two or three-two or two-three. However, in some games the fast break can be used almost exclusively.

combating a fast break

There are two choices open to the coach in combating an effective fast-breaking unit. One would be to sustain as much pressure on the offensive board as possible, thereby delaying the defensive rebound and the outlet pass and subsequently the fast break. In that case he has to hold two or three men under the offensive board. The alternative is to concede the offensive rebound and tell the men to drop back as quickly as possible in order to assume a defensive posture or delay or stop the fast break.

fast-break drills

The following drills are fundamental drills in incorporating the fast break into a team offense. We feel that the fast break is the most important single offensive attack that a team may have; therefore, players should perfect the fundamentals in early season practice.

A primary drill is a simple rebound drill.

Diag. 5-1, "BALL" DRILL

A rebounder stands on either side of the basket. The coach shoots the ball, and the rebounder who rebounds it calls "ball" as he obtains possession. Calling "ball" to alert teammates is the first fundamental on obtaining the ball off the defensive board. Managers are stationed near the twenty-eight-foot hash marks in outlet position, and the rebounders must look for them and

DIAG. 5-1

make the toss out as quickly as possible in good pass form, using a two-hand overhead, hook, or baseball pass. After the pass, rebounders should change positions. At first no opposition should be on the court. However, once rebounders are used to calling "ball," a defender should be put on the back of each rebounder to make the drill more realistic.

Diag. 5-2, BASIC THREE-ON-TWO DRILL

This is one of the most important drills in teaching the fast break. One coach stands near the head of the circle at one end and another coach stands on the side of the court at the far end, at the foul line extended. Two defenders, X_1 and X_2, position at the far end. At the near end are two rebounders, R_1 and R_2, and an outlet man, O_1. The coach shoots and the player who rebounds calls "ball." The outlet man goes to the side of the court the rebounder is on, as close to the hash mark as he can get. He is always coming from behind the rebounder, therefore the rebounder has to pick him up visually before he can make the outlet pass. He must *see* him before he throws, he cannot throw to a voice. O_1, the middle man on the break, after receiving the outlet pass dribbles toward the center circle as R_1 and R_2 fill in the wing lanes, running in a straight line. The dribbler should use a high dribble as long as he does not meet any opposition. Occasionally, X_1 should dart out to challenge O_1. When O_1 comes into penetrating area near the top of the key, he must control his dribble and be under complete control himself. He should move the defenders, X_1 and X_2, so that he may pass off to either R_1 or R_2 without the receiver having to make another pass or dribble.

Initially this drill is used with just the three attackers against the two defenders. After the players become familiar with the movements, the coach at the defensive end adds a third defensive player. When he is added, the three fast break men must immediately recognize that the defense is matched man-to-man and can play a man-to-man defense. At this time the middle man must make a two-on-two or three-on-three play, either dribble in and screen for either side man, or pass to his left and screen to his right. He should not wait until the other two offensive players and the other two defenders can get into the play.

The third defensive man should be sent in before O_1 approaches the head of the free-throw circle so that all offensive players may recognize that they are matched defensively and will go into some type of simple play pattern. It is much easier to get a good shot under three-on-three half-court conditions than it is when the defense is back and balanced in the five-on-five situation.

The coach at the initiating end will occasionally add a fourth man as a trailer during this three-on-three situation, calling a player by name from the group underneath the basket or the group on the side. Since the trailer comes up completely blind on the middle man, the trailer must give O_1 a verbal signal so that he can move the defenders to give the trailer a clear shot to the basket. From this drill, coaches learn which players intuitively know how to move the defensive players to set up the trailer or to pass to a wing man in such a way that they do not have to dribble or make another pass. Occasionally, use all guards at the O_1 position, not only designated middle men. This gives insight into their potential.

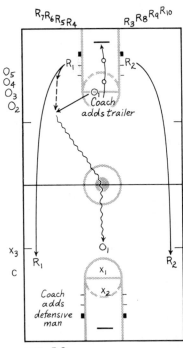

DIAG. 5-2

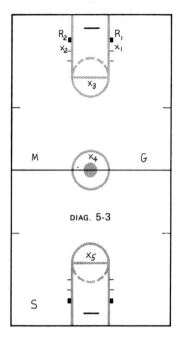

DIAG. 5-3

Diag. 5-3, FAST-BREAK DRILL, FOUL-LINE PLAY

When the opponents are shooting a free-throw the best re-bounder-passer, R_1, should be stationed in the right offensive lane. R_2 the second best rebounder, should be in the left lane. M, the designated middle man, should be at mid-court on the side, opposite R_1. The best-shooting big man, S, should be in the deep corner on the same side as the middle man, and the other guard, G, should be at mid-court.

The purpose of this drill is to initiate a fast break by beating the foul shooter, X_3, downcourt or to obtain a good jump shot for S. As soon as the ball reaches him, he should take any shot that he can take from twenty feet in.

Probably, seventy percent of the shots that the foul shooter takes will go in. Therefore, the first fundamental this drill teaches is quick retrieval of the ball by the best rebounder-passer, stepping out-of-bounds and getting the ball in to M. R_1, as the best passer-rebounder, will be the pass-in man. He must take the ball out-of-bounds, immediately, and throw it in to M, taking into consideration the position of X_4. If X_4 has moved towards M, R_1, who is normally the strongest passer and best long passer, should look for G cutting downcourt and may throw the ball long to him beyond half-court. (If the foul shot is missed and R_1 is the rebounder, he will pivot to the outside and pass immediately up to G.) G looks downcourt for S, who moves to the ball side. G passes to S if he is open. If S is not free, G may assume the middle man's role. However, in most situations M should be given the ball.

We feel that the important ingredients of fast-break basketball are all involved in this foul-line play. Therefore, we teach it as a drill in skeleton form first, later put a defensive team in to passively resist, then put in a team that will actively and aggressively attempt to stop the break.

Diag. 5-4, BOTH-ENDS THREE-TWO DRILL

This is a fairly complicated drill to initiate with the players; but it is such a complete action, rapidly moving drill, we feel that any team—especially one that wishes to incorporate the fast break in its offense—should put it into use as soon as the players can learn it. Players X_1 to X_{16} are placed at six spots around the court: at one end of the court at each foul lane extended; at the hash mark to the right of the first spots, at the far end of the court at both foul lanes extended; and at the hash mark to the right of these foul lanes. X_1, with the ball, X_7, to his right, and X_4, the other under man, step on the court, ready to attack in a three-on-two situation. X_{12} and X_{14} are defenders in tandem position front and back at the far end of the court. X_1 initiates the drill by passing to X_7. X_7 dribbles to the middle as X_1 and X_4 fill the fast-break lanes. X_7 penetrates and attempts to make a scoring pass to X_1 or X_4. Only one shot is allowed. X_1, X_7, and X_4 do not rebound. X_{12} and X_{14} attempt to break up the fast three-on-two break coming at them. If they cannot, they rebound the shot. X_{10}, at their right at the hash mark, steps in bounds. If X_{12} has rebounded, he immediately turns to his outside and pitches to X_{10}, who assumes the middle man's role. If X_{10} observes the rebound going to the opposite side of the court to X_{14}, he must

184

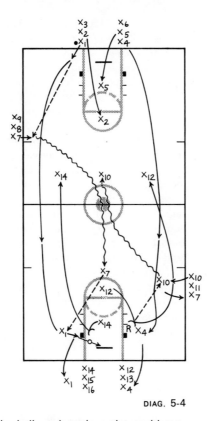

DIAG. 5-4

move cross-court, calling for the ball, and get in outlet position to
receive a pass from X_{14}. X_{10} takes the ball to the middle with rebounders X_{12} and X_{14} filling the wing lanes. The two defenders
waiting are X_2 and X_5, who have stepped in on the court in front
and back tandem position to attempt to stop the fast break. X_{10}
penetrates. X_{14} and X_{12} run their lanes looking for good position to
get a shot. X_2 and X_5 rebound, and X_8, at the right hash mark,
steps inbounds to become the middle man. X_{15} and X_{13} at the far
end have now stepped on the court to defend against this break
with X_8 as a middle man and X_2 and X_5 as the wing men.

This extremely good continuous-motion drill contains all the fundamentals of three-two fast break basketball. Coaches should not
run this drill for more than ten minutes at a stretch. However, it is
especially effective from the seven- to ten-minute mark, when the
players become a little tired as they would late in a game. As this
drill is used periodically in the daily practices during the preseason
and season, the players will be able to sustain themselves longer
and longer.

Preferably the middle men in the fast break should be at the
hash mark position so that they may be the ones who are handling
the middle on the break most frequently in this drill. However, at
times coaches can place the middle men underneath so that they
may have experience playing defense against a three-on-two break.
For a change of pace, they can sometimes allow one of their big
men who fancies himself a ball handler to assume the outlet position and handle the ball coming up the middle. This shows players
that certain players make better middle men than others.

185

Diag. 5-5, ONE-TWO-THREE DRILL

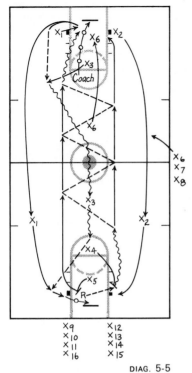

This drill starts at the far end of the court. The coach is in the free-throw circle. X_1 and X_2, the rebounders, and X_3, the middle man, are in the classic triangle rebound position. The coach shoots. X_1 or X_2 rebounds, turns to the outside, and looks for X_3, who must move to the proper side for the outlet pass. When X_3 obtains the ball, he dribbles hard to the middle, with X_1 and X_2 as wing men in the classic three-on-two break. X_4 and X_5 defend against them at the other end as they come downcourt and attempt to score. Only one shot is allowed. X_4 and X_5 rebound. X_6, who is at the right side mid-court area moves onto the court, near the center circle. X_4 and X_5 move up the court with the ball, attempting to score against X_6 in a two-on one posture. After a shot, X_6, X_4 and X_5 stay at that end, returning the ball to the coach. X_4 and X_5 assume the roles of rebounders, and X_6 becomes the middle man, setting up the rebound triangle. X_9 and X_{12} step on court at the other end to act as defenders. The coach again initiates the three-on-two phase of the drill by shooting.

Next to our Both-ends three-two fast-break drill, this is our favorite continuous action drill. Practicing it frequently is extremely beneficial, as it gives big men experience in the two-on-one attacking postures.

types of offenses against man-to-man defense

The following principles must be incorporated into all basic man-to-man offenses, whether they be set pattern or free-lance play. The offense should keep the middle open. If a pivot man is being used, he should play opposite the ball side as much as possible. If a double pivot is being used, cutters should be able to move towards the basket without moving into the pivot area.

installing the offensive system

The offensive system from a set pattern should be installed by diagraming each play on a blackboard, breaking down the options on each play, and explaining them thoroughly. (Each player should be given a copy of the diagram for reference.) The best method is to have a movable blackboard on the court, outlining the play as it unfolds. Then the coach should have five players walk through the set play on the court, without opposition. If necessary, the coach can lead the players through the play initially during this walk-through period. After each aspect of the play has been completely covered, the coach should leave these five players at one end of the court, then walk a second group through the play at the other end. The first group, led by an assistant coach or a captain, should be going through the play pattern slowly as the coach is working with the second group. The coach must insist on correct movement initially, since proper implementation of the play depends

186

on accurate movement and timing. The coach should hold a player if he is going too soon or tap him lightly to start him on his way at the correct juncture.

On the first day that a play pattern is given to a team, the coach should identify it by a number, a name, or a recognizable key signal. He should use this name, number, or key signal repeatedly during his explanation of the play in the walk-through and slow motion period.

On the second day, the coach should repeat the procedure, explaining the play to the assembled squad, outlining it schematically on a blackboard on the court, going over the play repeatedly in the walk-through and slow movement procedures (again doing it at both ends) and at all times referring to the play by name, by number, or by the recognizable key. On the third day the coach should use passive defense against this play pattern. The defensive players should usually be the weaker players on the team and they should be told to maintain passive defensive positions on their men. They should not use their hands and they should not switch. It is imperative that the team gain confidence in the play, therefore, coaches should not defense their offense out of existence early in practice. Aggressive defense may make the players lose confidence in the play.

The fourth day the players should move more aggressively. Timing should be checked as the pattern movement speeds up, and constant constructive criticism should be offered. Once the players understand the play and the options completely, the coach should break the play down into its fundamental ingredients, for drilling. (Of course, the coach will probably inaugurate other play patterns periodically during these four days.)

Offense teams should have the proper deployment, or spread, against man-to-man defense. First, try to beat the opponent's weakest player one-on-one. Second, if the opponents adjust defensively to help this weaker defender, work through the weakened area after a feint towards the weak defender. Third, use inside screens to cut men free for a close-in shot, screening away from the ball or at the ball. Fourth, use beat-the-switch tactics and offensive rolls to negate the effectiveness of switches. Fifth, use outside screens in the set shot area, to obtain good shots for percentage shooters, especially against teams which use sloughing or sagging principles in their man-to-man defense.

The following are suggestions for offensive players in specific situations.

When played against an opponent who is playing closely man-to-man, run your opponent into your teammates or his teammates. You can screen effectively away from the ball while being played closely, as your guard usually concentrates on you so completely that he abandons team

187

defensive principles—for example, he may neglect the switch or he may neglect to drop off from the weak side to help teammates.

When playing against a team that jump switches, the passer-off should cut directly to the basket as soon as he hands off. The receiver should anticipate the jump switch and stop immediately on receiving the ball, remaining alive, alert for possible double-team situations, and in a position to return the ball immediately to the teammate who passed it to him if he's free on his cut to the basket. If the receiver cannot pass back to his teammate, he should reverse pivot when the jump switch is used and dribble away from the jump switch towards his original direction.

When playing against a defensive opponent who uses floating or sagging tactics, dropping back to the basket at all opportunities, look for medium shots that are in a high-percentage area to keep him close to you. Try to divert his attention from the focal point, and look for lateral screens from teammates away from the ball. If the defender is a long way off, walk into him towards the screener. If he doesn't move, use a change of direction or pace as you approach him and cut tight off the screen to open yourself near the ball. If he retreats, continue to take him in closer. If there is no screen, a quick fake towards the basket and a quick step back will open you for a short or medium shot.

If your team is using a pivot offense and the pivot player is being fronted, teammates should clear the weak side. This action increases the possibility and effectiveness of a lob pass by taking a possible floating defender away from the area of defensive help. If the closest defender insists on staying in the double-team area to prevent the effectiveness of a lob pass to a pivot, the weak side offensive player clearing should go immediately to the best intermediate shooting area. He'll get an easy shot, or he can pass in to the fronted pivot player himself if his defender leaves the pivot area and moves towards him.

All pivot players must be able to use evasive tactics in moving towards the ball, and the passer-in should be able to tell the offensive pivot player the location of his guard by passing to the hand farthest from this defender.

Every offensive pattern used against man-to-man defense must spread the offense to spread the defense. Such spreading can be effected first, by use of screens; second, by movement without the ball away from the ball; and third, by good passing and ball handling. The passer must always see the guard of the man he passes to, see options for the man he's passing to, and know the limitations of the man he's passing to. If the potential receiver is a good shooter who normally looks for shots when he receives the ball, the passer shouldn't pass to him unless there is a good shooting opportunity. If the player is a poor ball handler on

188

low passes, don't bounce pass to him. If he's a poor dribbler and must dribble more than one bounce in order to obtain a favorable offensive position, hold the pass.

We will discuss play situations and set patterns from six types of offensive systems:

1. A single-pivot type of offense in which there are two guards out front (normally the ball handlers), two forwards, and a strong, big pivot man who takes care of the pivot area. In a second single-pivot-type of offense, the pivot man is used as a screener. A third uses a basic screening figure eight movement between the three inside players who are fairly agile, big men, none of whom have more outstanding pivotability than another. This offense keeps the three big men in close to the basket and allows a good offense rebounding potential.

2. A double-pivot type of offense, either from the one-three-one structure or the three-two structure. In the one-three-one structure, one pivot player (the better ball-handler) would always be in the high position or middle position, while the less agile pivot or the better rebounder would be the low man under the basket. In the three-two structure, a continuity pattern with the two pivot men starting from a medium post position will be shown.

3. A basic type of free-lance offense, first from the three-two structure with three men out front and two men wide underneath, second from a two-one-two structure with two guards out front ball handling—two agile forwards in the corners, and an agile pivot man who can move from low to medium to high position at random.

4. An overload, in which four players on the same side of the court make use of a continuity type of movement, or shuffle.

5. A basic stack offense in which four offensive players are placed within ten feet of the basket, two along each of the foul lanes facing each other. This is an excellent offense for cutting down the number of bad passes, in keeping with the margin of error theory.

6. Specially designed offenses that show the latitude that the thinking coach may have in designing an offense to fit his personnel.

Following are basic rules for running plays from all offensive formations.

1. Fake the first pass to check and hold the defense.

2. Pass to the man on his outside shoulder, away from his defender. The man receiving the pass should meet and protect the ball.

3. Cut to basket sharply, leaving no daylight if using a screen.

play situations and set patterns from man-to-man offensive systems

189

4. Unless the coach gives orders to the contrary, set the screen facing the basket whenever possible.

5. Proper timing in running plays is the key to successful execution.

6. When making the pass or using a screen and receiving the ball, always keep yourself alive by maintaining your dribble.

7. The men not involved directly in the play should continue movement. (For example, exchange positions to discourage floating by defense.)

8. If defense overplays the switches, be prepared to exercise play options immediately.

9. Utilize a change of pace, whenever the man is cutting without the ball.

single-pivot attack

A single-pivot attack may be the type in which one player in a two-three offense is designated as the pivot man primarily. This player should be a tall, strong, mobile player who can get good pivot position. He must move in an area from the basket to sixteen feet away, constantly maneuvering for position to his advantage, breaking from a low or away position to meet the ball.

If a pivot man is to be interchangeable with the forwards, normally he will be used to screen away, setting screens opposite, rebounding, and cutting at times off a low or opposite screen set by a fellow forward. The evasive moves of the player in the single-pivot position are of prime importance. He must be able to pivot away when closely guarded, reach the designated position at the correct time, break away from the ball position and cut back, keep the defender on his back as the ball changes from one side to the other, turn the defenders away from the position of the ball by using all possible evasive tactics, and have a variety of shots from the inside position. The pivot player must realize that it's very difficult to get the ball into him when he's in a low pivot position, but if he can get the ball he must score himself, since it is hard to cut off a low pivot player towards the basket. Cuts from away from the ball are good moves when the ball is in this position.

The pivot player must be able to protect the ball, keeping the basket area clear and staying on the side away from the ball initially so that cutting players can take advantage of the middle. He should never dribble more than one or two bounces, unless he is forced to dribble out away from the basket in a protective position. He must always be in good offensive rebound position, being able to roll off opponents, spin, slide, or exert pressure, without letting the opponent feel his position. He is used as a screen frequently, and he is always the key rebounder offensively.

190

Diag. 5-6, SINGLE PIVOT, TWO-THREE ALIGNMENT, PLAY NUMBER 1

A and B, the guards, have brought the ball into attack position at approximately even with the hash marks on the side of the court and just to the outside of the foul lanes. D and E, the forwards, are even with the second foul-lane marker (the first lane marker after the buffer zone), a little wider than the guards. The center, C, started in a low-pivot position, opposite the ball position. The possible plays in single pivot, two-three alignment, will each have a number. The key ball handler initiates a play by calling the number or by making a finger signal. As C, the pivot man, moves up to the high pivot, B passes to him and follows his pass, setting a double-screen at the foul line with C at the side to which he passed. A fakes a movement down the left sideline and cuts sharply behind the double screen set on the foul line by B and C. As B makes the pass, E, the forward on the same side, clears to the opposite side, opening the whole right corner of the court. C has the option of giving the ball to A for an eighteen-foot jump shot over the double screen set by C and B or passing it to A on a tight cut to the basket. D, the weak-side forward, sets a screen on that side for E. A has the option of taking the shot or continuing on to the basket with the ball. The rebounders would be D on the strong side, C in the middle (if A continues to the basket), A on the right side. E, the intermediate rebounder will move back toward B, the deep defender, as soon as A shoots or goes by. If A takes a jump shot, the rebounding would be done by D on the left, C on the right and E in the middle, with A the intermediate rebounder.

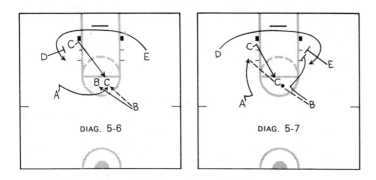

DIAG. 5-6   DIAG. 5-7

Diag. 5-7, PLAY NUMBER 2

This play is a direct follow-up to Play Number 1. The play starts in basically the same fashion with B passing the ball into C, who has moved up after a preliminary fake. A makes the same basic move, faking away and then heading towards C's position. D, the corner man, opposite the original ball position, clears. A fakes his movement towards C and changes direction towards the basket, receiving a pass. B, after faking towards C, moves to his right, and sets up a double screen with E along the right foul lane. D circles behind the double screen. The rebounding would be done by A on the left, C in the middle, E on the right, and D in the intermediate position. B would come back quickly if A shoots or after D shoots over the double screen.

191

Diag. 5-8, PLAY NUMBER 3

B passes into C, coming high. E clears the right side, B fakes toward C and reverses towards the basket to receive a pass from C. A, after faking in, sets a double screen on the left side of the foul lane with D. E circles behind this double screen. Rebounders would be D on the left, C in the middle, B on the right, and E in intermediate position. After a shot, A retreats quickly to a safety position.

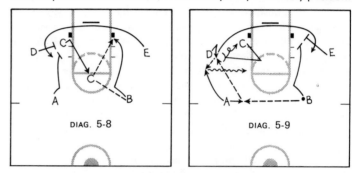

DIAG. 5-8   DIAG. 5-9

Diag. 5-9, PLAY NUMBER 4

With all players in their basic starting positions, B passes to A. A moves to meet the pass. D fakes to the baseline and moves out to get the pass. A passes to D. C starts towards the foul line area and reverses direction towards the ball. A cuts behind D for a return pass. After D returns the pass, he clears to the baseline under the basket. C sets a rear screen for A. A dribbles off the rear screen towards the center. C uses an offensive roll into the basket from the left side. A has the option of driving into the basket, stopping for a medium-jump shot, passing to C on his offensive roll, or passing to D, who has circled under the basket and come behind a double screen on the right foul lane, set by E and B. If any shot is taken, C will rebound the left side, E will rebound the right side, D will rebound the middle, A will be the intermediate rebounder, and B will retreat into a safety position.

Diag. 5-10, PLAY NUMBER 4

(An option of Play 4 in Diag. 5-9.) A receives the pass from B and passes to D after D's fake. A clears through, indicating to D that he will be able to use C's screen. C sets a rear screen for D. D dribbles off and has the same options as A in the previous play. C rolls to the basket. A goes behind the double screen set on the right foul lane by E and B. C again rebounds the left, E rebounds the right, D rebounds the middle, B is the intermediate rebounder, and A retreats for defensive purposes.

DIAG. 5-10

Diag. 5-11, PLAY NUMBER 40 OR 41

Guard B has the ball before the preliminary movement. On observing the defensive stature of the man guarding E, B has two options. After a pass to E, he may cut to E's inside between E and his defender to receive an inside hand off or he may cut outside E and receive an outside hand off. (40 is outside, 41 is inside.) He can then dribble into the basket for a shot. The rebounders would be C in the middle, D on the left, E, the intermediate position and B on the right. If B's shot is not a driving lay-up, E would rebound the right, and B would be the intermediate rebounder with A moving back on defense.

DIAG. 5-11   DIAG. 5-12

Diag. 5-12, PLAY NUMBER 5

B passes to E and fakes to the center. C starts up from the low side opposite the ball and reverses direction to a medium pivot. E passes to C, follows his pass, and sets a screen just above the foul line on the right side of the circle. B reverses, cuts off the screens set by E and C and receives a pass from C. He may take a short jump shot or drive into the basket. D and A deploy their men away from the point of attack. D rebounds the left side, C the center, and B the right. E is the intermediate rebounder, and A falls back.

Diag. 5-13, PLAY NUMBER 6

B passes to C moving into the high-pivot position. B moves as though to set a foul-line double screen. E clears. A fakes and deploys to his right. C has the option of turning and taking a jump shot or turning to the open side and driving into the basket with his man guarding him one-on-one. D moves in, and he and B set a double screen on the left side for E, who is circling around. C has the option of passing to E if his movement towards the basket is stopped. For rebounding, C is on the right side, D on the left side, E in the middle, and B in the intermediate position. A moves back on defense.

DIAG. 5-13

Diag. 5-14, PLAY NUMBER 7

C moves up into high-pivot position and receives a pass from B. B fakes towards C and deploys to his right. E fakes and deploys to the baseline, keeping his man occupied. A fakes towards the ball and moves in to a low screening position. C fakes and dribbles to the offensive left, setting up a double screen for D on that side. D fakes towards the baseline and comes back off the double screen. C, after his screen, makes an offensive roll to the basket from the left side. D has the option of shooting, driving, or passing to C. C rebounds the left side, E the right side, and D the middle. A is the intermediate rebounder, and B falls back on defense.

DIAG. 5-14

Diag. 5-15, PLAY NUMBER 8

B passes to A. A starts as though to dribble into the middle, changing direction to the left. C cuts through. C starts from the low position, opposite, towards the high pivot and reverses. D fakes and C and D set a low double screen for B. A passes to B behind the double screen. B has the option of a drive or jump shot. E moves into the middle to deploy his man and to be open if his man sags towards the ball. A drops back on defense. D will rebound the left, C will rebound on the right, E will rebound the middle, and B is the intermediate rebounder.

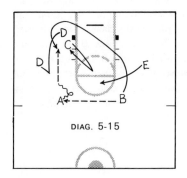

DIAG. 5-15

The following series of plays involves a figure eight movement, under the basket from a two-three alignment. No name or number has to be called to initiate a play in this series. Each play is predetermined by the offensive team, and it is initiated by the movement of the guard with the ball (B in these diagrams).

194

Diag. 5-16, BASIC PATTERN

B passes to E, the forward. E should fake to the basket and come back to receive the pass. B cuts outside E. C sets a rear screen away from the ball for D. D fakes to the baseline and cuts off C's screen. E has the option of passing to D on the cut, passing to C if there is a switch, passing back to B in the corner, or passing to A, moving across, out front.

DIAG. 5-16

Diag. 5-17

(This is a continuation of Diag. 5-16.) E passes back to A, who dribbles the ball towards C, the original low-pivot man. C has moved out to receive the pass after screening for D. A cuts to the outside into the corner. C has moved from the opposite corner back towards the outside. D sets a rear screen away from the ball for E. E may cut to the ball. In this diagram, E has run into the screen, and as the men have fallen off, he has dropped back. C may pass across the court to E. In Diags. 5-16 and 5-17, C, D, and E are the rebound triangle under the basket taking the position nearest their placement on the court. The guard in the corner is the intermediate rebounder, and the back guard is the safety man.

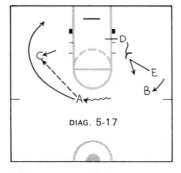

DIAG. 5-17

Diag. 5-18

B passes to E, then sets an inside screen. E dribbles off B's screen, and B rolls to the basket. E has the option of driving to the basket; shooting a medium jump shot; passing to B on the roll; passing to D, who has cut off C's position; or passing back out to A.

DIAG. 5-18

195

Diag. 5-19

B passes to E and signals the initiation of the offense by moving into the outer half of the free throw circle. C moves from his low position, opposite, to a medium pivot on the ball side. E passes to C. A cuts off a screen set by B and follows E to the outside as E cuts over the ball position to the inside. D deploys his man away from the point of attack. The rebounding would be done by D on the left side, E, in the middle, C in the intermediate position, and A (if he's the shooter) on the right. B falls back on defense.

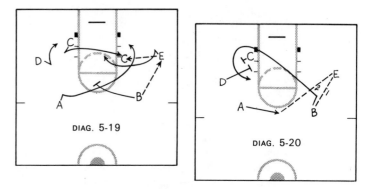

DIAG. 5-19

DIAG. 5-20

Diag. 5-20

B passes to E, takes one step towards the pass, and cuts diagonally across the court, his movement signalling the play. A moves to the head of the key. C and D set a double screen away from the ball, and B cuts around it. E makes a pass to A at the head of the key. A looks for B coming around the double screen. If there is a switch, D can roll to the basket. Rebounding positions are C on the left, E on the right, and D in the middle, with B the intermediate rebounder. A plays defense.

Diag. 5-21

B passes to A and holds position. Holding position is the signal for the play. A passes to D, then moves diagonally to the opposite foul lane area. B moves as A moves to set a double screen for E. E cuts off the double screen, and C deploys his man away from the foul lane area. D may pass to E or to B who has rolled back towards the ball into the foul line area. A retreats as a defensive safety factor. B, C, D, and E rebound the offensive board with B in the intermediate position.

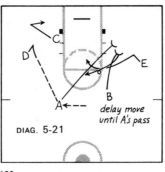

delay move
until A's pass

DIAG. 5-21

Diag. 5-22

B passes to A and cuts behind A to receive a return pass. As A returns the pass, D moves in and sets a screen for C. C rolls around the screen to the basket. A cuts diagonally and sets a screen for E, who fakes away and then cuts back over the screen. The timing is such that B's first option is to pass to C or (if C is not open) to pass to D on his roll to the ball. B's second option is to pass to E or (if E is not open) to pass to A on his roll back. B will retreat for defensive purposes while A, C, D, and E rebound with A as the intermediate rebounder.

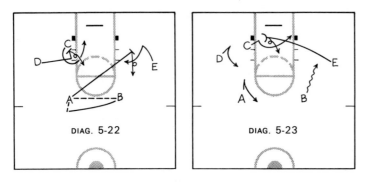

DIAG. 5-22   DIAG. 5-23

Diag. 5-23

B dribbles in towards E's position as the signal for initiating the offense. E fakes and reverses. If E is open, B may pass to him. If E is not open, he continues his movement, screening for C. C cuts off the screen to the basket. E may roll back towards the ball after C's cut. A and D deploy their men away from the point of attack. D, C, and E rebound inside, B is the intermediate rebounder, and A moves back on defense.

Diag. 5-24

B starts to dribble towards A, then passes to A as the keying maneuver. A dribbles off the inside screen set by B. E fakes to the ball and reverses. If he cuts clear into the basket, he may receive A's pass. If not he V's out to the ball and receives a pass from A. A and B set a double screen along the left lane for D. D fakes towards the basket and cuts off the double screen to receive a pass from E. C deploys his man away from the point of attack and then moves into rebounding position. C rebounds left, E right, and D in the middle, and B moves back into safety position. A is the intermediate rebounder in this shot.

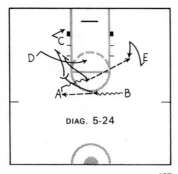

DIAG. 5-24

197

B passes to A and sets an inside screen for E. D sets a screen for C, who is in a pivot position. C cuts back to the ball. D sets up in pivot position. E cuts to the basket. A has the options of passing first to E, cutting off B's screen; second to B, rolling back to the ball after screening; and third to C, moving back off D's screen. If C receives the ball, he may pass into D in the pivot position, and A and C may scissor off D's position. B moves back into defensive position in this case. If E, B, or C takes the shot, A moves back while the others rebound, B being the intermediate rebounder.

DIAG. 5-25

double pivot offense

A double pivot offense is excellent for a team with two taller players and three smaller more agile players. Normally players A, B, and C can be interchangeable in this offense. Good jump-shooting and set-shooting opportunities for these players appear frequently. The double pivot offense is usually a tandem pivot, with one pivot man in a high position and one in a low position. D and E may exchange positions if they are fairly equal in ability. However, if one is less agile than the other and not as good a ball handler, he should be placed low, away from the ball in position E, to be used as a screener for a cut to the ball and to be in good rebound position. Screens off this player may result in a mismatch that will allow E to receive the ball for an easy shot. The more mobile pivot player can play on the foul line, as he will have more latitude and will be able to move into the basket for rebounds with more agility than the slower player. If the two pivot players are of equal ability, it is possible to play a three-out with a double medium-pivot system, with the players playing side by side and interchanging frequently.

A double-pivot offense lends itself very well to a disciplined style. It is easy to teach, has good balance, excellent continuity, and good ball control potential. It puts personnel in their best offensive positions, and it is very adaptable as a zone offense, without much adjustment. It has good inside and outside offensive threats, it puts pressure on the defense (since they must play two pivot men) and it gets good high percentage shots. It is excellent for taking advantage of one-on-one situations or two-on-two free-lance basketball. As in most offenses, there are good scissoring opportunities off either pivot player. It is hard for defensive players to sag effectively against this offense, as it gives good quick intermediate shots when ball movement is reversed. When defensive players overplay wing men, good back-door and screening opportunities result.

The double-pivot is an excellent offense to use when one tall player is uncoordinated or slow or is not a good ball handler. He can be placed to advantage (see E in Diagram 5-26) without affecting the offensive maneuvering to any great extent. The double-pivot is also a good offense to use when trying to slow down the tempo of the game. It can be used very effectively against zone and combination defenses.

Diag. 5-26, DOUBLE PIVOT, TANDEM PIVOT POSITION USING THE ONE-THREE-ONE ALIGNMENT, BASIC PATTERN

A, out front, is normally the best ball handler. B and C are smaller, quicker, more agile players who are good ball handlers. In this alignment, D is the more mobile of the tall men. E is used basically as a low screening pivot. A passes to C and cuts quickly off D to the side of the ball. If A is open, C will pass to A on this cut. The rebounding would be done by D, E, and A inside, and the coach would designate either B or C (preferably C) as the intermediate rebounder, with the fifth man dropping back on defense.

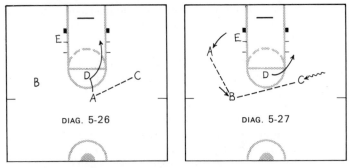

DIAG. 5-26   DIAG. 5-27

Diag. 5-27

This play follows Diag. 5-26. If A cannot receive the pass on the cut, C would dribble towards the head of the key, and B would adjust up from his wing position. C would pass to B and A would circle underneath and cut back out to the ball, using E as a stationary screen. B would pass into A if A were open, with D deploying to the right. If there is a switch between the defenders of E and A, A may pass into E immediately, as E will have the smaller defender guarding him.

Diag. 5-28, A CUT, SCREEN, AND ROLL PLAY

A passes to C, cuts off D, and if he does not receive a return pass, screens low for E. E cuts off the screen towards the ball. A makes an offensive roll into the under-basket area. C can pass to E or A. In this diagram E, D, and A would rebound under, C would be the intermediate rebounder, and B would go back on defense.

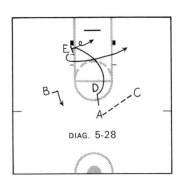

DIAG. 5-28

199

Diag. 5-29, DOUBLE PIVOT, ONE-THREE-ONE, DOUBLE SCREEN

A dribbles towards Wing Man B, passes to B, and moves inside towards the left corner. B dribbles off A. This signals a double screen on the low right side, with D moving in with C to set the double screen. E moves around behind the double screen. This keeps the big men, D and E, in low position for good rebounding balance. If E has the shot, he will take it after a pass from B.

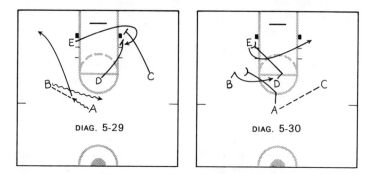

DIAG. 5-29   DIAG. 5-30

Diag. 5-30, DOUBLE PIVOT FROM ONE-THREE-ONE TANDEM ALIGNMENT, SCREEN AWAY

A passes to C, starts towards D, and cuts away, setting a screen away from the ball for B. B cuts off the screen into the foul-line area. D fakes towards the ball and cuts away, setting a screen for E. E cuts off the screen. C may pass to B or E after the cuts. A would come back for defense; E, D, and B would be the three inside rebounders; and C would be the intermediate rebounder. This positioning also gives good one-on-one opportunities to C against a weaker defender.

Diags. 5-31 through 5-35 show three play situations from the one-three-one tandem alignment that are keyed to the movement of Guard A with the ball.

Diag. 5-31, DOUBLE SCREEN

A's dribble to the right signals the play. As A dribbles, C, the right wing, reverse cuts towards the basket. If he is open, he may receive a pass quickly from A. If he is not open, B and E set a double screen low on the left side. D, the high pivot, moves out to the right at the head of the key to set a block for A, who pivot dribbles off this block. As A dribbles back, A may (1) pass to C, if he is open behind the double screen, or (2) pass to D, who has used an offensive roll off of the screen towards the basket.

DIAG. 5-31

200

Diag. 5-32 (following Diag. 5-31), SCISSOR AFTER DOUBLE SCREEN

A passes to C, who does not have the shot. B moves into the left offensive corner. E turns into pivot position from his double screen position. C passes into E, and C and B scissor cut off E's position. D has moved out after not receiving a pass on his offensive roll in Diagram 5-31. B, C, and E would rebound in close to the basket, D would be the intermediate rebounder, and A would drop back on defense.

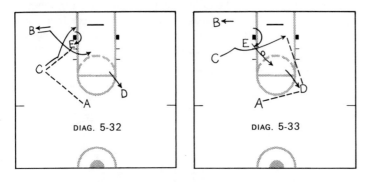

DIAG. 5-32   DIAG. 5-33

Diag. 5-33 (following Diag. 5-31), SHUFFLE CUT

If A cannot pass to C, he passes cross-court to D, who has moved out to the head of the key at the right. B moves into the left corner, E rolls into medium pivot position, C cuts off E in a shuffle cut towards the basket, and E makes an offensive roll into the lower half of the free-throw circle. D may pass to C on his cut or to E on E's offensive roll. Again, B, C, and E should rebound in close to the basket, D would be the intermediate rebounder and A would be back on defense.

Diag. 5-34, DOUBLE PIVOT, ONE-THREE-ONE, TRIPLE SCREEN

A bounce passes to B, the left wing. On the bounce pass, E, D, and A form a triple screen along the right foul lane. C may cut to either side of this screen hoping for a shot. If none materializes, B and C may play two-on-two on the left side, with A rolling back towards the ball. The signal is the bounce pass to the wing on the left.

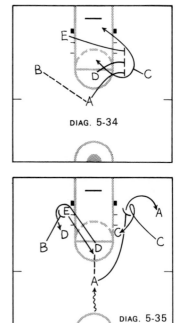

DIAG. 5-34

Diag. 5-35, DOUBLE PIVOT, ONE-THREE-ONE, HIGH-LOW EXCHANGE

A dribbles and waves towards the basket to signal the play. On the hand wave, D and E exchange positions, E coming up strong from his low pivot position, receiving a high pass from A, and pivoting towards the basket. At the same time, B moves in and screens low for D. D circles around behind B's screen. C moves into a low position on the right as D and E are exchanging. A sets a screen for C, and C rolls back. The timing is such that D will be open for a pass first and C second. If neither pass is possible, C should roll through the pivot area, going to the left. A, who has moved to the right corner after his screen, would receive the pass from E for a one-on-one move towards the basket.

DIAG. 5-35

Diags. 5-36 through 5-40 are a double pivot, three-two continuity.

All players keep moving and each has several shooting opportunities as he goes through the continuity movement.

Diag. 5-36

A initiates the play movement by dribbling to his left. As he dribbles, E moves out of his medium-pivot position and sets a rear screen for C, who cuts to the outside toward the basket. D makes the same movement on the right side and B cuts off D towards the basket. If C is open, A can pass to him. C and B continue their movement, cutting off each other on their right side, C moving out to the right side, B continuing to the left side. A may pass to B.

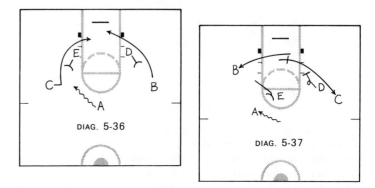

DIAG. 5-36

DIAG. 5-37

Diag. 5-37

After B cuts by D, D rolls and sets a block for C, coming out. C should be in good medium-range shooting territory after this second block. E rolls to the left end of the foul line to set a block for A, who may reverse his dribble off E's block for a jump shot from the foul-line area. A may pass to B in this movement, for a one-on-one move, if B is open.

Diag. 5-38

A passes to B. E moves back towards his original position, and D rolls and cuts to the basket after screening for C.

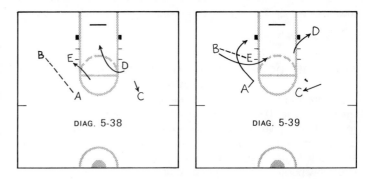

DIAG. 5-38

DIAG. 5-39

Diag. 5-39

B may now pass into E in the medium pivot position on the left, and B and A scissor off the E pivot position. C moves back towards the middle as an outlet man or as a defensive safety man. D rolls towards the right side, low, in good rebound position.

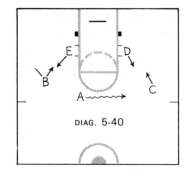

Diag. 5-40

If the play (5-39) is not available, B will pass back to A, who will dribble towards the right. B and C are now back in the wing positions on opposite sides of the court from their original positions, D and E move back into their medium pivot positions, and as A moves to the right, the continuity continues to the right side.

free-lance, or incentive movement offense

Free-lance offenses use play patterns as outlined in Chapter 4, and unless players are completely familiar with all of the movements of these play patterns and with their teammates' habits and movements with or without the ball, they should not be considered as a team offense. However, if players know each other's movements well and are good ball handlers, a great deal of satisfaction is derived by all playing in such an offense, since it allows latitude for intuitive and instinctive movement. Of course, all players must be aware of the basic principles in team free-lance movement.

The first type of movement that is used frequently in this type of offense is a weave, or figure eight movement. This is basic ball movement in weave fashion, cutting to the basket using inside screens to delay or impede opponents defensively so that receivers may cut free, using give-and-go plays, and cutting off the ball whenever the ball is between your defender and the basket. Give-and-go requires excellent fundamentals by all five offensive players—smooth ball handling with continuous movement, excellent screening and use of screens, and good movement without the ball. In using a free-lance offense, all players must be aware of audible and visual signals that their teammates may use; for example, hand claps, peculiar vocal sounds such as ''beep-beep,'' head and eye signals, and finger pointing.

The weave is used for circulation and for preliminary movement prior to the inception of free-lance plays. Set-pattern teams as well as free-lance teams make good use of the weave movement. Receivers cut close to and outside the ball. The passer usually uses a short, one- or two-hand underhand pass with good fingertip control. He follows his pass, and the receiver moves towards it. The passer may inside screen or outside screen (usually the latter).

If players move too close together in a weave, the man with the ball should skip a man and the man who did not receive the ball should cut for the basket. Players must move.

Weaving is very effective against close guarding, but it is ineffectual if the players are cutting towards the sidelines habitually and if the defenders are playing zone. It may be used by three, four or five men. The circulation may be deep from the basket—as in a four- or five-man weave movement—or it may be flat, parallel to the mid-court line—as in a three-man weave.

A necessary essential of weaving is excellent ball handling, with the passer always crossing in front of the receiver. If there is no pass, the man with the ball may stop and pivot in front of his teammate, who may cut off the ball, or run around the ball, to the basket, cutting tight off the player screening with the ball. The middle in a five- or four-man weave must be kept open at all times. When the weave is used with a three-two free-lance offense, the player who passes off cuts down the middle towards the basket expecting a return pass. If he does not receive a pass, he cuts to the corner on the same side he passed to. Constant effective weaving can retreat defenders toward their basket so that the offense can obtain easy medium jumpshooting opportunities.

In a three-two free-lance pattern, the middle man out front with the ball should be an excellent quarterback, dribbler, and ball handler. The wing men should be good ball handlers and outside shooters. The corner men must be mobile, good ball handlers who are able to move in and out of the pivot in a flash pivot maneuver. In a five-man pattern, all the players offensively are in constant movement. In practice, this helps your defensive unit as each player is defending against opponents in all postures—near the basket, in the medium areas, in the corners and out front. Regardless of the deployment used in a free-lance offense—whether it's a two-one-two or a three-two—the floor must be kept balanced, the player with the ball must determine the play, and all must compound the defensive problems as much as possible.

The following rules should be enforced in the free-lance movement. The player with the ball always determines the play. He should be facing the basket at all times, he should be alive, and he should be in triple threat position where he can pass, shoot or dribble. For best results, he should see all offensive and defensive positionings.

The passer off, on cutting towards the basket, should set an inside screen for the player he passes to if possible.

The offensive players must be well spaced. If they are

too close, a player moving towards a teammate who has the ball should reverse direction towards the basket.

Players should dribble minimally, and only as a protective reaction against a good defensive move by an opponent, for good shooting position on driving to the basket, or for offensive balance when the team position is poor.

Initial probing passes should be used; however, a penetrating pass should be made immediately, if possible. When players are bringing the ball upcourt on the side, they should pass into the corner man immediately and work a two-on-two play on that side, rather than pass the ball back to the middle and have two or three initial probing passes before the offense moves into a penetrating position.

It's possible to work the ball in close for shots. Therefore, long shots against man-to-man are not needed unless the defense is in a complete floating or sagging posture.

Players should not hold the ball. If they do not have a play, they should pass it to another player and continue the movement.

In playing without the ball, offensive players should use deceptive moves and fakes. First they should determine where the player with the ball wants them to position themselves. Second, they should screen weak side away, using inside screening and roll techniques. Third, they should cut to the basket, using either a back-door or inside cut to the ball or weak-side cut off the screen, tight, towards the ball. A cutter should always stop if he is the second cutter and is not open. If he is the second cutter and is open, he should make an audible sound to alert the man with the ball that he is open away from the point of attack.

Players receiving a pass should **V** away and come back to the ball. In reversing direction to the basket, they should make a **V** towards the ball and then push off towards the basket.

Players using a free-lance offense should never shoot a hurried shot or a forced shot under pressure.

In using two- and three-man plays as described in Chapter 4, all players should know their teammates' moves. The man with the ball has five options. First, he may pass and not move, telling the receiver and the three other teammates he is relinquishing the pattern selection to the receiver. Second, he may pass and screen away with teammates moving the ball to the best area for open passing lanes to the cutter. Third, he may pass and screen towards the ball, with the receiver driving off the screen towards the side the screen came from. Fourth, he may pass and go behind the receiver, indicating that he expects the receiver to return the pass, move away, and screen. Fifth, if the passer wants the ball back on an inside hand-off (for example, a wing man passing to a corner man), he should nod his head as he passes to signal the hand-off, then cut between the man with the ball and his defender so he may get the hand-off and drive to the basket.

The position replacements should always be from the weak side, out front, away from the ball. Players should never go to the area near the ball too quickly. In a three-out-two-in offense, a corner man should never cross both foul lanes when moving towards the ball. He may move and cross both foul lanes when screening away from the ball.

If you are a primary receiver and cannot get open for the pass, reverse and go to the basket. If you are a cutter off the ball and open for a pass, cut off the ball towards the basket quickly. Cutting off the ball puts an extra pair of defensive hands near the ball and it puts the ball in a very dangerous position if your movement is not quick, fast, and towards the basket. Movements must be balanced, deceptive, quick, and varied. Footwork and feints must be used to put the defender at a disadvantage that should be readily discernible and understandable to teammates with the ball.

When using an inside screen, a good procedure to follow when defenders switch is to stop and screen for the screener after you cut off him. This generally will open the cutting screener for a shot. If both defenders follow the cutter, you will be open for a medium shot yourself.

Three-Two Free-Lance Offenses. The rebounding aspect from a three-two free-lance offense is a most important consideration. Each player must be looking for the shot to come to him and take only good shots so that his teammates know when to start to move into rebounding position. The back man should always go back in a defensive posture. The second man in the back should be the intermediate rebounder, unless he is a shooter, in which case he should follow his shot.

Diag. 5-41, THREE-TWO OPEN MIDDLE OFFENSE, BASIC ALIGNMENT AND MOVEMENT

A, with the ball, should be at the head of the key or four or five feet behind it. B and C, the wing men, should be deployed to the sides, just in front of the hash marks. D and E, the corner men, should be about even with the first lane marker after the buffer zone, fairly close to the lower half of the foul circle, about eight feet from the sideline, and slightly to the outside of B and C. D and E must never be deep in the corner, as it would limit their movements in the offense. No one is within twenty feet of the basket in their original position. Initial movement is as follows: A passes to C, moving into the pass. A fakes towards the ball, then cuts straight down the middle towards the basket, coming out on the right, the same side he passed to. C dribbles across towards the head of the key. C passes to B. B holds position until the pass is on its way, then steps to meet it. (He fakes away before coming back to receive the ball.) B would dribble slowly towards the middle. C, after passing, steps towards B and cuts directly towards the basket, looking for a return give-and-go pass if he is open. (If players cutting toward the basket are open, they should raise the hand closest to the basket as a signal and a target to the man in possession of the ball.) D and E move from their corner positions straight out, staying at least eight to ten feet wide of the foul lanes as they come out to the ball. They should not bend in towards the keyhole as this will narrow and shorten the three-two movement, which should be fairly long and wide, unless a tight weave is being used in order to get a short jump shot. This movement can continue, and basic patterns can evolve from it.

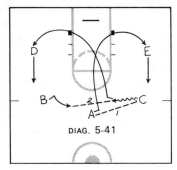

DIAG. 5-41

The movement of the player with the ball determines the type of play. Beginning with Diag. 5-42, A's movement will determine the play in each diagram. We will name each play so that players can identify it in a game situation.

Diag. 5-42, THREE-TWO OFFENSE, "OPPOSITE"

A passes to C and cuts away from C (not going down the middle) to set a screen for B. This movement by A tells teammates the play. The best way to get the ball into B on his cut is from the low side. Therefore, after a faking move, C passes into E. E fakes and comes back to receive the ball. B fakes away and cuts off A's screen into the middle towards the basket. A continues into the corner to screen for D. D is a second cutter and should come out in the lower half of the free-throw circle. If B does not receive the pass, he may set a screen for E, who may drive off the screen towards the basket. C would be the man back in defensive position.

DIAG. 5-42

Diag. 5-43, THREE-TWO OFFENSE, "CORNER"

A passes to B (1) and moves toward B for a return pass. B passes back to A (2) and moves in, setting an inside screen for D. D fakes to the baseline and cuts tight off the screen. After the cutting move by D, B steps back towards the corner. Normally, B will be momentarily open for a good shot, as defensive players guarding D and B will both be alert for the cut. A may pass to D (3b) if D cuts open or pass back to the corner to B (3a), who has stepped back after his inside screen. D, if he does not receive the pass, continues over and sets a screen for E. E fakes to the baseline and cuts off the screen. C would be the back man on defense.

DIAG. 5-43

Diag. 5-44, THREE-TWO OFFENSE, "CLEAR OUT"

This is an excellent move when a defensive team is sagging to clog the middle to prevent cuts to the basket. A calls the clear out and passes initially to B (1) to determine the side to be cleared. B fakes towards D and returns the pass to A (2), cutting diagonally across the middle as though anticipating a return pass. As B starts his cut toward the opposite corner, D starts in the same direction, making the defense expect possible movement to the right side. A fakes a pass to B, who is cutting through the middle. (He may actually be able to pass to B on this diagonal cut, if B's defender is lax.) D, on hitting the foul lane, pivots up the foul lane, setting up in a medium pivot position. A passes to D (3) and cuts to the outside left of D. D may return the pass to A on his cut, take a one bounce dribble to the opposite side for a move on his own, or turn and take a short jump shot. In this movement D, E, and C must keep their defensive men busy.

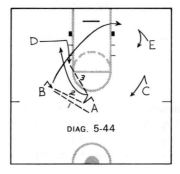

DIAG. 5-44

Diag. 5-45, THREE-TWO FREE-LANCE OFFENSE, "BEHIND"

A, in the center, passes to B (1), the left wing, then cuts behind B's position. (This move is the key to the play. Anytime an offensive player passes and goes behind the receiver in a free-lance offense, he should receive a return pass.) B returns the pass to A (2) and immediately cuts to the right, to the opposite end of the foul line. He opens a clear passing lane towards D with his movement, and A passes into D (3) after D fakes and comes back to the ball. B sets a screen near the far end of the foul line. C sets up his defender by faking a cut towards the baseline and then cutting back off B. B then continues into the far right corner, screening for E, who is the second cutter in the play. D has the option of passing to either C or E.

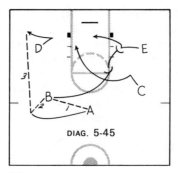

DIAG. 5-45

208

Whenever the middle man in a three-two free-lance offense passes to either side and doesn't move, he is indicating to the other four teammates that he wishes the receiver to make his own play, usually a two-on-two play with the corner man on that side. This offense also readily allows each player a "Get One For" shooting opportunity (see Chapter 4).

Diag. 5-46, THREE-TWO OFFENSE, "DOUBLE FOR D"

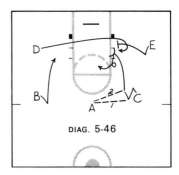

DIAG. 5-46

The double movement starts to the right. A passes to C (1) and receives a return pass (2). E sets low along the foul lane to the right. C sets a double screen with him. D times his cut behind the screen to receive a pass from A. If he doesn't receive the pass he continues around the double screen towards the basket. A must pass to B so that B may make the easier pass-in on D's move. B has a good back-door opportunity during these maneuvers. C makes an offensive roll back to the ball. After his pass, A would be on defense.

Diag. 5-47, "DOUBLE FOR C"

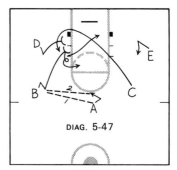

DIAG. 5-47

On the call "Double for C," the initial pass goes away from C to B (1). The second pass comes back from B to A (2), both players using fakes before the pass. D and B set a double screen along the left lane for C. C cuts behind. A may pass to C for a short jump shot behind the double screen or pass to B on an offensive roll towards the ball. C continues to cut through towards the basket and right corner if he does not receive the pass behind the double screen. A drops back in defensive position, with D, C, and E responsible for rebounding. B is the intermediate rebounder after his roll back.

Diag. 5-48, THREE-TWO OFFENSE, "SCRAMBLE"

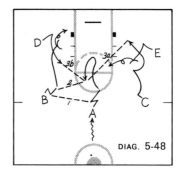

DIAG. 5-48

A dribbles into position and passes immediately to B (1), fakes down the middle, then buttonhooks back to the foul line, taking a high pivot position. B passes to A (2) on the foul line and moves in, setting an inside screen for D. D fakes to the baseline and then comes back off B's screen. E sets a screen for C, who fakes and cuts outside off E's screen towards the basket to the right. A may pass to C (3a), on his cut towards the basket, or to D (3b), cutting back for a medium jump shot. Both E and B use offensive rolls, B moving towards the basket, E moving back towards the ball. After his pass, A would drop back in defensive position.

Diag. 5-49, THREE-TWO OFFENSE, "BACK DOOR"

DIAG. 5-49

A, dribbling up into position, observes X_2, B's man, moving back with him in halfhearted defensive position. On observing this, he calls the back-door movement. D fakes and comes up to the left side of the outer foul circle. A passes to D. B fakes towards D then reverses direction, going directly to the basket. D would pass to B on B's cut. C and E deploy away from the point of attack. This is an excellent play to use, also, whenever B or C are overplayed to the ball.

Diag. 5-50, THREE-TWO OFFENSE, "REVERSE"

This is a four-man weave movement. A passes to C (1), fakes towards C, and cuts towards the basket, *cutting away* from the side he passed to. C dribbles across the top of the key towards B. B fakes toward the basket and comes back, moving into the pass from C. C passes to B (2), then clears through following A's movement. B dribbles slightly towards the head of the key. E, the fourth man in the weaving movement, fakes to the basket, comes back as though to get in the weave pattern, and immediately reverses direction, pushing off the left foot and cutting hard to the basket. B's pass (3) leads E into the basket on a reverse movement. B would be the back man on defense.

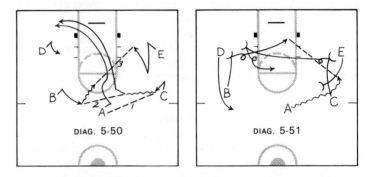

DIAG. 5-50   DIAG. 5-51

Diag. 5-51, THREE-TWO OFFENSE, "LOW"

This is a five-man set play. As A starts to dribble towards C, C moves in and sets a screen for E. E moves out off the screen and screens for A. A continues to dribble off E's screen. As A starts to dribble to the right, B moves in and sets a screen for D. D cuts back to be the safety on defense. After C screens for E, he rolls and changes direction to the left across the court and screens for B. B, after screening for D, rolls off C's screen and cuts to the basket. A, after cutting off E's screen, passes to B on B's cut. C makes an offensive roll back to the ball, and in any switching maneuver he may be open to receive a pass and take a shot in the lower half of the free-throw circle.

In three-two free-lance basketball there is ample opportunity for any type of play. It would be impossible to list all the possibilities. Plays that have not been outlined, such as "scissors off a post" (see Chapter 4), are simple plays to incorporate in a three-two free-lance offensive, with D and E moving quickly into pivot position and either A and B or C and A scissoring off them.

Diags. 5-52 through 5-56 outline a three-two roll-back continuity type offense in which all cuts are away from the ball and players must cut off their screens. In the basic three-two, free-lance, open middle, offensive pattern, A is the middle man with the ball, B and C are the wing men, and D and E are the corner men, with all players outside a twenty-one-foot radius facing into the basket. A initiates the offense.

210

Diag. 5-52

A passes to B (1), then cuts away and screens for C. B may pass to C (2). If C does not receive the pass on his cut, he continues into the right corner, screening for E. B may pass to E (3) if E opens. A buttonhooks back towards the ball after his screen for C. B passes back to A (4).

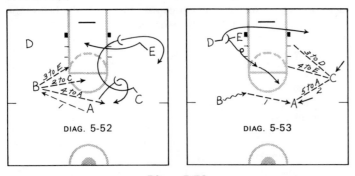

DIAG. 5-52   DIAG. 5-53

Diag. 5-53

A receives the pass back from B (1) and passes to C (2). E has continued across the lane and has screened for D. D cuts to the baseline side off E's screen. C can pass first to D (3); second to E (4), who rolls back towards the ball after screening for D; or third, back to A (5).

Diag. 5-54

C passes back to A (1) and cuts to the right corner around D. A passes to B (2) and steps into the outer half of the free throw circle, screening for E. E cuts off A's screen. B has a pass to E (3) cutting towards the basket, or he may pass to A (4) who has rolled back.

DIAG. 5-54

Diag. 5-55

B passes back to A (1), then moves in and screens in the corner for E. E cuts off B's screen across the middle. A may pass to E (2) or to B (3), who is rolling back.

DIAG. 5-55

211

A passes to B (1). B may pass to D (2), who is cutting along the baseline off E's screen; to E (3), who has rolled back towards the ball after screening in the right corner for D; or back to A (4). If B passes back to A, the players are back in their original positions (5-52)—E rolls back to the right corner, D (if he does not receive a pass) moves into the left corner, and A has the ball at the head of the key. B and C are the wing men.

DIAG. 5-56

This is a good continuity offense based on the roll back to the ball for a good jump shot or a medium set shot after screening. It requires good circulation, with the middle of the court constantly open for good cuts without the ball. All players must know the open spot to go to if they do not receive the ball, and they must be alert for shots by teammates so as to be in the most advantageous rebounding positions. Many open lay-ups result from this movement.

Two-One-Two, or Two-Three, Free-Lance Offense. The following procedures should be understood and followed in running a two-one-two free-lance offense. The pivot should be low opposite the side on which the ball is brought up. There should be a good back-door movement possible between the guards. There should be a back-door or reverse movement for the forward on the ball side. Anytime there is a play off the pivot, the corner man must be alert to clear the side from which the ball was passed in. This opens that side for the second cutter coming through off the high pivot. When the ball is passed into the pivot player in the outer half of the free-throw circle, guards and forwards should be deploying to their best advantage, setting screens to allow free cuts to the basket, and looking for back-door movements. A pivot low opposite affords a good lob opportunity if his man is playing in front of him and is attempting to keep him from getting the ball in the high pivot position. If the pivot receives the ball in the high pivot position, he should turn and face the hoop, looking for the strong-side forward, who will make a back-door movement if he is being played tight. The pivot will pass quickly to this forward if he is loose. The forward should clear through if no pass is made. The center should then look for the strong-side guard, cutting to the basket if his defender has floated in towards the pivot position to harass the ball. The pivot,

212

if neither play appears, may drive by his man to the open side, or shoot over him. If the strong-side guard cuts, the other guard will replace him to that side. If the weak-side guard floats into the pivot position, the strong-side guard should screen him so that he can come off the screen for a medium jumper or a cut to the basket.

If the ball is not passed into the high pivot, with the guard alive, the guard should drive off a screen set by the strong-side forward, with the forward rolling and going to the hoop. He clears through if there is no switch or pass. The center should delay his movement and screen for the weak-side forward. The weak-side forward should cut to the middle off this screen, looking for the open spots and going all the way if the opening is there. The pivot should roll low to the ball side after his screen. The weak-side guard should replace the strong-side guard, moving to the ball side so as to be an outlet for the guard with the ball or to be ready to go back on defense. If the guard with the ball has used his dribble, he should pass to the strong-side forward and cut off his screen.

All players are constantly looking for reverses without the ball, and the guards are looking for two-on-two opportunities with a forward away from the pivot. Anytime a guard is overplayed to the forward's side, when the guard has the ball and the pivot man cannot come up, he should pass to the weak-side guard. The pivot man may hold his defender if he is being played in front to the ball side and roll to the basket to be open for a pass. If the weak-side guard's defender has sagged off, the guard should penetrate to the circle looking for a shot, a pass to the pivot, or a pass to either forward. There are many opportunities for two-on-two plays or three-on-three plays with scissoring off the pivot if the players keep the ball moving, if the guards and forwards remember that they are going to one of four spots, and if the pivot is mobile and circulating, using evasive tactics in the pivot area.

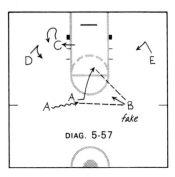

DIAG. 5-57

Diag. 5-57, TWO-ONE-TWO FREE-LANCE, BACK DOOR FOR THE GUARD

C, the pivot, is low opposite the ball. B, the guard, having received a pass after A dribbled partially across the court, fakes to A. A reverses and goes to the basket on a give-and-go movement with B, C, D, and E are using deploying tactics to keep their guards away from the point of attack.

Diag. 5-58, TWO-ONE-TWO FREE-LANCE, GUARD AROUND THE WEAK-SIDE FORWARD

A has the ball, and C is low on the opposite right side. C fakes and comes high for the ball. X_2, B's guard, has floated in to harass the center. E on observing this, moves up to screen X_2. B cuts around E's screen. C, feeling the pressure, knows that there should be an open man to the pressure side and passes to B.

DIAG. 5-58

213

Diag. 5-59, TWO-ONE-TWO FREE-LANCE, BASIC

A passes to Pivot C, who moves up from the side opposite the ball position, turns, and faces the basket. D, the strong-side forward, has moved up towards the ball as if to fake the back door from A, or reverse from A. Options: As C turns, D pushes off and goes to the basket. C passes to D, if D is open. A second possibility is for C to drive or shoot over his defender if he can. If A's defender sags towards the ball, A should cut to the open corner, with B replacing A. If B's defender sags towards the ball, either E can screen and B can cut outside or A can screen and B can cut off A's screen to the open side with D clearing that corner.

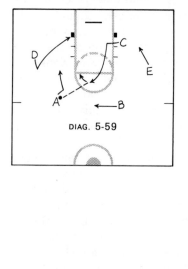

DIAG. 5-59

DIAG. 5-60

Diag. 5-60 (CONTINUATION OF Diag. 5-59)

If D does not receive the ball, he continues through and sets a screen for E. E cuts off D to the baseline side. C looks for (1) E under the basket, (2) D on a roll if there is a switch, and (3) E as he hooks out for a short jump shot if his man leaves him after he cuts through. A and B deploy in the back court waiting for an outlet pass. Options: C may pass back to A for a free-lance two-on-two by A and E, C and D clearing away.

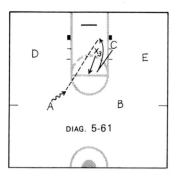

DIAG. 5-61

Diag. 5-61, TWO-ONE-TWO FREE-LANCE, LOB PASS

C is low, opposite the ball. X_3 his defender, is in front of him, attempting to beat him to position on the foul line to stop the free-lance movement. A dribbles slowly towards the circle as C moves quickly up towards the foul line. X_3 assumes his fronting position. A lobs the ball over X_3 to C, who has reversed back towards the basket. This is the safest position for a lob pass, as D's defender cannot float because he is on the strong side and would allow an easy shot by D. It is too long a float for E's man as the pass should be in front of C. This is an excellent play to use whenever the pivot is being pressured high. One lob pass allows all of the two-one-two offense emanating from the high pivot position to be used freely, because once X_3 is beaten on the lob, he will become cautious and not fight for the position as C goes high.

214

Diag. 5-62, TWO-ONE-TWO, FREE-LANCE, DOUBLE SCREEN

A, dribbling slowly to the left, looks for a reverse cut by D. If the cut is not forthcoming, A passes back to the opposite guard, B (1), who is moving towards the head of the key. B calls a double screen for E, and D and C move into position low at the left foul lane. A moves back towards the ball, using evasive tactics. E cuts to the baseline side, off the double screen. B returns the pass to A (2). A passes to E (3) behind the screen. Options: (1) E may continue around the double screen into the basket. A would then pass back to B for a better passing lane into E's cut. (2) B may go back door or reverse to the weak side, receiving a quick pass from A.

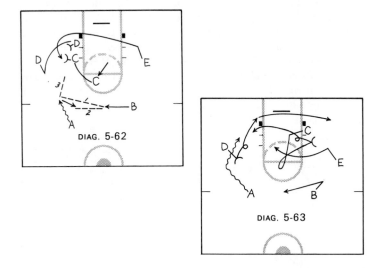

DIAG. 5-62

DIAG. 5-63

Diag. 5-63, TWO-ONE-TWO, FREE-LANCE

C has moved to the high pivot. A dribbles slowly to the left. D moves up and sets a lateral screen. A dribbles off the screen, and if he can go all the way, he does. If he cannot, D makes an offensive roll to the basket. If D does not receive a pass, A pulls off the left side. After D clears through, C moves from the foul line and sets a screen for E. E fakes to the baseline and cuts off C's screen into the lower half of the free-throw circle. If he is open, A passes. C makes an offensive roll to the low pivot on the ball side after E moves over his screen. A will pass to C if there is any switch on the move. B deploys back in good defensive position.

Diag. 5-64, TWO-ONE-TWO, FREE-LANCE

C has moved up to the high pivot. A cannot make any move as he has used his dribble. As soon as D sees that A has used his dribble, he fakes into the basket and comes back strong to the ball to receive a pass. A then sets an inside screen for D, who dribbles off the screen, taking a shot if it appears. A rolls into the corner, looking for a pass and shot if there is a switch. C seeing the movement, moves back low opposite, setting a screen for E. E fakes to the baseline and cuts off the screen into the center at the lower half of the free-throw circle. If E is open, D passes to him. C rolls low toward the ball side, looking for a pass. B deploys back in good position defensively.

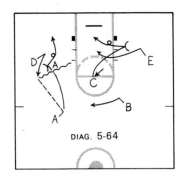

DIAG. 5-64

215

overload offense

This offense overbalances on one side of the court at the inception of each play, then moves to the other side. Players use rear screen cuts away from the ball, scissor moves off the ball and off the post, and several secondary screens to exploit switching or sagging tactics. All types of shots will appear from this type of offense.

Diag. 5-65, OVERLOAD OFFENSE, GUARD THROUGH

In basic positions, A, a guard, is on the left side of the court, with B, the second guard, at the head of the key. The forward, C, is close to the sideline below the medium pivot, D. E is in low-pivot position opposite. A initiates the play by passing to C and cutting off D to the basket. C has the following options: (1) He may pass to A if he appears free after his cut off D. (2) He may drive to the baseline. (3) He may drive over a screen set by D and take a jump shot, or drive into the basket if the lane is open. (4) He may pass to D on D's offensive roll to the basket.

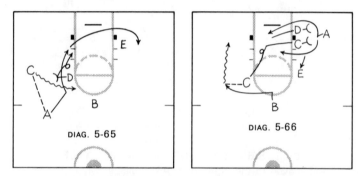

DIAG. 5-65

DIAG. 5-66

Diag. 5-66, OVERLOAD OFFENSE, DOUBLE SCREEN (CONTINUATION OF Diag. 5-65)

C passes to B. E has moved up the right foul lane. D and C have moved across the foul lane setting a double screen for A. B may drive into the basket if he is open, or he may pull off to the left and look for A's cut either to the low side or into the middle off the double screen set by D and C.

Diag. 5-67, OVERLOAD OFFENSE, SCISSOR

This play starts from the alignment shown in Diagram 5-65. If A does not cut, after pass in to C (1), C may pass to D (2). C and A may scissor cut off D.

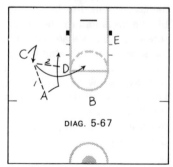

DIAG. 5-67

216

Diag. 5-68, OVERLOAD OFFENSE WITH A HIGH-LOW EXCHANGE BY THE PIVOT MEN

As A passes to C, D moves towards E's position and screens. E moves off the screen into D's former position in medium pivot on the ball side. D rolls off his screen, low on the ball side. After the exchange of high-low pivot, B screens for A. A cuts. The options: (1) C may pass to E as E moves into the medium pivot for a pivot shot. (2) C may pass to D in the low pivot. (3) C, D, or E may pass to A, opposite, after his cut off B for a quick shot or a one-on-one move. This play for A will appear on the weak side, as the defense is concentrating on the overloaded side of the court.

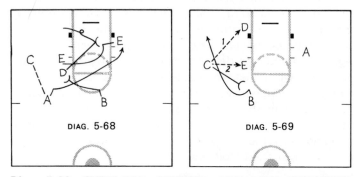

DIAG. 5-68   DIAG. 5-69

Diag. 5-69, OVERLOAD OFFENSE, HIGH-LOW EXCHANGE (CONTINUATION OF Diag. 5-68)

C has passed to D (1) or E (2) and screens for B, who can cut left into good medium shooting area. After the pass in to D or E, the opportunities for an open shot after a screen are magnified, because the defense concentrates in the pivot areas.

Diag. 5-70, OVERLOAD OFFENSE, TO THE RIGHT

A and B are the guards. A is a little off center at the head of the key, B is to his right between him and the sideline, C is in a high pivot, and D and E are in forward positions. This play frees A, the tall guard, along the baseline where he can rebound offensively and, after the play movement, go one-on-one. A, passes to B (1) and cuts off C's screen on the high pivot. B passes to E (2). E may pass to A if A is open, he may reverse the ball by passing back to B, or he may pass to C, who has rolled into the medium pivot after A's cut and the pass to E. If E passes back to B (3), B has two options. (1) He may pass to D for a pass to E, who is cutting off C's medium pivot position. (2) He may pass into the corner to A for a one-on-one move by A from the corner. A may pass to C, now in the medium pivot, then scissor cut off him with B or fake towards C and make a backdoor cut to the basket.

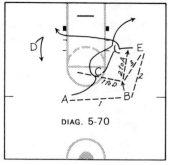

DIAG. 5-70

217

the stack offense

The basic offense used by the authors is the stack offense. We believe that it has many advantages in modern basketball. Primarily, it cuts down the margin of error, as the best ball handler (A) generally handles the ball most of the time and brings it into scoring position. It is more difficult for teams using pressure-type defense (especially from the man-to-man posture) to pressure one outstanding dribbler and ball handler into offensive mistakes.

After the ball is in the offensive set position, the only person who is required to dribble the ball is A, whose dribbling movement keys the offense. By observing the defenders, he can determine which play to use in a given situation. Against man-to-man defense, he can call the plays by name or he can let his teammates determine the correct play by watching the defensive deployment. After one or two short passes, a team should get a good shot at the basket from this offense—either a high-percentage medium-jump shot or a shot from the low pivot area. Other advantages of the stack offense are as follows:

1. It should neutralize any defense, forcing it to play man-to-man and match players man-to-man.

2. Setting up double teams against one opposing star is difficult. If the defense doubles up on one player, an open man is usually in position close to the basket for an easy shot.

3. The coach can easily arrange mismatches by altering the starting position of the men.

4. It can take advantage of any individual defensive weakness.

5. Setting a defense against the stack is difficult. The offense can go left or right quickly from the starting position, and all players interchange positions, with the possible exception of the A man.

6. It is excellent with big men. Once a shot is taken all of the big men jam the offensive boards for a second and third effort at the basket.

7. It is not a tiring offense, and its simple patterns are easy to understand.

8. Players can easily work away from the opposition's defensive strength.

9. Options show up immediately, which forces defensive players to stay honest if they try to realign for better protection.

10. It's impossible to keep this offense from getting a good shot if it is properly timed and executed.

11. The one-man front is the hardest type of offense to press man-to-man.

12. When two big men are not adaptable to a forward position, you can use this offense effectively, keeping them in their

best rebounding positions and shooting positions with a minimum of movement.

13. Most teams practice defense against the normal set systems; for example, a three-two offense, a two-three offense or a one-three-one offense. The use of the stack presents added defensive difficulties.

14. There is no defense against a good reverse movement.

The stack offense also has the following disadvantages.

1. If the ball is stolen from the outside man or the team cannot control the offensive board consistently, it is susceptible to a fast-break team.

2. It is not as effective when used as the only offense for the entire game. However, all teams should have a secondary offense. (We try to use our fast-break offense at all times. penetrating against the defense whenever possible, even if the defense has three men back against our three men. Our primary set offense is the stack, and our secondary set offense is either a two-one-two free-lance type or a two-three single pivot type.)

3. If the entire team does not move together on the outside man's keys, the offense will fail. Timing and surprise are essential in this type of offense.

Basic Qualifications. A is the quarterback, the best dribbler, the best ballhandler, the play-maker who has speed and is a threat from the outside. He should be able to take defensive pressure, and he must always be able to get back on defense quickly.

B should be a big, strong, tough offensive player, probably the best scorer among the big men. He should have a good hook shot and move well from the low pivot, with his back to the basket. Whenever he gets the ball in the low pivot position, he should be good for a basket or, if he is double-teamed, a pass-off to E on the weak side if E's man leaves him to help double team. He should be a good one-on-one man in this low position, with excellent moves close to the basket.

C is the best shooter facing the hoop. He should be an excellent short- to medium-jump shooter and a very good feeder from the side or corner into the pivot. He should be capable of playing two-on-two basketball with B, and should be able to move one-on-one from his side position. C's position is good for a left-handed shooter.

D is usually a smaller man than C. He should be an excellent jump shooter from the medium shooting area. D's position is good for a right-handed jump shooter or for the second guard if there is a good shooting forward to play in the C position.

E, usually the second big man, should be a strong rebounder who can block out well. He must be alert for all movement when he is away from the ball, as he will open frequently, since his defender is often called in to help a teammate towards the ball.

A will always be back as the defensive safety in all plays except those in which he moves to the basket. On those plays, either C or D (depending on the movements) will assume A's defensive position. B, D, and E, the best rebounders, are normally in a triangle arrangement moving to the board whenever a shot is taken, with C the intermediate rebounder in most situations. After the initial movement to the left or right, A, the best ball handler, is in position to pass to B, C, D, or E from either side off his dribble, depending on the defensive alignment and position.

Starting Positions. The starting positions as outlined are planned to operate mainly to the right side. The positions would be reversed if you were working to the left. A is at the top of the key in possession of the ball. All inside men in the stack (see Diag. 5-71) place their feet close to the foul lane, and each side faces the other. C and D are approximately four feet from the basket, just outside the buffer zone. C's left foot should be behind B's right foot. D's right foot should be behind E's left foot.

The distance of the inside men from the baseline will be determined by B's position. He will pivot counterclockwise on his right foot after initial movement to his side to assume a low pivot position with his back to the basket. Once he has found a low pivot position he prefers, he will always set up where he can make his pivot into this position, and everyone else will set up accordingly. It is possible to be closer to the foul line than the original positions indicate or anywhere from one to four feet farther back from the foul lanes if the offense works better from this alignment.

Basic stack positions (A is No. 40; B, No. 50; C, No. 10; D, No. 42; and E, No. 22).

The position varies slightly, but normally B's left foot will be about even with the broken line of the lower half of the free-throw circle.

Keys to the Offense. The big men, B and E, must get into position on the lanes as quickly as possible. If they can't set up on the lane, they should set up as close to the lane as they can. The timing and execution are important. All players must move together as A makes a definite penetrating move to the right or to the left after bringing the ball up to the head of the circle. Quick passing is important, particularly hitting the open man as soon as he is free.

Basic Stack Offense. Everything described will be on the right movement. (Reverse procedures for left movement.) As A dribbles to the right, the following moves are made simultaneously: C pops out from ten to fourteen feet, continuing to face the hoop, moving towards the ball at a forty-five degree angle from the basket, adjusting position depending on the way his defender plays him. B pivots on his right foot into a low pivot position. D moves behind E to the foul-line area, adjusting position for best advantage. E adjusts position depending on the defense, usually maneuvering towards the basket.

Basic Options. A may hit C for a medium to short jumper as soon as C opens. A may hit D coming around E's screen to the foul line. A may hit B in his low pivot position if his defender is behind him. A may pass to E across the court if E's defender is in front, lobbing the ball to him, or possibly bounce passing through the opening that may appear after defensive deployment. A may go one-on-one for himself, taking a medium or outside shot if the defense sags to jam the middle or cut off the pass.

C may shoot a medium or short jump shot. C may pass into B for a pivot shot or one-on-one movement in the low pivot. B may hand off to C, cutting off his pivot position from the outside. B and C may use any number of two-on-two moves as outlined in Chapter 4. C may pass to D after he has come around E's screen. C may play one-on-one against the weak defender. D may take a shot from the foul line area. D may make a quick pass in to B or E if their defensive men try to help out against D.

There are many alternate options on special calls by A. C may cut behind a double screen set opposite by D and E to receive a pass from A and make a short jump shot. If C is not free, A and B may work two-on-two on the open side of the floor. This is particularly effective if the defense is setting itself to play C to drop out to the right initially as the ball goes in towards the right side.

At a special call by A, C and D can pop out simultaneously while B and E crisscross to low pivot on opposite sides of the foul lane from their original position. A may pass to B or E, depending on the defensive switching. This play

221

allows a two-on-two possibility for either C and E on one side or B and D on the other, depending on the side that A passes to.

All coaches can find many other possible variations. For example:

1. If B is being double-teamed, he may exchange positions with C. This should leave a man alone underneath.

2. If C has a small opponent, he may exchange movements with B and work on his opponent in the low pivot as B moves out for the initial pass.

3. If B has a big man who can't move, he may change positions with C to take the big man outside for one-on-one moves facing the basket.

4. If the defense is keying on B, by placing him in C's position and running the plays to the left, your best shooter will be able to get the ball at the foul line at the top of the key where the defense will have more trouble defending against him.

The following diagrams will help explain many of the moves available and the basic alignments.

Diag. 5-71, STACK OFFENSE, TEAM ALIGNMENT

A is outside with the ball. B and C are along the right foul lane with C's left foot behind B's right foot. D and E are along the left foul lane with D's right foot behind E's left foot. The pairs are facing each other along the foul lanes. These positions are adjustable out towards the foul line or back away from the foul lane depending upon defensive alignments.

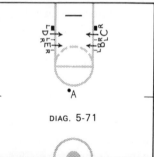

DIAG. 5-71

Stack offense team alignment.

Basic move offensive right.

Diag. 5-72, STACK OFFENSE, STRONG-SIDE PIVOT MOVEMENT BY B AS C MOVES OUT FOR THE BALL

C has moved out to receive a pass. B pivots on his right foot, counterclockwise, and ends up with his back to the basket. The original position shows him facing across the lane; his final position shows him facing C and the right sideline. B's position is adjustable towards the foul line if he wishes to obtain a higher pivot position. C, D, and E will adjust with B's position.

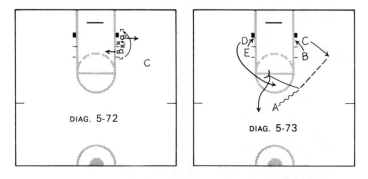

DIAG. 5-72

DIAG. 5-73

Diag. 5-73, STACK OFFENSE, BASIC MOVEMENT

The play is keyed by A's penetrating dribble to his right. C moves out at a forty-five-degree angle and receives a pass. B pivots on his right foot to the low position on ball side. D has moved around E's screen. If C's reception of the pass is without great defensive pressure, A slides back toward D, setting a secondary screen at the foul line for D and then rotating back into defensive position or into position as the safety outlet if the ball is tied up. E's position is adjustable along the left foul lane. C's options after receiving A's pass: (1) shoot if open; (2) pass to B in the low pivot; (3) pass to D in the outer half of the foul circle after a screen.

223

Stack offense "one" for point man (to left—E screens)

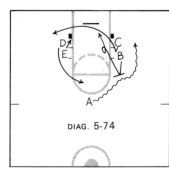

DIAG. 5-74

Diag. 5-74, STACK OFFENSE, "ONE"

A calls "one" and dribbles to the right. C fakes towards the ball and then cuts across the foul lane behind D and E. B moves up to set a screen at approximately the foul line extended. A dribbles off his screen. B makes an offensive roll to the basket after A cuts off his screen. D makes his normal move to the foul line and is the back man defensively if a shot is taken. E adjusts along the left foul lane. E adjusts along the left foul lane. A may also pass into B and use B as a screen, cutting off him for a return pass.

Diag. 5-75, STACK OFFENSE, "CLEAR FOR A."

On the clearing movement, C taps B and both C and B clear baseline to the opposite side, leaving the whole right side open for an offensive move by A. D makes his original move to the foul line, and E adjusts along the left lane. C will fall back into defensive safety position.

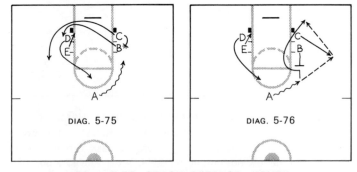

DIAG. 5-75   DIAG. 5-76

Diag. 5-76, STACK OFFENSE, "CUT"

If C's position or A's position is being overplayed, a cut off a stationary pivot is possible. A dribbles as though to start the offense, and C cuts out a sharper angle and deeper than usual. B sets a stationary screen at the right end of the foul line. A cuts to the inside off this screen to receive a return pass from C. D and E make their normal basic maneuvers.

Diag. 5-77, STACK OFFENSE, "GET TWO FOR D"

A starts his dribble to the right and then quickly reverses to the left, setting up a double screen along the left foul lane for D. D cuts tightly behind the double screen of E and A and receives a back pass from A for a quick short jump shot. C's move is similar to the move of D in the basic pattern, with B moving into rebounding position. If the shot is taken, C's move starts him back into good defensive position.

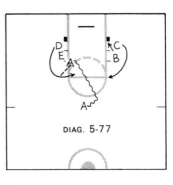

DIAG. 5-77

Diag. 5-78, STACK OFFENSE, "BACK DOOR"

X_3 has played between B and C, trying to overplay C's move out to the ball to prevent the pass. On observing this, A calls "back door" and dribbles over normally. B will immediately come up to the high pivot position on the ball side, bringing his defender, X_2, with him. C will come out into his normal position, being overplayed by X_3, and D and E make their normal moves. If C opens, the normal pass on this play would be for A to make the pass directly to C on his reverse move. The options: (1) A may pass to B, who may pass to C. (2) After C's cut, if the reverse doesn't show, A may pass to B and go "back door." (3) D may hold his position and C may continue to cut around D and E for a double screen.

DIAG. 5-78

Diag. 5-79, STACK OFFENSE, "SPLIT"

Some defenses will attempt to play a defender in front of B to guard C and in front of E to guard D. X_3 is guarding C and X_4 is guarding D. To counteract this defense, A calls "split" and dribbles opposite C, the man he wants to pass to. E breaks to the foul line, taking his defender, X_5, with him. D breaks to the left side, his defender, X_4, moving with him. On this movement, C fakes and cuts left on the low side, opposite, under the basket. A dribbles left and passes, timing C's cut. X_3, C's defender, cannot effectively guard C. If X_2 picks up C, A can make a quick lob pass to B, who will have X_3 on his back as he moves into the basket area. X_3 is normally a smaller defender, giving B the height advantage in the in-close area.

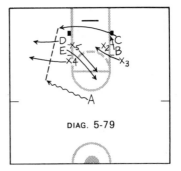

DIAG. 5-79

Stack offense "split." Defender playing outside D (24). A calls "split" and dribbles right.

Stack offense. Pivot defender fronts B with ball in right corner (C). Pass back to A opens B.

Diag. 5-80, STACK OFFENSE, "OVERPLAY"

Many defenses will attempt to put X_2, the defender guarding B, high, between B and the ball. When A observes this while dribbling, he calls "overplay." C, instead of coming out at a forty-five-degree angle, uses a more direct path towards the sidelines, paralleling the baseline. A passes to C. B, instead of pivoting counterclockwise on his right foot, will step into the pivot lane with his left foot, pivoting in a clockwise fashion so that he will be facing the basket with X_2 on his back. C simply has to pass the ball to the front of B for B to receive an easy shot, defeating the defensive alignment of X_2.

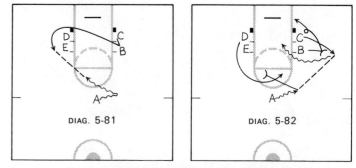

DIAG. 5-80

Diag. 5-81, STACK OFFENSE, "DOUBLE"

A starts his dribble to the right and changes direction on the call. C fakes a move out to the ball on the right side, then goes behind the natural double screen set by D and E on the left side. As he comes behind the double screen, A passes to him. If C is not open for the pass, A and B have an excellent two-on-two opportunity on the right side.

DIAG. 5-81   DIAG. 5-82

Diag. 5-82, STACK OFFENSE, "HELP C"

The offense moves as originally planned, C coming out to the ball and receiving the pass after A's penetrating dribble towards his right. B then sets a rear screen for C. C dribbles off the screen, and B offensively rolls to the basket. C may shoot, drive into the basket, pass back to B on his offensive roll, or to D, who is making his normal movement off the stack alignment.

226

Diag. 5-83, STACK OFFENSE, "LEAVE C ALONE"

A dribbles, and C moves out to receive the ball. B clears to the opposite side, allowing C one-on-one opportunity on the open side. D and E make their normal movement, D cutting off E's screen and taking advantage of A's screen in the outer half of the foul circle. (The plays in this diagram and in diagram 5-82 can also be used with B popping out to receive the ball.)

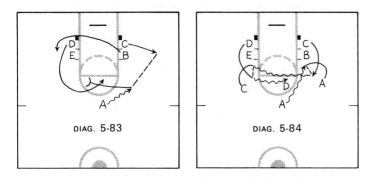

DIAG. 5-83   DIAG. 5-84

Diag. 5-84, STACK OFFENSE, "WEAVE"

It is possible from the stack alignment to have a tight weave using A, C, and D. On the weave call, A dribbles in. C comes around B and behind A, receives a hand off or flip pass from A, and dribbles across the foul line. D, timing his movement with that of A and C, comes around E and behind C, receiving the hand off from C. A and C both buttonhook back to continue the weave if a good shooting opportunity has not appeared. B and E will normally move into the basket for offensive rebound position.

Diag. 5-85, STACK OFFENSE, "SCISSOR"

A passes to C (1). B pivots for best position. C passes to B (2). C cuts first, A second, in a scissor move off B's pivot position.

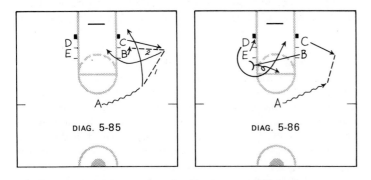

DIAG. 5-85   DIAG. 5-86

Diag. 5-86, STACK OFFENSE, "OPPOSITE"

A passes to C. B moves across the lane next to E. D cuts around the double screen set by E and B opposite the ball and drives into the basket. B makes an offensive roll into the lower half of the free-throw circle to be open on his roll back towards the ball if there is a switch. C passes to D, if open, or to B rolling back if defense switches.

227

Diag. 5-87, STACK OFFENSE, "PICK LOW"

A dribbles to the right, passing to C. E cuts around B, who moves as though to set up the opposite play but screens low for E. E cuts off B's screen to the basket and B rolls back towards the ball to be in position to receive a pass if a switch is made. C may pass to E on the first cut, to B on his roll back to the ball, or to D coming over E and A's screen.

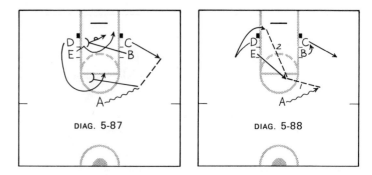

DIAG. 5-87   DIAG. 5-88

Diag. 5-88, STACK OFFENSE, "FLOAT"

Many times the defenders on the weak side, guarding D and E, will attempt to float towards the strong side as A moves. This play counteracts a float towards the B and C side and anticipation of D's movement around E's screen. As C pops out to position with A's dribbling movement to the offensive right, D starts around the screen that E would normally set. Simultaneously, E moves to the foul line. A quickly passes to E (1). D reverses and is usually open for an easy shot on a pass in from E (2).

Diag. 5-89, STACK OFFENSE, "QUICK"

Observing that D's defender assumes the usual cut around E in the basic stack movement, A calls "quick." As A starts his dribble, D cuts quickly between E and his defender into the area just below the foul line as the other players make their normal offensive moves. Usually, D's defender will be anticipating normal movement (around E), and a quick pass from A to D will give D a short jump shot.

DIAG. 5-89

Diag. 5-90, STACK OFFENSE, "LOB LEFT"

E is being played in front by X_5, either for position or to help defensively from the weak side. The play starts towards the right, as usual, with players making their normal moves. E, however, takes a step as though to come to the foul line, forcing X_5 high. As X_5 steps towards the foul line, E quickly reverses and A makes a lob pass over X_5 into the basket. It is essential that D make his normal move, staying a little wider than usual, however, to deploy X_4 with him and that B and C make their normal offensive moves on the right side.

DIAG. 5-90

Stack Offense Drills. Players work on all phases of the stack offense, drilling from three skeleton positions. A coach should be with each group.

228

Diag. 5-91, LEFT

D and E are in their stack positions at the left of the foul lane, and the point man, A, is in position. From this stack and point position, they work all the plays that have been outlined in this chapter on stack offense. This is a fundamental drill that we work on daily in the preseason practice.

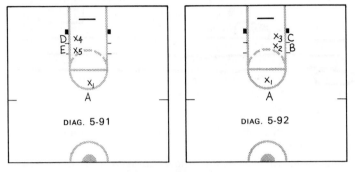

DIAG. 5-91   DIAG. 5-92

Diag. 5-92, RIGHT

B and C are on the right, and A is at the point. All phases of the stack offense are worked from these three positions. The play should be called by the point man or coach, and the players should react. Normally these drills are used only in early preseason practice.

zone offense

In determining what type of a zone offense to use, the coach should consider, first, his personnel and, second, the man-to-man offense he has designed. The closer the two offenses are in principle and in movement, the better the zone offense will be. He next should consider why the opponents are using a zone defense. Normally, they are doing so because their personnel is best suited for a zone. Other reasons include the following:

1. To institute an aggressive offense.

2. To disrupt a team that has a good set pattern against a man-to-man defense.

3. To protect players who are in foul trouble.

4. To protect a lead.

5. To change the tempo of a game.

6. To protect defensive players incapable of good man-to-man defense.

Since the reason for using the zone defense is negative rather than positive, the offense should attack it from that point of view. If the opponents are protecting players in foul trouble, the zone offense should move at those players if possible, using fakes and feints with the ball to force them to commit another foul.

There are two important factors in attacking a zone defense: (1) the players must be patient and (2) they must get a good shot every time they have possession. The basic facts to remember about a zone defense are that the zone moves with the ball, leaving areas away from the ball position open, and that the defensive rebounders are not in good blockout positions due to their slides. Offensive players must take advantage of this situation. First, the offensive players should get the ball in good shooting position. (Any shot within sixteen feet of the basket should be a good percentage shot if it is not under pressure.) Second, they should move away from the ball position. All men must be in their most advantageous position. They should never be near a defensive man, and they should split defenders. Third, all players should know what they are going to do with the ball before they receive it.

fundamentals

In zone offensive play the following fundamentals must be adhered to.

Dribbling. Dribble with caution against a zone, as dribbling generally tends to stabilize the defense. Never dribble between men unless they are very widely spread or over-extended. There are only two times when a player should dribble: (1) when he is driving with a lane to the basket either along the baseline or at a forty-five-degree angle, or (2) when he is moving back towards mid-court for protective purposes in order to keep the ball in play.

Cutting. When cutting against the zone, split defensive men. No more than two cutters should go in the same direction at one time. Attack a zone with player movements that counter defensive moves, cutting parallel with the path of the ball and constantly using a directional pattern towards the uncovered zone areas. Purposeful movement of men and the ball is essential. Cutting into the zone from behind the back men is effective. Fake without the ball while cutting in order to split men better.

Passing. Pass into the zone. Return the pass to the teammate you received it from. He will be open, because the zone moves with the ball. Never use routine or stereotyped passes or passing lanes. As any zone focuses attention primarily on the ball, accurate, quick, precise ball movement is essential in spreading the zone. Good ball movement increases the zone's vulnerability. Passes should be short, if possible, and bounce passes are extremely effective. Passes should be against the flow of the zone at all possible times.

Screening. It is possible to screen against a zone. You may screen inside or outside the perimeter of a zone, preventing an opponent from sliding defensively and permitting the teammate to shoot over your screen. Screens should normally be toward the sideline and baseline, screening the defensive man in from his outside, taking advantage of his defensive position. Screens require quick reversing actions in the flow of the ball.

SPL it DEF. MEN.

230

Rebounding. Offensive rebounding against a zone is of paramount importance. The players must aggressively move into rebounding position. As the zone defense slides, it sometimes takes the defenders away from the offensive players, so the offense should be able to get good rebounding position inside opponents if they are quick and aggressive. Slap or deflect the ball if possible.

Ball Control. Good ball handling is extremely important against a zone defense. Only good shots should be taken. Any hurried, deflected, or poor percentage shots hinder the zone offense's effectiveness. Players should take only high percentage shots without defensive pressure. Players should not expect to get this high precentage shot immediately against a good zone, but they must take it as soon as it appears. Primarily, a team must score from outside the periphery of the zone in order to penetrate it. If outside shooting is successful, the zone must extend away from the basket, opening the center of the zone for quick cuts, passes, or drives into this area. When the ball can be passed into the crucial middle-zone area effectively, the defense must collapse towards the ball, opening the intermediate shooting areas on the side of the pass-in and perhaps freeing cutters in the area away from the pass-in.

Danger Areas. Two areas are dangerous for offensive men playing against a zone defense—the corners and the pivot area. If a player is in the corner, defenders can double-team him. In addition, he has only two passing lanes: back out or into the middle of the zone. Therefore, a player who receives the ball in the corner should pass it out immediately unless he is an exceptionally good ball handler. In any instance, the ball should never be held in the corner for more than the count of two. Corner men, unless they have a baseline move to the basket, should never dribble the ball.

The pivot area is dangerous because the zone collapses back towards the ball. Therefore, before he receives the ball, the pivot man should know what he will do with it. He should know where the shooters are, and consider passing to a wing man. If his back is to the basket, the passer must tell him if he has a shot himself. He should never dribble the ball under any circumstances.

Overloading. Overloading the zone aids team maneuverability. Overloading can be from the stationary position at the outset or it can be from a moving stature after the ball has been passed one or two times.

Defensive Balance. All zone offenses must have built in safety factors. One man must always be moving back into a defensive position during movement of the ball against a zone defense to prevent an easy basket by the opponents from a turn-over or a fast break.

attacking principles

The following attacking principles should be incorporated into all offensive planning against zone defense.

Use the fast break immediately upon getting possession of the ball in order to get back before the defense can set up its zone. Even if the fast-break opportunity is not present, look for a high percentage shot before starting the offensive pattern, before the zone has time to set up.

Spread the zone as much as possible, attempting to overextend it, and then pass behind the overextended players for penetration. Attack the weak spots in the zone, using probing passes to determine who the weak players are and working through them. Using full-court pressure against a team playing a good zone may diminish the effectiveness of their zone.

Offensive players, except for a pivot man, should never have their backs to the basket when attacking a zone. If they do, teammates should seldom pass to them. A man in the foul line forces the defense to guard him, thereby controlling the structure of the zone. With the ball in the pivot, opportune baseline cuts and weak side cuts are possible. It is important that the zone offense shift with passes. Zone offense must be simple, but flexible. It must have a team offensive continuity with quick, coordinated team movement. Players should shuffle or rotate to outposition the zone, using an overload principle. Cutting through the zone is important in the zone offense.

An excellent maneuver is to use a good passer as the pivot man, regardless of his size. A small man (possibly a guard) in the center of a zone will be quick and more agile in his deploying movements than a bigger man. He will be able to find the openings between men and keep the pass low.

Fake from the back of the zone to the open areas when the ball is passed into the pivot area. With every pass, the offense should reposition themselves in relation to the adjusting defense, except for the defensive safety man. If a zone adjusts to cover up for an overextended defensive player, the offensive team should fake towards this shift and penetrate into the newly opened areas away from the shift. Cut into a zone to an open area or to the baseline, looking for openings in the defense as you cut. A cutter may delay momentarily to take advantage of a defensive slide in order to move between men.

Regardless of the original alignment of the zone, all zones tend to flex into similar postures after basic ball and offensive player movement. For example, one defensive player must be at the ball position; one defensive player must be positioned close to a pivot man; and one defensive player must be positioned under the basket defending

232

against lay-ups or weak-side movement. Therefore, in all zones at least three men are actually immobilized, and it is easy to determine their positions.

Against an attack defense, it is best to get the ball inside the front line. There is usually an opening between the front and back line, because the front line is attacking defensively and the back line is generally thinking about protecting the basket; therefore, good intermediate shots are possible. The floor should be balanced at all times.

Players should know and see the passing lanes. They should not make routine passes. It is best to move a zone from the inside with a quick fake rather than from the outside.

A player can pass to a man inside the perimeter of the zone with his back to the basket if he is not under defensive pressure. If he has a shot, the passer-in must call "two" or some such signal to alert the receiver to his shooting opportunity. If a player passes in without a call, the receiver knows he does not have a shot, and he should pass to teammates with good shooting opportunities as the defenders move towards him.

Offensive teams should be alert for changing defenses. If you are ahead, and the opponents are playing a zone, do not slow down the game; try to move the front line of the zone out so you can get good shots in the medium area. If the back line moves out, the weak side behind the back line is generally susceptible to cutting movements.

zone offense from a three-out two-in attack formation

When a three-two man-to-man offense is used, the offensive team should incorporate zone attack patterns from this alignment. These patterns should have a continuity, and be adaptable for use against any zone defense.

Diag. 5-93, ZONE OFFENSE, THREE-TWO ALIGNMENT
A dribbles to the right, indicating the direction of the movement against the zone. After one or two preliminary dribbles, he passes to B. As A starts his dribble, E moves from his low left position into a medium-pivot position on the ball side. B passes into E, if possible, and moves parallel with the sideline towards the baseline. D parallels E's movement, cutting quickly under the basket. E may pass to D, cutting under; to B, moving along the sideline; or to C, moving into the outer half of the free-throw circle.

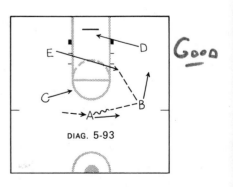

DIAG. 5-93

233

Good.

Diag. 5-94 (AN ALTERNATIVE TO DIAG. 5-93)

If B cannot pass into E, D will **V** out towards the corner, and B will pass into D (1). B then cuts immediately towards the basket. If he opens, he will receive a give-and-go return pass from D. After B's cut, E will slide from his medium-pivot position down to a low-pivot position on the ball side. A moves right as an outlet for the pass. C may move into the foul-line area or into the outer half of the free-throw circle in good shooting position for a possible quick pass from D. If D cannot pass to B, E or C, he will pass back to A (2) and A will pass to C (3), who will move to the head of the circle. B circles out to the left side to an open medium range shooting area.

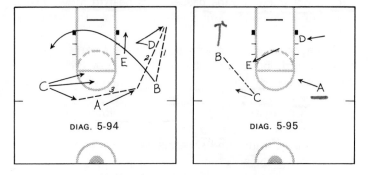

DIAG. 5-94   DIAG. 5-95

Diag. 5-95, THIS FOLLOWS DIAG. 5-94

C should pass quickly to B, as the opponents may have shifted to the offensive right, allowing B a good intermediate jump shot opportunity. E will move up from his low position into a medium-pivot position on the ball side. C moves towards B's side. D moves in under the basket, low, opposite the ball. A moves into the outer half of the free-throw circle, as he may be open because of the quick shift the opponents must make back to the offensive left.

Diag. 5-96, ZONE OFFENSE, THREE-TWO ALIGNMENT, SCREENING A ZONE

A passes to C (1), who moves to meet the pass. E moves up into high-pivot position. B moves towards the head of the key, getting a quick return pass from C (2). During this movement, D waits and times his positioning until the zone has slid to the offensive left. He screens the outside low man, farthest from the ball position. This player normally will be moving in to protect the area under the basket. D holds the screen. A, after his pass to C, cuts down the middle and hooks behind D's screen. B passes in to A (3).

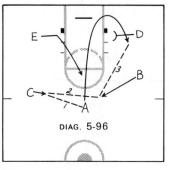

DIAG. 5-96

Diag. 5-97, ZONE OFFENSE, THREE-TWO ALIGNMENT, MOVE AGAINST A TWO-BACK ZONE

Teams using a three-two or one-two-two zone defense may be attacked as follows: A passes to B (1). At the same instant, D moves up into medium-pivot position from the right corner, and E, the opposite corner man, moves over into the position vacated by D and receives a pass from B (2). C is moving into the outer half of the free-throw circle. B may pass to D or C if either appears open.

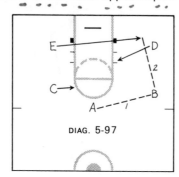

DIAG. 5-97

zone offense two-three

The two-three zone offense continuity is used by the authors as their secondary zone offense. We have also used this offense as a diversionary man-to-man offense attack *us match ups* and against match-up defenses. In this offense A is the best ball handler, the quarterback, who should have a good outside shot. He looks for openings in the front line of the zone near the key and for good outside shooting position. As he rarely penetrates in this offense, he is usually back as the defensive safety factor.

B is normally the other guard. He should be a good outside and medium jump shooter, tall enough to rebound, as he cuts through the zone on occasion. He should be able to pass into the pivot man, feed a wing man on a give-and-go movement, or pass out to A over pressure in the corner. C and D are usually the forwards, who move in a rocking motion from left side to right side and back. Normally, they are looking for plays inside. They are always primary rebounders with E in this zone offense continuity.

E is the center. He generally moves up and down along the foul lanes and across the lanes looking for good openings in the zone structure as he comes to the ball. If he receives it, he looks quickly for medium shots for B, C, or D or for shots for A in the outer half of the free-throw circle.

Diagrams 5-98 through 5-105 outline a complete offensive continuity against any type of zone defense.

Good

Diag. 5-98, ZONE OFFENSE, TWO-THREE CONTINUITY

B passes to C, as C moves up from his forward position at approximately the foul line extended. D cuts into the right corner. C returns the pass to B and cuts through the middle looking for a return pass from B. A and D adjust their positions towards the ball, A moving over to replace B. D moves up looking for good shooting position at the left side of the foul lane.

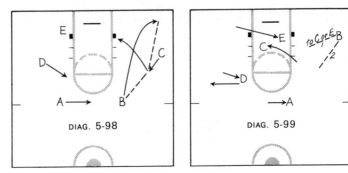

DIAG. 5-98

DIAG. 5-99

Diag. 5-99

B has two options with the ball in the corner. (1) He may execute a give-and-go pass to C, who is cutting through, or pass to E, who times his movement with C. As C is going away from the ball, E moves across the lane into low pivot position, looking for seams in the zone. B may pass to E as he moves into this position. (2) If B does not find E or C open, he will pass back out to A. D has adjusted over towards the end of the foul line. If he does not get a quick pass from A, he will move back into a position on the foul line extended, closer to the left sideline.

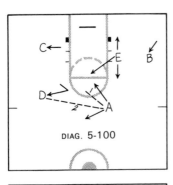

DIAG. 5-100

Diag. 5-100

As D did not have the good shooting position (1), he has moved back to position to receive the pass (2). As D moves back, C moves into the left corner. E may adjust his position into medium-pivot position on the weak side, going into the lower half of the free-throw circle if it appears open, because the zone must slide to the offensive left. B is moving back up towards his original position. A will adjust to the left with the ball movement. He may also break into the outer half of the free-throw circle for a quick return pass from D if the area is open.

DIAG. 5-101

Diag. 5-101

D, having passed the ball to C in the left corner, moves toward the ball and then cuts sharply across the middle. He may receive a return pass from C if he appears open. E comes across the lane, going on either side of D, looking for the open position inside the zone. Sometimes this position will appear higher than D's movement. As the zone drops back, the back line will drop back towards the basket to cover D's movement through. A adjusts to the offensive left. B moves out into his original position. B may move into the outer half of the free-throw circle if the opening appears for a quick pass from C to A to B.

236

Diag. 5-102

C could not make the pass to D or E. He returns the ball out to A. B, who could not get the pass into the outer half of the free-throw circle in the previous diagram, moves back into his normal position. E is now in his original position along the foul lane. C moves up to the position that D had at the beginning. D moves out to C's initial position. The ball may now be passed back from A to B and the offense started again.

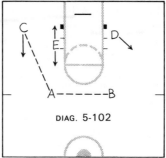

DIAG. 5-102

Options from these plays follow.

Diag. 5-103, ZONE OFFENSE, TWO-THREE

This is an alternative to the play in Diag. 5-101. D has the ball on the left side. A cuts through to the weak-side, and B comes back into original position. D fakes the pass to C as A calls the cut through, then D passes back to B at the head of the key. E moves down the right pivot lane. A will appear open in the right corner as a quick reversal of the ball back to the head of the key breaks normal continuity. This is a good maneuver for two reasons: (1) it breaks away from the routine stereotyped passing lanes that the defense may get used to, and (2) it gives A a chance to cut through, a move he does not normally make in this offense. As the zone is sliding from right to left quickly, this move will give A an open shot in a short jump-shot area along the baseline.

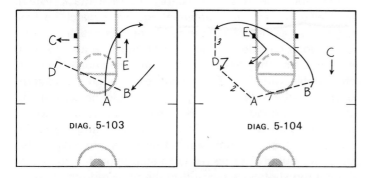

DIAG. 5-103

DIAG. 5-104

Diag. 5-104, ZONE OFFENSE FROM A TWO-THREE ALIGNMENT

Instead of passing into C in Diag. 5-98, B could pass back to A (1) and cut through diagonally. D fakes to the middle and comes back. A passes to D (2). E fakes as though he is going across and comes up into a medium position on the ball side. D passes to B (3) in the left corner after B's diagonal cut. B, D, and E form a good offensive triangle in an overload situation, as do D, E, and A.

Diag. 5-105, ZONE OFFENSE, TWO-THREE

This is a free-lance variation of movement in Diagram 5-104. A passes to D (1), who is moving up from his forward position. A follows through into the corner on the strong side. As D moves up, E moves up to a point approximating the left end of the foul line. B moves to the head of the key, and C moves into the right foul-lane area. C's position is adjustable up or down the foul lane or into either half of the free-throw circle if a shooting opportunity appears. D may pass to A. If A is covered by a back man, E may appear open within the zone perimeter in a pivot position. If neither A nor E appears open, and it is not possible to pass into C, D may pass to B (2), who may pass quickly to A running along the baseline. As the ball moves back from D to B, C should move out into good pass reception territory (3), looking for a quick pass along the baseline to A (4).

DIAG. 5-105

REAL
GOOD

zone offense, one-three-one alignment

One of the most popular zone offensive attack patterns, the one-three-one, is used as a basic pattern against man-to-man and zone. It is a formidable offensive attack system, as it also has excellent potential against a match-up type defense. A, at the head of the key, should be the best passer and a good outside shooter, and he must be able to diagnose holes as they appear in the zone. He should be interchangeable with B or C if he moves through the pattern. B and C—the side, or wing men—should be good jump shooters and good drivers, as many times they will have an opportunity to drive at a forty-five-degree angle into the basket. They should not expect to drive all the way in this situation, but should be ready to stop short for quick medium jump shots or a pass-off to the weak side of the back side of the zone (if the back line of the zone overshifts its position). D, on the foul line, is a pivot player who has good hands. He should be a fairly mobile person. E, the baseline player, should be more mobile, and a better outside shooter than D. If D and E have similar abilities, their positions are interchangeable.

Diag. 5-106, ZONE OFFENSE,
ONE-THREE-ONE CONTINUITY

A passes to B. E breaks out to the corner. E's position is adjustable; he may be either on the ball side or the weak side initially. Normally, the offense will start to the side on which E positions himself. B passes to E, who is moving out towards the corner. E's movement should be determined by the defensive alignment. He should only move out as far as he has to to receive the ball. Against some types of zone defenses (for example, a two-three, a wing man may move up to play B, which will allow E to stay fairly close in under the basket. E should be facing the basket when he receives the ball, ready to shoot if the opening occurs. B cuts through the zone looking for a return give-and-go pass from E. A has moved to the ball side. D, on the pivot, has turned toward the ball into a position where he may break down the right lane on the ball side as B clears through. C must take a step towards the basket as B cuts, because if E returns the ball to B, C should break for the baseline on the left side near the buffer zone marker. He will be open, because the zone will have to slide to stop B's shot. B knows that if he gets a return pass, C will be in this general area as a passing option. If the ball is not passed to B, he cuts through, away from the ball.

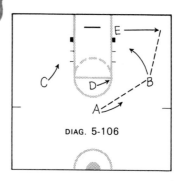

DIAG. 5-106

Diag. 5-107

E received the ball in the corner, but could not pass to B or D or shoot. He has to pass back out to A, who has moved from the head of the key into position as the outlet receiver. D has moved along the right foul lane into low-pivot position. C's position is now adjustable. He should look for an opening in the outer half of the free-throw circle for a quick shooting opportunity on a snap pass from A.

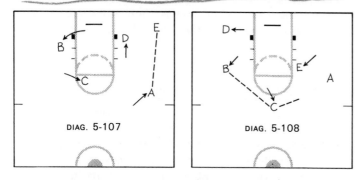

DIAG. 5-107   DIAG. 5-108

Diag. 5-108

None of the previous options have materialized. Therefore, C moves out to the head of the key and receives a pass from A. D now moves opposite to the left corner, anticipating movement of the offense to the left. E has moved from the corner position up into the foul line high-pivot area. C passes to B, who has passed into the left wing spot, and since D is moving out, the continuity offense is now ready to move through from the left. The positions of A, C, and B are interchangeable, as are the positions of D and E.

239

Diag. 5-109, ZONE OFFENSE, ONE-THREE-ONE ALIGNMENT, "OPPOSITE"

This works from the same basic formation, with A passing to B (1) and E and D simulating their movement in Diag. 5-106. However, in this play, B passes back to A (2) and cuts through to the opposite corner away from E, the underneath man. E and D anticipate this move as they **V** back towards the ball. C has faked his baseline move and has dropped back to get a pass (3). All the possibilities mentioned for Diag. 5-106 are available. Normally, B will cut through for a good quick shot, or C and B will find themselves in a two-on-one situation against the defense.

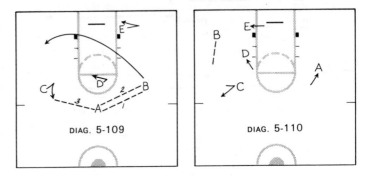

DIAG. 5-109   DIAG. 5-110

Diag. 5-110, ZONE OFFENSE, ONE-THREE-ONE, "OPPOSITE" CONTINUED

Many times when defending against a reverse movement, the defense overadjusts back toward the ball. B has received the ball from C. C now adjusts his position on the ball side. E has moved into low position, and D has moved into medium-pivot position, focusing the attention of the zone to the left offensive side. A may sneak down the right side to receive a pass over the zone from B or C for an open shot. While this play will not work often against a zone, and the pass is dangerous, if it works once it will help subsequent "opposite" moves, as the zone will be expecting the over-pass to A on the weak side and will not shift as readily.

a free-lance zone offense, the wheel

In this zone offense, four men are outside the zone perimeter with one man inside. If the four men who are outside are of comparable size and ability, and the inside player is a mobile, good-size pivot man, the Wheel is an excellent zone offense to use when players have good intuitive basketball sense and understand the precepts of good zone offense attack. There are no prescribed patterns or passing lanes; therefore, all players are able to move freely within the framework of the rules of the basic wheel pattern, making it extremely difficult for the defense to analyze offensive movement. This is a balanced offense with all five players moving according to a set plan, all five men having preknowledge of the movement of their teammates, and all five being able to pass the ball sharply and quickly.

We will describe the Wheel from the one-three-one alignment that we use most frequently. Four men form the perimeter of the wheel, rotating to the right or to the left, with the pivot man, D, as the hub. The passing lanes into and out of the pivot are the spokes. The pivot must constantly adjust position towards the ball as the players rotate left or right. Since he is inside the zone, he is the focal point of the offensive attack. If the ball can reach him and he can make a quick move, he should score.

Point Man A may pass to either wing, B or C, who should dribble towards the basket, shooting if open. If he is not open, he may dribble protectively as the wheel starts to turn. The underneath-the-basket man moves along the baseline, below the backline of the zone, stopping in good shooting position. The pivot man rolls to the ball side in the medium pivot, forming a spread triangle composed of the man with the ball, the baseline man, and himself. The opposite wing man will move down the opposite foul lane, towards the basket. A must delay at the outset to be sure that C, with the ball, has an outlet if he is in trouble. If the ball moves to the baseline man or to the pivot, A will move in the same direction as B, looking for openings in the zone. C shoots if he is open. If he is not, he tries to get the ball to the baseline man. The baseline man will shoot if open; if not, since the defense is sagging toward the ball, he may pass to the pivot, the opposite wing, his passer-in wing man on the same side, or the point man. If the pivot receives the pass from the wing man, he should shoot if open. If he can't shoot he may pass back out to the wing man who originally had the ball; pass to the opposite wing man moving in advantageous position along the weak-side foul lane; or pass back out to the point man, who has rotated away from the pivot side into medium shooting area at the opposite end of the foul line, or in the outer half of the free-throw circle.

The Wheel Offense may be started to either side, and it may rotate to the left or to the right. The offense must remain spread. The baseline man (who could be any of the four outside men) and the pivot man must know that their time with the ball is limited when the ball penetrates the zone; therefore, they must make their move immediately upon reception. They should know what their move is going to be before the ball reaches them. All outside players in the wheel should be alert for openings in the defense for quick movements into shooting position. If they do not receive the ball immediately, however, they should continue with their normal rotation in the wheel. All players in the outside perimeter should be able to maneuver from any one of the four outside positions. They must be alert for all possible defensive maneuvers that my tie the ball up so as to be in good safety outlet position to protect possession.

Diag. 5-111, ZONE OFFENSE, ONE-THREE-ONE ALIGNMENT, WHEEL

A passes to the left wing, C. A hesitates slightly to be sure that C is moving well with the ball, then moves away to the right. B also adjusts to his right. E moves over on the baseline side, close to the foul lane behind the back line of the zone defense. D rotates to the medium-pivot position on the ball side.

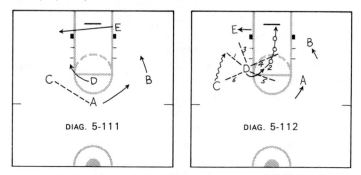

DIAG. 5-111

DIAG. 5-112

Diag. 5-112, WHEEL OFFENSE, CONTINUED

C dribbles probingly parallel with the left sideline as he did not have a good shooting opportunity. E moves out of the under-basket area, since C could not pass to him. C makes a quick pass (1) into D in the pivot. D now has five options with the ball: he may turn and shoot (C calls ''two'' for D) (2); he may pass to E as the zone moves towards D (3); he may pass across the lane to B (4); he may pass to A, who is at the right end of the foul line (5); or he may pass back to C (6).

overload offense

Basic movements against the zone defense will be similar to those in the man-to-man offense, omitting the inside screening and offensive roll techniques, which are negated by the zone defense positions, since no switching is necessary.

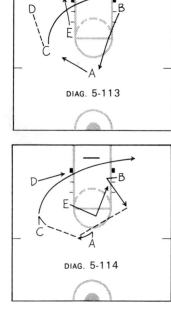

DIAG. 5-113

DIAG. 5-114

Diag. 5-113, OVERLOAD ZONE OFFENSE

C passes to D and cuts through the zone. E moves down along the foul lane. A rotates toward the ball from the head of the key. B moves out to the head of the key from his low position. The ball may now be passed quickly to the right, through A and B, to find C open. D has good triangle position on the left side with E and A.

Diag. 5-114, OVERLOAD ZONE OFFENSE

C fakes the pass to D and passes to A, who has moved towards him. C cuts through diagonally. B fakes into the foul lane and moves out right to receive A's pass at the foul line extended, approximately six feet from the foul line. He will pass quickly to C if C cuts through open. E has moved up to the foul line in a high-pivot position. B may pass to E. If E does not receive the pass, he moves along the right foul lane to medium-pivot position, forming a triangle with B and C. As E moves up to the foul line, he may draw a defender with him. D makes a quick move from the back side of the zone and many times a passing lane opens from B to D.

Diag. 5-115, OVERLOAD ZONE OFFENSE, SCREEN FOR C

This is a continuation of Diag. 5-114. B could not make any of the passes mentioned and dribbled out to his right. He passes to C (1) and cuts through to the opposite side. C passes back to A (2), who has moved right towards the ball. D has moved quickly out to the top of the key on the offensive left and receives a pass from A (3). If C is open, D can pass to him; if not, since the overload on the right is rocking back to the left, the zone defense is caught in two shifting moves and overadjusts back to the offensive left. D passes quickly back to A (4) who has moved in a few steps from his original position. E moves down the foul lane, screening the back weak-side defender. C moves in behind this screen, receiving a quick pass from A (5) for a screened shot.

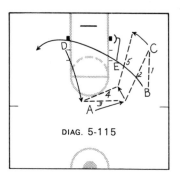

DIAG. 5-115

stack zone offense

The authors use stack offense as the primary attack weapon against all types of zone defenses. In using this offense against a zone, quickness of movement and timing are essential, as all moves must be made simultaneously when the defense is at its weakest posture. Basically the positions are the same as in the stack man-to-man offense. The moves are also basically the same, but in a zone, the point man, A, will dribble into a wing man in an odd-front defensive alignment and will dribble at a front-line man, being ready to change direction quickly on the dribble against an even alignment. A must reverse quickly so as not to be trapped by the even-front defense. Another adjustment against the zone occurs if the point is dribbling to the right. Instead of going behind E to the foul line area, D, the off-side man, cuts in front of E in a straight line cut to the foul line area. In offensive zone movement, the strong side pivot (B on the right and E on the left) must adjust his position between the defensive men in the zone structure. The man who pops out quickly (C to the right and D to the left) must pick the most advantageous position as he moves out. This again is determined by the type of zone.

Most teams resort to some type of man-to-man defense against the stack, because this offense quickly finds openings in most zone alignments.

Diag. 5-116, STACK ZONE OFFENSE AGAINST A TWO-THREE ZONE

A dribbles hard at X_2. If X_2 retreats, A looks quickly for C. If X_4 moves with C and X_2 has retreated at all, a passing lane opens immediately to B. If X_2 attacks A, A quickly passes to D, coming up the lane. Many times on this quick change he will find that X_4 has moved with C, X_5 has moved up to position on B, and X_3 has adjusted slightly towards D's position, allowing a quick, immediate lob opposite into E as E moves down the left lane.

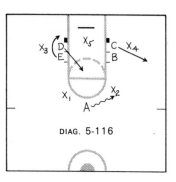

DIAG. 5-116

243

Diag. 5-117, STACK OFFENSE AGAINST TWO-ONE-TWO ZONE

A dribbles at the front man, X_2, again ready to change direction. Against the two-man front, A gets a lot of quick jump shots from the head of the key, especially if he is moving right and is a left-handed shooter or vice versa. C pops out normally, X_4 moving out with him. X_3 generally will overcompensate towards B, to cut off the pivot position. If X_3 moves quickly and X_4 moves out with C, the lob will show over X_3 into B along the right lane. D adjusts slightly, compensating for X_3's movement, positioning near the left end of the foul line. As X_3 expects X_1 to drop back, X_3 may move to the ball side. Sometimes, however, X_3 will not shift, opening the lane into B.

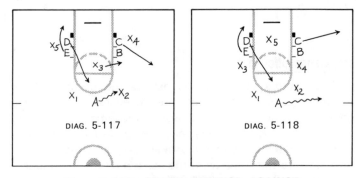

DIAG. 5-117

DIAG. 5-118

Diag. 5-118, STACK OFFENSE AGAINST TWO-TWO-ONE ZONE

A will try to dribble a little to the outside of X_2 if possible, because C will pop into the right corner, which is a good shooting area since X_4 is fronting B. A will look for a quick pass-in to C. If X_4 moves in that direction, A can pass into the pivot man, B, who should be adjusting up. B can shoot himself, pass back to A, pass to C in the corner, pass to D on the foul line, or pass to E, who has moved under the basket opposite.

Diag. 5-119, STACK OFFENSE AGAINST ONE-THREE-ONE ZONE

A dribbles right at the wing man, X_3. C moves into the right corner. B can move low, waiting for defensive adjustment until he sees how C will be covered. Normally C will be wide open. In this defense, X_2 will sometimes move over to front B, leaving C open. If X_3 falls back to cover C and X_1 shifts towards A, D will be open high on the foul line.

DIAG. 5-119

Diag. 5-120, STACK OFFENSE AGAINST ONE-TWO-TWO ZONE

A dribbles quickly towards the wing man, X_2. C pops out parallel to the baseline. B will adjust up slightly, giving X_4 the problem of covering B or C. Normally, C will be open for a shot from the right sideline, or B, in the pivot area, may receive a quick pass-in. Sometimes X_5 adjusts quickly across the lane, leaving E free on the weakside under.

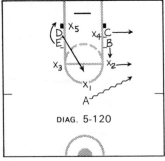

DIAG. 5-120

Diag. 5-121, STACK OFFENSE AGAINST THREE-TWO ZONE

A dribbles between the front men, X_1 and X_2, at X_2. C pops out and generally is open unless X_2 falls back. This gives A a good medium shot. B is in front of X_4 for a quick pass in, or D will be open quickly near the foul line.

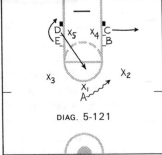

DIAG. 5-121

Many teams using a zone defense against the stack will attempt to double-team the point man as he moves into offensive position. To eliminate any risk and to attack aggressively from the stack zone offense stature, all players must be looking at the ball to see an attack movement by X_1 and X_2 as A dribbles into position. On this movement, a player (usually A) calls "Red." On the call, either B or E —generally the man on the side of the ball—moves up as high as he must to receive a high pass from A. The others deploy as shown in Diagram 5-122.

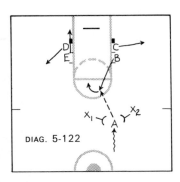

DIAG. 5-122

Diag. 5-122

X_1 and X_2 are attacking A. "Red" has been called. B moves up and receives a quick pass-in from A. B immediately turns to face the basket, taking a sixteen-foot shot if he is open. C moves into the right corner, D moves slightly to the left sideline in good shooting position, and E moves in directly to the basket. If the ball gets by X_1 and X_2, and B's pivot move is quick, one of the three players inside will have an easy, high-percentage shot.

245

attacking
match-up defenses

USE STACK
vs
MATCH UP.

A match-up defense—zone or man-to-man—attempts to force the pattern team out of its set patterns, getting the offense to stand still. Teams playing against a match-up defense should not congest areas away from the ball where one defender may guard two offensive players. Attackers should also omit inside screens, which are usually ineffective against this defense.

The offense used against a match-up defense must be a well executed, properly timed, intelligent moving offense that utilizes pre-knowledge of the defense's principles. Good ball handling and ball control are essential. We recommend the stack offense, which takes teams out of a match-up defense and forces them into a straight man-to-man or zone set-up, since it's impossible to match up the men when they are in a close-to-the-basket position.

The offensive team must determine the type of match-up defense being used and attack it. Primarily, the offense should beat it back to the set position by fast breaking and taking good high percentage shots quickly before the defense has a chance to align itself. Diagonal cuts make trading of men—essential in a match-up defense—difficult, and they confuse the defense. Long cuts on the same side as the ball and diagonal cuts opposite the ball are also effective. Cuts paralleling the path of the ball make trading difficult and force a small defender to make a difficult decision —whether to stay with the man paralleling the ball or to trade him to someone else. This defensive indecisiveness must become an offensive asset.

Passers should be alert for defenders playing intercepting angles and cutting off passing lanes, and they must move and receive the ball with assurance. Offensive players should shoot over outside screens. With quick ball movement it is possible to isolate an offensive player for a one-on-one situation. Since the primary receiver is usually overplayed, pass by him, using a safe passing lane. Moving in quickly without the ball behind a teammate's movement with or without the ball is a good trailing maneuver.

The offense should reverse the direction of the ball quickly against a match-up defense. Players should use back-door moves in the front line to combat overplaying outlets. Since defenders are normally overplaying to prevent a forward from getting the ball, a quick fake towards the ball and a reverse movement may open the offensive player. Simply reversing the ball movement may take advantage of two offensive players who are guarded by one man in a defensive area away from the ball. Smaller players should use bounce passes to penetrate past the big men who are kept inside by the match-up defensive deployment.

two-three and three-two offenses

Good cutting opportunities such as long cuts on the

246

ball side, diagonal cuts through the match-up defense, and back-doors should be incorporated into the two-three and three-two offenses against a match-up defense.

Diag. 5-123, TWO-THREE OFFENSE AGAINST MATCH-UP DEFENSE

B passes to A (1). D, the left forward, fakes and comes back to receive a pass from A (2). B makes a diagonal cut paralleling the path of the ball. B's cut makes it difficult for B's defender to trade off, as he would normally do on a normal passing maneuver from B to A to D. Therefore, B should be open for a shot. E moves behind B's cut into medium-pivot position. C makes a parallel cut to the weak side.

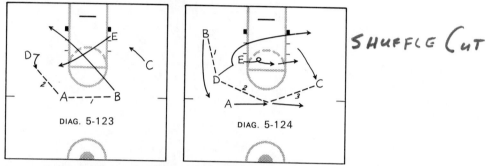

DIAG. 5-123

DIAG. 5-124

Diag. 5-124, TWO-THREE OFFENSE AGAINST MATCH-UP DEFENSE

If B does not have a shot, he passes back out to D (1). D passes to A (2) moving away from the ball, and A passes to C (3) who has V'd back out. D makes a diagonal cut off E to the opposite corner. A trade is possible here, with the big man switching from D to E. E (now being guarded by a small man) makes an offensive roll to the ball for possession and a shot if possible. It's also possible that D may open. A continues moving toward the ball. B, after his pass, moves out of the corner as a safety man.

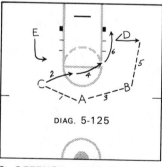

DIAG. 5-125

Diag. 5-125, THREE-TWO OFFENSE AGAINST MATCH-UP DEFENSE

C passes to A (1) and parallels the pass with his cut (2), moving into the outer half of the free-throw circle. As A passes to B (3), C parallels this pass, cutting (4) to the right end of the foul line. D makes a V and moves out for a pass from B (5). C parallels this pass along the foul lane (6). E moves out of his position, alert for rebounding on the weak side if a shot is taken from the right and ready to move into good offensive position.

247

Diag. 5-126 (CONTINUATION OF DIAG. 5-125)

Since D cannot pass into C's movement. B **V**'s out and receives a return pass from D (1). E has moved into the high-pivot area. C moves across under the basket (2) paralleling B's pass to E (3). E passes out to A (4). C moves out from underneath (5), again paralleling the path of the pass. A good parallel path causes the defensive man to move through with the offensive player. Any player may make this paralleling cut. E, after passing back to A, moves down the middle in a give-and-go movement and cuts out to the left offensive corner to resume position to start the offense again.

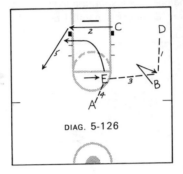

DIAG. 5-126

one-three-one offense

Along with the stack, the one-three-one presents the best opportunities against a match-up defense.

Diag. 5-127, ONE-THREE-ONE OFFENSE, ROCKER MOVE AGAINST A MATCH-UP DEFENSE

C initiates the offense by passing to A. A passes to B, then moves to the right of the head of the key. B must be alert for C's cut, diagonally paralleling the path of the passes, to the right corner. B has three options: (1) he may pass to C if C cuts free on his movement; (2) he may pass to E in the low pivot on the ball side if there is a trade between C's man and E's man; and (3) he may pass back to A, who has adjusted position. (This rocker movement may be made in both directions. If it were made from right to left by B in Diag. 5-127, E would adjust across the pivot lane as the passes were being made to allow B to cut off him.)

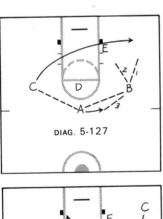

DIAG. 5-127

Diag. 5-128 (CONTINUATION OF DIAG. 5-127)

As soon as D sees B pass back to A, he moves out and screens A's defender. A dribbles tightly off D's screen and has many good jump shooting opportunities at the left end of the foul line. A may continue all the way to the basket if it is open. If a switch is made, D makes an offensive roll to the basket, moving along the left lane, away from the defensive congestion to the right.

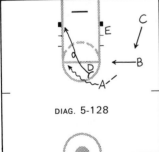

DIAG. 5-128

248

Normally a stack offense negates the effectiveness of a combination defense against an outstanding player. If the player is put on the point, it is difficult to double-team him. The defense must play some type of a two-man front zone, which will allow the offense to penetrate and take advantage of the stack alignment. If the man being played man-to-man is put inside in a stack offense, natural screens are set up. Since the zone defenders are concentrating on double-teaming this star, they will leave lanes open for easy shots from basic stack movement.

The defense does not want the outstanding player to get his normal share of points or to handle the ball if possible. Therefore, the offense must concentrate on getting the ball to him. A big man may be inside in the stack, on the baseline, low on a one-three-one offense, or in pivot position. A small man should move according to plan.

The team should plan to cause defensive confusion, setting screens for the outstanding player and getting him open away from the zone for a one-on-one situation against his man-to-man guard. Teammates may pass directly to him when he cuts into the seam of a box or diamond zone.

Diag. 5-129, COMBINATION OFFENSE AGAINST A ZONE-AND-ONE

A, the outstanding player, has the ball but is bothered by his defender and is double-teamed. A passes in to C (1) in the corner and moves off D's screen. B has moved into receiving position to the right side of the head of the key. C has these options: he may pass to A cutting off D's screen to the basket (2); he may pass to A behind D's screen for a shot (3); or he may pass back to B (4). He passes to B, who dribbles in, pivots, and sets a post at the foul line. A reverses direction, cuts off D and B, receiving a hand back or flip pass from B. A dribbles into the open area, left, for a one-on-one maneuver against the man playing him man-to-man.

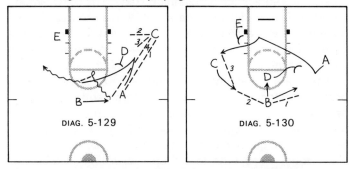

DIAG. 5-129   DIAG. 5-130

Diag. 5-130, COMBINATION OFFENSE USING ONE-THREE-ONE AGAINST A ZONE-AND-ONE

A, the outstanding player, has the ball without being able to move on the right side. A passes to B (1). B passes to C, who has V'd out (2). D, at the pass A to B, sets a screen. A runs his defender into the screen. E, low on the left side, moves up and sets another screen. A maneuvers his man into this screen. C moves out, receives the pass from B (2), and relays the ball to A (3) for an offensive move.

249

Diag. 5-131 (CONTINUATION OF DIAG. 5-130)

If A does not have the shot, he passes back out to C (1). C and B have moved to the right in this offense, rotating away from the ball. E moves up from the low position on the left side and sets a screen. A maneuvers his defender into this screen. D sets a low screen on the right. The ball moves from C to B (2) to A (3), who cuts off the two screens trying to elude his defender. C steps into the outer half of the free-throw circle. If B can't get the ball to A, C may appear open for an easy shot. This is a rocker type of offense that can be moved from side to side, with B and C rotating opposite the flow of the ball and D and E switching from the foul line in a high-pivot position to the buffer zone in low pivot. D and E are always opposite each other, setting continual high-low screens for A to run off.

attacking pressure defenses

A predominant part of current defensive planning in basketball defies the old theory of keeping a man defensively between his man and the basket. That is being discarded for an aggressive new theory. In man-to-man defense, men play between the ball and the men they are guarding, force reverses, force longer passes, and try to intercept the ball. When playing zone, they invite long passes and attempt to harry the offensive team into difficult situations by the threat of double-teaming and by using zone techniques full-court, three-quarter court or half-court. This type of basketball defeats the old offensive tactic of passing to a man and screening away—first, the defenders won't allow the pass, and second, they will jump switch on the crosses.

Modern defensive maneuvers require a great deal of intelligent offensive planning and coaching innovations. They require an aggressive offensive tactic of quick penetration.

One of the most important aspects in preparing for defensive pressure is the preplanning stage. The coach should be ready for the defense. He should have scouted the opponent, be abreast of modern trends, and know the principles of the defense he will be attacking. Preknowledge makes the attacking plan easier to put into effect.

There are several theories concerning playing against pressure defenses. The first one recommends having the nearest man pass the ball in quickly, as soon as it is out-of-bounds after a basket or foul shot. The speedy pass-in takes advantage of the fact that pressure defenses—especially zone—need time to set up. According to a second theory, however, hurrying may result in an intercepted ball if the wrong man takes the ball out-of-bounds.

The coach must prepare his team psychologically not to be upset by pressing tactics. He should tell the players that structurally and theoretically pressing defenses are the weakest defenses in basketball, because they overplay or double-team opponents. Overplaying leaves openings that an offensive team can attack and take advantage of if it plays with poise, confidence and preknowledge. If the ball can successfully escape the double-team, the attackers have a one-man advantage at the other end of the court when the ball is moved up court quickly. Man-to-man press and zone press attempt to do in a full-court area what it is difficult to do in the area within twenty-one feet of the basket—prevent the opposing team from scoring baskets. Teams must understand that with preparation and confidence, they can discourage this type of defense.

team offense against man-to-man press

Against man-to-man press, work within the margin of error theory, allowing the best dribbler and ball handler to dribble the ball up. Most good dribblers have little difficulty alone in the back court dribbling upcourt against one opponent. If the best dribbler does have difficulty the most mobile offensive player with a weaker defender—perhaps the other guard or a forward—can dribble the ball upcourt alone. Against man-to-man pressure, a good dribbler will use a controlled dribble, change of direction, and reverse dribble.

The good dribbler can beat most defenders one-on-one if he can control his defensive man until he gets to the front court. If he is double-teamed there, he should try to pass into the pivot. The pivot must protect the ball and pass it quickly, usually to a weak-side cutter or back to the man who passed it in.

Players must know the intent of the team playing man-to-man pressure defense full court in order to prepare to combat it. The usual reasons for playing this type of defense are as follows:

1. To intercept the pass by overplaying the men on the court

2. To prevent penetration by the good ball handler by double-teaming him and forcing the ball towards a weaker ball handler, playing intercepting angle to prevent the ball from being passed back to the good ball handler

3. To harass the receiver for a violation or a misplay

4. To invite the long pass for interception

5. To deter the offense in the back court for a ten-second violation.

Diag. 5-132, ATTACKING FULL-COURT MAN-TO-MAN DEFENSIVE PRESS, BEST DRIBBLER TAKING THE BALL UP
C, D, and E are upcourt. A, the best dribbler, takes the ball from out-of-bounds, passing it inbounds to B (1). B immediately returns the pass to A (2). Both B and A use defensive fakes to deploy the defensive men away from their intended positions. A dribbles upcourt, using reverse dribbles and protecting the ball. B moves away from A. The positions of A and B may be reversed.

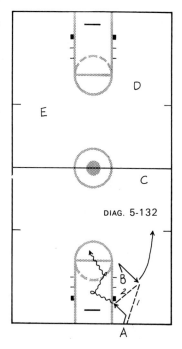

DIAG. 5-132

251

Diag. 5-133, ALLOWING A GOOD BIG DRIBBLER TO BRING THE BALL UP ALONE AGAINST A WEAK DEFENDER

B, the best ball handler, has been double-teamed in the back court by X_1 and X_2. A cannot pass the ball to B. E has the weakest opponent in the man-to-man defensive structure. D **V**'s to the ball and moves away downcourt. C fakes to the ball, then breaks to the middle as though to receive a pass. A moves along the end line so that the basket will not interfere with his pass-in. E, who has a weak defender, deploys a step up, then comes back to the ball, receiving A's pass-in. All players now clear E so that he may dribble up without being double-teamed. As soon as it is safe, E will pass the ball back to Guard A or Guard B in the front court.

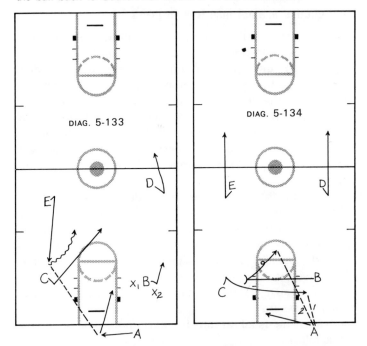

DIAG. 5-133   DIAG. 5-134

Diag. 5-134, BACKCOURT SCREEN PLAY AGAINST FULL-COURT MAN-TO-MAN PRESSURE WITH ALL FIVE OFFENSIVE PLAYERS IN THE BACKCOURT

A has the ball out-of-bounds. D and E, near mid-court, fake to the ball and pull their men upcourt. B moves across the foul lane, setting a screen for C. C **V**'s away, then comes back and receives the pass-in from A (1). If there is a switch on the play, A may pass to B (2) after B executes an offensive roll moving upcourt. If a switch is made, B will often have a slower defender on him, as C's defender may be a forward. A full-court three-on-two break is possible if B gets ahead of the switching defender on his offensive roll. A should be in protective position to get a return pass from B or C.

attacking zone-pressure defenses

Before structuring an offense against various types of zone presses, we should examine the uses of zone press.

    1. The zone press is a psychological attempt to disrupt an offensive routine.

2. It is an offense itself, attacking to intercept passes and to fast-break on steals.

3. It is used when a team has good pressing personnel defensively.

4. It is used by smaller teams against bigger, less coordinated opponents.

5. It is used to upset the poise of the opponents, especially inexperienced teams.

6. It is used to upset a team offense, attempting to force opponents to use lob passes, cross-court passes, and long passes to get the ball upcourt with either more than one man moving the ball or one man trying to bring the ball upcourt alone.

7. It attempts to force the opponents into double-teaming situations that affect the peripheral vision of the man with the ball, delimits his passing lanes, and negates his dribbling ability.

8. It attempts to force misplays and violations.

9. It changes the offensive stratagem and patterns, as it overplays and plays in the passing lanes, using intercepting angles.

10. Since it is usually well conceived and well coached, it requires a well conceived and well coached offensive attack to beat it.

11. It forces hurried, poor, low percentage shots.

12. It forces turnovers, or loss of possession, and mistakes that upset the confidence of a team, especially when that team is leading.

13. It is an excellent late game defense when the leading opponent is tired or the game is close, as it forces physical and mental errors.

14. It upsets and determines the tempo a game will be played at.

15. It takes calculated risks to force the opponents to hurry.

The following points should be incorporated into a team's zone pressure offense. The team should attempt to keep the ball in the middle of the court at all times. Therefore, players should never pass to teammates moving into a corner, towards a sideline or at a hash-mark, except in desperate circumstances. A jump ball may be preferable. When players are double-teamed near a side line, the side line becomes in effect a third defender. Get the ball over mid-court safely and quickly. Once the ball is over mid-court, the guards should get over the mid-court line quickly so that they can help the forwards and centers in the front court who haven't been able to penetrate to the basket, and to negate a back-court violation.

If a dribbler is being double-teamed he should never turn his back to his own basket in the back court. He should anticipate a double-team with the ball, see as much of the court as possible at all times, and know his primary outlets.

If he has dribbled by an opponent and the man is behind him, he should push the dribble far in front of him or change hands immediately on the dribble to prevent a rear flick by the defender. Players in possession of the ball should always expect pressure from behind and from the blind side when the ball has broken by the front line of a zone press defense.

After a basket, a team should get the ball in play quickly, before the press can set up. The near man should retrieve the ball before it hits the floor after going through the basket, step out-of-bounds, and inbound it to his offensive advantage.

Players should go to the basket in attacking a zone pressure defense. A fast-break situation is always possible when a player is double-teamed, as the offensive team has a one-man advantage. Players should be able to sense a double-team moving towards them. They should practice defeating it every day. A teammate of a man being double-teamed should approach within his visual field, using a recognizable voice signal and spreading wide so that he is not close to another defensive player.

It is difficult to tell a man who is about to be double-teamed when he should pass. He should try to maintain control of the ball until he is attacked; but if the double-team trap can be sprung on him, he should pass early rather than too late.

IMP. ☆

Zone offenses against pressure need a series of release men. One man should always be behind the ball handler in the backcourt, serving as a safety outlet. The ball should always be returned to the best ball handler quickly. If forwards or centers are handling the ball, they should know the good ball handlers, their position, and where to look for them. Conversely, the ball handlers should always be coming to the ball, in keeping with the margin of error theory. They are less likely to make ball handling mistakes.

Players normally should go away from the pressure after they have passed off. All players should fill fast-break lanes when the ball has penetrated by the front line of the opponent's zone press defense. Players with the ball should fake, then pass quickly, because a fake freezes most defenders momentarily.

The offense must organize well and set up quickly. It must be practiced daily. A team must know its offense and have confidence in it. Practicing against inferior defenders at first will instill this confidence.

Teams should remember when they are moving the ball upcourt against a pressure zone defense that ten seconds is a long time and they need not fear the ten-second rule unduly. In practicing, a team should first walk through their zone press offense, delineating each position, its responsibilities, and its options. Then they should move through the offense at half speed in skeleton form. Next they should play against stationary defenders, then against slow-moving defenders, then against a defensive team whose players are not allowed to use their hands. Finally, to perfect timing and coordination and to instill confidence, the offense should be used against weak defenders. Drills should cover good vision, handling the ball while moving, and playing against outnumbered defenses. All players must recognize the defenses that they are practicing against and their positions and deployment, making their own moves counter to the defensive moves. After a team has mastered fundamentals of the zone offense, and can move through its various maneuvers smoothly and with good timing, coaches may use extra defenders in practice sessions to give offensive players poise and confidence. It is also useful in practice to forbid dribbling when moving the ball upcourt against a zone press defense. Practice time should also be given to using a controlled dribble—bouncing a dribble into a trap purposefully so as to get the defenders moving towards the ball and then passing.   *go to trap.*

Coaches should seek questions. The players must be interested and intent. They must know the how, what, where and why of their zone pressure offense. Coaches should also question the players, especially those who are making mistakes, for mistakes in this offense always lead to an opponent's basket. Mistakes should be corrected immediately or the player should be replaced. A player should never make a cross-court pass unless he is one-hundred percent certain of success.

It is easy to double-team a man who has used his dribble; therefore, players should use the dribble effectively and purposefully. Good ball handlers should dribble if they are in the middle lane and the ball is by the front line. They may also dribble to avoid trouble, to drive to the basket, and to decoy a double-team.

Players must meet passes. They should make sure they have possession of the ball before they attempt to make a pass themselves. Some players try to catch and pass in the same motion to hurry the offense upcourt. This is disastrous. Deceptive deployment prior to meeting the pass is a must for all offensive players.

The zone press offense must get by the front line and attack. It must attempt to distort the front line. A player should move up behind one of the front-line defenders and try to draw him away so as to get the ball by the front line quicker. Once the ball gets by, the guards must sprint upcourt to get it back in order to bring it quickly into position for the good high-percentage shot. A positive, aggressive attack is necessary against any zone press. Dribble under control towards the trap with your head up. As the defenders approach, make your preassigned move to gain a one-man advantage as the ball moves upcourt. Know that you can pass back in the backcourt. There should always be a teammate behind the ball. If a ball handler passes back, he must drop back as a safety outlet for the teammate he has passed to, or he can angle towards the ball to a position behind the defenders and in front of the teammate who has received his pass for a quick pass splitting defenders.

Players must be prepared for zone pressure tactics at any time in a ball game, especially after a time-out or the insertion of substitutes with known speed and good defensive ability. They should also be prepared for zone pressure when they are ahead in a ball game.

The following three passes are available to players in a zone pressure offense: (1) back to a trailer; (2) to a man in a predetermined position upcourt in the ball handler's field of vision; and (3) between a double-team to a teammate moving behind double teamers into a position to get the ball. A long diagonal pass is possible if all defenders are accountable and the possible receiver can get into good scoring position without defensive pressure. This means that you must know the exact location of the five defensive players before making the pass. With extreme caution, a long two-hand lead pass may be made to a teammate moving downcourt away from the ball, the pass travelling over a defender. Never use a lob pass.

Players should remember the following important factors. Coaches would rather have a jump ball in a pressure situation than have a player throw the ball away. A player may dribble when no double-team is coming at him, but his head must be up. He should never try to dribble unless he has room to dribble, and he shouldn't stop once he has started unless he has to. Dribble when no good pass can be made, using it as a penetrating dribble. It's important to spread the defense as widely as possible in a full-court posture according to the preconceived offensive plan. Players should never leave the ball in the backcourt in the possession of a teammate by himself. Players should never cluster in one area; stay spread.

If a player is pressured on the end line, he may back up, run the end line, or pass to a teammate out-of-bounds. If he passes to a teammate along the end line out-of-bounds, he should move towards the ball for a return pass, using deploying tactics so he will be open.

To be successful against a zone press attack, each player must break towards passes when he is the primary receiver, and he should not stop until he has received the ball. If he receives the ball with his back to their offensive basket, he should pivot immediately and look upcourt with-

256 —

out dribbling. He should pass to an open man and cut quickly to his assigned area, being certain that there is good offensive floor balance.

The team should stay as close to the prescribed method of attack as possible. While there are times when players may use some extemporaneous move, it is best for all if the practiced method of sifting through a zone press defense is used.

Diag. 5-135, SPLITTING A POSSIBLE ZONE DEFENSE TRAP WITH A DRIBBLE

A, the best ball handler, has passed the ball in bounds to B (1). B has **V**'d away and come back to the ball to receive A's pass. B uses a controlled dribble to draw the trap of X_1 and X_2. As X_1 and X_2 move into trapping position, B passes back to teammate A (2), who has timed his move from out-of-bounds so as to be as close to B as necessary without allowing X_1 an intercepting chance. A will drive hard at X_3's position through the attempted trap by X_1 and X_3 before X_1 can double team. This is a good maneuver with a strong dribbler.

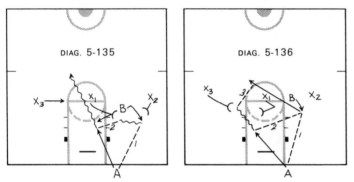

DIAG. 5-135   DIAG. 5-136

Diag. 5-136, SPLITTING THROUGH A ZONE DEFENSE AFTER THE TRAP AND ANGLING TO THE BALL

A passes into B (1). B passes back to A (2). A dribbles under control into X_1 and X_3's trap. B angles sharply to a position in front of A, behind X_1, so that he is in A's field of vision. A splits the trap with a quick pass (3). A should be the best ball handler.

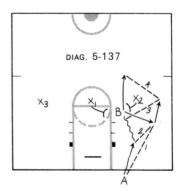

DIAG. 5-137

Diag. 5-137, SPLITTING A ZONE DEFENSE TRAP AFTER PASSING

A, the best ball handler, passes from out-of-bounds to B to the side (1). B return passes to A (2). A uses a controlled dribble into X_2 and X_1's trap. Just as X_2 makes his move for the trap, A passes quickly to B (3), who is moving up the right side line, and breaks through the trap, receiving a return pass from B (4).

257

Diag. 5-138, ONE-ONE-TWO-ONE ZONE PRESS OFFENSE

A is out-of-bounds with the ball, whether the opposing front is odd or even. B is near the foul line or the foul line extended, usually starting behind X_1 for greater deception. C and D are near the mid-court line, with C having the responsibility of moving a front line defender (X_3 in this case) away from the front line so that the offense can control its initial pass-in for its advantage. As A is to the right of the foul lane, X_4, the deep defensive player, will probably favor this side so as to be fronting the ball. Therefore, X_3 will have to move back to be certain that C cannot receive a pass beyond the front line. C must keep X_3 aware of his presence so that he will be more inclined to move back towards C than to attack the ball. B, the best ball handler, fakes and moves toward the ball, A passing the ball inbounds to B (1). As soon as A has passed to B, A moves into the court, away from the side that B is on. B uses a controlled one- or two-bounce dribble to lure the trap of X_1 and X_2 towards him and passes back to A (2) as quickly as feasible. A drives directly towards the position that X_3 is moving back into. As X_3 moves away from him, C comes back to receive a pass. A passes to C (3), because X_4 cannot cross the court to stop the pass. As soon as A passes he breaks up the middle as an alternate receiver. Without dribbling, C passes to B (4) who has broken up the middle through the trap. C must be aware of X_4's coming across the court hard at him, but as C's pass is backward (B being behind C), it is usually a safe pass. Either A or B must have the ball for a drive down the middle to obtain a fast-break basket.

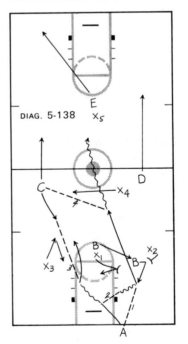

DIAG. 5-138

Diag. 5-139, ONE-ONE-TWO-ONE ZONE PRESS OFFENSE AGAINST AN EVEN DEFENSE FRONT

B is in the center. A passes to B, who takes a controlled dribble and passes back to A. A dribbles hard to the right, where the defense wants him to go. As X_4 and X_2 react to trap A, B will break up the middle of the court to receive a return pass from A (1). If X_2 overplays on the side of A so that A feels he can't get the pass to B, he may pass to D (2), who will take a step towards A to receive the pass as X_4 comes up quickly. B would continue upcourt and receive a pass from D.

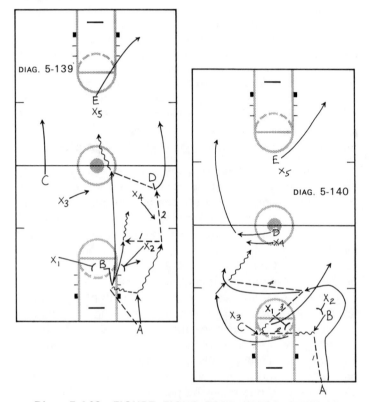

Diag. 5-140, FIGURE EIGHT ZONE PRESS OFFENSE FROM A ONE-TWO-ONE-ONE ALIGNMENT

This is a little used and hardly ever mentioned offense against zone pressure, yet, it is one of the most practiced fundamental drills in the game of basketball and is an easy, effective method of moving the ball upcourt against any type of zone press. A player simply passes and goes behind the receiver, who passes to a third teammate. The first player looks for a pass from the third player as he cuts into the player's field of vision. D should always go opposite the first pass in this type of zone press offense. A passes into B (1) and cuts behind him. B takes a controlled dribble left to lure X_1 and X_2 to trap him. B passes to C (2). B cuts behind C. C knows that A, the first cutter in the figure 8, will be moving from right to left into his field of vision. C takes a controlled dribble, then makes the third pass to A, splitting X_1 and X_3. C cuts behind A. A now knows that B will be cutting into his vision left to right and may make a fourth pass to B. When either guard, A or B, has broken the front line of the zone press, he should be the middle man in a fast-break thrust.

We incorporate the following three drills into our practice sessions with excellent results.

Diag. 5-141, FULL-COURT, FIVE-ON-FIVE DOUBLE WHISTLE DRILL

DIAG. 5-141

Whenever the coach sees any obvious mistake on the court from which all players in a full-court five-on-five situation can profit, he double whistles. At that signal, all players must instantly freeze in position, so that the coach can point out and correct the mistake for the benefit of all. We use this drill frequently with excellent results. The diagramed play is an example of a situation calling for a double whistle. Offensive players are O_1, O_2, O_3, O_4 and O_5, and defensive players are X_1, X_2, X_3, X_4, and X_5. O_1 passes upcourt to O_3, who dribbles, stops, and shoots with X_3 in good defensive position. O_4 is in the left corner. Once O_3 started to dribble we would double whistle. As soon as he received the ball, he should have passed to O_4. If O_4 had received the pass and dribbled towards the basket, either he or O_5, coming in from the other side, would get a lay-up.

full-court, five-on-five no-bounce drill

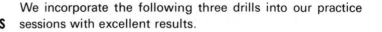

This fun drill works to greatest advantage during the regular season, although it may be used occasionally in preseason. No player may put the ball on the floor, except to bounce pass, on penalty of losing the ball. Dribbling is a violation, except in two situations: When an unopposed player is within 15 feet of the basket, one bounce is allowed for a lay-up. One bounce is also permitted to clear a rebound if the rebounder is tied up.

This is a very interesting drill to use with players at any level, especially young players. It is amazing how difficult it is for players to advance the ball up the court without bouncing. At first, they will stand in one place when they can't dribble. Through this drill, players learn to pass the ball upcourt, and players without the ball learn the importance of moving into receiving position.

full-court, two fast break units alternating against one set pattern unit.

To properly inculcate fast-break instinctiveness in squad members, almost daily use of this drill (described on p. 164, Chapter 5) is essential.

part three
the defense

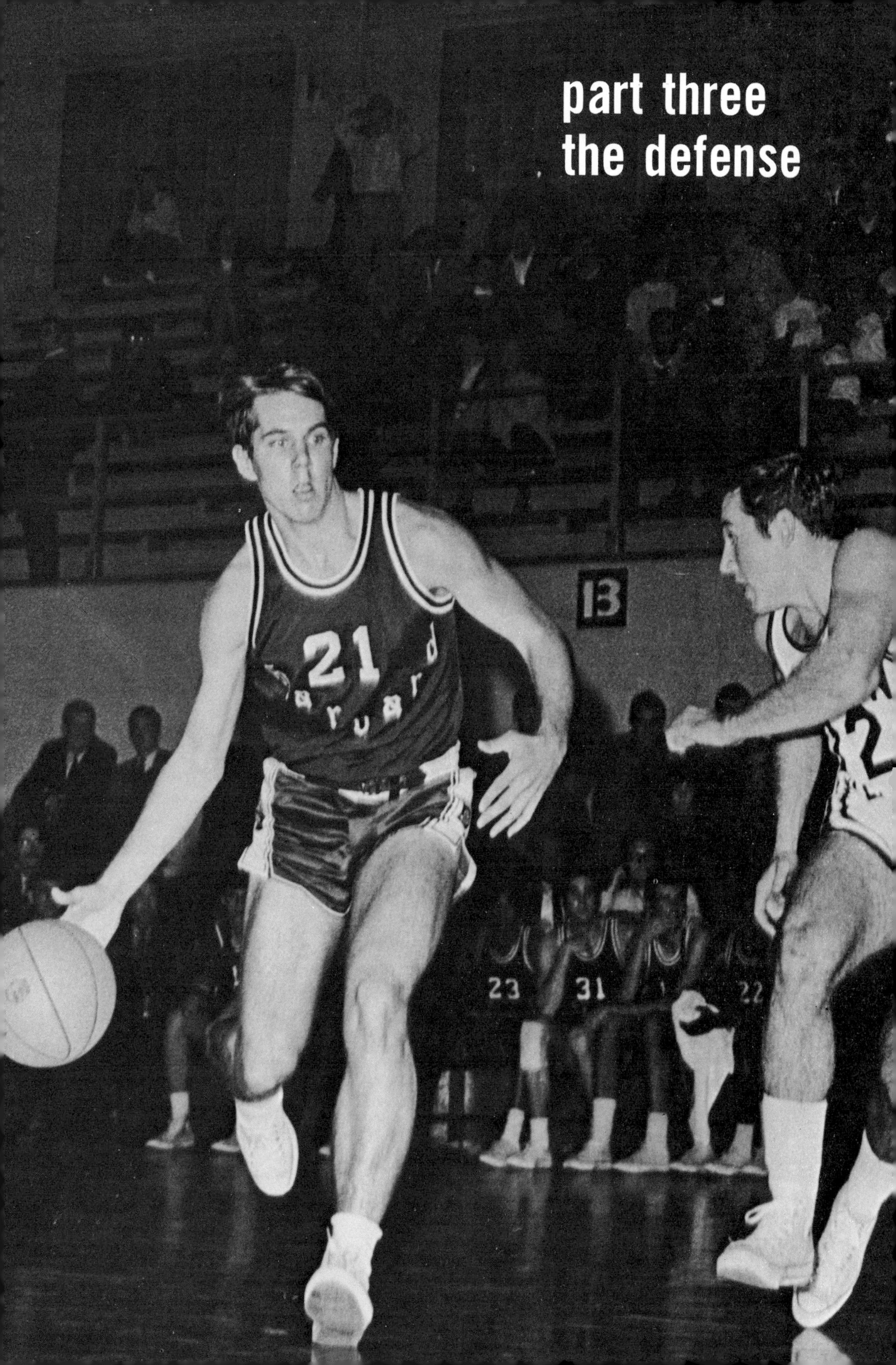

6

basic
defense

All defensive basketball team plans are only as effective as the individual ability of each player. Attributes to be sought individually are speed, quickness, and mental alertness, aggressiveness, desire, pride, anticipation, and adaptability.

1. Speed and Quickness. Sheer running speed enables a defensive player to move from one court position to another more rapidly than other players. It allows him to recover from defensive mistakes and assume a new defensive position with little overall team danger. Quickness, usually of feet, hands, and arms, enables a defensive player to keep the offense in a protective attitude by individual harassment. It effectively neutralizes an opponent's superior speed. Because the normal defensive distance from the basket is between eighteen to twenty-two feet or less, quickness of reaction and reflex may be more of an asset than speed; however, both are essential for good defensive posture.

2. Mental Alertness and Aggressiveness. The player who reacts immediately to a change from offense to defense will be in position to cover unguarded opponents, prevent the surprise offensive maneuver, and place the offense at a disadvantage. This mental alertness, coupled with aggressiveness (the ability to attack defensively) and defensive faking, can actually force an opponent into a defensive posture while he is in control of the ball.

3. Desire and Pride. Regardless of how fundamentally sound a player may be, he cannot play effective defense without desire and pride, because defense requires hard work and determination, while offering very little praise or recognition. Hustle springs from desire, which includes the determination to play defense well, to concentrate wholly on an assignment, and to work tirelessly. The extra effort expended when tired is the keynote to success.

Pride is the satisfaction a person feels when he knows that he did his part to the best of his ability while receiving little or no credit.

4. Anticipation and Adaptability. Anticipation is the ability to predetermine offensive patterns—to decide whether a pass can be intercepted or whether to exchange offensive men with a teammate before the situation presents itself. Adjusting to changes with the correct defensive action indicates adaptability. This ability is not entirely based on instinct but rather on the intelligent study of an opponent's individual and team offensive moves from the moment a game begins.

There are two basic defensive stances for playing the man with the ball. The first is the staggered, or stride, stance (boxer stance); the other is the parallel, or square, stance (wrestler's stance).

staggered stance

For the staggered stance, the feet should be spread approximately the width of the shoulders, with either foot forward. Right-handed players seem more comfortable with the left foot forward; left-handed players prefer the right foot forward. The foot spread varies slightly with the player. A taller player may be more comfortable with a slightly wider foot spread than a smaller player. However, there are dangers in having the feet too close together or too widely spread. The closer together the feet, the less balance the player has. The wider the base, the slower the initial movement. The body weight must be distributed evenly on the balls of the feet, never forward on the toes, with the heels touching the court. If body weight has to be shifted to maintain balance, it should be shifted back, never front. The knees must be flexed to facilitate movement. Hips and buttocks should be low to maintain a low center of gravity, with the trunk slightly forward, shoulders approximately above the knees, and head held high. Head, shoulders, and back are in a straight line and stationary. Any movement of head and shoulders will destroy body balance and give the offensive man with the ball an advantage.

The arms and hands should be carried in a comfortable position and moved or waved in direct proportion to how

Basic defensive stance—staggered.

this action affects body balance. The hand above the front foot should be up and moving from side to side; the other hand should be at the side or reaching backwards. Over-extension of the hands and arms is a deterrent to basic defensive principles, since it shifts the player's balance and prevents mobility.

The amount of movement expended on defense varies greatly in different persons. Many players waste a great deal of energy and motion. Every defense move should be made with a specific purpose in mind.

parallel stance

In the square, or parallel stance, the feet are parallel and normally spread wider than the shoulders, weight is evenly distributed, the knees are bent, hips and buttocks are low, the trunk is more erect than in the staggered stance, and hands and arms are held low. This stance is primarily used when aggressively attacking a player who has finished dribbling. Functionally, this is the position in which defenders find themselves when guarding a dribbler who is moving downcourt or when guarding a cutter who is away from the ball.

Basic defensive stance—parallel.

use of sight, hearing, and speech

Three important adjuncts to fundamental defense are sight, hearing, and speech. A player must see everything around him, either directly or with peripheral vision. He should never concentrate solely on his opponent when he does not have the ball unless the coach has instructed him to do so. Normally, while he should be primarily concerned with his man, he should still be aware of the position of the ball and any lateral screens that may be set.

The defensive player guarding the man with the ball should always be alert to teammates' vocal warnings. The

266

voice must be used constantly on defense to warn team-mates of the offensive screening possibilities, to signal an intention to switch, for encouragement, to upset and dis-concert opponents, and to improve team morale and alert-ness.

Four foot movements are essential to good individual de-fense. The first is running backward; the second is the de-fensive shuffle, or boxer's slide; the third is running and stopping full stride; and the fourth is the wheel and guard maneuver.

All defensive players should be able to run backward as easily and as effectively as they run forward. Running back-ward is an unnatural physical ability requiring constant practice and perfect body balance. The weight must be centered above the foot spread and slightly forward to counteract the backward momentum. If body weight shifts to the rear, the player will fall on his back.

The *defensive shuffle* is the basic footwork involved in maintaining proper position defensively. When an offensive player moves cross-court, the first defensive movement is a short step with the foot to that side. The other foot is quickly brought to within six to nine inches of the first. The player repeats the short, fast, sliding steps, maintaining bal-ance and position on the man with the ball and forcing him to the sideline or towards a teammate. The feet never cross in the defensive shuffle.

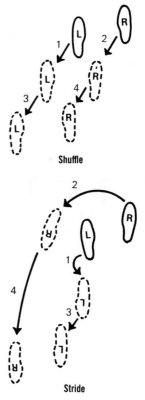

Shuffle

Stride

When defending a dribbler who is moving vertically to-ward the basket, the defender begins the shuffle with the foot on that side, forcing the man to the end line or towards a defensive teammate. However, if the offensive player gains an advantage, the defensive man must cross his legs and run full-stride to regain his defensive position.

When a defensive player is running in full stride, he must stop by planting his lead foot hard and dropping his hips low to maintain a low center of gravity, regain his bal-ance, and immediately assume the fundamental defensive position.

A good defensive player must be conditioned mentally and physically to start quickly and change direction instan-taneously. The start is initiated by a short step with the nearest foot in the direction the player wishes to go and a push off the far foot. Simultaneously, the rear arm and shoulder are swung in the same direction. The change of direction is begun by a balanced stop, without loss of time, and a reversal of the starting procedure.

The *wheel and guard* maneuver is the best way to pick up your opponent when he dribbles by you after you have committed yourself forward on to the right foot. When an opponent with the ball is driving opposite the defender's direction of commitment, the defender must make a 360 degree pivot turn by pushing off the over extended right foot, pivoting quickly on the rear foot, wheeling 180 degrees away from the dribbler, pushing off the left foot, pivoting on the right and wheeling another 180 degrees to regain defensive position facing the dribbler. Reverse the procedure if the defender's left foot is forward.

individual defensive techniques

All defenders must be well versed in their individual defensive techniques, as one poor defender greatly weakens the team defensive structure

guarding the man with the ball

Players must be proficient at defending opponents with or without the ball, regardless of their court position.

The Backcourt Man. The backcourt man, or guard, with the ball in scoring range (under thirty feet from the basket) is a potential shooter, passer, or dribbler. The advance scouting report should indicate if he is a good set or jump shooter; if he is an individualist who always dribbles when in possession, looking for his shot; if he is a play-maker who will be looking for a teammate to set up for a shot; if he has a favorite hand when dribbling; if he uses fakes and feints before shooting, passing or dribbling; if he cuts to the basket after passing, etc. If no report is available, the defensive player must adapt his defensive maneuvers to the guard's offensive tactics, assessing his opponent's potential quickly. He should maintain the fundamental defensive position with his front hand up and waving.

If the backcourt man is dribbling, the defensive player fakes with the hands, feints with the feet, and utilizes the sideline or a teammate to stop the dribbler and to force the dribbler away from his passing or shooting objective. The longer a player dribbles in a balanced offensive situation, the more help the guard's defensive teammates can give him.

A good dribbler with a strong hand should be overplayed one-half a man to the strong side to force him to his weaker side. Many left-handed players are completely one-handed and should be played a full-man to his left defensively. If the dribbler uses both hands well, he should always be forced to the middle where the guard has more team help.

When the dribbler has gained an advantage, the defensive player must get in stride with him, maintaining good defensive balance, and harass him with an upward scooping motion of the near hand. The upward motion contributes to good balance and lessens the danger of fouling. The majority of fouls committed against dribblers are the result of the downward motion of the defender's hands and arms.

Defender in step with dribbler.

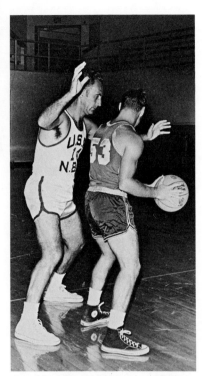

Attacking when dribbler stops dribble.

When the dribbler has been stopped, the defensive man should attack him aggressively with arms moving and maintain strong pressure on him until he releases the ball. He should be forced into a poor shooting position or into a passing situation where his only outlet is a ball-control pass to a teammate in a poor shooting area. The defender may touch or deflect a pass being made, but rarely intercepts it. Poor balance and reaction leaves the defender susceptible to a quick cut and a return pass inside (give-and-go).

After the ball is released, the defensive man should drop back quickly in the direction of the pass to defend against a cut by the passer, to maintain defensive position on his man in the eventuality of continued team movement, or to be in good defensive rebound position if a shot is taken.

The most difficult dribbling situation is the one-on-one

Defender drops back after pass.

Defender drops back after pass.

play guarding the basket alone when the defender must prevent the offensive player from getting past him for an unopposed basket. This opportunity arises most frequently after a pass interception, a long rebound, a long bat during a jump-ball, or recovery of a loose ball. The lone defender may be a guard, a forward, or a center. A retreating, delaying defense should be played, and the dribbler should be forced toward the sideline or baseline. When a man is dribbling, he must stop to shoot, except on a lay-in; therefore, stay away until he stops. Never move in aggressively on a dribbler in this situation as a change of direction will allow an unopposed lay-up.

When an offensive player in the backcourt fakes, the defender's initial move is a backward slide with the rear foot, with the front hand coming up quickly. This movement is a deterrent to an outside shot and keeps the defensive player in good position.

Backcourt opponent fakes shot.

Defender's back foot slides back—front hand comes up.

270

Caution must be used in approaching a backcourt man with the ball who has not dribbled. Slide the front foot forward eight to twelve inches, keeping the body balance on the balls of both feet, and follow with a quick, short, forward slide of the rear foot, with the weight shifting to the rear foot. It is always better to be caught with the weight back rather than forward.

Any time an offensive man who has dribbled is strongly pressured defensively, all defensive men *must* cut off all outlets in order to intercept the desperate pass, or to force a held ball.

The Forward, or Corner Man. The forward, or corner man, with the ball is in a dangerous offensive position. He is in

Guarding the baseline, foot nearest baseline forward.

Guarding the baseline on fake. Rear foot slides back.

Guarding the baseline. Step to baseline closes it to drive.

Defense against low pivot. (Defender may be entirely in front, also.)

shooting range, can drive the baseline for a lay-up, and can feed the low or medium pivot effectively. The defensive man must be close enough to prevent a clear shot at the basket and should be half-a-man to the baseline side to prevent a move in that direction. The foot nearest the baseline should be forward, and on a fake, the rear foot should be dropped back and a side step with the front foot must close the baseline drive. The arms and hands should prevent an easy set shot or a pass to the pivot man. Any dribble by the corner man should be forced to the middle area where teammates and congestion help the defensive player.

Center, or Pivot Man. There are three pivot, or post, areas. Low-pivot position is within nine feet of the basket; medium-pivot position is between ten and fourteen feet from the basket; and high-pivot position is fifteen feet or more from the basket. Normally, the low and medium positions are on the sides of the foul lane area, and the high-pivot position is in the outer half of the foul circle or higher, nearer the middle of the court. Each area requires a different defensive technique.

Low pivot. An offensive man receiving the ball in the low-pivot area is primarily a scorer who will use quick, deceptive fakes and then take the shot that presents itself. The man guarding the low pivot must prevent the ball from reaching this position. The initial defensive position is between the ball and the pivot man, three-quarters of the way in front, with the front hand outstretched and the rear hand lightly touching the offensive man. The defensive player's back is to the sideline, and his feet are to the outside of the low pivot man. When the ball is in the left corner, the left arm and foot are advanced; if it is in the right corner, the position is reversed.

The corner positions are the best areas from which to

272

pass into the low pivot; if the ball cannot enter the low-pivot area from one corner, the offensive players will try to enter from the other corner. This necessitates a minimum of two passes to get the ball to the opposite corner. When these passes are being made, the low-pivot guard must keep between the ball and the pivot man, for if he goes behind the low pivot, the ball can easily be passed in from the backcourt area. With the ball reversing from right defensive corner to left corner, the defender maintains position, stepping forward with the baseline foot and fronting the low pivot man to prevent him from moving up the free-throw lane. He feels him with the left hand as the pivot crosses to his left, using the boxer's defensive glide to maintain his fronting position and dropping his right foot back to regain a three-quarter fronting position at the left low-pivot position. The right hand is pointing towards the ball during this movement.

If the defensive player is behind the pivot man when the pivot receives the ball in the low area, the defensive man should loosen his position slightly so that the pivot man cannot ascertain his exact location by pressure. Give the pivot man the first fake or move, turn with him, and attempt to deflect or tip his shot. If the low pivot is a good hook-shot shooter, the defender must attempt to alter the hook-shot trajectory by forcing it higher, using the same hand the pivot is shooting with. Using this hand prevents fouling, and better rebound position results, since both men are turning with bodies parallel, and the defender is inside. If the other hand is used it crosses the defender's body and may force him into the shooter. Another reason for using the near hand is that the defender can jump higher than he could if he used the far hand. The defender must maintain this inside position for rebounding. The defensive jump should be timed with the ball's release, and a deflection or bat at the height of a straight-up jump is a deterrent to further shots of this type.

When the low pivot out-positions his defender, the defender must alert his teammates with a loud vocal warning. Near teammates must immediately attack the ball in possession of a low pivot opponent to help their outpositioned teammate and prevent an easy scoring opportunity by the low pivot man. If the pivot man fakes, there is an excellent opportunity for an alert collapsing defender to force a held ball.

Medium pivot. It is difficult to defend against the medium pivot, for he is in excellent position to fake and one-bounce drive, shoot, hand off to cutters, or return a pass quickly to a teammate for intermediate jump shots if defensive men attempt to help his guard. All defenders should recognize the dangerous potential of the ball reaching the

Defense against medium pivot.

273

medium pivot and attempt to close passing lanes to this area. The man guarding the pivot should play one-half a man to the ball side, with his front hand out to deflect or deter a pass and his feet straddling the foot of the pivot that is closest to the basket.

When the ball reverses direction outside and the pivot player crosses the foul line, the medium-pivot defender must slide behind his man to a new one-half a man defensive position. He is extremely vulnerable to a lob pass if he crosses in front. During this defensive transition, the defending teammates must prevent a direct pass-in to the pivot player.

If a pass-in to the medium pivot is successful, the defender should drop one foot behind the pivot, watching for cutters and forcing the pivot to the outside or to the sidelines if possible. If the guard is too close, the pivot can feel him and move accordingly. When attempting to block a shot by the pivot, the defender must stay on the floor until his opponent leaves the floor. If he jumps or moves with a fake, he allows the pivot an easy scoring opportunity.

High pivot. The basic function of a high pivot is as a screener or feeder. The defensive man plays a high pivot two to three feet behind the pivot, between the man and the basket. Anticipating his opponent's probable maneuvers from the scouting report or the pattern of play, the guard should attempt to close passing lanes to the cutters and call out if he thinks the high pivot is going to be used as a screen. If the high pivot receives a pass and turns to face the basket, the defender must play him as a backcourt man would. He should allow the sixteen- to eighteen-foot shot, unless the pivot man has proven his ability to score from this range.

guarding the man without the ball

When you are defending against a man without the ball, the distance you may drop off him varies, depending on the position of the ball, your man's distance from the basket, his shooting range, and the offensive deployment in the basket area. No offensive player should be allowed to handle the ball within sixteen feet of the basket. If he does gain possession in this dangerous area, the defense must exert extreme pressure on the ball.

One Pass From the Ball. The ball is one pass away from the man you are guarding when he may receive a pass from the man in possession without danger of interception.

Backcourt man. When guarding a backcourt man with the ball one pass away, in the other guard's possession, your team's man-to-man philosophy determines the defense. In a normal defense, the defender should drop off his man and open toward the ball, within the triangle formed by the man with the ball, the basket, and the man being guarded. Both the ball and the man being defended should be visible. The defensive man's stance should be a little higher than when he is playing an attacker with the ball, and he should be mentally aggressive and anticipatory. His hands should point in the direction of the ball and the man he is guarding. From this position, he must close passing lanes to the high post and anticipate a cut to the basket by his man. The cut to the basket usually occurs simultaneously with a pass by his man to the other guard (give and go). Interceptions generally are made by the defender of the man being passed to or a third defender who is aware of the offensive passing lanes.

If the team defensive pattern is an aggressive man-to-man technique, and the other guard has the ball, the defender positions himself between his man and the ball, inviting the cut behind and the return pass. Teammates behind the backcourt defenders must anticipate this move and float to the middle to minimize the opponents' opportunity to carry it out. If the guard cuts, his defender must open to the ball and retreat with the man, staying close to him, between him and the ball. The defender must challenge every pass aggressively, intercepting or deflecting it whenever possible. If the backcourt man is to receive a pass, he should be forced to move away from the basket.

When the near forward has the ball, the man defending against the near guard should drop back two steps, opening his stance toward the sideline so that he is standing in the triangle formed by the ball, the basket, and the man being guarded, with both the ball and his man in sight. He must be ready to defend against the forward drive to the middle area and to deflect or intercept a pass to a medium or high pivot. If the guard goes away from the ball, his defender must maintain the same relative position within the ball-basket-man triangle. The farther the guard goes from the ball, the greater the distance between him and his defender. Since any cut by the guard will be away from the ball, the defender should keep between the ball and the man, close enough to the man to prevent pass reception. He must anticipate a quick stop by his man that may afford him a good shooting opportunity, or a change of direction that will allow him easy pass reception.

If the guard cuts outside toward the corner, his defender should overplay slightly to the sideline to prevent him from working a two-on-two play with the corner man.

When the medium or high pivot has the ball, the backcourt guard should drop back and pressure the ball as far as his man's outside shooting ability will allow.

The forward, or corner man. When the ball is in the backcourt, the defender against the corner man on the

Overplay defense against corner man.

same side may assume one of two basic positions. He may overplay with the right hand and foot forward on the defensive left side (and vice-versa) to challenge or prevent a pass to this position. Usually, reception in the mid-court area should be allowed, as it removes the corner man from his strongest offensive position and puts him in an unfamiliar position with the ball. However, some forwards are able to fake to the ball, then reverse direction.

When preliminary information indicates the offensive man possesses this ability to a high degree, the defender can assume the alternate defensive position, in which the left hand and foot are forward on the left defensive side. This second position makes possible a cut to the ball in front of the defender. As a corner man receiving the ball on this move is in excellent position to go towards the basket, the defender must take every precaution to prevent this reception. The corner man can now receive the ball more readily, so the defender should challenge each pass to move the man farther from his normal position.

If the forward has good shooting range, but is not a good ball-handler or does not like to move without the ball, the first position is preferable. If the forward reverses well, and does not have a long range, use the alternate stance.

The defensive man, either from scouting information or from personally analyzing his man's moves, should anticipate cutting moves by legally moving into his man's path, thereby either preventing the cut or hindering it to the point where it becomes ineffectual.

When the defender loses his defensive advantage to a cutter behind him, he should turn quickly towards the basket and attempt to stay between the man and the ball. If possible, the turn should be to the inside, so he will not lose sight of the ball. After turning, he should keep active and low, ready to deflect a bounce pass, the usual pass in this situation.

If the cut is between the defender and the ball, the guard should turn in the direction of the cut and run hard to regain a legal defensive position as soon as possible. He should not attempt to use his hands or arms, as such movement will slow the recovery and result in fouls. The defender may receive help from a teammate in the area, who may switch assignments with him by picking up his man.

The pivot man. The defender of the high pivot man should be to the ball side, with the near hand moving in front of the pivot to discourage a pass in from the backcourt man. If the ball is passed cross-court, the defender goes behind the pivot and assumes the same position on the other side. When the ball is passed to the front court, the defender should step up with the near foot and play one-half a man to the ball side, the near hand waving actively to discourage a pivot roll and reception of the ball in the medium-pivot area.

When his opponent is in the medium-pivot area, the defender should position himself one-half a man on the ball side to prevent the pass in, if possible. Since the medium-pivot man usually changes position frequently, using fakes, feints, sudden directional changes, and quick pivots, the defender must be alert for these moves, basing his movement and position on the actions of the man with the ball, and the ball's location. When a medium pivot moves away from the ball area and his guard is overplaying him to the ball, the danger of a lob pass should be compensated for by the alert positioning of the far defensive forward.

A pass to the low pivot area usually comes from the corner position; therefore, the pivot's defender should play him three-quarters front or full in front. Since the low pivot is constantly looking for good shooting position, there is

Guarding the high pivot who is a good shooter. (High to ball side.)

277

more body contact in this area than in any other on the court. The defender must never allow himself to be pushed or moved under the basket behind the pivot man, as that is a very poor position from which to prevent a pass-in or to rebound another's shot. If he is extremely alert, anticipatory, and mobile, the defender should be able to maintain a solid fronting position. When a team relies primarily on a pivot man as the focal point of its pattern or as its scorer, defending the pivot requires constant and complete concentration, and even then the defender may require help from his teammates. However, if the pivot position is defended properly, the defender can be responsible for stopping the opponent's team offense almost completely.

Two Passes From the Ball. The ball is two passes away from the man you are guarding if it can be intercepted by any defender other than the guards of the passer and receiver.

The guard, or backcourt man. When the ball position is two passes away from the backcourt man being defended against, usually in the possession of the far corner man or the low or medium pivot on the far side, the backcourt defender should open his stance toward the ball and back off from his man towards the middle of the court near the foul-line area to aid in team defense. He should watch both his man and the ball, preventing the man from cutting to the ball and taking any good opportunity to intercept a pass or cause a held-ball situation. Of course, he must always be ready to return quickly to his man if the situation warrants it.

Forward, or corner man. If defending against a corner man when the ball is held by the far guard, the defender should open towards the ball, seeing both his man and the ball, and move toward the foul-lane area, in line with his man (this line being parallel to the base line). He should point one hand at his man, the other toward the ball, and be ready to prevent his man from cutting between him and the ball. If the ball is passed cross-court, he should return to basic defensive position. If the pass goes to the far corner man, the defender retreats two steps into the foul lane area, keeping alert for a lob pass to a low or medium pivot man and anticipating movement by his man toward the ball. When the defender is opposite a low pivot, he must realize that his forward may move to the foul-line area to receive a quick pass for a short jump shot. At all times he must look for interceptions, guards cutting without the ball, and held-ball opportunities.

Center, or pivot. Normally, the high-pivot man is never more than one pass from the ball. In the medium-pivot and low-pivot areas, the pivot man may be more than one pass away, but quick movement on his part and lack of anticipation or alertness by his defender can allow the pivot to

278

obtain excellent position on the ball side. Any offensive player, regardless of size, can play the pivot, and if he receives the ball in the low area easily, he has a good scoring opportunity. Therefore, the best method of defending the pivot areas is to prevent the ball from getting in to the post man.

If prevention is not possible, the pivot man should be forced into reception in positions where a good shooting opportunity is difficult—on the base line, ten or more feet from the basket, or two or three steps from the foul lane, near the free-throw line. Always challenge the pivot for position, anticipating his moves. Know his favorite areas and beat him to these spots.

The man guarding the pivot should only help teammates defensively when an unopposed scoring opportunity arises. When the man defending the low or medium post picks up an offensive man who has shaken his guard, that guard must sprint to an intercepting position between the free pivot man and the ball to prevent an easy return pass to the open pivot area. As this situation usually involves a big man switching to a small man, the big defender can try to block the shot. In attempting to block shots, never bring the blocking arm down or jump into the shooter, as fouls always result. Try to deflect the shot or distract the shooter with arm movement. Do not leave the floor until the shooter has left the floor or the ball has been released.

The man guarding the low- and medium-pivot areas is in excellent position to observe the opponent's offensive patterns, and he should shout instructions constantly to his teammates.

If the pivot moves away from the basket, he is not very dangerous. He usually moves away from the ball to clear the middle for a cutter or driver, or to screen for a teammate. The alert defender should remain in the pivot area to hinder the driver or cutter and should play the screening or clearing pivot man loose.

defensive drills

Defensive drills are worked one-on-one, two-on-two, three-on-three and in full team alignment. In all of the drills, the coach must insist on the following fundamentals. Players must maintain good body balance and good position, bothering the men they are guarding. Whenever possible, they must use peripheral vision to watch both the man and the ball, and they must always be alert to help teammates. They must keep pressure on the ball and on potential receivers, without being overly aggressive and causing fouls that hurt their team. The men must be able to recognize when an opponent is not in position to make a good offensive play.

279

Blocking a shot. Defender blocks with same hand as shooter to prevent fouling.

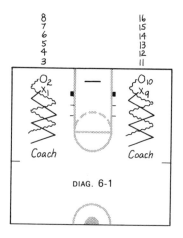

DIAG. 6-1

Diag. 6-1, INDIVIDUAL DEFENSIVE FOOTWORK DRILL

The squad splits into two eight-man groups, one on each side of the court, with one coach observing each group. The first and second man in each group step out onto the court. The first man maintains good defensive position on the second man, who dribbles a ball. The defender should shuffle from side to side as the dribbler changes hands. He must constantly attempt to shuffle in front of the dribbler to force a change of direction dribble or draw an offensive charge. At first this drill should be used at half to three-quarter speed so that the coaches can observe and criticize the movements.

The defender must not spread his feet too wide or cross them, and he must keep his buttocks as low as possible with his body in a fairly upright position, bent a little bit over the thighs. He cannot use his hands. While many coaches have the defensive player clasp his

280

hands behind his back, we prefer that he keep his hands on his belt or lightly touching his thighs. We feel he maintains better body balance that way.

The dribbler should be limited in space to less than half the width of the court. After he has dribbled, changing hands several times, he should, if he beats the defensive player, dribble hard into the basket. The player who is on defense should then turn, get in stride, and run to an intercepting position on the dribbler, keeping defensive pressure on him as he goes in for a lay-up. After the drill, the players should exchange positions so that the defensive player is on offense, and vice versa.

This drill should be used frequently in preseason practice and periodically during the regular season.

Diag. 6-2, ONE-ON-ONE DRILL, BALL SIDE

DIAG. 6-2

This drill is used in preseason practice. The passer, P, can be either a good passing guard or one of the coaches. X, the defensive player, is guarding O, the offensive player, attempting to prevent him from receiving the ball in good offensive position. The offensive player wants to reverse direction and go back door. If he cannot get the ball near the basket with constant use of footwork, head fakes, and feints, he comes out toward the passer to receive a pass. However, X should force O out from the basket to where he is not in an advantageous offensive position with the ball, so that he must pass back to P. As soon as the ball is released back to P, O continues his jockeying while X tries to maintain good defensive balance and prevent the ball from reaching O. If O does beat X and goes back door, X must make the following move, because he will have committed his weight forward to his left foot. He should push off the left foot, transferring his weight back to the right foot, and pivot on the right foot to the inside so that as he retreats he is facing the passer. As he makes this movement, his inside hand should be low, as the passer will normally lead the offensive player in with a bounce pass. The pivot technique is reversed on the other side of the court. This drill should be used at both ends (and from both sides) of the court so that all players can work often. After the first two players have worked the drill two or three times, they go to the rear of the line, and X_1 and X_2 step on the court. X_1 becomes the defensive player, and X_2 becomes the offensive player.

Diag. 6-3, ONE-ON-ONE, BALL AWAY DRILL

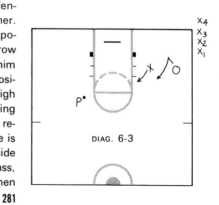

DIAG. 6-3

The passer, P, is on the left side of the court, with X, the defensive player, and O, the offensive player, on the opposite side corner. X's responsibility is to prevent O from getting the ball in scoring position. O will try to cut in front of X to get the ball in the free-throw circle area, or he may try to turn in to the basket with X facing him and catch a lead (dummy type) pass from P. X should open his position so that he sees both the ball and the man. He must float high enough on O to prevent a cut between himself and the ball, staying almost parallel to O in relation to the baseline. If X allows O to receive the ball, he should be sure that O is in a position where he is not an offensive threat—going toward the head of the key or outside the head of the key. The passer should not make a long lob pass, but should try to make a pass after O fakes to the baseline and then comes back quickly. X should realize that there is a possibility of a pass over his head, and he should never be too far from O to prevent it. After two or three defensive attempts have been made, the players should go to the rear of the line on the right, with X_1 coming on the court as the defensive player and X_2 assuming the position of O, the offensive player. Use both ends and both sides.

Diag. 6-4, ONE-ON-ONE GET IN STEP WITH A DRIBBLER DRILL

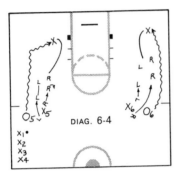

DIAG. 6-4

On the left side of the court, Defender X_5 allows O_5, the dribbler, to gain a momentary advantage on him. When O_5 starts his dribble down the left side of the court, X_5, in full stride, attempts to get in step with him. He does this by pushing off on the left foot, stepping back for balance slightly on the right foot, and pivoting on his right foot toward the sideline so that both men are now facing the end line, and X_5 is running in stride with O_5. After gaining balance, usually in two or three steps, X_5 can attempt to harass the dribbler with an upward motion of his outside hand, the hand nearest the dribbler. The motion should never be down, or he will break stride and give the dribbler an advantage or be more prone to foul. It is not essential that the defender harass the dribbler with his hand; primarily, he should sprint toward the baseline to retain good defensive position so he can make the dribbler stop. The defensive player must get back in position facing the dribbler as soon as possible, without giving him an advantage to the basket.

The same drill is used on the right side of the court. X_6, the defender, allows O_6, the dribbler, to get a slight advantage on him. X_6 has overplayed with his right foot. He pushes off the right foot, steps back on his left foot, and pivots on this foot so that his right side is facing the dribbler and he and the dribbler are both heading toward the baseline. Again the defensive player must match stride for stride with the dribbler and attempt to get in front of him before he can make a turn to the basket.

An alternative use of this drill is to allow the dribbler to go by the defender so that the defender can (1) use the "wheel and guard" technique or (2) flick the ball away from behind. The latter is an excellent tactic if a defender is completely beaten. He should use a left-hand flick when beaten to his right side and vice-versa.

Diag. 6-5, TURNING DRIBBLER DRILL

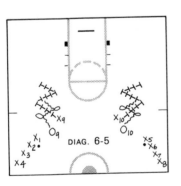

DIAG. 6-5

X_9 is on defense and O_9 is dribbling. The purpose of this drill is to teach players to turn the dribbler by sliding sideways with a good boxer's shuffle, getting in front of the dribbler and forcing a turn. As he turns, the defensive player should shuffle in the opposite direction. The coach should be sure that the defender does not cross his feet, maintains low balance, and uses his hands as little as necessary, as hand movement may throw the player off good defensive balance. X_9, on the left, should attempt to turn O_9 two or three times, while X_{10} and O_{10} perform the drill on the right side of the court. The players should alternate sides so that they work on both sides. If the dribbler beats the defender, the defender should pivot behind the dribbler and attempt to flick the ball away from him from the rear, using the same hand the man is dribbling with.

282

Diag. 6-6, DEFENSIVE POSITIONING DRILL AGAINST A LOW OR MEDIUM PIVOT MAN

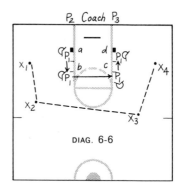

DIAG. 6-6

The pivot defender, in a man-to-man defense, is in the low left pivot position with the ball in the hands of X_1. The ball may pass from X_1 to X_2 to X_3 to X_4, who may move closer together or spread farther apart, if necessary. These four men are in the basic positions on the court from which a low- or medium-pivot man can be fed. A defensive player is depicted by a three-quarter circle (the body) and two straight lines (the arms). The pivot defender in the low position area (a) should be three-quarters of the way in front of the pivot man on the low side, ball side, when X_1 has the ball. As the pivot man moves medium (b), and X_2 has the ball, the defender should overplay from the strong side, half a man. If the ball is passed across to X_3 as the pivot man moves across to medium pivot position on the right (c), the defender should assume a fronting position on his man. His back should be almost to the basket, but he should feel the pivot man so that he can move with him if he goes to the basket on a lob pass. When the pivot man is in the low position on the right (d), and X_4 has the ball, the defender should stay in a fronting position prior to his assuming the proper relative defensive position, three-quarters in front on the baseline side.

This is a very important drill and should be used frequently for big men, especially in preseason practice. If the pivot man were to slide across the foul lane low (a to d), as the ball passed to that side, the defender would front the man and reassume position low on the opposite side. He would step forward with the left foot at a so that he would be in front of the pivot man. As the pivot man crossed, the defender would stay in front of him. At d, the defender would step back with the right foot, keeping his left arm and left foot in front of the pivot man.

The purpose of this drill is to give the pivot defender practice in correct technique. He should be close enough to feel the offensive pivot man with his body or arm so that when the pivot man moves he will feel the move and move with him immediately. This minimal contact must be maintained at all times when it is advantageous to defense.

Diag. 6-7, DEFENSIVE DRILL, TWO-ON-ONE

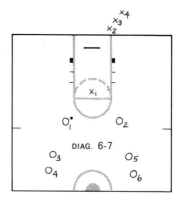

DIAG. 6-7

O_1 and O_2 are on offense. O_1 has the ball. X_1 is retreating towards his basket. As O_1 and O_2 approach, X_1 should make defensive fakes at the ball to stop its progress. If the defender can stop the ball outside the foul-lane circle or the foul line, forcing O_1 to take the shot from beyond the fifteen-foot area, he has done an exceptionally good job defensively.

This should be a competitive type drill, with the players taking pride in their defense. The defensive man has to be open so that he can see both offensive men approaching, and his attempts to stop the ball should be made chiefly by faking, yelling, and playing for time so that eventually a second defender may come back. Usually, he should fake at O_1 to make him pass. On occasion, he can fake backward movement to bring O_1 in closer to him, take a calculated risk, and move quickly to steal the ball.

Diag. 6-8, DEFENSE DRILL, TWO-ON-ONE, BIG MEN

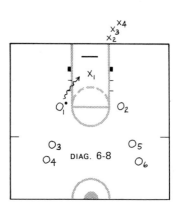

DIAG. 6-8

A big man is placed under the basket to perform relatively the same defensive assignment as in Diag. 6-7. However, in this drill O_1

and O_2 should penetrate farther in than in Diag. 6-7 and try to fake X_1 up off his feet. X_1 should not jump until O_1 has left his feet. X_1 should fake at O_1 as he comes in with the ball, try to anticipate a pass or a shot, and block the shot. A great deal of team enthusiasm can be derived from this type of drill, as small men vie against big men.

blocking out defensively

Defensive guards (except the man guarding a low or medium pivot) almost always have inside position on their men initially, and their first duty is to retain this advantage. Defenders must assume that all shots will be missed, and then prevent their men from obtaining possession of the rebound by blocking them from the defensive boards or getting the ball themselves. The best fast-break opportunity results from a defensive rebound possession and the proper clearing out of the ball to an attack position.

Defensive box out.

Defensive box out.

When a shot is taken, the shooter is in the best position to judge the eventual area in which the rebound will fall; therefore, his guard must block off the path the shooter attempts to take to retrieve the ball.

Basic rebounding position.　　*Two-hand rebound.*

backcourt man

If the shooter is in the backcourt, the defender remains face to face with him no more than one step away until he makes his first move after the shot. If this move is to the outside, the defender pivots on his outside foot so that he is facing the basket in the path of the shooter and maintains this position, using the defensive shuffle to move the shooter away from his intended path to the rebound area. (If the shooter moves to the inside, the defender pivots on his inside foot.) If the defender has a chance for recovery, he should go to the ball immediately from this blockout position. If the ball is rebounded by a defending teammate he must quickly go to an area clear of an opponent, towards the near sideline, to receive an outlet pass. If the offensive team regains possession, he must pick his man up quickly in good defensive position.

The man defending against the other guard drops back two or three steps after the shot is taken and remains facing his man. Normally, an offensive team never rebounds both men farthest from the basket; therefore, if the shooting backcourt man moves in to rebound, the remaining guard will start back to defend. If the second guard does not break

285

toward his offensive backboard, his defender should count one thousand and one, one thousand and two after the shot is released (this count allows for the flight of the ball before striking the rim or backboard and rebounding), turn quickly to face the defensive basket, looking for the rebounding ball, and ascertain who will obtain possession of it or whether he has a chance to retrieve it himself. If he can rebound the ball he must get it immediately. If a teammate rebounds the ball, he should go to the near sideline to receive a clearing pass out. If offense rebounds the ball, he must immediately revert to a defensive stance on his man.

corner man

When the shot is taken by a corner man or a pivot man, the backcourt defenders, whose positions may be some distance from this man, should take one step back towards the basket, concentrating face to face on their men, count to two slowly, then proceed as described above. An alert backcourt defender, by reacting quickly on defensive rebounds recovered by a taller opponent, can often cause a held-ball by attacking him aggressively.

The defensive man guarding a shooting corner man, a dangerous offensive rebounder, must keep him from following up his shot. He should allow his first move to the basket, then pivot in front of him, moving with his movement (determined by feel) and keeping in front of him. He can maintain front position by bracing himself firmly, arms up, elbows at shoulder height, knees slightly flexed, ready to jump if necessary.

Although the distance may vary, ideally, the blocker should turn and make his contact when the offensive rebounder is within an eight-foot radius from the basket. Anything out farther than this gives the offensive rebounder a better opportunity to defeat the block. Anything in closer may result in the blocker being forced too far under the basket to get the rebound himself.

When defending a corner man in the corner opposite the shooter, the defender's normal position is several steps away from his man. He moves one step toward him after the shot, allows him to make his initial move, then pivots in his path, anticipating a change of direction by him. If the man reverses direction, the defender steps in that direction (but toward the basket to minimize danger of a foul for illegal blocking out) and goes to the ball aggressively when slight contact takes place. He must take care that his man does not get inside him.

pivot man

Usually the high-pivot defender is his team's best rebounder. Guarding a high-pivot he is stationed fourteen to sixteen feet from the basket, between his man and the basket. If he waits for the offensive movement, he may be too late in getting to the ball. Therefore, unless he has been specifically instructed otherwise, he should turn with the shot and go to the rebounding ball as soon as he judges where it is likely to fall. He has a rebound advantage on his man, and after his turn, he is in good position to move in, hold, or move laterally to his left or right to get the ball, if his teammates have reacted to the shot with good defensive rebounding techniques. When a high pivot shoots, he will always follow his shot. Therefore, the man guarding him should vary the above technique slightly and turn into the path the shooter takes. He then rebounds as instructed above.

The man guarding a low or medium pivot is generally at a disadvantage in defensive rebounding, as he may be one-half a man to a full-man in front of the pivot man when the shot is taken. If he is one-half a man in front of the medium pivot (ball-side) when the shot is taken, the defender should pivot on the rear foot and establish a strong position, feet spread, arms and hands up, elbows at shoulder height, and hold position momentarily before going to the ball. If the defender is between his man and the ball (the shot taken from the far side of the court from the medium pivot), he should use the boxer's shuffle to maintain his advantageous position between his man and the basket, hold position, and then go to the ball strongly.

When the pivot is low, the defender will almost always be in a disadvantageous, rebound position ball-side, as the offensive man will usually be inside him. Therefore, he must work aggressively to neutralize his man's position advantage. The defender should turn to the middle area and attempt to move into a siding position, shoulder to shoulder with his man, to his inside if possible. If the defender finds himself directly behind the offensive pivot, he should crowd him, attempting to force him farther in under the basket so that he is too far in to rebound effectively. If this maneuver is not successful (the pivot may lean back with his back and shoulder to counteract the crowding tactic), the defender should attempt to slide around his man into better rebounding position.

When the low or medium pivot shoots, his defender must block him out of the rebounding area. Usually the defender attempts to block or deflect the shot with extreme pressure, and both men are off their feet. The defender's jump should be up but not into the man. If he jumps toward the pivot shooter or the ball, he will take himself out of the rebounding action and possibly commit a two-shot foul. Upon landing, the defender must quickly turn into the path of the shooter and maintain this position.

defensive rebounding

The primary function in rebounding is gaining possession of the ball. The defensive man (except for the pivot defender) is usually closer to the basket. For his team to have a chance to obtain possession, he must maintain this position advantage, blocking his man from the rebound. If the shooting team rebounds the ball, the defender is still in excellent position to guard his man. Should the ball be batted or lost by the players in the rebound area, the defender is in position to recover or to prevent his man from recovering. If a teammate recovers the ball, they should switch to offense immediately.

As more shots are missed than made, the defensive rebounder should assume that every shot will miss and be ready to rebound after each shot. He should also assume that his opponent will try to rebound and that every rebound will come into his area; therefore, he must maintain position on his man, while watching the ball's flight, and be prepared to meet the ball aggressively. In moving toward the rebounding area, his hands should be held high, with elbows spread in anticipation of the recovery. As he steps in, before his jump to gain possession, he should mentally note the relative positions of his teammates so that when he obtains possession, he knows the best area for a quick pass out.

Defensive rebounder pulling ball down away from pressure.

When the complete turn to the basket is made, the rebounder must establish a wide, braced base from which to operate. This wide base will prevent his man from easy access to the ball, and the bracing will allow him to be jostled or leaned on without losing balance. The feet should be spread as wide as comfort and balance will allow. The knees should be slightly bent; hips lowered; the elbows wide, at shoulder level; upper arms parallel to the floor. The forearms and hands should be held high, parallel to the body, with fingers widespread and palms facing the basket. The body balance should be slightly forward, with the weight on the balls of the feet for quick movement to retrieve the ball.

Two defenders box out while third gets rebound.

Several physical factors affect every rebound—the force and distance of the shot, the angle of the shooter with respect to the basket, the spot the ball hits (the backboard, or rim, or roll around the rim), the resiliency or deadness of backboard and rim, the impetus and arch of the shot, and the spin imparted to the ball by the shooter. These components vary with each shot attempted and have a direct effect on timing. Players must consider all these factors when judging the rebound, remembering also that most shots rebound to the side of the basket opposite the side from which the shot is taken.

Excellent timing is a greater attribute for a rebounder than jumping high. He must spring into the ball, attempting to secure it with both hands as he approaches maximum

Offense timing jump, going up as defensive man inside (boxing out) comes down, to steal rebound.

jumping height. His elbows and legs should be widespread, his buttocks slightly extended rearward for maximum protection. While in the air he should turn the ball over slightly so that one hand is above, the other below the ball, which should be held strongly for protection.

He should land with the feet and elbows wide, buttocks extended slightly rearward, and the weight balanced. As he comes down, he should turn his head slightly toward the nearer sideline to ascertain whether or not a teammate is in good outlet passing position. On alighting, he must protect the ball before the pass by bringing it strongly to chest height or higher in both hands. If pressured, he should use quick fakes, holding the ball strongly, and pivot or dribble, if necessary, to prevent a held ball. The passout is usually to the outside on the side on which the rebound is recovered. It should rarely go across the free-throw lane at the defensive end.

Tall rebounders, holding the ball firmly in two hands, must keep it above shoulder height and decide quickly whether to release it or protect it further. A small man obtaining possession of a rebound must bring the ball close to the floor, protecting it with body and elbows, and pass it out immediately, if possible, or dribble rapidly away from the congested area.

In our rebounding drills, we are looking for aggressiveness, determination, and position in obtaining possession of the ball, as well as for correct fundamental techniques. Defensively, a player must remain in position between the man he is guarding and the basket, pivoting in front of him properly, and blocking him out. After the ball has hit the rim or the backboard, if he has any chance of getting the ball, he must time his leap, keeping the boxed out man behind him so that he obtains possession of the ball at the height of his jump.

rebounding drills

Offensively, we feel that the most important single fundamental is that rebounders must know when their teammates are shooting. Therefore, players must take good shots that evolve from the pattern they are using so that rebounders may maneuver for position as soon as one of their teammates is going to shoot. This gives them a split-second advantage in obtaining position. They must be able to time the flight of the ball so that they can get at least one hand on it to slap it back out to one of their guards.

Diag. 6-9, HAMBURGER DRILL

In this drill, one of our favorites, the coach is at the head of the key with the ball, and three players face him, within five feet of the foul line.

The players should not turn to the board until the ball has left the coach's hands. Then they should pivot, raising their hands, and go aggressively to the ball. Normally, the ball will fall near one of the three players, and the other two men will have to attack him aggressively without fouling in order to tie him up so that he cannot get a clean point. (A player receives a point each time he makes a clean rebound and gets away from the other two.) Usually, no more than two or three clean points per five attempts are made.

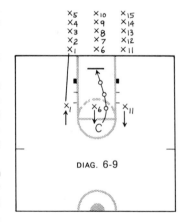

DIAG. 6-9

Both ends of the court should be used for effective results from this drill. Caution should be taken not to use the drill too long or with the same groups too often. Any fouling action should be called immediately. If a foul occurs when a rebounder has the ball cleanly, he gets a point. This drill evokes a great deal of enthusiasm and competition. We use it frequently.

Preseason jumping drills are essential for every basketball team. Have the managers attach adhesive tape, marked off in inches, to the sides of each backboard. The strip of adhesive tape is three feet long. As the bottom edge is nine feet from the floor at the lower corners of the backboard, the upper edge of the tape will be twelve feet from the floor. Wide markings can be used to indicate 3, 6, 9, and 12 inches.

jumping drills

291

Marked adhesive tape on backboard edges.

The following is a simple jumping drill at each backboard. Two players stand with their backs to the basket. (If eight baskets are available, the entire squad can do this at once.) On a signal, they pivot, face the backboard, jump, and touch the tape as high as possible with both hands. The pieces of tape can be left on the backboards as long as you want, except on the two main boards that are used for the games.

There is an incentive-giving element of competition in this drill. The players attempt to increase the height they can touch on the tape to better their own previous jumping height and go higher than the teammates with whom they are paired. Players should be paired with teammates who are jumping to approximately the same height.

The back-to-the-basket drill is useful because it involves a pivot and a spring. The pivot is similar to the pivot that a defensive rebounder would have to take to box out before jumping. A manager should record the height of the boys daily in preseason practice. This drill should not be used too long. It should be a quick change of pace from some of the other preseason conditioning drills.

DRILL 6-10, CONSECUTIVE JUMPING FACING THE BASKET

The player jumps five times, touching the rim each time, alternating hands. If he cannot touch the rim, he should touch as high up on the netting as possible. The same drill should be repeated using either hand then both hands, gradually increasing the number of consecutive jumps to fifty. Tall men should touch the sides of the rim with both hands as they jump—if possible, they should touch the rim with the inside of the wrist or the forearm. This is an excellent preseason conditioning drill and many players use it during practice sessions when they are on the sidelines or in pregame practice to loosen up and to improve jumping.

coordinating individual defense techniques against the offense

Individual defensive techniques must be coordinated so that defending teammates function as a unit whether evenly matched with the attackers or not. It is essential that each defender be aware of his team responsibilities against every offensive thrust. Mental alertness, aggressiveness, hustle, and anticipation are attributes that enhance the defensive posture in varying situations. Players must know when to retreat purposefully and when to counterattack expediently from the defensive structure. Only through constant practice can satisfactory results ensue.

defensing against screens

Several maneuvers are appropriate for all defenders in defensing against screening techniques of their opponents. If the screener has the ball and is in a dangerous scoring area, the following methods of defense are possible. The screener's guard may step back and allow through a defensive teammate guarding a cutter off the ball. This teammate may discourage a shot by waving his hands at the screener so that he will try to protect the ball. A second method is for the man guarding the screener to stay tight and direct his teammate behind him. A third maneuver is for the man guarding the cutter to fight between the screener and his man, applying hard pressure on the ball so that the man in possession must protect the ball. The cutter's guard can also overplay to the side of the screen to force the cutter away from the screen. The main determinant of which method to use depends on the scoring ability of the screener with the ball and the cutter. These are coaching decisions.

The most common method to neutralize a possible offensive advantage obtained in screening or blocking is to exchange defensive responsibility (switching). Of course, assignments should never be exchanged unless absolutely necessary. It is the responsibility of the man guarding the screener to warn his teammates loudly of the potential

294

screen ("screen left," "screen right," "watch the pick," etc.). After his clear vocal warning, he should step back to allow his teammate to slide through the screen, directing him through by shouting "Slide, slide."

If an exchange of men is necessary, the man guarding the screener must call "switch" and quickly exchange assigned men with the teammate.

After an exchange of men, each defender is responsible for the man exchanged to. However, if in switching there is a decided mismatch in the comparative height of the offensive and defensive men, a switch back must be made as quickly as possible. If it is not made, a taller offensive player will move into the low-pivot area with a shorter defender. A shorter offensive player will have a distinct maneuvering advantage from the side areas against a taller opponent. If the opportunity to switch back does not arise, however, it should not be forced, as many times this results in an offensive player being left completely free. The switches should remain until the play is over or the defenders' team gets possession of the ball.

Any time a defender picks up a loose opponent, he should call out loudly the exchange in assignments; for example, "I have 22, take 15." This warns the man originally assigned to guard Number 22 that his man has been picked up by an alert teammate and his assignment has switched to opponent Number 15. On this type of exchange, the defender looking for the new assignment must sprint to a position six to eight feet in front of the basket and then look to the outside for his new man.

When defending in an area where screening maneuvers are probable, the defender should feel to the rear with one hand in the direction from which a potential screen may come, and listen for any vocal instructions from a teammate.

A defensive man should never let himself be screened when his man is two passes from the ball. He should have dropped off his man and be opened towards the ball so that he can see any potential screen without relying on a verbal warning.

lateral, or cross-court, screens

In a lateral, or cross-court, screen, the defender being screened can see his man and the screener. When offensive guards cross with each other outside the top of the foul-line circle (twenty-one or more feet from the basket), the man guarding a screener always steps back to allow his teammate to pass through. If either guard has excellent shooting range (twenty-one to twenty-five feet) and is screened for with the ball, the defender must fight over the screen to stay with the dangerous scorer. The man guarding a screener without the ball should be high to the side of his man towards which the potentially dangerous shooter is moving with the ball. This defender's hand and arm movement and the possibility of a switch should discourage a shot. The man guarding the screener must be alert for a quick cut to the basket by his man. An alternative to the above maneuvers is to overplay the good long-range outside shooter one-half a man to the side of the lateral screener and force him away from the screen. In this usage, the defender must watch for a reverse cut without the ball or a drive with the ball. Inside defensive teammates must be cognizant of these possibilities and be prepared to help out if necessary.

inside, or rear, screen

The inside, or rear, screen, in which the man being screened cannot see both the screener and his man, is used in the following five positions.

1. A backcourt man can dribble or cut tightly off a screen set by the other guard (who has the ball) in or near the outer half of the free-throw circle. The man guarding the cutter must force him to the middle; he must never allow him to go to the outside, as the offense usually clears that corner for this maneuver. The man guarding the screener must overplay to the open side, shouting instructions to his teammate, indicating that the left or right corner is cleared and telling him the location of the screen.

2. A backcourt man has the ball and dribbles off his strongside corner man positioned near the end of the foul line or foul line extended. In this case, the dribbler's guard must receive loud voice warning from the screener's man and attempt to overplay the dribbler strongly on the outside, forcing him to the middle. If he cannot force his man to the middle, the defender must try to fight his way between the screener and the dribbler.

If an exchange of men must be made, the screener's guard calls "switch," and forces the dribbler to the end line to stop his dribble. He then attacks aggressively, both hands held high, to prevent a pass to the forward moving towards the basket with a smaller defender guarding him. The smaller defender must get between the ball and the forward to prevent a bounce pass to the forward. The ball is being attacked in such a way as to prevent a high pass, and the smaller defender must be in position to stop the bounce pass.

If the screening action takes place beyond the twenty-foot area, the screener's defender should call for the guard to slide through between screener and defender.

3. The backcourt man passes to the corner man positioned near the end of the foul line or foul line extended

and cuts off him toward the baseline or basket. When this screen occurs, the screener's man must alert the cutter's guard, who must force the cutter to the middle. The guard keeps between the cutter and the ball and does not allow a return pass.

4. A corner man has the ball, and the guard can cut off a high- or medium-pivot screen. The man guarding the screening pivot must loudly warn the guard's defender of the screen. The defender should open to the ball side and stay between the cutter and the ball all the way from the outside starting position of the cutter to the basket.

5. The pivot screens for the corner man in possession and alive fourteen to eighteen feet from the basket. The screener's defender must warn the corner defender so he can protect the baseline to prevent an easy dribble-in lay-up. The men guarding the backcourt offensive players must fall back in position to help out on a drive off the screen to the middle. The man guarding the screening pivot should drop off his man a step toward the middle, to also discourage a dribble in that direction. He has to make the forward believe he will remain in this position to stop the dribble or shot in the middle, and still cover the screener on a roll to the basket. The corner defender remains responsible for his man, unless the screener's defender calls switch. If "switch" is called, the defending forward must get between the screener and the ball as the screener rolls to the basket. Defense of a lob pass from the corner man becomes the responsibility of the weak-side corner defender.

double cuts (scissors)

There are two types of double cuts that must be defensed against: (1) a double cut off a high pivot by the two guards (either passing to the pivot) and (2) a double cut off a medium pivot by the forward (who passes in to the pivot) and strong side guard. Both of these offensive maneuvers are extremely effective, producing open cuts, double-screened jump shots, or drive-in lay-up opportunities for the forward and/or guards and hook shots, drive-in lay-ups or short jump shot scoring possibilities for the pivot.

Preventing Double Cut off High Pivot. The defense must first prevent the ball from reaching the high pivot man. To discourage a pass, the defender of the guard with the ball must play him with the inside foot and hand forward, and the other guard's defender should drop off his man towards the high pivot. The second defender should be opened toward the ball, one hand pointing to the pivot to prevent the pass, the other toward his man. If the ball is passed cross-court, the defensive procedure is reversed.

If the pivot man receives the pass-in from either guard, their defenders can remain close to their men, one-half a man towards the middle of the court, discouraging the guards from crossing if possible and fighting over the pivot if the cut is successful. The defenders must try to force a wide cut from the guard position and must be alert for a change of direction by either guard. When a change occurs, the offensive corner man on the same side as the reversing guard will clear to the opposite corner. The defending corner man must warn his teammates loudly if this happens. When the first cutter screens for the other guard, the second cutter's defensive man should attempt to force his man high above both the screening guard and the high-pivot man. Neither defending guard must ever drop to a position behind the pivot man, as this affords the offensive guard an easy jump shot over a double screen of pivot man and other guard.

The alternative defense is for the defensive guards to drop back from their men and in toward the high pivot with the ball. They should try to exert defensive pressure on the ball so that the pivot man has to pass it back out quickly to prevent a loose ball or a held-ball situation. If the offensive guards cut, they must be forced to go outside the defensive guards, never between guard and pivot man. If the defending guards must switch, the man guarding the first cutter or screener calls "switch." The guards now must be alert for both cutters heading for the basket on the same side of the pivot. Anticipating this maneuver will help to counteract its effectiveness.

The man guarding the high pivot should overplay his man one-half a man to the ball side to prevent a pass-in from either guard. If the pass-in is successful, the pivot defender should step back one step and line up between his man and the basket. He must alert both guard defenders of potentially dangerous moves, and he must be aware of his own man's potentialities, as the pivot can turn for a fifteen-foot jumper or fake the shot and drive in. If either cutter is open, the pivot defender, calling "switch," must quickly pick up the free man with the ball and prepare to block the cutter's lay-up shot or deter a return pass to the pivot man.

Preventing Double Cut off Medium Pivot. When the forward passes to a medium pivot, the strong-side guard and forward may double cut off the pivot. Again, preventing the pass-in to the pivot is the first line of defense. The defending guard on the side of the ball should drop off toward the baseline and ball, and the pivot should be played a strong one-half man on the ball side. If the pass-in is successful, the far side defensive guard, who has dropped far off his man, should attempt to tie up the pivot man. Both the far-side defensive guard and forward must float protectively towards the ball position.

The forward passing in, usually the first cutter, cuts to the middle. The guard cuts to the outside off the forward. Defenders guarding either cutter can attempt to tie up the ball or prevent the cuts by legally maintaining defensive position in the cutter's path. All defenders should be alert for a "switch" call.

double screens

Individual defensive players must be alert for two types of stationary double screens used effectively by many offenses. The first type results when two offensive players set a screen side by side at the foul-line area or to the side away from the ball. The cutter comes from the outside, away from the ball, off the double screen towards the basket. Players defending against the screeners and the cutter should drop off their men toward the middle in the direction of the ball. If they do this simultaneously with ball movement, the screen should be ineffectual, and switching and congesting the cutting area will be relatively easy.

The most difficult stationary double screen to defend against is set along the foul lanes, and the cutter goes behind the screen on the baseline side, cutting out to the ball from the inside for a short jump shot. Usually, the cutter is moving in the same direction as the ball is being passed, and the man defending the cutter must play between his man and the ball. The defenders guarding the potential passers should be alerted to the double-screen by shouted warnings of its position by the screeners' defenders. The passers must be played with extreme pressure so that a pass-in is difficult.

Several times during a game, defenders retreating after losing the ball will find themselves outnumbered by the offense. The player who has made the physical error of losing the ball should not commit the mental error of following the ball when it has been intercepted by the intended receiver's defender. His best defensive move is to drop back quickly for defensive position. If he moves toward the ball he will give his defender a clear, unopposed break to the basket. There is no defense for this one-on-none break except to hustle back for a rebound in the event of a missed shot.

The most common offensive advantages are the two-on-one, three-on-one, three-on-two, four-on-two, four-on-three, and five-on-four situations.

The primary defensive strategy when outnumbered is to slow down the advance of the ball until teammates can recover and help out and, if possible, to prevent the easy lay-up shot and the good percentage shot. Defenders should use realistic fakes to stop the dribbler, and feint and

**defensing the
offensive advantage**

299

shout loudly to make offense commit itself. When outnumbered with more than one defender back, practical zone defense principles must be used to delay, to force the least advantageous shooting opportunity, and to help position the defenders in the best possible rebounding position. A defensive player who can intercept the ball, deflect the pass to the cutter, delay the attack until help arrives, or force a shot beyond the sixteen-foot range has done an outstanding job of defending.

two-on-one

When one defensive player is retreating and must defend against two fast-breaking opponents with the ball, he must run backward to a position at the top of the free-throw circle, keeping the ball and both men in view. If the front man has the ball, the defender, while retreating, must delay him as far out as possible. When a cutter is ahead of the ball-handler, the defender must open his stance toward the cutter, since he is the more dangerous man, keep the foul-line area covered, and attempt to stop the dribbler without allowing him to make an easy pass to the cutter or execute a stop-and-go or change-of-pace dribble.

Knowledge of the abilities of the two fast-breaking opponents is important. If the cutter is a tall man, he may not be as good a ball-handler or passer as the dribbler. In that case, the defender should attempt to force a pass to the cutter, then attack him aggressively to cause a fumble, violation, or poor return pass. The shot will generally be taken by the player on the right side, and the better shooter will look for the shot himself. If the ball is being brought down either side, the defender should try to keep it on the side, as the sideline and baseline can be utilized in defense, and the influencing maneuver tells fast retreating teammates where to position themselves.

Never try to take the ball away from the dribbler unless he makes a careless tactical error. If the ball is being passed back and forth between the attackers, retreat to the foul line and then fake at the man nearer the middle to force a hurried pass or a hesitancy in the passing continuity. Never allow the lay-up shot, and challenge any good shot without giving away rebound position or a better shooting opportunity.

three-on-one

In the three-on-one break, the defender must retreat to the foul line and determine by preknowledge or judgment where the pass will go. If the dribbler stops, the defender must retreat back to within eight feet of the basket, allowing the foul-line shot. He must attempt to influence the dribbler to his weak hand to prevent the easy lay-up or pass. If necessary, he should foul the dribbler for a one-shot opportunity rather than give an unopposed lay-up.

three-on-two

There are two methods of defending against a three-on-two offensive advantage. The first method is a front and back defensive alignment, with the front man in the outer half of the free-throw circle and the back man between the foul lanes, six to eight feet in front of the basket. The front man must stop the dribbler as far out as posible and force a pass. (The more passes the attackers make, the greater the chance for errors on their part.) The back man must react to the side of the pass, but he cannot start until the ball has left the passer's hands. Moving before the release commits the defender to that side, and a good fake will leave the third man free for an easy lay-up. After the pass the front man opens towards the side of the pass and drops back to the side opposite the pass. The back man should attack aggressively after committing himself, trying to step in and draw an offensive charge or to prevent the cross-court pass. If the dribbler does not stop or pass, the front defender influences him to one side or the other to limit his passing opportunities. If he succeeds, the back man should favor the opposite side, and the front man must retreat on the same side he forced the dribbler towards. A third retreating defender should come back to the foul-line area and cover there.

The second method of playing a three-on-two break is for the defense to play side by side, parallel to each other. The only time this method is preferable is when the middle man is not a good ball-handler or when the opponents are not a good fast-break team. The two defensive men should take positions near the ends of the foul line, approximately fourteen feet apart, and open towards their respective side-lines, keeping the ball and the cutter on their side in view. The distance between the defenders should not be so great that the offensive man can dribble between them for the lay-up shot. The man on the side of the dribbling hand must try to stop the dribbler, using defensive fakes and feints and shouting to disconcert him, while retreating. When the dribbler stops, each man should fall off towards the cutter on his side, waving his hands and yelling to discourage a pass-in and make the middle man take the shot. If a pass is made to a cutter, the defender on that side must move with the pass to get position between the cutter and the basket to prevent the easy shot. The other defensive man opens toward the pass and must be alert for a rebound or a pass attempt to the cutter on his side. The third defensive man catching up takes the middle man.

four-on-two

On a four-on-two disadvantage, the defenders should play parallel at the ends of the foul line and attempt to slow the offensive man with the ball until other defenders can retreat to help out. They must try to force the outside shot, if possible, or foul advantageously to prevent the easy basket.

four-on-three

Against the four-on-three and five-on-four offensive advantages, the same basic principles mentioned previously apply. The defenders should use basic zone defense techniques. The maneuvering area is lessened for the offense by the additional defensive man.

In the four-on-three defensive situation, a triangular zone should be formed, with a front man in the outer half of the foul circle and the two rear men six to eight feet in front of the basket with their inside feet on the foul lane on their side. The three defenders should have their arms outstretched and moving to cover as much area as possible and must face the ball until their teammates can get back in defensive positions. The front man should force the ball toward the side with the fewer attackers and follow the pass. The defender away from the pass turns with the pass and steps into the foul lane, facing the ball. He must protect against a cutter coming down the middle and a pass underneath the basket on his side. The back defender on the side to which the pass was made turns with the pass to a man moving into the strong-side pivot area. The three men should cover the good percentage shooting areas to prevent the good offensive thrust, trying to keep the offense passing the ball by maintaining a shifting triangular defense until defensive help arrives. When defensive balance is achieved, the defender should return to man-to-man cautiously, being certain that all offensive players are matched closely in size.

five-on-four

The five-on-four defensive principle is similar to the four-on-three, except that the zone used initially should be in the form of a diamond when the ball position is in center court: one man in the outer half of the foul circle, two side men stationed fifteen feet apart one step below the foul line, and the back man six feet in front of the basket in the foul lane. The zone shifts from a diamond to a box with ball movement left or right.

Many times during the course of a game an offensive man will start towards his basket after receiving a pass-out only to discover that he is far ahead of his offensive teammates, and there are two defenders back. In this situation, one defender should play the man to stop his dribble, and the second defender should attack aggressively from a blind side to force the offensive player into making a bad pass or into a held-ball situation. The defenders must be certain that no other offensive player is in scoring position.

When two offensive players attack three defensive players the nearest defender stops the dribble and a second defender attacks aggressively. The third defender plays between the second offensive man and the ball.

Present-day basic defensive philosophy has changed the defensive player from the retreating, passive, stay-between-your-man-and-the-basket prototype into a daring, aggressive attacker. When a defensive team elects to challenge the offense at any point—full-court, three-quarters court or half court—much of its defensive strategy is based upon methods that previously were considered to be extremely poor defense, such as over-guarding or deliberately playing out of line to the basket. Constant defensive pressure has a twofold purpose. It disrupts the offensive team's preferred style of play, and it incorporates this aggressive defense into its own offensive pattern.

interceptions

When bringing the ball upcourt, many backcourt men pass routinely from one to the other before reaching the offensive attack position. An aggressive guard should be encouraged to try to intercept a pass during this advance. If this attempt fails, and the defender is in poor defensive position because of his effort, his backcourt teammate, who is open towards the ball, should switch quickly to the man with the ball, calling out the exchange in responsibility, and the player who is out of position should recover as rapidly as possible and run to the defensive foul-line area to pick up the attacker left open. At the same time, defenders near the basket should move into position to prevent an easy cut to the basket and a return pass.

Defensive fakes can be passive as well as aggressive. As an attacker approaches the offensive maneuvering position, he is intent on the pattern he wants to put into operation. A defender can lure an unaware dribbler into thinking he is retreating routinely, then make a quick thrusting move to the ball and slap it free for a clean steal. A defensive player who is quicker than his man can entice the offense by falling farther off his man to invite a pass and reacting to an intercept-

303

ing position. A corner defender can over-play to allow a reverse cut and react quickly to the ball when the pass is made to the cutter. A pivot defender can seemingly play behind his man until the pass is on its way, then quickly step in and flick it away. The determining factor on taking such defensive chances should be whether help is possible; if it is, take any good opportunity. The closer the play is to the basket, the less team help can be expected.

double-teaming

Doubling up on opponents, especially on the sideline or baseline after a dribble, is very effective as a defensive chance maneuver. When a dribbler is forced to the sideline by an aggressive defender and stops, the defender should overplay strongly to the sideline side, necessitating a pivot towards the mid-court line by the dribbler to protect the ball. The other guard should anticipate this pivot and charge the man with the ball from his blind side to effect a held ball, a violation, or a bad pass. The same tactic can be used when a good defensive forward seemingly allows a baseline drive attempt, then quickly closes the baseline and attacks the driver on the baseline side forcing a pivot toward the near sideline. The backcourt defender on that side can approach from the forward's blind side to force an offensive mistake.

Defenders who double up on one man must aggressively attack the ball without fouling, using quick hand movement and outthrust feet to prevent a damaging pass out. Do not deliberately try to steal the ball in any double-up situation, as fouls usually result. Be aware of the status of the man with the ball on a defensive double-team. If he has not dribbled, the defense can be hurt.

On all ball-exchange crosses by offensive men, guard to guard or guard to forward, a quick switch (jump switch by the screener's defender) into the path of the man receiving the ball, and a rear follow-up by the receiver's guard can put the offensive man at a disadvantage. The purpose of these double pincer movements is a resultant offensive mistake—an off-line pass that can be intercepted, a held-ball, or a violation. Many times the next closest defender to the double-teaming jump-switch can help, since the man being double-teamed will instinctively attempt to pass immediately to the man left unguarded. Anticipating this pass, the next nearest defender should leave his man and try for the interception.

In many offensive screens, the man guarding the screener can jump-switch into the path of a dribbler driving hard off the screen and draw an offensive foul. The same technique can be used on hard-running cutters at the end of a fast break.

An aggressive defensive player will occasionally be beaten by a good dribbler, but with a quick recovery he can turn his defensive lapse into a possible ball-stealing situation by coming up fast behind the dribbler, getting in a stride with him, and (using a darting, flicking hand thrust) attempting to tip or deflect the dribble. The same play can be used in overplaying a dribbler's strong side to force a pivot in order to retain the dribble. After the turn, a hustling defender can tap the ball free by pivoting behind the dribbler and swinging the far hand and arm with a sickle-like movement from behind. With all other defenders within the defensive triangle of ball, their man, and basket, a clean steal can result.

The defender guarding a screener must constantly be alert to overplay (hedge) to the ball side when an opponent cuts off the man he is guarding. He must be prepared to defend against three situations: (1) when the opponent using the screen has the ball, (2) when the screener has the ball (usually a post, back to basket), and (3) when a third player (other than the screener or cutter) has the ball.

overplaying strong side of screener (hedging)

cutter has the ball

When an opponent with the ball is using dribbling maneuvers to force his defender into a screen, the player guarding the screener must move up towards the dribbling opponent on the strong side, approximately beside the screener, giving loud vocal warnings. The defender guarding the screener should be aware of the offensive potential of the dribbler. He must first be prepared to stop a drive-in if the dribbler's guard is rubbed off by the screen. Second, he must be prepared to impede a shot if the dribbler stops and jump shoots. Third, he must be able to maintain a fronting position on the screener to prevent a pass to him if he rolls to the basket anticipating a defensive switch.

The overplay must force the dribbler to take a wider path, thus allowing his guard to go over the top of the screen and regain good defensive position without giving an offensive advantage. With good anticipation, the screener's defender may cause an offensive charge by the dribbler. If a switch is necessitated, the screener's defender (the back man) calls it. (This defensive team play requires constant practice.) Weak-side teammates must help in defending against a lob pass if the screener rolls to the basket.

The distance the screener is from the basket also affects the defense. Beyond eighteen feet of the basket, the guard playing the dribbler must force over the screen, while the

305

screener's defender fakes a strong-side overplay to slow down or stop the dribbler without committing himself. Within twelve feet, the hedger must overplay so completely it is impossible for the dribbler to shoot or pass. Passing in this area becomes increasingly more difficult because of the limited passing lanes.

screener has the ball

When the screener has the ball, his distance from the basket is the most important consideration for his defender in determining how to overplay to the strong side. If the screener is within his effective shooting range, his defender must play close to him, anticipating the cutter and feinting quickly at him, but not losing defensive position on the screener. If the cutter's strong side is outside, the screener's guard must concentrate his defensive attention on his man, as any overt reaction to the cutter would allow a post screener to pivot and dribble into the basket unimpeded. If the cut is to the inside, off the screen, the hedger can more effectively overplay to this side without giving the screener with the ball too great an offensive advantage.

The man guarding the cutter must always try to go over the top of the screen, slashing at the ball as he retreats to force the screener to protect the ball. If the cutter is not a good outside shooter, his defender should go behind the screener's guard, not in front of him, because if the screener's guard had to step back to allow him through, the screener could then shoot. If the screener is in a low- or medium-pivot area, his defender must concentrate on him exclusively until a pass-off is made, and then react quickly to the cutter.

third player has the ball

When a third player has the ball, the screener's defender should overplay strongly to the ball side, denying the cutter a good path towards the ball and forcing him as far out from the basket as possible without giving an offensive opportunity to his own man (the screener). Good basic defensive position (balancing to the ball) by both defenders away from the ball should negate any offensive attempts by their opponents.

defensing the outlet pass against the fast break

The first line of defense in stopping the fast break is at your offensive end of the court. The team breaking must first rebound at its defensive end and make an outlet pass. If the breaking team relies on one or two key rebounders to initiate the break, pressure must be exerted aggressively to tie up the rebounder or make him dribble. If the key fast-break rebounder has inside position on a rebound, and he recovers the ball, the man behind him should try to prevent a high pass out by positioning himself to the outside of the rebounder with his hands and arms held high and moving to effect a possible deflection and to cause the rebounder to be protective. A second man can be assigned to help in harassing the rebounder, but both should retreat immediately if the player passes out. If the rebounder must pivot to protect the ball, the original pressure man should stay and the other man retreat. If the key rebounder is guarding an offensive pivot, he will usually be outside the pivot man when a shot is taken. The pivot must aggressively maintain this inside rebounding position. He should not move to get the ball, but hold off the other team's key rebounder to prevent the fast break. He only rebounds if he is certain of possession. A delay of only a few seconds is enough to impair the effectiveness of the organized fast break.

Coupled with the attempt to diminish the rebounding potentiality should be an effort to stop the effective outlet pass. For their first outlet pass, teams look to the sideline area near mid-court on the side on which the rebound is recovered. A quick guard should play an intercepting angle on the outlet receiver, forcing him to adjust his position or come back toward the rebounder for safe reception, thus slowing the initial thrust of the fast break. Overplaying this outlet to force him deeper towards the mid-court area will reduce the rebounder-passer's passing range, as a two-hand over-hand pass or a quick hook pass cannot be thrown accurately for too long a distance.

If the outlet pass is made, the assigned backcourt defender should try to keep the receiver from dribbling the ball to the middle or passing it to a teammate cutting to the middle lane. He should concentrate on forcing the ball up on the outside lane if possible.

There are two accepted methods in defending against the inbounding passer on out-of-bounds plays. The first is a challenging, aggressive approach, with each defending teammate playing between the ball position and his man, forcing him away from the pass-in area so that any pass-in must be to a man retreating from the basket area. The player guarding the man making the pass-in stands directly in front of him and waves his arms, kicks with his feet, and yells loudly to disconcert the passer and prevent an effective pass.

The second method in popular use is for the defender of the passer-in to play between his man and the basket, keeping this position after the pass-in. All other defenders drop off their men toward the ball and the basket and open their position to enable them to see both their men and the ball.

defense against the passer-in on out-of-bounds plays

The man guarding the passer-in does not play too close to the passer and tries to cut off any pass-in to a cutter coming into the foul-line area or a possible pass-in to a pivot player. When the passer comes in bounds, the defender should force him away from the basket area to prevent a pass-and-cut situation.

group defensive drills

In the two- and three-men drills, players should show a lot of enthusiasm, talking and encouraging teammates so that all defenders acquire a sense of individual and team pride in their defensive accomplishment.

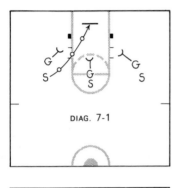

DIAG. 7-1

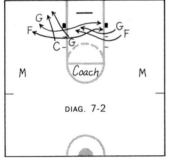

DIAG. 7-2

Diag. 7-1, THREE-ON-THREE REBOUNDING DRILL

This drill involves three guards and three attackers. The defenders allow one of the shooters to shoot after a dribble or two without too much opposition. They must take a step back, watch the path of the three shooters who are following the shot, and then box them out. This drill should be used early in the season to inculcate good fundamental techniques in the basic rebounding position areas. Coaches should also look for evasive tactics by the attackers as they approach the boards. This drill can be performed at both ends of the court at the same time. Don't spend too much time with it.

Diag. 7-2, MOVING THREE-ON-THREE REBOUND DRILL

An offensive center and two forwards and three defenders move in position close to the basket. We like to have one of the offensive players in the foul-lane area and the other two in the forward areas to the left and right of the foul lane. The coach, in the outer half of the free-throw circle, passes to and receives return passes from the players on offense, as they are moving. If one of them gets an unopposed lay-up he should take it to impress on the defenders that they have to be in good guarding position throughout the movement of the drill. Any of the three offensive players or the coach may shoot. As the shot is taken, the offensive players should look for good offensive rebound position, and the defenders should immediately box out, attempt to secure the rebound, and pitch out to managers stationed at the outlet areas. The manager passes back to the coach. The players should interchange after five or six rebounds. This drill should be used at both ends of the court in preseason practice. It is an excellent positioning drill against a moving type of offense and teaches proper offensive and defensive rebounding techniques.

Diag. 7-3, TWO-ON-TWO OFFENSIVE CROSSING DRILL

Three two-on-two situations are illustrated in the diagram. O_1 and O_2 are on offense; X_1 is guarding O_1 and X_2 is guarding O_2. In the first situation, O_1 passes to O_2 and screens for him. As the screen takes place, X_1 slides to his right and steps back, telling and allowing X_2 to slide through.

In the second situation, O_1 passes to O_2 and begins screening on X_2 for O_2. X_2 goes over the top of O_1's screen and stays close to O_2.

In the third situation, O_1 again passes and screens for O_2. X_1 guarding the screener, calls the switch and picks up O_2 as X_2 drops back and picks up O_1. The two offensive men continue crossing

308

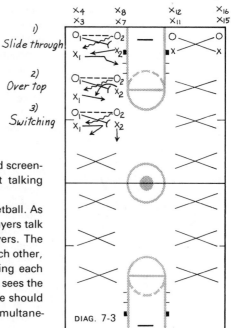

1)
Slide through

2)
Over top

3)
Switching

DIAG. 7-3

down the court and back, alternately passing, dribbling and screening. A coach should watch for defensive mistakes. (Not talking enough is a most common fault.)

This is an excellent fundamental drill at all levels of basketball. As the players progress down the court, the coach and the players talk constantly, shouting encouragement to the defensive players. The defensive players should talk to each other, encouraging each other, talking each other through screens, calling switches, telling each other what to watch out for as the screen is coming. If one sees the other dropping his hands from good defensive position, he should call "hands up." Both sides of the court should be used simultaneously.

Diag. 7-4, HALF-COURT OVERPLAY TO STRONG SIDE OF SCREEN DRILL

On the left side, O_1 (a forward) and O_2 (a guard) are defended by X_1 and X_2. O_2 passes to O_1 and goes to the outside behind O_1, looking for a return pass so that he can dribble or take a jump shot. As the ball is passed back to O_2, X_1 moves to the strong side of the screen in order to move O_2 off a good turn-in path to the basket. He cannot move too soon, because if he does he will allow O_1 a direct dribble to the basket. From his new position, X_1 must still be able to maintain a good fronting defensive position on O_1 if O_1 cuts to the basket. X_1 also has to attempt delaying action to give X_2 a chance to go over the top of the screen and get in good defensive position on the man with the ball, O_2.

On the right side of the diagram, O_3 and O_4, offensive men, are almost parallel, within shooting range. X_3 and X_4 are guarding them. O_4 passes to O_3 and sets a screen on X_3. X_4, guarding O_4, moves to his left, keeping ready to move O_3 away from a good shooting position by stepping into his path legally as he dribbles off the screen. X_3 goes over the top of the screen. Should O_4 cut to the basket, X_4 will be in position to pick him up, maintaining position between O_4 and the ball.

These two plays should be practiced so that players guarding the screener become aware of their responsibility to help their defensive teammates. The players should take turns being on offense and defense and working on the left and right sides of the court.

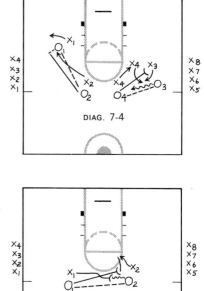

DIAG. 7-4

DIAG. 7-5

Diag. 7-5, SWITCH AND JUMP-IN DEFENSIVE DRILL

This excellent drill should be practiced to combat a team with a set pattern type of offense in which the guards routinely exchange positions and cross over. The technique can be used either to draw an offensive foul on the man who is dribbling or to double-team the

309

ball. O_1 has passed to O_2. O_1 moves to his right and screens X_2. X_1 follows O_1 across, and as the screen is set he jumps into the path of dribbling O_2, looking for the offensive charge and trying to stop the opponent's planned offense. This drill should be practiced cross-court and moving vertically down the court.

Diag. 7-6, THREE-ON-THREE DOUBLE-TEAMING BALL DRILL

This drill calls for aggressive double-teaming of the ball in the backcourt, and incorporates some of the other fundamental techniques we have practiced in defensive drilling. O_1 dribbles away from O_2, the other guard. X_1 assumes an aggressive shuffling defensive posture and turns O_1 in his dribble back towards the middle. X_2 should slide toward O_1 as he loses sight of X_2 by turning toward the sideline in a protective dribble. When O_1 turns to the middle, X_2 should move in as fast as he can from the blind side and stop any cross-court pass, if possible. A third offensive player, O_3, and a third defensive player, X_3, are in position on the weak side. Normally when a man is double-teamed or feels defensive pressure from one side, his immediate reaction is probably to pass to the side of the pressure. As X_3 sees X_2 slide rapidly toward the ball, he should move up into position to overplay O_2 so that he cannot receive a pass. X_3 should lay off O_2 until he sees O_1 tense to make the pass. If accurate, X_3's timing will allow him to come from an out-of-sight position into the path of the pass. If he picks the ball off, he has an unopposed path to the far basket.

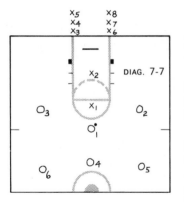

DIAG. 7-6

Diag. 7-7, DEFENSIVE THREE-ON-TWO DRILL

O_1 has the ball in the middle, O_2 and O_3 are offensive wing men. X_1 must stop O_1 as high as he can. X_2 should remain back and go to the side to which a pass has been made. If O_1 passed to O_2, X_2 would slide to his left. He would not go out to attack O_2, but would use defensive faking and feinting motions at him. X_1 would drop back opposite (right). If the ball were passed from O_1 to O_3, X_1 would drop back to the opposite side (left) and X_2 would attack O_3.

First, X_1 must attempt to stop the man with the ball. Second, he must try to influence him. If X_1 can direct O_1 to X_1's left, X_1 will stay with him, going to the basket with him if he goes there, and X_2 will drop opposite. Forcing the middle man to commit himself left or right while in possession of the ball allows X_1 to play both the ball handler and the other offensive player to that side.

X_1 and X_2 must have good defensive positioning, and they must prevent easy lay-up shots. If they can force the offensive players to use more than one pass, teammates should have time to come up from the far end of the court.

DIAG. 7-7

team
defense

The primary purpose of a team's defense is to limit the opponent's scoring opportunities, preventing them from using a fast-break or predesigned offensive patterns by disrupting their continuity and efficiency. The coach selects the type of team defense to be used, basing his selection on several factors, the most important being the personnel available.

The correct defense is that which best limits the primary offensive thrusts and procedures of the opponents. A good team defense incorporates the strong points of both zone defense and man-to-man defense. The primary focus in man-to-man defense is the man, and the secondary objective is the ball. But teams that use man-to-man as a primary defense also use such zone defense features as playing loose away from the ball, weak-side collapses towards the basket to prevent penetration of the crucial area, and compacting the defense in the basket area and in the middle. Conversely, zone defensive players, who play the ball first and the man second, must be able to defend against the opponent with the ball on a man-to-man basis. Zones today do not cover just certain areas. They flex with a man-to-man attitude at the focal point (the ball), attacking the man with the ball and preventing reception in the pivot area.

the coach's defensive philosophy

A coach must insist that his players never allow the offensive team to advance the ball to their point of attack without strong defensive pressure. (The offensive point of attack is the point at which they wish to put their set offensive pattern into operation.) The coach cannot use a single defense in his overall team preparation. He must adopt whatever defensive style is best suited to counteract the opponent's offensive moves. It is important that he understand the type of defense he wishes to use and that he be able to teach it to his players.

All coaches work hard at improving the defensive posture of their teams. The defense must be sound, both individually and as a team; it must be flexible; and it must be simple enough for the players to learn, yet complex for the opponents. Defensive ability is based on hard work, determination, dedication, discipline, concentration, responsibility, cooperation, physical and mental coordination, speed and quickness, willingness, and pride.

By scouting, opponents preview each other's defenses. Showing multiple defenses allows you to employ a defense that will give them difficulty. This forces them to use practice time to prepare themselves for your defenses, playing against substitutes or freshmen who must be taught each defense in order to act as opponents. If there has been no previous scouting, the coach should prepare defenses for any defensive contingency and be able to adapt mentally during the progress of the game using his time-outs strategically and making good use of his half-time discussion period. The coach should make adjustments quickly, as soon as weak points are discovered. For example, if a good player is in foul trouble, the coach can keep him on the court by changing from a man-to-man to a zone defense. It is easier to defend against a team with one inflexible set style. If they do not vary their offense, you may implement double-teaming tactics.

The coach should pressure teams holding the ball for the last shot at the end of a quarter, at the end of a half, or at the end of the game. They are concentrating on maintaining possession and generally are not looking at the basket; therefore, it might be easy to force them into a violation or cause an interception or a held ball. Teams that are ahead should not become relaxed or passive defensively; they should maintain pressure. All teams must be able to press to some degree, especially in the late stages of the game. Defensive aggressiveness will cause the opponents to move out of their normal pattern so that the defensive team has a chance to obtain possession of the ball.

Defensively, a team should change game pace to their own advantage, concentrating on their opponents' strengths and covering up their own weaknesses. They must surprise and confuse the opponents. Surprise was the deciding factor in an NCAA regional game that the authors' team played. With 40 seconds to go, we changed from the basic tight man-to-man defense the team played for 39½-minutes to a half-court zone-press defense. By double-teaming the ball handler of the opposition, our players were able to intercept the ball and make an easy basket, resulting in a one-point win in an important closely played game.

Saving some practiced defensive variations for the second half that were not shown in the first half is another good surprise maneuver. You could also use a defensive variation in the last few minutes of the first half so that the opposing coach will use much of his valuable half-time period discussing methods of attacking a defense that will not be used again in the course of that game.

The winning team in basketball is frequently the team with the quickest transition from offense to defense; therefore all teams must maintain defensive balance while attacking offensively. In case they lose possession of the ball, they must have offensive players in a defensive safety position so that they may hinder or stop the opponents from scoring an easy unopposed basket. A team should have three offensive rebounders; one man who is half offensive and half defensive going to the ball only if he is certain of possession and one player who is back on defense. Efficient transition from offense to defense is the most important single factor in maintaining a good team defensive posture in the course of a ball game.

defensive preparation

Defensive preparation starts the first day of practice. Team defensive fundamentals are of prime importance in early season drills, and coaches should constantly review them during the season. (The coach should have a five-man offensive skeleton group run the patterns. During each play, he should point out the offensive players who should be moving back as safety men for defense or to fill outletting areas to relieve pressure at the ball position when the play situation does not result in a shot. After a basket is made, he should have the five men on offense break quickly back on defense.)

The coach must practice double-teaming opponents, working on the double-teaming aspects for man-to-man, zone, or zone press defensive alignments. He must teach baseline defensive techniques and how to play men who do not have possession of the ball. If he wants an aggressive defense, he will have his men overplay. If not, he will have them play loose or sag back when the man is one pass away. He must teach his players never to allow an opponent to cut in front of them to the ball, especially not a corner man who wants to cut to the keyhole area with the ball out front or on the opposite side.

He must teach players to force opponents away from their favorite shooting spots by forcing them off course or by stepping into their path. (This action is especially useful when defensing against a fast break.)

The most important technical function of the basketball coach is making his players understand the importance of team defense. Defense in basketball is a constant, offense is a variable; therefore, the coach should motivate the players to work to acquire proper defensive techniques. Each player must be made to understand the necessity of giving his all defensively for the good of the team. This we might call the perfect approach or perfect factor. Also, the player should know he will not be allowed to play if he cannot contribute to the team defense. This we might call imperfect motivation or the imperfect factor.

Each squad member should be made to understand that

the greatest burden to a team is a weak or indifferent defensive player, and that the coach, would prefer an aggressive defender who is uncoordinated offensively to a good shooter with a blasé attitude.

In emphasizing the necessity for good defense, the coach must follow these eight guide lines:

1. Convince the squad of the necessity for a cohesive, positive defensive policy.

2. Insist on adherence to detail when implementing the defensive philosophy.

3. Break the defense into component fundamental techniques.

4. Practice group defensive techniques each practice sessions, and develop rules and guidelines for each phase of defense.

5. Allot as much practice time daily to defense as to offense.

6. Disperse defensive drills discriminately through daily practice (at the beginning of one practice session, halfway through another, at the end of a third) so as to obtain maximum results by simulating playing conditions effectively. The tiredness of a player varies in the course of a game, and this factor must be taken into consideration during defensive practice.

7. Never allow improper, careless, or slovenly defensive practices. Correct poor defensive procedure immediately.

8. Place a premium on good defensive play by praising individuals both privately and publicly for outstanding defensive accomplishment. The stability and reliability of a good team defense must often counteract the inconsistency of poor offensive accomplishment.

team characteristics

The following characteristics should be intrinsic in all teams when playing defense.

1. A Positive Mental Approach. Since defense must be played at least fifty percent of the time in every game, the team must be completely prepared mentally. A good mental approach is made up of confidence, poise, mental aggressiveness, anticipation, and pride.

Confidence. The coach must convince the players that a selected method is the best possible defense. Both coach and team must have complete confidence in the strategy.

Poise. Good defensive players must be poised. They must not get upset, rattled, or unduly concerned over opposition moves; they should be emotionally prepared to overcome them.

Mental aggressiveness. (We use the term mental aggressiveness because we do not wish players to get physically aggressive to a point where they overextend themselves or foul.) Players must play within their limitations and understand the overall team philosophy of defense so that they can always make the right play at the right time.

315

Anticipation. Intelligent anticipation and reaction to this anticipation are important factors in team defense. Players must understand the philosophy of the offense that they are defending against so that they can prevent the opponents from getting the position they want or making the type of play they wish to make.

Pride. Pride in individual accomplishment and, more important, pride in team accomplishment on defense is an important mental aspect in the team defense posture.

2. Adaptability. The team must be able to vary its defense depending on the following five factors.

1. The team's capabilities
2. The coach's understanding of the defense and his ability to teach it to his players
3. The physical appurtenances of the home court
4. The type of opposition that will be played against in the course of the team schedule
5. The level of competition
    (The lower the level of competition the more difficult it is to inculcate all of the proper fundamentals and team techniques necessary in building a complete team defense. At lower levels of competition we strongly recommend the use of man-to-man team defense for the best interests of the players.)

3. Good Floor Position and Floor Balance. Since the team must protect the goal, defense must be built from the basket out. The focal point of all defenses must be the ball position and its distance from the basket. Also to be considered are the type of defense and the relation of the floor position of the man you are guarding with respect to the ball position. Consider the man in your area if the team is playing a zone defense.

4. Physical Activity. Offense must be balanced, with one offensive player moving into good defensive position during all offensive maneuverings. All players must be able to change quickly from offense to defense, getting back down the court so that they can play defense from the basket out. They must be able to stop the ball's progress once the basket area is defended and be able to prevent penetration after stopping the ball movement.

5. Flexibility. The defense taught must be able to meet all types of offensive challenges, and it must be able to move into action at all times of the game from any court position. The defense used depends on the type of opposition, the game situation (whether the team is ahead or behind, the time left in the game), and special situations (out-of-bounds plays, foul shots, and last second situations).

basic team types

When determining a team's defense, basic team types should be considered. These are usually categorized by the heights of the players. High school guards generally range from quite short up to six foot or six foot one, while in college they will range up to approximately six foot three. Forwards in high school will be between six foot one and six foot three; in college they will probably range from six foot three to six foot six. Centers, generally the tallest boys on the squads, will be six foot three or taller in high school and six foot six or taller in college.

Each squad will be one of the following six types with respect to the height of the team members:

1. Five tall men

2. Four tall men and one small man

3. Three tall men and two small men

4. Two tall men and three small men

5. One tall man and four small men

6. Five small men

We will discuss the six types of teams and the type of defense we feel is best suited to the personnel involved.

Five Tall Men. If the team is playing man-to-man it should play a loose man-to-man. If the coach prefers a zone defense, a passive type of zone would be best, especially if the team has two tall boys who are extremely awkward. In this type of defense they can defend the goal area. If pressure is needed, a type of half-court pressure is best, with one fast, tall man forcing the ball up towards the ten-second (mid-court) line as quickly as possible and then exerting the pressure in the half-court area.

Four Tall Men and One Small Man. This team should play a loose man-to-man defense or a one-two-two zone in which the one small man is given latitude to move to anticipate and intercept. Half-court pressure should be used.

Three Tall Men and Two Small Men. We recommend regular man-to-man defense. The team could also use a two-one-two zone or a two-three zone, a combination type defense, or a pressure defense of the type that could be extended to full court (probably a two-two-one type of full-court pressure).

Two Tall Men and Three Small Men. This team can use any type of man-to-man defense the coach wishes. For a zone defense the coach should use a three-two zone, a one-two-two zone, or a one-three-one zone. A combination defense is also a possibility.

One Tall Man and Four Small Men. We recommend a switching type of man-to-man defense in which the four smaller players are allowed to switch men on every lateral cross or movement towards the basket staying with their men only on diagonal cuts. The best zone would be a two-two-one or a one-three-one in which the big man is left in the basket area at all times. The pressure defense should be either a man-to-man pressure or a zone pressure using a one-two-one-one type of press with the big man as the back man.

Five Small Men. This team should use a tight man-to-man in half court, with the double and turn procedures, or a full-court man-to-man. A zone press type defense could be used, with five men crashing the defensive boards, or an aggressive type of two-three zone defense in which pressure is put on the ball at all areas of the front court.

team principles

All good team defenses are based on the following six principles.

1. **Reduce the Frequency of High-Percentage Shots.** This may be done by maintaining a good team balance defensively and by harrying the opponents, forcing them to take off-balance shots. The defenders should also allow the ball to be passed to the less accurate shooters, permitting them to take low percentage-shots, and frustrate the good shooters by denying them the ball or by harassing them when they have the ball.

2. **Decrease the Number of Close-in Shots (the Shots under the Eighteen-Foot Area).** The more shots a team gets from the close-in area, the weaker the team defense structure is.

3. **Diminish Second Shot Possibilities.** Prevent the offense from position by using good rebounding and blocking-out techniques. Be alert, active, and aggressive near the defensive basket.

4. **Eliminate Give-Away Baskets.** Fight to maintain ball possession when your team has possession. All players must be aware of the importance of possession of the ball.

5. **Attack the Ball with Controlled Aggressiveness.** The defensive point of attack must be predetermined by the coach, depending on the type of team defense he feels is best for his players. The minimum defensive attack point is the twenty-one-foot area. The reference point for this distance from the basket is the head of the free-throw circle. If the team is to attack here, then the front man should attack the ball when his feet are on the outer rim of this circle. By maintaining good defensive balance from this position, the defenders will cause the opponents to shoot from twenty-four feet or more from the basket. This is the first area of attack, and usually a loose man-to-man defense is used.

The second attack point is the mid-court line. Attacking from here the defenders would use a half-court pressure defense, either man-to-man pickup or aggressive zone. This leaves openings closer to the basket that must be filled by the team in its defensive reaction. One movement on defense by one player should result in four immediate reactions by his defensive teammates.

The third point of attack for the ball could be three-fourths court or full court, using pressure from a zone or man-to-man defensive alignment. The purpose of this defense is to cause the opponents to make mistakes in the backcourt while they are bringing the ball up. Although a three-quarter press spreads the five man to a point where penetration is possible in many areas, if the team functions as a cohesive unit, it should be able to cut down the number of shots, make enough interceptions, and cause enough violations to make the gamble worthwhile.

6. Discourage the Opponents from Penetrating the Defensive Perimeter. Defensive players should never allow a free opponent under or near the basket, and they must prevent easy reception of the ball in this area. It is incumbent on all defenders to close off the keyhole area initially, then work the team defensive structure from the basket out. The coach must decide whether each defense (except the full-court and half-court pressure defenses) is to be played aggressively or passively. His choice will be determined by the physical makeup of his team and by the game situation. If he wishes to play an aggressive defense, the team must attack the ball at all junctures in the front court while overplaying passing outlets. Complete team alertness is necessary for intelligent aggressiveness. Two players should double-team by forcing a turn-and-pivot movement or by trapping a man at the side line, at the juncture of the front-court hash-mark, or near the mid-court division line. Two of the remaining teammates should play intercepting angles on the two near receivers, while the fifth man zones the two opponents farthest from the ball, concentrating on the more dangerous of the two.

A passive defense in the front court permits perimeter movement and allows perimeter pass reception outside the twenty-one-foot area. It closes passing lanes away from the ball and passing lanes into the pivot. It prevents the lob pass to the pivot over a fronting defender and it attacks the ball from the front when the ball is in possession of a low or medium pivot opponent.

types of team defense

There are four types of team defense: man to man, zone, combination and pressure.

man-to-man defense

Man-to-man may be played in five ways: in a normal manner (about three feet from the man with the ball), tightly, loosely, as an aggressive defense in which the man with the ball is turned from the basket and double-teamed by the nearest defender, and as a switching man-to-man. The coach determines how the team defense will be played, and the position of the ball determines each individual's position in the defense.

Normal. In normal man-to-man defense each defender has two duties—to guard the opponent assigned to him by the coach and to cooperate with teammates to prevent structural weaknesses. His first duty is his man, and normally, he should expect a minimum of help from his teammates, who have their own basic responsibilities.

The basic position for defending man-to-man is a stance with the weight back, body crouched low, and hands up and moving, pointing to the man and the ball (when the defender's man does not have it). Each defender is stationed within a triangle formed by his designated opponent, the ball, and the basket.

When guarding a man who is dribbling, the defender must never lunge; he must move the man away from the advantage he is seeking.

When playing a man who is cutting off a screen the defender has four options.

1. He may "go over the top" if his man is a good outside shooter or is dribbling with the ball in good scoring position.

2. He may fight through the screen with the help of the screen's guard, who steps back to allow him by and talks him through.

3. He may go behind his teammate in order to maintain defensive position on his opponent. (This is the weakest position.)

4. He may switch.

The back man or the man guarding the screener should call every switch, and the players should talk their way through the maneuver. Both players should be aggressive, staying with the men they have switched to without retreating. In case of a mismatch, where a smaller defender must cover a taller opponent, a defensive teammate should collapse in to help him. The small man should play in front of his man in a pivot position, knowing he will get weak-side help from alert, defensive teammates. The men should switch back to their original opponents as quickly as possible under safe conditions, again calling the switch.

Men away from the point of attack should be ready to collapse towards the screen to help. To coordinate his movements to those of the team, each player has the following responsibilities in a normal man-to-man defense.

1. Force the opposing dribbler in a predetermined direction. This is called influencing the offense and the dribbler. There are four directions in which a defender can turn the man who brings the ball up-court. Each coach should teach his team the strategy he believes is most effective. The player guarding the man with the ball can influence him to

320

Influencing the dribbler to the left side.

the sidelines. Advocates of this maneuver feel that the side-lines are a help to the defender, since the dribbler has only one direction—back towards the middle—in which to make an outlet pass, unless he wishes to throw the ball towards the division line.

A second philosophy recommends forcing the player to-wards the defensive strength (usually, but not always to the middle.) This strategy is essential in the baseline area, for the defensive player cannot allow his offensive opponent to go between him and the end line where there is no help.

The third method of influencing is to force a player to dribble the ball with his weak hand by overplaying on the strong side.

The fourth direction in which to influence the ball han-dler is away from the good shooter.

2. If possible, watch both the designated opponent and the ball when another opponent has possession. Although the defender should concentrate primarily on his man, he should open towards the ball so that he can see it with peripheral vision. If he must give up one, he should give up the ball position to maintain proper defensive alignment on his man.

3. Be prepared to pick up opponents who are free com-ing off a screen or after a reverse cut.

4. Collapse to the middle to prevent easy reception in the pivot area or under the basket when the ball is away from your designated area.

5. Be vocal. Encourage and warn teammates, and dis-courage opponents.

6. Get back on defense quickly after the ball is lost of-fensively. Defenders should play defense from the basket out, sprinting to a position within six or eight feet of the basket to determine if there are any opponents in that area,

then picking up the first loose opponent if he is in a scoring position or attacking the ball to stop its penetration into the scoring area.

7. Be alert to double-team opponents, and move in to overplay the man left open when a teammate doubles-up on the ball.

8. Be mentally and physically alert to avert any opponent's scoring opportunities. Defenders should get inside rebound position on every opponent's shot.

9. Help the pivot defender in the following three ways. First, do not allow a pass-in to the pivot area; second, float into this area to discourage the ball from being passed when your man is on the weak side; and third, try to tie up a good pivot player from the front by following the pass-in if the ball does get to him.

10. Improve team defensive strength by playing towards the vital penetrating areas, going as far from your man as his floor position with respect to the ball allows.

11. Know your man's strengths and weaknesses and play him accordingly. Know your other opponents' individual strengths and weaknesses so that you can help teammates guarding these opponents.

12. Intercept or deflect if possible. The intercepter or deflector rarely guards the passer. The passer's defender forces bad passes.

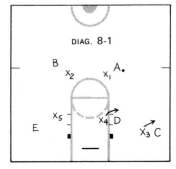

DIAG. 8-1

Diag. 8-1, NORMAL MAN-TO-MAN DEFENSE AGAINST A TWO-THREE OFFENSE

A, a guard, has possession of the ball. X_1, his defender, is playing him normal, close to him, in line between him and the basket. The corner defender, X_3, guarding C, is up a little bit towards the ball but still close to C. X_2, defending against B, has dropped off a step towards the ball and in line with B. Pivot Defender X_4 has taken a half fronting position towards the ball in guarding D. X_5, defending against the far forward, E, has loosened normally and has moved up to prevent E from cutting up to the high-pivot area to get a pass. He is also in position to help defend against D if the ball should pass to the corner player, C.

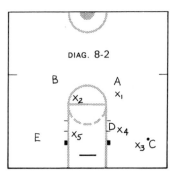

DIAG. 8-2

Diag. 8-2, THE BALL HAS BEEN PASSED FROM A TO C, THE CORNER MAN

X_3 is playing C to the baseline side to prevent a drive in that direction. X_1 has moved to a position where he is overplaying slightly towards the ball. X_2 has dropped off B considerably, into the foul-lane area. X_5 has dropped off E, the opposite forward, into the area between the foul lanes. X_4 is fronting D in a low-pivot position to prevent him from getting an easy pass into the pivot area.

Diag. 8-3, NORMAL MAN-TO-MAN DEFENSE AGAINST A THREE-TWO OFFENSIVE ALIGNMENT

A has the ball and is guarded by X_1, who is in straightaway position between A and the basket. B is guarded by X_2, who has

322

dropped off slightly and is playing a little bit towards the ball in line with the basket. X_3 has dropped off C. X_5 has dropped off E and is a little high on him so that he cannot get good pivot position at the outer half of the free-throw circle. X_4 has moved closer to D to prevent a direct pass-in or to pick him up if he cuts along the baseline without the ball.

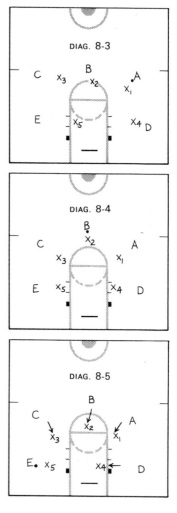

DIAG. 8-3

Diag. 8-4, THE BALL IS PASSED FROM A TO B

X_2 is guarding B between the man and the basket. X_1 has dropped off slightly from A. X_4 has dropped off and up on D. X_5 has dropped off and up on E. X_3 has dropped off and towards the ball against C. Note, defenders are inside the man-ball-basket triangle.

Diag. 8-5, THE BALL HAS BEEN PASSED-IN TO CORNER MAN E

X_5, guarding against E, must prevent a baseline drive. X_3 has dropped off C slightly towards the ball position. X_2 has dropped off a distance from B, as B is two passes from the ball. X_1 and X_4 have dropped off A and D, since A and D are far from the ball.

Tight Man-to-Man. In tight man-to-man defense players play closer to their men than normal, aggressively challenging them if they have the ball. The man playing the dribbler would force him to his weak side, not attempting to steal the ball but maintaining proximity to the man and faking and jabbing at him to stop the dribble. As soon as the dribbler stops, the defender moves in as close to the man as possible, waving his arms aggressively to block his vision, and attempts to overplay him without fouling, to prevent an easy pass. The two defenders nearest the ball-handler should overplay their men to prevent their receiving an easy outlet pass. The other defenders should maintain position in their men's passing lanes to prevent them from receiving a pass. If the dribbler does pass off, his defender should immediately drop directly back towards the basket and in the direction that the pass was made, to prevent a reverse cut to the basket by the passer. This is basically a half-court defense, but it can be extended to full-court if the situation warrants.

The tight man-to-man is a good defense for a quick, small team. It would be used first to move the offensive point of attack farther out from its normal position, thus distracting and upsetting offensive movement. It is an excellent late game defense when trailing. Tight man-to-man could be used effectively against a team that has poor ball handlers or against inexperienced teams.

Diag. 8-6, TIGHT MAN-TO-MAN DEFENSE AGAINST A TWO-THREE OFFENSE

A has possession of the ball and is dribbling. X_1, his defender, is closer to A than normal and forcing him towards the sideline to cut down on his passing lanes. All other players are guarding their men

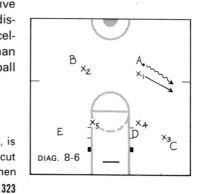

DIAG. 8-6

323

closely, except X_5, who is guarding E, the man farthest from the ball. X_5 has moved off to be in good intercepting position and to be able to help X_4, who has fronted D, in case of a long lob pass to the basket. X_3 has overplayed C to the ball side to prevent C from receiving the pass. X_2 has overplayed B to the ball side to prevent B from receiving a pass.

Diag. 8-7

DIAG. 8-7

C has moved from his position in Diag. 8-6 and has come back up towards the ball and received a pass from A. X_3, his defender, has closed in on him aggressively. X_1 is overplaying A on the ball side. X_4 is still in a fronting position on D between D and the ball. X_5 has dropped down to stay between E and the ball, far enough off so as to help X_4 in the event of a lob pass into D over the head of X_4. X_3 has dropped off B, who is two passes from the ball, towards the position of the ball to prevent a cut by B, primarily, and to help X_1 if A should use a reverse cut to the basket. X_3 is in good position to intercept the pass.

Loose Man-to-Man. The loose man-to-man defense is played, as the name suggests, in a looser fashion than normal man-to-man, with the players collapsing, or sloughing, towards the penetrating area in order to prevent the ball from reaching this area. The normal pick-up point for any player in a loose man-to-man defense should be at the twenty-one-foot area (indicated by an imaginary semicircle on the court.) (See Diag. 8-4.) The head of the key is twenty-one feet from the basket. The dead corners are twenty-five feet from the basket, and a player who is within or close to the twenty-one-foot semi-circle can effectively cover a player in these shooting areas.

The loose man-to-man is an excellent defense to use against poor outside shooting opponents, a good cutting team, a team that changes direction to the basket well, or a faster team. It is also good for a taller team that is playing man-to-man defense for good rebounding strength. It places a burden on the offensive team to score from the outside.

DIAG. 8-8

Diag. 8-8, LOOSE MAN-TO-MAN DEFENSE AGAINST A TWO-THREE OFFENSE

A has the ball. X_1 is on the twenty-one-foot circle, playing A. X_4, playing the corner man, D, has floated off, allowing pass reception. X_5 is fronting the pivot man, E. X_2 has dropped back and is playing B loosely. X_3 is playing C loosely.

Diag. 8-9, D HAS RECEIVED A PASS FROM A

X_4 is playing close to the perimeter, on the baseline side of D. X_1 has dropped off A and is on the ball side, closer to the basket. X_2 has dropped farther off B and is in the foul-line area. X_3 has dropped off C and is in the foul lane. X_5 maintains a fronting position on E.

DIAG. 8-9

324

Turn-and-Double Man-to-Man Defense. The turn-and-double man-to-man defense is an aggressive double-teaming defense used in the front court in which the man guarding the dribbler influences him towards a sideline. As this influencing is taking place, the near defensive guard will cheat towards the dribbler between the man he is guarding and the ball. As soon as the dribbler stops his dribble, his guard forces him to pivot back towards the mid-court line. The guard who is cheating should sprint towards the man with the ball as he is pivoting and attempt to double-team him with the dribbler's defender.

Normally, a player who is double-teamed will attempt to pass in the direction the pressure comes from; therefore, the forward closest to the man who is leaving to make the double-team should move into an intercepting angle between the ball and the teammate's free offensive player. The near forward should play at an intercepting angle. The center should zone between the remaining two offensive opponents, staying closer to the more dangerous of the two.

If the ball is passed to a forward, the double-team would take place between the defensive forward and a guard. Normally, we expect that the two guards or a guard and a forward will be the double-team men, with the center in the middle area using zone defense principles to protect the area near the basket. Intercepting angles are played on offensive players who are one pass from the double team. A zone is played in the basket area by the fifth defender.

If the dribbler can get the ball to a teammate successfully, each defender must pick up the nearest man. The passer must be played by his original defender, and the double-teamer should sprint in towards the basket, because the loose opponent is usually the player farthest from the ball. To negate the offensive opportunities from the mismatch of a small man playing a big corner man, a switch may be necessary between the forward who has come out to pick up the man of the double-teaming guard and the guard who has picked up the far-corner offensive forward.

The best way to effect this switch is to allow the ball to be passed back to the original passer and have the men switch on the pass. This will not hurt the defense because these men are so far from the ball and the basket, and it will allow the defensive team to adjust to this situation and again attack in the turn-and-double stature. Rather than attacking this double-up defense, the offensive team is likely to bring the ball back into a defensive posture in front court. The hashmarks in the front court, the sidelines, and the mid-courtline all act in favor of the defense, and forcing a five-second held-ball violation is a distinct possibility using this type of double-teaming. Good intercepting angles and intelligent play by either defensive player guarding the two offensive players closest to the ball result in many interceptions. If the ball reaches one of the men in the off-side area and they have a shot, the defenders should fake at them and allow the shot rather than give up an easy lay-up underneath.

The turn-and-double is an excellent surprise maneuver that is very effective against a taller team with poor ball handlers. It upsets the opponents' planned offensive system and increases the pace of the game. It is an excellent defense to use when behind in the late stages. While turn-and-double defense is a departure from man-to-man defense as it has been played in the past, we feel that it is an asset in certain situations, as it implements the best parts of an aggressive man-to-man defense with some of the thinking of zone defense.

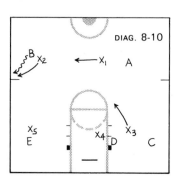

DIAG. 8-10

Diag. 8-10, TURN-AND-DOUBLE MAN-TO-MAN DEFENSE AGAINST A TWO-THREE OFFENSE

Player B has crossed the mid-court line and his defender, X_2, forces him to dribble towards the sideline. X_1, guarding A, starts to cheat towards the same sideline. X_3 coordinates his movement with X_1 and starts to cheat up towards A's position. E is guarded by X_5 in an intercepting position. X_4 is guarding D, the pivot man opposite the ball, in an overplay position towards the ball.

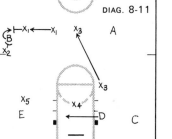

DIAG. 8-11

Diag. 8-11

B has stopped his dribble on being forced to the sideline by X_2. As B pivots back towards mid-court, X_1 charges from his mid-court position to double-team him with X_2. X_3 has moved up to an intercepting position between the ball and A. X_5 has over-played E towards the ball. X_4 has moved to the center of the foul lane at the lower half of the free-throw circle to be in position to defend against D, who is moving across the foul lane, or C, who is the farthest player from the ball.

Diag. 8-12

B passes to E, who has faked or made a **V** into the basket and come back in order to relieve the pressure. Immediately upon this reception. X_5 plays E strongly on the baseline side to make E pivot, and E should be attacked from above by X_2, who immediately leaves B to effect the double team. X_1 overplays B on the ball side and X_4 overplays D, who is in the low pivot on the ball side. X_3 has fallen back from his position at an intercepting angle on A to the lower half of the foul circle to discourage a lob pass to D while still having an intercepting angle between A and C in case the ball is thrown cross-court.

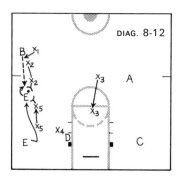

DIAG. 8-12

Switching Man-To-Man. A switching man-to-man defense is one in which the defensive players switch on every offensive cross, except for a pivot defender. (They never switch on a diagonal cut or a reverse cut, since they would have to stay with the cutter.) If offensive guards are crossing

326

laterally in the back court, a jump switch is very effective. The switching men are usually guards or forwards. If the center must switch while playing a pivot man against a two-three offense, he should call the switch, because his team-mates will not be expecting it. If the opponents use an offense with three men out and two in, switch on all crosses with all five players.

The switching man-to-man is an extremely effective defense against the weave or an offense using good guard-to-guard or guard-to-forward screens. It confuses the offense, as it looks like a zone defense. The weak-side men would be sagging towards the middle and playing their opponents loosely, with the ball on the weak side. The switching man-to-man is excellent for a team that has one big man and four smaller men. Since the smaller men are constantly exchanging opponents, they are not going to be hurt badly by any disparity in height.

Diag. 8-13, SWITCHING MAN-TO-MAN DEFENSE AGAINST A TWO-THREE OFFENSE

Offensive Guards A and B exchange the ball in the back court area. X_1, guarding A, and X_2, guarding B, move together as A dribbles and hands off to B, who is cutting behind him. X_2 and X_1 automatically switch, with X_1 picking up B, who has begun a dribble, and X_2 picking up A. (There is also a good opportunity for X_1 to make a jump switch into the path of B. X_3 is playing an intercepting angle on C, X_4 is defending D in the low pivot on the ball side, and X_5 has floated towards the center and a little higher, guarding the opposite corner. If B attempts to pass in this situation, there is a good opportunity at interception.

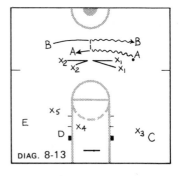

DIAG. 8-13

Diag. 8-14

A passes to C, who moves out to meet the ball. A cuts behind C. X_1 moves along the path that A is cutting. X_3 has moved out to guard against C. C starts to dribble, and as A and C cross, X_1 and X_3 automatically exchange guarding assignments, X_3 defending against A and X_1 picking up the dribbler.

DIAG. 8-14

Advantages. The following are positive attributes of the man-to-man defense.

1. It fixes responsibility, issuing a challenge to each player.

2. It enables individual match-ups of opponents based on size, strength, speed, and height.

3. It can force the opposition when they are stalling or when you are behind.

4. It permits effective double-teaming.

5. It affords excellent defensive rebound position, since in most cases the defensive player is inside his offensive opponent.

6. It permits better preparation of each individual, since the coach can tell him the strong points and weaknesses of the single opponent he is to guard.

7. It makes good use of the fundamentals, providing they were taught properly.

8. It places high premium on good conditioning.

9. Pressure man-to-man defense allows for good fast-break opportunities.

10. It is adaptable to any opponent's offense, especially a delayed or wide-spread offensive system.

11. It can be used full-court to increase the game tempo.

12. It can be used in all situations during a game or during a season, changing only the team attitude (that is, tight, loose, half-court, full-court, etc.).

13. It makes it possible to recognize good individual defensive play, so the coach can credit the player publicly for his efforts.

Disadvantages. Before choosing man-to-man defense, the coach should assess the following negative characteristics in relation to his personnel.

1. It is much tougher on the individual physically, requiring excellent stamina and top condition.

2. Mismatches in size during switching maneuvers or an inability to match the opponents individually hurts the team.

3. It is ineffective against a good screening and cutting team.

4. It requires excellent fundamental ability and mental attitude on the part of each player.

5. Players are more prone to fouls using this defense.

6. It allows the opponents to exploit the poor defensive man by isolating him.

7. It requires flexibility in men who must switch during screening tactics.

8. In addition to their individual responsibilities, players must be aware of team responsibilities.

9. It requires extremely good knowledge of defensive fundamentals.

10. A normal or loose man-to-man defense may not be a good fast-break defense.

11. Overconcentration by a player hurts the team posture, as does a weak overmatched man.

12. It requires a great deal of teaching time.

zone defense

The basic philosophy of zone defense is that every defensive player is responsible for a designated defensive floor area, primarily determined by the position of the ball. Each player faces the ball and moves in unison with each ball movement, adjusting position continuously as the ball position moves. Though the ball is of primary importance, position of offensive players must also be considered. A cut through the zone towards the ball, or an offensive player stationed in the low- or medium-pivot area inside the zone perimeter would alter basic defensive movement.

Defensive movement depends on player reception of a pass. If the potential receiver is in a position to score, the nearest defender should prevent him from getting the ball, intercepting it, if possible. All players should position themselves where they will give the opponent the least advantage, defending from the basket area out. When the ball is passed to a position behind one of the front-line defensive players, he should move towards the basket until he can regain sight of the ball, at the same time concentrating on offensive player deployment in the immediate area. He should always permit the outside shot rather than allowing the ball to go to a player behind him in better shooting position.

The fundamental stance taken by a player in a zone defense is higher than the basic man-to-man boxer crouch, and the arms are widespread and windmilling to present an apparently impenetrable barrier to the attacking offensive player.

The zone defense lends itself to ideal placement of defenders according to physical and mental attributes. Taller, less agile players can be positioned near the basket to cut down their defensive movement, improve the defensive rebounding effort of the team, limit pivot playing by tall opponents, and negate the cutting opportunities of smaller opponents. The faster, usually smaller players, can be placed in the outside positions of a zone where they may have a wider defensive latitude in forcing the ball, attempting interception, and harassing the opponent more aggressively than they would if they were in a standard man-to-man defense.

The zone defense is easier to teach and it can cover up weak man-to-man fundamentals in individuals that cannot be overcome due to lack of coordination or lack of speed. It allows room for intelligent, aggressive defensive imagination in the quicker players. Players in a zone defense are less afraid of mistakes, as they feel there is somebody behind them to help minimize the effects of a mistake. Each player has a chance to intercept the ball and gain an offensive advantage. All zone defenses have inherent weaknesses and vulnerable areas. It is incumbent on the defensive team to limit vulnerability to areas outside the zone perimeter and to influence the offense into the less vulnerable areas.

The penetration of the perimeter of a zone defense is the first sign of weakness in any zone. Because of the shifting essential to floor coverage, the zone loses its original shape after the first or second pass and all types of zones tend to look alike. Thereafter, coordinated team movement is essential to maintain the restrictiveness of the zone. Zones contract and expand with ball and offensive player movement.

Zones have a tendency to overextend towards the ball in the corners and at forty-five degree angles from the basket, allowing the offense to penetrate the back line by maneuvering from the side away from the ball or by cutting inside the zone paralleling the path of a pass. The back men must vocally warn overenthusiastic teammates when they overextend and distort the zone making it unnecessarily pregnable to these maneuvers by opponents.

Important Factors in the Use of a Zone Defense. The basic principle of protecting certain territories while shifting and concentrating on areas attacked is intrinsic in the zone defense. The zone allows much more liberty defensively. All players must move continuously, using their hands or feet to block passes that attempt to penetrate the zone. The player who is closest to the ball in good offensive territory must attack it aggressively, using good fundamental man-to-man principles and attempting to force a pass back to a protected area far from the basket or to hurry the shot. The change from defense to offense coordinates quickly, and a team can fast break immediately from the basic defensive zone positions. The equally important change from offense to defense can also be effected quickly.

Players in a zone defense can play in front of or to the side of a player close to the basket on the ball side, as a defensive teammate is behind this opponent. Moving offensive players are guarded successively by various defenders as they sift through the zone. A player may leave his area open to protect a territory or uncovered offensive player close to the basket. Intelligent anticipation leads to interceptions. Offensive players moving away from the ball may seem to be weakening their position, while actually they are anticipating the ball's movement to the other side of the court. With good defensive anticipation alert defenders may intercept passes, creating many good fast-break opportunities.

Zone defenses may be aggressive or passive and should be used with caution when a team is behind in the score, or against good long shooters or good ball handlers. If the zone is to be used when behind, it must be aggressive to force ball handling mistakes and hurried shots.

Whether a zone defense is aggressive or passive generally is determined by the personnel, the opponents, the score, and the time remaining. A zone allows the most advantageous positioning of players, with the tall players under the basket and the quick players chasing in good position to inaugurate the fast break. The front line of a zone should be fast and aggressive; the back line taller with

330

the better rebounders. A zone may send three, four, or five players to rebound at the defensive backboard. If five players are sent, the zone is passive, or defensive.

If four defensive players move aggressively to the defensive backboard, maintaining position in front of offensive players and blocking them out, and the fifth defender sneaks towards the offensive end when the opponents shoot, at least one (normally two) offensive player will fall back defensively. Since only three opponents will be rebounding, the defenders will have an advantage. If the ball is rebounded by the defensive team and gets up the court fast, good penetration is possible at the offensive end.

Interceptions and steals by aggressive front-line players (who normally are the fastest) lead to quick baskets by the front-line players. Back-line defenders must stay close to an opponent near the ball. They should never let offensive opponents split them defensively near the ball. No player in a zone defense should ever guard an empty area or zone. It is important that the back men act as quarterbacks, directing the zone vocally to the strong or overloaded offensive side. All players defending in a zone should be aware of the imaginary semicircle twenty-one feet from the basket. Defenders should stay within this semicircle or on its circumference with arms extended, either up or to the sides, to deter and upset opponents, because twenty-one feet is the limit of the high percentage shooting range for the majority of basketball players, unless an aggressive zone is called for.

The floor markings help pinpoint areas that are twenty-one feet from the basket.

1. The head of the key is twenty-one feet from the basket.

2. A player taking two defensive slides and a step from either end of the foul line will be twenty-one feet from the basket.

3. A player taking three defensive slides and a step from the middle of either foul lane restraining lines will be twenty-one feet from the basket.

4. Both deep corners are twenty-five feet from the basket.

A disadvantage in a zone defense is that a moving, aggressive offensive rebounder can outmaneuver stationary defensive players for position. Many times defensive players in a zone backline turn in position and expect the rebound to come to them. If they do not look for a player on the offensive team to box out, the moving opponents will outposition defenders.

Types of Zone Defense. Zone defenses are classified by the alignment of the players from the front of the line in the area towards mid-court back towards the basket. The one-two-two zone, for example, has one player towards the center of the court, two players in the back line near the basket, and two players between the front line and the back line. The two types used today are those that have an odd front and those that have an even front.

The odd front type of zones include the one-two-two zone, a one-three-one zone, and a three-two zone. The even zones are the two-two-one zone, the two-one-two zone and the two-three zone.

One-two-two zone defense. The one-two-two zone defense has strength in the middle- and low-pivot areas. It is simple to use, as the slides are basic and uncomplicated.

In Diag. 8-15, X_1, the quickest player, should be given latitude of movement within this zone setup. X_2 and X_3 should be agile and fairly tall. X_4 and X_5 should be the best rebounders, with X_5 the least coordinated of the two. Players X_1, X_2, or X_3 must maintain rebound position when the opponents shoot. There are good sneak away opportunities for X_1 when the opponents shoot. The possibility of this maneuver will take one or two offensive players away from the backboard. X_4 or X_5 must take the medium-pivot man in the opposite pivot area during ball movement. This leaves the one-two-two zone vulnerable from behind or from the weak side unless quick adjustments are made.

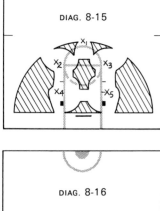

DIAG. 8-15

Diag. 8-15, ONE-TWO-TWO ZONE DEFENSE
Shaded areas indicate vulnerability. The initial positions are X_1 at the head of the key, X_2 and X_3 at the ends of the foul lines on either side, X_4 and X_5 straddling the foul lanes approximately six feet in front of the basket.

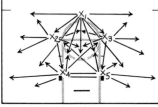

DIAG. 8-16

Diag. 8-16, ONE-TWO-TWO ZONE DEFENSE
The arrows indicate the slides the defenders must make for good coverage.

Diag. 8-17, ONE-TWO-TWO ZONE DEFENSE
The slides made by each defender as the ball is passed from A to B (1) to C (2) to D (3) are numbered.

DIAG. 8-17

One-three-one zone defense. The one-three-one zone defense attempts to keep three defensive players in line between the ball and the basket by flexing with the passing movement of the ball. This zone is strong in all pivot areas, under the basket, and against medium jump shooters. It is weak against good outside angle shooters and in the corners and is susceptible to baseline drives. Because of the positioning of the two big rebounders, there are rebounding difficulties in this zone.

Diag. 8-18, ONE-THREE-ONE ZONE DEFENSE
Shaded areas indicate vulnerability. X_1, the first guard, should be very quick and aggressive and should be given latitude for imaginative anticipation. He can sneak away when offense shoots. The

wing men, X_2 and X_3, must be active. X_3 should be the second guard; X_2 the quickest forward; X_4 the slower, taller forward; and X_5 the center. X_5's position is good for big, uncoordinated players who are good rebounders.

Diag. 8-19, ONE-THREE-ONE ZONE DEFENSE

Arrows indicate slides each defender must make for good coverage.

Diag. 8-20, ONE-THREE-ONE ZONE DEFENSE

Slides by defense are numbered as (1) A dribbles; (2) A passes to E; and (3) E passes to B. Each movement is indicated by an arrow with a number on the line. X_1, X_2, X_3, X_4, and X_5 are the defense; A, B, C, D, and E are the offense.

Three-two zone defense. The three-two zone defensive strength lies in the mobility of its front line, which must attack opponents aggressively, attempting to cause misplays, violations, and bad passes. It is an excellent defense to fast break from. In Diag. 8-21, X_1, X_2, and X_3 should be the quickest players, because they are expected to make the most defensive movements and slides. X_1 is responsible for the foul-lane area. X_2 and X_3 are responsible for the weak side medium and low areas near the basket when the ball is on the opposite side of the court. Against taller teams, X_1, X_2, and X_3 should play to the ball, doubling up when possible. This zone is weak in the medium-pivot areas and in the side areas when there is a pivot player. It needs rebound help from X_1, X_2, or X_3, and the back of the zone is vulnerable to quick movement from the corners. This zone is weak underneath, in the corners, and behind the front line if retreating movement by the front line isn't forthcoming. X_1 should be the quickest forward, as he has to drop into the middle foul-lane area frequently and he is the front line player likely to be in best rebound position. X_2 and X_3 should be the guards; X_4, the second forward; and X_5 the center.

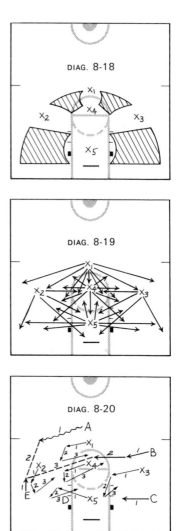

DIAG. 8-18

DIAG. 8-19

DIAG. 8-20

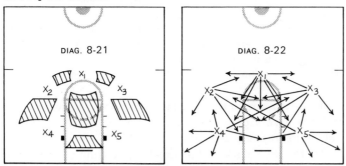

DIAG. 8-21

DIAG. 8-22

Diag. 8-21, THREE-TWO ZONE DEFENSE

Shaded areas indicate vulnerability.

Diag. 8-22, THREE-TWO ZONE DEFENSE

Arrows indicate slides defenders must make for good coverage.

DIAG. 8-23

Diag. 8-23, THREE-TWO ZONE DEFENSE

Slides by defense are numbered as ball is passed from (1) A to B, (2) B to E, and (3) E to D. The arrows indicate slides by the defensive players X_1 through X_5.

Two-one-two zone defense. The two-one-two zone defense is strong underneath the basket, in the rebounding triangle area, against good pivot men, and in the foul-line area. It is a good defense from which to fast break, as it allows one man, usually X_1, to break as soon as the offensive team shoots. It is vulnerable from the weak side along the baseline, from jump shooters on the side at forty-five degree angles, from medium shooting areas, and from the top of the key.

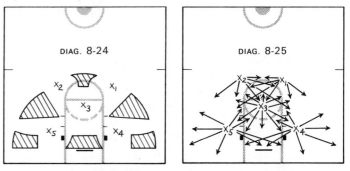

DIAG. 8-24

DIAG. 8-25

Diag. 8-24, TWO-ONE-TWO ZONE DEFENSE

Shaded areas indicate vulnerability. X_1 and X_2 are fast, aggressive guards, X_3 is the center, X_4 is the best rebounding forward, and X_5 is the more mobile forward.

Diag. 8-25, TWO-ONE-TWO ZONE DEFENSE

Arrows indicate slides defenders must make for good coverage.

Diag. 8-26, TWO-ONE-TWO ZONE DEFENSE

Slides by defense are numbered as the ball is passed. Initial adjustments by defensive players X_1 through X_5 are indicated by an unnumbered arrow. Arrows numbered 1, 2, and 3 indicate the slides they make during each pass. Movements by offensive players are also indicated by arrows. A, with the ball, has started at the offensive left side area. The ball is passed (1) from A to B; (2) from B to C, who has moved into the high pivot area; and (3) from C to E, who has moved up from the baseline side offensive right corner.

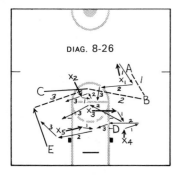

DIAG. 8-26

Two-two-one zone defense. The two-two-one zone defense is a very good basic defense from which to employ half-court trapping procedures.

There are excellent fast-break opportunities from this zone, and it is good against close shots and jumpers. It is weak at the top of the key, so the two front men must sag to prevent good shooting opportunities from this area. This is an aggressive defense that can be used well by a small, fast team with one big rebounder.

334

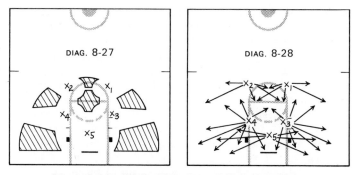

DIAG. 8-27   DIAG. 8-28

Diag. 8-27, TWO-TWO-ONE ZONE DEFENSE

Shaded areas indicate vulnerability. X_5 should be a big man and a good rebounder.

Diag. 8-28, TWO-TWO-ONE ZONE DEFENSE

Arrows indicate slides defenders must make for good coverage.

Diag. 8-29, TWO-TWO-ONE ZONE DEFENSE

Arrows numbered 1, 2, and 3 indicate the defensive slides as the ball is passed (1) from B, backcourt at the offensive right side of the zone, to A; (2) from A to C; and (3) from C to D. D has moved from the foul line to a low-pivot area on the left offensive side. The unnumbered arrows originating at the defensive players indicate initial adjustment by the defense from their original positions to compensate for the ball being on the offensive right side backcourt.

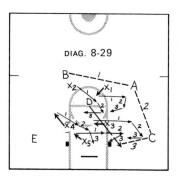

DIAG. 8-29

Two-three zone defense. The two-three zone is an excellent rebounding defense with good sneak-away possibilities for X_1 or X_2. The zone lends itself to a fast-break type of offense. It is very strong in the low- and medium-pivot areas against a good pivot player. It is weak at the side, at the foul line, and in the high-pivot areas, especially against jump shooters at the top of the key.

Played passively by a team that is ahead or wishes to protect a key player who has four fouls, this defense prevents offensive penetration into good medium or close-in shooting position. Good outside shooting is the only offense that can beat it. It presents excellent double-teaming opportunities if the guards are aggressive.

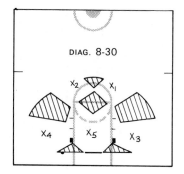

DIAG. 8-30

Diag. 8-30, TWO-THREE ZONE DEFENSE

Shaded areas indicate vulnerability. X_1 and X_2 are aggressive guards. X_3 and X_4 are the forwards, X_3 being the better rebounder. X_5 is the center.

Diag. 8-31, TWO-THREE ZONE DEFENSE

Arrows indicate slides defenders must make for good coverage.

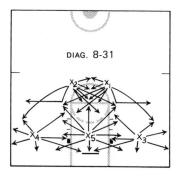

DIAG. 8-31

Diag. 8-32, TWO-THREE ZONE DEFENSE

Arrows numbered 1, 2, and 3 indicate slides by the defense as the ball passes (1) from B to C; (2) from C to D, and (3) from D to A. D has crossed from one side to the opposite side medium-pivot posi-

335

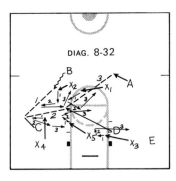

DIAG. 8-32

tion. The unnumbered arrows leading from defenders indicate their initial adjustments to the offensive right necessitated by B's dribbling to his right before passing.

X_2's first sliding move is made at right angles, towards the baseline, to the pivot position, paralleling the foul lane before moving out towards C's position with the ball. If X_2 had taken a direct route to this position, he would have left a passing lane open into D, who moved quickly and assumed the pivot position. As X_2 moves, X_1 slides from his position on the far side at the top of the key to a cut-off position on D, thus negating the possibility of a pass into this area. X_2 and X_1 should move in when they are in a balanced position at the top of the key, because the greater danger emanates from the ball penetrating the perimeter rather than from an outside shot from C, who is approximately twenty-one feet from the basket.

Two-three zone aggressive defense with traps. The two-three aggressive zone with traps requires determination, intelligent anticipation, and vigorous execution of the necessary slides. Players must be active and animated— their arms and hands held high, ready and probing, closing the passing lanes—and they must use vocal commands and warnings to teammates. The back line must direct the front-line players to the strong side of the offensive formation to prevent a high-pivot player from getting the ball. (In this type of zone the high pivot must be pinched from in front and in back.) The men in the front line have great latitude in forcing the ball. They can move out towards the center and influence the ball handler to the left or right side so that the initial pass will be made into a sideline area, allowing for double-teaming or trapping situations in these areas. When a trap is sprung in a corner, the far defensive player must anticipate a pass by observing the arm and head movements of the player in the trap with the ball. The back-line men must be constantly aware that this defense starts from the basket out, and never allow anyone in the low basket area who is not covered by a defender.

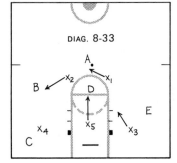

DIAG. 8-33

Diag. 8-33, TWO-THREE ZONE AGGRESSIVE DEFENSE USING DOUBLE-TEAMING

Defenders are in their original positions, X_1 and X_2 at the head of the key area, X_5 just below the broken line of the lower half of the free-throw circle, and X_3 and X_4 in the low-wing positions. A has the ball out front at the top of the key. X_3 sees that there are four defensive players to his left and calls "strong side left." X_1 immediately shifts to the head of the key and X_2 moves toward B. X_4 maintains his position. X_3 slides up towards the foul-lane area, and X_5 comes up to cover D. Arrows indicate this movement. X_1 should drop off from his position so that D is pinched from the front and the back.

DIAG. 8-34

Diag. 8-34, AGGRESSIVE TWO-THREE ZONE (CONTINUED)

A has passed to B. The arrows moving into the defensive posi-

336

tions indicate the sliding maneuvers of the zone to shift with the ball position. X_1 moves from the top of the key to front the pivot man, D, on the ball side. X_5 moves from the foul lane to the medium-pivot area. X_4 drops back as C drops back. X_2 moves towards B to challenge the ball. X_3 plays an intercepting angle on E. If D slides to medium- or low-pivot position, X_5 fronts him. X_4 is positioned to help X_2 at the ball location and to play C should he receive a pass.

Diag. 8-35, AGGRESSIVE TWO-THREE ZONE (CONTINUED)

B has passed to C. C's corner position indicates a good trapping situation. On C's reception X_4, the baseline trapper, and X_2, the side trapper, are in trapping position, X_2 having moved with the pass. X_1 moves from the free-throw circle area to an overplaying position on B to deny him a pass. X_5 fronts D in the pivot area. X_3 should anticipate C's pass-out direction by observing his eye or arm movement. X_3 has good intercepting angle if he can anticipate a pass from C to A, but if he miscalculates, a pass to E will result in an easy basket. The trap will be effective if all five defenders coordinate their movements.

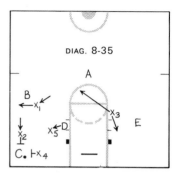

DIAG. 8-35

Diag. 8-36, AGGRESSIVE TWO-THREE ZONE (CONTINUED)

C has made an outlet pass to D who has moved from the medium-pivot area to the high-pivot area in the outer half of the free-throw circle. X_1 pressures the ball, moving from the position he had on B (8-35) to a high position on D. X_5 has slid up the foul lane to a low, aggressive, attacking position. X_4 must drop towards the foul lane to protect against movement in this area by D, if he can get around X_5. X_2 and X_3 must be alert. X_2 has moved from the double-team on C to a position inside of B. X_3 must be aware of the weak-side potential of E and his under-the-basket possibilities.

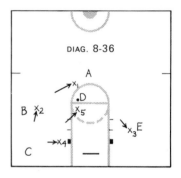

DIAG. 8-36

Diag. 8-37, AGGRESSIVE TWO-THREE ZONE (CONTINUED)

D passes to E at a weak-side outlet position. X_3 moves out cautiously on E. X_5 moves from the high-pivot position to a low, protective pivot position on the ball side. X_1 moves across the pivot lane, continuing to front D, the pivot player. X_5 must be conscious of the open low-pivot area. He is alerted by X_4, who calls that C has moved to the opposite low-pivot position. X_2 moves high towards the ball side. X_4, moving protectively into the center of the foul lane, low, must be aware of the possibility of B's cutting behind him to the basket or splitting the zone defenders by moving into the middle area to the medium pivot on the strong side.

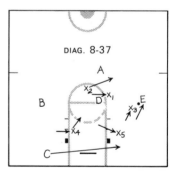

DIAG. 8-37

Diag. 8-38, AGGRESSIVE TWO-THREE ZONE (CONTINUED)

E, on the left side offensively, has passed to C, who has moved from the low-pivot position to the corner. Normally, C would receive this pass moving towards the sideline with his back to the basket area and would have to pivot to make a move towards the basket. His corner position indicates a good trapping situation. X_3 moves to the baseline trap position with the pass. His responsibility is first to prevent the baseline drive and second to apply the baseline low trap. X_1 moves off the high pivot quickly to assume the sideline high-trap position. X_2 moves to cut off a passing lane to E. X_5 delays his move until X_3 reaches the baseline position then moves up on D, fronting him in this pivot position and cutting off a passing lane.

DIAG. 8-38

337

X_4, at the weak-side foul lane, anticipates a long pass to A and may move to intercept it. (Anticipate a long pass to A by observing C's arm or eye movement.) Since he is the last line of defense, he must be ready to drop back if X_3 does not contain C. X_5 moves up to front D.

Advantages of Zone Defense. Following are the positive attributes of zone defense.

1. It is effective against medium and close-in shots and against pass-and-cut moves.

2. Its compactness closes normal passing lanes and necessitates careful maneuvering and accurate passing; therefore, it is effective against a pivot attack.

3. It develops aggressiveness in intercepting the ball.

4. It can conserve the energy of tired players.

5. It is an excellent defense from which to obtain good offensive fast-break opportunities.

6. It is an excellent defense against a poor ball-handling team and poor outside-shooting teams.

7. It is effective against teams using a set pattern, screening type offense.

8. It is effective against teams using a free-lance type of offense.

9. It reduces the number of fouls.

10. It is a good defense if the court space is restricted.

11. Rebound position is assured.

12. It is adaptable for tall, uncoordinated men who cannot play good man-to-man defense.

13. It is easier to teach from a team structure than man-to-man defense.

14. It protects players who are in foul trouble.

15. It is a good psychological defense against some opponents. They become cautious or take bad shots.

16. It hides weak defensive players.

17. Beating it requires a planned attack that must rely on accurate medium or outside shooting primarily.

18. It is an effective surprise maneuver, especially if the team can play different types of zones from the initial zone structure.

19. A passive zone protecting the keyhole area forces a trailing opponent to take outside or low percentage shots.

20. It is easily adaptable to a well schooled man-to-man defensive team as an auxiliary defense.

21. It is effective against a team with an outstanding driver, as it tends to immobilize the team and restrict the driver.

Disadvantages. The negative characteristics of a zone defense are as follows:

338

1. It is weak against side and long shots and in the areas behind the back men when opponents move in from the weak side away from the ball.

2. It loses its compactness if it is spread or if players do not coordinate their sliding movements.

3. Overshifting weakens the offside or backside of a zone.

4. It is weak in the foul-line area and the short jump-shooting areas if the front line overextends or players don't coordinate their movement.

5. Sometimes players forget man-to-man principles when the team is behind and they must leave the zone posture to pressure the ball.

6. It tends to weaken individual responsibility as no match-up of men according to height, speed, and ability takes place.

7. Normally it cannot increase the tempo of the opponents' attack.

8. It is not good at the end of a losing game, because it does not attack the ball as well as man-to-man or pressure defenses.

9. It is ineffective at times against overloading one side of the zone defense, a strategy that tends to get good shots for the offensive team.

10. Smart ball handlers can probe the zone, shift it, tire the defenders, and fake them out of position to pass inside the perimeter for good short shooting opportunities.

11. It is ineffectual against a good fast-break team or a team that penetrates quickly before the zone can set up.

12. It can make a game dull for players and spectators.

13. Defenders may become listless or complacent.

14. In some zones, if the rebounders do not block out their opponents, they can be out-hustled under the boards.

combination defenses

Combination defenses utilize the strengths of both man-to-man and zone defenses.

Combination defenses fall into three categories. The first includes two types of match-up defenses in which both the man and the ball are focal points. In one type, the defense starts as a zone front then switches to a man-to-man pickup strategy. In the second, the defenders guard the opponents man-to-man, determining match-ups according to the type of offense being used. After the first pass, they switch to zone techniques.

The second category includes combination defenses in which three of the men play one type of defense while the other two play another type. The back three men may play zone in a triangle while the front two men play man-to-man, or three men in front play man-to-man while the back two men play zone, either side by side or one in front of the other.

The third category includes defenses in which four men play zone while one plays man-to-man against the outstanding player on the opposing team. The zone men may position themselves so that together they form a box, a diamond, or a **T** (the back three play triangle, the fourth plays in front of the point man).

The Match-Up Defense. The match-up defense consolidates cogent features of man-to-man and zone into a defense that is sound, facile, and flexible and that stymies most basic offensive patterns. The match-up defense decreases the effectiveness of offensive screens and cuts, eliminating the necessity of switching and allowing floating from the weak side or from vacated offensive areas. It also permits cutting off passing lanes to the pivot areas.

The defense uses the following man-to-man tactics: Pressure on the ball at all times, close defensive play on men adjacent to the ball, overplaying or forcing opponents out of position for pass reception when they are close to the ball, and fronting and closely guarding the men in under-the-basket areas. It diminishes the chances of being badly hurt by outside shooting as can happen in a zone, because defenders are close to and aggressively playing the man with the ball and other players in near pass-reception areas. The match-up can neutralize the advantage of a superior opponent and is an excellent surprise maneuver. The defense can force passes to weak ball handlers by closing the passing lane to a good ball handler, overplaying aggressively between him and the ball. The only place the defense allows the outstanding players to receive the ball is near mid-court, and then it double-teams him for a quick release of the ball.

The match-up defense keeps specific personnel in their most advantageous defensive areas while apparently changing team identity frequently. This defense gives the appearance of a zone primarily, making many offensive teams resort to the traditional zone attack of patient perimeter passing, probing on cuts, and finally, taking poor percentage shots.

Zone origin. The first match-up discussed is zone in origin and converts to man-to-man coverage after the first pass that goes by the head of the key. It is described here from the two-one-two posture, although it could be a one-two-two zone origin or a two-two-one zone origin.

Diag. 8-39, MATCH-UP DEFENSE, ZONE ORIGIN, SWITCHING TO MAN-TO-MAN COVERAGE AFTER THE FIRST PASS

A has the ball at the head of the key, approximately twenty-three

feet from the basket. A passes to B. The arrows show the movement
as the defense adjusts to man-to-man pickup coverage. The initial
defensive alignment is X_1 and X_2 at the head of the key at the foul
lanes extended, X_3 in the middle area a step below the foul line,
and X_4 and X_5 approximately five feet from the basket with their
inside feet touching the foul lane. This zone structure is in effect
until the ball goes past an imaginary line extended across the head
of the key to the sidelines. The defense keys on allowing opponents
to shoot long outside and preventing pivot penetration. If the ball
reaches a high pivot, defenders must be alert for cutters. The personnel should be placed as follows:

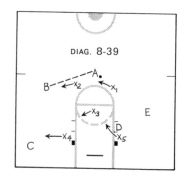

DIAG. 8-39

X_1 should be the quickest player on the team with the best anticipation. After the offense's initial movement, he should have free-
lance defensive latitude in the keyhole area. X_2 is usually the second
guard. X_5, normally the best rebounder, plays on the right defensive
side, because shots taken from the opposite side will rebound in
his direction. X_4 and X_5, the slower men, must quarterback the
flexing of the zone using vocal warnings to keep teammates in position on the strong side. X_3, the quickest of the tall men, plays the
pivot man on the strong side in all three pivot areas. He must box
the pivot player on all shots, holding his block-out position and
never moving for the ball. His lack of height may be a hindrance
at times, but his quickness, agility, and aggressiveness should neutralize the opponent's height advantage.

For several reasons, the front-line men should influence the ball
to the side. This movement limits the offensive possibilities—they
may pass in through the defensive perimeter, they may pass to the
corner, or they may pass back outside the twenty-one-foot radius,
at which point the defense would revert to the two-one-two zone.
Influencing the initial pass to the side allows the defense to match-up
quickly in a man-to-man alignment and it allows them to pick up
the pivot man, if there is one, quickly. It also allows X_5 or X_4, the
back men, to give audible signals from the weak side directing the
front men or X_3 into proper position.

The initial responsibility of the back-line men is to protect the
baseline. They should influence to the middle where they may obtain help from X_3. If they force the man fairly high, X_2 or X_1 must
react to the ball, and together with X_3, may double-team.

Diag. 8-40, MATCH-UP DEFENSE, ZONE ORIGIN

B has the ball, having received a pass from A. The arrows
indicate the movement of the defensive players in assuming their
man-to-man position. X_2 has moved to the left to pick up B, with
the ball, man-to-man. X_4 has moved to pick up C overplaying slightly
to the ball side. X_3 has moved from the center of the foul lane into
a medium-pivot protective position. X_1 has dropped off from his
position on A into the upper half of the foul circle, and X_5, who has
moved up to cover D, moves to the middle as D crosses the lane.
X_5 must give an audible signal to X_3 that D is assuming this low
pivot position, so that X_3 can front him. X_5 would be responsible
for D until X_3 picked him up. A pass from B to D would be difficult,
so X_5 would not have to be extremely close to D. X_5 remains in

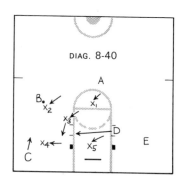

DIAG. 8-40

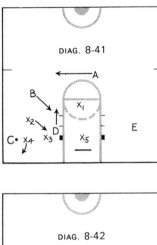

DIAG. 8-41

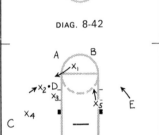

DIAG. 8-42

position in the middle of the free-throw lane. He is primarily responsible for E, but E is on the weak side, far removed from the position of the ball.

Diag. 8-41, MATCH-UP DEFENSE, ZONE ORIGIN

B has passed the ball into the corner to C. C is guarded by X_4, whose initial movement is towards the baseline to prevent a baseline drive. B is cutting through the pivot area. X_2 is playing an intercepting position between B and the ball, shutting off the passing lane until B enters the foul lane area. B then remains strong-side. X_3 has fronted D in the pivot. X_1 has dropped just slightly below the foul line to be ready to double-team or pick up B if B **V**'s out high with X_2 switching to A. X_5 has maintained his position in the center of the foul lane. The arrow indicates that D is moving up to a medium-pivot area.

Diag. 8-42, MATCH-UP DEFENSE, ZONE ORIGIN

C has passed the ball to D in the medium-pivot area. X_3 is playing D from behind. X_4 is overplaying C slightly towards the ball. X_2 has allowed B to cut through the foul-lane area, and B has moved out to A's original position. A has moved over to B's position. X_2 and X_1 are attacking D from the front to cause a tie-up or to prevent a good shooting or passing opportunity by D. X_5 is moving up with E to prevent a pass to E. If D were to pass the ball defensively back out to A or B, who are retreating into the back part of the front-court area, the zone alignment two-one-two would be reshaped. If the ball were passed from D to A, X_2 would play A man-to-man, and X_1 would play B.

Man-to-man origin. This match-up defense puts a defensive man in position on every offensive player regardless of the offensive pattern used. If the offense comes down in a three-two, the defense is in three-two man-to-man position on each player. The diagrams show the offense in a two-three alignment.

The defense should be playing zone when the offense is geared to man-to-man defense, and it should appear to be in man-to-man when the offense is expecting a zone. Disguising the defense will confuse the offense and perhaps get them into a zone offense pattern.

In man-to-man origin match-ups, the front line and back line influence the ball movement as they do in zone-origin match-ups. Defenders play men man-to-man in the area of the ball. When an opponent tries to cut through the defense to an area away from the ball, the defender guarding this cutter should allow him to go through, playing between him and the ball to a point where he cannot receive a pass. Trading men is an important factor in this defense. Each player is actually responsible for one man, but sometimes two offensive men will be close together in one area making it possible for one defensive man to play both. However, the nearest defensive teammate must be prepared to pick up one of the men if he leaves the area. If one defender cannot play two, he must call to the nearest man for help.

Diag. 8-43, MATCH-UP DEFENSE, MAN-TO-MAN ORIGIN, TO ZONE COVERAGE AFTER THE FIRST PASS

DIAG. 8-43

A has the ball in the front of the offensive two-three alignment. D, in low pivot with X_4 playing off him to the ball side, moves up to a high pivot position. X_4 follows him up to this position, guarding aggressively. X_5 adjusts towards the ball as though playing C in a normal man-to-man position. X_2 and X_3 move into intercepting angles on B and E, both one pass away from the ball.

DIAG. 8-44

Diag. 8-44, MATCH-UP DEFENSE, MAN-TO-MAN ORIGIN

A has passed the ball to B. A makes a long diagonal cut through the defense to the opposite side. X_1 should follow A through the defense to a point where B cannot pass to A—usually to the foul line. X_1, X_2 and X_5 should trade responsibilities. X_1 should move to pick up B, X_2 should move to pick up C, and X_5 should pick up A. X_4 has overplayed D at the high pivot, and X_3 has moved into an intercepting position in the middle area since his man, E is far removed from the ball position.

Diag. 8-45, MATCH-UP DEFENSE, MAN-TO-MAN ORIGIN

A passes to E and cuts through the defense on the ball side. X_1 follows A, positioning himself at a point where he can prevent a return pass to A. X_1 and X_3 trade responsibilities. D has moved to a low pivot position opposite. X_2 has taken a long float off B. X_4 has moved long off D towards the ball position. X_5 has moved into the foul lane and can cover D. Now the defense appears to be in a zone structure.

DIAG. 8-45

Diag. 8-46, DOUBLE-TEAM FROM MATCH-UP DEFENSE. MAN-TO-MAN ORIGIN

E has passed the ball to A. A's position in the corner presents a good double-teaming situation. X_4 moves quickly from a low position in the foul lane guarding the basket to the corner to double-team on A. X_3 covers A on the baseline side. X_1 plays an intercepting angle on E as E moves away. X_5 adjusts to the middle of the foul-lane, five feet out from the basket. X_2 is in position to intercept a long pass across the court to C or out to B.

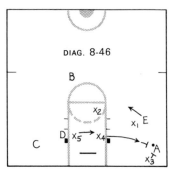

DIAG. 8-46

Diag. 8-47, MATCH-UP DEFENSE. MAN-TO-MAN ORIGIN

A passes to B, who has moved out for the ball. A cuts through away from the ball position. X_1 plays between A and the ball as A cuts down the lane. Just below the foul line X_1 realizes that a

343

DIAG. 8-47

return pass to A would be intercepted by X_4 or X_5, therefore, X_1 can leave A. X_3 has fallen into the foul circle to assume a zone defensive position. X_5 moves to front D. X_4 is low enough to go to the basket to help if a lob pass is thrown from B to D. With A away from the ball it is possible for one man, X_4, to guard two, A and E. If an exchange had to be made, X_3 would drop down to pick up A. X_1 now has defensive latitude but must be alert to pick up a free opponent if warned verbally by a teammate.

The Triangle and Two Combination Defense. In this defense, two defenders play man-to-man against the two outstanding opponents while the three back-line men use a triangle zone defense near the basket against weaker or uncoordinated big men who are not basically good ball handlers. The zone players should permit outside shots but prevent close-in shots, preserving the defensive rebound triangle. The two men playing man-to-man should pressure and cut off all passing lanes. They can switch on crosses by the good offensive players, unless game plans indicate different defensive coverage. The triangle men should double-team these men when they are in their zones. When pressure is applied man-to-man at half court, the three men in the zone should be close enough to opponents to cut off passing lanes to them without leaving the basket unguarded. If one of these opponents receives the ball, his defender should pressure him to cause a ball-handling error.

This defense is weak against good shooters, and opponents can penetrate the back line from the weak side. It is also weak if a good pivot player is one of the three being played zone.

This is a good basic defense against a weak-shooting team with two good ball handlers, and it presents good fast-break opportunities. It allows for defensive chances and aggressive play by the two men who are playing the man-to-man defense. Of course, caution should be used on defensive chances in close-to-the-basket areas. The unorthodox quality of this defense makes it an effective surprise maneuver, and it has the good team defensive elements of backboard control, ball pressure, and good defensive coverage near the basket and in the pivot area.

The alignment of this defense may vary so that three men play man-to-man in the front, with a two-man zone in back, or the front can play zone while the back line plays man-to-man. Coaches can improvise, using different combinations.

The initial zone alignment should have X_3 standing on the foul line and X_4 and X_5 standing with their inside foot on the foul lane, approximately six feet from the basket area. (X_1 and X_2 play man-to-man.)

Diag. 8-48, TRIANGLE AND TWO COMBINATION DEFENSE

B is dribbling the ball towards the head of the key. X_2 is moving

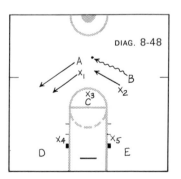

DIAG. 8-48

344

in good man-to-man position on B. X_1 is guarding A man-to-man. X_3, X_4, and X_5 are in their original alignment in a triangle zone. X_3 is a little higher, blocking C from the ball.

Diag. 8-49, TRIANGLE AND TWO COMBINATION DEFENSE

C has moved higher for a pass from B. X_3 has allowed this reception. B cuts through to the corner, and X_2 guards him man-to-man. A moves out towards the head of the key, and X_1 guards him man-to-man. X_4 has played in front of D, who is low. X_5 is in position to stop any movement by E. If C takes a shot, which would be allowed, the triangle is in excellent rebound position.

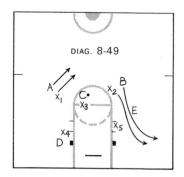

DIAG. 8-49

Box-and-One and Diamond-and-One Combination Defenses. The box-and-one and the diamond-and-one defenses will be discussed together as they are basically the same defense after the initial movement of the zone formation once the offense passes or dribbles. The box-and-one defense has one man playing man-to-man defense against an opponent and the other four players in a box arrangement, the diamond-and-one has one man playing man-to-man and the other four players in a diamond arrangement near the keyhole area.

The primary use of the two defenses is to limit the effectiveness of the high-scoring opponent. Cutting down greatly on the point production of any outstanding scorer hurts the opposing team in more ways than one; it can cause disharmony among them, with the star blaming the others for not getting the ball and the others perhaps blaming the star for taking bad shots.

The one free man (X_1) may be used in two ways. First he can be used to play man-to-man defense. Playing against a fast player who is an outside shooter and driver, the man-to-man defender should not let him get the ball. Playing against a good player who goes to the backboard strong offensively and is a good shooter, but is not a good driver, the defender would allow him to have the ball under pressure, boxing him at all times to keep him away from the rebound area.

The second method of using the fifth man is to allow him to move freely, especially if he is an aggressive defender with excellent stamina and good ball sense and anticipation.

The two front men (X_2 and X_3) in the box, should be quick with good reaction; they can be rovers on defense, covering the intermediate area and the high-pivot area. One must rebound at all times. The two back men (X_4 and X_5) should be the best rebounders; they are responsible for the pivot areas and the medium baseline area. Whenever the opponent who is being played man-to-man has the ball in a vulnerable area, all zone members must be prepared to double-team him. If the fifth defender is a floater or rover, not given man-to-man responsibilities, zone members should attempt to force the opponent's offensive patterns into movement than can be anticipated by the floater or by the rover. In the diamond-and-one alignment X_1, usually a guard, is assigned man-to-man. X_2 is normally the second guard. X_3 and X_4 are the forwards, with X_4 the better rebounder and X_3 perhaps the quicker. X_5 is the center.

If the fifth man is a floater or rover, he can sneak away. If he is assigned to play man-to-man, he cannot sneak away as he must keep close check on the good opponent, harassing him as much as possible. In that use, we would recommend that the second guard, X_2, be used to sneak away. He will have good opportunity to do this, because the good offensive player will be intent on going to the boards to get the rebound offensively.

The sliding movement in this type of defense must be extremely quick and the anticipation factor is essential. The single man and a zoner should double the star whenever possible, and two of the zoners may double-team the others. The four men in the zone posture must always be alert to shut off the weak areas—the foul-line area, the medium-side areas, and the pivot area. They also should be aware of the passing lanes into the difficult areas, closing them inside and opening them outside, laying off just enough for interception.

The four members playing zone should never overextend. They should give the outside shot when overextension is a factor. When playing a star with a box-and-one or a diamond-and-one defense the four men in the zone alignment should use all available means and influencing tactics to deploy the ball away from the outstanding player.

Diag. 8-50, BOX-AND-ONE COMBINATION DEFENSE, INITIAL ALIGNMENT

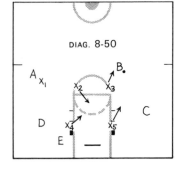

DIAG. 8-50

X_1 plays A, the opposing star, man-to-man. X_2 and X_3, the front men in the box position, are slightly above the foul line straddling the circle area. X_4 and X_5, the back men, are rebounders, straddling the foul lane approximately six feet from the basket. B has the ball at the offensive left side. X_3 moves towards the ball, X_2 adjusts back in the lower half of the free-throw circle, X_4 adjusts slightly into the lane, and X_5 adjusts up outside the lane towards the ball position and C.

Diag. 8-51, BOX-AND-ONE COMBINATION AFTER INITIAL SLIDE

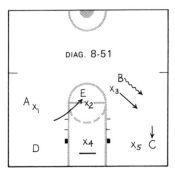

DIAG. 8-51

Diagram shows the flexing of the zone defense as B dribbles to his left and X_3 follows the ball. X_2 moves to the foul line as E comes up into a high-pivot position. X_5 moves towards the sideline, but not overextending in the area of C as the ball moves into that vicinity and C moves into the corner. X_4 adjusts to the center of the foul lane, approximately three feet in front of the basket. X_1 stays man-to-man with A.

346

Diag. 8-52, DIAMOND-AND-ONE COMBINATION DEFENSE, INITIAL ALIGNMENT

Again X_1 is playing A, the outstanding opponent, man-to-man. X_2, the point man in the diamond, is just below the outer circle at the head of the key. X_3 and X_4 are just below the foul line straddling the foul lane. X_5 is in the center of the foul lane, approximately six feet in front of the basket. B has the ball. X_2 adjusts to the ball position. X_3 moves towards the middle of the lane. X_4 moves towards C. X_5 moves up in front of E, who is low. There is a great similarity between diagrams 8-51 and 8-52 after the initial flexing of the zone.

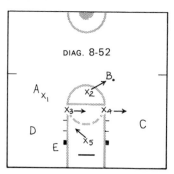

DIAG. 8-52

Diag. 8-53, DIAMOND-AND-ONE COMBINATION AFTER THE INITIAL SLIDE

B again is shown dribbling to the offensive left. X_2 is moving in position with him. E has moved up to the foul line again, and X_3 has adjusted his position up on the foul line. X_4 has moved to his right to be in position on the ball side with C in the vicinity of the ball. X_5 has dropped back to an under-the-basket position in the middle of the lane, about four feet in front of the basket. X_1 is guarding A man-to-man. Again there is a close similarity between Diagrams 8-51 and 8-53.

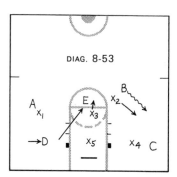

DIAG. 8-53

T-and-One Combination Defense. The T-and-One combination defense derives its name from the similarity between the letter **T** and the pattern formed by the four men playing zone-principle defense. X_1 plays the opposing star man-to-man. X_2, the more mobile forward, is in front. Since he is tall, the opponents will probably be unable to shoot over him effectively. X_3 is the quickest zone player with the best anticipation. He is used most to double-team and has the greatest range of movement of the four zoners. Usually he is the second guard. X_4 and X_5 are the remaining defensive players, X_5 being the better rebounder. X_2's initial position is in the outer half of the free-throw circle. X_3's initial position is in the inner half of the free-throw circle. X_4 and X_5 are approximately five feet in front of the basket with their inside feet on the foul lanes.

This defense has good double-team potential. X_2 double-teams on A, the outstanding opponent, with X_1 in the front and side front areas. X_3 double-teams on A with X_1 to the sides and at 45-degree angle areas. X_4 or X_5 will double-team on A with X_1 in the corner or pivot areas on their sides. The men playing this defense should be careful not to overextend.

The purposes of this combination alignment are to lessen the scoring efficiency of the outstanding opponent; to prevent close-in scoring opportunities for the other opponents; to encourage outside shooting opportunities by the other opponents, expecially those beyond their range; and to get good rebounding position. X_2 will move closer to the basket after offensive movement and will be in good re-

347

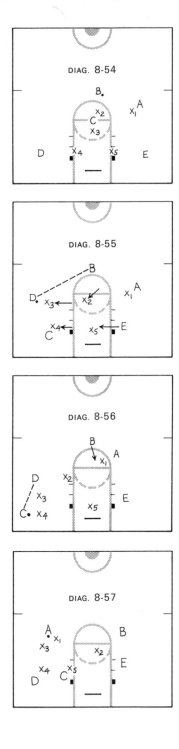

DIAG. 8-54

DIAG. 8-55

DIAG. 8-56

DIAG. 8-57

bound position after a shot. Usually X_2 forms the rebounding triangle with X_4 and X_5, as X_3 shifts to the ball areas. X_3 is the player who should break on a sneak-away attempt, as X_1 must remain in position on the outstanding opponent. Another reason to allow X_3 this sneak-away opportunity is as a bonus for his necessarily aggressive play. It is possible in this defense to interchange X_1 and X_3 if their defensive abilities are similar.

Diag. 8-54, T-AND-ONE COMBINATION DEFENSE

A, the outstanding opponent, is to the offensive left, guarded man-to-man by X_1. B has the ball at the top of the key. X_2 is in position in the outer half of the free-throw circle. X_3 is in position in the lower half of the free-throw circle. X_4 and X_5 are straddling the lanes in position approximately five feet in front of the basket. After the flexing of the zone defense, X_2 is closer to rebound position than X_3, hence he should be the third rebounder with X_4 and X_5.

Diag. 8-55, T-AND-ONE COMBINATION DEFENSE

B passes the ball to D. With the pass the defensive alignment flexes towards the ball. X_3 moves directly towards the ball, challenging D. X_2 drops down into the lower half of the free-throw circle. X_4 overplays C. X_5 moves into the center of the foul-lane area. X_1 plays A man-to-man.

Diag. 8-56

D passes into the corner to C. X_4 has moved into position on C to prevent a baseline move. X_3 has dropped into this area. X_2 has moved to the side of the foul lane on the ball side. X_5 has remained in position. X_1 is still playing man-to-man at an intercepting angle on A.

Diag. 8-57, T-AND-ONE COMBINATION DEFENSE WITH A DOUBLE-TEAM ON A

A has moved towards the ball and has received a pass. X_1 and X_3 are double-teaming him. X_4 is still overplaying in the corner on the side. X_5 is overplaying in the pivot. X_2 is in good position between B and E.

Advantages. Coaches should assess the following attributes of combination defense to determine whether they are suitable for existing personnel to use against the teams to be played.

1. It is an extremely good defense by which to influence the ball away from an outstanding opposing scorer.

2. The defender guarding the outstanding player can overplay him to prevent his getting the ball, and he can be confident of help from his teammates.

3. It tends to confuse opponents, because combating it requires special offensive preparation.

4. It utilizes the best attributes of man-to-man and zone defenses.

348

5. It is a good double-teaming defense.

6. It is excellent against a good dribbler or a good dribbling team.

7. It is excellent against poor outside shooting.

8. It often prevents ball penetration to vulnerable areas.

9. It negates the effectiveness of a good screening and cutting opponent, as it eliminates the necessity of switching.

10. It places defensive personnel in their most effective areas.

11. It has good rebounding positions.

12. It permits good fast-break development.

13. It incorporates collapsing from the weak side.

Disadvantages. The negative factors in a combination type defense are as follows.

1. It is vulnerable to good ball handlers.

2. It is vulnerable to diagonal cuts in the match-up structures as it weakens or confuses defenders during the exchange of men.

3. It can be overloaded.

4. Overextension leaves combinations vulnerable to good short and medium shooting opportunities by opponents.

5. It is not effective against good outside shooting.

6. It leaves certain floor areas vulnerable to a deliberate probing team.

7. Teams must revert to a pressure defense if they are behind late in the game.

8. It requires specialized defensive abilities that not all teams or players may possess.

9. It requires time to set up, making it vulnerable to fast-break and quick-ball movement upcourt.

10. It requires a great deal of practice time.

11. It confuses individual defensive players at times, even when it is used as a primary defense.

pressure defenses

The best time to initiate a pressure defense is after a basket or a foul shot made by your team. There are two types of pressure defenses—man-to-man and zone. Each type can be implemented in a full-court posture, at three-quarter court, or at half-court. Full-court pressure can begin with the man out-of-bounds or with the front defensive men at the backcourt foul line. Three-quarter pressure would be enforced at or behind the outer edge of the far keyhole area. Half-court pressure should be initiated one step before the division line at mid-court in the opponents backcourt.

The term "pressure defense" implies use of advancing,

349

attacking tactics by a forcing defense. Its purpose is to force misplays or bad passes by the opponents, taking advantage of the ten-second rule and overplay tactics. Successful execution of this defense requires fine conditioning and thorough knowledge of the fundamentals.

Pressure defense should be used within the framework of the available personnel. Teams need good bench strength to sustain such a defense over an extended period of time during a game, plus much practice time on both man-to-man and zone presses. Full-court zone pressure in most instances is better than man-to-man pressure, as one good dribbler can defeat the man-to-man defense. A weak man-to-man player—usually the least mobile forward defender—can even be beaten by a dribbler who is only fair.

An all-out press is demanded when the situation requires forcing opponents in order to gain possession of the ball. Possession is essential when a team is one or two points behind with only seconds left to the game and the opponents are stalling. While shooting is improving (the shooting percentage is the highest today in the history of basketball) the quality of ball handling is decreasing. Therefore, pressure defense can counteract improved shooting (especially by jump shooters) by increasing the number of losses-of-possession by the offensive team.

Teaching Pressure Defensive Tactics. The coach should outline both man-to-man and zone pressure on paper and give each player a copy to be kept for reference. After the squad members have had time to study the outlines, the coach should present both defenses in a lecture, using a blackboard at the court, if possible, to diagram the tactics. He should cover each detail before moving on to actual demonstrations and insist that the assembled squad ask questions. After the diagraming, the coach should walk through the defensive movements on the court; then go through them in slow motion; and finally, use them at half speed against weak reserves, junior varsity players or freshmen.

The squad should practice the press every day, using it in an actual game only after it has been perfected. Then the coach should try it out in a game situation where the team cannot be hurt by its use or as a last resort in a losing game when a surprise change in tactics is required. Normally, players master man-to-man press faster than zone press.

Man-to-Man Pressure Defense. Preseason practice drills and stressing of fundamentals are extremely important in the man-to-man pressure defense. It should be practiced one-on-one, two-on-two, three-on-three and full team, picking up at full court. The coach should have a team of good man-to-man pressure defenders available for insertion in a game at the proper time.

Coaches may vary the pickup point of a man-to-man pressure defense. At full-court, the strategy is to cut off outlets, assuring that the pass will be received in the backcourt by a weaker offensive ball handler. The defender must harass the inbounder, distracting him, preventing him from passing to a good ball handler, and forcing him to hesitate so that he may incur a five-second violation.

An alternative strategy is for the man guarding the passer-in to fall off and double-team the best on-court dribbler with his defender, forcing the ball to a less capable ball handler, then returning to pick up his out-of-bounds opponent.

If the press is applied at three-quarter court, at the head of the foul circle, the inbounder can pass the ball in. The three-quarter pickup allows the defense to assess the situation and take advantage of the opponent's necessity to bring the ball up-court over the mid-court line within ten seconds. This press is a good surprise tactic.

Picking up at half-court, one step in the opponent's back-court, again takes advantage of the ten-second rule. It is effective because there is less area to cover than in the three-quarter or all-court man-to-man situation and it can be used to force the opponents out of their positions for their set offensive attack. When the ball does go into the front court, the defensive team can use turn-and-double techniques.

In man-to-man pressure the defender should approach an alive opponent quickly, but under control, faking or feinting to make him start his dribble, then forcing him to his weak hand. It is possible to spring a surprise man-to-man press with two men pressuring at mid-court just as the opponents are bringing the ball over the division line. This tactic is used to force mistakes, loss of ball, or a backcourt violation; to trap opponents; and to pick up a loose opponent who may otherwise have eluded them. While two men are double-teaming on the ball, other teammates should play intercepting angles, watching both the ball and the men they are guarding. A corner defender should move up to play this intercepting angle so that a potential ball receiver will have to reverse, moving farther from the passer.

To make the long pass, the ball handler will have to draw back his arm, thus alerting the defenders. If an opponent gets out of his defender's sight by moving behind him, that defender should immediately go to the basket area, about a step inside the lower half of the foul circle, in the middle of the free-throw lanes, and try to pick up this man by moving out from the basket area.

Defenders should jump switch on all offensive team crosses. If a defender jump switches into the path of a teammate's opponent, that teammate should switch immediately to defend against the jump switcher's man. In some situations, the coach may decide to have the teammate stay to double-team with the jump switcher. If the double-teaming fails, the teammate will then pick up the loose man. Guards should jump switch at every opportunity.

When using man-to-man pressure defense full court, the near man should aggressively attack a rebounder or a retriever of a jump ball to force him into a defense posture in the backcourt, slowing the movement of the ball upcourt so that all defensive teammates may pick up a man quickly before the ball penetrates. It is a good defensive tactic to turn the man with the ball, if possible, so that his back is to the basket. This maneuver causes him to lose sight of his teammates, allows his defender to move in on him, and makes double-teaming possible.

The man-to-man defender should force the dribbler to his weak hand, to the middle, or to the sidelines as instructed. If the dribbler gets even with or past his defender, the defender must turn and run in stride with the dribbler, forcing him towards the sidelines and striking up at the ball with his inside hand. He should use defensive fakes to attempt to stop the dribbler; he should not foul or try to steal the ball. If the dribbler stops, the defensive opponent should attack him aggressively to force a poor passing situation. If an offensive man dribbles by a defender some distance from the basket, that defender should quickly pivot behind him and attempt to deflect or bat the ball forward to a teammate, using a flicking motion from the rear. When a player who has stopped dribbling and has been aggressively attacked by his defender passes off, the defender must react instantly, dropping back towards the basket in the direction of the ball.

Players who are guarding teammates of a dribbler who has been stopped should play an intercepting angle on their opponents, being alert for a reverse movement. The defenders in a man-to-man pressure defense should attempt to force the ball to weaker offensive ball handlers by opening the door and allowing them to obtain possession of the ball. The center should overplay high on the opposing center to invite lob passes; however, as he is the back defender he must remember his primary responsibility of allowing no easy lay-ups. At times, opponents with the ball will sift through a man-to-man pressure defense and move in on this last defender in a two-on-one situation. If they do, he should zone the two, using delaying tactics to stall until a teammate can help him.

Zone Pressure Defense. The zone-press type of defense uses basic zone principles in forcing opponents over full-court, three-quarter court or half-court areas in order to confuse and disrupt them.

Defensive positioning and movement are based on offensive ball and player movement. Rather than sliding, the defensive players must in many instances sprint to their new positions, since a defender playing zone press covers a far greater area than the player in a normal zone defensive alignment.

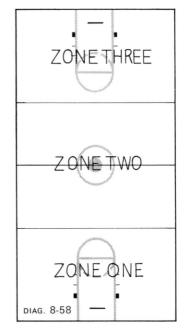

Diag. 8-58

This diagram outlines defensive reference areas for full-court zone pressure. Zone 3 is from the endline to the backcourt hash mark, Zone 2 is from the backcourt hash mark to the front-court hash mark, and Zone 1 is from the front-court hash mark to the basket.

Even if a team does not have occasion to use zone press often, two advantages accrue from perfecting it. First, by practicing the defense in actual game situations, the players learn to understand its principles so that they can attack an opponent's zone press defense effectively. Second, it is a good secondary defense that must be used as a primary defense under certain circumstances.

Other advantages include the following:

1. It compensates for a height disparity when the defensive team is smaller than their opponents.

2. It is effective for a team with a speed advantage.

3. It is an excellent team conditioner.

4. It generates enthusiasm and a good team defensive attitude.

5. It forces the opponents into a running, pressure type of game.

6. It helps a fast-break offense by speeding up the game.

7. It simulates team defensive play by making players aware of its importance.

8. It discourages opponents if they misplay.

9. If used for a few minutes near the end of a half, it is an effective deceptive tactic. The opponents may use valuable intermission time postulating attack methods for a defense that may not be used again.

Zone press should be used at the following times:

1. When a team is behind

2. When big men on the opposition are defensive problems

3. When the opponents play a set pattern to force them out of the basic offense

4. When playing against a poor ball-handling team

5. When quick baskets are necessary

6. When a team has small, quick personnel

7. When aggressive pressure must be applied continuously

8. When opposing teams have a good pivot attack

9. When playing against slower, poorly conditioned teams

Coaches should not expect an immediate or quick return from zone-pressure tactics. Returns may be slow in coming but they will accrue when the tactics become effective.

Teams should keep zone pressure on opponents after they make mistakes so that other mistakes will ensue. As setting up a zone pressure defense takes time, the defense should only be initiated at the following points in a game:

1. After a basket or successful free throw by your team

2. When the opponents have the ball out-of-bounds and are slow in getting into position to inbound it

3. After a time out, especially if it has not been used before

4. At any time as a surprise maneuver
   (It is very effective at the beginning of a game, at the quarter or at the half.)

Zone pressure defense is used (1) to surprise the opponents; (2) to upset their poise; (3) to make them cautious and protective of the ball; (4) to disrupt their basic patterns; (5) to lure them into trap or double-team situations; (6) to force misplays or mistakes; (7) to distort the opponents patterns, and force bad shots; and (8) to speed up the pace of the game when the opponents wish to set a slower game tempo.

Zone pressure defense, like normal zone defense, can be played from an odd front or an even front. The odd fronts possible at full-court, three-quarter court, or half-court position include a one-two-one-one zone press, a three-one-one zone press, a three-two and a one-two-two. The even presses are the two-two-one, two-one-two, and two-three zones. All zone presses will flex into similar structures after the ball has inbounded. We will outline an odd-front zone pressure defense, an even-front zone pressure defense, and a half-court odd front zone pressure defense.

One-two-one-one three-quarter or full-court zone press basic alignment. X_1, the middle man, is usually a guard. He should be a smaller player with good speed and quick hands for both defensive and offensive opportunities. He forces the opponents to move to the advantage of his team. The middle man is limited to double-team movements or lateral movements in the backcourt, and he must get back to the head of the key quickly whenever necessary.

The wing men, X_2 and X_3, are taller players, usually the forwards. The more maneuverable forward should be placed in the X_2 position, as the defensive team wishes to force the attack in his direction. X_2 or X_3, depending on the position of the ball, must go back to the defensive basket area frequently to protect underneath the basket from the weak side.

The four man, X_4, should be the quickest player on the team, with good court sense and anticipation. Whenever possible, he is the taller guard. He is given a great deal of latitude, as he has the greatest range of responsibility and must be overprotective of the middle area. The back man, X_5, is usually the center, the biggest man and best rebounder. The last line of defense protecting the basket, he is primarily responsible for preventing an easy shot by the opponents.

Diag. 8-59, ONE-TWO-ONE-ONE ZONE PRESSURE, FULL COURT OR THREE-QUARTER BASIC ALIGNMENT

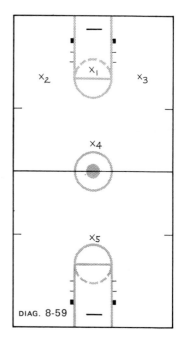

DIAG. 8-59

All players in a pressure defense should be identified by position as well as by number for easy reference. X_1, the middleman, positions himself initially in the front half of the near foul circle. X_2 and X_3, the wing men, are on opposite ends of the foul line extended, between the actual edge of the foul line and the sideline. X_4, called the four man, is at the front of the center circle, and X_5, the back man, is at the head of the far key.

Following are play-by-play procedures for each player as the ball moves from the out-of-bounds position towards the basket.

Middleman, X_1

1. Direct the first pass-in, usually to defensive left. If necessary, move to your right to effect this pass-in.

2. Prevent a return pass to the inbounder by cutting off the passing lane to the foul-lane area.

3. Double-team with either wing, closing the backdoor trap.

4. If the wing man forces a dribble turn, attack the ball aggressively as the opponent turns, denying the dribbler the alley between the wing man and your own position.

5. If the ball is returned to the inbounder, use the same trapping techniques to the other side, trapping with the other wing. This trap will take longer to spring because of the distance the other wingman must travel back to initial position. Be patient.

6. When the ball passes over the front line, sprint to the defensive end, determining the most advantageous position by observing the offensive and defensive deployments and anticipating open passing lanes.

7. If the ball goes to the middle of the high-pivot area at the defensive end, attack it aggressively to force a pass back towards mid-court, a misplay, or a double-team situation.

8. If the ball goes to a front court corner, protect the medium-pivot area on the ball side.

Wingmen, X_2 and X_3

1. If the pass-in is allowed to be made uncontested, it should be in front of X_2. X_3, if no opponent is in front of his initial position, drops back towards the nearest offensive player on his side or into the middle of the backcourt to prevent a pass over X_1 and the other wing.

2. Allow reception in your corner, standing back far enough to prevent a pass-in to the backcourt sideline area behind

you. If the inbounder hesitates on his pass-in, delaying for a few seconds, attack the near-corner opponent aggressively to force a five-second violation or a long, hurried pass.

3. If reception is made on your side, approach the alive or dribbling opponent quickly, but under control, using good fundamental man-to-man defensive approach techniques.

4. *Never* allow the dribbler to get between you and the side-line.

5. Attack aggressively if the dribbler stops, preventing a good upcourt pass opportunity along the sideline passing lane. Arms should be up to force a lob or deflection.

6. If the ball is inbounded opposite your position, drop back into the center of the floor in the opponent's backcourt, between mid-court and the foul circle. Anticipate and play intercepting position on the inbounder and any other opponent in the backcourt away from the trap area, decoying the ball handler into an apparently safe pass. Intercept cross-court or lob passes.

7. If the ball is passed back to the inbounder from the side opposite you, double-team with the middle man, being careful not to overextend your defensive position. Getting into position hurriedly may prevent an effective double-team. Be sure to protect your sideline against the dribbler.

8. If the first inbound receiver on your side passes up your sideline while you are double-teaming him, react immediately, following this pass along the sideline for a possible double-team with X_4.

9. Continue following the ball to the deep defensive corner if it is passed there. Double-team with X_5.

10. Cover the under-the-basket area as quickly as possible if the ball is in the opposite defensive corner. Cover in the middle of the foul lane if the ball is in the opposite sideline area near the hash mark or at the point of an imaginary extension of the foul line.

11. Anticipate and try to intercept a centering pass to the high pivot if the ball is just over mid-court at the opposite side-line. (Wingmen can read the offensive zone pressure pattern after it is used a few times and make invaluable contributions through imagination and hustle.)

12. Sprint back under the basket if the ball breaks the frontline of the press quickly on the opposite side.

13. If the ball is passed over the frontline on your side, react immediately for possible double-teaming with X_4.

14. If you intercept, call "ball" and look immediately for a guard, usually X_1. Give him the ball and break. Be aware of a ten-second violation possibility. Dribble only if you have a clear path to the basket.

Four Man, X_4

1. Know how the opponents position themselves to attack the zone press. Prevent a pass over the front line by playing

an intercepting angle on an opponent near the mid-court area. The arm and body positions of the opponent's inbounder signal his intention. If he turns sideways, he may be preparing to make a long pass; if he is square to you with the ball in both hands, the pass normally will be a short one.

2. When the ball comes in-bounds, move towards the sideline on the side it comes in on, approximately in line with the ball.

3. Be in intercepting position on a man in the mid-court area near that sideline, but be alert for cutters coming up in the middle and for cross-court lobs or short passes.

4. If there is a good double-team at the front line, anticipate the most likely passing areas and try to intercept or deflect the pass.

5. If a dribbler gets through on a sideline past your near wing, approach cautiously and anticipate a pass. If the pass is made, bother it or deflect it. If the dribbler continues, attack to stop him and double-team with the near wing man beyond the hash-mark in the backcourt, as X_1 and the other wing man might become uncertain of floating responsibilities.

6. Attack the ball if it is passed to the middle from the mid-court side area on your side. This is a dangerous territory.

7. If the ball gets past your position on the far sideline, sprint to the pivot area ball-side and anticipate.

8. If the ball gets past your position on the near sideline, sprint to the pivot area on your side, observing the offensive opportunities as you move.

9. If the ball passes to a defensive corner, sprint to the lower medium-pivot position on that side and front an opponent in this area. Stay on the side of the ball in low position if there is no pivot. Be prepared to box anyone in the pivot area on a shot.

Back Man, X_5

1. Never allow a long pass to go over you to an opponent.

2. If there is no offensive player in front-court, move up to mid-court opposite the ball position. X_4 should be covering on that side to deny a pass over the front line into the mid-court area.

3. Double-team the ball in either front-court corner with a wingman.

4. Cover a pivot man to discourage a pass to him from the side mid-court area.

5. Protect the basket from quick, offensive penetration, never allowing a lay-up. Use good defensive delaying tactics when outnumbered two-on-one or three-on-one. Fake and feint, allow the outside shot, and rebound.

6. Intercept long passes with caution. If you mistime the pass or misjudge it, the opponents score.

357

7. Analyze ball movement, offensive player movement, and double-teaming by teammates to determine your most advantageous position. Go to passes in your area that you can intercept.

8. Play to the side of the foul lane as the ball crosses mid-court on that side and anticipate a corner double-team if the ball goes there. Use swarming, aggressive tactics, but protect the baseline, as the ball handler is probably more agile than you.

9. Play a pass into the pivot aggressively, but be alert for free cutters to the side who can receive a dropdown pass for a lay-up. Use delaying zone tactics in this case, giving up the outside shot if necessary.

Diag. 8-60, ONE-TWO-ONE-ONE ZONE PRESS, FULL COURT, MOVEMENT AFTER THE INITIAL PASS

A, out-of-bounds, passes in to B. X_1 steps towards A, then moves left towards the ball position. X_2 approaches B cautiously as B dribbles with the ball, initiating a double-teaming movement by X_2 and X_1. X_3 adjusts position slightly towards A, then—after B makes his move—drops back into the middle as a floater. X_4 overplays C in intercepting position. X_5 adjusts slightly towards E.

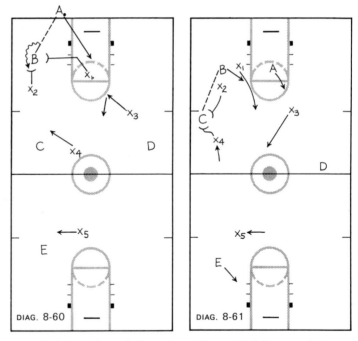

DIAG. 8-60 —   DIAG. 8-61 —

Diag. 8-61, ONE-TWO-ONE-ONE ZONE PRESS, FULL COURT, MOVEMENT WHEN B PASSES UP THE SIDELINE TO C

B passes from the trap position to C, near the backcourt hash mark. C has eluded X_4 or X_4 did not get in cutoff position quickly enough. X_4 approaches cautiously and sets the rear trap. X_2 follows the ball along the sideline and traps with X_4. X_1 becomes a floater in backcourt, guarding against a pass back to B or over to A. X_3 adjusts up in intercepting angle on D. X_5 moves over as the ball reaches C so that he can cut off a pass to E if necessary, without allowing a long pass over his position.

358

Diag. 8-62, ONE-TWO-ONE-ONE ZONE PRESS, FULL COURT, MOVEMENT WHEN BALL IS PASSED BACK TO THE INBOUNDER

This is a continuation of Diagram 8-60, an alternative to the offensive tactics shown in Diagram 8-61. B passes the ball back to A, who has come inbounds. X_1 adjusts from his position, staying on the side of A and forcing him, if possible, towards X_3 at the opposite sideline. X_3 adjusts back towards the sideline and up, cautiously, in an attempt to cut off A. X_1 and X_3 will double-team A. X_2 who had stepped up as B received the ball, retreats back towards the middle to become the floater as B passes back to A. X_4 quickly adjusts towards the opposite sideline in line with the ball. X_5 moves to the head of the key, still playing deep intercepting position on E.

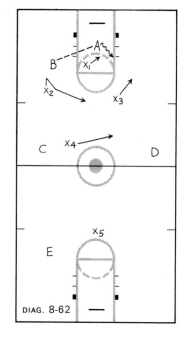

DIAG. 8-62

Diag. 8-63, ONE-TWO-ONE-ONE ZONE PRESS, TRAP ON B NEAR THE HASH MARK PRELIMINARY TO A PASS ALONG THE SIDELINE TO C

X_1 and X_2 have trapped on B after a return pass from A in Diagram 8-62. In this diagram the trap is higher than normal. X_1 and X_2 are trapping after the dribble, and X_4 has positioned on C. X_3 has adjusted back over half-court with the movement of D. If B passes back to A, X_3 can assume position on A to the outside, trapping with X_1. X_5 is low on E.

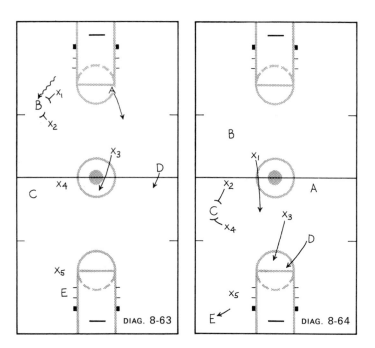

DIAG. 8-63   DIAG. 8-64

Diag. 8-64, ONE-TWO-ONE-ONE ZONE PRESS, TRAP ON C IN THE FRONT COURT NEAR THE SIDELINE

B has passed along the sideline to C. X_4 is the low trapper. X_2 is moving into position as the high trapper. D has moved towards the high-pivot position and is cut off by X_3. X_1 has come back inside the front-court area to cut off A who has come over mid-court. E is cut off by X_5. It is impossible for C to pass back to B, who is in the back-court, because it would be a violation.

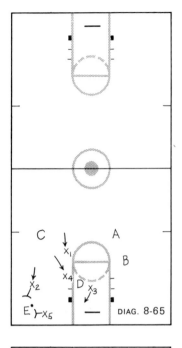

DIAG. 8-65

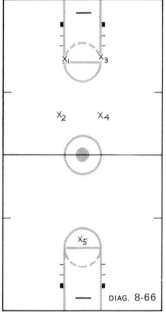

DIAG. 8-66

Diag. 8-65, ONE-TWO-ONE-ONE ZONE PRESS, CORNER TRAP ON E

E has received a pass from C. X_2 continues his movement along his sideline to become the high trapper. X_5, the low trapper, must close off the baseline to E. X_4 has dropped from his trapping position to overplay D in the pivot area. X_1 is at the end of the foul line on the side of the ball, ready for any pass. X_3 is in the under-basket area with the ball in the opposite corner.

After a one-two-one-one zone press. If the one-two-one-one doesn't end in a shot or misplay, the defenders should be prepared to fall back in the predetermined defensive alignment. Normally an outlet, safety pass towards mid-court after the opponents have attempted to attack a full-court or three-quarter court zone press is the signal for the defense to deploy into an aggressive two-three zone alignment with X_1 and X_4 as the front men, X_2 and X_3 as the back men, and X_5 in the middle. However, the coach may prefer that his men remain in the one-two-one-one zone press, using half-court principles. In making his decision, the coach considers factors such as personnel playing on both teams, time left, score, where the game is being played, and fouls on the players on his team.

Two-two-one zone press, full or three-quarter court. Placement of the players is shown in Diag. 8-66

Diag. 8-66

The front men, X_1 and X_3, position in front of the near foul line, with their feet straddling the lane, to influence the ball coming in to the sides and prevent the initial pass from going down the middle of the court. The left front, X_1, is usually a small, quick guard, with good speed and hands. His duties are similar to those of X_1 in the one-two-one-one zone press. The right front, X_3, is perhaps the taller of the forwards. His basic duties correspond to those of one of the wing men in the one-two-one-one press. He must get back extremely fast if the ball goes over the front line on the opposite side. X_2 and X_4 position themselves in backcourt between the hash mark and the mid-court line, approximately in line behind X_1 and X_3. X_2, the left trapper, is a fairly agile forward. X_4, the right trapper, is generally the second guard. As he has a lot of moving to do, he should be the quickest player, with good anticipation and speed and good stamina and range. X_5, the backman (positioned in the top half of the far free-throw circle), is the center. His primary responsibility is protecting the basket, for he is the last line of defense.

If the initial pass-in can be influenced properly, this defense is played in a similar fashion to the one-two-one-one zone press. A change in alignment for defensive variations and change in the structure of the zone offense is desirable at times. If the coach wishes, X_1 and X_3 can change sides, as can X_2 and X_4, and the influencing of the ball will be up the opposite side of the court with the players maintaining the same basic responsibilities. X_4 always backs up X_3, and X_2 is always behind X_1.

360

If the area guarded by X_1 and X_3 is secure, X_3 may adjust position near an opponent on his side to direct the pass-in to the defensive left. If the initial pass comes into the defensive left, X_2 cheats up and moves to the ball. X_2 and X_4 may adjust their initial position, depending on the situation. They must never allow a pass up the middle. They must adjust slightly to prevent a long pass to either side that X_5 cannot prevent, since he must be back protecting against a baseline opponent. Either X_2 or X_4 may adjust to prevent a pass over X_3, as long as the adjustment doesn't permit a down-the-middle pass.

If the ball is influenced in to the defensive left, X_1 and X_2 trap as in the one-two-one-one press, and the other players also move as they do in the one-two-one-one. If the pass comes in to the defensive right, X_3 and X_4 are the trappers. X_1 assumes the duties held by X_2 in the one-two-one-one press, and X_2 assumes X_4's responsibilities. X_3 assumes the responsibilities of X_1 as the low trapper, and X_4 assumes the responsibilities of X_3 in the one-two-one-one press as the high trapper.

This exchange of duties weakens the structure of the two-two-one zone press somewhat, because of differences in basic abilities; therefore, defenders should influence towards the more advantageous area whenever possible.

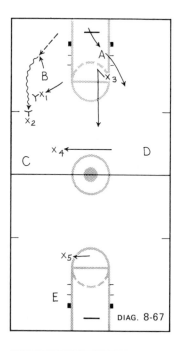

Diag. 8-67, TWO-TWO-ONE ZONE PRESS, FULL COURT, MOVEMENT AFTER THE INITIAL PASS

A, out-of-bounds, has passed in to B. B has started to dribble up the sideline. X_1 waits until B has moved by his position, then follows him. X_3 has taken an initial step towards the out-of-bounds area to prevent a quick return pass to A. When B starts his dribble, he moves up-court to become a floater. X_2 moves from his initial position to become the high trap, stopping the dribble by B. X_1 closes the trap from the rear. X_4 has adjusted across court, taking an intercepting angle on C to prevent a pass. X_5 has adjusted to overplay E.

Diag. 8-68, TWO-TWO-ONE ZONE PRESS, FULL COURT (Cont.)

B has passed the ball to C, near the mid-court. X_4 becomes the high trap, and X_2 continues along the sideline, trapping from the rear. X_1 moves into the middle to become a floater between the ball position and A. X_5 has moved to overplay E in the deep corner. X_3 maintains an intercepting angle on D all the way to the basket, if necessary. As the trap is closed on C, D moves deep into the corner position or deep into front court opposite E. X_3 must adjust back to the outer half of the free-throw circle to cut off a possible pass to D. On this movement, X_1 must adjust towards mid-court and be in position to overplay anyone that the ball is passed to in this area.

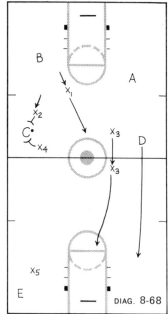

One-two-one-one half-court press. The basic responsibilities of the personnel and the names of the positions are the same as in the full-court one-two-one-one zone press, but the initial positions are different.

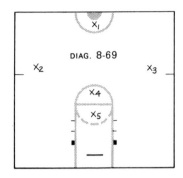

DIAG. 8-69

Diag. 8-69, ONE-TWO-ONE-ONE HALF-COURT ZONE PRESS, BASIC ALIGNMENT

X_1 is in the front court, in the center circle, ready to step forward to influence the direction of the ball. X_2 and X_3, the wing men, are back near the hash marks on their respective sides. X_4 is at the top of the outer half of the free-throw circle, and X_5 is in the lower half of the free-throw circle. The basic alignment is almost one-three-one. If the ball gets by the front line on the strong side, X_2 and X_4 double-team. If it is returned cross-court and towards the center line, X_1 and X_3 double-team. The play continues as in the one-two-one-one full-court zone press until a shot is taken, an offensive mistake is made, or the coach decides to change the defensive structure when the ball is passed back towards the mid-court line.

Diag. 8-70, ONE-TWO-ONE-ONE HALF-COURT ZONE PRESS

A, influenced by X_1 dribbles across mid-court line towards the defensive left. This causes X_4 to move, staying head-up on the dribbler. X_3 adjusts towards the center area. X_2 moves quickly and aggressively from his initial position as A is dribbling and traps him with X_1. (If the dribbler had been influenced to the right, X_3 would trap with X_1.) X_4 should now be in position to intercept if the ball is passed to C or E. X_3 is in position to intercept if the ball is passed to D or E. Since the most dangerous pass from A is into E in the pivot position, guarding the pivot area should be the first consideration of X_3 and X_4. X_5 is in position to guard the basket yet close enough to discourage a pass into E.

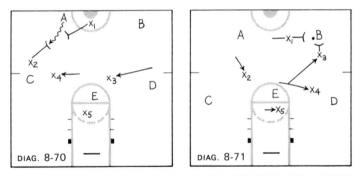

DIAG. 8-70   DIAG. 8-71

Diag. 8-71, ONE-TWO-ONE-ONE HALF COURT ZONE PRESS

A passes cross-court to B. The arrows show the movement of the defensive players during the pass. X_1 and X_3 become the trap men at the ball position. X_4 adjusts back across court to play intercepting angle on D. X_2 reacts back to shut off E in the pivot. Again, the position of X_2 and X_4 are determined by their primary responsibility of keeping the ball out of the pivot. X_5 has adjusted slightly to the ball side behind E.

Diag. 8-72, ONE-TWO-ONE-ONE HALF COURT ZONE PRESS

From Diag. 8-70, A has passed to C. X_4 has adjusted position to be the low trapper. X_2 follows the ball to become the high trapper. E has moved into a corner position. X_5 must move towards him, delaying slightly to check the positions of X_1 and X_3. X_1 has dropped from his trap position to cut off D in the high-pivot position. X_3 drops back under the basket, on the side away from the ball, to protect this area.

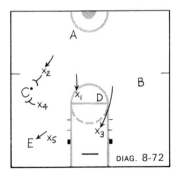

DIAG. 8-72

362

Diag. 8-73, ONE-TWO-ONE-ONE HALF-COURT ZONE PRESS

C has passed to E. X_2 follows the movement to become the high trapper. X_5 is the low trapper, closing the baseline. D, has moved from the high pivot to a low-pivot area, so X_4 moves back to protect this area. X_1 has adjusted towards the end of the foul line to be in position to intercept if the ball is passed back out. X_3 has moved over to hamper D's movements from the rear if the ball should get to him and to be in rebound position under the basket should a shot be taken.

DIAG. 8-73

Tactics Requiring Special Drilling. To perfect the zone press, constant drill is essential in four areas of the defense.

1. All men must drill on quick alignment. Players must get into position quickly to implement the zone press with any degree of success.

2. All men must drill on cutoff positions for long initial passes so that they know the danger areas and are prepared to adjust their positions at a call from the back man, X_5, or from X_4. Teams should practice this initially in almost standstill position, with the coach realigning the offensive team indiscriminately to put players in positions where they may be able to make an initial long pass from out-of-bounds, over the front line, into Zone 2.

3. The big man should practice two-on-one and three-on-one situations while moving back towards the basket so that he may improve his delaying tactics and sharpen his ability to block a shot or give the outside shot.

4. Players in the front line should practice realigning when an offensive player passes out-of-bounds along the baseline.

Coaching Decisions. The coach is responsible for fundamental game strategy. Following are some of the decisions he must make concerning zone-press defense.

1. Whether to pressure the inbounder. If the coach decides to pressure, he must then decide whether to use a small man to distract the inbounder or upset his poise or a big man to jump in front of him. In making this decision, the coach must remember that the ball may be passed or carried out-of-bounds behind the baseline after a basket or a foul shot. A big man will be slower in reacting.

2. Where to influence the direction of the pass-in. The decision depends primarily on the basic abilities of the defenders and secondarily, on offensive player alignment.

3. How to align the back two defenders if three men are up. Should they be side by side or one in front of the other? The offensive positioning generally determines this alignment.

4. Whether to apply pressure full-court, three-quarter court or half-court. The coach must consider his team's personnel, their speed, their quickness, and their reaction time.

General Tactics. Players must be alert to the following tactics, which are fundamental to a good zone press. (Many

363

of these points have been mentioned previously, but since they are so important, we feel they should be summarized for easy reference.)

1. The defensive alignment must be set up quickly. Never help an opponent get the ball after a basket. Leave it alone. Let them pick it up, as this gives you time to get into position. Since the back man is usually a big man, he may be slow getting to his position under the basket. If so, the 4 man, a guard, can take the back man's position until he gets back himself. It is better for the 4 man to leave his own position uncovered momentarily than to give up an easy basket.

2. Players must force the first pass from out-of-bounds to go into an area in front of the front line. This can be done (1) by playing close to offensive players behind the line and (2) by having one player drop off the front line.

3. Defenders must force the offense into positions advantageous to the defensive press. Accordingly, defenders should prevent long initial passes.

4. Defenders should never allow a pass over a zone (for instance, a pass from out-of-bounds to Zone 2 or from Zone 3 into Zone 1.)

5. Front-line players must execute quick reaction movements when the ball gets upcourt, sprinting to predesignated positions.

6. The back line, generally X_4 and X_5, should watch the passer-in. If he has a square stance with the ball in two hands, normally the pass will be a short one. If he turns so that he has one foot in front of the other and the side of his body is to the court, he normally will attempt to make a long pass. The movement of eyes and the tensing of an arm are also passing tip-offs.

7. When trapping initially with the zone press, it is a good idea to allow two or three less advantageous passes so that the opponent becomes complacent and dependent on this passing lane, then close it quickly.

8. Defenders should trap quickly, to make a dribble ineffective. Since an offensive player feels secure when he is dribbling, he may dribble when defensive men move towards him, wasting the movement. Cutting an alive player off may make him put the ball to the floor quickly for balance, again using his dribble up. Never let a man dribble out of the trap, because the result is a basket.

9. The man approaching a dribbler in the backcourt to close a double-team trap should advance cautiously, using the boxer's shuffle and good fundamental stance. He should force the lob pass, if possible, and he should never try for a steal.

10. Players must never run away from a potential double-up. If a defender is moving back and a teammate has stopped the ball, he should immediately double-team the ball.

11. A defender stopping the dribbler should try to make him turn his back to his teammates, then attack aggressively.

12. If a dribbler breaks the trap, the man in the high trap position should follow him to try and knock the ball away with a rear flicking movement. A dribbler shouldn't be allowed to penetrate the zone's perimeter over or through the front line.

13. All defenders must move with ball movement and player movement. Immediate anticipatory reaction is essential. Intelligent anticipation forces certain play situations. All players should know the possible passing lanes from pressure points and position for interceptions.

14. Cross-court or lob passes should be intercepted.

15. Defenders must beat the ball back to the basket when it is upcourt in front of the front line.

16. The wing opposite the ball should be in the best intercepting position possible when he is the floater. If the ball beats the front line he must sprint back under the basket on the weak side.

17. Defenders should keep the ball on the side and out of the middle. First, you can recognize passing lanes better. Second, there is no indecision on double-up techniques. Third, from the middle area the ball can be passed in several directions for an easy score.

18. Defenders should drop back to prevent a pass into high-, medium-, or low-pivot areas, allowing a cross-court pass or a sideline pass if necessary.

19. Defenders must sprint back on a long penetrating pass.

20. The farther the offensive man is from the ball the farther a defender can be from him.

21. Defenders must verbalize and apply continual pressure.

22. Defenders must make the ball move. The more passes the offense makes the greater the possibility of error, as no team has five outstanding ball handlers.

23. Protecting the under-basket area prevents lay-ups. The wing man opposite must be under the basket if the back man is pulled towards a corner.

Advantages. The following positive attributes of pressure defense should be considered by the coach in his determination of whether to use it with his team.

1. It makes the opponents increase their tempo.

2. It forces teams in poor condition to move more; therefore, they make more mistakes.

3. It is effective against slow teams, inexperienced teams, and teams with poor ball handlers.

4. It is effective late in the ball game when the defensive team is behind.

5. If it is known that a team has a good zone-press defense, opponents will spend a great deal of their practice time preparing to combat that defense, necessarily neglecting other drills.

6. It is an extremely good psychological weapon, even against good teams. Teams sometimes panic when faced with a good pressure defense. They lose their poise and take hurried shots.

7. It changes the opponent's offensive strategy, especially when the opponent is a slowdown-pattern type team.

8. It blends with aggressive offense, as it leads to many interceptions, steals, mistakes, and misplays which can be turned into quick, fast-break baskets.

9. It lends itself to easy baskets from the backcourt position.

10. It is excellent for team spirit.

11. It is a strategic defense.

Disadvantages. The negative characteristics of pressure defense are as follows:

1. It may give up easy baskets as it involves anticipation and taking chances, and it is widely spread.

2. All players on the team must be in excellent condition and have speed, together with mental and physical aggressiveness.

3. Players are susceptible to excessive fouling, especially on away-from-home courts and in sections where pressure defense is not played as a general rule.

4. It requires complete team coordination.

5. It is mentally demanding on the players, as there are no hard and fast rules for many situations.

6. It requires good reserve personnel to sustain pressure over a long period of the game.

7. It necessitates hard drill work.

8. The breakdown of one player kills a pressure defense.

9. Man-to-man pressure is weak against the exceptional dribbler.

10. Zone pressure is weak when the ball gets by the front line quickly.

11. A man is always free somewhere when two defenders double up.

12. Anticipating all eventualities is difficult.

13. It makes defensive rebounding difficult. Especially when opponents penetrate quickly.

14. It is tiring.

drilling Daily drilling of the selected team defensive alignments is essential. It is strongly recommended that the coach incorporate frequent half-court team drills using (1) man-to-man defense with double-ups, (2) aggressive two-three zone with double-ups, and (3) one-two-one-one zone pressure. Full court pressure defenses must also be practiced often so that the team will be prepared to use them at critical times, and so that team members can practice playing offense against them. Coaches should make up teams of specialists who can best get the ball when possession is of the essence.

part four
the game

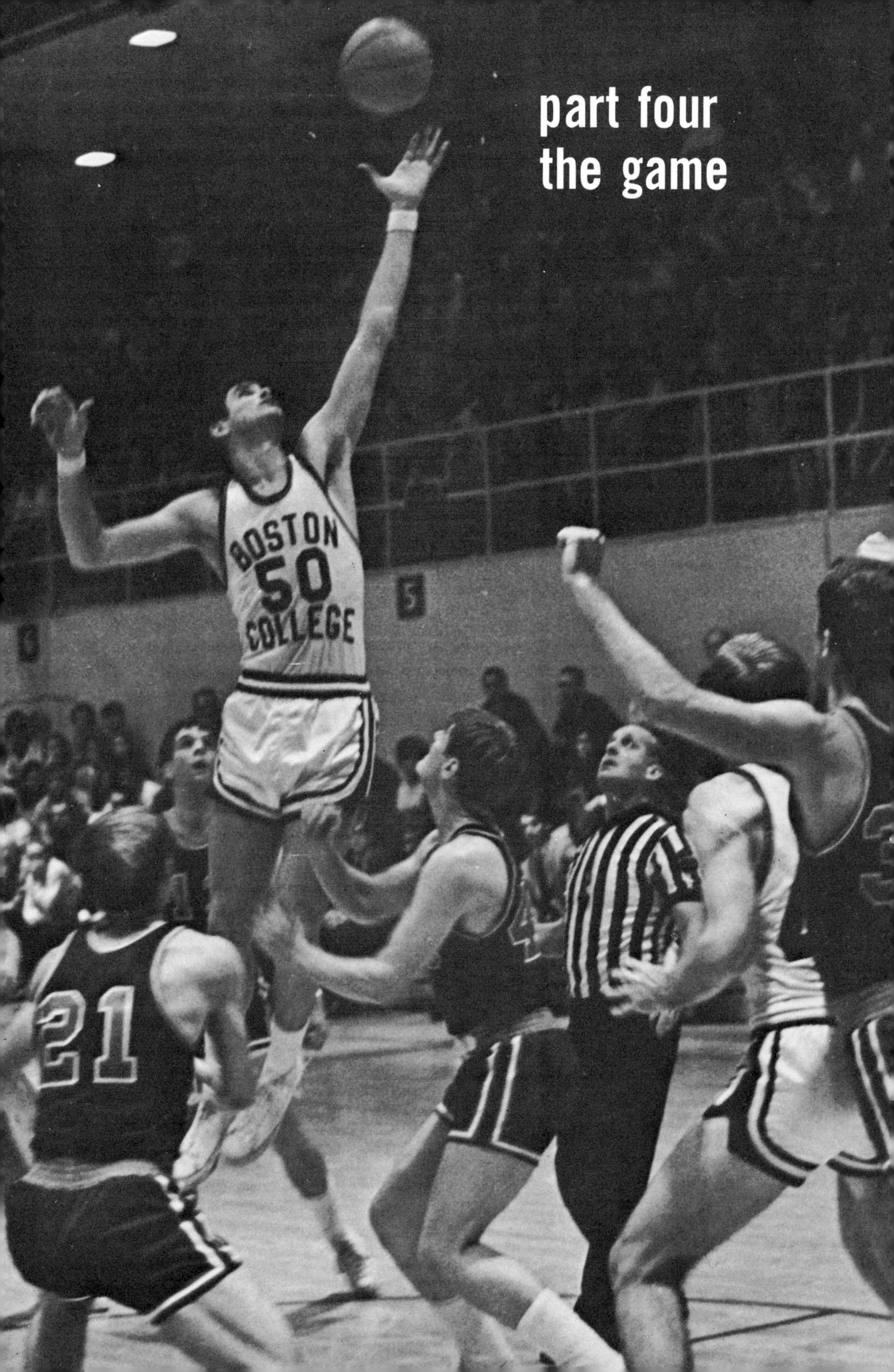

9

special game situations

A coach should prepare thoroughly for all special situations that occur in basketball—free-throw situations, jump balls, out-of-bounds plays (both under basket and sideline), end-of-game situations, deliberate fouling when ahead or be-hind, stalling, and last second situations. Preparedness for these situations is the essential difference between winning or losing in close games, as approximately eighty percent of all basketball games will go into the final three or four minutes undecided, with one team ahead by five points or less.

A coach should analyze and practice for all contingen-cies, even situations that may occur only once or twice during a season. If the coach waits to explain a situation until it occurs late in an actual game, the players will be in no condition—mentally, emotionally or physically—to carry out an unfamiliar pattern efficiently. Winning a close game by a successful late game strategem has an extremely high psychological impact on a squad or a team.

Drilling these late-game situations also affords a good change of pace during a routine preseason practice session.

free-throw situations

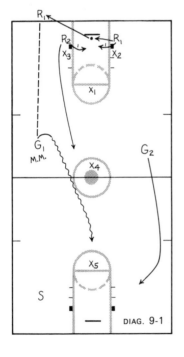

DIAG. 9-1

When the opponent is shooting a free throw, we normally set up in our fast-break foul-line play situation, with the two best rebounders at the inside position (See Diag. 9-1). They must step into the foul-lane with the outside foot (the foot nearest the man in the second lane position) to block their opponents from the ball in case of a missed foul shot. The best rebounder-passer should be on the right lane, and if the shot is successful, he should catch the ball before it hits the floor, immediately step out-of-bounds to his left, and pass in quickly to the middle man who is on the left side near mid-court. The two guards are in the mid-court area, near the side lines. The best shooting forward is in the deep corner on the side of the middle man.

When the ball is inbounded quickly after a successful free throw, it puts considerable pressure on the opponents. The free-throw shooter must be thinking of defense, as he has probably been alerted to defend against the foul-line fast-break play.

We work on the law of averages in planning this play. Game statistics over a period of years tell us that approximately seventy percent of all foul shots will be made and that over eighty percent of missed foul shots fall to the inside men. Therefore, less than five percent of all foul shots are normally retrieved by the shooting team. The fast-break foul line play forces a defensive compensation which further lessens retrieval by the shooting team.

If one of the inside men retrieves a missed free throw (See Diag. 9-2), he turns to the outside and passes to the middle man, if possible. If he must pass to the second guard instead, the designated middleman should immediately break to the middle of the court to get the ball. The object is to get upcourt quickly in a three-on-two or three-on-three fast-break situation to capitalize on the three-on-two advantage, to obtain a good shot with minimal team opposition (three-on-three), and to keep the biggest opponents from rebounding a missed shot.

When the opponent is free-throw shooting and the situation warrants it, other men should be put in defensive rebounding position. You might do this when a change in strategy is necessary near the end of a game to obtain or keep possession of the ball, or when a scouting report precludes using the fast break and recommends a controlled type or game.

In these situations, the best two rebounders will be inside, with the best rebounder on the same side as the opponent's best rebounder, as close to the restraining buffer zone as possible. He must box this man from the inside on a missed shot, stepping into the foul lane with the outside foot. The third and fourth best rebounders will be in the third lanes, as close to the restraining line as possible, crowding towards the best opposing rebounder to prevent his getting the ball. One of these rebounders must be designated to step in front of the shooter to prevent the ball from rebounding to him. The arms and hands of the rebounders must be up in ready position, primarily to try to get the rebound, but also to disconcert the foul shooter. The fifth man will be behind the shooter. After the shot, he will go to the corner on the side on which the ball is taken out-of-bounds, or the rebound is retrieved to receive an outlet pass.

When you are shooting a free-throw, you want your two best rebounders in the second lane positions. They must step in with the inside foot (the one nearest the baseline), attempting to end up at the side of the opponents who have inside position on them. They should not let themselves be boxed out behind their opponents. Against an exceptionally strong rebounder, the player in the second lane position can fake to a middle siding position by making a

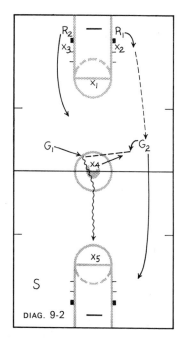

DIAG. 9-2

373

jabbing step into the lane with his *outside* foot as though trying to get side position, pushing off that foot when the opponent steps in to box him, and swinging around the strong rebounder to his baseline side.

If playing against an exceptionally strong rebounder when your team is shooting a free throw, you can sometimes station a teammate three feet behind the strong rebounder, towards the baseline. As soon as the ball hits the rim or the backboard, he slides on the baseline side to the inside to pinch the rebounder from the front. When shooting a foul shot, the shooter and the other men who are back can expect a tip out if the inside men are crowded but can get a slap at or a hand on the ball. If a tip-in is not possible, players may still control a tip of the ball back to the foul shooter or another man.

the jump ball

During a basketball game, there are many times when two opposing players must jump for team possession. Jump-ball situations can occur up to eight to twelve times in the course of a ball game. In college there are always at least two jump balls (at center court at the start of each half), and in high school there are always at least four (at the start of each quarter). They can occur at any one of three locations—at your own foul circle, at the center circle, or at the opponents' foul circle. Jump-ball plays should be simple and flexible. In all cases, players must be alert and aggressive to deflect the ball or get a hand on it. Players should be allowed to free-lance and to move before the ball is tossed to distract the opponents. Many times, players instinctively determine the right move. When control of the ball is doubtful, or when jumping for a defensive tap, the greatest defensive strength should be between the ball and the opponent's basket.

Organization for possession on jump balls is an important factor in coaching success. The team that has the taller jumper should usually gain control of the jump ball. Therefore, that team should, first, think about obtaining possession in this situation and, second, have an organized play in which a scoring opportunity is possible.

Predetermined plays are essential for control of the ball in the following situations:

1. A jump-ball situation in which one player or team is sure of control

2. A jump-ball situation in which the jumpers are even in height and jumping ability so that there is a good possibility of either team getting the ball

3. A situation in which teams want to take defensive measures when the opponents have the taller jumper

The jumper must be certain that he is ready for the toss

by the official, not stepping into jumping position until he has relaxed (if the game has been in progress) and can step in with good balance. Before getting into position, he must know where he is going to tap the ball. He should also look over both teams' alignments and recall pertinent scouting information regarding an opponent (such as the type of movement he has used in previous games in jump ball situations).

Normally, a jumper should tip the ball high and away from the defender guarding the best retriever, who should be in front of and facing the jumper to receive the tapped ball. If the opponents have massed in front of the jumper, he should tap the ball back to a position between two of his teammates who can screen their opponents away. Possession of the ball is thus assured, even though the massed opponents prevent a scoring play.

The jumper may also tap the ball to a predetermined spot on the floor. A designated teammate must know that the jumper is going to put the ball in this area and sprint into position to receive it. There are three different ways to signal where a ball is to be tipped to.

1. The jumper or captain can call a number or a name. Many coaches depict the jumping area as a clock, with the jumper facing 12. When a number is called, the jumper taps the ball to where that number would be on a clock, and a designated player moves towards that spot to take the ball.

2. The jumper or captain may use a hand signal.

3. The team may determine the tap by the position of the official who is tossing.

Four other basic jump-ball alignments are possible:

1. A box position

2. A diamond position

3. A Y position

4. A special formation in which one man moves far away from the jumping circle

The diagrams show the alignments from the center position, but they are the same at the foul-lane circles. In scouting diagrams, we use the first letters of our players' last names to indicate tapping positions on the court, and opponents' numbers. In the following diagrams, the players are A, B, C, D, E.

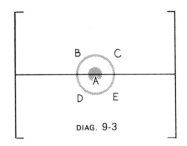

DIAG. 9-3

Diag. 9-3, JUMP-BALL BOX ALIGNMENT
A is jumping and B, C, D and E are in a box alignment.

375

Diag. 9-4, JUMP-BALL DIAMOND ALIGNMENT

A is jumping and B, C, D, and E are in a diamond around the jumper.

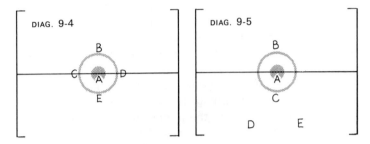

DIAG. 9-4

DIAG. 9-5

Diag. 9-5, JUMP-BALL, Y ALIGNMENT

B is facing the jumper, A. C is directly behind A, and D and E are in a defensive position. This is the most common defensive jump ball alignment. It is an excellent alignment for tipping the ball back to obtain possession when the opponents are crowding B, the best retriever.

Diag. 9-6, JUMP-BALL, INVERTED Y ALIGNMENT

This alignment is used when defensive tap is called or possession at the center circle is doubtful. A is the jumper, and B is facing him. C and D take positions around the circle, forming a triangle with E, who is back as a safety man. In a doubtful tap situation, A should try to tap back so that C and D can hold men on their outside near the mid-court line and the sideline and the tap can go between them to E. From this inverted Y formation it is possible to rotate clockwise or counterclockwise in a defensive jump-ball situation with B, C, and D rotating and E back as the safety man.

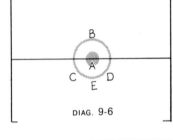

DIAG. 9-6

Diag. 9-7, JUMP-BALL, SPECIAL ALIGNMENT

B is in front of the jumper, A. D and E are a little to the rear and to the side, and C, the best shooter, is deep in the corner. Since an opponent will have to defend against C in this position, there will be one less opponent in the tapping area, giving a better chance of possession.

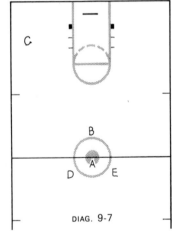

DIAG. 9-7

After positioning themselves in their pre-designated basic positions, the players may move in a preplanned team pattern to help obtain possession and to confuse the opponents. Movement of players not on the circle can begin on a signal from a teammate; movement of players on the circle starts after the official tosses the ball. There are three types of movement—clockwise, counterclockwise and knifing.

Diag. 9-8, CLOCKWISE AND COUNTERCLOCKWISE ROTATION FROM A BOX FORMATION

A is the jumper, and B, C, D, and E are in a box formation. The movement is depicted by the arrows. The same movement can be obtained from the diamond formation.

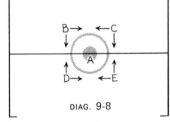

DIAG. 9-8

Diag. 9-9, JUMP-BALL KNIFING FROM A BOX FORMATION

D is knifing hard to his right towards X_1. E is knifing hard towards X_2. The players make this knifing movement after the official has tossed the ball to try to prevent X_1 or X_2 from receiving the tapped ball.

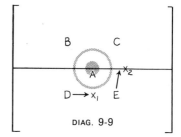

DIAG. 9-9

Jump-ball situations involve five men in a cohesive team action; synchronized team movement is imperative. The coach must cover jump-balls completely in the preseason practice sessions, explaining all the possiblities and the alternatives. Since all members of the team at one time or another can be involved in a jump ball situation, each must be given the opportunity to jump several times in practice at all three jumping areas. There can be as many as twenty players on the court divided into two groups of five offensive and five defensive players with a coach for each group. One group can jump at the center circle while the other group is at a free-throw circle. Players must also practice being a non-jumper in a jump-ball stituation. Each player must understand all positions perfectly and be able to act unhesitatingly.

The coach should explain that many officials have tossing idiosyncrasies; no two toss the ball exactly the same way. Some do not toss the ball high enough; others toss too high. Still others do not toss the ball straight; they toss it towards one player. Some officials toss it closer to themselves or far away from themselves.

Players should be aware of the alternatives that they have in jumping for a defensive tap. A jumping player can crowd in closer to get his opponent off balance. When he is jumping straight up directly under the ball, with his hands towards the wrist of the opposing jumper, he may touch the wrist accidentally, possibly deflecting the ball from its intended path so that his teammates may obtain possession. In a defensive situation, the four nonjumpers should align themselves behind their opponents, pressuring them on one side and then going quickly to the other, so that the opposing jumper does not know on which side they are going to be and becomes confused. Normally, a coach will tell a jumping player not to back tap at his defensive end but to try to go forward. In a defensive or a doubtful jump, an intelligent team will take advantage of their opponents' reluctance to tap towards their own basket.

The diamond formation is best at each jumping circle under normal conditions, with the best jumper jumping at the beginning of each half (in high school, the beginning of each quarter) and the best retriever in the B position facing the jumper. The ball should always be tapped to B. If it is tapped high, B can go up high and get the ball, negating the possibility of the opponent's knifing in to stop the catch.

377

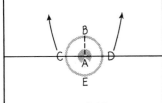

DIAG. 9-10

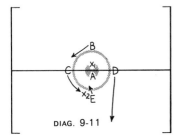

DIAG. 9-11

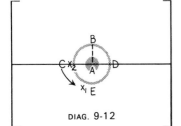

DIAG. 9-12

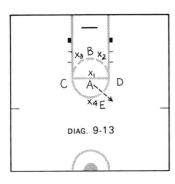

DIAG. 9-13

If the opponents were putting extreme pressure on B, E would keep an opponent to one side and A would tap back between teammates. If a defender were to the left of E, A would tap back between D and E.

Normally a team tries to score a quick basket when it has sure control of the tap.

Diag. 9-10, CENTER TAP SURE

A taps the ball forward to B. When B has the ball, C and D, the two best shooters, break in straight lanes to the basket, receiving a pass for a shot if free. Usually when a team is sure of the tap, the opponents are in an inverted **Y** formation, attempting to put pressure on B. If opponents fall off B, he may pivot and dribble towards the basket looking for a shot or an open man.

Diag. 9-11, CENTER TAP, DEFENSIVE

Normally, the opponents tap forward in this situation. Therefore, assume they will tap forward and leave the back position open, unless the scouting report indicates that they will tap backwards. Two forwards, C and E, and a guard, B, will pinch both opposing forwards, using the knifing technique. The second guard, D, will fall back on defense. If you have preknowledge of the opponents' tap ball play when they are sure of the tap, attempt to steal, using aggressive tactics.

Diag. 9-12, CENTER TAP, DOUBTFUL

C, the strongest wing, plays in back of an opposing side man, X_2. E is in a similar position behind X_1 to confuse him. C, on the same side as the tapper's strong hand, knifes towards X_1, their strongest opposing retriever. (When the tapper is left handed, C will be on his left hand.) D knifes towards a near opponent, attempting to obtain the ball. Try to tap to B.

Sure tap—our basket. Tap back between guards for certain possession.

Diag. 9-13, YOUR BASKET TAP, SURE

When playing for offensive possession without using a set play, assume a diamond position. Tip where two of your men do not have an opponent between them. In this diagram D and E are together. Therefore, tap into their area. B, the best retriever, is at the front of the circle facing the jumper. Since the opposition must double-team B, they must leave an opening somewhere.

378

Diag. 9-14, YOUR BASKET TAP, SURE

A attempts to tap to B. If there is no extreme pressure on B, it is possible for C, the best shooter of C, D, and E, to fake towards the basket to move a defender away and buttonhook back to receive a pass from B for a quick jump shot. However, if B can move to the basket himself without pressure, he should go.

A word of caution on a play of this type. Try to predetermine if the opposition is permitting a tap to B so that they can tie the ball up by jamming B or double- or triple-teaming him.

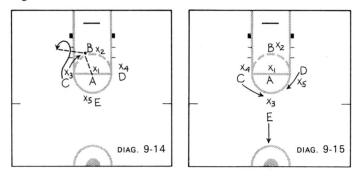

DIAG. 9-14   DIAG. 9-15

Diag. 9-15, YOUR BASKET TAP, DEFENSIVE

At your own basket, when one of your small players is jumping against a taller player, a defensive tap is necessary. First, the team should confidently assume a diamond position. Second, the jumper should attempt to legally impede the tap of the opponent, who will always tap forward at this end. If he can, he should tap to the side with two teammates in position to retrieve the tap. The wings, C and D, should knife aggressively towards X_3, the opponent's best retriever. E, a guard, should go back quickly on defense. If you have preknowledge of the type of play the opponents attempt to use, you can try for a steal with B, your front man.

Diag. 9-16, YOUR BASKET TAP, DOUBTFUL

The opponents must double-team B, your big man. Therefore, try to tap to an open spot or between two of your men who have position on the opponents. Possession is the important factor in this type of tap.

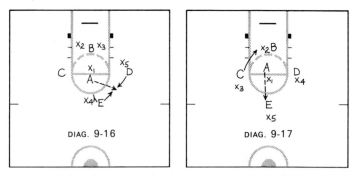

DIAG. 9-16   DIAG. 9-17

Diag. 9-17, OPPONENTS' BASKET TAP, SURE

E, the best retriever, is facing the jumper. The jumper should try to tap forward to E, making sure that the opponents don't get the ball for an easy basket. Be defense conscious at this end, because a misplaced tap, stray tap, or a surprise retrieve by an opponent may put him in good shooting position.

Diag. 9-18, OPPONENTS' BASKET TAP, DEFENSIVE

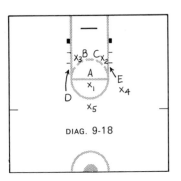

DIAG. 9-18

You don't want to give up the back tap uncontested, but if the opponents do get the tap, you want it to go back. The two best non-jumping retrievers, B and C, should take inside positions in the foul lane, forcing the opponents, X_3 and X_2, to take outside positions. B and C would pinch up front if one opponent gained a center-lane position. You want center-lane positions primarily to force the tap away from the basket so that even if the opponents do gain possession, they do not get an easy shot. Players should be extremely alert and aggressive, trying to deflect the ball so that they might gain possession in a scramble.

Diag. 9-19, OPPONENTS' BASKET TAP, DEFENSIVE

B and C have inside position on X_2 and X_3. When your players are in this position, with D and E pinching on X_2 and X_3, the opponents will normally back tap. Therefore, D and E must fake towards X_2 and X_3 to make the opponent back tap. As soon as the official has tossed the ball up, D and E should knife inside X_4 and X_5 in order to get the ball or deflect it.

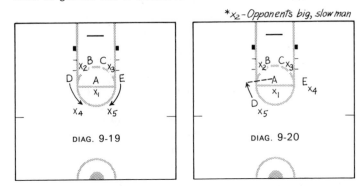

DIAG. 9-19   DIAG. 9-20

Diag. 9-20, OPPONENTS' BASKET TAP, DOUBTFUL

This is perhaps the toughest of all jump-ball situations, because a stray back tap could be turned into an easy score by the opponents. B and C, your biggest non-jumpers and best retrievers, have to be in a defensive, inside position to defend the basket in case the opponents control the tap. If your jumper can control the tap, he should tap forward to the side of X_2, the opponents' big, slow man, so that you can obtain possession of the ball.

Many jump-ball plays from any alignment may be used, if they are well designed and contain defensive safety factors, at any of the three jump-ball areas.

offensive out-of-bounds plays

All intelligent, well-coached teams should have a series of reliable out-of-bounds plays from different areas of the court so that offensive players may execute them quickly and without hesitation. The number of different out-of-bounds plays given to a team should be as few as possible, and they should be simple to learn and to execute. Every play must start from the same basic position to be effective. Each must have perfect timing, and coaches must practice constantly to attain this timing. All out-of-bounds plays must have a safety outlet and at least one player going back on defense.

The first objective in an out-of-bounds play is possession; the second is getting the ball to the best shooter with one pass for a high percentage shot. Naturally, the coach should select plays that will take advantage of the available personnel. Working again on the margin of error theory, a designated player (normally the best passer) should always inbound the ball, and one or two big men should be in position near the basket in case a missed shot presents a rebounding situation. It is imperative that the players on the court set up in position as quickly as possible, because from the time the official hands the ball to the inbounder they have only five seconds in which to get the ball in play.

All out-of-bounds plays must include safety factors—one man must move into a defensive position while another deploys as an outlet man so that the team can maintain possession even if the good shooting opportunity does not appear. Another good tactic when a shooting opportunity does not appear is to return a pass to the inbounder, if his defender is ignoring him to double-team or assist a teammate. The designated inbounder should call the play before taking the ball from the official, then take his time in getting to the spot where the ball is to be inbounded so that his teammates can get into their predetermined positions to execute the play.

The inbounder should be back far enough from the sidelines so that his arms do not extend over the plane of the boundary line. This position has a twofold purpose. First, it protects him from the defensive player guarding him, since that player cannot break the plane of the boundary line without committing a violation. Second, it gives the inbounder psychological security, as he does not feel defensive pressure being exerted on him.

The inbounder should initiate the play either by a verbal signal, by slapping the ball, or by raising the ball over his head.

The player inbounding the ball should never inbound from directly under the basket and backboard (officials will not normally give the ball to a player in this position). He should stand to either side of the foul lane so that the backboard will not interfere with the pass-in.

If the offensive players use the basic alignments several times, they may lull the opponents into expecting those alignments. Then one of the offensive players may deviate his movements to get a quick basket. There are times also when one of the offensive players feels that he can fake and cut by his man for an easy basket. If a player plans to fake, he should inform his teammates at a time-out so that the play can be carried out. Players must be absolutely certain about this faking maneuver before they try it.

Many times teams do not get good results from their out-of-bounds plays because they have not spent enough time practicing them or because the play is not basically sound. Therefore, all players must practice every out-of-bounds play from every position so that they know the responsibilities of each spot. In preseason practice the coach should designate at least three inbounding players. If the first designated player is on the court, he will always inbound the ball for all out-of-bounds plays. If he is not on the court, the second designated player will inbound the ball. If neither the first nor the second man is on the court, the third man will inbound.

Several types of basic out-of-bounds plays may be used under the basket or at the side-court areas from the hash marks in. All these plays should be practiced from both the left and right sides of the court. The basic out-of-bounds plays close to the basket include screen and roll plays, cuts off a post, a box formation, one-on-one plays, a continuity play, and a double screen away from the pass-in area. Options in these plays depend on the positioning of the defensive players. Coaches should devise out-of-bounds plays that best suit their player's abilities.

Diagrams 9-21 through 9-28 describe the out-of-bounds plays that the authors have used successfully over a period of years. On these plays, we work within our margin-of-error theory by cutting down the number of times the ball must be handled. The best shooter takes the shot, the big men stay in the best position to rebound, and men move into defensive position in case the pass is deflected or the shot is missed and the opponents rebound. Exact timing is extremely important for these plays. Normally, the best passer will inbound the ball in these plays, identifying the play by calling the number or by signalling with his fingers. He must call the play before accepting the ball from the official so that his teammates have time to get into position.

DIAG. 9-21

Diag. 9-21, OUT-OF-BOUNDS PLAY, OUR SERIES, UNDER, PLAY ONE

A is the inbounder. B, C, and D set up as close to each other as they can in approximately the second and third foul lanes on the same side as the ball. E is approximately at the foul line extended and closer to the sideline (ball-side) than B, C, and D. When A slaps the ball to initiate the play, E cuts off D to decoy his defender away from the area of the play. D the best shooter, then cuts quickly to the baseline ball-side, getting an inbound pass from A (1) for a short jump shot. As D initiates his movement, C steps back to administer a slight brush block to momentarily delay D's defender.

If anyone tries to get between B and C, B immediately goes to the under-basket area. Many times E can cut off D to either side and be open for the shot (2).

An option of this play is to have D, the designated shooter, tap C, a good shooter. As E cuts off D, C pops out right to get the quick pass in from A for the shot.

A second option is for E to cut to the corner on the same side as the ball to receive a pass. A will then cut as close to B, C, and D as he can, coming up the foul lane. He will receive a quick pass back from E and take a shot.

The movement of the defensive players will determine the play. In using any play we are working within our margin-of-error theory, because the best passer makes a single pass that results in a good jump shot for one of the best shooters.

Diag. 9-22, OUT-OF-BOUNDS PLAY, OUR SERIES, UNDER, PLAY TWO

A, the best passer, inbounds the ball. B, C, D and E line up shoulder to shoulder in the lane, approximately even with the second free throw lanes, as close together as possible and facing the basket. As the play is initiated, E breaks quickly out to the ball-side corner to receive a pass-in from A. As soon as E receives the ball, B pops out, getting a pass from E for a short jump shot. C, leaning left, administers a slight brush block to impede the progress of B's defender. The option on this play is for B to tap C lightly on his buttocks as they line up to signal him to pop out. B and D will then pinch together to prevent C's defender from getting between the block. E again moves quickly to the side of the ball, receives a pass-in from A, and passes to C for a quick shot.

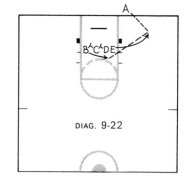

DIAG. 9-22

Three play from out-of-bounds. Only pass receiver's legs visible as he cuts. Man at right about to step behind screen for pass and shot.

Diag. 9-23, OUT-OF-BOUNDS PLAY, OUR SERIES, UNDER, PLAY THREE

The alignment is the same as for Play Two. When A slaps the ball to initiate the play, B cuts behind C, D, and E to get the pass. C steps behind D and E as B receives the pass, ready for a pass from B and a quick short jump shot.

DIAG. 9-23

383

The option on this play is for B to pass to D popping back for the shot. (C will tap D to let him know he is expected to step back to receive B's pass.)

Diag. 9-24, OUT-OF-BOUNDS PLAY, OUR SERIES, UNDER, PLAY FOUR

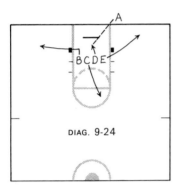

DIAG. 9-24

This is a one-on-one situation for the tall player, D, if his defender is shorter or less agile than he is. The alignment is the same as in Plays Two and Three. When A slaps the ball, E cuts quickly to the corner on the same side as the ball. B will fake and cut opposite, and C will drop back as though he is going to receive the ball as in Play Two. This clears the whole foul-lane area, except for D, who is near the basket with his defender. If the defender is face guarding, A should lob the ball to D, who will jump, catch the ball in the air, and shoot in the same motion. This dummy play is usually most effective against a smaller player. D could out-maneuver a less agile defender by faking and then going opposite or by faking away from the ball and then coming back to it.

Diag. 9-25, OUT-OF-BOUNDS PLAY, OUR SERIES, UNDER, PLAY FIVE

DIAG. 9-25

This is a tight box formation that varies somewhat from the other plays, but all players are still in or near the foul lane. It is a pick-and-roll play. A is the designated inbounder. B and C, the two biggest men on the court, have their inside feet on the buffer zone at the foul lane. D and E are at the foul line extended, just outside the foul lane. At the signal, E moves across the foul lane to set a screen for D, and C moves across the lane to set a rear screen for B. D cuts off E's screen and towards the corner on the side from which the ball is being inbounded. E moves back in defensive position, and D becomes a safety outlet. B cuts off C's screen to the outside into the foul-lane area. C executes a screen and roll maneuver. A has the option of passing either to B, if no switch is made, or to C, if a switch is made putting C inside on the pick-and-roll maneuver.

Diag. 9-26, OUT-OF-BOUNDS PLAY, OUR SERIES, UNDER, PLAY ONE, DIAMOND

DIAG. 9-26

Many times teams line up in different defensive formations from the ones expected. Any time a defender is outside our alignment (between one of our players and the side line in Play One alignment) we immediately call, "Diamond." In this diagram, A is guarded by X_1, B is guarded by X_2, and C is guarded by X_3, who is between C and the sideline. D is guarded by X_4, and E is guarded by X_5. As soon as the inbounder calls "Diamond" and slaps the ball, the players move as follows: B moves to the corner on the same side as the ball taking X_2 with him. E holds position. D moves back towards the foul line, taking X_4 with him. C now has an open move to the basket with X_3 on his back, and he can receive a pass-in from A for an easy shot.

384

Diag. 9-27, OUT-OF-BOUNDS PLAY; OUR SERIES; UNDER; PLAYS TWO, THREE, AND FOUR; DIAMOND

A is guarded out-of-bounds by X_1. B is guarded by X_5, C by X_4, and E by X_2, D is guarded by X_3, who is behind D. As soon as A calls "Diamond" and slaps the ball, the players move as follows: E moves to the side on which the ball is to be inbounded, taking X_2 with him. B moves to the opposite corner, taking X_5 with him. C moves to an underneath position opposite the ball. If X_4 stays to guard D, C will be open. If X_4 goes with C, D steps directly towards the basket with X_3 on his back, receives an easy pass, and shoots.

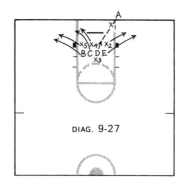

DIAG. 9-27

Diag. 9-28, OUT-OF-BOUNDS PLAY, OUR SERIES, SIDE

B, C, D, and E line up along the foul line. A, the best passer, inbounds the ball. On A's signal, B, the best shooter, moves behind C, D and E's screen to receive the pass (1). If B's defender stays behind C, D and E, B takes a high percentage shot from the outer half of the free-throw circle. If B's defender comes with him to prevent the shot, B passes back to A (2) for a drive-in basket. (To receive the pass, A starts towards the ball, then reverses to the open corner on the side from which he inbounded the ball.)

DIAG. 9-28

Diag. 9-29, OUT-OF-BOUNDS PLAY, OUR SERIES, SIDE, DIAMOND

Because X_3 is behind D to negate B's movement to the ball, A calls "Diamond." On the initiation of the play, E cuts as quickly as possible to the corner, taking X_2 with him. B steps back as he normally would if he were going to get the ball, taking X_5 with him, and C moves down the opposite lane, taking X_4 with him. D then moves down the near foul lane towards the basket and receives a lead pass from A. D's left hand should be up as a target for A. If X_4 attempts to stay with D, he will leave C alone on the opposite side.

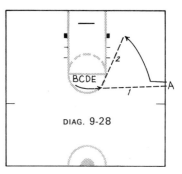

DIAG. 9-29

Many teams use a zone defense to protect against out-of-bounds plays.

Diag. 9-30, OUT-OF-BOUNDS PLAY, UNDER, AGAINST A TWO-THREE ZONE DEFENSE

A, the best passer, takes the ball out. The other players assume their Play Two alignment across the foul lane just in front of the broken line free-throw circle, with E, the best shooter, on the same side as the ball. E moves quickly to a position ball-side, 16 feet from the basket along the baseline, perhaps taking X_3 with him. If X_3 does not cover E, E is in position to receive the pass and take the shot immediately. D and B are the big men. D steps into the right side of the lane in front of the ball, and B moves into the opposite lane position. Their movement puts extreme pressure on X_2, so he will need help from X_4. C, the second best shooter, cuts to the right, in line with the ball. If X_3 goes with E and X_4's attention is diverted by D, C is in excellent position to take a short, high-percentage jump shot. B's position inside X_1, underneath on the weak side, negates X_1's defensive position. E circles back in outlet position if the shot does not show for him immediately. B and D must be cautioned

DIAG. 9-30

that they cannot remain in the three-second area if the safety outlet pass is made to E.

DIAG. 9-31

Diag. 9-31, OUT-OF-BOUNDS PLAY, UNDER, AGAINST A ONE-THREE-ONE ZONE DEFENSE

E, the best shooter, breaks to the corner. If X_3 does not go with him, A passes to E for a quick jump shot from as close to the basket as possible. D steps straight in towards the ball, C steps straight towards the basket, and B, the second best shooter, cuts behind C and D. C and D's movement will freeze X_2 and X_4 and B should be in front of X_5. If X_3 is guarding E, A may pass to B. If E cannot receive the pass-in, he should circle back to become a deep safety outlet in case the ball cannot be passed to a teammate in good shooting position.

defense against out-of-bounds plays

When defending out-of-bounds plays under the basket, the man guarding the inbounder should position himself between that man and the basket, aggressively preventing him from passing in towards the basket. He should force the ball away from the basket or towards the corners, where the shots are more difficult to make. Other defenders should protect the underneath area primarily but remain alert for screening maneuvers that will set up a good outside shooter for a high-percentage shot. A man guarding a weaker shooter should step back into the middle of the foul-lane area in a man-to-man defense so that he can help out in double-teaming or in preventing a pass from coming into the close-in area, forcing the ball to be passed back out to the weak shooter he has left.

If scouting shows that the opponents have one man that they can one-on-one with or have a very good series of pick-and-roll plays, we may go to a zone defense to prevent those plays, giving up the outside shot rather than giving easy inside shooting position.

When defending against an out-of-bounds play on either sideline in front court, players must force the pass to go towards the mid-court line; therefore, the man guarding the opponent inbounding the ball should be between his man and the basket. He should not allow passes into the inside penetrating area but rather should make the ball go back out towards mid-court. Players should maintain aggressive pressure on their men from the basket side, retreating if screens are set to prevent inside shots.

out-of-bounds plays from the backcourt

A team should not work an out-of-bounds play from the backcourt unless it was a last shot attempt and a time-out could not be taken. Normally, if you are working from deep in the backcourt or from the far end line it is best to attempt to get the ball in front court quickly, using only one pass, and call a time-out. Then you may pass the ball into scoring

386

position using a front-court sideline play rather than one from the deep backcourt or far baseline. This procedure takes only a second or two. However, it must be practiced. If a play from the backcourt is necesary, it can be executed from two positions—either sideline or the far end line.

There are two important aspects to consider when determining whether to use a backcourt to basket play. The first factor is the type of defense the opponent is using, and the second is the length of time left to play. If the opponents are behind, they must press. If the score is tied or the opponents are ahead, they will not play tightly in the backcourt. If the ball is deep in the backcourt with no time-outs remaining (less than five seconds left), a back-court to basket play should be used. Remember, it is possible to call a time-out to stop the clock when the ball goes through either basket after a floor shot. However, it is always best to work from your basic set pattern, as normally the defense will be alert for a backcourt-to-basket play in a late game situation.

If the ball is at a sideline position closer to front court, and time is a factor, a team should go to its strength. It should go to its practiced pattern first, to its height second, and to its best shooter third. Normally, when a team goes to its pattern in this last-shot situation, the players should play to the defensive weakness of the other team, trying to get the best shooter in position to get a shot at the weak defensive position. They also may go to an opponent with four fouls, as despite the shortness of time remaining, he is psychologically aware that he is in foul trouble.

Diag. 9-32, LAST-SHOT PLAY, MID-COURT SIDELINE

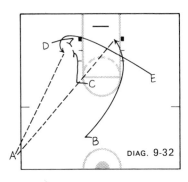

Basically, this play presents itself from our single stack pattern. A, the best passer, inbounds the ball. D is in the corner on the same side as the ball, and C is on the same side in the outer half of the free-throw circle. B, the fastest player, fakes to the ball and cuts in a direct line to the basket, trying to outrun his opponent. D fakes to the basket and sets a screen. C steps to the ball and then sets a low double screen with D. E, the best jump shooter, starts as B fakes, cutting to the basket and around the double screen. B must time his movement so that he is cutting momentarily after E has made his initial movement. If B can outrun his man to the basket, A should pass directly to B for the shot. We cannot start from the original stack positions in this situation as it would place defensive men too close to the basket initially for B to cut clear. The other option is for E to receive a pass as he cuts behind the double screen, putting him in position to take the last shot in the ball game.

Diag. 9-33, LAST-SHOT PLAY, FAR END LINE

After the opponents score a basket, the pass-in may be made from anywhere along the end line, and a pass may be made out-of-bounds along the end line. B, C, D, and E line up opposite where A has the ball. B fakes to the ball and steps out-of-bounds. C and D

387

cut towards the ball, and E fakes towards the ball, then cuts behind C and D to the mid-court area in the backcourt on the same side as A. If no time-out is left, A passes along the end line to B. A, the fastest player, cuts diagonally downcourt to receive a front-court pass from B. The clock will not start until the ball touches A's hand. If C, D, and E can decoy their defenders, A may be able to outrun his man to the far end of the court and get the last-second shot. However, if a time-out is remaining, we would prefer to have A pass to E at the mid-court area so that we may call time-out, then use either last-second play outlined in Diag. 9-32 and Diag. 9-34.

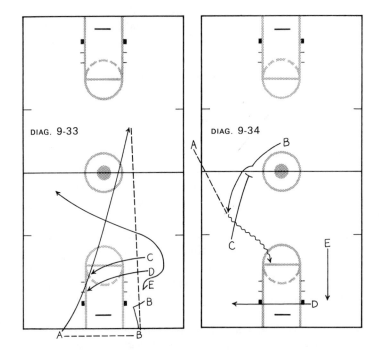

DIAG. 9-33

DIAG. 9-34

Diag. 9-34, LAST SHOT PLAY, SIDELINE, BACKCOURT

If the ball is on the sidelines in the backcourt with three to five seconds remaining, you may try to set up a fast-break, a three-on-two situation, or a three-on-three situation at the offensive end. The best ball handler should have the ball so that he can get it to the good shooters. A, the second best passer, has the ball out-of-bounds on the sideline. D is a big man who is underneath. B, the best ball handler and designated middle man, is in backcourt as though to receive a pass-in there. Normally he will be closely guarded, as will C, a big forward near the ball. C moves up as though to receive a pass but sets a screen at about the mid-court line for B. B cuts off this screen to either side, but preferably between the sideline and the screen. A bigger, less agile opponent should switch to B. As soon as B receives the ball, he dribbles into the outer half of the free-throw circle, attempting to set up a three-on-three situation and looking for a shot from E, the best shooter. Many times, E's man will be so intent on guarding him that B can drive all the way to the basket. Even if this is a three-on-three situation, there is time for a pass and a screen to get a good shot off.

388

When defending out-of-bounds plays from the backcourt or at the far end line with the score tied or down a point or two in last-second situations, players should never allow an easy shot. They must keep pressure on the ball and be extremely aggressive, as officials are reluctant to make the foul call in this situation. They should try to make the passer-in make a short pass in the deep backcourt where they can attack the ball and double-team. A long pass to an open man precludes double-teaming and may lead to an easy basket.

The farthest man back should be cautioned that he must not let himself be decoyed away from the basket he is defending, because he must defend against any opponent cutting to the basket.

If the opponents are more than two points behind, players should not foul, which would allow a three-point play. Therefore, they should take good defensive position without getting too close to their men.

Coaches should practice all last-second situations during preseason practice and intermittently during the regular season so that all players on the team know their responsibilities and are acutely aware of the game situation.

The outcome of most close games that go into the late stages with less than five points separating the teams is determined by the ability of one team to control play as time is running out. Offensively, players can control the play by controlling the ball, using time-consuming tactics (such as a slowdown or a freeze) to protect the lead, and remaining alert for the unopposed high-percentage basket. Defensively, players may use a forcing, aggressive, pressure type defense to harass, confuse, and upset the opponent into making mistakes when in possession of the ball.

Late in the game when the situation is tense and the men have played between thirty-five and thirty-eight minutes of extremely difficult basketball, the players will be physically, mentally, and emotionally weary. The team that is in the best physical and mental condition will have a great advantage in this late-game situation.

tactics when a team is ahead

When a team is ahead in the latter stages of a close basketball game, stalling tactics force opponents to come to the ball in an attempt to intercept or steal it, thus opening under-basket areas and affording good offensive opportunities for the team that is ahead. The defensive team is foul prone late in the game, and the teams are usually in a one-on-one foul-shooting situation. A team must never give up

389

the ball except after a sure shot or a foul by the opponent. Giving up the ball should mean you scored two points.

As the team that is behind must defend aggressively, thereby becoming mistake prone, reverse or back-door movements are excellent tactics to use. Defenders, when behind, are trying to steal the ball. As soon as a defender guarding an offensive player makes any movement in the direction of the ball, that player should immediately cut directly to the basket. The poised, prepared team can do well against this type of desperation pressure.

The best ball handlers must be in the game when a slow-down or complete freezing tactics are being used, and the stalling team must move continuously to present a constant offensive threat. The movement and positioning of players and the decoying of opponents must be adjusted constantly to prevent opponents from doubling up.

The most difficult thing for a coach to determine is exactly when his team should go into a stall. A team should go into a stall when there is not enough time left for the opponents to gain momentum to win the ball game. This point varies, depending on the type of opponent.

The team that is ahead when stalling tactics are put into effect must be prepared for pressure. This pressure may be full court, three-quarter court or half court, and it may be man-to-man or zone.

The team that is ahead must be constantly aware of several important factors. After an opponent's score, the ball may be inbounded from any point along the end line. Therefore, players must practice passing the ball along the end line to a teammate who is also out-of-bounds to relieve pressure at the ball point or to take advantage of an open man who may be upcourt on the side opposite the ball.

When a team is ahead in a stalling type of a game, the best passers and ball handlers should be in the game. Normally, they or the best dribblers should always have control of the ball.

The players must prevent opponents from double-teaming. Therefore, when a team is ahead and is stalling, teammates must never cross. When a pass is made, the passer should cut away from the man he has passed to. The players who are not involved in the ball-handling, dribbling, or passing should move constantly to decoy their defenders away from the area of the ball, attracting their complete attention so that they cannot double-team the ball.

Player movements must be definite, sharp, and quick. Short, safe passes must be used; never lob passes or soft passes. A bounce pass is excellent as a lead pass on a reverse. It is better to have a held ball situation than to make a bad or uncertain pass.

The receiver of a pass must meet the ball, never making any movements which would obscure his intent and confuse the passer. The passer must see both the man he is passing to and his defender. Players must keep the ball out of the corners and the sides of the court, especially near the hash marks or mid-court line, as double-teaming usually occurs in these areas. Players on offense should keep wide, spreading defenders, keeping them busy.

All offenses used in late game situations when ahead must be a constant threat, relying on extremely high-percentage shots that are good in-close shots. (Only take unopposed lay-ups if the coach desires.)

A player must dribble under control in late game stall situations, and he should expect to meet pressure. If he is forced to pivot during his dribble, he should expect double-teaming tactics. Therefore, he should not get himself into a position where double-teaming tactics can be costly. If a player is double-teamed while dribbling, he should know that the safety outlet is generally positioned in the direction from which the double-team pressure was applied.

When a defender leaves his man near the basket to go double-team the ball, it may be impossible or impractical for the man with the ball to pass to the teammate who has been left undefended in the basket area. Therefore, the open teammate must vocally alert the man with the ball and go to an outlet area where the handler may pass to him safely. Trying to score at this time is not the most important consideration, possession and control of the ball is. It is the open teammate's responsibility to relieve pressure on the ball by getting himself into a safe position in the passer's visual field.

When receiving the ball in a slowdown or stall situation, the player must be aware of his court position before he uses his dribble. He should remain ''alive'' until he is sure what is in front of him.

Good team technique dictates that you do not gamble when you are in the lead, but you must continue to penetrate with the ball so that you may take advantage of all good scoring opportunities in the late game stages. These are usually better than the ones that presented themselves early in the game. Many coaches believe that a sound tactic when you are ahead in late game situations is to press the opponents as soon as they begin pressing you. Of course, you should not let the game become wild or unmanageable. Controlled aggressiveness is a positive team action which may force the opponents to make mistakes.

tactics when a team is behind

When a team is behind at the end of a game and the opponents are using stall tactics to control the tempo of the game, the team that is behind must force the ball upcourt fast. They must pressure the ball, over-playing opponents meanwhile. It is best to apply pressure from a zone structure rather than man-to-man. In zone pressure someone will always be guarding the basket against an unopposed lay-up if defensive mistakes are made. It is a good tactic to allow opponents to pass to a weak ball handler and then exert extreme pressure on him.

Defenders must not allow lay-ups or easy shots. They should be aware that while they must be aggressive in pressing the ball, fouling will hurt the team, as normally a one-on-one foul shooting situation exists. If an opponent is trapped or cornered, players should not try to steal the ball but harass the opponent so that he will make a bad or uncertain pass or be called for a violation or jump ball. They should encourage outside shots, especially when the ball is in the hands of an opponent who likes to shoot or is a high scorer. To encourage a shot, players should yell "shoot, shoot." At the same time, they should harass the player by waving their arms wildly and faking at him.

It is important that all defenders in late game situations understand and implement the predetermined team pattern. Any time opponents cross at or near the ball, a double-team of the ball should take place. The man with the ball should be harassed relentlessly in order to force mistakes. It is best to let the player with the ball start his dribble then attempt to force him towards a teammate so as to get double-up pressure.

When the team that is behind obtains possession of the ball it is imperative that they get good shots as quickly as possible, as the time factor is against them.

In preseason practice, the coach must practice both end-of-game situations—when the team is ahead and when the team is behind. These can be practiced together daily, using the clock and the scoreboard. The coach should allot a minimum of forty-five minutes of preseason practice time per week to this type of situation. He should put his players in special units, combining the best pressers on one team to be used when behind and combining the best ball handlers, passers, and dribblers on a team to be used when ahead. In early preseason practice these pressure-defense and ball-control units should be balanced to make the teams as equal in ability as possible so that coaches can find the players who react best to pressure situations.

The situation should simulate game conditions as much as possible. First, these conditions sustain player interest during practice; second and most important, they help players acquire the mental, emotional, and physical poise necessary in late game situations; and third, they teach players what they will have to do and why in an actual game.

In practice, the coach should outline the game situations, breaking them down into five-, three-, two-, and one-minute situations and last-shot situations. (For example: (1)

Team A is six points ahead with five minutes remaining on the clock, and team B in possession of the ball. (2) The score is tied with five minutes remaining and the ball is in possession of team B.) It is best to make the better group behind in the score, giving the ball to them when they are more than four points behind. Give it to the weaker team when the score is closer. The clock and the scoreboard should be used for all strategic, simulated game conditions.

When simulating last minute conditions, the coach should be certain that he uses his special situation out-of-bounds plays. It is also imperative that late-game or last-minute situations be officiated. If regular officials are not available, managers or coaches should officiate. At times, let the players handle these simulated situations themselves. The coaches then should observe who is making the recommendations, as this indicates a leader, and how well these recommendations are put into effect. They should also determine which players are calm and unemotional under stress, relying on their mental as well as their physical ability.

The coach should explain all of the alternatives before these simulated game-condition pressure situations start. Notes should be taken and criticisms and observations given at the end of each session. As soon as a player makes a mistake, he should be told what he has done wrong, and he should be praised when he makes a good play.

Three types of stalls can be used: A five-man continuity, a dribble stall, and a pattern type of freeze. Using a five-man continuity, we prefer an open-middle three-two type of stall. When the ball is passed, the passer cuts away from the receiver toward the basket, clearing to the corner in the direction in which he has passed. This still should be a continuous motion, making use of all five players and looking primarily for a back-door or reverse cut if an opponent attemps to double-team.

In a dribble stall, one, two, or three good dribblers will constantly handle the ball. A pivot man moves up and down along the foul lane away from the ball, coming as high as necessary to relieve the pressure in case a dribbler is double-teamed.

In a pattern type of freeze, three or four men will control the ball, screening away from the ball and then coming to it. The pivot man will be moving along the foul lane on the opposite side. Passing lanes must be kept open on the strong side so that if an opponent on this side does double-team the ball it is possible to make a lead pass to the free teammate if he has a break away or if he has reversed direction.

Diag. 9-35, BASIC THREE-TWO STALL

In this offense, the players are spread and the ball is "long," which means it is out at least twenty-eight or thirty feet from the basket. A and E are wide in the corner positions. They should be decoying to keep their men occupied. B and D are in the front wing positions wide. C has the ball approximately thirty feet from the basket. He will pass to D. D should make a good fake away from the ball and come back to it to receive the pass, moving into the ball. C should not pass without making a preliminary fake and making sure that D is open as a receiver. After C passes, he cuts down the middle towards the basket and comes out on the right, the side the pass was made to. D dribbles the ball under control towards the opposite side, keeping it as long as possible from the basket. B makes a **V** fake to the basket, then comes to meet D's pass. D then cuts down the center. The ball is now in the approximate center of the court, still long from the basket. As C goes through and cuts right, he will relieve E, who will come out and take D's place. After D passes and goes down the middle, he will relieve A in the left corner, A will come out in B's place, and the process will continue.

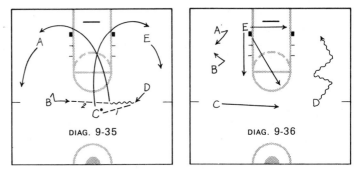

DIAG. 9-35   DIAG. 9-36

Diag. 9-36, DRIBBLE STALL WITH SEMI-ROTATION

This is a stall that the authors have used with success. A, B and C are on the side of the court opposite the ball. The pivot man, E, is in a low position and has latitude in movement. He should remain opposite the ball. However, E breaks to the basket, under, any time his defender leaves him to double-team the dribbler. He can move up along the lane setting screens for A, B or C as they approach the ball, or he can come high to the head of the key to relieve the pressure on D. D's job is to keep his man occupied while dribbling the ball on the right side of the court. He is going to drive to the basket in a one-on-one situation if possible, or he may pass to E in the pivot position in the outer half of the free-throw circle and cut to the basket using a back-door type of move. When D's dribble is stopped, C should use evasive tactics to get into position to take a safety outlet pass. C would continue dribbling, with D replacing C. Generally, designate two or three players to dribble in this situation. Normally, the forwards (A and B) should not dribble in this type of stall. However, it is a good technique to allow a good dribbling forward to handle the ball if he is guarded by a less agile opponent.

Normally in a stall situation, you are looking for the sure-shot quick basket that takes advantage of defensive mistakes (unopposed lay-ups after a good reverse or defenders leaving a man open underneath).

394

scouting

A scout is a qualified observer who studies a future opponent to learn their players' strengths and weaknesses on both an individual and team basis. When properly analyzed, objective data and subjective impressions obtained through scouting can help a team prepare for an upcoming game against the scouted opponent. Many coaches also have their own team scouted every game to check their own strengths and weaknesses. The coach's ability to assimilate the information obtained from the scouting report and to transmit it to his team is a great determinant in the team's success.

Perhaps the most important single value of scouting is that it helps to determine the immediate game plan. It also improves player confidence, preparing the team mentally for each game by giving members an accurate perspective on the opponent's strength.

Scouting is a personal thing. Preferably, it should be done by a member of the coaching staff, and the coach who does the scouting should report to the team as simply as possible. If the scout is not a member of the coaching staff, his basic basketball philosophy and thinking should parallel that of the staff. He should know the makeup of the team's personnel—their capabilities, their strengths, and their weaknesses. As a final resort, if a member of the coaching staff or a person who knows the team cannot scout, a reliable recommended scouting bureau can provide the report. However, since the scout from the bureau does not know your team, the report should not be given in complete detail. (Many scouting bureaus give complete analyses that are sometimes many pages long. While they are excellent scouting reports, the scout is giving more of an objective report than a subjective report, because he does not understand or does not know the personnel of the team he is scouting for.) Even though these reports are made by knowledgeable experts, they should be used with caution. Always put an agreement with a scouting service in contract form. If you are planning to take a scouting report from an agency that you have not had personal contact with, preview the bureau's work before using it.

When an upcoming opponent is to be scouted, there are several factors that should be taken into consideration in deciding which games to scout. First, it is best to scout them against a team whose philosophy of play, both offensively and defensively, is similar to yours. The distance the scout has to travel should also be considered. If time permits, it is best to have the same person scout an opponent more than once. Always scout opponents as close to your game with them as possible.

Before leaving for a game the scout should take care of several preliminary requirements. First, he should acquaint himself with the team that he is to scout. If there is a previous report on the team from the last season, he should go over it to recollect the salient points of the team's offense and defense. He should also look at any films of the team, paying special attention to the personnel who will be playing in the game he is about to scout. It is important that he review the philosophy of the opposing coach and the type of play that he presents. He should also go over any notes that may have been picked up through newspapers, from publicity brochures, or from statistical reports from sports information directors of the school that he is about to scout.

All material to be used on the scouting trip should be collected and put in one place, usually in a file-folder or briefcase. Essential material includes a clipboard with a pad of paper (or a stenographer's notebook), several colored pencils and pens, several mimeographed half courts for diagraming play patterns, and jump balls. If more than one person is going, include the large, reproduced full court shot charts which the second scout will keep. Well in advance of the trip, the scout should contact the home team of the game to be scouted to be certain that tickets are available. Travel arrangements should ensure that he will get to the place of the game in plenty of time.

A scout should plan to arrive at the gym at least an hour and fifteen minutes to an hour and a half before the scheduled start of the game he is to scout. This allows time for any unfamiliar procedures—a parking space a long way from the gym or a difficulty with the ticket arrangements—and avoidance of the rush before the start of the varsity game.

When a scout arrives in the gymnasium early, he should go immediately to the seat given to him by the home team. If no seat has been designated, he should sit as high above the court as possible, preferably at a corner. From that spot he can see the offensive and defensive patterns evolving, for he sees the full court at all times. (One of the worst seats to scout from is a seat directly at the court level, because you do not get a good picture of what is happening on the court.)

In order for any scouting report to be effective, the maximum amount of accurate information must be obtained; therefore, as much information as possible should be analyzed and summarized in the pregame period to supplement the scout's understanding of the strategy during game time. He should pay close attention to a preliminary game, since all teams from one school will normally incorporate the same basketball philosophy into their pattern of play. Observing a freshman or junior varsity game allows the coach to diagram out-of-bounds plays and jump-ball plays.

The scout should check local newspapers for information concerning the team he is scouting. If he does not reveal his identity, he may also obtain valuable information by talking to spectators before the game. Normally the people who are at games early are very interested in the team that they are following, and they are very happy to discuss injuries, morale, team conflicts, basic characteristics of players, and other important items.

During the pregame time, the scout should observe the physical setup of the court that the game is being played on—the type of floor, the type of backboards, the type of supports on the backboard, the tightness or looseness of the rims, and the lighting. These notes are especially pertinent when the game with the scout's team is to be played on this court. The type of ball to be used should also be ascertained, as well as the proximity of the crowd to the court and the crowd reaction at certain times of play (for example, when players are shooting foul shots, when the ball is out-of-bounds). Many times at games all scouts are seated next to each other. Exchanging ideas and comparing notes with other scouts, some of whom may have already seen the team play, may help in early organization of notes. A perusal of a program that lists player's name, number, height, weight, and year in school is essential for the scouting report, and this information can be put down during the pregame observation.

When the team being scouted comes on the court, the scout should be especially observant of the type of warm-up followed—the type of shots the players take, their favorite shooting spots, their favorite shooting hands, their attitude.

game procedures

Game procedures are the most important part of the scouting report. All scouts should have a definite method for arranging and taking notes. The jump-ball arrangement should be marked on the jump-ball chart immediately, since the players will normally move to the center of the court and get in position before the first toss-up of the game takes place. The good scout will put this arrangement down quickly. For the next four or five minutes, he should try to get a good picture of the game before starting to annotate and draw conclusions. Concentrated attention in the first minutes of the game is vital, because that is when the team is following the coach's basic instructions; free-lance pat-

398

terns have not yet developed. If the players are going to run a pattern, that is when they are going to set it up. Once the scout has determined the pattern, he should note the personnel and place them in their respective positions, writing down who is handling the ball the most, who is inside, and who is outside. While many people believe that note-taking while the ball is in play is incorrect procedure, we feel that pertinent information should be written down as soon as it occurs so it won't be forgotten.

Scouts should take full advantage of any time the clock is stopped. It is usually stopped for a held ball, an out-of-bounds violation, or a time-out. A scout should record why time-outs are taken in the first half, and should be alert for changes in offense or defense.Time-outs can be used to fill in personal summaries and to make a resumé of the game to that point. If the clock was stopped for a jump-ball, the scout should ascertain the positions of the players on the jump and diagram and annotate the play as quickly as possible. He should also note the positions of personnel on an out-of-bounds play.

Strategic changes often occur during time-out. A scout should watch for changes in personnel; he should note the times that substitutes enter, and for whom, and try to determine why the coach made the substitutes at that time. He should also observe whether a change in defense or offense takes place after a time-out. Such changes give an insight into a coach's philosophy. When defenses or offenses are changed, the scout should observe, if possible, how the changes are made. Sometimes they are made by arm signals or a sign held up from the bench; at other times a player on the court may institute this change in strategy. The best way to keep track of changes is to make slight symbolic notations as they occur and then elaborate on them at a time-out.

Many ideas should be incorporated in the game scouting report. The scout should note the team's physical and mental characteristics: Is it big? Is it fast? Is it aggressive? Is it in good condition? Are the members pulling together? Do they have great competitive spirit? A very important factor is the ability of the substitutes. If they are good, your coach may change the game strategy. If they are not good, he may use full-court pressure or some type of defense which would attempt to tire out the opposing team.

observing team offensive characteristics

Some teams will use more than one type of attack. The scout should ascertain first the type of pattern that a team is going to use. Is it a 1-3-1 or 3-2 or 2-3? Do they depend on a post man? Are they trying to get the ball into this post man? Do they rely on the outside men for a good deal of

399

their scoring? Do they use plays going down the side of the court? Do they attempt to get the ball into the middle? Is the offense balanced?

The fast break, if it is used, should be analyzed. Do the players attempt a fast break after a field goal is made or after a successful free-throw try? Do they attempt the fast break and run all the time or just part of the time after a well-cleared rebound? Do they try to go full court? Do they try to make an extremely long pass? Is it an organized break by which they go to an outlet man and fill the lanes properly? Do they leave the ball in the middle or do they pass it back and forth? How frequently does the ball go into the pivot man? Is the pivot man primarily a shooter or a feeder who is used to cut off when he has the ball? Where do the passes to the pivot man come from? Is the team a good ball handling team? Are they a deliberate team or do they attempt to score fairly quickly after setting up a basic pattern? Are the cutters good? Do they move well when they don't have the ball? Do they pass and go using give-and-go plays? Do they look for screens of each other? Do they attempt to dummy the ball into the big man or lob it in? Which men shoot the most? Which men seem to take the bad shots? What type of shots do they take? Will they attempt to tap an offensive rebound back up or will they try to slap the ball out? Are the guards or the men who handle the ball prone to excessive dribbling? Are the patterns determined by the type of pass that is used to initiate the play, by a called name or a called number, or by fingers?

observing team defensive characteristics

The scout should determine the type of team defense used before he breaks down the individual abilities of the players. He should observe if the team uses any type of defense after they make a successful foul shot or a basket. Some teams, without a signal, will press full court man-to-man, or full-court zone, depending on the type of score that is made. That is a prearranged defense that should be noted.

Sometimes it is very difficult to ascertain a combination defense. Therefore, the scout should follow cutters on the team opposing the team he is scouting to see if men are chasing them through and how the men are setting up their defense—whether they are meeting the offensive team at half court or three-quarter court. As soon as individual defensive mistakes are made, they should be jotted down.

The scout should observe the type of defense—man-to-man, zone, or press—where the defense picks up, and whether it is an active defense. When the defense picks up does it maintain pressure on the ball and on the outlet of the ball or is it a passive type of defense by which the ball is allowed to advance up to a certain point before the defensive posture is assumed? (Many teams will pick up strong defense at half court, others at full court, others at three-quarter court, some at the head of the offensive key of the team attacking.) Does the team react quickly on going from offense to defense?

It is important for the scout to know where the defense is being set up in order to determine the type of offense his own team will use against this team. The point of pickup determines how far the offensive team can penetrate before they meet the defense. Are the defenders working as a team to slide behind screens or to go over the top of screens? Do they switch well, allowing for a roll to the basket? How do they play the roll to the basket? Do they play between the man and the ball or the man and the basket when they switch men? Are they an extremely aggressive defensive team? Are they the type of team that is constantly trying to steal the ball defensively? Which men on the defensive team is it best to keep the ball away from if they are using any type of combination defense? Which type of men are most apt to be moving in on the ball? Is one side of the defense weaker than the other side? Does the team's defensive philosophy indicate that they want the pivot man completely fronted or played on the side, or do they play behind the pivot man?

The scout should know where the team's front line in a zone picks up and who plays the front line of the zone defense, who plays the back line near the basket, which men are the easiest to penetrate against, how they react getting back on defense, whether they are an easy team to run the fast break against or if they are fast getting back, and what type of pressure defense they use when they are behind in a ball game.

general individual characteristics

The individual characteristics of each player on a team that is being scouted should also be noted. These include height, weight, position, number, condition, reaction in a team posture, speed, and the type of player. There are many offensive characteristics to look for. How well does he react when he does not have the ball? Does he move well without the ball? Does he keep his defensive man occupied when other teammates have the ball? Basically, is he a good overall offensive player? (Normally, we think of a good overall offensive player as one who reacts well when he has the ball, but the work of a man without the ball is much more important, because if he is a cutter without the ball, then he must be covered at all times. When he does not move without the ball, then it is easier for the man guarding him.)

Is he a good dribbler? When he dribbles does he penetrate towards the basket or is he more lateral in his movements, trying to keep the ball until he can move it to someone else? Is he a good passer? If the pass is not a good one does he handle the ball well or receive the ball well on the move? Is he looking for a teammate when he is cutting? When he cuts, does he go straight for the basket? Is he lazy offensively? Is he deceptive? Does he use a change of direction or a change of pace? Does he attempt to run the man guarding him into teammates or into opponents? Is he a good screener? Is he a good scorer? What position on the court does he generally take his shots from? Is he a good outside shooter? Does he shoot with both hands in close? Is he predominantly a one-handed ball player, mostly right or mostly left? Does he take good shots? Is he a good foul shooter? (This is an important item, because if the scout knows who the good foul shooters are, he'll know who must be fouled if his own team must get possession of the ball.) What is his posture on the offensive backboard? Does he attempt to gain control of the ball? Does he attempt to tap the ball back up on offense or does he attempt to tap the ball out offensively? Is the player an individualist? Does he only pass the ball when he has to, and then pass it off balance or to a teammate who has no idea the ball is coming to him?

individual characteristics by position

The scout should find answers to all these questions: What type is the center? What is he doing when he is in the pivot? What type of shot does he take? Does he take hooks? Does he take turnaround shots? Does he fade away from the basket when he shoots? Which side does he prefer? Is he agile and active attempting to get position? When he is at the high post is he used as a screener or does he hand the ball off? How good a rebounder is he when he has to move from a position away from the basket, and how does he fight a good rebound position? Does he fight a boxer—is he passive or does he try to jump over the man who is boxing him?

What side of the court is each forward on? Does he step to the ball for pass reception or does he wait for the ball to come to him? Does he reverse well when he is overplayed? Is he a good driver? Does he look for position as soon as a shot is taken? Can he be boxed from the board?

Is the guard fast? What type of dribbler is he? Quick? Straight ahead? Does he use good change of direction? Does he dribble well with both hands? Do both guards bring the ball up or does the better ball handler bring it up? (If he does, the coach will naturally plan to have the other guard take it up.) Does the good ball handling guard shoot well from the outside or is he reluctant to take a shot?

Would he prefer to make the play than take the shot?

Defensively, the scout is looking for both positive and negative individual characteristics. Naturally, the first thing he looks for is the aggressiveness of a player on defense. Is he a good defensive player? Judgment is based more on his position and his defensive attitude than anything else. Does he get back fast on defense? Does he react to fakes? Is he easy to move out of position? Does he turn his head in man-to-man defense to follow the path of the ball? Does he watch the ball when a shot is taken? Does he switch well? Does he talk when a switch is necessary? How does he react on defensive rebounds? When he rebounds does he protect the ball and make sure that a good outlet pass is possible? Does he box out well? Does he try to steal the ball? Does he stay on his feet until the man with the ball has jumped? Will he dive for loose balls? Does he protect the baseline if he is playing the forward? Does he work hard when he is screened off by an offensive man? Does he attempt to go through a screen? Does he stop when a screen is set? Does he fight over it or attempt to slide through? Does he double up well? Does he talk when he is being screened or when his man is screening someone?

Negative factors should also be noted. Does the person leave his feet when someone fakes? Does he foul unnecessarily? Is it easy to drive baseline against him? Does he box his man out after a shot is taken? Does he pay attention to his man when his man does not have the ball? When the ball is near him, does he lean toward it? Does he cross feet when he is moving or when he is shuffling on defense? Does he attempt to see the man and the ball at the same time? Does he talk on defense and point out to his teammates the man he is guarding? Does he leave as soon as an opponent shoots without waiting to ascertain possession?

At half-time, the good scout replays the first half mentally and records his impressions, diagraming the pertinent **half-time** offensive and defensive alignments while they are fresh in his mind. He should review his notes and jot down doubtful items for checking in the second half. He should also get first-half statistics if they are available, and if someone else has kept a shot chart he should check it against his own. He should fill in as many individual personnel observations as he possibly can at this time.

The scout should watch the players as they warm up for the second half, noting especially whether the players who did not perform well in the first half seem listless or dejected because of their play or whether they are enthusiastic and attempting to build up enthusiasm in their teammates. The attitude at half time sometimes indicates the type of ball player a person is, and sometimes it indicates how he will perform during the second half.

second half In the second half, the scout again lists the starting lineups, making a point of observing which of these five players started in the first half. The jump-ball arrangement should be diagramed, noting any defensive or offensive adjustments that the coach may have made based on his observations of the first half of the game. As the second half progresses, many changes may take place. One change might be the use of reserve players for starters. This may indicate a change in the coach's opinion of the player who has been replaced, and it may change the scout's thinking in regard to the game coming up with his team. As the game nears the end, he should note whether there is a slow down in the offensive if the team he is scouting is ahead, or the type of pressure that is exerted on the ball if the team is behind. In a stall game he should know exactly what time in the second half the players started to slow down the tempo of the game, and what type of stall they are using. Is it a definite freeze or is it a semi-stall when they are still looking for a shot at the basket? Is it a team type of movement or does one man usually control the ball? The scout should determine if they can be double-teamed while they are using this type of stall attack and at what time they could be expected to stall if they are ahead in the coming game with his own team.

The scout should follow the same procedures he followed in the first half, writing down impressions, making personal observations of the players, and noting the time that the substitutes enter. All out-of-bounds plays should be completely diagramed as soon as possible, noting if they are organized and if they are progressive. (Does one play follow in the same setup as the one that has preceded it?) If the play is under the basket, does the same man take the ball out? Do they have a signal—do they slap the ball or call a name or a number to start the play? Are they looking for the same player—the big man or their best shooter? Do they have a safety outlet on their out-of-bounds plays if the man to whom they wish to pass is covered? What type of play is used from the sidelines? The scout should try to learn whether this play is going to the basket for the score or if the intention is to get the ball in play to start the regular offense. Do they have a systematic method of putting the ball in from the far end when the opponent is putting on a full-court press? Are they trying to penetrate or just maintain possession?

after the game The scout should notice turning points in the game, the method by which a team was able to obtain the lead and

404

gain control of the game, and the conditions which may have changed the outcome. Immediately after the game, he should check his diagrams to make sure that they are clear. Complete game statistics are usually available from the home team at the close of the game. At this time the scout should start to plan his post-game analysis and the procedures he will follow in writing his report.

To write his report, the scout should coordinate all of the information that he has. Statistics and play-by-play summaries may be available to help him in his final analysis of the game. He also should speak with any other scouts who were watching the same team so that they can compare notes. If the scout is driving home he should write as much as possible before he starts to travel. If he is going home by public transportation he can write his final draft during the trip.

The final draft should include, first, the individual characteristics of each starting player and each substitute who played—height, weight, relative speed, quickness, overall condition, team playing ability, and individual ability. All positive factors and negative factors that were observed by the scout should be recorded. It should reflect his own personal observations. Other scouts' comments and suggestions should be added in parentheses.

The report should be a brief account of the game as he has seen it—the way the game went, why the scouted team won or lost, what strategies were used, the type of offensive and defensive play used, and all special plays used. Primarily, the scout should report whether the team he is scouting can be played man-to-man and suggest defensive matchups for his team, giving reasons for his choices. He should also suggest specific offensive patterns for his team and maneuvers that he feels will be successful against the scouted team. He should include a summary of the statistics he has received and, if possible, clippings of local newspaper accounts of the game.

The scout should base all of his observations on fact, being positive and objective in the conclusions he comes to. However, he should state any intuitions that he may have had and any opinions that he may hold. The relative strength of the team opposing the scouted team should also be considered when writing the report.

The coaches review the scouting report and question the member of the staff who did the scouting. If the report was done by a scouting bureau, then important decisions regarding the individuals on the opposition should be made collectively by the coaching staff. The staff should analyze each opponent in terms of his offensive and defensive ability, and determine which players (both starters and re-

coach's use of scouting report

405

serves) on their own team will play him if using man-to-man defense.

Normal defensive strategy demands that your team (1) place as much pressure as possible on a good shooter at every opportunity and (2) play away from the strengths and to the weaknesses of each opponent. If one opponent is an outstanding shooter, normally you will play your best defensive player on him, and you will try to help him as much as possible by leaving a weaker opponent unguarded momentarily. If the opponent is a good outside shooter but not a good driver, he should be overplayed when he has the ball at all distances from the basket. Normally when a player is an outstanding shooter, it is wise to keep the ball from him because (1) it makes the offensive team work harder to get shots for this player on whose scoring ability the team depends, and (2) when he does get the ball, he will be more apt to take a poor shot than he would if the pressure were not exerted on him.

In all instances, players should be taught to play the percentages against their opponents. If an opposing team depends on getting the ball into the pivot area for their offense, stress should be placed on floating or dropping off the men who are designated to make the pass-ins to that area. This maneuver will cut down the passing lanes into the pivot area and will allow the passer-in to shoot. Normally, players do not take this opportunity if penetration to the post area is a fundamental in their offensive game strategy. Therefore, your team must be told of the peculiarities in the opponent's offensive play.

If an opponent is not a good shooter but a good driver, his guard should be told to stay off him to allow the outside shot and to take away his drive to the basket. If an opponent maneuvers well in only one direction, he should be overshifted so that you are playing to his strong side instead of directly in front of him. If he is a good shooter but must have the ball before he can make his offensive move, he should be played so that he does not receive the ball except in a disadvantageous position. He should be made to move as much as possible without the ball, making him work to obtain possession of the ball.

If a certain opponent must have the ball all the time, it would be well to remember that in a close ball game he will attempt to make the play himself. Therefore, when he has the ball in this situation, players near him should realize that they can double-team him.

When an opponent is a poor ball handler, more defensive chances can be taken against him. If an opponent lacks confidence—and this is especially true of a sub—it is best to try to force him to take shots in a position that is not to his advantage and to talk to him, yell at him, and fake rushing at him in an attempt to upset or confuse him. It is important to take advantage of all weaknesses observed by the scouts. When a coach finds an opponent who is an especially weak defensive player, he should not try to beat him all the time, as the opposing coach will replace him with a better defensive player if the situation is obvious. Therefore, in the normal course of events the coach should attempt all of the offensive patterns which he feels will be to his advantage. If he does have one weak defensive opponent there may be a crucial time in the game when the coach must get a basket and he can get it against the weak player.

The type of offense to be used against the opponent naturally is based on the type of defense he plays. However, game strategy must always be within the framework of the fundamental offensive and defensive patterns that have been used during the year. No great change in basic procedure should be made, because any game plan that has any practical impact must be practiced, and there is not enough time to practice it in the day or two prior to a ball game.

Usually the best defensive players are matched against the best scorers on the opposing team, and size is a factor in matchups of men who will be close to the basket. Normally, you play tall men against tall men, but a good strategy against a pivot man is to use a smaller, quicker defender who can outposition the good post opponent, especially if the post man is the type who shoots, or looks for his shot, when he gets the ball. Not allowing him to get the ball is the best defense.

Many idiosyncrasies appear in individual opponents' offensive maneuvers. Some good shooters must always fake after they receive the ball. Therefore, the defenders should be told not to move with the first fake. Other shooters must bounce the ball once after they get it in order to obtain body balance. Their defenders should be told to move in quickly as the players receive the ball to prevent them from putting the ball to the floor, thus making them take the shot in a posture that is not to their best advantage.

Players who are not playing the first, second, or third strongest offensive opponents should know the latitude that they have in helping to double-team the better opponents. Many times, for example, when a pivot player gets the ball and he is to be double-teamed, the strong side forward comes in to help the double-team. Often it is best for one of the guards to drop off to help double-team, especially if the pivot man has outmaneuvered his defender and his defender is behind him. Again, the relative outside shooting ability of this player guarding an opponent on the strong side must be considered. If the guard is the stronger outside shooter, then the defensive forward should drop back to double-team. If the forward is the better shooter, or is in a much closer position relative to the basket, then perhaps the guard should drop back.

In the pregame determination of strategy the scout must be as objective as possible in his appraisal of the opponent's strengths and weaknesses, because players sense whether they are being given accurate information, and it is imperative that the team have complete confidence in the ability of the coaching staff.

Appendix D contains a complete game scouting report.

game organization and team strategy

Each game presents a challenge to the coach. The pre-game plan must be well organized and presented in its entirety to the assembled squad. Offensive and defensive adjustments must be explained in detail. The time has passed when players can simply be told to do something a certain way. You must explain why, and like a good salesman, sell them the positive idea. They must believe in what they are doing.

planning for the game

Choose offensive patterns that are most likely to be successful against a particular opponent and explain why they will probably be successful. Defensive match-ups must be predetermined if man-to-man is to be used. The scouting reports, listing the individual tendencies of each starting opponent and each first-line substitute, must be discussed. Then every aspect of each pattern must be presented for the squad and the player concerned. The whole squad must understand the strategy, because conditions may necessitate another squad member's taking over the assignment at any time during the actual game. If a type of zone or combination will be used defensively, each man's responsibility must be outlined. Nothing must be left to chance. Within reason, every possible eventuality must be explored, taking human nature into consideration.

presenting the game plan to the team

After making the individual defense assignments and determining the team's game strategy, the coach and his assistants should commit the basic game plan to paper. (See Appendix E for a sample of the authors' game plan.) The plan should be presented to the players as follows: One assistant, using the basic game plan and a copy of the scouting report, should select personnel from the freshman or reserves whose physical attributes resemble closely those of the players on the opposing team. Then the assistant should acquaint these players with the personal characteristics of the players they are to imitate. Next he discusses the opponent's offensive and defensive play patterns. Fi-

410

nally, their out-of-bounds plays and jump-ball plays are discussed.

The presentation to the squad is made before the first practice session prior to the game. In most instances no more than two practice sessions can be devoted to the game plan report, since many teams will play a game in the middle of the week and a game on a weekend. If two consecutive games are to be played on a weekend, the scouting report for the first game only should be given before the first game is played (unless compelling factors dictate otherwise). If games are to be played on the coming Friday and Saturday, and there are no previous games that week, then the report for the Friday game will be given on the Monday and, if necessary, a partial report for the Saturday game will be given on the Tuesday. The partial report will cover only the essentials that require on-court practice. Practice time then must be allotted to both reports. However, as games are taken on a one-at-a-time basis, emphasis must be placed on the first game, and the players should never look beyond that to the second game. Normally, in a back-to-back game situation, it is important that a full pre-game mental skull session be scheduled Saturday morning so that the scouting report for the Saturday night game can be evaluated when the team can concentrate on it.

Available movies of previous games played against the upcoming opponent should be shown to the squad when the scouting report and game plan are presented. The movies should be marked so that it is easy to get to the pertinent parts that will highlight what the scouting report shows, if the opponent is still performing in a similar manner. The person who scouted the game should give the report. He should have written up the individual characteristics so that the notes can be passed around and discussed briefly by the coach, then he should outline on a blackboard the pertinent offensive and defensive maneuvers, out-of-bounds plays, and jump-ball plays. After this presentation, which should be as brief and inclusive as possible, the squad should be asked if there are any questions. When all questions have been answered, the head coach should discuss the game plan with the assembled squad, while the assistant goes to the court to continue to work with the freshmen, junior varsity, or reserves who are going to be the opponents in the practice sessions.

When the squad reassembles on the court after going over the game plan, the coach who did the scouting and is handling the freshmen-junior varsity-reserve group should present the opponents' individual characteristics, and their offense and defense in skeleton form. As each junior varsity or freshman opponent comes to the court, the assistant coach should list his capabilities as described in the scout-

411

ing report. After the five players are on, the offensive pattern should be walked through, first without opposition and then with minimal pressure. The same procedure should be followed in outlining the opponent's defense.

After the individual defensive strengths and weaknesses of the opponents have been discussed, the assistant coach goes over the team's defensive patterns. The team should be cautioned not to be too aggressive against the freshman or junior varsity group. The purpose of the practice game is to acquaint the players with the offensive and defensive structure and the individual strengths and weaknesses of the upcoming opponents, not to stop the practice opponents. Therefore, minimal pressure should be used at first. After the reserve group is a little familiar with the offensive and defensive structure that they are using, stronger pressure can be applied. To reiterate, game strategy must always be within the framework of the team's offensive and defensive patterns, and great changes should never be made. The overall game plan must include second-half offensive and defensive stratagems. Defensively, a team may play the first half man-to-man, using man-to-man pressure on occasion. In the second half, perhaps after a score, a pre-practiced type of zone and zone pressure can be used.

team strategy

The most important factor in team strategy is to play your own game. Therefore, the opponent must be forced to play within the framework of your thinking. If an opposing team likes the fast break, it may be advantageous to you to be able to slow the ball down as a team, even though you are a running team. You do not want the opponent to do what he wants to do, but rather what he does not want to do. It is important, therefore, that the team be prepared to meet any contingency on the court. All possible maneuvers must be completely discussed and practiced so that when the time comes to use a procedure, players will not have to attempt an entirely unfamiliar pattern.

A team should have one or two secondary defenses in addition to its primary defense, because a situation during a game may require a change from the primary defense. Normal strategy is to play a pressing or forcing defense against a bigger team, a slower team, or a mechanical team that uses many set patterns and wishes to control the ball. A team that is not in good condition should always be pressured and played aggressively. A team that dribbles frequently should also be pressured, because it is easy to double-team a player who is bouncing the ball frequently, and it is very difficult for the player to start passing the ball in the course of a game after he has been used to dribbling throughout the season. Any team that does not have good ball handlers should be forced aggressively at all times.

412

Offensively, screens should be used against any team that guards closely or uses a tight man-to-man defense. Not only is it easier to screen for a teammate if your opponent is guarding close, but it is easier to rub a man off any screen set by a closely guarded teammate.

Any team that attempts to get the ball into a post area should be played with a floating defense to prevent the ball from getting in and to force the outside shot. The same tactic should be used against a driving team.

A change of strategy is normally advisable after a time-out. Certain plays should be saved to use when you have the ball following the time-out. Many teams also change their defense after certain maneuvers on the court. For example, following a successful basket or a free throw, many teams will change to some type of pressure defense or perhaps zone defense. As we said previously, against an excellent fast-breaking team or a team that is much bigger it is normally best to play a slowed down, deliberate ball control game. Your players should be conditioned to step in on the lane men as they come down on a fast break, because they are looking for the pass and are not anticipating this type of defensive maneuver.

The coach has the responsibility of getting a team prepared mentally for a game. Usually you do not need a great deal of mental preparation for the players in a game that is going to be extremely close or one in which you are the underdog. A good scouting report and a good game strategy plan should be enough. However, for games which you are expected to win, or should win, much mental preparation is necessary.

The coach should arrive in the locker room approximately forty-five minutes before the start of the game, physically and mentally rested and thinking positively. He should check with the trainer and the team, indulging in basketball small talk to discover the team's frame of mind. Then he should confer ten or fifteen minutes with his staff to review the game strategy and to discuss the starters and the early substitutes. The game plan should include projected opponent reaction to proposed strategy so that countermeasures may be thought out in advance. If there is no trainer, the coach should take care of any training duties at this time, assisted by the manager.

At home, the managers should arrive at least an hour and a half before game time to supervise game arrangements. They should take care of the scorer's and timer's necessities and make certain that the game officials' room is in order. One manager should stay with the game officials before the game. At half time, and after the game, he should conduct officials to their room, and open it for them. Other managers should make certain that statistical

organization for the game

413

reports and programs are available for visitors or newspapermen, that the statistical recorders are placed, and that bench equipment is in order. One manager should check the home locker room to make sure that it is clean and has all the proper equipment. The manager assigned to the visiting team should check the cleanliness of their room and supply them with towels, blackboard and chalk. He should let the visitors know that they may consult the home team's trainer when necessary if their own trainer did not come with them. For away-from-home games, the managers who are making the trip should arrive at the point of departure at least three quarters of an hour before the scheduled leaving to make certain that all trip arrangements have been taken care of.

The players should eat their pregame meal at least four hours before the start of the game. After the meal they should exercise and get a little rest. Players should arrive at the site of the game about an hour and a half to two hours before game time. They can spend some of this time watching a preliminary game if one is scheduled, but should report to the locker room in time to have all preparations complete forty-five minutes before the scheduled starting time of their game. At this time, the trainer tapes the players and checks the emergency equipment he will be taking to the court.

The trainer renders great psychological support to the players before the squad assembles. It is his job to relax them and get them in the best frame of mind for the upcoming game.

the pregame warm-up

A pregame drill, about twenty minutes long, should be discussed and integrated into practice sessions before the first game. That eliminates confusion when the team goes out on the court and ensures efficient use of pregame practice time. Initially, use a dribble and passing lay-up drill to loosen up, then go into a three-line pass, cut, and shoot drill with all three men shooting and all three men rebounding. All players should practice shooting from their normal positions and take at least six practice shots from the foul line, with the starting team and the first line substitutes doubling this number. All must practice their foul shooting for rhythm.

We prefer to have a ball for every two men in the pregame warm-up (or, at most, a ball for every three players), which means six balls should be available for a twelve-man squad. The players should remove their warm-up pants and jackets as their body warmth increases.

Along with the Basic Lay-up Drill, Lay-up and Medium Jump Shot with Defensive Pressure Drills, and the Pass, Pick, Pop Drill (Chapter 3), the following drills may be used

414

as pre-game warm-up drills. They are excellent for loosening up and getting ready for practice or competition.

Diag. 11-1, MOVING LINE PASS, SCREEN, DRIBBLE, CUT, PASS DRILL

Each of the players in the line to the right has a ball. X_9, the first man in the line, passes to X_1, the first man in the left line. X_9 screens for X_1, who dribbles off the screen. X_9 rolls to the basket, receives a bounce pass from X_1, and shoots a lay-up. X_1 rebounds and they switch lines. X_1 dribbles back behind X_{16}, and X_9 runs to the opposite side behind X_8. The next two players in line do the same thing. When X_9 rebounds the ball, he will dribble it back to the left line so that the balls will end up in that line for the next round. Thus, players will get lay-ups, screens, passes and cuts from both sides.

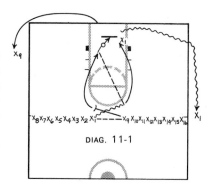

DIAG. 11-1

Diag. 11-2, ALTERNATE BALL LAY-UP

Alternate players (X_1, X_3, X_5, etc.) in a sixteen-man line have basketballs. X_1 dribbles in and lays the ball in from the right side. His partner, X_2, rebounds and passes to X_1, and they form the line on the left. All other pairs follow rapidly. All pairs repeat this procedure from the left. After rebounding the left lay-up, X_2 retains possession of the ball and begins another line of the right with X_1 trailing him. The other pairs repeat this procedure, alternating from left to right and taking turns dribbling in, rebounding, and shooting. This drill should start at approximately half to three-quarter speed, and as the players get the continuity of the drill, it should speed up.

DIAG. 11-2

Diag. 11-3, THREE-LINE PASS-AND-GO-BEHIND DRILL, ALL THREE SHOOT

The middle men, X_2 and X_5, each have basketballs. X_2 looks at the line to his right, and X_3 moves forward towards the free-throw circle. X_2 passes to X_3 and cuts behind X_3. As X_3 moves forward, X_1 moves forward from the left. X_3 passes to X_1 and cuts behind X_1. X_1 passes to X_2, who drives in for a lay-up. X_3 rebounds the shot and feeds to X_1, who is moving in from the right for a lay-up. X_2 rebounds X_1's shot and feeds X_3 cutting in from the left for a lay-up. X_1 moves under the basket, rebounds X_3's shot and passes to X_2 (beyond the right sideline), who brings the ball out and passes to X_8 in the center line. X_4, X_5 and X_6 continue the drill. Each player shoots, each player rebounds. Players should alternate lines.

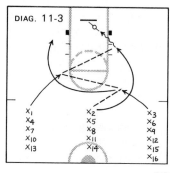

DIAG. 11-3

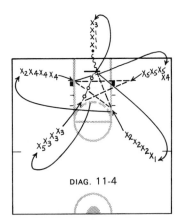

DIAG. 11-4

Diag. 11-4, FIVE-SPOT MOVEMENT DRILL

This drill, while it may look a little complex, is very fast moving and entertaining and not difficult to teach. The players form five lines, each line designated X_1, X_2, X_3, X_4 and X_5. Each line is positioned on the spot the players in that line might assume for a two-three offense. X_2 and X_3 are out front. X_4 and X_5 are deep in the two corner spots. X_1 is underneath the basket with the ball. To initiate the drill, X_1 should dribble out one or two bounces towards either X_2 or X_3. In this example, he dribbles out towards X_2. He passes to X_2 and moves on the left side of X_2, going behind the X_2 line. X_2 catches the ball in movement and the diagonal corner, X_4 moves towards X_2. X_2 passes to X_4 and moves to the left-hand side, going behind the X_4 line. X_4, when he receives the ball, passes cross-court to X_5 who is moving out of the opposite corner. X_4 goes to the left of X_5, going behind the X_5 line. X_5, moving towards the X_3 line, passes to X_3 and goes to the left of X_3, to the end of the X_3 line. X_3 shoots a lay-up. The next X_1 in line rebounds, and the drill continues with players exchanging lines each time they make a movement so that they are approaching the ball from a different angle at all times. If you wish the lay-up to be made by X_2, all that must be done is to change the movement of the ball. X_1 will pass to X_3 and follow through on the right of X_3. X_3 will pass to X_5 and go through on the right of X_5. X_5 will pass across court to X_4 and go to his own right. X_4 will pass to X_2. Each player goes to the end of the line he has passed to.

game arrangements for the first half

The coach and his assistants must exchange ideas frequently during the game. One assistant or a manager, sitting next to the coach, must keep track of team and individual fouls on both teams, time-outs, opponent substitutions, and pertinent commentaries of the coach. Ideally, another assistant should be high above the court, in direct communication with the bench, for court level is one of the poorest locations from which to watch a game. This coach should check continually for any errors in the pre-game plan and relay necessary adjustments immediately.

Seating should be arranged so that the first-line substitutes sit nearest the coaches, ready to enter the game. They should be close enough to listen to the coaches' comments as the game progresses. The bench should be constructively vocal, shouting encouragement and warning players on the court of any up-coming plays that they may see. They should participate in the game—concentrating on their part of the game in particular and the overall game in general—so that when they are called upon physically, they can enter the game without any loss of momentum for the team.

When considering substitution, the coach should take into consideration the fact that the substitute will be shooting cold. If a player on the court is taking and missing good shots and he is generally a good shooter, he should be encouraged before a substitute is sent in. If he is taking poor shots, he should be cautioned. Substitution should be made for team impetus if the team has a nonstarter who is an outstanding sixth man. The players on the court should be certain that the incoming replacement receives the ball immediately so that he feels he is a part of the game and loses the anxiety that all substitutes have.

During time-outs for psychological or strategic purposes, the team should remain standing or bent over slightly, hands on hips or knees or relaxed at the sides, grouped around the coach with the reserves behind the participants. *All* players and nonparticipants should concentrate on the advice of the coach.

time-outs

A coach should interject his thinking into all parts of the game strategy during the playing of the game. He determines when his team will call time-out and how it will handle substitutions. A team should have a general method for calling a time-out. Normally it should not call any time-outs (never more than one) in the first half, except for extreme emergencies—for example, to take care of a severe injury, to interrupt the momentum of an opponent who has scored several quick successive baskets, or to discuss what to do if the opponents have used a strategy which you have not been prepared to meet. In most circumstances, however, time-outs should be preserved so that a team has three or four going into the very last minutes of the ball game, when they can be used to advantage.

A time-out is a good strategic move when it is called to prevent loss of ball when a player is about to be tied up or cannot bring the ball upcourt late in a game. One can also be called in the late stages of a game when a player on the opposing team is about to shoot a crucial foul shot. The time-out will give him time to worry about the importance of making the shot. The coach can use a time-out late in the game to determine what the last play will be in a tie game when his team has the ball, and he can call another one within the last ten seconds to set up the play he wants the team to use. Both players and coaches should always be aware of the number of time-outs that each team has remaining. Remember, a time-out can be called when *you* score a basket.

substitutions

A coach should substitute purposefully. Primarily, he takes men out for instruction, rest, in case of an injury, or to prevent them from fouling out early. He should immediately substitute for any player who is hurting the team defensively.

The coach should always make essential defensive

417

changes as soon as possible, either inserting substitutes or rearranging starters. Substitution during the game is one of the most important aspects of coaching strategy. A coach should insert substitutes frequently and early, because they will hustle when they are in the game if they feel they have the coach's confidence. A time-out should never be used to rest a player. Fatigue normally is recognizable by slowness of a player—diminished reaction time, loafing on defense, and not hustling. If a player wishes to conserve his energy, he should do it on offense.

Taking themselves out of a game should be recommended to the players as a good team effort. Taking himself out to let a fresh player come in should be automatic to a player, and he should be commended for informing the coach that he is tired on the court. Normally it is the coach's responsibility to determine the condition of the players during the game.

Place of game is another factor in substitution. Some players play better at home; others are better away from home. The coach should be alert to a player's reaction to spectator response. If the player starts to get upset because he is the object of an away-from-home crowd's derision, then taking him out and talking to him is advisable.

The score is also an important factor when considering substitution. Normally, don't substitute when you are ahead. If you are falling behind, you can insert two or three substitutes for aggressiveness and hustle. The question now is whether the substitutes should be allowed to remain in the game after they obtain the lead or whether they should be replaced by the players that the coach thinks are the best players. We feel that you should have your five best players on the court whenever possible. Therefore, if you feel that the best players are rested and that their mental attitude is good, you should reinsert them. A coach who does not keep his five best players on the court at all times is second guessing himself. If the substitutes have gained the lead and the coach goes with them, he is telling the spectators that he made the mistake of not starting them as his five best players.

A coach should not lecture a substitute when putting him into the game. Anything he had to say to the player should have been said in his scouting and pregame strategy meeting. A long lecture will tend to confuse a sub. All the coach should do is pat him on the back and give him a few words of encouragement as he goes to report to the player he is replacing.

The coach should never talk to a player as soon as he comes out. The player should take the bench position of the teammate who replaced him, cover up to retain body warmth, towel himself dry, and rinse out his mouth. Let him relax a bit and then go over the reasons he was replaced if they are not perfectly obvious to him. The coach does not owe an explanation to a replaced player, and one should not be demanded. However, we do feel that one should be given, and it makes its greatest impact when it is given immediately. After the coach or assistant has given him constructive advice, the replaced player should quickly get back in the game mentally.

A coach should protect a player from fouling out too early in the game. Normally he should allow his best players to have at least two fouls remaining at the start of the second half. If a key player has two fouls and there are only two or three minutes left to the half, it is a good idea to substitute for him in the time remaining so that he will start the second half with at least three fouls left and he will not lose any of his hustle or aggressiveness.

Never let a starter with four fouls remain out of a ball game too long. Many coaches will replace a player who has only one foul left and then reinsert him at a time when the game is perhaps out of reach. If you are behind in the second half and one of your best players has his fourth foul called, do not replace him, especially if he is cautiously aggressive. However, do substitute if he is overcareful of his position and allows an opponent easy shots.

When substituting, always maintain team balance of size and speed, unless there is a compelling reason to alter this balance. The opponent's defensive tactics may alter this arrangement. When you are behind, and you are pressing, you must go with speed and aggressiveness. If the opponents have sprung a surprise zone defense on you, then you might go with a good shooter.

A coach should always be prepared to substitute for a special situation. For example, for a jump-ball, offensively or defensively, he can insert a player who is extremely aggressive and intuitively comes up with a loose ball on a tap situation. He should insert big men for a crucial foul shot recovery. He may substitute each time his team scores in order to slow down a good fast-break opponent.

A coach should never embarass a player by putting him in for just a few seconds at the close of a game that is either completely lost or obviously a victory. If the coach wishes to elicit the plaudits of the crowd for a player who has played an outstanding game, he may replace him in the last few seconds, but if he does so, he should substitute a player who has previously been in the game.

A coach must always be cognizant of the number of fouls that each player on his own team has, and perhaps more important, the number of fouls that each player on an opposing team has. He should play at these men if they are key opponents. It is also a good idea to remind players which opponents have fouls so they can talk to the men who are in danger of fouling out to make them overcautious and then take advantage of their caution.

half-time procedures

High school half time is ten minutes; in college it is fifteen minutes. Efficient use of this time is extremely important.

Players must go straight to the locker area at the half, use the lavatory if necessary, put on warm-up jackets, and relax, either lying or sitting. They should discuss the game quietly and constructively with the other players and non-participants until the coach is ready to discuss the first half happenings and the second half strategy with the assembled squad.

At this time the managers do not join in the discussion, but rather take care of the needs of the players and the coaches quietly and efficiently. They give the players sliced oranges (for saliva), bits of chocolate (for energy), and a prescribed drink (for a fluid reserve). They should have towels available and any training aids that are necessary. One manager should collate the available statistics for the coaches.

The trainer should administer any necessary first aid. He should check the physical condition of each player and rub them down slightly, concentrating on shoulders, arms, back, legs, and back of the neck.

The coaches should confer privately for about two or three minutes near the team's locker room. They should review the first half, perusing the score book and statistics and discussing alternative strategies. The first half strategy report (see Appendix F) should be used to assess the team game plan during the first half. When the managers and trainers have completed their ministrations, the coaches should discuss individual criticisms with the players concerned and make a group critique including suggested corrections and strategies. If a blackboard is available they should diagram maneuvers to be used in the second half, basing them on what has occurred in the first half. They should discuss the first half with the team, praising what has been done well and correcting mistakes. The discussion should be brief so that the players will have three to five minutes to warm up for the second half.

An inspirational pep talk has far more value at this time than before the game, for most of what is said pertains to what has taken place on the court in the first half. The coach must see that any momentum achieved in that half carries through to the second half. Victory often depends on the half-time instructions.

Offensive adjustments to the opponent's first half defensive tactics must be made. The coach should be prepared for possible defensive changes by the opponent, as indicated on the scouting report. If the coach's out-of-bounds plays have been successful, perhaps an option will be a good strategy, as the opposing team similarly adjusts to his play in the first half. Different jump-ball plays can also be incorporated if necessary.

The second half offensive adjustments should include a discussion of who your best scorers have been and what type of offensive patterns have been successful, because the opponents are going to attempt to shut off the best scorers and the best offensive patterns in the second half. Therefore, though the coach should stay with his strength, he should be alert for possible opponent defensive changes. During half-time, he should discuss the possibility of using a good scorer as a decoy, waiting for a defensive adjustment, and then taking advantage of the adjustment.

Defensive adjustment to the play of the opponent in the first half must also be made. The coach should stress what patterns have worked best for them and discuss the various defensive techniques to counteract these moves. He should also name their best shooters and tell the team how to play them to cut down on their point production.

second half

The second-half arrangements on the bench should be similar to those used in the first half. The first-line substitutes should be placed close to the coach so they can listen to his comments.

When the game outcome seems assured, the coach may substitute reserves to give them valuable game experience. As a morale factor, he should give playing time to as many players as possible. Generally, he should not take starters out as a group, and he should observe the performance of reserves with starters.

He must try to avoid playing a substitute in a situation that may be embarrassing. For example, he shouldn't put a player into a game when the team is way ahead and there are only a few seconds of playing time left.

Time-outs become more strategic as the game progresses. A coach should call time-outs in the second half to change the defensive posture. For example, he might switch from man-to-man to a pressure zone to upset the opponents. That is especially effective after the opponents have called the time-out. He should be aware of key players who may be tiring, and try to substitute for them as quickly as possible so they may conserve energy and be at full strength in the final stretch. Also, he should be alert to insert key reserves with special ability. If the team is losing control of the backboards, he could insert a good rebounder. He should also call time-outs in the second half to implement prepracticed late game strategy. The coaches must keep track of the time-outs and fouls left for both teams. If a key opponent has four fouls, the team should try to foul him out if it is part of the overall strategy and the game situation warrants it.

late game strategy

Important strategies that must have been preplanned and prepracticed for second half implementation are the tactics for controlling the game if you are ahead. The coach will decide if or when to slow the game down and what type of offense to use to slow it, depending on the second-half play and the time remaining in the game. The coach should also indicate when a complete freeze is to be used. If a team is behind, it is important that the players know who the weaker foul shooters on the opposing team are so they can foul them when they need the ball. Normally one does not foul the best ball handler and certainly not the best shooter, but they are usually the players who have the ball most in team offense. Therefore, it is important for the coach to have stressed which opponent he wants to take the foul shot and to have discussed methods of forcing the ball toward him so that he may be fouled in a strategic situation.

If a team has not used the number of fouls allotted per half (six in college or four in high school) before the bonus situation, they should know how to use strategic fouls, allowing the weak foul-shooting opponent to get the ball and then fouling him and taking a less than 70 percent chance of his getting one point so that they may obtain the ball. (Normally, a team shoots no better than 70 percent from the foul line as a game percentage.) Possession of the ball is approximately 0.9 points, based on a 45 percent average shooting percentage, and is fast approaching one point per possession of ball.

Other tactics that should have been practiced and included in the pregame plan in case they have to be used in the second half are the last shot and the strategy when the opponent has the ball late in the game when you are ahead three or more points. You do not want any fouls with less than half a minute to go, and you want strong but unaggressive pressure on the ball with all your defenders playing a defense that will force opponents away from the basket if they are to receive a pass. You want five men boxing out for the defensive rebound. (Don't cause a three-point play.)

If you are behind three or more points with possession of the ball late in the game, you must strive to have a good driver take the shot, looking for a three point play.

If you are more than three behind, naturally you must bring the ball upcourt quickly in order to get it to a good

422

shooter and have him take the best available shot while the other men crash the offensive boards.

If you are one or two points behind and have the ball, then you are looking for a good shot from your basic pattern with your best shooters taking the shot if possible, and you must have strong offensive rebounding from at least four of your players.

If you are one or two points ahead, and the opponents have the ball, you must try to pressure the opponent with the ball, leaving no good openings for other players, and you need five men to go strong to the defensive boards when a shot is taken. If the opponents penetrate your defense in this situation then it is important that all players retreat immediately toward the defensive basket to help out, because if an opponent has penetrated someone else is going to have to pick him up, and there is the possibility of an open man under the basket.

If the score is tied and you have possession of the ball, you want the last shot so that you will finish the game with a victory or, at worst, with a tie game and an overtime period in which to win it. To make sure that the last shot is a good one, you should take a time-out with ten to twelve seconds left to discuss what play to use and who is to take the shot, if possible.

A defense should have been perfected for occasions when the score is tied and the opponents have the ball. Players should attempt to force a pass by the opponent's best ball handler, who normally will have possession of the ball, back toward mid-court to some other player, then keep the ball from getting back to the good ball handler, if possible. When the ball goes backwards they should attempt a double-team for a possible jump ball or interception. If you sit back and allow the other team to move the ball until the last ten or twelve seconds, you are losing the possibility of ball possession, taking a chance of losing or at best ending the regulation game with no better than a tie score. You should not allow the long freeze for the last shot.

Psychologically, you should allow the opponents to go into a freeze, for when they are thinking in terms of freeze, they are not thinking of penetrating until a certain number of seconds are left on the clock. Normally, a team feeling pressure will try to pass back when they are freezing rather than passing into scoring area. By allowing them to start the freeze, you lull them into thinking you are going to allow the type of offensive that would give them the last shot. After they have been lulled, attack in a surprise maneuver. Of course, the inside scoring area must be covered to prevent an easy shot.

When you are behind ten or more points in the second half, a time-out must be taken to change strategy and personnel. A pressing, aggressive type of defense is called for, and the coach must make personnel changes for morale purposes and to change the course of the game. When a team is ahead ten or more points in the second half, the team must keep pressure on the opponents offensively because two or three quick baskets at that point will make it impossible for the opponents to catch up, and if they are discouraged, the game will change from a fairly close game into a game that will become an easy victory. It is psychologically important to keep a double digit lead on the score board.

Special situations, Chapter 9, must be thoroughly inculcated for late game use so that minimal explanations are necessary during the game.

after the game

The coach has many post-game responsibilities. First, he should meet on the court briefly with the opposing coach to exchange gracious congratulations and condolences; then, he should go to the locker room with the team. He should be positive in any remarks he makes to the team, whether or not they have won the game.

The coach should see that either he or a staff member remains in the locker room vicinity immediately after every game. His presence prevents horseplay after a victory and wards off bitterness or vindictiveness after an extremely difficult loss. The coach should then meet privately with his assistants. This gives him time to recover from post-game exhilaration or depression. He should see the press as soon as his duties to the players are completed and he has control of his game feelings, always remembering the press's deadlines. He should be objective and positive in his comments, never criticizing players, opponents, the opposing coach, or officials.

postgame reports

All games played should be reviewed by the coaching staff and the team. A written report should include the coach's impressions of his own team's game (determined from the strategy reports) and his opinion of the effectiveness of the pregame scouting report on the opponent. It also covers how the game was played, whether or not the tactics conformed to the pregame strategy, where and why strategy was weak, where and why the strategy was effective, and any other pertinent comments. Game statistics and post-game notes, together with the scouting report, should emphasize positive and negative factors and summarize the thinking of the players and assistant coaches after each game. The coach's own observations belong at the end of the summary. Underscore what is especially pertinent and accurate; put question marks through anything that was erroneous, and revise the scouting reports in light of the game as it was played.

part five
coaching aids

12

the use of statistics in basketball

Statistics in basketball are relevant, objective data, which are observed, recorded, and compiled to serve as a constructive basis for measuring relative individual and team performance in order to derive meaningful conclusions pertaining to the individual or the team.

Certain minimal statistical standards are essential. The minimal standard in scoring is simply keeping total points scored by both teams. At the lowest levels of basketball, where the game is played primarily for recreation, total points is the only statistic kept in a game. At the lower levels of team basketball, where the budget does not permit hiring officials or where court-time is very limited, usually only the number of baskets scored by each player and the number of foul shots scored by each player are tallied. These minimal standards suffice at those levels. At the lower levels of organized basketball, it is essential to have a scorer to record the baskets made, the foul shots made, the personal fouls charged against each player and team, the number of team time-outs, and an accurate running score.

At levels where complete statistics are not kept, the single most relevant statistic is the number of individual mistakes made—the number of times a team has had possession of the ball without getting a good shot at the basket. At the lowest levels of organized competition this vital statistic would normally have to be kept by the coach. Using a small index card listing each player, he should note the number of violations, bad passes, or errors in ball handling which cause the loss of the ball. He should also record the number of bad shots taken by each player and poor defensive efforts by individuals.

All basketball coaches recognize that the mere scoring of points is not a valid measure of a player's worth. A player must be measured in terms of his defensive ability, his ball-handling ability, his ability to rebound, his shooting average (the percentage of scoring opportunities that he makes), and so forth. We know that the pertinent facts, as recorded statistically, or on a chart, are measurable quantities in basketball that will help the coach determine the relative ability of players.

Statistics are valuable to four groups of people in basketball: the coaches, the players, the news media, and the fans.

Primarily, they are important to the coach. He can obtain

an objective comparison of his players and their abilities through the intelligent interpretation of statistics. In many cases, he can determine the relative value of a player by statistically comparing his ability with that of another player in the same category. Therefore, when scouting an opponent the scout should include as much objective data as possible in his scouting report along with his subjective analysis of the team. Coaches may use statistical information to help determine starting team members and those who will be in key substitute positions. It is often very easy for a coach to determine who his best three or four players are; but he may have to think about the fifth man and the order in which the substitutes should be put into the game. It is possible for the coach to determine which players deserve to be on the court during a game by objectively analyzing statistical reports of preseason practices.

Shooting percentages alone, derived from the number of shots taken and made, the areas from which the shots are taken, and the types of shots taken, are of value to a coach. A shooting chart shows what areas a given opponent may be strongest from, what areas he is weaker from, and what areas he takes most of his shots from. This information gives the coach an insight into the effectiveness of the offensive pattern that the team is using. It tells if a player is a good driver (depending on the shots that he takes in close to the basket) or if he is weak as an outside shooter. The coach can also use the shot chart analytically for his own team to show a player where he should not have taken certain shots because his percentage is not good from that area, or where the ball could have been passed more effectively because teammates have been shooting consistently in that area.

Free-throw information is valuable because it tells him who the strong and weak opposing foul shooters are in case his players must foul an opponent late in the game to obtain possession of the ball. It also tells him which of his own players need more work in shooting foul shots.

Rebound information, offensively and defensively for his own team and for his opponents, is essential. If certain opponents are strong rebounders, he might hold them off the boards to allow his other rebounders to move into the boards to try to rebound. Rebound statistics will also tell him which of his players is not doing a good job when his opponent rebounds effectively.

Information regarding loss of ball is perhaps the most important single factor in the amassing of statistics. Under present day standards, the value of the ball in team possession is approaching one point per possession when a shot is taken. Therefore, possession of the ball is more important to a team than a foul shot, because a foul shot has a value no greater than .7, the national average. It is essential to pinpoint the player who constantly violates the travel procedures in the game, or the player who loses the ball for his team by passing badly, or passing to a player in a position where he is not able to control the ball. If the coach cannot correct their bad habits, then he must replace them. The proper use of statistics can tell him which players are doing the job efficiently.

Team shooting percentages have gone from approximately one in four in the late 1930's to approximately one in two today. Of course, this percentage increases as a player gets closer to a basket for a shot. Since this fact applies to their opponent as well, it is imperative that teams in possession of the ball get a good shot during each possession.

We define a good shot as a shot that a player takes (1) when he is shooting from an area where he consistently makes the greater percentage of his shots; (2) when he has teammates in position to rebound if he misses, giving his team a chance at regaining possession; and (3) when no teammate has a more advantageous shooting position. The third factor must be considered in light of the position of the shooter, and the open teammate who is closer to the basket. If a shooter is within ten feet of the basket, it is perhaps to the team's advantage if he takes the shot, because he is in a high-percentage area (over 60 percent). If the teammate is open with no one between them, naturally, the shooter should pass to him. But if the pass must go by an opponent, because the area for the pass is limited and the passing lane is almost closed, it is better percentage for the man in the ten-foot area to take the shot, because his team has a two to one chance to rebound against the opponent. The margin of error is great in limited passing areas; therefore, under normal conditions, the first good shot that appears should be taken.

The fewer the personal fouls a defender accumulates the more advantageous it is to his team. Personal foul statistics will help the coach to determine how effective his players are on defense. If a good offensive player, assigned to guard an easy opponent, fouls frequently, the coach should check the types of fouls committed by the player in order to prevent them. Naturally the coach does not want an outstanding offensive player to be in foul trouble. If he has three or four fouls the first half with quite a bit of time remaining, the opponents are going to play towards him to try to foul him out of the game.

It is obvious that the players are the chief beneficiaries of statistical analysis. The primary reason for accumulating statistics is to improve the individual techniques of the players and the team techniques of the squad. The analysis and the subjective observations from scouting are most important in determining how a team will play an opposing team, and how each individual player should perform against his opponent. If a player has the desire and the attitude for self-improvement, his own self-analysis of obvious statistics will be the best step towards improvement.

Statistics can be used to advantage by the sports information director, the athletic director, or the person who relays the accumulated statistics to the news media. If statistics are accumulated and compiled in orderly, readily interpreted fashion, the team, the coach and the school can disseminate the information to interested radio, television and newspaper men. More and more, newsmen are crediting players for outstanding rebounding or assists. They are also placing greater emphasis on the number of losses of possession, or turnovers, as they are more commonly called by the news media. A standard practice for news media people is to determine the number of points scored by each team after a turnover by the opponent. This information, compiled by qualified recorders, should be given to newsmen as quickly as possible after a game.

The other individuals who welcome and absorb statistical information are the basketball fans. Statistics gives them a better understanding of the contributions of team members who are not high scorers, but who have superior rebounding, passing, or defensive abilities. Spectators can derive a far greater appreciation of all aspects of the game by being made aware of the statistics on the games.

The final score is the simplest, most essential statistic in basketball, and the scorekeeper is the most important statistical keeper. Therefore he must be a competent person who is familiar with the duties of scorers, as outlined in Rule 2, Section II of the rule book. At a junior high-school level, an interested, qualified teacher could be asked to keep score. At the high-school level any impartial adult who knows the scoring rules should be the scorekeeper. At the college level a paid, impartial expert should be the official scorer.

The rules of scoring are outlined in the rule book and the official scorer and his assistant must be alert to all the intricacies of these rules. Minimal recorded facts about both teams are essential in organized basketball. The scorekeeper must list the names and numbers of the members of each team, and keep track of the number of baskets made by each individual and each team, the number of foul shots taken and made by each individual and each team, a running score, the number of personal fouls credited to each player on each team, the number of team fouls each half, the number of technical fouls charged to each team, and the number of time-outs that are charged to each team during the course of the game and in any overtime period. He must notify the officials when a player gets his fifth personal

keeping score

431

foul, because the player must be excluded from the game at that point. He must also tell the officials and the team when it is charged with its last allowed time-out. In high school after the fourth foul and in college after the sixth foul in each half, a foul shooter gets a bonus attempt if the official calls a one-shot foul. Therefore, the scorers must be accurate. The official NCAA Basketball Scorebook, published and distributed by the National Collegiate Athletic Association, is unquestionably the finest, most complete scorebook that can be used. It should be used by all organized teams in junior high school, high school, college, and clubs so that scoring and recording will be uniform at all levels.

The scorer and an assistant scorer should both keep a running score, comparing their scorebooks with each other, whenever possible, after each goal, at time-outs, and when the officials come over to talk to the scorers. The scorers should check their books first for the accuracy of the running score, second for the accuracy of the fouls against each individual player and each team, and third for the number of time-outs charged to each team.

The following statistical information should be kept.

complete shot chart

standard statistical information

A carbon copy of this chart should be made for the opponents. A shot chart is a diagram of an entire court with certain areas semicircled. The first semicircle indicates an area within ten feet of the basket. In this area, the recorder notes short field goal attempts by each player using the player's number to represent each attempt. Succesful scoring attempts should be circled. A second semicircle encloses the intermediate field goal area, the area ten to twenty-one feet from the basket. Again, the recorder puts down a player's number to record an intermediate field goal attempt, circling the number if the basket is made. Long field goal attempts should be recorded in the area more than twenty feet from the basket, and a succesful scoring attempt should be circled. For clarity, we feel that shots within four feet of the basket should be recorded outside the endlines on the diagram. Otherwise, the diagram would become cluttered and difficult to interpret, since most shots are in close to the basket. The team shooting to the left is noted at the top left of the shot chart, and the team shooting to the right is noted at the right top. Where and when the game is being played is also noted at the top of the chart, as well as the period covered by the chart.

Diag. 12-1 covers the first ten minutes of the first half. The number of shots attempted, the number of shots made, and the shooting percentage are noted at the bottom of the chart. At the half time the two shot charts for the first half can be added together to get the first half shooting percentage.

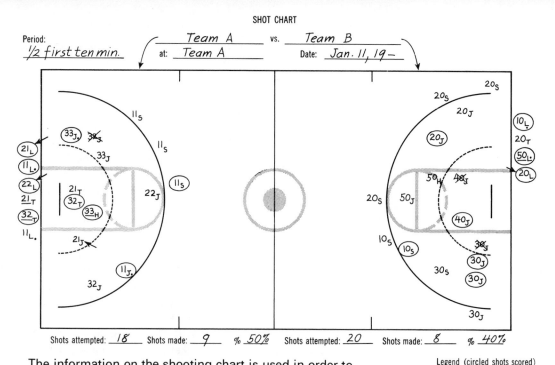

Period: ½ first ten min.

Team A   vs.   Team B
at: Team A   Date: Jan. 11, 19 —

Shots attempted: _18_ Shots made: _9_ % _50%_   Shots attempted: _20_ Shots made: _8_ % _40%_

The information on the shooting chart is used in order to show where the shots came from and the type of shots that your team and the opponents are taking. All shot attempts should be noted.

In the center of the shot chart on the court diagram, we list the legend. The following symbols are used: All shots which score a basket are circled. *J* means a jump shot; *S*, set shot; *L*, lay-up or driving shot; *H*, hook shot; *T*, attempted tap-up. Underscore indicates that a player was fouled on his shot attempt, and *X* through the player's number indicates that his shot was blocked. We put a dot at the bottom of a shot to indicate that it was obtained as a result of a good fast break. We indicate a drive-in by an arrow.

Diag. 12-1 shows eighteen shots by Team A. (Actually there are nineteen shots, but one tip taken by Number 21 was not counted in the percentage since the shooter was fouled.)

To the left of the court, 21 *L* in a circle indicates that Player 21 scored on a lay-up. The arrow indicates that the shot was a drive-in. The next shot, taken by Player 11, was a successful lay-up that resulted from a fast break.

In the short field goal area, Player 21 tipped without scoring, 32 tipped and scored, and 33 took a successful hook-shot and was fouled. Player 21 *J* drove to the basket, stopped, and took a jump shot.

In the intermediate area Player 33 scored on a jump shot as a result of a fast break, and Player 32 attempted a jump shot which was blocked.

Thus we can see from the shot chart that Team A attempted ten shots in the "in-close" area, six of which

Legend (circled shots scored)
J — Jump shot
S — Set shot
L — Lay up
H — Hook shot
T — Tip
— — Fouled (underlined)
X — Blocked
• — Fast break shot
← — Drive-in

scored (one not counting as a shot because the shooter was fouled.) The team took six shots in the intermediate area, two of which scored, and one of which was blocked. Player 11, took three shots, one of which scored, from the long-shot area.

These statistics indicate that Team A was moving the ball into the in-close area for the most part and was scoring primarily on in-close shots. This means that the fast break was working well, as indicated by the dots on the shots, and the ball could be moved into good shooting area by Team A.

Team B is diagramed on the right of this chart. Four inside shots are listed beside the court, two of which are results of fast breaks. Player 10 scored a lay-up at the end of a fast break, 20 missed on a tip, 50 scored on a lay-up at the end of a fast break and was fouled in the attempt. Player 20 scored on a driving lay-up. A jump-shot by 40 and a jump shot by 30 were blocked in this area. Player 40 scored on a jump shot. Player 30 scored two jump shots from the right side of the basket and missed a set shot from the intermediate area. He also missed on a jump shot from the long shot area to the right side.

This disbursal of shots is generally the result of shooting attempts by a team playing against a zone defense. Two of the shots scored in the in-close area were the results of fast breaks. One was a drive, and another was a tip. Two of the inside shots were blocked, indicating that there probably was a massing of the defense in this area. Most of the shots are disbursed over a great area and are taken from the intermediate area, or the outside area. Five shots, none of which scored, were taken from outside. Shot charts are not used for game statistical purposes. They are used by the coach for analytical purposes after the games and are kept by scouts to help prepare their teams for upcoming games. A summary of the four quarters should be transcribed neatly onto one master diagram. Then an individual shot chart should be made for each player, showing the type of shots he has taken, made and missed, the shots he was blocked or fouled on, and the types of shots the team is scoring on at the end of the fast break.

The shots shown on charts for individual games should be compiled game by game on a master chart for each player. At the end of the season this makes an excellent summary for a coach to use in order to discuss a player's shooting ability, strengths and weaknesses with him.

game statistics summary (table 1)

The teams playing, the place and the date are listed at the top. The first two columns on the left list the names and numbers of the players on Team A and Team B.

TABLE 1. GAME STATISTICS SUMMARY

Team A vs. Team B   At Team A   Date: Jan. 11, 19____

Team A Player	No.	Time Played	Total	Shots Att. and Made	T	Assists	T	Turnovers	T
Smith	21	20-11, 9-2 9+7 20-11, 3-0 9+3	16 28 12	IIXIIX 6-2 IIX 3-1	9-3	IIII 5 III 3	8	III 3 I 1	4
A. Jones	23	20-16, 8-0 4+8 20-16, 13-4 4+9	12 25 13	XXIII 5-2 IIIX 4-1	9-3	II 2 III 3	5	I 1 II 2	3
B. Jones	25	20-4 16 20-17, 8-0 3+8	16 27 11	IXXIIIX 7-3 IXIIXX 6-3	13-6	I 1	1	I 1 II 2	3
Kelly	31	20-0 20-0	20 40 20	IXIIXXIX 10-5 IIXIIXXIIIX 11-5	21-10	I 1 II 2	3	II 2	2
Hart	33	20-18, 13-0 2+13 16-8, 2-0 8+2	15 25 10	IXII 4-1 IXXII 5-2	9-3	II 2	2	I 1 III 3	4
Jasper	35	18-13 5 17-4 13	5 18 13	IX 2-1 IXIXIXI 7-3	9-4	I 1	1	I 1	1
Hunt	41	16-8 8 20-13, 11-3 7+8	8 23 15	X 1-1 XXXIXI 6-4	7-5			I 1	1
Johnston	43	11-9, 2-0 2+2 4-0	4 8 4	IXI 3-1 IXIIIX 6-2	9-3				
Leftowitz	45	4-0 4-2	4 6 2	II 2-0 III 3-0	5-0				
Arthur	51		0						
Totals		100 200 100	100	40-16 51-21	91-37	10-10	20	9-9	18
Team B									
Green	10								

Team Shooting	First Half			Second Half			Final		
	Att.	Made	Pct.	Att.	Made	Pct.	Att.	Made	Pct.
Team A	40	16	40.	51	21	41.2	91	37	40.7
Team B	35	18	51.4	40	17	42.5	75	35	46.7

435

There are enough spaces on the chart to list the players on both teams, including the starters and the frequently used substitutes. If there are more substitutes than spaces, seldom-used players should be doubled-up in the lower spaces at the bottom of each team's list.

The next column lists time played. In this column the recorder writes the number 20 after the five starters. When a substitute replaces a starter, the recorder puts the time that the player comes out after the 20. The time that the second player enters becomes the first number after his name. Since breaking the time into fractions of minutes would be confusing, recorders should go to the nearest minute. If a player is replaced with 11 minutes and 23 seconds left in the half, the recorder would put down 11. If it were exactly 11 minutes and 30 seconds, he would go to the nearest even number, 12. The figures for the first half are kept in the upper area of the allotted box, and the second half figures are in the lower area. This procedure is illustrated in Table 1.

On Team A, Smith (Number 21) started the game; therefore, a 20 is placed on the upper half of the box. He was replaced at the eleven minute mark so 11 is listed after the 20. Johnston, the man who replaced him, started at 11 and stayed in until 9. Johnston was then replaced by Smith, the starter. Johnston replaced Smith again at the two minute mark, so the time played column reads 9-2 for Smith and 2-0 for Johnston. The numbers to the right are the minutes played. Smith played 9 minutes the first time he was in and 7 minutes the second time. The total, 16, is placed in the total column at the top of the allotted space for the first half. The total for the second half (12) is recorded at the bottom of the space. The sum of the two totals is put in the middle. The sum of the totals in each half should total 100 minutes. This figure must be accurate, because it is used in postgame summaries in the NCAA Scorebook.

The fifth column indicates shots attempted and made. The recorder makes a line for each shot attempted and crosses it when a player scores. Smith took six shots in the first half and made two, as the markings show. The shots taken by all the players are totaled for each half. In Table 1, forty shots were taken, sixteen shots, or 40 percent, were made. Every shot that a player takes should be recorded unless he was fouled on a shot that did not score. Blocked shots and a successful shot in which a player is fouled are counted. All taps on the offensive end must also be counted as shots, as they are actual attempts at scoring a basket.

The totals of the attempts and made shots for each half are listed in the sixth column (T).

The team shooting percentages are kept at the bottom of this statistics summary. Team A attempted forty shots in the first half and made sixteen for a shooting percentage of 40 percent. In the second half they attempted fifty-one shots at the basket and made twenty-one for a percentage of 41.2 percent. They attempted a total of ninety-one shots and made thirty-seven for a final shooting percentage of 40.7 percent.

Assists are recorded in seventh column. An assist is credited to a player whenever he makes the important pass which leads to a score. Assists are not given for every basket; they are only given for a major contribution by the passer, thus information in the assist column is subjective. It is not necessarily the last pass made that deserves credit for an assist. The major pass might have been an excellent hard pass to a person who was moving in toward the basket, and the second player may have passed off to a teammate in a better position. If, in the opinion of the statistician, the first player made the important contributing pass leading to the basket, then he should be given credit for the assist.

The total number of assists goes in the eighth column (T).

Turnovers are listed in the ninth column. These occur when a team loses possession of the ball without obtaining a shot at the basket. The player who causes the loss of possession should be charged with the turnover. If a player is tied-up when he has possession of the ball and a jump ball ensues, he is only charged with a turnover if his team loses possession of the jump ball. While turnovers are not used in the NCAA game summary, they are used in most other statistical game summaries and are an important factor in game analysis for both the coach and the representatives of the news media.

rebound chart (table 2)

Records of rebounds are one of the most important statistics. The rebounds for the first half of the game are marked and totaled in the upper half of the box. The rebounds in the second half are shown in the lower half of the box. We break down offensive and defensive rebounds in our statistical summary, but total rebounds only are shown in the NCAA Scorebook.

A rebound must be credited to someone each time a field goal is attempted or a foul shot is missed. A team rebound is credited to the team that puts the ball in play, if a field goal or free-throw attempt misses and goes out-of-bounds, if a violation or foul is called after an attempt, or if a shot is blocked and goes out-of-bounds. A rebound is also credited to a team for recovering a held ball tip after a missed shot. If a shot is blocked and stays in bounds, the rebound is credited to the player who gains possession. A player who tips the ball is credited with a rebound as well as a shot attempt, as he is the one who has actually obtained at least partial possession of the ball. If a rebound is deflected to a teammate, the player who tips it is credited with the re-

TABLE 2. REBOUND CHART

Team A _____ vs. _____ Team B

At: Team A _____   Date: Jan. 11, 19___

Player	No.	Off.		Def.		T.	Player	No.	Off.	Def.	T.
Smith	21	II	2	III	3	5 / 13 / 8	Green	10			
		II	2	⟋⟋⟋⟋⟋	5						
A. Jones	23						Black	12			
B. Jones	25						Hoar	14			
Kelly	31						Irving	22			
Hart	33						Wright	24			
Jasper	35						Seegrove	32			
Hunt	41						Roth	34			
Johnston	43						Phillipman	44			
Leftowitz	45						Raska	52			
Arthur	51						Hansen	20			
							Loudenville	50			
							Brady	54			
		First Half		Second Half					First Half	Second Half	
Team Reb.							Team Reb.				
First Half							First Half				
Second Half							Second Half				
Game Total							Game Total				

bound. The rebounds for the first half and the second half are totaled together and a game total is listed at the bottom of the rebound chart. The number of missed shots equals the total number of rebounds (individuals plus team).

TABLE 3. TURNOVER CHART

Team A vs. Team B   At Team A   Date: Jan. 11, 19___

Violations		Legend		Passes
T—traveling	X—10 sec. viol.	B—back court viol.		P—passer's error
3—3 sec. viol.	O—out of bounds	D—dribbling viol.		R—receiver's error
5—5 sec. viol.	K—kicking viol.	H—held ball		S—ball stolen on dribble

Team A	No.	Loss of Possession					Recovery of Possession				
		Viol.	Pass	Foul	Jump	Total	Viol.	Int.	Foul	Jump	Total
Smith	21										
Team B											
Green	10										

turnover chart (table 3)

This chart is important to the coach for game analysis purposes. The recorder who keeps it must be a basketball expert. The chart includes the number of violations made by each team, the number of bad passes or losses of possession made by each team, and the recoveries made. The total turnovers are kept for use on the game statistics summary sheet. The violations are listed at the top. *T* means traveling; *3*, a three-second violation; *5*, a five-second violation; *X*, a ten-second violation; *O*, ball out-of-bounds; *K*, a kicking violation; *B*, backcourt violation; *D*, a dribbling violation; *H*, a held ball when the player in possession is tied up. If a bad pass is considered by the recorder to be a passer's error, he puts a *P* in the loss of possession column. If it is the receiver's error, the recorder puts an *R* next to that player's name. An *S* indicates a ball that is stolen on a player's dribble. Both teams can be listed but it is most important that the players on Team A, or the home team, be compiled accurately.

Loss of Possession falls into four cateogries. Under violations, the recorder lists losses of possession caused by violation of rule. If a player on Team A is traveling with the ball, the letter *T* would be put in next to his name. If a player made a bad pass, a *P* would be put in the pass column next to his name. If an offensive foul or a technical foul is committed while in possession, a loss of possession occurs and is designated by a vertical line in the foul column. If a player is tied up while his team has the ball, an *H* is put in the jump

439

column. If the ball is recovered by that team on a jump, then the recovery is also recorded in the recovery of possession box.

Recovery of Possession also falls into four categories. The first is "violations." If a player causes an opponent to violate a rule, that player should be credited with a recovery. An interception or a steal should be noted in the second column. In the third and fourth columns the recorder notes who caused an offensive foul, and who recovered a jump ball.

This chart, while not a part of the official scoring summary, is an important adjunct to any good coaching situation, because it tells who lost the ball, how the ball was lost, and under what circumstances. For example, if Team A loses a ball because of a traveling violation, and a Team B player had caused this by stepping in his path quickly so that the player could not stop in time to avert traveling, then the Team B player would be given a violation recovery, and the Team A player would be given a violation loss. In this way the coach can pinpoint vital loss of possession mistakes. At the same time credit can be given for recovery of possession by an alert defender.

drill statistics

All statistics that are to be recorded during a ball game should also be recorded in practice so that recorders, observers, and statisticians can practice under simulated game conditions, preparing themselves for the season ahead. Statistical records of practice sessions also give coaches valuable objective information that can be used to help determine weakness in players and to better evaluate players whose abilities seem close in personal observation. At times some drills should be analyzed from an objective point of view. For example, a chart for our basic three-on-two drill could simply list the names of the players, the number of bad passes made, poor ball handling, poor defense, and bad shots. A manager or a recorder keeps this chart.

recorders

All of the above statistics should be recorded whenever possible. At the high-school and college levels, at least four statistical recorders, not including the scorer, should cover each game. The first recorder should make the shot chart, starting a new chart at the ten-minute mark in each half of a college game and at each quarter in a high-school game.

The second recorder should keep the Game Statistics Summary.

The third recorder keeps the rebound chart, noting offensive and defensive rebounds for both Team A and Team B.

The fourth recorder keeps the turnover chart.

440

All statisticians, scorers, and recorders should be close to each other during a game or scrimmage so that all statistics compiled during the first half can be compiled quickly and put onto one master chart that can be used for half-time analysis. The recorders should bring this to the coach in the locker room area as soon as possible. As a courtesy, duplicate copies should be made so that the opponents may also use these statistics. Many schools will run off ditto copies of half-time statistics for use by the sports media. At the close of the game the same procedure should be followed. After the official scorer has totaled up the necessary columns, the other recorders should give him the statistics in orderly fashion so that he may complete the summary of the NCAA Scorebook. Then all summary statistics should be placed on a final master ditto page and run off for dissemination to the sports writers and other news media representatives who may wish a copy, to the visiting team, to any scouts of future opponents of both teams in the game, to the coaches, and possibly to the players.

training
and
conditioning

Training is the regimen used to prepare players physically and mentally. It includes proper diet; adequate sleep; routine daily habits; the prevention, treatment, and rehabilitation of basketball injuries; and conditioning, a systematic program for working the body into a state of physical fitness so that it is capable of efficiently and effectively performing the strenuous muscular actions required of it in basketball.

medical examinations

The team doctor must examine every athlete before the start of practice or training camp to make certain he is physically capable of playing the game. Players at all levels should be examined, and the doctor should ask about possible old injuries. If there is no team doctor, a statement from the family physician should be obtained. In cases where this is impossible, the person responsible for the team should make arrangements for the players to be examined at a nearby medical clinic.

The examination should be thorough. If possible, a complete medical history form should be filled out by parents or the family doctor. The coach should check the student's school health record and investigate any suspicious areas. If playing will jeopardize his health, the individual should not be allowed to try out for the team.

responsibilities of the player, coach, trainer, and team doctor

During training, the athlete, coach, trainer, and team doctor must function as a close-knit team. Each must understand the areas of responsibility of the others, working cooperatively for maximum team efficiency.

players

The athlete is the focal point of attention of the coach, trainer and team doctor. He must work himself into maximum physical condition and try to maintain that level, reporting all illness and injuries, no matter how slight they may seem. He must adhere to sane living habits, eating properly, sleeping enough, abstaining from alcohol and tobacco, and maintaining a healthy outlook. To prevent injuries, he must report worn out and faulty equipment so it can be replaced.

coach

The coach is the coordinator of the cooperating team. Most colleges and many high schools have qualified trainers

444

and team doctors; when they are not available, the coach shoulders the grave responsibility of training and conditioning single-handedly. Of course, they should remember that they are not qualified to diagnose or treat an athletic injury or to prescribe internal medication. Some coaches, either unwittingly or purposely, have played injured athletes without proper diagnosis or prognosis, in the hope of winning a game. Especially at lower levels of competition, these improperly cared for ankle, knee, or shoulder injuries may become chronic conditions that necessitate later treatment—possibly corrective surgery—or result in permanent incapacitation. Coaches must never play an injured athlete without medical clearance.

A coach, especially one without a trainer and doctor available daily, must be emminently well-qualified for his duties. Primarily, he must know basketball thoroughly, and he must be capable of transmitting his knowledge effectively. He must also understand the psychological factors governing the age group he is working with so that he knows who to praise and when, who can accept criticism, etc. Any coaching aspirant on an organized (junior and senior high school or college) level should take courses in anatomy, physiology, kinesiology and first aid, for he must be prepared to function as a trainer. He has to understand the physiological limitations of the group he is working with and be able to outline guidelines in healthful living for his charges.

The coach is responsible for setting up safeguards against faulty equipment or improper use of equipment and against accidents in practice facilities, especially in the locker room area. He must insist on cleanliness there to prevent athlete's foot, skin infections, boils, etc., and he must insist that players shower daily. At all times, the coach must anticipate probable injuries and be prepared to deal with them immediately using proper methods. The coach must know the location and telephone number of an available doctor, ambulance service and hospital.

trainer

The trainer must have the complete confidence of athlete, coach and doctor. He should devise the off-season conditioning programs with the coach and prescribe and supervise corrective and developmental weight programs. He also supervises treatment prescribed by the doctor and initiates the recommended rehabilitation programs. He must be expert in first aid as well as in taping and bandaging, and he must see that the players obtain proper attention mentally and emotionally as well as physically.

The trainer should be a positive psychological factor for team morale, acting as a father-confessor and confidant to the players. The training room is his domain; its friendly, close atmosphere changes when an outsider—even a doctor or coach—enters.

The trainers must recognize and respect the authority of the team doctor in all medical matters. At the same time, the doctor must recognize and respect the contribution of the trainer. Many times, the two men's duties overlap. Giving a capable trainer added responsibility relieves the coach and doctor of many problems while increasing the trainer's sense of importance and increasing the players' faith in the trainer.

Student-Trainers. If no trainer is available, the coach should make provisions for training interested nonathletic youngsters as student-trainers. Organizations such as CRAMER of Gardner, Kansas, have a free summer correspondence course for student-trainers. It consists of six weekly lessons and a student-trainer manual. This course would also be beneficial for a coach. By taking advantage of this service, the coach will improve his program, while allowing himself more time with the team.

Nurse. If no trainer is available at the junior or senior high school levels, the school nurse may play an important role in training and conditioning. If properly indoctrinated by the coach or team doctor, she can become an integral part of the program. Her closeness with student athletes, her ability to help in filling out essential but tedious athletic injury reports, and her ability to glean vital information concerning a boy's actual condition, demand close rapport between her and the coach.

team doctor

Orthopedic specialists generally make excellent team doctors, as the majority of injuries are in their specialized area. However, the most important considerations for the team doctor are, not his specialty, but his interest, knowledgeability of athletic injuries, and availability. He should enjoy competitive team athletics. Besides understanding the game he must recognize that competition is essential to an athlete. He must be expert at devising extensive rehabilitation programs to be implemented following injury. A competent athletic physician is indispensible to the team. Athletes generally make excellent patients, as thorough conditioning gives them a high threshold for withstanding pain. This attribute allows them to compete effectively under conditions that would probably incapacitate the average man.

The team doctor must be the final judge of an athlete's status. To compete or not compete is solely his decision. He must base his decision on the following rule: if further aggravation or permanent disability is possible at any time, the injured player, regardless of his ability, must be kept inactive, even if pressure from all sources—athlete, coach, alumni, etc.—is overwhelming. The doctor's decision must be binding and final.

However, it is incumbent on the team doctor that he base his treatment and rehabilitation of an injury not only on his clinical knowledge but also on his interest in returning the athlete to competition as soon as possible. Many nondisabling injuries, (for example a pulled muscle, a sprained finger, or a turned ankle) will correct themselves, given sufficient time and rest. Therefore a disinterested physician, perhaps unconcerned about or unaware of the months of torturous conditioning highly competitive athletics demands, may allow nature to take its course when treatment and rehabilitation could return the injured competitor to action in a few days. Because of their excellent physical condition, young athletes usually have above average recuperative powers, and their incentive to recover quickly makes them cooperate fully in corrective and rehabilitative programs.

The most important attribute in the athlete-doctor relationship is confidence. The players must instinctively sense that the team physician is "with them" when they need him most.

When no trainer is available, the coach and student-trainers should use a clean area near the locker room as a training room. This area must be large enough for basic taping requirements and first aid procedures. Minimum furniture requirements include a heavy, long table for taping; a refrigerator to make and store ice and to hold supplies that must be kept cold; a bench for athletes waiting for treatment; a foldaway cot; and a locked storage compartment.

minimal essential trainer—first aid equipment when no trainer is available

The following supplies and equipment are essential:

Bandage scissors, regular scissors, sponge rubber, fever thermometer, instant cold packs, an oral screw, tongue seizing forceps, tongue depressors, felt padding, tape cutters, large bucket or pail, weight scale and daily weight chart, elastic ankle wraps, adhesive tape (in 1 inch, $1\frac{1}{2}$ inch, and two inch rolls), skin toughener, gauze rolls, 2×2 gauze pads, ammonia inhalants, absorbent cotton, band-aids, analgesic balm, green soap, vaseline, foot and body powder, and first-aid cream.

Proper rest and sleep habits help maintain the condition of the body and keeps athletes alert. The amount of sleep necessary for good health varies from person to person. Eight hours is the recommended norm, but some people require more and others require less. Young people generally require more sleep during their period of growth. Each player should determine how many hours of sleep he requires to maintain a feeling of health and vitality and

sleep

get that much sleep every night, going to bed at approximately the same time each night. The athlete who abuses his sleeping hours cannot play to his full potential, regardless of his natural abilities.

Players should be encouraged to rest after hard workouts and—for at least an hour—before a game. If possible, a coach should supervise rest periods before games to cut down on horseplay and to alleviate mental or emotional strain brought on by anticipation of the game.

diet One of the first things the coach should do each year is to call the team together for a lecture on good living habits and proper nutrition. If there is a trainer, he should give this lecture; otherwise, the coach or a health education teacher should handle it. On a high school level, it would be ideal to invite the parents, because it is at this level that coaches have the most trouble controlling the diet of their charges.

The lecture should cover the following information:

Food influences the physical condition of the player. A diet must contain protein for growth, iron for blood, calcium and phosphorus for teeth and bone, and vitamins for strength, energy, and good eyesight. Meat, fish, eggs, milk, fruit, and fresh vegetables build red blood and firm muscles, and they prevent constipation. Rough cereals and bread provide iron and the B vitamins. Pie, cake, chocolate, fried foods, candy, carbonated beverages, and plain "junk" foods are not good for athletes.

An athlete should drink a lot of water daily, especially with his meals, but water intake during practice sessions and games should be limited to a few sips at a time. Cold water on the hot stomach of a person who has been running has an adverse effect. Actually, an athlete in excellent condition doesn't need much water during practice or a game, but he should be allowed what he needs. Usually, trips to the water fountain to rinse out his mouth are more from habit than from need.

A solution to the water problem is found in new formulas such as "Take-Five" by Cramer, of Gardner, Kansas, or "Gator-Ade," by Stokely-Van Camp. These are instant salt-dextrose mixtures which are absorbed by the human system twelve times faster than water, thus putting back body minerals quickly and making players stronger. They come in instant dry packets which are mixed with a gallon of water. This citrus-flavored sodium chloride mixture replaces salt, fluid, dextrose and ascorbic acid lost during practice sessions and games, and it is not necessary to limit intake. Several gallons can be made very easily daily. The mixture also improves eating habits of players, because it quenches their thirst without bloating.

448

Today's athlete has to watch his weight very carefully. Speed is a prime requisite for playing basketball, and the athlete with weight problems will lack full speed, quickness and endurance. Athletes should not exceed five pounds over their normal playing weight during the off-season so that it isn't too much of a chore to attain their regular weight quickly when the practice sessions start. An athlete who has to go on a crash diet is going to be weak for the rest of the season. Of course, allowances must be made for normal growth during adolescense. If an athlete loses an excessive amount of weight during a season, he should see a doctor, as there might be something seriously wrong.

weight

Players should eat four hours before the game, then take a good walk (at least one-half mile) so that the digestive system is working. The walk should be followed by a rest period of approximately one hour, during which time the players lie down and relax completely.

pre-game meal

The problem on the high school level is that coaches usually cannot control the players by supervising the pre-game meal, walk, and rest period. A good solution is to get the team together at the gymnasium at least two and one-half hours before game time. In this way the coach is certain of minimal digestive time and can control an enforced rest period.

We suggest the following pre-game meal: fruit juice or fruit cup; toast (1 slice) with honey, steak, baked potato, green vegetable, jello, tea with lemon or sugar (no cream). No milk should be consumed with the pregame meal. Liquids at that meal should be readily absorbable and low in fat content.

Coaches should safeguard the health of their players. In case illness or injury does occur, the coach and trainer must know what to do.

prevention and treatment of illnesses and injuries

colds

Colds and flu continue to harass mankind, even though many years of medical research have gone into finding a cure. Prevention is still the best antidote. Coaches should insist that their players abide by the following rules.

1. Get cold or flu shots as early as possible in the school year, with doctor's approval.

2. Take vitamin C daily in pill form or in twelve ounces of orange juice.

3. Maintain a proper diet, take vitamins, and drink fluids in abundance.

4. Ensure regular elimination of body wastes.

5. Build resistance by being out in the air every day.

6. Avoid warm stuffy places and drafts.

7. Taper off the daily shower so that you finish with a cold spray.

8. Dry hair and body thoroughly. Wait awhile before going outside.

9. Dress warmly in cold weather. Wear a hat.

10. Keep temperatures in the gym about 60 degrees.

11. Keep living temperature at 68 to 70 degrees.

12. Avoid people who have colds.

If preventative measures fail and a cold develops, it should be treated by the doctor. Any medication taken internally should be prescribed by him.

staleness

Staleness is a very common, sometimes exaggerated athletic phenomenon for which there is no medical explanation. It is a psychological phenomenon that many people say is nonexistent. However, as any physician will tell you, if something exists in the mind of an individual it is real to that person.

Basketball players, more than any other athletes, are vulnerable to this condition. The basketball season is long, and players must "get up" for many games. The physical drain, coupled with the emotional pitch, depletes the athletes' resistance.

Staleness can be averted if the coach is sensitive to the following symptoms.

1. Sleep does not eliminate fatigue.

2. The player is moody, irritable, and sluggish.

3. The player loses his appetite and loses weight.

4. The player is tired yet restless.

5. The player is not in strong condition at the end of practices and games.

6. The player is not up to par mentally or physically. His game is "off."

7. The player has no enthusiasm. His mind and body do not return to normal eagerness for mental and physical activity.

Staleness has many causes. A coach must know his personnel well so that the cause of each case can be pinpointed and cured. Following are four possible causes.

1. Boredom caused by monotony is the chief culprit.

2. The victim may be studying too hard or doing too much outside work. Perhaps he is worried about exams or personal problems. He could also be suffering from lack of sleep.

3. Practices may have become too long and strenuous, not allowing the body to adjust. "Too much basketball."

4. The player may have become impatient with his progress and development.

A good coach will conduct his practice sessions with an eye to avoiding staleness. Practice should be enjoyable, not unbearable. Variety is a keynote. It pays to have fun at practice. A pleasurable drill or game and a little laughter promote a feeling of comradeship, which is so important to a team. We believe in allowing players at least a day or two a week away from basketball.

As a change of pace, the coach should arrange for a team practice or intra-squad scrimmage on a different court occasionally, if possible. He should also arrange for the team to have a meal in a new environment.

For cases of extreme staleness, a complete rest is in order. Generally, shorter practices, without strict regimentation, and a change of drills, diet, or scenery will relieve the players' tensions. Using drills such as big men against small men, a no-dribble scrimmage, or a scrimmage with a no-bounce basketball relieve monotony in practice.

care of the feet

A basketball player should keep his feet in condition at all times so that when he begins practice his feet are tough. Each day during the first week of practice, the trainer or coach should check the players' feet carefully. If the feet become irritated or blister, the trainer should pinpoint the cause, treat the foot, and lessen the players's activity if necessary. A skin conditioner should be available to the players for daily use. This gets their feet ready for strenuous exercises and workouts.

Players should wear two pairs of socks, preferably two pairs of heavy sweat socks. They should use clean socks daily, both for dress and practice. Another preventative measure is to rub soap *inside* the *inner* sock, coating the sole and heel. When the player's feet perspire, the soap dissolves and creates a film that eliminates all friction points.

Athlete's Foot. Athlete's foot, a highly contagious skin disease, is caused by a fungus that thrives on a damp, hot environment. Players must dry their feet carefully, especially between the toes, and sprinkle their feet with antiseptic powder daily. Prevention is the best cure, but if athlete's foot does develop, the player should see the doctor immediately. He will prescribe something to dry it up.

Blisters. If a blister develops, it should receive attention immediately, because blisters are very susceptible to infection.

The primary causes of blisters are shoes and socks that do not fit properly, too much practice before the feet are conditioned, a hole in a sock, and lack of physical conditioning before the start of the season.

To treat a blister, sterilize the area around the blister, puncture it with a sterile instrument if it hasn't broken, and

451

allow the fluid to seep out. With sterile surgical scissors, remove the dead skin, holding it with tweezers. Cover the area with a medicated cream to prevent infection. Bandage with sterile gauze and tape. The area should be uncovered, dressed and cleansed every day until healing is complete.

Calluses. A callus is a hard, thickened skin area, usually on the foot, that forms wherever there is pressure and friction. A callus can cause very sore feet if the area under it becomes inflamed. Consult a doctor immediately if this occurs.

A callus file, available at any drugstore, is used to shave down a thick callus. Never use a sharp cutting instrument for this purpose. It is a good idea to have the trainer supervise the filing, because if a callus is filed too thin, live tissue can be cut, creating a possibility of blisters and infection.

shoes

A basketball player's shoes are the most important part of his equipment. In no other sport do the feet of the athlete take such a tremendous amount of wear and tear. Consider the pounding on a hard floor, the quick starts and stops, the sudden turns, and the constant running, accelerating and decelerating continuously. The fit of the basketball shoe is all important. Sneakers must be comfortable over two pairs of socks. There is no advantage to wearing high cut sneakers rather than low cut ones, because the upper part of the high sneakers is made of flimsy canvas material that provides no support to the ankle.

ankles

Ankle injuries are the most common basketball injury. All turns, sprains, and possible fractures should be examined by the doctor. If no break is present, he will prescribe treatment and rehabilitation. First aid for an ankle injury is as follows: Help the injured player to the training area so that he does not have to put any weight on the injured foot. Submerse the ankle in a large pail filled with cold water and ice for approximately half an hour. Call a doctor. Wrap an elastic bandage tightly around the ankle, after covering the sorest area with a piece of sponge rubber.

An athlete's ankles should not be taped until he receives his first sprain. To prevent reinjury after that, he should be taped daily for all games and strenuous practices for the remainder of the season. Taping doesn't weaken the ankles, as it is not worn for long periods. All tape should be removed daily. Normal usage and walking strengthens the injured ankle.

The doctor should advise trainers and coaches or student-trainers on taping procedures for each injury. Although most sprains are taped from medial to lateral side, some may have to be taped lateral to medial. Incorrect taping procedures usually further incapacitate athletes.

452

Before taping, benzoine or a skin toughener should be sprayed on the area to be taped. Then guaze pads should be placed on the instep and behind the heel over the Achilles tendon. The entire area to be taped should be covered with gauze. The basket-weave taping has proved most successful for us. (The open basket-weave allows for swelling.) It is very easy to learn, and once the doctor has okayed its use, the coach can proceed on his own.

The coach-trainer must supervise rehabilitation as prescribed.

nosebleeds

Nosebleeds occur frequently on the basketball court and are usually the result of a blow on the nose. If a player has repeated hemorrhages, or if he continues to bleed for more than fifteen minutes in spite of first aid, he must be examined by a doctor. The first aid treatment of a nosebleed is as follows:

1. Place the player flat on his back and pack his nostrils with a cotton wad saturated with nose drops that shrink the tissues.

2. Place cold towels or ice bags against the back of the neck, forehead, or lips.

3. Gently pinch the lower part of the nose.

4. If the player seems to be swallowing a great deal of blood, turn his head so that his nose is pointing downward.

5. When a fracture is suspected, call a doctor.

finger injury

Finger injuries are a common occurance in basketball. Jamming of a joint, spraining of joint ligaments, or a fracture may occur when the extremities of the extended fingers are struck by the ball or are banged into by another player. If a too long fingernail is struck, a painful blood blister may form under the nail. Proper paring of fingernails is a must to prevent this.

When an injury occurs, use ice packs immediately. If a doctor's examination shows no fracture, continue treatment using constant ice packs. When the doctor allows the athlete to play, the injured finger should be taped to an adjoining finger, which serves as a splint. The splint finger will take the brunt of any blow so that the sore finger won't be abused. Placing a one-eighth inch thickness of felt between the fingers minimizes friction and prevents irritation. If a shooter feels this method may affect his touch, a molded pliable cast can be fitted and taped to the injured finger. A third method of treatment is to powder the finger, apply a layer of one-inch tape loosely, sticky side up, then add another layer, sticky side down. This tape cast should limit joint movement. It gives good protection, can be removed and reused constantly, and psychologically doesn't give the player a bound up feeling on his shooting hand.

floor burns

Floor burns are injuries where the skin is partially destroyed by a player sliding on the floor. Usually these wounds are not too deep. A floor burn should be washed with soap and water, dried thoroughly, then cleaned with an antiseptic and covered with a dressing of zinc oxide. This process should be repeated daily until the burn is healed.

shin splints

Shin splits are a very annoying and painful condition in the front lower leg area. They can be caused by excessive running on a hard surface, or by switching from an outdoor court to an indoor court or vice-versa. Players making these transitions should start slowly on the different surface, building themselves up to full speed over a ten day period, thereby not putting undue strain on their shins.

If shin splints do occur, use ice packs until they are seen by the doctor. For a severe condition, the doctor may recommend taping.

muscle pulls and spasms

Muscle pulls or spasms result from abnormal contractions. Common causes are fatigue, a blow, overstretching untrained muscles, cold, or loss of saltwater balance when perspiring excessively. Apply ice to a muscle pull as soon as it occurs. The doctor should prescribe treatment and rehabilitation, determining how to tape or wrap the injury and when the athlete may start to play again.

During a muscle spasm, the muscle should be grasped firmly and squeezed until the cramp is relieved. Then the area should be massaged. The athlete should exercise the muscle as soon as he is able to do so.

conditioning

Competition is the essence of sport, and conditioning is essential to competition. Improved performance in competition requires hard work. A competitor must drive himself with desire and determination towards his goals. Excellent condition is a team's most valuable asset.

Basically a basketball player needs stamina and endurance. He must use a conditioning program that places stress on his body beyond his fatigue level, raising that level higher and higher to condition himself for optimum body performance. A prime reason for a high level of physical conditioning is that it minimizes the chance of injury. Fatigue reduces a player's speed and agility, making him more prone to injury.

The basketball player must condition himself to be able to make all the movements of the game easily—stopping, starting, sprinting, changing direction, jumping, moving backwards, etc.

The conditioning program for basketball players must be a year-round process. Off-season, players should participate in some type of sport whose movement approximates that of basketball. We suggest tennis, handball, squash, and volley ball. In addition, such basic exercises as rope-skipping, rope-climbing, squeezing a rubber handball, push-ups, pull-ups, and passing and catching a medicine ball from a kneeling position strengthen the hands, wrists, arms, and shoulders. The off-season program should be planned to increase such factors as strength, endurance, coordination, and agility.

A well-balanced conditioning program for the off-season should include a forty-five-minute daily program. The coach should keep a check-off list of things to accomplish. He should also check the players' weight chart daily. Four days a week should be enough for the formal off-season program.

The EXER-GENIE Exerciser, available from sporting goods dealers, has an excellent conditioning program for basketball players in the off-season. The program combines isotonic and isometric exercises with a prescribed series of exercises using different resistances.

Of course, an athlete cannot be in top shape all year round, because the body will not respond. The important thing is that he maintain muscle tone, wind, and weight, and keep his legs in shape.

An athlete should arrive at the first practice in good mental and physical condition and get himself in progressively better shape through the basic drills and scrimmages so that he is in top condition for the first game. There will be no time for basic conditioning work.

Warming Up. Warming up before a game, a practice session, or an off-season conditioning workout is extremely important. To prevent muscle pulls, an athlete should go through a series of muscle stretching exercises to warm up all parts of his body gradually. About ten minutes of light jogging and mild exercises are recommended.

Weight Training. Only a moderate, carefully prescribed and supervised weight training program should be used by basketball players. Otherwise, a player could become too muscular in the shoulders or arms, thus affecting his "touch," or coordination. We recommend a program designed to increase speed, suppleness, rhythm, and endurance by using less weight with more repetition. Use of the overload principle, gradually increasing the weight to a prescribed maximum, will also increase strength. Weighted devices to strengthen the hands, arms, legs, knees, and ankles is recommended (e.g. weighted jacket, weighted sneakers, etc.).

Isometric Exercises. Isometrics should be an integral part of a basketball training program as they can develop essential strength quickly and easily without increasing muscle bulk that could be restrictive.

Calisthenics. Except for knee bends, full squats, or duck walks, which place strain on the knee joint and weaken the knee structure, calisthenics can be beneficial for stretching muscles in the warm-up period. They usually help develop agility and flexibility. By increasing the number of repetitions of each exercise and the length of exercising time, a player can increase muscle tone and build up cardiovascular efficiency gradually.

Running. The best conditioner for athletes is running, as it builds up their cardiovascular-respiratory fitness. While long-distance running is a good conditioner, basketball players benefit most from short windsprint running. Sprinting fifty yards, walking back, and repeating the process to the point of fatigue is most beneficial.

conditioning and running drills

Conditioning and running drills are used primarily as pre-season drills. As they involve a great deal of movement and running, they should be used with caution early, increasing the number of times the drill is repeated as the player's condition improves. The diagrams show a sixteen-man squad.

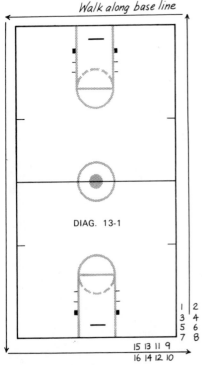

DIAG. 13-1

Diag. 13-1, INTERVAL LAPS

This is generally used as a warm-up drill before practice. The entire squad starts at the right-hand corner of the court in pairs, the captain generally being in the first pair. (Running in pairs provides a competitive element to the drill.) The first two players sprint along the right sideline. The other pairs follow, allowing approximately twenty feet between pairs. They walk along the far baseline, sprint down the left-hand side of the court, then walk the near baseline until they reach the starting position. Players generally start with five laps and gradually build up to a point where they can do twelve to fifteen laps. This drill can be varied as follows to relieve the monotony.

1. Each pair has one basketball. One of the pair dribbles during his sprint down the sideline and his walk along the far baseline, then hands the ball to his partner, who dribbles up the other sideline and along the near baseline and hands the ball back to the first player. One of the pair may run backwards, simulating defensive position against the dribbler.

2. During the sprint period, the two players may pass the ball back and forth, allowing them to improve their ball handling at full speed.

Diag. 13-2, RUNNING BACKWARD AND DEFENSIVE SHUFFLE DRILL

Starting one after the other in the right hand corner, the players, led by the captain or one of the outstanding players, run backwards to the mid-court line. At the line, they stop and then shuffle to their right, using the boxer's defensive shuffle. When they reach the opposite sideline, they run backwards to the far corner of the court, then shuffle to their left to reach the far right corner. At the corner, they make a reverse pivot on the right foot and sprint back to the starting point. From the starting point, they file across the baseline to the opposite corner and repeat the drill from that end. They run backwards to mid-court, shuffle to the left to the opposite sideline, run backwards to the far end line, shuffle to the right, to the far left corner, pivot on the left foot, and sprint back to the second starting point.

This drill is excellent for teaching players to run backward in good balance. The coach should be on the inside of the court, observing the movement of the players at all times and shouting encouragement and criticism to those who are not moving properly. The coach should look for good balance when players are running backwards, good shuffling techniques, and proper pivoting in the corner. This drill should never be repeated more than three times, as it can become monotonous. When it is used a few times, the players enjoy it, shouting enthusiastically as they run backwards and shuffle to their left and to their right and racing with each other when they sprint back to the starting point.

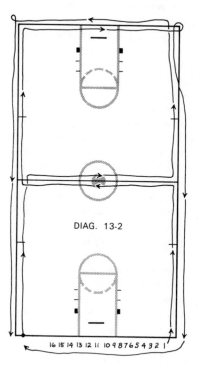

DIAG. 13-2

16 15 14 13 12 11 10 9 8 7 6 5 4 3 2 1

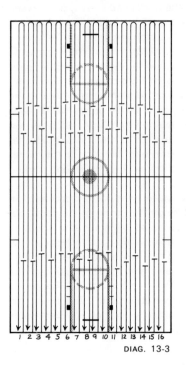

1 2 3 4 5 6 7 8 9 10 11 12 13 14 15 16

DIAG. 13-3

Diag. 13-3, WHISTLE SPRINTS

We generally close our practice with whistle sprints, because the best conditioning takes place when the players are tired and must push themselves. When the players are as tired as they should be at the close of a practice, the drill simulates game conditions during the last few minutes of a ball game.

All players line up along one end of the court. One of the assistant coaches starts the drill by blowing a whistle. All sprint as fast as they can, anticipating the next whistle blast. When the whistle sounds again they must stop in position immediately, with as little loss of body balance as possible and without any forward motion, assuming a crouched position in order to stop quickly and effectively. They remain in this crouched position until the assistant coach sounds his whistle again. Usually the players are stopped two or three times before they reach the far end of the court. After they touch the endline, they run backwards towards the starting line. The whistle stops and starts them at least once, with the coaches watching for balance and good stopping techniques. Repeat this drill five to eight times.

A variation is to have players do ten situps or run in position when the stop whistle sounds. This drill generally creates a great deal of enthusiasm. Extra whistle sprints can be used as a penalty if players have not shot accurately during foul shooting practice or if they are the losers in the competitive drills.

Do not repeat this drill too often at the end of a hard practice, and use it with extreme caution on days before games.

458

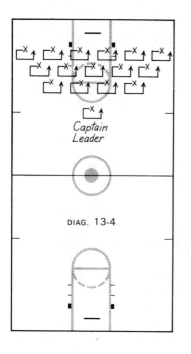

Captain
Leader

DIAG. 13-4

Diag. 13-4, GROUP DEFENSIVE SHUFFLE, FOOTWORK DRILL

Players form three lines, four or five to a line, six to eight feet apart, facing the captain or the leader. All players assume the boxer's stance, with one foot in front of the other. On the command of the group leader, they move in unison left to right, front, right to left, and back, following the leader's movements. He should move quickly three or four shuffles to the left, three or four back, three or four right and three or four front, then repeat the drill, changing the sequence.

This is an excellent conditioning drill, and players generally perform it enthusiastically. Occasionally the leader should have the players slap the floor with both hands and yell to increase the enthusiasm.

This drill promotes good defensive balance, good stance, and quick movement. When performed properly, it is one of the players' favorite drills in any team's early season practice. However, it should be used cautiously—the group will tire within one or two minutes.

A good jumping drill can be executed from the same player alignment that is used in Drill 4.

The group faces the captain or the leader with hands on hips or held loosely at the sides. The players hop on one foot twice, land on both feet, then slap both hands on the floor. They straighten up, bringing their hands up to shoulder height, and hop on the other foot twice. As their feet come back to the floor, they crouch again without slapping the floor and spring up as high as possible off both feet, arms spread and stretched overhead, body in jackknife position, using good rebounding technique. The players

459

execute a complete 360-degree pivot and then face the leader, shaking their arms to relax, and prepare to repeat the drill.

When they jump, they should get up in the air quickly, spreading and kicking the legs, the hands up, the elbows out. When they come back to the floor, their hands and bodies should be in good balance, with the hands close to the body, elbows still spread, and the buttocks extended. They should land in a low protective manner, as though holding the ball. Having the boys hop on one foot, slap the floor, and hop on the other foot gives the drill variety and keeps the boys a little off balance as they would be before going up for the ball. They must regain good balance in order to make the jump, simulating moving into position to rebound the ball and being bumped while attempting to box out an opponent.

Besides involving excellent fundamental techniques, this drill evokes a great deal of enthusiasm that is very good for team morale. It is a strenuous preseason conditioning drill that should not be used during a regular season. It is a good change of pace when used in conjunction with the defensive shuffle drill, but it should not be repeated more than five or six times.

The same groupings are used in a drill that simulates jumping on a jump ball situation. The players assume the crouch they would take prior to a held ball tap. As the leader jumps, all jump. Those who jump late should be corrected instantly, because all players at one time or another are involved in jump-ball situations. The coach should check with each late jumper to determine why he is not springing on the visual command. This drill, in conjunction with the preceding drills, takes four or five minutes in early preseason practice.

selected and annotated bibliography

Allen, Forrest C. *Better Basketball*. New York: Whittlesey House, McGraw-Hill Book Co., 1937.
A complete treatise in all phases of basketball by one of the game's most revered coaches. Still practical for the present-day coach.

Allen, Forrest C. *My Basketball Bible,* 7th ed. Kansas City: Smith-Grieves Co., 1928.
Covers material in all aspects of basketball incorporated in a later publication by the author. Excellent for reference.

Anderson, Forrest, and Albeck, Stan. *Coaching Better Basketball*. New York: Ronald Press Co., 1964.
Text incorporates all aspects of basketball for the coach, especially from an organizational point of view. Meticulous in all areas covered.

Anderson, Forrest, and Tyler, Micoleau. *Basketball Techniques Illustrated*. New York: A. S. Barnes & Co., 1952.
A short, well-illustrated book covering all individual fundamental techniques. Team defense and offense are presented in sketched outline form.

Angell, Lieut. E. D. *Basketball for Coach, Player, and Spectator*. New York: Thos. Wilson & Co., 1921.
Interesting and valuable as a reference and for historical information. Book was written for the Wilson Athletic Library.

Antonacci, Robert J., and Barr, Jere. *Basketball for Young Champions*. New York: Whittlesey House, McGraw-Hill Book Co., 1960.
A well-written short book focused on improving fundamental techniques in the beginning or younger basketball player.

The Athletic Institute—Basketball Instructor's Guide. Consultants: Dr. Forrest C. "Phog" Allen, Harold E. "Bud" Foster, Edward S. "Eddie" Hickey. Chicago, Illinois: The Athletic Institute, 1958.
A pictorial booklet dealing primarily with individual offensive techniques.

Athletic Journal. Evanston, Illinois: Athletic Journal Publishing Co.
Monthly publication containing informative articles on current trends in all areas of basketball. Should be subscribed to by all coaches to keep abreast with modern thinking.

Auerbach, Arnold. *Basketball for the Player, the Fan, and the Coach*. New York: Pocket Books Inc., 1957.
For everyone interested in basketball. No diagrams. Contains excellent information in free-lance situations. Approaches the game from a practical, workable point of view. Invaluable material for all coaches.

Bachman, Carl C. *Basketball for High School Players and Coaches*. Dubuque, Iowa: Wm. C. Brown, Co., 1955.
Primarily designed for high school coaches and players, but common sense approach is valuable at all levels of competition.

Baisi, Neal. *Coaching the Zone and Man-to-Man Pressing Defenses*. Englewood Cliffs, New Jersey: Prentice-Hall, 1961.
Good material on coaching multiple defenses. Methods of attacking zone press tactics and drills should be useful to coaches.

Balch, J. W. *California Offense for Basketball*. Santa Barbara, California: J. W. Balch, 1949.
Short book covers the author's version of California offensive theory.

Balch, J. W. *Theory for Basketball Offenses*. Santa Barbara, California: J. W. Balch, 1949.
Small booklet with basic offensive theory treatment. Informative for coaches building their own offense.

Baratto, John, and Krajewski, Bob. *Coaching Junior-High Basketball*. East Chicago, Ind.: M R Studios, 1960.
A fine text on beginning basketball at lower levels of competition. Covers the "feeder" system for the high school expertly.

Barry, Justin M. *Basketball: Individual Play and Team Play*. Iowa City: Clio Press, 1926.
Good reference material, presented by an outstanding coach of the 1920's, provides insight into how the game was played at top college level in that era.

Basketball Coaches Digest. Huntington, Indiana: Huntington Laboratories.

A free yearly publication for coaches, compiling excellent basketball articles from the previous season.

Bee, Clair. *Basketball*. New York: Townsend Publishing Company, 1939.
A short book on basketball as taught by the author at Long Island University.

Bee, Clair. *Basketball for Everyone*. New York: Ace Books, 1962.
An instructing pocketbook designed to appeal to spectator, player, and coach. Good individual techniques illustrated and explained.

Bee, Clair. *Make the Team in Basketball*. New York: Grosset & Dunlap, 1961.
Designed to help beginners improve their techniques. Illustrations use younger players in the development of these techniques.

Bee, Clair. *Winning Basketball Plays*. New York: Ronald Press Co., 1963.
A compilation of plays, including jump ball, out-of-bounds, and last shot situation, contributed by eighty outstanding college coaches.

Bee, Clair, and Norton, Ken. *Basketball Fundamentals and Techniques*. New York: Ronald Press, 1959.
Describes all phases of basketball fundamentals. Game situations present competitive aspect to learning techniques. One of a series of five books.

Bee, Clair, and Norton, Ken. *Individual and Team Basketball Drills*. New York: Ronald Press, 1959.
Well illustrated. Wide range of drills outlined allows the coach to select those best suited to his team's needs. One of a series of five books.

Bee, Clair, and Norton, Ken. *Man-to-Man Defense and Attack*. New York: Ronald Press, 1959.
Explains man-to-man defense and the variations. Methods of attacking man-to-man defense outlined with copious diagrams. One of a series of five books.

Bee, Clair, and Norton, Ken. *The Science of Coaching*. New York: Ronald Press, 1959.
Discusses the role of the coach in basketball today. Excellent coverage of all strategic situations. One of a series of five books.

Bee, Clair, and Norton, Ken. *Zone Defense and Attack*. New York: Ronald Press, 1959.
Thorough treatment of all zone defense alignments and offensive systems of attacking zones. Recommends several offensive formations in combating the zone defense. One of a series of five books.

Best of Basketball from the Coaching Clinic. West Nyack, New York: Parker Publishing Co., 1966.
Forty articles by many of the leading figures in basketball. Each article covers a different phase of the game. An excellent reference source for the young coach.

Bliss, James G. *Basketball*. Philadelphia; Lea & Febiger, 1929.
Written for coaches, players, recreation leaders, students and teachers of physical education. Good historical reference covers all phases of basketball.

Bonder, James B. *How to be a Successful Coach*. New York: Prentice-Hall, 1958.
Good practical information on dealing with the squad, public relations, and essential qualities and stepping stones in becoming a successful coach.

Brown, Glenn C. *Secrets of the Zone Press*. Danville, Ill.: School Aid Co., 1962.
Covers all phases of basketball with special emphasis on the zone press defense. Good material for the coach wishing to install team pressing tactics.

Brown, Lyle. *Offensive and Defensive Drills for Winning Basketball*. Englewood Cliffs, New Jersey: Prentice-Hall, 1965.
Contains 200 drills for all areas of team and individual basketball concepts. Diagraming easily understood and explicit.

Browning, W. *Basketball*. London: Sir Isaac Pittman & Sons, 1949.
Interesting publication by a founder of the Amateur Basketball Association of England and Wales. Change of pace reading for the basketball coach as it gives an insight into the game as played in England.

Buck, R., *Shuffle and Press Offense For Winning Basketball*. Englewood Cliffs, N.J. Prentice-Hall, 1969.
Based on current offensive thinking on attacking modern pressure defenses.

Bunn, John W. *The Art of Basketball Officiating*. Springfield, Massachusetts: M. F. Stibbs, 1948.
Good supplementary material for coach to help him better understand problems and techniques of the basketball official.

Bunn, John W. *The Basketball Coach: Guides to Success*. Englewood Cliffs, New Jersey: Prentice-Hall, 1961.
A theoretical yet practical approach to the science of coaching, written by one of basketball's better-known authors.

Bunn, John W. *Basketball Methods*. New York: Macmillan Co., 1939.
Complete text on all important general aspects and basic principles (especially good in the philosophy and methods sections).

Bunn, John. *Basketball Techniques and Team Play*. Englewood Cliffs, New Jersey: Prentice-Hall, 1964.
The result of the author's forty years of coaching, and his years as editor of the *Basketball Rules Book*. Advocates that the coach initiate and incorporate his own thinking and then test the validity of his theories.

Bunn, John W. *Scientific Principles of Coaching*.

New York: Prentice-Hall, 1955.
A technical coverage of laws and principles of physics as applied to all sports areas. Interesting reading for coaches who wish to understand why certain techniques are more desirable than others in athletics.

Carlson, Henry Clifford. *Basketball: The American Game*. New York: Funk & Wagnalls Co., 1938.
Contains good background material on the use of the figure eight as expounded by its best known advocate and innovator. Training, diet, and health references are applicable for today's coaches.

Carlson, Henry C. *You and Basketball*. Braddock, Pennsylvania: Brown Publishing Co., 1929.
Good historical reference because of the author's association with the figure eight five-man weave, discussed thoroughly in this book.

Case, Everett N. *New Pressure Game in Basketball*. Raleigh, North Carolina: Technical Press, 1948.
A short monograph dealing with pressure tactics in basketball. Coaches will find useful practical applications in this booklet.

Cathcart, Jim. *A Multiple-Continuous Offense For High School Basketball*. West Nyack, N.Y.: Parker Publishing Co., 1968.
A complete offensive continuity with options using a one-three-one pattern. Each position analyzed with personnel requirements.

Cella, George A. *The Young Sportsman's Guide to Basketball*. New York: Thomas Nelson & Sons, 1965.
Outlines the essential techniques for beginners. Good basic material for coaching younger players.

Chandler, Wm. A., and Miller, George F. *Basketball Technique*. (Publisher unknown) 1922.
Valuable as an historical reference.

Ciciora, Dale, and Sweet, Virgil. *Specific Drills for Basketball Fundamentals*. Valparaiso, Ind., 1966.
Fourth booklet in a series, the first three written by Virgil Sweet. Describes drills as used by the authors in their successful coaching careers at Valparaiso Junior and Senior High School.

Colbeck, Arthur L. *Modern Basketball—A Fundamental Analysis of Skills and Tactics*. 3rd ed. Kaye and Ward, 1966.
A British version of current basketball techniques from a fundamental point of view. Of interest to students of basketball.

Converse Basketball Yearbook. Malden, Massachusetts: Converse Rubber Co.
A free yearly publication for coaches. Covers all levels of basketball with interesting technical articles by the year's most successful coaches. Published since 1922.

Cooke, David C. *Better Basketball for Boys*. New York: Dodd, Mead & Co., 1960.
Outlines proper techniques for the young beginner.

Dean, Everett S. *Progressive Basketball*. New York: Prentice-Hall, 1950.
Good coverage of the system used by the author. Contains worthwhile material on individual defense and individual offense.

Dobbs, Wayne and Pinholster, Garland. *Basketball's Stunting Defenses*. Englewood Cliffs, New Jersey: Prentice-Hall, 1964.
Outlines several varying defenses evolving from offensive efforts to combat them. Unique training devices illustrated in text.

Driesel, Lefty. *Secrets of Offensive Basketball*. Charlotte, North Carolina: Meteor Publishing Co., 1966.
Short booklet with material designed to develop or improve the offensive techniques of the team and the individual.

Dwyer, Bob. *How to Coach and Attack the Zone Defenses*. Englewood Cliffs, New Jersey: Prentice-Hall, 1963.
Good coverage of diversified systems designed to penetrate zone defenses.

Eaves, Joel. *Basketball's Shuffle Offense*. New York: Prentice-Hall, 1960.
A presentation of the shuffle offense used by the author. Clarity and continuity of diagrams and accompanying text make this treatment easy to assimilate.

Edmundson, Clarence (Hec), and Morris, Robert (Bobby). *Basketball for Players, Officials, and Spectators*. Seattle, Washington: Frayn Printing Company, 1931.
Valuable as a historical reference.

Esposito, Michael. *Game Situation Strategy in Basketball*. Danville, Illinois: School Aid Co., 1966.
Good coverage of all strategic game situations. Uses different text organization, placing diagram on right hand page and explaining it on left page.

Esposito, Michael. *How to Coach Fast Break Basketball*. Englewood Cliffs, New Jersey: Prentice-Hall, 1959.
A thorough coverage of all aspects of the fast break from fundamental techniques and drills through complicated team patterns from all possible defensive postures.

Flack, Howard Watson. "Selected Basketball Systems Evaluated and Adapted for High School Coaching." Master's thesis, George Peabody College for Teachers, 1935.
Analyzes six methods of basketball theory by outstanding coach-authors. This is an outstanding research project that is not widely known. Second half of thesis discusses basketball as played in the early thirties. Extremely interesting material.

Fraley, Oscar. *Basketball in Action*. New York: A. A. Wyn, 1954.
Excellent photographic sequences of all areas of fundamental basketball techniques. Demonstrations and their analysis are beneficial to all coaches and players.

Gardner, Jack. *Championship Basketball with Jack Gardner*. New York: Prentice-Hall, 1961.
Covers all aspects of basketball as coached by the author. Sections on team offense and team defense adaptable to most systems of play.

Gill, Amory T. (Slats). *Basic Basketball*. New York: Ronald Press Co., 1962.
Unique instructional guide presenting a sound and thorough approach to offensive and defensive play Sequential checklists given for various phases of the game.

Gulick, Luther. *How to Play Basketball*. London: British Sports Publishing Co., 1907.
Reference material on the beginning era of the sport by one of the game's pioneers. One of the first books published on basketball.

Gullion, Blair. *Basketball Offensive Fundamentals*. Knoxville, Tennessee: The Author, 1936.
Contains primarily same material as author's *Basketball Offensive Fundamentals Analyzed*.

Gullion, Blair. *Basketball Offensive Fundamentals Analyzed*. St. Louis, Missouri: Universal Printing Co., 1954.
Contains a detailed analysis of all individual offensive fundamentals, well illustrated with sequence photographs demonstrating various steps for correct performance.

Gullion, Blair. *100 Drills for Teaching Basketball Fundamentals*. St. Louis, Missouri: Bardgett Printing & Publishing Co., 1953.
Deals with drills in all areas of basketball. Especially good selection in footwork, offensively and defensively. A practical book for coaches.

Gullion, Blair. *Techniques and Tactics of Basketball Defense*. St. Louis, Missouri: Bardgett Printing & Publishing Co., 1951.
Treats defensive techniques exclusively. Clear presentation makes this book an excellent source book for the coach.

Hager, Robert H. *Percentage Basketball*. Corrallis, Oregon: Oregon State College, 1926.
Good historical reference covers systems of play and fundamentals in an earlier era of basketball.

Harkins, Mike. *Successful Team Techniques in Basketball*. West Nyack, New York: Parker Publishing Co., 1967.
Develops team tastics to help the weaker team incorporate surprise patterns and spring the upset and to strengthen the team with a tendency to succumb to pressure in close games.

Harrell, Bill D. *Championship-Tested Offensive and Defensive Basketball Strategy*. West Nyack, N.Y.: Parker Publishing Co., 1967.

Offensive and defensive team strategies designed to keep a team in an attack position by confusing and upsetting the opposition.

Healey, William A. *Basketball's Rotation Offense*. Danville, Illinois: Interstate Printers & Publishers, 1964.
Describes in understandable terms the general theory outlining the basic positions, movements, and patterns of the rotation offensive.

Healey, William A. *High School Basketball (Coaching, Managing, Administering)*. Danville, Illinois: Interstate Printers & Publishers, 1962.
A necessary reference for every high school basketball coach. Includes excellent material on coaching and is invaluable for basketball management and administration.

Hepbron, George T. *How to Play Basketball*. New York: American Sports Publishing Co., 1904.
Valuable historical reference for basketball researchers. Written by one of the founding fathers of the sport.

Hickey, Eddie. *Basketball Drills*. New York: Coaches Press, 1955.
Small booklet contains an excellent variety of fundamental, continuity, weave, and fun game drills.

Hobson, Howard A. *Basketball Illustrated*. New York: A. S. Barnes & Co., 1948.
Fine basic book on basketball fundamentals for beginners. Covers aspects of conditioning and self-evaluation thoroughly.

Hobson, Howard A. *Scientific Basketball*. New York: Prentice-Hall, 1949.
First part deals with scouting and statistics; second part is a check list covering individual and team techniques.

Holman, Nathan. *Championship Basketball*. Chicago: Ziff-Davis Publishing Co., 1942.
Contains fine, useful material in individual techniques, especially man-to-man defense as performed and coached by one of basketball's legendary individuals.

Holman, Nathan. *Holman on Basketball*. New York: Crown Publishing, 1950.
Chronological treatment of author's years in basketball with reference to changes in the game from the early days of basketball to the modern era. Interesting for background material.

Holman, Nat. *Scientific Basketball*. Incra Publishing Company, 1922.
Short booklet discusses professional influence during formative stages. Interesting historical reference written by one of basketball's best known figures.

Holman, Nathan. *Winning Basketball*. New York: Charles Scribner's Sons, 1935.
Much of material outdated, but book has value for present day coaches in offensive and defensive systems.

Hundley, "Hot-Rod." *Basketball—Individual Offense.* Delray Beach, Florida: Gainsford Publishing, 1959.
Booklet covers the basic offensive fundamentals as illustrated by the author.

Hutton, Joseph W. *Learning How to Play Basketball.* Mankato, Minnesota: Creative Educational Society, 1964.
Covers the learning process essential in acquiring and developing the important techniques of basketball.

Hutton, Joe, and Hoffman, Vern B. *Basketball.* Mankato, Minnesota: Creative Educational Society 1966.
Designed to teach coordination and timing. Written for all stages of advancement—beginner to college. Appeals to player, spectator, and coach.

Jagger, B. *Your Book of Basketball.* London: Faber & Faber, 1961.
Written for young players in England by the National Basketball Coach of England. Interesting treatment of fundamentals from a different point of view.

Jourdet, Lon W., and Hashagen, Kenneth A. *Modern Basketball.* Philadelphia: W. B. Saunders Co., 1939.
Good analysis of eastern philosophy and principles of offensive and defensive play as expounded and played in the 1930's.

Jucker, Ed. *Cincinnati Power Basketball.* Englewood Cliffs, New Jersey: Prentice-Hall, 1962.
A description of the Cincinnati system of play that won two consecutive National Championships. Complete offensive and defensive techniques detailed.

Julian, Alvin F. *Bread and Butter Basketball.* New York: Prentice-Hall, 1960.
Covers team offense, with very useful material on free-lance aspect. Scouting hints and statistical information valuable.

Keller, Paul R. *Offense Efficiency Rating System.* Delaware, Ohio: The Author.
A widely used system designed to pinpoint causes of loss of possession. Remedial measures covered.

La Grand, Louis. *Coach's Complete Guide To Winning Basketball.* West Nyack, N.Y.: Parker Publishing Co., 1967.
A complete approach to basketball for the modern coach emphasizing a disciplined team attitude. Stresses psychological factors essential to team success.

Lai, William T. (Buck). *Winning Basketball: Individual and Team Strategy.* New York: Prentice-Hall, 1955.
An illustrated book explaining and diagraming fundamentals and techniques. Easy-to-read text makes the book more appealing. Discusses practical aspects in an interesting manner.

Lambert, Ward Lewis. *Practical Basketball.* Chicago: Athletic Journal Publishing Co., 1932.
An interesting, complete publication in an early era of basketball. Good reference material. Many suggestions applicable in today's approach to the game.

Lapchick, Joe. *50 Years of Basketball.* Englewood Cliffs, N.J., Prentice-Hall, 1968.
Summary of author's fifty years as a player and coach. Interesting account of early days of the game. Contains complete details of a successful professional and college coach's approach to basketball. An informative and enjoyable book for anyone interested in basketball.

Levitt, Bunny. *Basketball Handbook.* Neptune, N.J.: Bunny Levitt, 1963.
A thirty-six page pamphlet crammed with practical information for coach and player. Several pages diagramed with court outline only for inclusion of specific team patterns.

Levitt, Bunny. *Basketball Players Digest.* 707 Berkeley Lane, Neptune, N.J.: Bunny Levitt, 1964.
Helpful training manual for coaches. All aspects of basketball are professionally treated.

Lindeburg, Franklin A. *How to Play and Teach Basketball.* New York: Association Press, 1963.
A complete textbook on the methods of teaching all phases of basketball. The section on selection and purchasing of equipment is very good. Has good variation in the offensive and defensive team aspects.

Loeffler, Ken. *Ken Loeffler on Basketball.* Englewood Cliffs, New Jersey: Prentice-Hall, 1955.
Excellent instructional material, emphasizing man-to-man defense, is spiced liberally with bibliographical details and controversial opinions on rules, spectators, officials, etc.

McCracken, Branch. *Indiana Basketball.* New York: Prentice-Hall, 1955.
A thorough treatment of basketball as coached and played in the successful era of Indiana University. Well diagramed and illustrated.

McCreary, Jay. *Winning High School Basketball.* New York: Prentice-Hall, 1956.
Solid approach to high school coaching. Good technical coverage of all areas. Excellent for the young high school coach.

McGuire, Frank. *Defensive Basketball.* New York: Prentice-Hall, 1959.
One of the better treatments of all phases of defensive basketball. Expertly handled, especially the individual phase.

McGuire, Frank. *Offensive Basketball.* Englewood Cliffs, New Jersey: Prentice-Hall, 1959.
A good development of offensive basketball's individual techniques.

McGuire, Frank. *Team Basketball Offense and*

Defense. Englewood Cliffs, New Jersey: Prentice-Hall, 1967.
Coach McGuire divulges his coaching philosophy and includes a complete organizational check-off list as he discusses building a man-to-man and zone offense and defense.

McLane, Hardin, ed. *Championship Basketball By 12 Great Coaches*. Englewood Cliffs, New Jersey: Prentice-Hall, 1966.
Twelve outstanding coaches each develop a chapter covering one important aspect in basketball from either the individual or team point of view.

McLendon, John B. *Fast Break Basketball*. West Nyack, New York: Parker Publishing Co., 1965.
Completely oriented to the fast break as taught by the author.

Maravich, Press, and Steel, James C. *Basketball Scouting*. Author, 1949.
Pamphlet emphasizes the scouting chart.

Martin, William L. *The Shifting Ball Defense in Basketball*. Author, 1929.
Deals exclusively with team defense from the zone aspect. Valuable as a historical reference only.

Masin, Herman L., ed. *The Best of Basketball From Scholastic Coach*. Englewood Cliffs, New Jersey: Prentice-Hall, 1962.
A compilation of twenty-four outstanding articles covering all aspects of basketball selected from over five hundred articles appearing in Scholastic Coach Magazine.

Masin, Herman L. *How to Star in Basketball*. New York: Tab Books, 1958.
An elementary booklet on basketball designed primarily for players of pre-high school age.

Mather, Edwin J., and Mitchell, Elmer D. *Basketball*. Ann Arbor, Michigan: Charles W. Graham, 1922.
Contains hints to the player of 1922. Historical reference only.

Mather, Edwin J., and Mitchell, Elmer D. *Basketball: How to Coach the Game*. New York: A. S. Barnes and Co., 1925.
Outdated but has value historically.

Meanwell, W. E. *Basketball for Men*. Madison, Wisconsin: Democrat Printing Co., 1922.
Book by one of the successful coaches on the era, has value as a historical reference. Discusses one-hand push shot.

Meanwell, Walter E. *Science of Basketball for Men*. Madison, Wisconsin: H. D. Gath, 1924.
One of the outstanding early texts on basketball with fine fundamental treatment, especially in man-to-man defense. A good reference book for information on earlier day techniques.

Mears, Ray. *It's All in the State of Mind*. Springfield, Ohio: Mimeographed Notes, 1961.
Mimeographed booklet outlining coaching philosophy and principles of the author.

Covers all aspects of basketball.

Messer, G. N. *How to Play Basketball*. New York: American Sports Publishing, 1919.
Historical value. Booklet describes how to play various positions in basketball. Second section contains 1919 rules.

Meyer, Ray. *Basketball as Coached by Ray Meyer*. Englewood Cliffs, N.J.: Prentice-Hall, 1967.
Coaching methods and offensive system of one of the country's best known and most successful coaches.

Meyer, Ray. *How to Play Winning Basketball*. Chicago, Illinois: Wood Associates.
Designed to improve individual and team techniques.

Mokray, Bill. *Averages*. Boston: Potter Printing Co., 1967.
Invaluable book for the statistician. Gives instant percentages for quick summaries of pertinent game data.

Mokray, William G. *Ronald Encyclopedia of Basketball*. New York: Ronald Press, 1963.
A complete presentation of basketball records and performances from the beginning of basketball to the present era. Excellent reference book.

Morley, Leroy; Ave, Harold C., Beu, F. A., and Newtson, Lawrence. *Fundamentals and Techniques for Winning Basketball*. Danville, Illinois: School Aid Company, 1951.
Basic fundamental play and individual techniques developed from the experiences of the four authors.

Miller, William H. *Basketball of Tomorrow*. Tulsa, Oklahoma: Jordon Company, 1938.
Covers aspects of basketball from the amateur team post-college approach, the fore-runner of our professional game today. Actual experiences of author described.

Mundell, Chuck. *Triple Threat Basketball*. West Nyack, N.Y.: Parker Publishing Co., 1968.
A complete diagnosis of current basketball team techniques both offensively and defensively Outlines tactics designed to overpower the opposition.

Murphy, Charles C. *Basketball*. New York: A. S. Barnes & Co., 1939.
A short treatment of fundamentals with explicit illustrations. Question and answer section at the end of each chapter—a unique feature.

Naismith, James A. *Basketball—Its Origin and Development*. New York: Association Press, 1941.
Last basketball publication by the founder of the game. A treatise for all coaches for its content and for sentimental reasons.

Naismith, James A., and Gulick, Luther A. *Basketball*. New York: American Sports Publishing Co., 1896.
The first publication in basketball by the origi-

nator and his collaborator. First rules are included. Invaluable reference for all who love the game.

Newell, Pete, and Benington, John. *Basketball Methods.* New York: Ronald Press Co., 1962. Combines best techniques of modern day team offense and defense with excellent suggestions for training and conditioning and morale incentives.

Newsom, Herbert. *Basketball for the High School Coach and the Physical Education Teacher.* Dubuque, Iowa: William C. Brown Co., 1952. Covers all phases of individual and team offense and defense. Offers excellent material to the high school coach and teacher in areas of methodology and philosophy.

Nisenson, Sam. *A Handy Illustrated Guide to Basketball.* New York: Permabooks, 1948. Short book on fundamentals of basketball published in pocketbook form for public consumption.

Nucatola, John. *Basketball Officiating.* Flushing, New York: Republic Book Co., 1959. Pamphlet deals with techniques of officiating and is meticulously presented. An excellent reference book for coaches.

Odle, Don J. *Basic Basketball.* Upland, Indiana: A. D. Freese & Son, 1950. Compilation of ideas of author as a coach and player. Covers all aspects of the game.

Odle, Don J. *Basketball Around the World.* Berne, Indiana: Economy Printing Concern, 1961. Basketball book with international flavor. Part I discusses basketball around the world. Part II covers all phases of the game.

Osborn, Chuck, with McClelland, Marshall K. *Basketball for Boys.* Chicago: Follett Publishing Co., 1960. Booklet on basketball based on individual fundamental techniques. Develops shooting and offensive areas very well.

Peterman, Mark A. *Secrets of Winning Basketball.* Danville, Illinois: The Interstate, 1941. Written from aspect of training players for a specific system of play.

Pinholster, Garland F. *Coach's Guide to Modern Basketball Defense.* New York: Prentice-Hall, 1962. Completely covers defense for the individual and team, especially concealed and combination defenses.

Pinholster, Garland F. *Encyclopedia of Basketball Drills.* Englewood Cliffs, New Jersey: Prentice-Hall, 1958. The complete book on basketball drills. Should be one of the first books purchased by the new basketball coach.

Pinholster, Garland F. *Illustrated Basketball Coaching Techniques.* Englewood Cliffs, New Jersey: Prentice-Hall, 1960. Solid, fundamental approach to all aspects of-

fensively and defensively. Well-illustrated. Chapter on coach as a teacher very well conceived.

Pinholster, Garland F. *Pinholster's Wheel Offense For Basketball.* Englewood Cliffs, N.J.: Prentice-Hall, 1966. Describes a team offensive system designed to attack any defensive alignment without using a variety of team offensive patterns.

Presley, Bud. *Pressure Defense—West Coast Style.* San Carlos, California: D & G Sports Publications, 1962. Covers defense from the pressure concept as played in West Coast basketball.

Ramsay, Jack. *Pressure Basketball.* Englewood Cliffs, New Jersey: Prentice-Hall, 1963. A detailed approach to basketball based on building the defense as an integral foundation for the offense. Coach Ramsay's aggressive pressure defense paves the way to many quick scores.

Richards, Jack. *Scramble Attack For Winning Basketball.* Englewood Cliffs, N.J. Prentice-Hall, 1968. A presentation of offensive patterns designed to incorporate the offensive abilities of all players into a balanced scoring attack.

Ridl, Charles. *How to Develop A Deliberate Basketball Offense.* Englewood Cliffs, New Jersey: Prentice-Hall, 1966. Author's version of developing a modern offense based on the deliberate style of play prevalent in many sections of the country today.

Robertson, Oscar. *Play Better Basketball.* Cincinnati, Ohio: Oscar Robertson and Michael O'Daniel, 1964. Individual techniques as used by one of the game's foremost exponents. Photographs of Robertson in action with descriptive text by the author.

Rosenburg, John M. *Basic Basketball.* Dobbs Ferry, New York: Oceana Publications, 1962. Aimed at high school level player and below, material is divided into individual skills, team play, and organization and development.

Rubin, Roy. *Attacking Basketball Pressure Defenses.* Englewood Cliffs, New Jersey: Prentice-Hall, 1966. Covers various methods of attacking pressure defenses with excellent results. Good pictorial development of methods.

Ruby, J. Craig. *How to Coach and Play Basketball.* Champaign, Illinois: Bailey & Himes, 1926. Designed as a textbook and as an aid to coaches.

Ruby, James C. *Basketball Coaching.* Champaign, Illinois: Basketball Book Co., 1931. Book has value for its insight into early style of play in midwestern section of country. Sound treatment of fundamentals.

Ruby, James C. *Team Play in Basketball.* Champaign, Illinois: Basketball Book Co., 1931.
Good treatment of team offensive and defensive play in midwestern college basketball.

Rupp, Adolph F. *Rupp's Basketball Guide Book.* New York: McGraw-Hill Book Co., 1967.
Designed for teaching fundamental techniques to young players by the game's most successful college coach.

Rupp, Adolph F. *Rupp's Championship Basketball.* 2nd Ed. Englewood Cliffs, New Jersey Prentice-Hall, 1957.
Covers all aspects of basketball as coached by the most successful college coach of all time. Seven cardinal principles of both offensive and defensive play are excellent.

Samaras, Bob. *Blitz Basketball.* West Nyack, New York: Parker Publishing Co., 1966.
A complete description and discussion of Blitz basketball as coached successfully by the author.

Santos, Harry G. *How To Attack and Defeat Zone Defenses in Basketball.* West Nyack, N.Y.: Parker Publishing Co., 1966.
A complete analysis of proven methods used in attacking zone defenses. Very helpful for coaches in designing their zone offense.

Scholastic Coach. New York: Scholastic Magazines, Inc.
A monthly publication that contains numerous articles on all aspects of coaching with emphasis on the in-season sport. Basketball material is copious, current, and informative. All coaches should subscribe to this publication.

Sharman, Bill. *Sharman on Basketball Shooting.* Englewood Cliffs, New Jersey: Prentice-Hall, 1965.
A masterful book covering all pertinent areas of shooting. Each phase of a shot is thoroughly explained by one of the game's outstanding shooters. Corrective measures are excellent.

Shublom, Walter R. *Tips to Titles.* Wyandotte High School, Kansas City, Kansas, Walter R. Shublom, 1960.
An instructive coverage of high school basketball authored by one of the country's most successful coaches.

Shublom, Walter R. *The Ways of a Champion.* 1010 N. Washington Blvd., Kansas City, Kansas 66102: Walter R. Shublom, 1964.
A complete manual for the high school coach.

Sports Illustrated, Editors, *Sports Illustrated Book of Basketball.* Philadelphia and New York: J. B. Lippincott Co., 1962.
An expertly illustrated book containing line drawings and accompanying text briefly outlining basic individual and team techniques.

Stack, D.H. *Basketball.* Englewood Cliffs, N.J.: Prentice-Hall, 1968.
Drills, methods, team patterns, and strategies as taught by one of the more successful college coaches.

Sweet, Virgil. *Specifics of Basketball Fundamentals.* Valparaiso, Indiana, 1966.
Booklet on basketball's fundamental techniques as taught successfully at Valparaiso High School, Indiana, by the author. One of a series.

Sweet, Virgil. *Specifics of Free Throw Shooting.* Valparaiso, Indiana, 1966.
Booklet on free throw shooting as taught by the author at Valparaiso High School. Experiments with hand placement on back and other theories valuable. One of a series.

Sweet, Virgil. *Specifics of V Offense.* Valparaiso, Indiana, 1966.
The type of offense taught successfully and used by the author at Valparaiso High School.

Tarleton, Tom. *Tips and Ideas for Winning Basketball.* Englewood Cliffs, New Jersey: Prentice-Hall, 1965.
Good coverage of sometimes overlooked or seemingly insignificant details. Text compiles thinking of several other coaches.

Toomasian, John. *Developing A Winning Offense for High School Basketball.* Englewood Cliffs, New Jersey: Prentice-Hall, 1964.
Covers all aspects of basketball essential to the high school coach. Excellent drill and play diagrams.

U. S. Naval Institute. *Basketball,* rev. ed. Anapolis, Maryland: V-Five Association of America, 1950.
A professionally prepared document compiled by outstanding basketball coaches while in the U. S. Navy for use in the naval aviation cadet physical training program. One of the finest basketball books available for organization and instruction in basketball.

Vanatta, Bob. *Coaching Pattern Play Basketball.* Englewood Cliffs, New Jersey: Prentice-Hall, 1959.
Basic play patterns are broken down and described. Such areas as pass and cut, pass and screen, and pass and drive, are set forth in clear and precise terms.

Van Ryswyk, Ron. *Ball Control Offensive and Disciplined Defense in Basketball.* West Nyack, N.Y.: Parker Publishing Co., 1967.
Approaches team basketball from a complete control point of view, emphasizing good offensive ball control while waiting for the high percentage shot and advocating aggressive man-to-man team defense.

Veenker, George F. *Basketball for Coaches and Players.* New York: A. S. Barnes & Co., 1930.
Still of practical value today. Coverage of fundamentals and man-to-man team play is excellent. Good source reference.

Verderame, Sal (Red). *Organization for Championship High School Basketball.* Englewood Cliffs, New Jersey: Prentice-Hall, 1963.
A complete book on the organization of a high

school basketball program designed for the high school coach.

Ward, Charles R. *Basketball's Match-up Defense.* Englewood Cliffs, New Jersey: Prentice-Hall, 1964.

A complete text on the defense that matches up the offensive formation used by the opponents. The offensive maneuvers to combat this unique defense are analyzed and effective counter-moves are detailed.

Wardlaw, Charles D., and Whitelaw R. Morrison. *Basketball: A Handbook for Coaches and Players.* New York: Charles Scribner's Sons, 1921.

Has value as a historical reference.

Watts, Stan. *Developing an Offensive Attack in Basketball.* New York: Prentice-Hall, 1959.

Complete coverage of all offensive individual and team techniques. Areas on shooting, coaching, and passing to the big man are very good.

Weyland, Alexander M. *The Cavalcade of Basketball.* New York: Macmillan Co., 1960.

Traces the development of basketball and records the accomplishments of the outstanding teams yearly. An interesting reference book.

Wilkes, Glenn. *Basketball Coach's Complete Handbook.* Englewood Cliffs, New Jersey: Prentice-Hall, 1963.

Covers completely all the essentials of basketball. Very good analysis of most patterns of offensive team play being used in modern basketball.

Wilkes, Glenn. *Winning Basketball Strategy.* New York: Prentice-Hall, 1959.

Detailed instruction for the individual player, the team, and the coach.

Winsor, Chuck, and Davis, Tom. *Garage-Door Basketball.* Danville, Illinois: School Aid Co., 1965.

An excellent treatment of off-season practice essentials for the squad when formal coaching cannot be given.

Winter, Fred (Tex). *The Triple-Post Offense.* Englewood Cliffs, New Jersey: Prentice-Hall, 1962.

Carefully prepared diagrams outline implementation of triple-post offense.

Wolfe, Herman. *From Try-Outs to Championship.* Englewood Cliffs, New Jersey: Prentice-Hall, 1964.

Covers all aspects of basketball involved in developing the basketball team from the start of a season to its completion.

Wooden, John. *Practical Modern Basketball.* New York: Ronald Press Co., 1966.

A complete analysis of the methods and philosophy of one of the most successful college coaches of all times. The book, covering all essential phases of basketball, is clearly dia-gramed. All coaches should have this in their library.

Yaksieh, Rudy. *Winning Basketball with the Free Lance System.* Englewood Cliffs, N.J.: Prentice-Hall, 1968.

Describes use of two-man and three-man maneuvers as a complete pattern for team offense. Individual initiative stressed.

appendix a

basketball outline

1. Go over rules and regulations—look for any rule changes.
2. School work:
   a. Main reason for being here.
   b. Attendance and attention in class. Your attitude reflects on basketball program.
   c. Tutoring available for those who feel they need it—don't wait until it is too late.
   d. If you fall below average you are jeopardizing your chances of making the team.
3. Basketball practice rules:
   a. Be on time to all practices and meetings. The team will not wait for you.
   b. If you must miss a practice or be late, notify me as far in advance as possible.
   c. Stop all activity on whistle. Everyone give undivided attention. There's too much to be done in a short period to repeat for certain individuals.
   d. Anytime you come onto the floor, you are expected to give out 100% effort. We will get pleasure and enjoyment through accomplishments and hard work.
   e. Avoid all forms of horseplay. It is dangerous and it spoils the team morale.
   f. Profanity has no place in our practice—an educated man can express himself clearly without resorting to profanity.
   g. Don't be careless, slouchy, or vulgar in your actions or appearance.
4. Our aim: To prepare ourselves *mentally, physically,* and *technically* as individuals and as a team so we can play the game to the best of our capabilities, constantly, day after day.
   a. Mental attitude:

   The mental attitude of each of us is the most important factor in the success of our team this year. It is always the most important single factor. Our mental attitudes are determined by how we react to our environment—our ability to get along with each other without conflict under stress and strains.

   It is not the things that happen to us that make or break us, it is our mental reaction to these influences that counts. Consequently, it is better to be logical and sensible than to be emotional and impractical.

Make wisdom your partner in all you think about and do. The normal, well-adjusted person is endowed with certain character traits:

1. He is emotionally mature. He thinks and behaves as a grownup should. He has a definite aim in life. He knows where he is going.
2. He accepts the hard knocks of life philosophically.
3. He keeps himself too busy to be unhappy.
4. He is able to get along with almost everyone, has a flexible personality and is humanly understanding.
5. He goes about his life's business without too much complaining.
6. He does not act impulsively—he learns to control his emotions, exercises wise judgement and is able to make intelligent decisions.
7. He is not a cynic, nor does he harbor neurotic prejudices.
8. He keeps his nose out of others' affairs.
9. He is tactful and not argumentative; tolerant and unselfish.
10. He is not oversensitive and is able to accept criticism.
11. He has a sense of humor and radiates self-confidence.
12. He has faith in mankind and possesses a healthy attitude toward people and the world around him.
13. He acquires wisdom through the experience of the past. He profits by his mistakes.
14. He has achieved a desirable way of life—one that makes living pleasant instead of a struggle and painful. He has acquired an ability to relax—*a capacity to enjoy life.*

The proper mental attitude is essential—a prerequisite to a successful basketball season.

1. *Emotions*—Your mental health is affected greatly by your control over your emotions. Recognize your own emotional status. If you can recognize your problem then you may be able to do something about it. Then make up your mind to face it head on.
2. *Confidence*—A mental state which is necessary for success in any phase of life. We can't win games and establish a winning tradition unless we believe in ourselves, our teammates, our coaches, our system, etc. Confidence breeds confidence. If you believe in yourself, and act it, others will believe in you. Don't lose your confidence when you are criticized. Understand that constructive criticism is often a sign of interest by the coach. Coaches will seldom waste their time on a player they are not interested in. Don't see a "dig" or double meaning in every remark that is passed—don't be oversensitive.
3. *Victory Spirit*—To be a successful basketball player you must have a tremendous desire to win, coupled with a willingness to work hard and sacrifice for victory. You must be a great competitor, hustle constantly and radiate confidence.

4. *Loyalty*—No basketball player will ever be great unless he has learned the importance of loyalty. It is more than giving all as far as physical effort goes. It involves a devotion to a cause.

5. *Respect*—The respect of a player for his coach, faculty, and teammates is invaluable. I cannot demand your respect. I will do all I can to earn it.

6. *Physically*—Training and conditioning.

   When you report on the floor today it is assumed by me that you are prepared to make personal sacrifices and deny yourselves many of the social activities and pleasures which other students may have. You cannot function to your fullest potential unless you are in the best possible physical condition. Basketball is hard and strenuous, and condition counts more in this game than any other. It cannot be forced upon you— you've got to get into the best possible shape because *you* want to. Don't deceive your teammates, don't let your school down, don't deceive your coach, and mainly, don't deceive yourself by false condition because in the final analysis you will find you have deceived yourself most of all.

7. *Training Program*—Based on common sense:

   1. Diet—Regular meals on athletic training table. Don't eat between meals. Fruit and fruit juices are all right.
   2. Sleep—Offers the best and only means of recuperation.
      a. Arise at a regular hour, regardless of early morning fatigue.
      b. Stay awake all day.
      c. Determine the number of hours sleep usually required to produce a feeling of absolute rest upon awakening. Calculate the hour of retirement accordingly; establish the habit of retiring regularly each night at this hour.
      d. Avoid eating or drinking too much of anything before retiring.
   3. Colds—One of our worst enemies.
      a. Don't be careless regarding undue exposure—dry thoroughly after taking shower.
      b. Drink lots of fruit juices and water.
   4. Drinking—Cannot and will not be tolerated in any degree. Violation of this rule will result in immediate dismissal from the team.
   5. Smoking
      1. Doctors say smoking affects some of the physiological functions of the body.
      2. Morally—The player who smokes is untrue to himself and his teammates and is doing something that wrecks his conscience because he is cheating and breaking a trust. Strong team morale cannot be built upon the willful violations of our training rules.
      3. *Don't smoke!*

Responsibility—You are in the public eye—live up to your position, attend classes, make effort, be on your best behavior, respect others. Don't break training rules; it has a detrimental psychological effect and spoils team morale and confidence.

Technically—The smart coach realizes the real answer to successful coaching does not lie in the development of some super-strategy or super-play or in brilliant direction from the bench during the game. The key to successful coaching appears to lie in the realm of the effective teaching of fundamentals.

As players, you must realize that your natural ability can take you only to a certain level—whether or not you go beyond that level will depend on mastery of fundamentals. A player has learned a fundamental when it becomes so much habit that he will perform it instinctively, at the right time in the game.

If we practice the proper mechanics and techniques day after day, there will be an increase in the skill and efficiency of performance.

By practicing the proper fundamentals in the proper sequence and continually repeating them, nervous patterns are being established. The greater the number of times that impulses are sent over these nervous pathways, the more firmly established they become, until what has been practiced becomes habit and automatic.

This explains why proper execution is important. It also explains why bad habits, once formed, are hard to break. It is also true that the more a skill is practiced *properly*, the better you learn to use only the muscles involved in performing this particular skill. Thereby, you reduce the amount of energy necessary to perform a given amount of work. An increase in skill and efficiency will probably be the first changes which occur as a result of our practice sessions. "Practice makes perfect" is true only if the proper mechanics are being practiced. Bad habits can be practiced as well as good ones so it is important that you begin building good habits from the start—"Don't be careless."

Our practice sessions will be designed to give you the technical know-how of the game—to condition you physically, mentally, emotionally and technically.

The final thought I leave with you is that if you give me 100% effort, I will return 150% to you. On the other hand, if you give less than your best, you won't find a place on our team.

Coach Bob Cousy

appendix b

pre-season practice first week

Time: 1 hour and 30 min. (Have manager time each drill.) 30 min.—Chalk talk and drill explanation. First day—Rule changes (explain). Coaches work each day 15 minutes prior to practice with
(a) Big men—Kane, Adams, Vernon, Payne, Royer, and Carr.
(b) Small men—Shooting, passing, dribbling, individuals and pairs.

Objectives

1. Development of Basic Skills
   Offense:
       Passing
       Shooting
       Dribbling
       Rebounding and clear out
   Defense:
       Stance
       Movement
       Position

2. Development of Basic Team Concepts
   Offense:
       One-on-one—teach fakes
       Two-on-two—pick, roll, etc.
       Three-on-three
       Changes of direction—from stack alignment—from free lance.
   Defense:
       One-on-one
       Pressure
       Check advance
   Two-on-two
       Switch and slide
       Double up
       Check cutter—charge play—jump in
       Overplay pass receiver

Three-on-three
Overplay
Two-on-one
Double up
Three-on-two
Double up

Finish up with fast-break team drills.

appendix c

daily
practice
schedules

In First Week

Work before practice (15 minutes) on low stack moves.
Williams, Payne, Adams, Kane, Doll

  a. regular stack position with turn—Def.— fake left, go
      right
  b. come across lane and meet ball—Def.
  c. simulate overplay on B and E with reverse to basket
      and high lob pass (use Kunz and Evers)
  d. cutting through middle—pass from side—trailer
      move

Drills

Explanation time for drills (20)*

  A. 5 Interval laps around court—3 backward laps and
      shuffle around court—capt. lead (10)
  B. Lay-ups with bounce pass from middle (5)
  C. Stationary parallel passing lines—chest, bounce,
      overhead. Fake first, snap wrist, follow through—
      outside shoulder (5)
  D. 2-lane passing lanes—full court—side line to foul (5)
  E. Full-court dribble drill—down right, back left—side
      and front (5)
  F. Long pass drill—2 hands (10)
  G. Group shuffle drill—(Captain lead) very low, palms
      up (touch floor with palms), *growl* (2); shuffle com-
      pletely around the court (1); group jump drill (2)
  H. Hands on belt "D" drill—both sides of court (match
      up positions) (5)
  I. One-on-one—D overplays—off. Looks for backdoor
      —pass to outside, must return (side drill using coach
      as passer) (5)
  J. Two-on-two—full court (5)

477

Foul Shooting

K.   Shoot (5) at each basket—Total 40—manager record (10)

L.   Drive in drill— side and front   { side to side / Rocker fake—with "d" (10) / roll

M.   21—jump shots stack positions A, C, D (small men)— Rebound and box out drill with pivot and clear out positions (B and E) big men. (10)

N.   Fast-break drill—3-on-2—full court—rotate (10)

O.   Whistle sprints (5)

*(   ) indicate minutes per drill.

Daily Practice Schedules:

Day Before Early Season Game

Before practice (varsity) (30)
a.   Review films (last years) predetermined points for emphasis on U. of F. offense
b.   Go over U. of F. individual reports again
c.   Go over U. of F. jump ball and o.o.b. plays
d.   Basic game plan review

On court (freshman) (30)
a.   Use frosh as U. of F.
b.   Have Frank go over individual reports with frosh identified as U. of F. players
    1) Each frosh knows what he's capable of—oral report
c.   Slow motion (½ speed) skeleton U. of F. off. and def.
    1) ditto o.o.b. and jump ball

BASIC GAME PLAN REVIEW

Preparation for U. of F.

Defense—must step in.
Review movement on box-and-1 and 2-3 defense also; 3-1-1, demonstrate again position on defense and foul line step. Don't let ball in middle or low. If so, top men collapse and double team.

Rebounding
4 men in—must box out and go for ball. Don't start on break before we have ball.
(Review individual players on U. of F.)

Offense—Patience
1.   Look for break each time, get ball downcourt quickly. However, don't force if play is not there.
2.   Start with plays if its man—1R and 7 should work.

478

3. Review our Box-and-1 offense.
4. In shuffle work "Get one for Joe," if man overplays wing man.
5. If Bobb on Jones, put on post and send low off shuffle.
6. Set up tap-ball alignments.
7. Go over U. of F. out-of-bounds.
8. Pick up man-to-man and stay until play is finished.
9. Put ball on ground whenever possible.
10. Step in whenever opportunity arises.
11. Box out every time.
12. *Patience on offense.*

On Court Work
1. Work against 3-1-1—one-half-court press. (5)
2. Work against box-and-1 with our alignment. (5)
3. Df. work with triangle-and-2—stressing boxing out and rebounding, jabbing at man with ball. Don't commit too far. (5)
4. Df. work on using 3-1-1 press. (5)
5. Work on possible use of 2-3 zone. (5)
   N.B. This lineup should use plays on offense.
   Stress—stepping in; boxing out; patience on offense. Only good shots should be taken after everyone handles. (5)
6. Work 3-2 and shuffle using these principles. Everything on ground. (5)
7. Shooting (teams) and foul shots. (15)

appendix d

Scouting Report—Forsyth University

*Included in complete final scouting report folder on Forsyth University are:

1. Team offense—with diagrams—(vs. Leslie College)

2. Team defense—with diagrams—(vs. Leslie College)

3. Individual personnel reports—with individual shot charts—(vs. Leslie College.)

4. A supplementary report (by second scout) vs. another team (D. U.).

5. A Post game report (including game statistics summary and shot chart) vs. B. C.

6. A frosh game report (including game statistics summary and shot chart) vs. B. C.

7. The half-time strategy report (from B. C. Game).

8. Included but not shown for space reasons are:

   A. Statistics and charts for 5 and 6 and 7 above.

   B. Forsyth University basketball brochure, game program, scout's rough notes, game play-by-play report, game shot chart, final game statistics vs. Leslie College.

Forsyth University Team Offense

1. *Very patient*—looked for good shots (only took 49 in game).

2. *Many offensive taps*—cf. shot charts.

3. *Used several offenses*—stack, 2-3 regular shuffle, 1-3-1 shuffle, 2-3 low shuffle, 1-4 off., and stack with open side.

4. Stack and 2-3 regular and low were used most.

5. Looked for screens from opposite ball to ball, also looked for screens off low man out to ball (Inside-out screens).

6. Team moved fluidly and with precision vs. man-to-man for their first game.

7. *Took only 19 shots in second half—only five from beyond 10 feet.

8. Corr (22), Stein (32), Mann (23) *took 37 of 49 shots;* other 4 players took twelve shots between them.

9. Leslie's man-to-man did not disrupt the continuity of Forsyth University's patterns.

10. This is the best *team* that Forsyth University has had in several years.

11. Forsyth University back tapped on side tapped for possession and did not look for basket.

12. Used several out-of-bounds plays, primarily for possession.

13. Against full court pressure Forsyth University looked for high middle (Crane #31 or Smylie #24) and then under to Stein #32. Corr went into back court to help guards up with ball.

FORSYTH UNIV.   TEAM OFFENSE

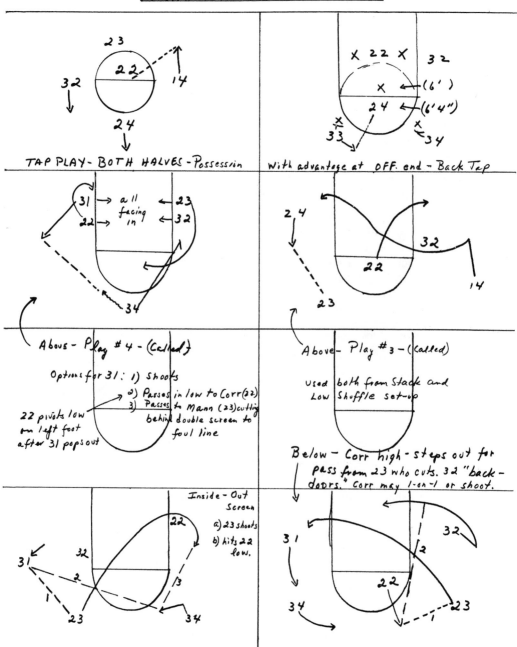

TAP PLAY- BOTH HALVES - Possession

With advantage at OFF. end - Back Tap

Above - Play #4 - (Called)

Options for 31: 1) Shoots
2) Passes in low to Corr(22)
3) Passes to Mann (23) cutting behind double screen to foul line

22 pivots low on left foot after 31 pops out

Above - Play #3 - (called)

Used both from Stack and Low Shuffle set-up

Below - Corr high - steps out for pass from 23 who cuts. 32 "back-doors." Corr may 1-on-1 or shoot.

Inside - Out Screen
a) 23 shoots
b) hits 22 low.

482

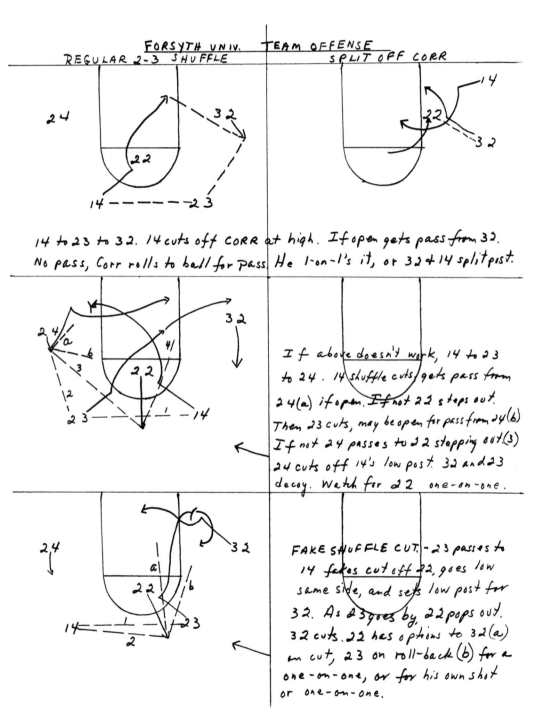

REGULAR 2-3 SHUFFLE

SPLIT OFF CORR

24   32   22   14

22   32

14 - - - - - - 23

14 to 23 to 32. 14 cuts off CORR at high. If open gets pass from 32.
No pass, Corr rolls to ball for pass. He 1-on-1's it, or 32 & 14 splitpost.

24 a b 3 2 23   41 22 32   14

If above doesn't work, 14 to 23
to 24. 14 shuffle cuts / gets pass from
24 (a) if open. If not 22 steps out.
Then 23 cuts, may be open for pass from 24 (b)
If not 24 passes to 32 stepping out (3)
24 cuts off 14's low post. 32 and 23
decoy. Watch for 22 one-on-one.

24 22 a b 32 14 - - - 23 2

FAKE SHUFFLE CUT. - 23 passes to
14 fakes cut off 22, goes low
same side, and sets low post for
32. As 23 goes by, 22 pops out.
32 cuts. 22 has options to 32 (a)
on cut, 23 on roll-back (b) for a
one-on-one, or for his own shot
or one-on-one.

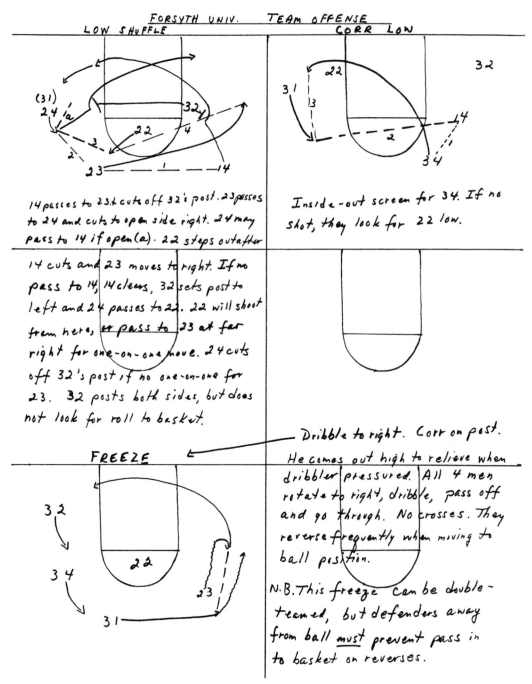

LOW SHUFFLE

CORR LOW

14 passes to 23, & cuts off 32's post. 23 passes to 24 and cuts to open side right. 24 may pass to 14 if open (a). 22 steps out after

14 cuts and 23 moves to right. If no pass to 14, 14 clears, 32 sets post to left and 24 passes to 22. 22 will shoot from here, ~~or pass to~~ 23 at far right for one-on-one move. 24 cuts off 32's post if no one-on-one for 23. 32 posts both sides, but does not look for roll to basket.

Inside-out screen for 34. If no shot, they look for 22 low.

FREEZE

Dribble to right. Corr on post. He comes out high to relieve when dribbler pressured. All 4 men rotate to right, dribble, pass off and go through. No crosses. They reverse frequently when moving to ball position.

N.B. This freeze can be double-teamed, but defenders away from ball <u>must</u> prevent pass in to basket on reverses.

484

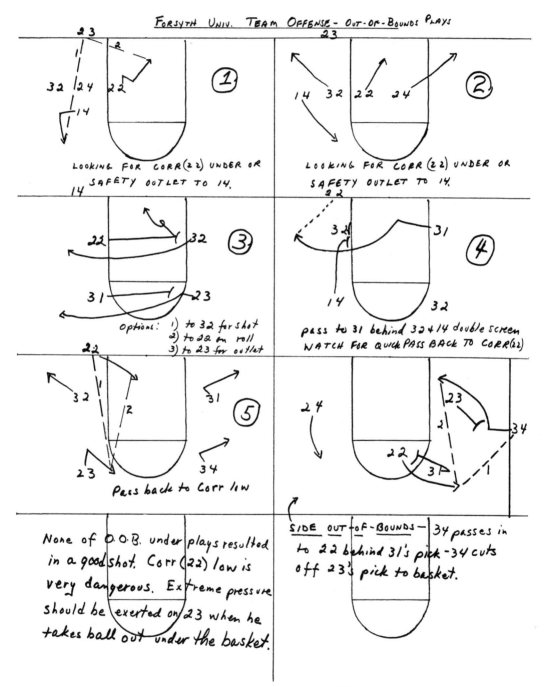

LOOKING FOR CORR (22) UNDER OR SAFETY OUTLET TO 14.

LOOKING FOR CORR (22) UNDER OR SAFETY OUTLET TO 14.

Options: 1) to 32 for shot
2) to 22 on roll
3) to 23 for outlet

pass to 31 behind 32+14 double screen WATCH FOR QUICK PASS BACK TO CORR (22)

Pass back to Corr low

None of O.O.B. under plays resulted in a good shot. Corr (22) low is very dangerous. Extreme pressure should be exerted on 23 when he takes ball out under the basket.

SIDE OUT-OF-BOUNDS — 34 passes in to 22 behind 31's pick - 34 cuts off 23's pick to basket.

485

Forsyth University Defense

1. Used a 2-3 zone as basic defense against Leslie.

2. Zone was aggressive with front men Meeny (14), Mann (23), Fish (34) waving arms and using quick thrusts and fakes to the ball—the latter two were most vocal.

3. The front men and corner man attempted to extend so as to trap at the 28' hash mark. (Sometimes it was the two front men all the way to left or right sideline.)

4. The corner and front men on the sides attempted to trap in the corners. (Sometimes Corr and the forward trapped.)

5. There were weak side openings in the Forsyth University zone.

6. Corr and the forwards overextend high from back line.

7. Corr particularly will go to top of key from middle spot.

8. The guards are extremely aggressive coming back to ball when it goes into low middle or corners for steals.

9. The forwards and center go up in the air on shot fakes close in.

10. Forsyth University went man-to-man for 6 to 8 minutes vs. Leslie, longer vs. D. U. They are ball watchers man-to-man, do not switch well, but boxed quite well from man-to-man.

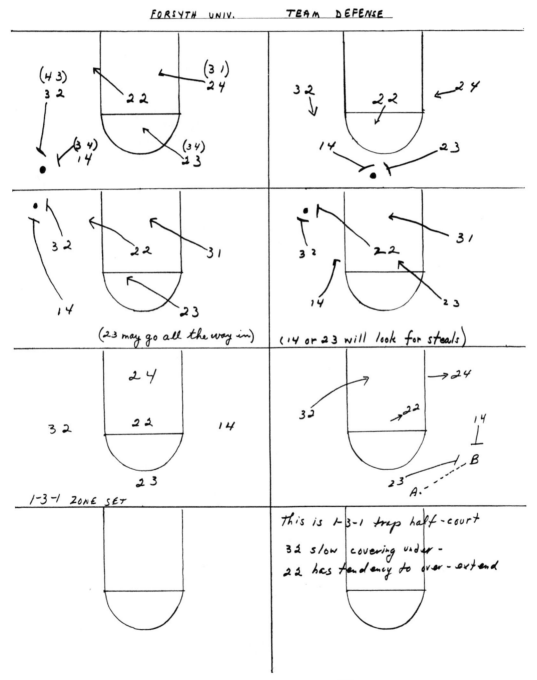

(23 may go all the way in)

(14 or 23 will look for steals)

1-3-1 ZONE SET

this is 1-3-1 trap half-court

32 slow covering under -
22 has tendency to over-extend

487

Forsyth University Personnel

c *#22, Corr, 6-7, 190, right hand.* Extremely quick and aggressive; excellent speed; a clean type of rebounder who twists and knifes to position rather than "bulls" his way in. Threw elbows repeatedly with effective results after getting ball; is shooting outside with fair accuracy— 18-22 ft. range. Comes high on defense from 2-3 zone center but recovers quickly. Also goes to corner on def. occasionally. Helps up with ball vs. man-to-man pressure. He dribbles well, but stops with feints. Reaches rather than steps to receive pass under pressure and an alert defender can deflect the ball with anticipation— 4 or 5 second half Forsyth U. turnovers were the result of this. He is playing higher this year offensively and is going outside from foul line to receive pass. He will shoot or feed Mann (23) an open right side for a 1 on 1— *Corr holds the ball in low or medium pivot and guards can come off men to the ball. He is the best Forsyth University reb.* Corr is extremely susceptible to ball fakes and he goes up in air with them. Against a smaller man he should be boxed. It's to our advantage to have his outside or high offensively. Corr gives pivot position low on man-to-man defense. Fair foul shooter.

f *#24, Smylie, 6-4, 185, right hand.* Smylie is a transfer from Stark State. Used a good base move in left corner and went up with jumper. While he didn't hit outside, he shot with confidence and was consistent in warm-up practice. Speed seemed fair to good. Played C or D man in their stack. Was first man subbed for. Like Corr, Smylie jumped at ball from left low position in zone. In man-to-man he did an adequate job. Position fair on rebounds. He tended in too far defensively on rebounds and looked for tap offensively. Ran offensive patterns well while in there. Hands suspect.

g *#23, Mann, 5-10, 170, right hand.* Good speed and was man they looked for as middle man in break situation. He is all right hand when dribbling; will wheel to left one bounce then right back to his right. Can dribble left but slowly. He looks to trap at 28' hash mark with other guard or forward. Drops a long way back from front for defensive steals. *He is a definite outside offensive threat.* Forsyth U. looked for him on 1 on 1's and outside shooting opportunities. Did not react well to pressure. Can step in for offensive charge especially when he wheels to left and back to right. Good hands def. and will take chances. Initiates all offensive patterns. They look for him on Inside-Out screen from underneath. *On a fast break, Mann took 25' jumper with the lanes filled* when the defender fell off him. This boy really hustled throughout the game both ways. He sees the play fairly well, but likes to shoot.

f #32, Stein, 6-3, 215, right hand. Speed only fair, but has *excellent timing and strength on rebounds.* His position is good and he has that knack for getting his hands on the ball. Not a real leaper. He is also a garbage man. Always in the right place at the right time. See shot chart. Defensively he is aggressive, with no glaring weakness or strong points. He recovered slower than the other 4 men in the zone (plays near right corner). He is a hustler and determined. Fairly sure with ball but he seemed to have a limited shooting range, perhaps because he was inside all the time. Always the back man vs. pressure where he picked up 3 unopposed "chippies." Was the pick man on the shuffle low. Did not roll to basket after cutter went by. Moved left to right to set up the block. He will look up for break from def. rebound. Seems to be a smart player. While speed only fair his moves are quick. A definite threat. Solid for his limitations. Moved well without ball. Excellent foul shooter.

g #14, Meeny, 6-3, 180, right hand. Good to above average speed. Has good long first step both with and without ball. Cut off picks without ball very well. Kept out a lot, but was in foul trouble. Seemed to have only fair range (16-17 feet) for guard. Both taps at half went to him on left side. Was guard they wanted to leave in. Did not shoot much and also didn't see a lot of the ball. Hustled on "D." Usually was first cutter on shuffle. Dribbled right protectively with ball under pressure quite well.

SUBS

f (for Smylie) #31, Crane, 6-4, 195, right hand. Aggressive—good speed and hands—*gets up well and strongly.* Good jump shooter 15-16 feet, but still has football muscles. *Looked for the play every time he got ball* (hit Stein twice under vs. pressure for lay ups). Good rebound position and excellent timing. With more practice he'll start for Smylie. Very aggressive on "D" and slides and reacts quickly from rear left zone position. Plays extremely sound and aggressive man-to-man. Moves are right.

g (for 23 first) #34, Fish, 5-9, 170, right hand. Short—*fair speed*—all right hand but *spirited, aggressive hustler.* Wants ball on offense and should have it. A pounding dribbler. Goes left on wheel motion but ineffective. Looks for pass. No shots in almost 1/2 of playing time. Reacted poorly to pressure. Worked extremely hard in front of zone. Both 34 and 23 sagged deep from zone position. Poorest foul shooter.

N.B. #12, McNair, 6-1, 183, right hand. Injured guard—may be ready. cf. last year's notes on him.

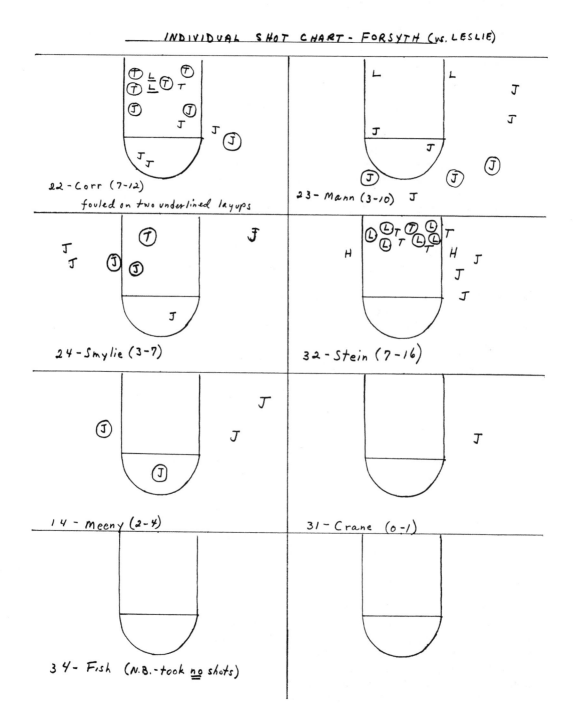

22 - Corr (7-12)
fouled on two underlined layups

23 - Mann (3-10)

24 - Smylie (3-7)

32 - Stein (7-16)

14 - Meeny (2-4)

31 - Crane (0-1)

34 - Fish (N.B. - took no shots)

(Supplementary report, second scout, italicized items our reaction to report)

Vs. D. U. Used 1-3-1 zone—*practice vs. it.*

Attack through 32. He's slower and the last one back on defense. *Foul line play to his side.*

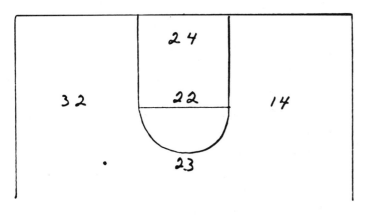

Forsyth University had poor penetration vs. 2-2-1, 3/4 trap of D. U.—*practice pressure.*

Forsyth University used 3/4 trap and 1/2 trap from 1-3-1 zone—*incorporate in daily practice.*

Forsyth University used two guards plus Corr (*see Leslie report*) to bring ball up—*force guards left.*

Corr gets in too close rebounding—*crowd him under.*

Forsyth University did not show fast break from 1-3-1 zone —*crash off board.*

Shots showed behind (3) line of 1-3-1 as they came up beyond foul line—*look low.*

Corr extended to the sides too far—*go to corners and bounce pass to low post.*

@12 min. ½ half Forsyth Univ. went 2-3 zone—*back line of (3) still too far out.*
Corr tries to block close shots—*fake him up.*

Forsyth Univ. getting fast break from 2-3—*less off. board pressure vs. this zone.*

@8 min. ½ half (3) line deeper-cutting off underneath— *take medium shots* side jumpers and foul line shots showing.

#14 Meeny shooting well—18-20 ft. (Taped leg may be bad) *Revise Leslie report.*

D.U. attacking 2-3 Forsyth Univ. zone with 1-3-1—good shots show from wings.

#43 Burke, 6-8″, rt. hand. Looks good but used sparingly.

Good 15-18 ft. touch. Runs well. Not aggressive. *Add to individual reports.*

Corr puts ball to floor all the time—*try to tie him up.*

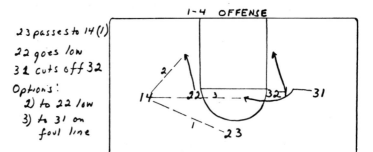

23 passes to 14 (1)
22 goes low
31 cuts off 32
Options:
   2) to 22 low
   3) to 31 on
      foul line

Forsyth Univ. using 1-4 attack vs. D.U. 2-3 zone—*discuss this offense.*

#23, Mann, not a good passer—*pressure him.*

Forsyth Univ. passes backwards in back court vs. press. A young team. Seems to be tight.

Forsyth Univ. man-to-man @12 min. 2nd half.

#14, Meeny, tries to double team man-to-man (his man scores). Meeny poor movement man-to-man (his leg?). Meeny weak vs. give-and-go, man-to-man.

#23, Mann, turns head on def. man-to-man.

#31, Crane, left man—pass under to him.

#24, Smylie, good offensive rebounder.

Forsyth Univ. poor switching team, man-to-man.

Forsyth Univ. acted as though D.U. was a set up (they were 3-20 last year and WE beat Leslie). Corr didn't put out until there was only six minutes to go. Too little, too late.

B. C.—Forsyth Univ.—19___ Post Game Report

Def. vs. our Stack was 1-3-1.

Shots appeared in 12-15 ft. range as Forsyth Univ. wanted to close off Doll and Kane under.

Forsyth Univ. was patient offensively—used #32, Stein, exclusively in low shuffle as pick man. He pushed every defender off stride on cuts. (Literally, with both hands.) He never rolled after cut but went opposite to pick again.

Corr stayed outside, except to cut off pick.

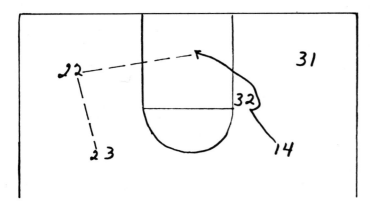

Corr hit #23, Mann, for 4 first half baskets when Evers doubled on him outside—only double low and medium. Evers moved laterally rather than penetrating from point. Lob right or left showed after initial ball movement vs. zone. They used Corr low series in 2nd half. Vs. zone, they looked for Corr inside. He went to basket. Corr has good shooting range.

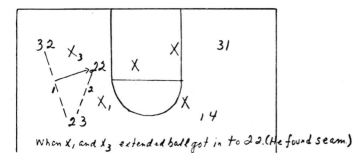

When X_1 and X_3 extended ball got in to 22. (He found seam.)

When we extended, they got it into Corr who scored. *When we sluffed* in zone, and *boxed* Corr, they took poor shots and we got ball. *DON'T EXTEND.*

Forsyth Univ. used cards to change def. from bench. All def. resolved into 1-3-1 slides after initial passes.

They gave Evers 12 to 15 foot shots, playing him to pass.

Used a new O. O. B. play for Corr.

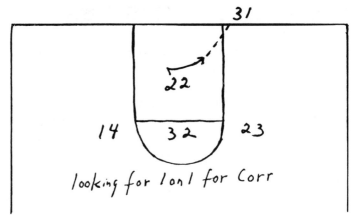

31

22

14   32   23

looking for 1 on 1 for Corr

We were too slow attacking on turnovers.

Adams did a poor job boxing #31, Crane.

#14, Meeny, showed good range shooting and he drove very well from left with left hand and he cut extremely well off Low Shuffle pick. He was open several times and didn't get pass.

#31, Crane, beat Adams on left hand drive from right sideline at midcourt and down the middle all the way to basket.

#23, Mann, shot well from outside.

#22, Corr, hit one from dead left corner and one from top of key.

#32, Stein, again got the garbage. He must be boxed.

Forsyth Univ. was stronger than anticipated because they handled better against man-to-man pressure than expected. We did a poor job in defending their Low Shuffle because we did not balance def. to ball position quickly enough. Forsyth U. tried to send men through zone to weak side, but were reluctant to take 20-foot shots. These shots showed, but were discouraged by faking rush at shooter and retreating to double upon Corr.

N.B. Review game movies with team prior to next practice. Point out strengths and weaknesses as noted.

Forsyth University Frosh—19___

Best player—#15, McCarey, 6' 2", right hand. Did an excellent job 1 on 1, but went right all the time. Excellent shooter from 22 feet and in, good fake and control when off balance—give him first fake if he has ball. Try to deny him ball as he doesn't have enough moves or speed to free himself. He cut off screen very well right to left and shot well off this move. He boxed effectively and had nose for ball on offensive board. A good prospect, but is too small for a forward and his ball handling is suspect for a guard. Defensively, he is fair. Passed well without pressure. We played him poorly (*Stock*).

494

Best rebounder—#43, Huber, 6' 5", left hand. Must go left. He was used as a pick man in Shuffle after original movement and he fouled on moving picks, but weren't called. He's a *HATCHET MAN TYPE*. Hit with jumper from 18 and 20 feet, but was inconsistent. Gets up real good. Must be boxed. Not a good man-to-man defender. We played him well (*Carey*).

Best guard—#22, Yates, 6', right hand. Too slow for top level, but aggressive. Good range, intelligent, excellent imagination. Went right dribbling well, but slow left. He played very well vs. Frosh; especially at the end when they pressured us. Had good moves and passed well.

Other Players

G #12, Bird, 5' 11", *right hand*. Good shooter. No moves. Fair speed. Fancy passer. Overrated.

C #24, Hogarty, 6' 5", *right hand*. Good rebounder, awkward, poor ball handler. Didn't look for or take open shots. He'll have trouble playing in their Conference.

Subs

#21, Carp, 6' 1", *right hand*. Good range. Went both ways. Good speed. Poor defensively except when pressuring us. He could be a good prospect with work.

#40, August, 6' 7", *left hand*. I liked him as a prospect —thin, but agile with a good range (16 to 18 feet). Very unsure of himself, and not aggressive. Should come strong in junior year. Watch him.

#33, Vallely, 6' 3", *right hand*. Good shooter. We had literature on him. Not a college player.

N.B. Their best player Glass did not play.

The Game—B. C. Frosh 91 vs. Forsyth University 87

We were tight beginning and it was even for 15 minutes. We opened to ten and ended 35–27 at the half. They were weak man-to-man and Oates went by his guard and fed well underneath. Carey read the Forsyth University offensive well and stole two or three passes for layups. Stock was weak defensively on #15.

They picked us well on Shuffle because:
1) We allowed passer to make play without pressure.
2) We were poor balancing to ball when it was opposite.

We had a 70–51 lead with nine to go when Fallon and Carey tired and Stock had 4 fouls. Oates took over, but he had many turnovers, mostly because of poor anticipation by our men. We were ahead 13 with 1½ to go and by 6 with 50 seconds.

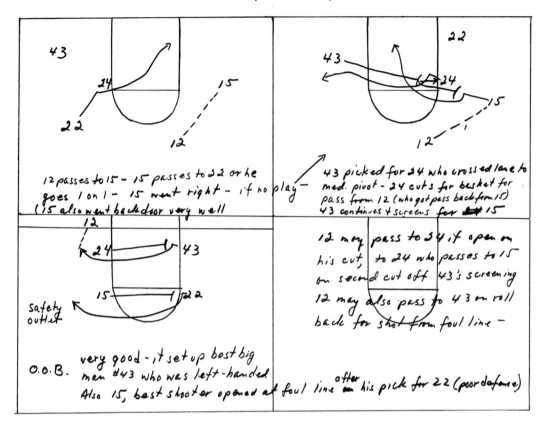

12 passes to 15 – 15 passes to 22 or he goes 1 on 1 – 15 went right – if no play – (15 also went backdoor very well

43 picked for 24 who crossed lane to med. pivot – 24 cuts for basket for pass from 12 (who got pass back from 15) 43 continues + screens for ~~24~~ 15

12 may pass to 24 if open on his cut, to 24 who passes to 15 on second cut off 43's screening 12 may also pass to 43 on roll back for shot from foul line –

O.O.B. safety outlet

very good – it set up best big man #43 who was left-handed Also 15, best shooter opened at foul line after his pick for 22 (poor defense)

appendix e

a game plan

U. L. N. O.—1-27-19____

Tap, go for wrist, wings knife (Doll jump) and get back with Anadore.

Def.—¾ ct. pickup. *Everyone responsible for his own man.* Stay close with or without ball—especially forwards. *Get back quickly on "D".*

1 on 1—no weak side help or center help. No *double teaming*.

*Possible strong side slough.

*Doll—Get back quickly after foul shot (ours). Don't let Anadore beat you down.

*U. L. N. O. shooting foul—4 men on lines.

Offense
1) No foul line play
2) Doll go quickly to ½ court and be ready to return
3) No fast break
4) vs. agg. full court pressure—explain (wings)
5) vs. agg. ½ court pressure—release to middle
6) vs. sagging man
7) start single stack vs. (man)
8) double stack (widened) vs. zone

Must look for free man over ½ ct.

Reb.—Explain—1 shot philosophy

Evers, Kunz, Dole vs. Press
1) Evers and Kunz alternate with Kunz mostly taking ball up alone.
2) Utilize bounce pass to get ball in
3) Look to bust through on dribble or release to Anadore's man.
4) Keep head up over ½—be aware of double team and hit wing in shooting area
5) If bringing into line, take all the way to Anadore (be careful of pursuit at all times after initial pressure penetration).

Offense
1) Be aware of your shooters (Adams, Duca, Dole, Kunz);

we must look for good shots.
2) If break doesn't develop for jumper, take as much time as necessary setting stack.
3) Work away from Anadore and bring his man to line. Adams, Kane, Doll, Kunz in B-C-D-E spots.
   Take Ware off point if necessary (Evers, Kunz exchange at point) (Man—Start).
4) Single stack with Adams and Doll (Doll setting pick).
5) Zone—Double stack with 4 passes.

Defense
1) Stay solid on Ware and Asten. Pick up Ware as early as possible and fake and retreat.
2) Don't look to double or steal. Stay with men with and without and box.
3) Reb. all go strong to bds.

U. L. N. O. Notes

1. Anadore—don't allow hook shot (esp.). Force turn away jump shot.
2. Forwards and center hit off bds; gds. ready to get back. Everyone must get back quickly after transition.
3. Kunz find Ware as quickly as possible and exert pressure. Pick up and don't allow to get started.
4. Evers or Kinder don't under any condition leave man (Asten) without ball. Don't double from weak side, and box Asten.
5. Adams on Lane must overplay initially on high post and pressure with ball, not allowing easy pass to Anadore.
6. Doll on Anadore—with ball on side must be ½ man to outside and jump back to force jumper after reception; with ball on foul line play directly behind.
7. Stafford—must be played tight with and without ball and boxed.

Def.—¾ court pickup with constant def. faking. Trying to force 1 on 1 situations. Will not get help from Doll. Everyone is on their own. Do not under any circumstances take your eye off your man without the ball. Don't try to double team Anadore.

Reb.—Every forward and center must turn and immediately make contact *before* going for ball. Man guarding Anadore must not go for ball at all but simply hold. Guards must immediately go to bds. for rebound. Asten guard may have to make contact first. This policy must be adhered to all game.

3 men stay on offensive boards as long as possession still in doubt, then get back quickly.

Offense—vs. agg. full pressure.
1. Guards always take ball out. With Adams and Kane in game go back to guard Kunz or Evers and bust through

with dribble; with 3rd small man go to wing and let him take middle quickly. Wings must bust down court and get in position for short jumper. Man with ball must take ball full speed right to Anadore before passing to either wing.

2. vs. agg. ½ court pressure after Doll comes high keep ball moving out of 2-1-2 alignment until good shot shows (preferably for Doll with Adams). If ball goes to forward release to Doll (must make passes with ball over head).

3. vs. sagging man to man. Go 2-1-2 with forward setting pick and clearing through to weakside bd. Shot taken by guard or pass to post (Doll moving to ball) and shot on Anadore. (Must try and draw Anadore away from hoop.)

4. vs. agg. full pressure we want to penetrate and take first good shot open by our *shooter* on the wing. Agg. ½ court pressure—make them work and keep ball moving.

vs. sagging man. Work 2-on-2 with forwards (forward set pick and roll out and under with Doll rolling to ball).

vs. zone. Stack with 4 passes.

Fast break only vs. pressure; otherwise, 5 men going to bd. for box or rebound.

appendix f

half-time
strategy report

1. Who controlled opening tap? If opponent, where did
   they go with it? If they stole it, how? Subsequent taps?
   Diagram.

2. Is opponent switching defenses? If so, what are they
   keying on? What is their pickup point? Where is defense
   giving us most difficulty?

3. Is our man-to-man doing the job? If not, where or who
   is breaking down? Suggested changes? Is pressure high
   enough?

4. Is our zone press accomplishing our aim? If not, where
   or who is breaking down? What outlet are they going
   to on first penetrating pass? How high is he (or they)
   coming? At what point in the pressure are we having
   most success?

5. What type of game (offensive) is opponent trying to
   play? Are we letting them play their game? If so, suggestions for shutting off key men—speeding up, slowing down, etc.

6. Offensive comments: Is our break working? Why not? Are we getting shot from stack? What options will work best against their defense? What about 2-2-1 or 2-1-2?

7. Board control: Are we controlling "D" board? If not, what changes? Offensive boards are we getting our share? Who should we box if necessary?

8. Individual comments:

   a. Def. matches re: speed, hgt., strength, etc. (suggest possible changes).
   b. Are we stopping dribbler? Who isn't giving outlet pressure?
   c. Is everyone getting back on "D"? Who is tiring?
   d. Who isn't doing reb. job? Not boxing out if called for?
   e. Williams and Kane—are they shooting properly? Going out too far on their men?
   f. Are shooters getting good shot?
   g. Are we overshooting, passing, and dribbling?
   h. Too many long passes? Can we send men down sooner?
   i. Foul line play—diagram the defensive coverage. Who is covering deep man, guard, or forward?

index